THE EIGHTY-SECOND ANNUAL MEETING OF THE AMERICAN ACADEMY OF POLITICAL AND SOCIAL SCIENCE

APRIL 7 AND 8, 1978
THE BENJAMIN FRANKLIN HOTEL
PHILADELPHIA, PENNSYLVANIA

The Annual Meeting will be addressed at each session by prominent scholars and officials and will be devoted to

PLANNING FOR THE ELDERLY

Approximately 800 persons will be in attendance sometime during the two days of sessions, representing a wide variety of cultural, civic and scientific organizations.

Members are cordially invited to attend and will automatically receive full information.

- Proceedings of this 82nd Annual Meeting will be published as the July issue of THE ANNALS

- **FOR DETAILS WRITE TO: THE AMERICAN ACADEMY OF POLITICAL AND SOCIAL SCIENCE • BUSINESS OFFICE • 3937 CHESTNUT STREET. PHILADELPHIA, PENNSYLVANIA 19104**

VOLUME 435 JANUARY 1978

THE ANNALS

of The American Academy *of* Political *and* Social Science

RICHARD D. LAMBERT, *Editor*
ALAN W. HESTON, *Assistant Editor*

AMERICA IN THE SEVENTIES: SOME SOCIAL INDICATORS

Special Editor of This Volume

CONRAD TAEUBER
Director
Center for Population Research
Georgetown University
Washington, D.C.

PHILADELPHIA

Library of Congress Card Number 77-22914

Marion M. Williams, *Copy Editor*

The articles appearing in The Annals are indexed in the *Reader's Guide to Periodical Literature*, the *Book Review Index*, the *Public Affairs Information Service Bulletin*, *Social Sciences Index*, and *Current Contents: Behavioral, Social, Management Sciences* and *Combined Retrospective Index Sets*. They are also abstracted and indexed in *ABC Pol Sci*, *Historical Abstracts*, *United States Political Science Documents*, *Abstracts for Social Workers*, *International Political Science Abstracts* and/or *America: History and Life*.

International Standard Book Numbers (ISBN)

* ISBN 0-87761-223-4, vol. 435, 1978; paper—$6.00
* ISBN 0-87761-222-6, vol. 435, 1978; cloth—$7.50

Issued bimonthly by The American Academy of Political and Social Science at 3937 Chestnut St., Philadelphia, Pennsylvania 19104. Cost per year: $18.00 paperbound; $23.00 clothbound. Add $2.00 to above rates for membership outside U.S.A. Second-class postage paid at Philadephia and at additional mailing offices.

Claims for undelivered copies must be made within the month following the regular month of publication. The publisher will supply missing copies when losses have been sustained in transit and when the reserve stock will permit.

Editorial and Business Offices, 3937 Chestnut Street, Philadelphia, Pennsylvania 19104.

* These prices are for this special issue only. See back cover for regular prices.

CONTENTS

BOOK DEPARTMENT

PAGE

UNITED STATES

SOCIOLOGY

ECONOMICS

PREFACE*

This is the third time that THE ANNALS has devoted a special issue to the subject of social indicators. In May 1967, a two-volume edition appeared under the title, *Social Goals and Indicators for American Society*. In January 1971, a volume on *Social Information for Developing Countries* was published. The title of the present volume, *America in the Seventies: Some Social Indicators*, reflects a recognition of the fact that, though many new statistical series have been developed, it is not possible to set forth a single or even a small number of summary indicators of social welfare which would meet with general acceptance.

Robert Parke and David Seidman's contribution to this issue describes some of the efforts that have been devoted to the development of social indicators since Raymond Bauer, in 1966, issued his volume under that title and THE ANNALS devoted its May 1967 issue to an exploration of objectives and of data availability and data needs.

There has been a growing recognition that statistical reports are not normative indicators; that in fact they often are ambiguous. Ida Merriam illustrates this when she writes: "An increase in expenditures for unemployment insurance signals both a weakness in the economy that should disturb us and a strength in the protection of individuals and families that marks an effective social welfare system."

The report *Social Indicators, 1973*, issued by the Office of Management and Budget clearly recognized this ambiguity and made no effort to draw conclusions for policy from the numerous series which were presented. The successor report, *Social Indicators, 1976*, observed the same limitation.

Nevertheless the data presented have a significance that goes well beyond the description of trends and patterns which is given by the tables and charts in that report. The present issue of THE ANNALS was planned to provide insights into the significance of these patterns and trends. The authors were invited to interpret the data, to give their own views of the significance of the trends to American society, and to observe interrelations as well as implications for policy and for the future. They were not limited to the assumptions which underlay the choices of particular series presented in *Social Indicators, 1976*. They were encouraged to criticize the choices that had been made and to draw attention to other data, presented in the text of the article, if it was their conclusion that such data would have provided greater insights into significant developments.

The readers of these articles will want to refer to the recently issued *Social Indicators, 1976* for more detailed sets of data and for comments on the

* A grant from the National Science Foundation (SOC 76-80262) helped make publication of this volume of THE ANNALS possible. The American Academy of Political and Social Sciences is grateful for this support. However, any opinions, findings, conclusions, or recommendations expressed herein are those of the authors and do not necessarily reflect the views of the Foundation.

methodology and limitations underlying the series.[1] The matching tables and charts presented at the end of each article are drawn from that source. *SI, 1976*, was intended to provide a body of comprehensive statistical information from which individual readers could draw their own conclusions. It is the hope of the editors of this volume that these articles will assist readers to arrive at their own assessments of the trends which are portrayed.

The cooperation of the editors of *SI, 1976*, in providing advance copies of the data presented in that volume and in facilitating the preparation of these articles in other ways, is gratefully acknowledged.

Selecting from the large body of statistical information which is available from official and nonofficial sources is a major task. But many readers will feel that the available data are not sufficiently comprehensive or that they are not appropriate to the current needs and perceptions of problems. If these articles help to direct future data gathering and to initiate efforts for a clearer and more relevant portrayal of current conditions and trends, they will have served to improve future efforts to present social indicators for the United States.

CONRAD TAEUBER

1. U.S. Department of Commerce, Office of Federal Statistical Policy and Standards and Bureau of the Census, *Social Indicators, 1976*. For sale by the Superintendent of Documents, Washington, D.C., 20402. Price: $7.00; Stock #041-001-00156-5.

ANNALS, AAPSS, 435, Jan. 1978

Social Indicators and Social Reporting*

By ROBERT PARKE and DAVID SEIDMAN

ABSTRACT: Doubts about the easy equation of economic growth and social progress led, in the 1960s, to a renewed interest in social measurement and to the birth of the "social indicators movement." *Social Indicators, 1976*, a product of that interest, can be read as both a report on social conditions and trends in the United States and a progress report on social indicators research. The volume is best understood against the background of the social indicators movement and of the research it has stimulated.

Several research traditions are joined together in the social indicators movement, but they share a concern for measurement, analysis, and the reporting to a general audience of aspects of social conditions. The tradition best reflected in *Social Indicators, 1976* stresses the monitoring and reporting of social change. Research work in this tradition emphasizes conceptual and methodological development of measures, improvements in the available data base, the development of social indicator models, and social reporting. In its data selection, treatment of data, organization, and commentary, *Social Indicators, 1976* is an improvement over its predecessor, *Social Indicators, 1973*, though the analysis it contains is notably insufficient. Most of the improvements which should be found in future editions depend upon continued progress in the development of social indicators.

Robert Parke, M.A., Washington, D.C., is Director of the Social Science Research Council's Center for Coordination of Research on Social Indicators. A de-

* This article draws on Eleanor Bernert Sheldon and Robert Parke, "Social Indicators," *Science 188* (May 1975), pp. 693–99. The views expressed are not necessarily those of the Social Science Research Council or its Center for Coordination of Research on Social Indicators. Preparation of this article was supported by Grant No. SOC 74-07148 from the National Science Foundation.

mographer, he taught at Brown University and Muhlenberg College, served in the Population Division and as Program Planning Officer, U.S. Bureau of the Census, and was Deputy Director of the U.S. Commission on Population Growth and the American Future. He is Chairman of the Joint Ad Hoc Committee on Government Statistics and has published articles on demographic aspects of marriage and the family and on social indicators.

David Seidman, Ph.D., Washington, D.C., is a Staff Associate of the Social Science Research Council, at the Council's Center for Coordination of Research on Social Indicators. A political scientist, he taught at Princeton University and has published articles on social indicators, crime statistics, administrative structure, statistical methodology, and the regulation of pharmaceuticals.

IN THE 20 years between 1949 and 1969, median family income in the United States doubled and the Gross National Product more than doubled (in constant dollars). Yet the same period was marked by crime, drugs, racial unrest, demonstrations, the urban crisis, the discovery of environmental degradation, and the rediscovery of poverty in America. These events prompted doubts about the easy equation of economic growth and social progress and a widening sense that economic indicators alone no longer sufficed to measure that progress. Among social scientists and public administrators there arose a renewed interest in social measurement more broadly conceived. In the mid-1960s this interest emerged in the writings and speeches of social scientists, social commentators, and policymakers in the form of calls for the development of "social indicators," "social accounting," "social reporting," "measuring the quality of life," and "monitoring social change."

Impetus toward the development of social indicators was provided by a handful of social scientists and public administrators. Their enthusiasm elicited responses from economists, who saw a role for their skills as theorists and measurers of welfare, sociologists, who saw the relevance of their own research tradition in the measurement of social trends, political scientists, who sought ways to rationalize government programs, social workers, bureaucrats, and other researchers and practitioners. Their collective efforts came to be known as the "social indicators movement," an apt designation in that, as in other movements in their early stages, the participants were ill-defined as to membership, had little organization, and shared few specific objectives, but sensed great needs and opportunities for change and celebrated shared but necessarily ambiguous ideas.

Social Indicators, 1976, the subject of this special issue of THE ANNALS, is one of many concrete manifestations of the efforts to measure and report social change resulting from that movement. A brief review of the field of social indicators will serve to place *Social Indicators, 1976* in perspective.

SOCIAL INDICATORS

Many of the concerns of the social indicators movement are not new. An important precursor of much that is valuable in social indicators today is the work of William F. Ogburn, research director of President Hoover's Research Committee on Social Trends, which in 1933 published the monumental *Recent Social Trends.*[1] Ogburn was fascinated by social change and committed to the application of social science to the elucidation of social trends and thus to the guidance of social planning. In 1929 he set forth his view of the significance of research on social trends:

> . . . there is a continuity in cultural change; one event grows out of another . . . the knowledge of what has occurred and of what is happening is the safest guide we have. With more complete statistics and with better measurement we shall obtain fuller knowledge of what is happening to us and where we are going. Only with these shall we be in a position even to begin to speak of control.[2]

The term "social indicators" became widespread following publication in 1966 of a book by that title edited by Raymond A. Bauer.[3] Seeking to find ways to assess the social impacts of the space program, Bauer brought together several prominent social scientists whose work came to be focused instead on broader questions of social measurements and their use in assessing the state of society relative to national goals. A chapter by Albert D. Biderman showed that pertinent statistical indicators were available for only about half of the goals identified by the President's Commission on National Goals in 1960. Bertram Gross's influential chapter on "Social Systems Accounting" called for the development of comprehensive models describing the structure and performance of entire social systems. Such models might serve to counter what Gross called the "new Philistinism," the tendency of hard measurements, usually in dollars, to dominate equally important, but softer, measurements.

In the same year, the President's Commission on Technology, Automation, and Economic Progress called for the development of a system of social accounts that "would give us a broader and more balanced reckoning of the meaning of social and economic progress . . . that would enable us to record not only the gains of social and economic change but the costs as well . . . ," and eventually might provide a "balance sheet" useful in "clarifying policy choices."[4] A proposal by (then) Senator Mondale for a council of social advisers and an annual social report from the President to Congress, contained in several versions of his "Full Opportunity and Social Accounting Act," likewise relied on this analogy to the national income accounts and their role in the policy process. In 1967, two issues of THE ANNALS were devoted to discussions of social indicators.[5]

These early documents present diverse views of what social indicators are or should be. But they share common themes: concern for the de-

1. President's Research Committee on Social Trends, *Recent Social Trends in the United States* (New York: McGraw-Hill, 1933).

2. William F. Ogburn, "The Responsibility of the Social Sciences," in *William Ogburn on Culture and Social Change*, ed. Otis Dudley Duncan (Chicago: University of Chicago Press, 1964), p. 101.

3. Raymond A. Bauer, ed., *Social Indicators* (Cambridge, Mass.: MIT Press, 1966).

4. President's Commission on Technology, Automation, and Economic Progress, *Technology and the American Economy* (Washington, D.C.: USGPO, 1966), quoted in Daniel Bell, "The Idea of a Social Report," *The Public Interest*, no. 15 (Spring 1969), p. 78.

5. Bertram M. Gross, ed., *Social Goals and Indicators for American Society*, vols. I and II; *The Annals* of the American Academy of Political and Social Science, vol. 371 (May 1967) and vol. 373 (September 1967).

velopment and use of statistics measuring the social state of the nation, emphasis on measures of noneconomic dimensions of well-being, and commitment to the idea that better social information will improve public policy.

These ideas were noticed throughout the federal government. Under the supervision of Assistant Secretary William Gorham and his successor, Alice Rivlin, the Department of Health, Education, and Welfare produced *Toward a Social Report*,[6] an influential statement of the need for social indicators. Not a social report, but rather "an attempt, on the part of social scientists, to look at several important areas and digest what is known about progress toward generally accepted goals," the volume treated the areas of health, social mobility, the physical environment, income and poverty, public order and safety, and learning, science, and art. It was not a social report because, the authors said, the data needed for one did not then exist. For example, "We have measures of death and illness, but not measures of physical vigor or mental health. We have measures of the level and distribution of income, but no measures of the satisfaction that income brings."[7]

In outlining the need for social indicators in future reports, *Toward a Social Report* stressed the usefulness of statistics capable of being aggregated to allow diversity to be summarized into manageable form, and allowing disaggregation for purposes of more detailed analysis. It defined social indicators as "in all cases . . . direct measure[s] of welfare," and contrasted them with the more readily available measures of government expenditures and other "inputs" of various kinds (crime rates versus number of policemen, for example).[8] This distinction, roughly that between outputs and inputs, has been influential but controversial, because it is neither exhaustive nor unambiguous: the output of one social process is the input to another. Further, "direct measures of welfare" do not include many of the variables central to an understanding of social process. A broader definition of social indicators may be more useful.

The intellectual backgrounds of the participants in the social indicators movement are diverse. Not surprisingly, then, diverse types of work have been associated at one time or another with social indicators. The major research traditions are sketched briefly below.[9]

Evaluation research and social experimentation

Disappointment with the results of domestic social programs in the 1960s directed attention to the need for a more scientific approach to program testing and evaluation, as illustrated in the New Jersey Income Maintenance Experiment[10] and the evaluation of the Head Start Pro-

6. U.S. Department of Health, Education, and Welfare, *Toward a Social Report* (Washington, D.C.: USGPO, 1969).

7. Ibid., p. xiv.

8. Ibid., p. 97.

9. A typology of work on social indicators is presented in Wolfgang Zapf, "Systems of Social Indicators: Current Approaches and Problems," *International Social Science Journal* 27, no. 3 (1975), pp. 479–98.

10. David Kershaw and Jerliyn Fair, *The New Jersey Income-Maintenance Experiment*. Vol. 1: *Operations, Surveys, and Administration* (New York: Academic Press, 1976); Harold W. Watts and Albert Rees, eds., *The New Jersey Income-Maintenance Experiment*. Vol. 2: Labor-Supply Responses (New York: Academic Press, 1977).

gram.[11] In early discussions of social indicators, it was suggested that they could be used as a basis for program evaluation. Donald T. Campbell has long advocated this position.[12] But social indicators research and evaluation research have increasingly diverged, and recent thinking emphasizes the need for experimental design in program evaluation.[13] Nor is the direct use of social indicators likely to be fruitful for evaluation in the absence of experimental design because of the difficulty of showing that specific government programs, rather than uncontrolled exogenous variables, determined the outcomes measured by indicators.

Net national welfare measurement

The image of the national income accounts lay behind *Toward a Social Report*. Mancur Olson, principal author of that document, has written, "for all their virtues, the national income statistics don't tell us what we need to know about the condition of American society. They leave out most of the things that make life worth living."[14] One response to this possible shortcoming of the national accounts is to make them more inclusive. Economists in the United States and Japan have experimented with adjustments to the accounts to improve their adequacy as measures of welfare. Nordhaus and Tobin have incorporated into GNP such things as the costs of pollution and the benefits of leisure, and other economists have proceeded along related lines.[15] While this has been an area of major social indicators activity, there are limits to what the national accounts can absorb. *Toward a Social Report* noted that "the goal of a grand and cosmic measure of all forms or aspects of welfare must be dismissed as impractical. . . ."[16] There may also be costs to treating social indicators work as concerned with what "the national accounts don't tell us." The approach may lead to viewing the "social" aspects of life as a homogeneous residual category consisting of whatever is outside the realm of economics. In fact, of course, the economy is but one part of a complex society whose other parts—the educational system, the political system, or the family, for example—differ one from another as much as they differ from the economic system. They must be under-

11. Lois-ellin Datta, "Design of the Head Start Planned Variation Experiment," pp. 79–100; Marshall S. Smith, "Evaluation Findings in Head Start Planned Variation," pp. 101–12; and Carol Van Deusen Lukas, "Problems in Implementing Head Start Planned Variation Models," pp. 113–26, in *Planned Variation in Education: Should We Give Up or Try Harder*?, eds. Alice M. Rivlin and P. Michael Timpane (Washington, D.C.: The Brookings Institution, 1975).

12. Donald T. Campbell, "Focal Local Indicators for Social Program Evaluation," *Social Indicators Research* 3 (September 1976), pp. 237–56.

13. Alice M. Rivlin, *Systematic Thinking for Social Action* (Washington, D.C.: The Brookings Institution, 1971); Henry W. Riecken and Robert F. Boruch, *Social Experimentation: A Method for Planning and Evaluating Social Intervention* (New York: Academic Press, 1974).

14. Mancur Olson, "The Plan and Purpose of a Social Report," *The Public Interest*, no. 15 (Spring 1969), p. 86.

15. Economic Council of Japan, NNW Measurement Committee, *Measuring New National Welfare of Japan* (Tokyo: Economic Council of Japan, 1973); William D. Nordhaus and James Tobin, "Is Growth Obsolete?," in *The Measurement of Economic and Social Performance*, ed. Milton Moss (New York: NBER, 1973), pp. 509–31; National Bureau of Economic Research, *Annual Report, 1975* (New York: NBER, 1975), pp. 14–23.

16. U.S. Department of Health, Education, and Welfare, *Toward a Social Report*, p. 99.

stood on their own terms, and not simply viewed as "the rest."

National goals accounting

An early concern of some social indicators theorists was measurement and analysis of the achievement of national goals. Work in this tradition takes the form of national goals accounting—attempts to give explicit definition to national goals and priorities, to estimate progress towards the achievement of these goals, and to measure the cost of further achievement. Nestor E. Terleckyj, whose work is the principal current exemplar of this tradition, has developed a framework for estimating the possibilities for planned improvement in the quality of life in the United States. It includes (1) identification of social concerns and of indicators to measure relevant conditions; (2) projection of baseline trends in these conditions and in resources potentially available for altering them; (3) identification of the costs and effects of discretionary programmatic activities affecting social conditions; and (4) calculation of the maximum feasible impact of combinations of discretionary activities that can be undertaken, given resource constraints, taking into account multiple consequences of programs, nonadditivity of effects, and other complications. Estimates to date are highly tentative, in large measure because of data limitations. Following the publication in 1975 of Terleckyj's *Improvements in the Quality of Life: Estimates of Possibilities in the United States, 1974–1983,*[17] a consortium was organized to pursue related work.

Measurement of social change

A broader view of social indicators, advocated by many leading theorists and practitioners, sees the task as one of social measurement and analysis designed to improve our understanding of what the main features of society are, how they are interrelated, and how these features and their relationships change. Otis Dudley Duncan states the case well:

> What we must have, minimally, are quantitative statements about social conditions and social processes, repeatedly available through time, the reliability and validity of which are competently assessed and meet minimal standards. If such statements—"social measurements"—can be organized into accounts . . . so much the better. If some combination of measurements or quantities derived from elementary magnitudes can be shown to serve a clear interpretive purpose as "indicators," so much the better. As accounting schemes, models of social processes, and indicators are developed and tested, our idea of what to measure will, of course, change. But that does not alter the principle that the basic ingredients are the measurements themselves. We are talking about information, the processing of information, and the reporting of processed information.[18]

This view of social indicators has its roots in Ogburn's work and has been prominent since the early days of the social indicators movement. Social indicators as measures of changes in social conditions had

17. Nester E. Terleckyj, *Improvements in the Quality of Life: Estimates of Possibilities in the United States, 1974–1983* (Washington, D.C.: National Planning Association, 1975).

18. Otis Dudley Duncan, quoted in Eleanor Bernert Sheldon, "Social Reporting for the 1970's," in *Federal Statistics*, Report of the President's Commission on Federal Statistics (Washington, D.C.: USGPO, 1971), vol. 2, p. 430.

been discussed in Biderman's essay in the Bauer book[19] and in a few of the papers in the 1967 volumes of THE ANNALS.[20] Detailed reviews of conceptual and measurement problems in the delineation of demographic, social structural, and other types of change in the United States appeared in the late 1960s in work edited by Eleanor Bernert Sheldon and Wilbert E. Moore, and in other work sponsored by the Russell Sage Foundation.[21] These reviews, dealing with hard data, were followed in 1972 by similar treatments of subjective data on public aspirations, expectations, and satisfactions, which appeared in a volume edited by Angus Campbell and Philip E. Converse.[22]

Given the view of the social indicators enterprise as the measurement of social conditions and social change, development of the data base, and the development of social work toward the definition of measures of social conditions and social change, development of the data base, and the development of social indicator models. Social reporting is a fourth major task, implied not by the view of social indicators as the measurement of social change, but rather by the belief that one of the purposes of social indicators is to contribute to public enlightenment.

Conceptual and methodological development of measures

Social indicators work must extend to topics for which measures are now either inadequate or nonexistent, and so considerable attention is being paid to the development of new measures. Efforts to develop subjective measures of the quality of life, a topic central to the concerns of many social indicators researchers, are illustrative. Pioneering work in this area by Campbell and Converse[23] was followed by a study by Frank M. Andrews and Stephen B. Withey, who reported progress toward the development of "a rational empirical basis for measuring perceived quality of life."[24]

Recently, Campbell, Converse, and Willard L. Rodgers have published a major new work on measuring perceptions and assessments of the quality of life, in which they report the results of another survey-based investigation of perceived satisfaction, this one designed to

19. Albert D. Biderman, "Social Indicators and Goals," in Bauer, ed., *Social Indicators*, pp. 68–153.

20. Gross, ed., *The Annals*, vol. 371 and vol. 373.

21. Eleanor Bernert Sheldon and Wilbert E. Moore, eds., *Indicators of Social Change: Concepts and Measurements* (New York: Russell Sage Foundation, 1969); Abbott Ferriss, *Indicators of Trends in American Education* (New York: Russell Sage Foundation, 1969); *Indicators of Change in the American Family* (New York: Russell Sage Foundation, 1970); and *Indicators of Trends in the Status of American Women* (New York: Russell Sage Foundation, 1971). An outline of a program for monitoring social change was given in Sheldon and Moore, "Toward the Measurement of Social Change: Implications for Progress," in *Economic Progress and Social Welfare*, ed. Leonard H. Goodman (New York: Columbia University Press, 1966).

22. Angus Campbell and Philip E. Converse, eds., *The Human Meaning of Social Change* (New York: Russell Sage Foundation, 1972).

23. Ibid.

24. Frank M. Andrews and Stephen B. Withey, "Developing Measures of Perceived Life Quality: Results from Several National Surveys," *Social Indicators Research* 1 (May 1974), p. 24; see also Frank M. Andrews and Stephen B. Withey, *Social Indicators of Well-Being: Americans' Perceptions of Their Life Quality* (New York: Plenum Press, 1976).

serve as a baseline for trend studies.[25] The authors carefully consider the relationship between satisfaction in various domains and more global life satisfaction and examine the relation between objective conditions and subjective satisfactions. If, as Campbell suggests, "the quality of life lies in the experience of life,"[26] further developmental work will be required along similar lines. Such work is being done in a series of Canadian surveys by the Institute for Behavioural Research of York University, Toronto,[27] and in comparative studies of well-being based on surveys taken in various countries.[28]

Data development

While social indicators work requires data of many kinds, many of the necessary data come from sample surveys. Much of the developmental work, therefore, has been devoted to new surveys, to increasing the utility of old surveys through replication, and to making existing surveys more accessible for analysis.

New Surveys. In recent years, the federal government has begun major new survey programs which produce new kinds of data particularly suitable for social indicators purposes. For example, our knowledge of the levels and trends of crime in the United States has traditionally come from data on crimes reported to the police and by them to the Federal Bureau of Investigation for publication in the *Uniform Crime Reports*. But many crimes are not reported to the police, with the percentage of unreported crime varying widely for different types of crime; and police recording procedures are not always uniform. Furthermore, administrative records of this kind do not reveal much about the nature of public experience with crime, the experience of victimization. In recent years the National Crime Survey,[29] a continuing program which each month asks respondents in 10,000 households around the United States about their experiences as victims of crime, has been conducted by the Bureau of the Census for the Law Enforcement Assistance Administration of the Department of Justice. Analyses of the resulting data, as recommended by a National Research Council panel,[30] should substantially increase our under-

25. Angus Campbell, Philip E. Converse, and Willard L. Rodgers, *The Quality of American Life: Perceptions, Evaluations and Satisfactions* (New York: Russell Sage Foundation, 1976).

26. Angus Campbell, "Subjective Measures of Well-Being" (Paper presented at the Joint Seminar on Subjective Measures of the Quality of Life, sponsored by the Social Science Research Councils of the United States and Great Britain, Cambridge, England, September 1975); see also his "Poor Measurement of the Right Thing" (Paper presented at the Annual Meetings of the American Statistical Association, Chicago, August 1977).

27. Tom Atkinson, "Is Satisfaction a Good Measure of the Perceived Quality of Life?" (Paper presented at the Annual Meetings of the American Statistical Association, Chicago, August 1977).

28. Frank M. Andrews and Ronald F. Inglehart, "The Structure of Subjective Well-Being in Nine Western Societies" (Paper presented at the Annual Meetings of the American Statistical Association, Chicago, August 1977).

29. U.S. National Criminal Justice Information and Statistics Service, *Criminal Victimization in the United States: A National Crime Panel Survey Report* (issued irregularly). Other periodic publications of the National Crime Panel Survey report on victimization rates in selected cities.

30. National Research Council Panel for the Evaluation of Crime Surveys, *Surveying Crime*, Betty K. Eidson Penick, ed., Maurice E. B. Owens III, assoc. ed. (Washington, D.C.: National Academy of Sciences, 1976).

standing of the social reality of crime as well as of changes in the level of crime in society.

A similar concern for the experiences of individuals is in part responsible for the National Assessment of Educational Progress.[31] For years we have had abundant data on school attendance, school years completed, teacher-pupil ratios, bonded indebtedness of school districts, and the like. But who knew how much the children were learning? The National Assessment now provides this information, obtained by periodically administering a series of tests to probability samples of school children aged 9, 13, and 17, and of young adults and school dropouts. Changes in performance in such tests can tell us about overall changes in how much the students are learning.

The Annual Housing Survey,[32] conducted by the Census Bureau for the Department of Housing and Urban Development, devotes a major fraction of its interviewing effort to investigating how people feel about their housing and neighborhood, in addition to finding out about matters more traditionally investigated, such as structural and financial characteristics of housing. With this survey, we now have a means for learning, on a regular basis, how individuals themselves assess their residential environments.

Replication. Although new data sources such as these promise to improve the measurement of social change in the future, other means must be devised to measure past and current changes. Investigators have therefore adopted a strategy which Duncan calls "replication of baseline studies"[33]—the faithful repetition of important earlier surveys or of questions from earlier surveys. Duncan's own work has illustrated this approach: in 1971, at his request, the Detroit Area Study re-asked a number of survey questions originally asked in the 1950s. The results provide data on changes in the division of responsibility within families, racial attitudes of both whites and blacks, religious participation of the population, and school participation.[34] The General Social Survey of the National Opinion Research Center[35] uses periodic surveys to repeat questions selected from those asked in national surveys extending back to the early 1950s, thereby producing trend information on many significant aspects of the society. Perhaps the most notable example of this technique is the 1973 replication of the 1962 Survey of Occupational Changes in a Generation,[36] conducted by the

31. *Questions and Answers about the National Assessment of Educational Progress* (Denver: Education Commission of the States, June 1974); (National Assessment) *General Information Yearbook* (Washington, D.C.: USGPO, annual).

32. U.S. Bureau of the Census, *Current Housing Reports* (Series H–150); for occupants' subjective assessments of housing conditions, see *Indicators of Housing and Neighborhood Quality*, Annual Housing Report Series H–150–73B (Washington, D.C.: USGPO, 1975).

33. Otis Dudley Duncan, *Toward Social Reporting: Next Steps* (New York: Russell Sage Foundation, 1969).

34. Otis Dudley Duncan, Howard Schuman, and Beverly Duncan, *Social Change in a Metropolitan Community* (New York: Russell Sage Foundation, 1973).

35. National Opinion Research Center, *The NORC General Social Survey, Questions and Answers* (Chicago: March 1973).

36. David L. Featherman and Robert M. Hauser, "Design for a Replicate Study of Social Mobility in the United States," in *Social Indicator Models*, ed. Kenneth C. Land and Seymour Spilerman (New York: Russell Sage Foundation, 1975), pp. 219–51; Featherman and Hauser, "Changes in the Socioeconomic Stratification of the Races, 1962–

Census Bureau for Robert M. Hauser and David L. Featherman. It will result in measures, embedded in models, of trends in inequality of opportunity in the United States and the factors responsible for it.

Access to Data. Many existing data sets could be used for social indicators analysis if they were more readily available to researchers. The archives of the Inter-University Consortium for Political and Social Research provide a useful model of data accessibility.[37] A National Science Foundation grant will permit the existing files of the Current Population Survey to become more readily available for analysis, and a proposal for reconstructing public use samples from the 1940 and 1950 decennial censuses is under consideration.[38] Under a grant from Russell Sage Foundation, the Social Science Research Council's Center for Coordination of Research on Social Indicators, in cooperation with the Roper Public Opinion Research Center, produced an index to repeated questions in the Roper Center's archives, in order to facilitate social indicators uses of the data from early surveys.[39]

Development of models

This emphasis on data may leave the impression that the point of social indicators work is the production of masses of social statistics and nothing more, but this is not correct. Kenneth C. Land would require that the social statistics be placed and interpreted in the context of theories and models: "I propose that the term social indicators refer to social statistics that . . . are components in a social system model (including socio-psychological, economic, demographic, and ecological) or of some particular segment or process thereof. . . . The important point is that the criterion for classifying a social statistic as an indicator is its *informative value* which derives from its empirically verified nexus in a conceptualization of a social process."[40] A less

73," *American Journal of Sociology* 82 (November 1976), pp. 621–51.

37. Inter-University Consortium for Political and Social Research, *Guide to Resources and Services, 1976–1977* (Ann Arbor: University of Michigan Institute for Social Research, 1976). There is a vast literature drawing on the resources of the ICPSR. A recent example, which validates certain of the data as measures of political alienation, is James S. House and William M. Mason, "Political Alienation in America, 1952–1968," *American Sociological Review* 40 (April 1975), pp. 123–47.

38. "Planning, Pretesting, and Monitoring Production of Public Use Sample Files from the 1940 and 1950 Censuses of Population" (Proposal to the National Science Foundation from the University of Wisconsin. Co-principal investigators: Halliman H. Winsborough, Karl E. Taeuber, and Robert M. Hauser [January 1, 1977–December 30, 1980]); "Reconstructing, Redocumenting, Restructuring, and Archiving March Current Population Surveys from 1960 Forward" (Proposal to the National Science Foundation from the University of Michigan. Principal investigator: William M. Mason [Starting date: September 1, 1977]); and William M. Mason, Karl E. Taeuber, and Halliman H. Winsborough, eds., "Old Data for New Research" (Report of a Workshop on Research Opportunities and Issues in the Design and Construction of Public Use Samples from the 1940 and 1950 Censuses and from Current Population Surveys from 1960 forward, held in Madison, Wisconsin, June 28–30, 1976. Madison: University of Wisconsin Center for Demography and Ecology, October 1976).

39. Philip K. Hastings and Jessie C. Southwick, eds., *Survey Data for Trend Analysis: An Index to Repeated Questions in U.S. National Surveys Held by the Roper Public Opinion Research Center* (Williamstown, Mass.: The Roper Public Opinion Research Center, in cooperation with the Social Science Research Council, 1975).

40. Kenneth C. Land, "On the Definition of Social Indicators, *American Sociologist* 6 (November 1971), pp. 322–25.

formal statement would be that the transformation of social statistics into social indicators requires the development of greater understanding of the meaning of changes in indicators and a selectivity—inspired by theory and analysis—which reduces the mass of social statistics to a structured set of series and ultimately to a smaller number of important series worth monitoring. On either view, the development of analytic models is central to the social indicators enterprise.

Land's own work on an aggregate model of the American social process[41] illustrates this aspect of social indicators work. An example of social indicators modeling and analysis work, using crime data, has recently been published by Land and Marcus Felson.[42] Path analytic models of occupational mobility, as developed by Peter Blau and Otis Dudley Duncan, are another.[43] Further examples can be found in *Social Indicator Models*.[44]

A modeling approach closely linked to the notion of social accounting has been developed by Richard Stone under the auspices of the United Nations Statistical Office and the Conference of European Statisticians.[45] Stone's work applies notions of input-output analysis to the description of the processes by which people move into and out of various significant social states. The scheme is both a way of organizing data and an approach to analysis, particularly in a life cycle framework. Coleman has applied related models to a study of the achievement of occupational status by blacks.[46]

SOCIAL REPORTING

The full value of social indicators will not be realized if the results of data collection and analysis remain known only to professional social scientists, technical specialists, and other cognoscenti. Since Ogburn's time, social reporting has been central to social indicators work. In recent years, at least 29 nations have issued or have in preparation statistical compliations which in some sense are social indicators reports.[47] *Social Indicators, 1976*, like its pred-

41. Kenneth C. Land and Marcus Felson, "Towards a Macro Social Indicator Model of American Society: 1947–1974" (Paper presented at the Annual Meetings of the American Sociological Association, San Francisco, August 25–29, 1975).

42. Kenneth C. Land and Marcus Felson, "A General Framework for Building Dynamic Macro Social Indicator Models: Including an Analysis of Changes in Crime Rates and Police Expenditures," *American Journal of Sociology* 82 (November 1976), pp. 565–604.

43. Peter M. Blau and Otis Dudley Duncan, *The American Occupational Structure* (New York: Wiley, 1967).

44. Kenneth C. Land and Seymour Spilerman, eds., *Social Indicator Models* (New York: Russell Sage Foundation, 1975).

45. United Nations Department of Economic and Social Affairs, *Towards a System of Social and Economic Statistics*, Studies in Methods Series F, no. 18 (New York: United Nations, 1975); Richard Stone, "Transition and Admission Models in Social Indicator Analysis," in Land and Spilerman, eds., *Social Indicator Models*, pp. 253–300.

46. James S. Coleman, "Analysis of Occupational Mobility by Models of Occupational Flow," in Land and Spilerman, eds., *Social Indicator Models*, pp. 319–34.

47. United Nations Statistical Office, *Report on National Practices and Plans in Reporting Statistics of Levels of Living*, March 1, 1976, document ESA/STAT/AC.4/2. The list of country reports is reproduced in the introduction to *Social Indicators, 1976*. Overviews of social indicators work in several European countries are presented in articles by Stein Ringen, "Social Indicators Research in Nordic Countries," (March 1976) and Wolfgang Zapf, "International, Public, and Private Actors in Social Reporting," (September 1976), in *Social Indicators Newsletter*.

ecessor volume, *Social Indicators, 1973*,[48] is the American equivalent, produced by the Office of Management and Budget. Numerous more narrowly focused efforts have also appeared: the National Science Board produces a biennial, *Science Indicators*; the Department of Housing and Urban Development, an annual report on *Indicators of Housing and Neighborhood Quality*; the National Center for Health Statistics, *Health: United States*; and the National Center for Education Statistics, an annual report on the *Condition of Education. STATUS*, published from July to October 1976 by the Bureau of the Census and the Office of Management and Budget, was a short-lived experiment with monthly social reporting. All these reports are government products, but such reports are also produced in the private sector, an excellent example of the latter being a recent report about West Germany.[49]

The social reporting process has been the subject of much analysis and comment. The Social Science Research Council's Center for Coordination of Research on Social Indicators organized a critical review of *Social Indicators, 1973*,[50] and Statistics Canada organized a symposium on its social indicators report, *Perspective Canada*. There have been several sessions at meetings of academic professional societies devoted to commentary on the various American social indicator reports.[51] The National Science Foundation's program of research support for social indicators has funded a project designed to improve graphical presentation and communication of statistical information,[52] and has provided partial support for the publication of this volume of THE ANNALS.

Social Indicators, 1976

The publication with which this special issue of THE ANNALS is concerned, *Social Indicators, 1976*, is a report on "current social conditions and trends in the United States," and most of this volume is devoted to discussion of conditions and trends. But *Social Indicators, 1976* may also be viewed as an indicator of current conditions and trends in social indicator reporting and, to an extent, of the state of social indicators. We will examine it from this perspective, though we are handicapped by not having seen the final version, but only the table of contents, the introductory material, and two chapters in draft.

Social Indicators, 1976 is typical of government social indicators reports in that it consists mainly of tabular or graphical displays of standard social statistics, with mini-

48. U.S. Office of Management and Budget, *Social Indicators, 1973* (Washington, D.C.: USGPO, 1974).

49. Eike Ballerstedt und Wolfgang Glatzer, unter Mitwirkung von Karl-Ulrich Mayer und Wolfgang Zapf, *Sociologischer Almanach: Handbuch Gesellschaftspolitischer Daten und Indikatoren für die Bundesrepublik Deutschland* (Frankfurt: Herder and Herder, 1975).

50. Roxann A. Van Dusen, ed., *Social Indicators 1973: A Review Symposium* (New York: Social Science Research Council, 1974).

51. The most recent example is a session on social indicators, chaired by Abbott Ferriss, at the 1977 Annual Meetings of the American Sociological Association held in Chicago in September 1977. The papers reviewed *Health United States, 1975, The Condition of Education, 1976, Science Indicators, 1974*, and the criminal justice chapter of *Social Indicators, 1976*.

52. Barry M. Fienberg and Carolyn A. Franklin, eds. *Social Graphics Bibliography* (Washington, D.C.: Bureau of Social Science Research, 1975).

mal commentary. The questions to be considered are the adequacy of the data selection, the appropriateness of the treatment of the data, the usefulness of the overall organization, and the sufficiency of the commentary.

Data Selection. Like its predecessor, *Social Indicators, 1976* relies mainly on standard statistical products of the federal government. But as Otis Dudley Duncan noted, the 1973 volume also drew extensively on data that were either nonfederal, nonstandard, or both.[53] The new volume continues and extends this practice, drawing on the results of social science research, for example the Michigan research on subjective perceptions of the quality of life (Introduction), the General Social Survey data on attitudes toward marriage and divorce (chapter 2), James N. Morgan's longitudinal studies of poverty (chapter 8), John Robinson's data on time use (chapter 10), and the measures developed by Robert M. Hauser and David L. Featherman of trends in occupational mobility in the United States (chapter 11).

The new volume has a less constricted focus than its predecessor. *Social Indicators, 1973* selected data according to two main criteria: "That the indicators measure individual and family (rather than institutional or governmental) well-being and that they measure end products of, rather than inputs into, social systems." The volume was "restricted almost entirely to data about objective conditions."[54] *Social Indicators, 1976,* however, incorporates limited data on "system performance" and takes advantage of the increased availability of data on public perceptions.

These are encouraging developments, and they are perhaps in part attributable to a subtle shift in the definition of social indicators which has occurred between *Social Indicators, 1973* and *Social Indicators, 1976*. In the earlier volume, the notion of indicators was explicitly linked to that of "social objectives": "Ideally . . . an indicator would reveal . . . the status of the population in relation to a perceived social objective. . . ."[55] This parallels the idea of indicators as "direct measure[s] of welfare" found in *Toward a Social Report*, and it raises some difficult questions. For example, does a rising divorce rate move us closer to or further from a social objective? Divorce, after all, "may be an undesirable disruption in the continuity of development for the child of the marriage while it signifies the freedom of the spouses to terminate an unrewarding relationship."[56] *Social Indicators, 1976* removes the constraint of direct normative relevance and defines indicators simply as "statistics or statistical measures . . . which indicate the general status of the population with respect to certain aspects" of "certain topics of broad social interest. . . ." It has therefore become legitimate to include a broader range of statistical material concerning social conditions and trends.

Treatment of Data. To the professional social scientist, the language of tables and charts is familiar and easily understood, but this re-

53. Otis Dudley Duncan, "Developing Social Indicators," *Proceedings of the National Academy of Sciences* 71 (December 1974), pp. 5096–5102.

54. U.S. Office of Management and Budget, *Social Indicators, 1973*, p. xiii.

55. Ibid.

56. Otis Dudley Duncan, "Social Indicators, 1973: Report on a Conference," in Van Dusen, ed., *SI'73: Review Symposium*, p. 9.

port is intended for a broader audience. *Social Indicators, 1976,* unlike its predecessor, contains a useful section on how to read statistical tables and charts. It also provides considerably more discussion of problems of data quality and their implications for interpretation of data than did the earlier volume. This is progress, but we are still a long way from the "detailed discussion of the error structure associated with each of the indicators reported" advocated by Stephen E. Fienberg and Leo A. Goodman.[57]

Many of the indicators in *Social Indicators, 1976* are highly aggregated, referring to the entire population. Understanding of social conditions is increased when the data are disaggregated by characteristics of the population. Like its predecessor, and like American governmental statistical reports generally, *Social Indicators, 1976* disaggregates most frequently by age, sex, and color, and rarely in any other way. Natalie Rogoff Ramsøy[58] has noted that this practice contrasts with that of European reports, which frequently disaggregate data by some indicator of socioeconomic status as well—social class, social group, or occupation. The difference, as she points out, has consequences. Color and sex are relatively immutable characteristics of individuals, and age changes only at its own pace, beyond the reach of human intervention. The categories of disaggregation used by the Europeans, in contrast, embody the structural features of a society and invite speculation on "how things might be different if structural features of society were to change—occupational distributions, the relative positions of diverse occupational categories, productivity or prestige differentials, and so on."[59] Dynamics that work through the changing social definitions of fixed biological characteristics are less easy to visualize when examining charts and tables.

The choice of categories for disaggregation was determined not by the predilections of the editor of *SI, 76,* but rather by the normal operations of the federal statistical system, and it is to that system that calls for change must be addressed. If the claim to be working toward a system of social indicators announced in *Social Indicators, 1973* means anything, surely it suggests the desirability of altering standard statistical practice so as to incorporate disaggregations that tell us more than the current ones do about the nature of the society, how it has changed, and how it might be different in the future.

Overall Organization. Social Indicators, 1976 follows the by now conventional practice of national social indicator reports of dividing the full array of social conditions into a number of different "major social areas." With minor differences in titles, all the chapters of *Social Indicators, 1973* appear again, and there are three additions: the family, social security and welfare, and social mobility and participation. The additions, perhaps a result of the altered definition of social indicators, are to be applauded. But the conventional mode of organization, with chapters for the most part reflecting the policy

57. Stephen E. Fienberg and Leo A. Goodman, "Statistical Considerations," in Van Dusen, ed., *SI'73: Review Symposium*, p. 82.

58. Natalie Rogoff Ramsøy, "Social Indicators in the United States and Europe: Comments on Five Country Reports," in Van Dusen, ed., *SI'73: Review Symposium*, p. 47.

59. Ibid.

concerns and even the functional organization of governments, has its limitations even when so expanded. It serves to provide useful information in categories we are all used to. But it does not help us to develop understanding of social process, alert us to relationships across social areas, or introduce us to new concepts. Perhaps alternative organizational schemes for social indicators reports should be considered.

Within social areas, indicators have been organized by "social concerns," so that the volume has a residue of normative flavor and a sense of policy relatedness. The focus on social concerns presents some difficulties. Some social concerns are no doubt continuing, but others come and go. What is salient today may not be so next year, and vice versa. If only statistics related to current social concerns are reported, emerging problems that are likely to become matters of social concern may remain invisible until too late. A volume organized around social concerns will slight matters which either are not subject to policy manipulation or are not yet matters of concern, but which are important to an understanding of social process and change. Again, the method of organization is convenient, conventional, and useful. But it would be worth considering some alternatives.

Commentary. A study of the use of *Social Indicators, 1973* by federal executives found that "Practically all respondents stated that the *SI'73* information was stark . . . and that the report needed commentary and interpretation to increase its usefulness. . . ."[60] *Social Indicators, 1976* gives the reader more guidance than did the earlier volume. There are now brief chapter introductions which comment on inadequacies in the data, offer cautions on interpretation, and provide limited summaries of findings. And the reader who wishes to pursue matters further is referred to a list of references.

What *Social Indicators, 1976* does not do is go beyond general descriptions of data characteristics and limitations to draw specific conclusions about the trend evidence; explain why a series behaves as it does, and how this knowledge affects interpretation; highlight important relationships among series; and suggest the consequences that may reasonably be attributable to changes in a series. Data rarely speak for themselves, and this volume of THE ANNALS has been prepared in explicit recognition of this fact. But it is awkward to so separate data and analysis; *Social Indicators, 1976* would be a more useful volume if it contained more than the very limited text it now contains.

Improving social reporting

While *Social Indicators, 1976* is a useful and important publication, future social indicator reports should be better. Two kinds of developments must occur if we are to have better reports in the future.

First, there must be further development of social indicators. As the discussions in this volume make clear, we do not now have all the data required for description and analysis of important aspects of

60. Nathan Caplan and Eugenia Barton, "Social Indicators 1973: A Study of the Relationship Between the Power of Information and Utilization by Federal Executives," mimeographed (Ann Arbor: University of Michigan Institute for Social Research, 1976), pp. 22–23.

social conditions and trends. New data are necessary. Beyond that, however, social statistics must be transformed into good social indicators, through analysis, modeling, and use of the data. What is needed is the scientific work that alone can produce the infrastructure of consensual meaning about particular series that makes their presentation a self-evident necessity and their behavior over time laden with meaning for other related aspects of the society.

Second, there must be further development of the process of social reporting. *Social Indicators, 1976* represents the conventional format, and we have sketched its inadequacies. Two should be emphasized: First, the tables and charts of the conventional format do not communicate a scientific understanding of social change; there must be experimentation with ways of communicating the results of social scientific research on these matters to a broad audience; second, the overall organization of such volumes may not be ideal. There should be further experimentation with alternative forms of organization—forms which reflect a social scientific understanding of society rather than the administrative organization of government, and which link, rather than compartmentalize, social areas.

CONCLUSION

Considerable progress has been made since the mid-1960s toward achieving the diverse goals of the social indicators movement. The contrast between the statement of needs in *Toward a Social Report* and the solid accomplishments of *Social Indicators, 1976*, particularly when the latter volume is read together with this special issue of THE ANNALS, makes clear just how far we have come. But it should not be expected that we could move, in a single decade, from calls for a system of social indicators which would accomplish for the broad spectrum of social life more or less what economic indicators have accomplished for that relatively narrow area of the society, to the full blown operation of such a system. As de Neufville notes, the development of social indicators is a far more lengthy and complex process than many who advocate new indicators recognize.[61]

Social Indicators, 1976, then, is a progress report on both American society and the development of social indicators and social reporting. Both have a long way to go.

61. Judith Innes de Neufville, *Social Indicators and Public Policy: Interactive Processes of Design and Application* (New York: Elsevier, 1975), p. 10.

Table H
FEELINGS ABOUT PRESENT LIFE: 1971

Range of Feelings	1	2	3	4	5	6	7	Total	Mean	N
Boring to interesting	2%	2	6	16	17	21	36	100%	5.52	2151
Miserable to enjoyable	1%	1	4	13	16	27	38	100%	5.74	2147
Hard to easy	8%	7	11	29	15	13	17	100%	4.43	2149
Useless to worthwhile	2%	2	3	10	13	24	46	100%	5.87	2146
Lonely to friendly	3%	2	4	10	11	21	49	100%	5.85	2144
Empty to full	1%	2	4	12	15	22	44	100%	5.79	2143
Discouraging to hopeful	3%	2	3	11	13	23	45	100%	5.77	2146
Tied down to free	5%	4	6	17	12	20	36	100%	5.31	2148
Disappointing to rewarding	3%	2	4	13	16	25	37	100%	5.60	2148
Doesn't give me much chance to brings out the best in me	3%	3	6	21	18	23	26	100%	5.18	2147

Source: Angus Campbell, Philip E. Converse, and Willard L. Rodgers, *The Quality of American Life*, New York: Russell Sage Foundation, 1976, table 2-2, p. 38, (c) used by permission.

Note: Respondents were asked to check one of a row of seven boxes between each adjective pair. The percent checking either of the two boxes nearest the left-hand adjective are so classified; those checking either of the two boxes nearest the right-hand adjective are so classified; those checking any of the three middle boxes were classified in the "in between" category.

Chart H

Social Indicators, 1976—Introduction

FEELINGS ABOUT PRESENT LIFE, 1971

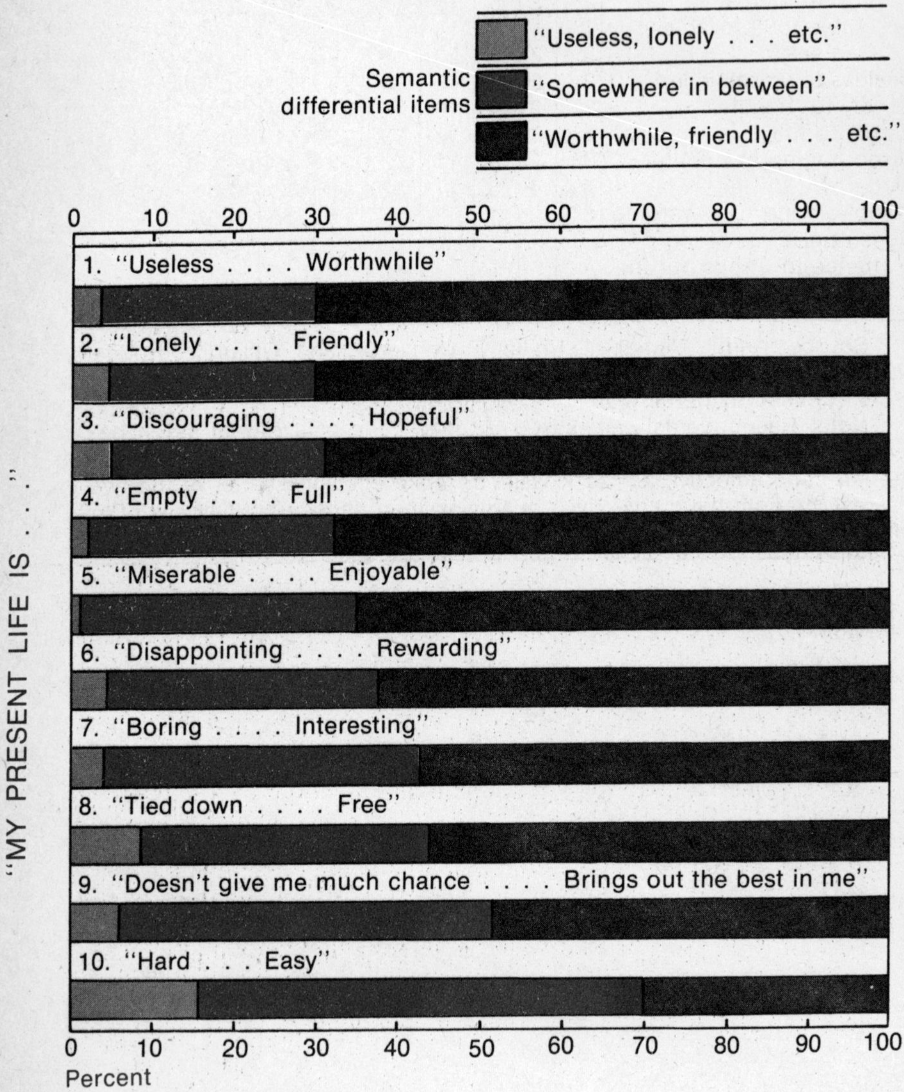

Source: see table H

Table K
MEANS AND DISTRIBUTIONS ON IMPORTANCE RATINGS OF DOMAINS, 1971

	Total	Extremely important 1	Very important 2	Quite important 3	Somewhat important 4	Not at all important 5	Mean	Proportion naming this as one of two most important domains
Being in good health and in good physical condition	100%	70%	24%	5%	1%	—%	1.37	35%
A happy marriage	100	74	17	3	2	4	1.44	55
A good family life—having family members you can enjoy being with	100	67	24	6	2	1	1.46	36
A good country to live in—a country with a good government	100	62	26	8	3	1	1.54	17
Having good friends, and the right number of friends	100	34	36	19	10	1	2.08	6
A house or apartment that you like to live in	100	35	34	19	10	2	2.10	8
An interesting job	100	38	32	13	7	10	2.19	9
A city or place where you like to live	100	28	40	20	9	3	2.21	3
Having a strong religious faith	100	38	22	16	16	8	2.35	23
Things you like to do when you are not working—hobbies, and things like that	100	14	28	28	25	5	2.79	2
A large bank account, so that you don't have to worry about money	100	16	19	17	30	8	2.94	6
Organizations you want to belong to	100%	3%	8%	13%	35%	41%	4.01	—%

Source: Angus Campbell, Philip Converse, and Willard L. Rodgers, *The Quality of American Life: Perceptions, Evaluations, and Satisfactions*, table 3-4, (c) 1976 by Russell Sage Foundation, New York, used by permission.
— Represents zero.

Chart K

Social Indicators, 1976—Introduction

Importance Ratings of Domains: 1971

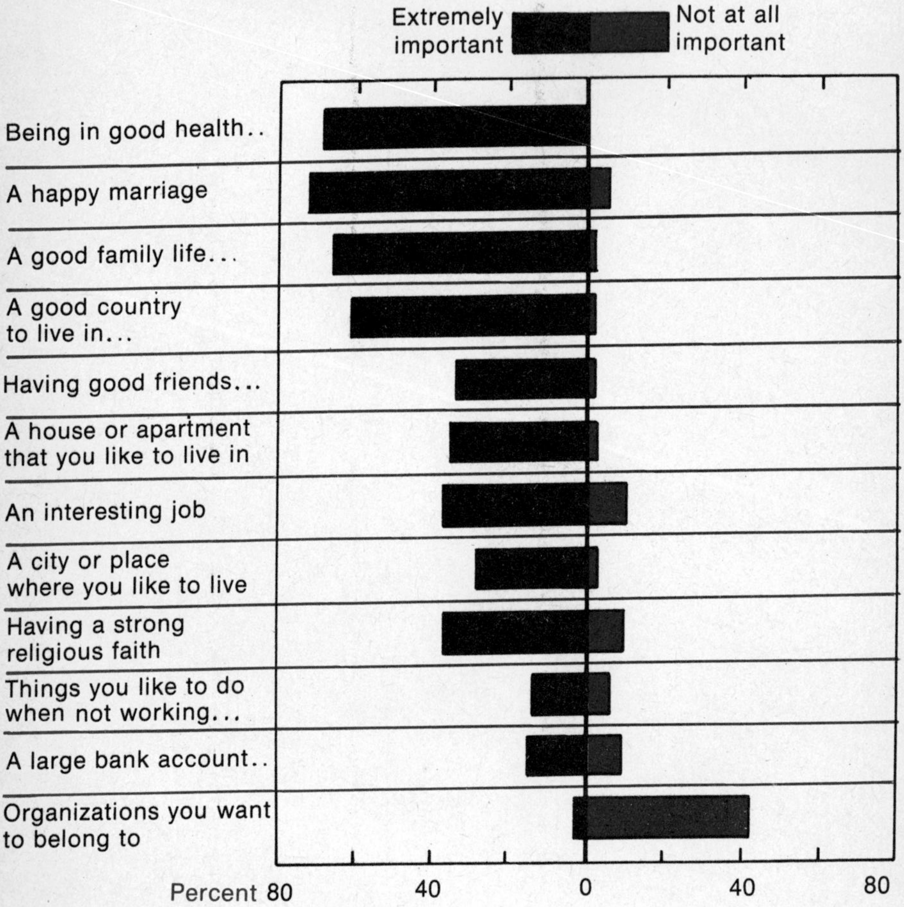

Source: see table K

Table U

ESTIMATED POPULATION AND PER CAPITA GROSS NATIONAL PRODUCT (GNP), MID-1973 AND PER CAPITA ENERGY CONSUMPTION, 1972, SELECTED COUNTRIES

Region and country		Population (mid-1973) in 1,000's	Per capita G.N.P. (mid-1973) (U.S. $)	Per capita energy consumption (1972)[1]
AFRICA	Nigeria	71,262	$ 210	66
	Egypt	35,619	250	324
	Ethiopia	26,550	90	35
	South Africa	24,265	1,050	2,770
	Zaire	23,438	140	86
ASIA	China	811,350	270	567
	India	581,911	120	186
	Indonesia	124,415	130	133
	Japan	108,350	3,630	3,251
	Bangladesh	74,000	80	32
	Pakistan	66,230	120	158
	Philippines	40,219	280	311
	Thailand	39,400	270	305
	S. Korea	32,905	400	827
	Iran	32,136	870	954
EUROPE	U.S.S.R.	249,750	2,030	4,767
	Germany (Fed. Rep.)	61,970	5,320	5,396
	United Kingdom	56,000	3,060	5,398
	Italy	54,890	2,450	2,796
	France	52,160	4,540	4,153
	Turkey	37,930	600	564
	Spain	34,740	1,710	1,765
	Poland	33,360	2,090	4,556
	Yugoslavia	20,960	1,060	1,610
	Hungary	10,430	1,850	3,279
	Greece	8,930	1,870	1,607
	Sweden	8,140	5,910	5,739
N. AMERICA	United States	210,400	6,200	11,611
	Canada	22,130	5,450	10,757
L. AMERICA	Brzail	101,051	760	532
	Mexico	56,047	890	1,318
	Argentina	24,282	1,640	1,728
	Colombia	22,500	440	610
OCEANIA	Australia	13,130	4,350	5,701
	New Zealand	2,960	3,680	2,887
	Papua, New Guinea	2,596	410	188

Source: World Bank, *World Bank Atlas*, *1975* (for population and per capita GNP); The Environmental Fund, *World Population Estimates*, *1975* (for per capita energy consumption).

[1] Quantities of energy consumption are in kilograms of coal equivalent. Data from United Nations *Statistical Yearbook, 1973*, table 137, (c) used by permission.

Chart U

Social Indicators, 1976—Introduction

ESTIMATED PER CAPITA GROSS NATIONAL PRODUCT (GNP) AND PER CAPITA ENERGY CONSUMPTION, SELECTED COUNTRIES, 1972–1973

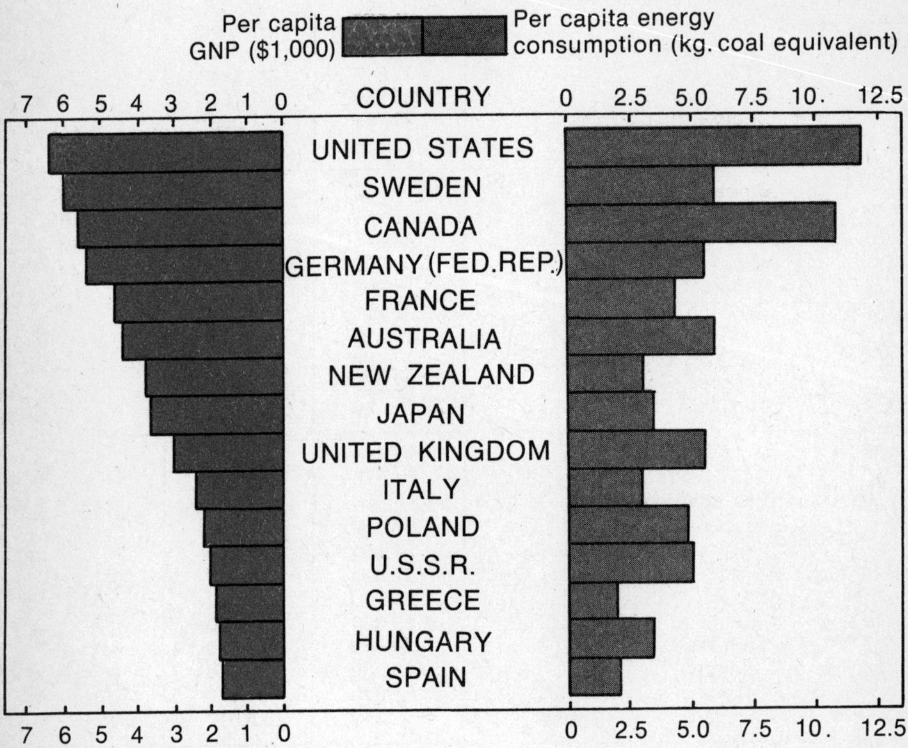

Source: see table U

ANNALS, AAPSS, 435, Jan. 1978

Getting and Spending

By SHELDON H. DANZIGER AND ROBERT J. LAMPMAN

ABSTRACT: The selected time series on income and consumption appear to give a clear picture of postwar change along the following lines: family incomes have grown substantially; consumption patterns have shifted away from necessities; income inequality has not increased; and poverty and intergroup income differences have declined. However, the broad indicators on which these conclusions are based do not illuminate the processes by which income is generated, consumption is shared, and costs are borne. The authors raise a set of questions related to the measurement and interpretation of the indicators. The answers to these questions suggest that a time series does not speak for itself and that a careful analysis of postwar changes awaits specification of the socioeconomic processes that generate the indicators.

Sheldon H. Danziger is Assistant Professor of Social Work at the University of Wisconsin-Madison where he is also a Research Associate of the Institute for Research on Poverty. His primary fields of research are the distribution of income, human resources, and public finance. His recent articles have analyzed the effects of government programs on the trend in poverty and income inequality.

Robert J. Lampman is Vilas Professor of Economics at the University of Wisconsin-Madison where he is also a Fellow of the Institute for Research on Poverty. He is the author of The Share of Top Wealth-holders in National Wealth *and* Ends and Means of Reducing Income Poverty. *He has also been a Research Associate at the National Bureau of Economic Research and a staff member of the Council of Economic Advisers.*

MOST presentations of social indicators put special emphasis on total money income received, and consumption outlays made, by households. This information about income and consumption constitutes the major overlap of social accounts and national economic accounts.

FIRST IMPRESSIONS

On first reading, the selected series on income and consumption seem to give a clear picture of postwar change along the following lines.

1. The median total money income, adjusted for inflation, rose by 88 percent for families and 104 percent for unrelated individuals. This would suggest that people are, on average, about twice as well-off now, in economic terms, as they were in 1947.

2. The pattern of consumption has altered over time, with the typical family spending a smaller proportion of its income on food and clothing and more on other items. This would seem to indicate that most people have more money to spend on nonessential or discretionary items, and to confirm the impression we get from income data that living standards are indeed rising.

3. The inequality of money income is slightly smaller than it was, that is, the top fifth of families now gets a somewhat smaller share of the national total, and the bottom fifth gets a somewhat larger share. The same change is apparent for the top and bottom fifth of unrelated individuals. This would seem to indicate that the disparity in living conditions and in opportunities between rich and poor is at least not increasing.

4. The number of people counted as having total money income below the official poverty lines—which are adjusted for price change and vary by family size—has fallen substantially. In 1947, 32 percent of the population was below these lines, but in 1976, only 12 percent was. Again, the impression is one of improvement in economic well-being.

5. Certain long-standing class or group differences in total money income were modified during this period. For example, the median income for nonwhite families increased from 52 to 62 percent of that of white families, and the median income of southerners, which used to be 78 percent of that of the nation, is now 89 percent. These examples support the impression of a trend toward equalization of income, and of consumption and satisfactions thereof.

Are these five impressions warranted, or do they fall apart when tested against other economic and social data? Are money income and consumer spending reliable indicators of changes that have normative significance, or do we need a broader set of indicators that reflect the process whereby production is managed, income is generated, consumption is shared, and costs are borne? In this paper, we seek to illuminate these questions and to point out some possible improvements in the reporting of income and consumption status. We proceed by asking how the sources, uses, and sharing of income changed during the period 1947 to 1975.

ARE PEOPLE TWICE AS WELL OFF NOW AS THEY WERE IN 1947?

"Total money income," as defined by the Bureau of the Census, includes money payments in return for the supply of work or the use of property, government cash transfers, such as social insurance and public assistance, and private cash transfers, such as pensions and alimony. This definition is both narrower and broader than what some would consider ideal. It is narrower in the sense that it leaves out undistributed corporate profits and their resultant capital gains and losses. It also leaves out, as its title implies, nonmoney income. Among the more important items of nonmoney income are imputed rent from owner-occupied housing, do-it-yourself home production and leisure. Also important are employer-paid fringe benefits, such as health insurance, and government-financed noncash benefits, such as education, health care, and food stamps. The total money income definition is broader than ideal in the sense that it makes no deduction for taxes paid, contributions made to other families, or certain expenses of earning income, such as payments for child care.

In table 1 we show some of the relationships between total money income and other concepts of income. Total money income is represented in this table by items 1, 2, 3, 8, and 9. It takes no account of nonmoney primary income. Most awkwardly, it combines "redistributed income" with "primary income," without accounting for payment for the redistribution.[1] By definition, redistribution, or transferring, means that what is received by some is given by others, and the giving up is not reflected in total money income.

The ratio of the 1975 to the 1947 amount of each component of primary and redistributed income is shown in the far column of the table. To the extent that redistributed money income has increased faster than primary income in money and nonmoney forms—and that it has is shown by the higher ratios for items 8 and 9 than for items 1–7—total money income overstates the gain in "income." At the same time, total money income does not reflect the total redistribution of income that occurs because it ignores nonmoney transfers, indicated by items 10 and 11. These transfers increase the consumption possibilities of households and should be accounted for in measuring the median level and distribution of income.

To know whether the median household is twice as well off now as it was in 1947, we need to know not only about taxes and in-kind transfers, but also about possibly offsetting reductions in home production and leisure (item 6—for which reliable estimates are unavailable) which result when work effort increases. Because of the expansion in the average number of earners per family (from 1.5 in 1954 to 1.7 in 1975), and the failure to account for this additional work effort, the trend in median income overstates the growth in economic well-being. For example, both a family whose income has doubled because the wage of a single earner has doubled, and a family whose income has doubled because an additional earner is now employed at the initial wage, experience equal increases in money income. But the second family had to reduce its leisure and/or consumption of home-

1. For a more complete discussion of this point, see Robert J. Lampman, "Social Accounting for Transfer," in *The Personal Distribution of Income and Wealth*, ed. James D. Smith (New York: National Bureau of Economic Research, 1975), pp. 31–44.

TABLE 1

SOURCES OF INCOME, 1947 AND 1975

	1947 (BILLIONS OF DOLLARS)	1975	RATIO OF 1975 TO 1947
PRIMARY INCOME			
Money			
1. Wages and salaries	$ 191	$ 807	4.2
2. Proprietors' incomes	35	90	2.6
3. Property income	17	152	8.9
Nonmoney			
4. Employer contributions to public and private transfers	10*	97	9.7
5. Net imputed rent of owner-occupied homes	4	13	3.2
6. Home production and leisure	n.a.	n.a.	
7. Corporate profits less dividends	25	70	3.1
REDISTRIBUTED INCOME (financed largely out of primary income)			
Money			
8. Public cash transfers	12	175	14.6
9. Private cash transfers (pensions and annuities)	1*	13	13.0
Nonmoney			
10. Public transfers (medical care and education)	7	133	19.0
11. Private transfers (employer paid health insurance)	3*	26	8.7

SOURCES: U.S. Department of Commerce, *The National Income and Product Accounts of the United States, 1929–1965* (Washington, D.C.: USGPO, 1966); U.S. Department of Commerce, *Survey of Current Business*, vol. 56, no. 11 (Washington, D.C.: USGPO, November 1976); Emil Sunley, "Employee Benefits and Transfer Payments," in *Comprehensive Income Taxation*, ed. Joseph Pechman (Washington, D.C.: The Brookings Institution, 1977).

*Estimates for 1955 by Emil Sunley.

produced goods and services when the second family member began working. In this example (and in actuality), the failure to measure the reduction in a source of nonmoney income—leisure and/or home production—means that economic well-being grows at a slower rate than money income.

On the other hand, it can be argued that median total money income understates the gain in per capita income since household size has been declining. There are now 2.7 times as many one-person households as there were in 1947, but only 1.2 times as many six-person households. Because median family income does not adjust for the composition of families, the trend in family income understates the trend in economic well-being.[2]

2. Some authors have argued that the changing composition of living units results from changes in available sources of income. In particular, they assert that the growth of government transfers has caused some families, that otherwise would have remained intact, to break apart. See Alice Rivlin, "Income Distribution: Can Economists Help?" *American Economic Review* 65 (May 1975), pp. 1–15; and Simon Kuznets, "Demographic Aspects of the Distribution of Income Among

TABLE 2

SELECTED USES OF INCOME, 1947 AND 1975

	1947 (BILLIONS OF DOLLARS)	1975	RATIO OF 1975 TO 1947
Purchases by households			
1. Food	$ 52	$ 210	4.0
2. Clothing	19	70	3.7
3. Housing services	12	137	11.4
4. Medical care	5	48	9.6
5. Education	1	14	14.0
6. Other	67	458	6.8
Nonmarketed consumption			
7. Net housing services of owner-occupied homes	4	13	3.3
8. Home production and leisure	n.a.	n.a.	
Purchases of medical care and education by governments and employers			
Governments			
9. Medical care	2	51	25.5
10. Education	5	82	16.4
Employers			
11. Medical care*	2*	23	11.5
Savings by households	7	84	12.0

SOURCES: Same as for table 1.
* Estimate for 1955.

Assume, for example, that there are two families. The first is composed of a couple with two children; a single member earns $5,000. The second is composed of a couple with two children and the aged parents of the family head; a single member earns $4,000, and the aged couple receives $1,000 of social security benefits. Median family income is $5,000. Now suppose that benefits are raised to $2,000, and that as a result, the aged parents can afford an apartment of their own. The behavioral response to the increased income actually lowers median family income to $4,000—there are now three families, with incomes of $2,000, $4,000, and $5,000. The increased social security benefits increase economic well-being, but produce a spurious decline in the economic indicator.

Families: Recent Trends in the United States," in *Econometrics and Economic Theory*, ed. Willy Sellekaerts (London: MacMillan Press, 1974), pp. 223–47.

How Has the Pattern of Consumption Changed?

Table 2 offers a broad view of how consumption patterns have changed in the postwar period. The standard method for reporting these changes confines attention to purchases by households, as shown in items 1–6. But total consumption by households exceeds what they personally purchase, since governments and employers also make purchases on behalf of households. Because these purchases are concentrated on a narrower range of goods and services, the actual distribution of consumption among categories differs from the distribution shown in items 1–6.

TABLE 3

PERCENTAGE OF POPULATION IN INCOME POVERTY, BEFORE AND AFTER TRANSFERS, SELECTED YEARS

	1947	1965	1976*
1. Before Transfer		21	21
2. After Cash Transfers	32	16	11
3. After Cash and In-kind Transfers		12	7

SOURCES: 1976: Harold Watts and Felicity Skidmore, "An Update of the Poverty Picture Plus a New Look at Relative Tax Burdens," *Focus: Institute for Research on Poverty Newsletter*, vol. 2, no. 1 (Fall 1977).
1965: Robert D. Plotnick and Felicity Skidmore, Progress Against Poverty (New York: Academic Press, 1975).
1947: Council of Econonic Advisers, *"The Problem of Poverty in America"* in Economic Report of the President (Washington, D.C.: USGPO, 1964).
*Fiscal year.

Items 9, 10, and 11 reveal the magnitude and growing importance of such purchases for medical care and education. A more comprehensive reporting (items 4 plus 9 plus 11; and 5 plus 10) underlines the significance of the shift toward spending on medical care and education. The increased importance of government spending for medical care suggests that the distribution of this service may have become less unequal among income classes.

HAS THE DISTRIBUTION OF INCOME BECOME LESS UNEQUAL?

As we mentioned earlier, the top fifth of families now gets a somewhat smaller share, and the bottom fifth gets a somewhat larger share of the national total of money income. Whether this trend remains after consideration of all taxes, contributions, and the receipt of nonmoney income is subject to some dispute. There is consensus, however, that these aggregate indicators obscure the processes that generate inequality. Increased government transfer payments and the earnings of married women contributed to a reduction in family income inequality. The declining progressivity in the tax system, increased inequality in the earnings of men, and the increase in the percentage of households headed by the young, the old, and women all contributed to increased inequality.[3] The stability of the trend results from these offsetting changes in socioeconomic relationships.

HOW MUCH HAS INCOME POVERTY BEEN REDUCED?

The official indicator for income poverty is total money income adjusted for family size. The guidelines for each family size are based on an arbitrarily selected base of $3,000 of 1962 purchasing power, or about $6,000 at today's prices. Table 3, line 2 shows that progress against poverty, thus defined, has been made, with the percentage of the population that is poor falling by about one percentage point a year up to the middle 1960s, and by about one-half a percentage point a year since then.

3. See Morgan Reynolds and Eugene Smolensky, *Public Expenditures, Taxes, and the Distribution of Income* (New York: Academic Press, 1977); Michael Taussig and Sheldon Danziger, *Conference on the Trend in Income Inequality in the U.S.* (Madison: Institute for Research on Poverty, 1977).

The slowdown in progress against poverty in recent years is explained in part by the failure of pretransfer poverty to fall at all after 1965 (see line 1). This concept is based upon what is called primary money income in table 1. We get another impression of progress against poverty, however, if we look at money income plus in-kind transfers (line 3), which shows that if food stamps, housing subsidies, and medical care are counted as income, then the frequency of poverty may be said to have declined sharply in the last decade.[4]

Poverty has declined for most socioeconomic groups, but there are significant variations in the rates of decline. Persons living in families with male heads (especially black male heads) or with aged heads, and persons living in the South have experienced the largest reductions in poverty. The group with the highest incidence of poverty, persons living with female heads, has experienced the smallest decline, despite increased government assistance.

HAVE LONG-STANDING INTERGROUP INCOME DIFFERENCES NARROWED?

Total money income measures indicate a narrowing of the difference between black and white families. Most of this narrowing occurred prior to 1967. However, once again the aggregate statistics obscure underlying changes. Consider the data in table 4 on the ratio of black median family income to white median family income for 1967 and 1976. The first row in panel 1 reveals that for all families the ratio remained at 59 percent during this period—the economic status of blacks did not improve relative to that of whites. But the rest of the data reveal that this stability results from two dramatic, but counterbalancing, changes in the relative situation of black families. First, black families with male heads gained relative to similar white families; the ratio of medians increased from 67 to 78 percent. Had other factors remained constant, the ratio of medians for all families would have increased. Second, the percentage of all black families with female heads increased rapidly from 28 percent to 37 percent. Had other factors remained constant, the ratio of medians for all families would have decreased. The ratio of medians remained constant only because of the coincidence that these two effects exactly offset each other.

But even the disaggregation shown in table 4 does not provide an answer to the more basic question: Has the economic well-being of black families increased relative to that of white families? Such an answer requires a model that can explain the changes both in incomes and family types. For example, if poor black males deserted their families so that their children could receive welfare benefits, then the median income of black families would rise relative to that of white families. Similarly, if black men received higher wage increases than white men, the ratio of the medians would rise. Which of these (or other) hypotheses explains the trend in the ratio can only be ascertained with a well-specified model.

Understanding the trend in other intergroup differences also requires

4. Since expenditures for in-kind transfers were small in 1947, we estimate that the entry in line 3 for that year would have been about 30 percent. Line 3, then, gives an impression of a substantial decline in poverty over the entire period.

TABLE 4

MEDIAN INCOME OF BLACK AND WHITE FAMILIES, 1967 AND 1976

	1967	1976
1. Ratio of Black to White Median Family Income:		
All families	59%	59%
Families with male head	67	78
Families with female head	62	62
2. Percentage of Families with Female Heads:		
Black families	28%	37%
White families	9	11

SOURCES: 1967: U.S. Bureau of the Census, *The Social and Economic Status of the Black Population in the United States, 1974,* Current Population Reports, Series P–23, no. 54 (Washington, D.C.: USGPO, 1975).
1976: U.S. Bureau of the Census, *Money Income and Poverty Status of Families and Persons in the United States*, 1976, Current Population Reports, Series P-60, no. 107 (Washington, D.C.: USGPO, 1977).

a disaggregation of underlying socioeconomic relationships. The incomes of prime-age heads of household (ages 45–54) have increased relative to those of other cohorts, but especially relative to those of the youngest (ages 14–24) and oldest (ages 65 and over) cohorts.[5] At first glance, then, these income changes suggest increasing inequality among age groups. But in this period there have been dramatic declines in labor force participation (hence, increases in leisure) as the young remained in school longer and the elderly retired earlier. Because these changes are not measured, the relative economic position of the elderly and the young is understated.

WHAT THE INDICATORS DO NOT INDICATE

Although we did not explicitly attach normative content to the five trends, we proceeded as if income growth, a shift in consumption away from necessities, and reductions in inequality, poverty, and intergroup income differences were desirable goals. We did argue that the trend in these indicators could not be understood without a specification of the processes by which they are generated.

There is, however, a further complication, which makes normative interpretations even more difficult. We have proceeded as if the indicators were independent of one another, and have neglected the possibility that an improvement in one indicator may lead to a decline in another. A familiar example of such a case is the presumed tradeoff between greater income equality and faster economic growth—that the higher taxes needed to redistribute more income would cause a decline in savings and work effort, and a consequent reduction in aggregate income.[6]

A similar conflict may exist between the goals of reducing income inequality and narrowing intergroup income differences. During the

5. The ratio of the median income of a specific cohort to the median income for all families fell from .77 to .67 between 1947 and 1974 for the youngest cohort and from .60 to .57 for the oldest cohort, but rose from 1.14 to 1.30 for the prime-age cohort.

6. See Arthur Okun, *Equality and Efficiency: The Big Tradeoff* (Washington, D.C.: The Brookings Institution, 1975).

period, the average earnings of females declined relative to those of males, and the income differences between families with female heads and male heads increased. The proportion of wives who worked increased, and the most rapid increases occurred for wives of men at the lower-middle and middle income ranges. The changes in labor force participation of wives, who now earn 15 percent of total family income, despite the growing male-female wage differential, contributed to the reduction in family income inequality.

It is possible that reductions in earnings differences by sex will induce increases in family income inequality. Because of assortative mating, high income men are likely to marry women with high earnings potentials. These women are now less likely to be in the paid labor force because of their husbands' high incomes and because discrimination against women denies them access to certain jobs (especially high income jobs). If full economic opportunity for women were to be achieved, these women would enter the labor market, acquire those jobs, and the male-female wage differential would be eliminated. The reduction of intergroup earnings differences would lead to an increase in family inequality.

To resolve this paradox we need an explicit ranking of goals and an equation that can weight a growth in family income, a reduction in intergroup differences, and an increase in inequality (or any other set of changes in the indicators). With such a weighting, the data could better be used to suggest whether economic well-being has increased or decreased.

CONCLUSION

Social Indicators, 1976 provides a set of time series that reveal a trend toward greater economic well-being over the past 30 years. The issues we raised concerning the measurement and interpretation of the data suggest that the indicators on income and expenditures are inputs for an analysis of social change, not outputs which can stand alone. Our first impressions of the trends, however, were generally confirmed even when confronted by the issues we raised. Income and expenditure data tell us what has happened, but not how or why.

Table 9/1

MEDIAN INCOME OF FAMILIES AND UNRELATED INDIVIDUALS, BY RACE: 1947–1975

(1974 constant dollars)

Year and period	Families: Total	Families: White	Families: Black and other races	Families: Ratio of black and other races to white	Unrelated individuals: White	Unrelated individuals: Black and other races	Unrelated individuals: Ratio of black and other races to white
1947	6,691	6,970	3,563	0.51	2,286	1,647	0.72
1948	6,529	6,781	3,622	.53	2,157	1,616	.75
1949	6,427	6,686	3,413	.51	2,345	1,695	.72
1950	6,800	7,057	3,828	.54	2,283	1,673	.73
1951	7,041	7,326	3,858	.53	2,387	1,764	.74
1952	7,227	7,643	4,344	.57	2,821	1,952	.69
1953	7,805	8,099	4,538	.56	2,716	2,136	.79
1954	7,657	7,961	4,422	.56	2,414	1,602	.66
1955	8,137	8,495	4,685	.55	2,579	1,722	.67
1956	8,679	9,060	4,768	.53	2,656	1,972	.74
1957	8,710	9,051	4,843	.54	2,799	1,779	.64
1958	8,676	9,039	4,624	.51	2,715	1,841	.68
1959	9,165	9,547	4,935	.52	2,815	1,818	.65
1960	9,358	9,716	5,379	.55	3,096	1,778	.57
1961	9,457	9,859	5,260	.53	3,108	1,908	.61
1962	9,710	10,168	5,429	.53	3,058	2,042	.67
1963	10,065	10,547	5,581	.53	3,040	2,086	.69
1964	10,444	10,903	6,102	.56	3,320	2,275	.69
1965	10,874	11,333	6,242	.55	3,509	2,559	.73
1966	11,445	11,890	7,128	.60	3,659	2,301	.63
1967	11,717	12,162	7,524	.62	3,648	2,696	.74
1968	12,236	12,668	7,924	.63	4,184	2,834	.68
1969	12,689	13,175	8,328	.63	4,140	2,919	.71
1970	12,531	13,000	8,275	.64	4,169	2,849	.68
1971	12,523	12,995	8,175	.63	4,219	2,831	.67
1972	13,103	13,614	8,376	.62	4,334	3,219	.74
1973	13,373	13,977	8,429	.60	4,738	3,541	.75
1974	12,836	13,356	8,265	.62	4,636	3,149	.68
1975[1]	12,570	13,073	8,540	.65	4,672	3,012	.64
Average annual percent change							
1947–1975	2.2	2.2	3.1	(X)	2.6	2.2	(X)
1947–1957	2.6	2.6	3.1	(X)	2.0	.8	(X)
1957–1967	3.0	3.0	4.4	(X)	2.6	4.2	(X)
1967–1975	.9	.9	1.6	(X)	3.1	1.4	(X)

Source: U.S. Department of Commerce, Bureau of the Census, *Current Population Reports*, Series P-60, No. 101.
(X) Not applicable.
[1] Figures for unrelated individuals of black and other races relate to blacks only.

Chart 9/1A

Social Indicators, 1976

MEDIAN TOTAL MONEY INCOME OF FAMILIES AND UNRELATED INDIVIDUALS, FOR WHITES, BLACKS AND OTHER RACES, IN CONSTANT 1974 DOLLARS, 1947 TO 1975

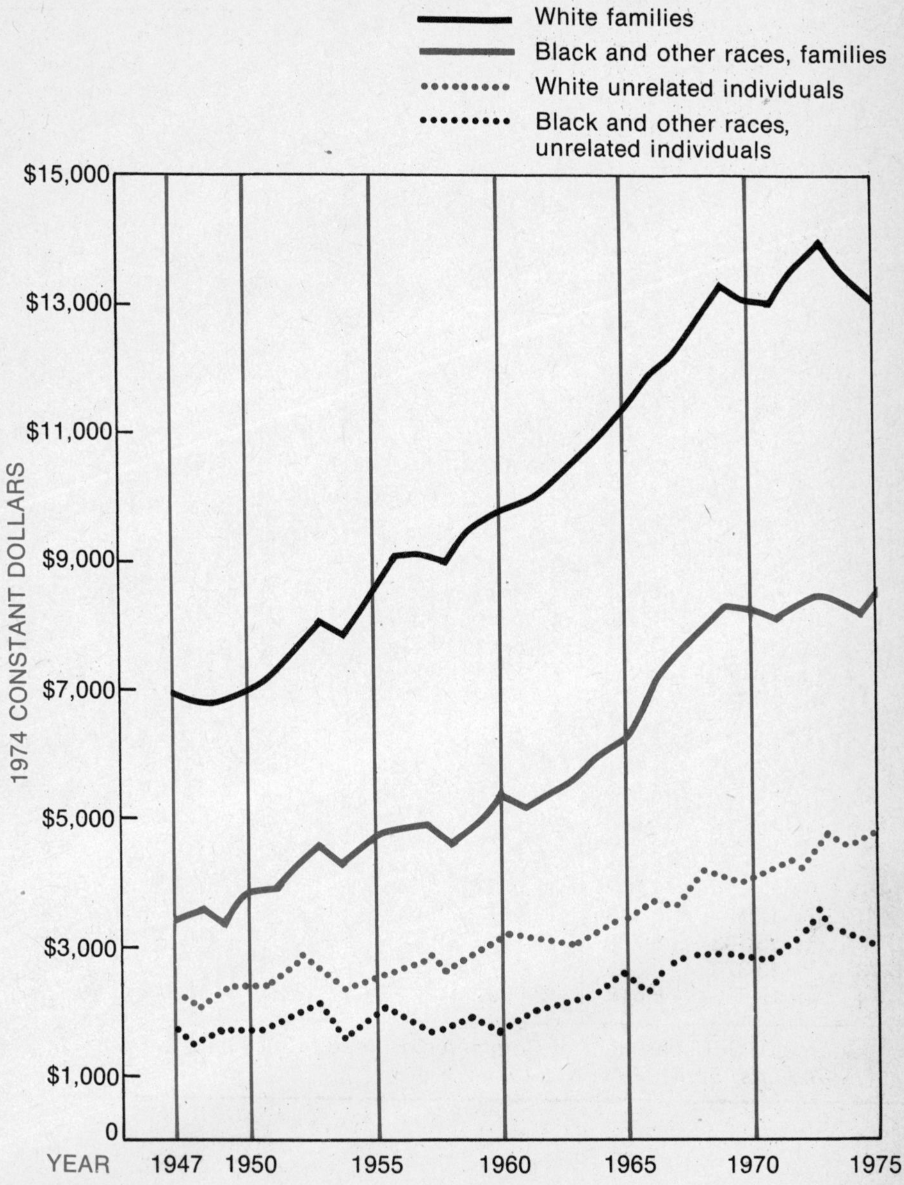

Source: see table 9/1

Table 9/3

MEDIAN FAMILY INCOME, BY AGE OF FAMILY HEAD: 1947–1974

(1974 constant dollars)

YEAR	ALL FAMILIES	AGE OF HEAD 14 to 24 years	25 to 34 years	35 to 44 years	45 to 54 years	55 to 64 years	65 years and over
	MEDIAN INCOME						
1947	6,691	5,177	6,470	7,269	7,594	7,068	4,035
1948	6,529	5,355	6,463	7,057	7,389	6,662	3,908
1949	6,427	4,894	6,619	6,892	7,176	6,518	3,899
1950	6,800	5,355	6,895	7,467	7,549	6,676	3,900
1951	7,041	5,854	7,269	7,721	7,715	6,934	3,712
1952	7,227	5,704	7,491	8,065	8,095	7,072	4,230
1953	7,805	5,830	8,050	8,487	8,987	7,640	4,124
1954	7,646	5,754	7,807	8,545	8,828	7,435	4,209
1955	8,137	6,112	8,278	9,055	9,370	8,057	4,284
1956	8,679	6,877	8,947	9,728	9,820	8,290	4,628
1957	8,710	6,813	9,054	9,730	9,760	8,359	4,361
1958	8,676	6,456	8,886	9,734	9,792	8,794	4,549
1959	9,165	6,540	9,347	10,391	10,384	9,203	4,790
1960	9,358	6,679	9,468	10,682	10,779	9,288	4,820
1961	9,457	6,970	9,593	10,750	11,058	9,586	4,985
1962	9,710	6,976	9,628	11,137	11,485	10,145	5,227
1963	10,065	6,758	10,184	11,403	11,940	10,435	5,398
1964	10,444	7,625	10,456	11,943	12,324	10,645	5,367
1965	10,874	8,388	11,056	12,489	12,933	10,977	5,491
1966	11,445	8,634	11,533	13,204	13,669	11,620	5,763
1967	11,717	8,616	11,911	13,572	14,195	11,827	5,773
1968	12,236	8,828	12,370	14,241	14,799	12,502	6,513
1969	12,689	8,970	12,785	14,754	15,607	12,985	6,464
1970	12,530	8,942	12,520	14,498	15,402	13,191	6,421
1971	12,523	8,415	12,509	14,473	15,708	13,385	6,642
1972	13,103	8,782	13,162	15,471	16,575	13,768	7,038
1973	13,373	8,895	13,547	15,879	16,896	14,185	7,132
1974	12,836	8,618	13,000	15,117	16,709	13,645	7,298

Source: U.S. Department of Commerce, Bureau of the Census, *Current Population Reports*, Series P-60, No. 101.

Table 9/3 (*Continued*)

YEAR	ALL FAMILIES	AGE OF HEAD: 14 to 24 years	25 to 34 years	35 to 44 years	45 to 54 years	55 to 64 years	65 years and over
	RATIO OF MEDIAN INCOME OF AGE GROUP TO ALL FAMILIES						
1947	1.00	0.77	0.97	1.09	1.14	1.06	0.60
1948	1.00	.82	.99	1.08	1.13	1.02	.60
1949	1.00	.76	1.03	1.07	1.12	1.02	.61
1950	1.00	.79	1.01	1.10	1.11	.98	.57
1951	1.00	.83	1.03	1.10	1.10	.99	.53
1952	1.00	.79	1.04	1.12	1.12	.98	.59
1953	1.00	.75	1.03	1.09	1.15	.98	.53
1954	1.00	.75	1.02	1.12	1.15	.97	.55
1955	1.00	.75	1.02	1.11	1.15	.99	.53
1956	1.00	.79	1.03	1.12	1.13	.96	.53
1957	1.00	.78	1.04	1.12	1.12	.96	.50
1958	1.00	.74	1.02	1.12	1.13	1.01	.52
1959	1.00	.71	1.02	1.13	1.13	1.00	.52
1960	1.00	.71	1.01	1.14	1.15	.99	.52
1961	1.00	.74	1.02	1.14	1.17	1.01	.53
1962	1.00	.72	.99	1.15	1.18	1.04	.54
1963	1.00	.67	1.01	1.13	1.19	1.04	.54
1964	1.00	.73	1.00	1.14	1.18	1.02	.51
1965	1.00	.77	1.02	1.15	1.19	1.01	.51
1966	1.00	.75	1.01	1.15	1.19	1.02	.50
1967	1.00	.74	1.02	1.16	1.21	1.01	.49
1968	1.00	.72	1.01	1.16	1.21	1.02	.53
1969	1.00	.71	1.01	1.16	1.23	1.02	.51
1970	1.00	.71	1.00	1.16	1.23	1.05	.51
1971	1.00	.67	1.00	1.16	1.25	1.07	.53
1972	1.00	.67	1.00	1.18	1.26	1.05	.54
1973	1.00	.67	1.01	1.19	1.26	1.06	.53
1974	1.00	.67	1.01	1.18	1.30	1.06	.57

Source: U.S. Department of Commerce, Bureau of the Census, *Current Population Reports*, Series P-60, No. 101.

Chart 9/3C

Social Indicators, 1976

MEDIAN FAMILY INCOME IN CONSTANT 1974 DOLLARS FOR SELECTED COHORT GROUPS 14–24 TO 35–44 YEARS OLD, 1949–1974

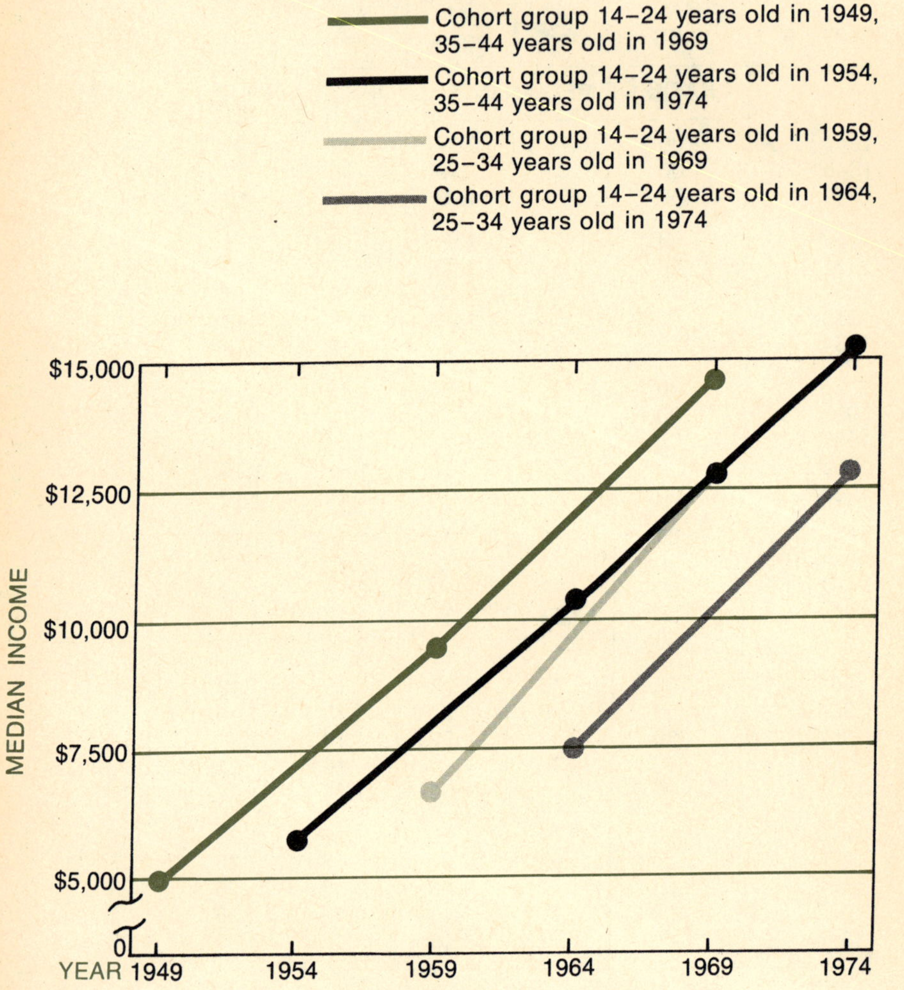

Source: see table 9/3

Chart 9/23 Social Indicators, 1976

CONSUMER PRICE INDEXES (1967 = 100) SELECTED YEARS, 1961–MAY, 1976—ANNUAL AVERAGES, EXCEPT FOR MAY, 1976

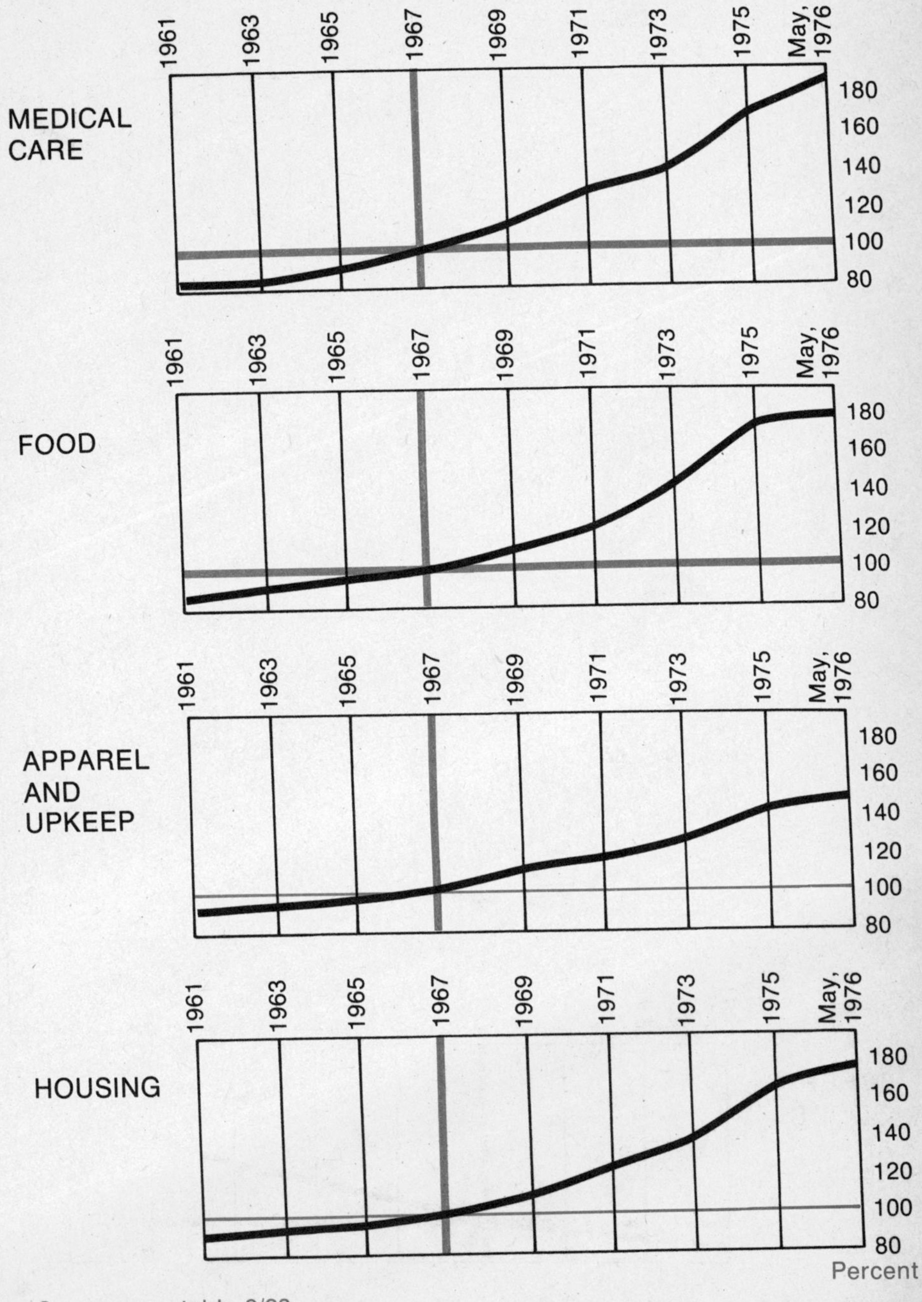

Source: see table 9/23

Chart 9/23

Social Indicators, 1976

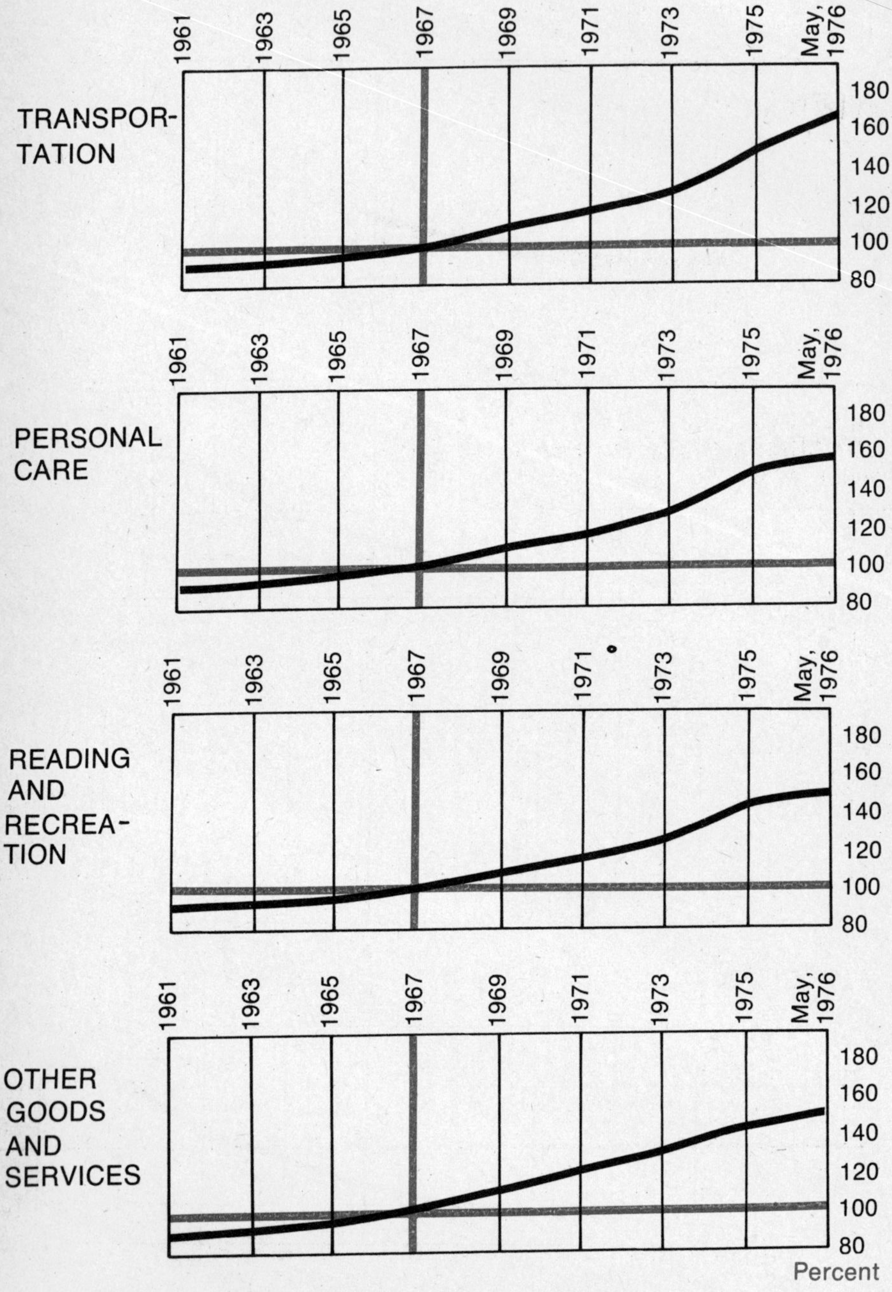

Source: see table 9/23

Chart 9/23 Social Indicators, 1976

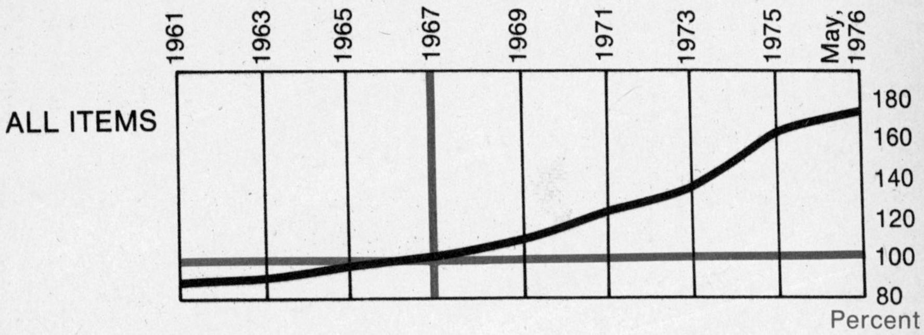

Table 9/23

CONSUMER PRICE INDEXES: 1940–1976

(Index: 1967 = 100; yearly data are annual averages)

Period	All items	All items less medical care	Medical care	Food	Apparel and upkeep	Housing	Transportation	Personal care	Reading and recreation	Other goods and services	All services
1940	42.0	(NA)	36.8	35.2	42.8	52.4	42.7	40.2	46.1	48.3	43.6
1945	53.0	(NA)	42.1	50.7	61.5	59.1	47.8	55.1	62.4	56.9	48.7
1950	72.1	(NA)	53.7	74.5	79.0	72.8	68.2	68.3	74.4	69.9	58.9
1955	80.2	(NA)	64.8	81.6	84.1	82.3	77.4	77.9	76.7	79.8	70.5
1960	88.7	89.4	79.1	88.0	89.6	90.2	89.6	90.1	87.3	87.8	83.8
1961	89.6	90.3	81.4	89.1	90.4	90.9	90.6	90.6	89.3	88.5	85.2
1962	90.6	91.2	83.5	89.9	90.9	91.7	92.5	92.2	91.3	89.1	86.2
1963	91.7	92.3	85.6	91.2	91.9	92.7	93.0	93.4	92.8	90.6	88.5
1964	92.9	93.5	87.3	92.4	92.7	93.8	94.3	94.5	95.0	92.0	90.2
1965	94.5	94.9	89.5	94.4	93.7	94.9	95.9	95.2	95.9	94.2	92.2
1966	97.2	97.7	93.4	99.1	96.1	97.2	97.2	97.1	97.5	97.2	95.8
1967	100.0	100.0	100.0	100.0	100.0	100.0	100.0	100.0	100.0	100.0	100.0
1968	104.2	104.1	106.1	103.6	105.4	104.2	103.2	104.2	104.7	104.6	105.2
1969	109.8	109.7	113.4	108.9	111.5	110.8	107.2	109.3	108.7	109.1	112.5
1970	116.3	116.1	120.6	114.9	116.1	118.9	112.7	113.2	113.4	116.0	121.6
1971	121.3	120.9	128.4	118.4	119.8	124.3	118.6	116.8	119.3	120.9	128.4
1972	125.3	124.9	132.5	123.5	122.3	129.2	119.9	119.8	122.8	125.5	133.3
1973	133.1	132.9	137.7	141.4	126.8	135.0	123.8	125.2	125.9	129.0	139.1
1974	147.7	147.7	150.5	161.7	136.2	150.6	137.7	137.3	133.8	137.2	152.0
1975	161.2	160.9	168.6	175.4	142.3	166.8	150.6	150.7	144.4	147.4	166.6
1976											
May	169.2	168.4	182.6	179.9	146.8	175.6	163.5	158.9	150.3	152.9	178.4

Source: U.S. Department of Health, Education, and Welfare, Social Security Administration, *Social Security Bulletin*, April 1976.

ANNALS, AAPSS, 435, Jan. 1978

Baby Boom to Birth Dearth and Beyond

By ARTHUR A. CAMPBELL

ABSTRACT: The processes of fertility change in the United States are structured in a way that exaggerates the upward and downward trends in annual measures of fertility, relative to underlying trends in the average number of children that women have during their reproductive years of life. In the 1950s, we witnessed a period of relatively inflated fertility; in the 1970s we are apparently going through a period of relatively depressed fertility. The childbearing expectations of young women suggest that annual fertility rates will rise in the near future, but do not provide any reason to believe that there will be a substantial increase in fertility comparable to that occurring between the 1930s and the 1950s. The causes of swings in fertility rates are not yet fully known, but some promising hypotheses have been proposed and are being tested.

Arthur A. Campbell is the Deputy Director of the Center for Population Research, National Institute of Child Health and Human Development, National Institutes of Health. He attended Antioch College as an undergraduate and did graduate work at Columbia University. Since 1955, his research efforts have been largely devoted to an understanding of trends and differentials in fertility-related behavior in the United States.

THE RATE of childbearing among women of reproductive age in 1976 was less than half the level recorded 19 years earlier in 1957. The decline over the intervening years was more rapid than that experienced by the United States in the 1920s and more rapid than any recent declines reported by other countries in the developed world. It brought the birth rate from 25 births per 1,000 population in 1957 to 15 in 1976. The annual number of births dropped from 4.3 million to 3.2 million in the same period. Both the decline in the birth rate and that in the number of births would have been greater if the population of childbearing age had not been rising at the same time.

These changes in the fertility of the United States population and their implications for future birth rates cannot be understood fully without considering the dynamic processes that gave rise to them and that will continue to affect fertility rates in the future. The description of these processes can be most easily accomplished by referring to two different measures of fertility: the completed fertility rate and the total fertility rate.

MEASURES OF FERTILITY

The completed fertility rate is the number of births that occur per 1,000 women during their reproductive years of life (generally taken as ages 14–49). A completed fertility rate of 3,000, for example, means that a group of women had three births each, on the average, by the time they reached age 50. The groups to which this measure refers are called birth cohorts; they comprise women born in a specified 12-month period. For technical reasons, cohorts are defined in terms of 12–month periods ending on June 30 of the year by which the cohort is identified. For example, the 1920 cohort includes all women who were born between July 1, 1919 and June 30, 1920. This cohort was assumed to have completed its childbearing by January 1, 1970, at which time its completed fertility rate was 2702.3 births per 1,000 women.[1]

Unlike the completed fertility rate, the total fertility rate is a hypothetical measure that expresses the level of fertility observed in a given calendar year. It can be interpreted as the number of births that 1,000 women would have if they continued to bear children at the rates observed for each single year of age during the year for which the rate is computed. For example, the total fertility rate for 1975 was 1770.3. This means that if a group of women were to bear children at the rates observed at each age in 1975, they would complete their fertility with 1770.3 births per 1,000 women. In brief, the completed fertility rate expresses the level of childbearing experienced by actual groups of women who have reached the end of their reproductive years of life. The total fertility rate expresses the level of childbearing observed in a particular calendar year.

It is often convenient to contrast the level of the total fertility rate with the presumed level of the completed fertility rates of cohorts currently in the reproductive years of

1. The total fertility and completed fertility rates cited in this paper are from the following source: National Center for Health Statistics, *Fertility Tables for Birth Cohorts by Color: United States, 1917–73*, DHEW Publication no. (HRA) 76-1152, April 1976. Rates for 1974 and 1975 are from unpublished tabulations by the National Center for Health Statistics.

FIGURE 1

Comparison of Completed Fertility Rates and Total Fertility Rates: United States, Cohorts of 1867–1958, and Calendar Years 1917–75.

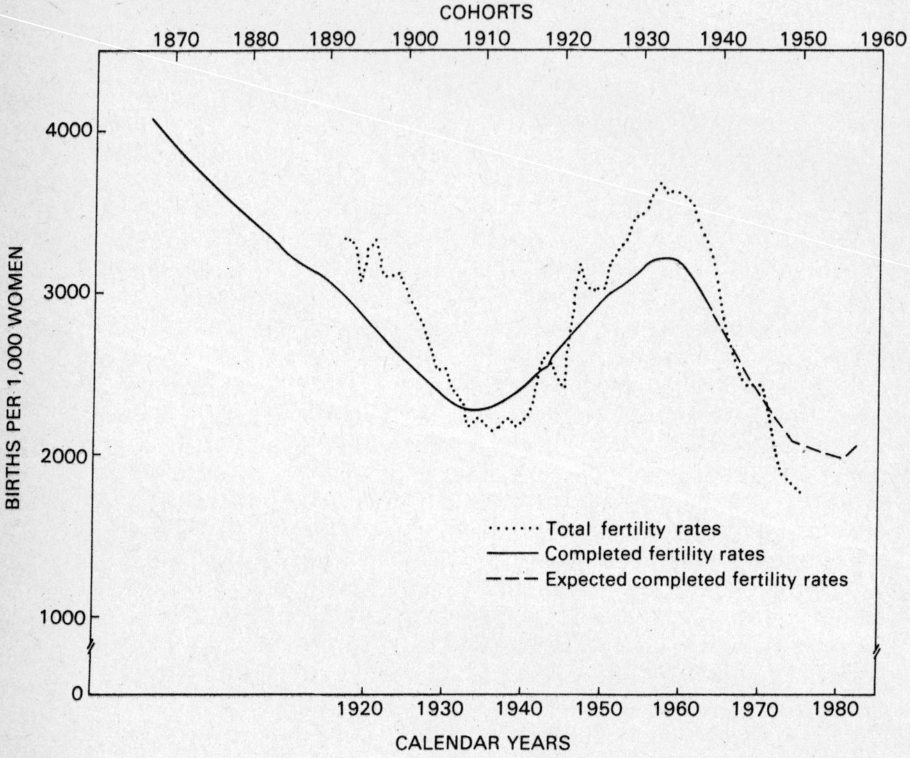

life. For example, in 1957, when the total fertility rate was 3,682, it did not appear likely that any cohort then in the reproductive years of life (which included the cohorts of 1908–43) would complete child-bearing with such a large number of children. Therefore, we say that the total fertility rate in 1957 was distorted upward, which means that it overstated the level of fertility that women then in the childbearing ages would experience over their reproductive lives. In more recent years the total fertility rate appears to be distorted downward—that is, it understates the number of children that women in the main reproductive ages will eventually have.

THE DYNAMICS OF FERTILITY CHANGE

Figure 1 contrasts the levels of the total fertility rate and the completed fertility rate for the historical series available from official statistics of the United States. The completed fertility rates go back to the cohort of 1867 which had over 4,000 births per 1,000 women. This measure reached a low turning point of 2,270 for the 1908 cohort, rose to a high turning point of about 3,220 for the 1933 cohort (an estimate based on reported births up to age 43), and appears to be reaching a new low around 2,000 for the cohorts born in the 1950s. The latter estimate is based on the number of births expected by women responding to a Census Bureau Survey in 1976.[2] Whether or not they will actually have this number of births is, of course, open to question.

The dotted line on figure 1 represents the trend in the total fertility rate from 1917 (the earliest year available) to 1975. The calendar years for the total fertility rate are plotted 25 years beyond the points for which the completed fertility rates for cohorts are plotted. This interval was chosen because the median age of childbearing in the United States in recent years has been about 25. Therefore, the observations for the total fertility rate appear at that point in the chart closest to the completed fertility rates of cohorts then in their 20s, which comprise the main childbearing ages. In this way, it is possible to estimate the extent to which the total fertility rate overstates or understates the completed fertility of cohorts then in the main reproductive ages of life.

Figure 1 shows that the amplitude of the total fertility rate is considerably greater than that of the completed fertility rate. For example, between the low of 1936 and the high of 1957 the total fertility rate rose by 72 percent. However, between the low and high cohorts of 1908 and 1933, the rise was only 42 percent. Similarly, the total fertility rate fell by 52 percent between 1957 and 1975, but the completed fertility rate will fall by an estimated 36 percent between the high cohort of 1933 and the cohorts of the late 1950s.

The reason for the greater swings in the total fertility rate is that the age distribution of childbearing is constantly changing from one cohort to the next. The unusually rapid rise in the total fertility rate between the 1930s and the 1950s was due to a combination of three factors: (1) the underlying rise in the completed fertility rate of cohorts; (2) the relatively late ages of childbearing of the cohorts of 1910–25; (3) the shift to relatively early ages of childbearing among the cohorts of 1925–40.

The relatively late ages of childbearing of the cohorts of 1910–25 was due to the fact that the women born in these years reached the main reproductive years of life in the period 1930–45 when young couples tended to delay marriage and childbearing, possibly because of depressed economic conditions and the absence of young men during World War II. After the war, these couples compensated for their previously low fertility by having relatively high birth rates at the later childbearing ages.

The cohorts of 1925–40, in contrast, reached the main ages of childbearing in the period 1945–60 when couples were tending to marry and have children at younger ages. Since both sets of cohorts were in the reproductive ages of life in the period 1945–60, relatively high rates at the older and younger ages combined with rising completed fertility rates to produce a strong upward trend in the total fertility rate.

In the 1960s and 1970s the three factors that caused the earlier rapid increase in the total fertility rate were reversed to bring about a rapid decline: (1) the completed fertility rates of the cohorts of 1935–55 were declining; (2) the cohorts of 1925–40 reached the older ages of childbearing by 1965 and were having relatively low rates at these ages

2. U.S. Bureau of the Census, "Fertility of American Women: June 1976," in *Current Population Reports*, ser. P–20, no. 308 (Washington, D.C.: USGPO, 1977), p. 9.

because they had had such high rates at the younger ages; (3) the cohorts of the 1940s and the 1950s were marrying and having children at later ages, which reduced their fertility at the younger childbearing ages. Thus, declining completed fertility and relatively low rates at the older and younger childbearing ages combined to bring about a sharp decline in the total fertility rate.

What will happen in the later 1970s and the 1980s is impossible to predict with any certainty. Future trends depend in part on whether the cohorts of the 1940s behave in a manner similar to that exhibited by the cohorts of 1910–25 and begin to show some increases in fertility as they reach the later childbearing ages. This would tend to raise the total fertility rate and may account for the tendency for fertility rates to have begun rising in 1977. In addition, there is a great deal of uncertainty about the trend in the completed fertility rates of cohorts now in the younger reproductive ages of life. Since these two issues are so important for forming an opinion about possible future trends in fertility, they will be examined separately in the next two sections.

THE TREND IN COMPLETED FERTILITY AMONG YOUNG COHORTS

Although it is impossible to predict with certainty how many children women now in the earlier reproductive years of life will bear, we can get some idea of the future trend in completed fertility rates from responses to questions on number of births expected. Such questions have been included in various surveys in the United States since 1955, and although the responses do not provide an accurate description of future trends, the general tendencies to have more or fewer children do seem to be reflected in the survey results.

Table 1 shows the number of births expected by currently married women in surveys conducted by the U.S. Bureau of the Census in 1967 and each year from 1971 to 1976. The rates shown for currently married women are not precisely comparable with the completed fertility rate because this rate is based on all women, rather than on married women only. In 1976, the Census Bureau included single and previously married women among those to whom it asked the questions on total number of children expected. The numbers based on the responses of all women are shown on the top line of table 1. These rates are directly comparable to the completed fertility rate. In general, they are 4 to 7 percent below the averages based on the responses of currently married women.

Table 1 provides strong evidence that the completed fertility rate is falling among the cohorts of the 1940s and 1950s. The high values of birth expectations are reported by women who belong to the cohorts of the late 1920s and the 1930s. For example, the 35–39-year-old women in 1967 belong to the cohorts of 1928–32. They expected to have 3,300 births per 1,000 women, on the average. In contrast, the 18–19-year-old women interviewed in 1976 belong to the cohorts of 1957–58. The married women among them expected only 2,163 births per 1,000 women, and all women interviewed in this cohort expected only 2,087 births per 1,000 women.

Table 1 also shows a tendency for currently married women in some cohorts to reduce their childbearing expectations as they become older. For example, in 1967, the 18–

TABLE 1

TOTAL NUMBER OF BIRTHS EXPECTED PER 1,000 WOMEN 18–39 YEARS OLD FOR ALL WOMEN IN 1976 AND CURRENTLY MARRIED WOMEN IN 1967 AND 1971–76: UNITED STATES

	AGE					
YEAR	18–19	20–21	22–24	25–29	30–34	35–39
			All women			
1976	2,087	1,989	2,022	2,098	2,445	n.a.
			Currently married women			
1976	2,163	2,122	2,145	2,202	2,536	2,994
1975	2,189	2,183	2,163	2,260	2,610	3,058
1974	2,189	2,142	2,170	2,335	2,724	3,090
1973	2,267	2,276	2,254	2,387	2,804	3,234
1972	2,229	2,210	2,282	2,452	2,915	3,218
1971	2,256	2,373	2,404	2,619	2,989	3,257
1967	2,719	2,916	2,856	3,037	3,288	3,300

SOURCES: 1973: U.S. Bureau of the Census, "Fertility Expectations of American Women: June 1973," in *Current Population Reports*, ser. P–20, no. 265 (Washington, D.C.: USGPO, 1974), p. 17.
1974: U.S. Bureau of the Census, "Fertility Expectations of American Women: June 1974," in *Current Population Reports*, ser. P–20, no. 277 (Washington, D.C.: USGPO, 1975), p. 15.
1975: U.S. Bureau of the Census, "Fertility of American Women: June 1975," in *Current Population Reports*, ser. P–20, no. 301 (Washington, D.C.: USGPO, 1976), p. 13.
1967, 1971 and 1976: U.S. Bureau of the Census, "Fertility of American Women: June 1976," in *Current Population Reports*, ser. P–20, no. 308 (Washington, D.C.: USGPO, 1977), pp. 9 and 17.

19-year-olds, who belong to the cohorts of 1948–49, said that they expected to have 2,719 births per 1,000 women. However, when the 1948–50 cohorts were interviewed at ages 22–24 in 1972, they expected only 2,282 births per 1,000 women. Part of this reduction was due to the inclusion in the later survey of women who had married at later ages and expected fewer births, but part of it was due to the fact that women reduced their family size goals during this period of time. This simply demonstrates that the childbearing expectations of young women are not immutable.

Since 1974, the birth expectations for the cohorts of 1950 and later have varied in the narrow range between 2,122 and 2,189 births per 1,000 currently married women. These values are consistent with completed fertility rates around 2,000 to 2,100. If such a low completed fertility rate were to be attained and continued indefinitely, it would, assuming no immigration, eventually result in the cessation of population growth because it would allow for the replacement of two parents by two children, on the average, and thus maintain successive generations at approximately the same size.

In the United States the cohorts of 1906–14 provide a historical precedent for low completed fertility rates. Although none of these cohorts had as few as 2,100 births per 1,000 women, the 1908 cohort did achieve the lowest recorded level of 2,270. However, this low rate was achieved in part by a high prevalence of childlessness among its members, 22 percent of whom had no births. This compares with a low of 8 percent childless among cohorts of the 1930s.

Unlike the cohorts of 1906–14,

TABLE 2

PERCENTAGE OF WIVES 18–39 YEARS OLD EXPECTING NONE, ONE, TWO, AND THREE OR MORE BIRTHS, BY AGE: UNITED STATES: 1967 AND 1971–76

AGE	1976	1975	1974	1973	1972	1971	1967
			Percentage of wives expecting no births				
18–19	3.7	2.4	4.1	3.4	3.4	5.5	1.0
20–21	4.0	4.3	4.8	4.3	3.5	3.0	0.4
22–24	5.3	4.5	5.4	4.0	3.6	4.1	1.7
25–29	6.4	4.9	4.7	4.1	4.0	3.2	2.2
30–34	5.5	5.2	4.9	4.6	4.1	4.7	3.8
35–39	4.7	4.2	5.4	4.4	5.0	4.8	5.0
			Percentage of wives expecting one birth				
18–19	12.4	12.4	13.1	10.7	12.0	8.6	10.9
20–21	11.4	11.9	13.8	10.4	10.0	9.0	5.4
22–24	12.2	10.6	10.7	9.0	9.2	8.1	5.2
25–29	11.2	11.7	9.5	9.1	7.9	6.8	5.1
30–34	10.3	9.8	9.0	7.8	7.3	6.6	5.8
35–39	9.3	9.3	8.7	8.2	7.1	7.6	7.8
			Percentage of wives expecting two births				
18–19	58.2	59.8	56.9	56.6	54.9	54.5	33.8
20–21	59.9	57.6	55.3	53.9	59.0	53.0	36.3
22–24	55.8	58.1	55.7	57.1	55.8	50.2	38.2
25–29	51.5	50.4	51.7	49.9	48.5	44.1	29.3
30–34	40.4	38.3	36.4	34.9	33.6	29.2	25.3
35–39	28.8	26.4	24.9	24.9	24.5	24.2	25.0
			Percentage of wives expecting three or more births				
18–19	25.7	25.4	25.9	29.3	29.7	31.4	54.3
20–21	24.7	26.2	26.1	31.4	27.5	35.0	57.9
22–24	26.7	26.8	28.2	29.9	31.4	37.6	54.9
25–29	30.9	33.0	34.1	36.9	39.6	45.9	63.4
30–34	43.8	46.7	49.7	52.7	55.0	59.5	65.1
35–39	57.2	60.1	61.0	62.5	63.4	63.4	62.2

SOURCES: 1967, 1971 and 1972: U.S. Bureau of the Census, "Birth Expectations and Fertility: June 1972," in *Current Population Reports*, ser. P–20, no. 248 (Washington, D.C.: USGPO, 1973), p. 19.

1973: U.S. Bureau of the Census, "Fertility Expectations of American Women: June 1973," in *Current Population Reports*, ser. P–20, no. 265 (Washington, D.C.: USGPO, 1974), p. 19.

1974: U.S. Bureau of the Census, "Fertility Expectations of American Women: June 1974," in *Current Population Reports*, ser. P–20, no. 277 (Washington, D.C.: USGPO, 1975), p. 17.

1975: U.S. Bureau of the Census, "Fertility of American Women: June 1975," in *Current Population Reports*, ser. P–20, no. 301 (Washington, D.C.: USGPO, 1976), p. 20.

1976: U.S. Bureau of the Census, "Fertility of American Women: June 1976," in *Current Population Reports*, ser. P–20, no. 308 (Washington, D.C.: USGPO, 1977), p. 25.

NOTE: Data are limited to currently married women reporting on birth expectations.

the cohorts of the 1940s and 1950s are not counting on childlessness to achieve low fertility, according to the Census Bureau Surveys shown in Table 2. Since 1974, only 2 to 5 percent of the currently married women in the cohorts of the 1950s expect to have no children. Between 11 and 14 percent of them expect to have only 1 child, 55 to 60 percent expect two children, and 25 to 28 percent expect three or more children.

The main difference between the

low fertility cohorts of the 1950s and the high fertility cohorts of the 1930s is in the proportion expecting two births and three or more births. Whereas over 60 percent of the women of the cohorts of the 1930s expected to have three or more births, only a quarter of the members of the cohorts of the 1950s expect that many births. In summary, the younger cohorts do not foresee any widespread return to childlessness. They expect more one-child and two-children families and far fewer larger families than were produced by the cohorts of the 1930s.

Table 3 compares the proportions of women expecting various numbers of births for all women and for currently married women interviewed in 1976. Between the cohorts of 1942–46 (ages 30–34 in 1976) and the cohorts of 1957–58 (ages 18 and 19 in 1976), the proportion expecting no births or only one changes very little; the proportion expecting two increases substantially; and the proportion expecting three or more declines.

Table 4 shows the completed fertility rates, by order of birth, that are consistent with these birth expectations. To summarize them briefly, the cohorts of the 1950s expect to have about 1,700 first and second births and 400 third and higher order births to give them a completed fertility rate of 2,100 births per 1,000 women. The number of first and second births is about the same as that recorded for the cohorts of 1931–35 (1,729). However, the number of third and higher order births (about 400) is only a fraction of the number reported by the cohorts of the early 1930s (1,473). The main areas of doubt about the birth expectations of the younger cohorts are (1) whether they will have as many

TABLE 3

PERCENTAGE OF WOMEN 18–34 YEARS OLD EXPECTING NONE, ONE, TWO, AND THREE OR MORE BIRTHS, BY AGE AND MARITAL STATUS: UNITED STATES, 1976

	Age				
Marital status	18–19	20–21	22–24	25–29	30–34
	Percentage expecting no births				
All women	11.6	11.0	9.8	10.2	9.0
Currently married	3.7	4.0	5.3	6.4	5.5
	Percentage expecting one birth				
All women	10.5	12.5	13.4	13.0	11.6
Currently married	12.4	11.4	12.2	11.2	10.3
	Percentage expecting two births				
All women	50.8	53.0	51.6	47.4	37.5
Currently married	58.2	59.9	55.8	51.5	40.4
	Percentage expecting three or more births				
All married	27.1	23.5	25.2	29.4	41.9
Currently married	25.7	24.7	26.7	30.9	43.8

SOURCE: U.S. Bureau of the Census, "Fertility of American Women: June 1976," in *Current Population Reports*, ser. P-20, no. 308 (Washington, D.C.: USGPO, 1977), pp. 13 and 25.

TABLE 4

TOTAL NUMBER OF BIRTHS EXPECTED AND NUMBER OF BIRTHS TO DATE PER 1,000 WOMEN 18–34 YEARS OLD, BY AGE OF WOMAN AND ORDER OF BIRTH: UNITED STATES, 1976

ORDER OF BIRTH	AGE 18–19	20–21	22–24	25–29	30–34
	Approximate cohort				
	1957–58	1955–56	1952–54	1947–51	1942–46
	Expected number of births per 1,000 women				
Total	2,087	1,989	2,022	2,098	2,445
1st	884	890	902	898	910
2nd	779	765	768	768	794
3rd	271	235	252	294	419
4th	102	69	68	92	185
5th	33	19	20	28	77
6th or higher	18	11	12	18	60
Summary:					
1st & 2nd	1,663	1,655	1,670	1,666	1,704
3rd or higher	424	334	352	432	741
	Births to date per 1,000 women				
Total	219	454	774	1,442	2,266
1st	179	327	486	725	876
2nd	n.a.	101	219	469	718
1st & 2nd	n.a.	428	705	1,194	1,594
3rd or higher	n.a.	26	69	248	672
	Percentage of expected births that have occurred				
Total	10.5	22.8	38.3	68.7	92.7
1st	20.2	36.7	53.9	80.7	96.3
2nd	n.a.	13.2	28.5	61.1	90.4
1st & 2nd	n.a.	25.9	42.2	71.7	93.5
3rd or higher	n.a.	7.8	19.6	57.4	90.7

SOURCE: U.S. Bureau of the Census, "Fertility of American Women: June 1976," in *Current Population Reports*, ser. P–20, no. 308 (Washington, D.C.: USGPO, 1977), pp. 12 and 14.

first and second births as they now think they will have and (2) whether they will be able to limit third and higher births to such a low number, in view of the fact that, even with improved fertility control, excess births are still reported.

In the next section we shall examine the recent experience of the cohorts of the 1940s and 1950s to see how consistent it has been with their reported birth expectations.

RECENT CHILDBEARING RECORD OF THE COHORTS OF THE 1940S AND 1950S

The various cohorts of the 1940s and 1950s are now at very different stages of their reproductive lives. As shown in table 4, the cohorts of 1942–

46 (aged 30–34 in 1976) had borne 93 percent of their expected total of 2,445 births per 1,000 women. However, members of the younger cohorts, who expect to have 2,000–2,100 births per 1,000 women, had borne a substantially smaller proportion of their expected total number of births by 1976.

If the cohorts of the late 1940s and the 1950s have as many births as they expect to have, they will have to increase their fertility rates at the later childbearing ages in comparison with rates observed for earlier cohorts. An approximate idea of the extent to which they will have to compensate for low fertility at the younger childbearing ages can be gained from figures 2 and 3, which show the age pattern of childbearing reported for the cohorts of 1931 to 1960, for first and second births separately.

Figure 2 shows that the cohorts of 1936–40 had the youngest age distribution of first births. By 1960, when they had reached ages 20–24, they had borne 525 first births per 1,000 women. The next set of cohorts (1941–45) had only 486 first births per 1,000 women by 1965 when they also reached ages 20–24. However, they had almost as many first births in the next five-year period as the earlier cohort group had at the same ages and actually had more first births between ages 25–29 and 30–34 than did the 1936–40 cohorts. In other words, after 1970 the 1941–45 cohorts began compensating for having had fewer first births at the younger childbearing ages.

Figure 2 also shows that the cohorts of 1946 and later will have to compensate to an even greater extent than did the 1941–45 cohorts for low first birth rates at the younger childbearing ages. For example, the 1951–55 cohorts had borne only 375 first births per 1,000 women by 1975, when they reached ages 20–24. This was 150 births fewer than the cohorts of 1936–40 had borne by the same ages. If the cohorts of 1951–55 complete their fertility with 900 or more first births per 1,000 women, they will have to distribute this deficit of 150 births over the remainder of the childbearing years of life. This is not impossible from a physiological point of view; but the major question is whether women who have postponed first births before age 25 will want to have them as they reach the later childbearing years. It is entirely possible that some of these "postponements" will become "cancellations."

Approximately the same observations apply to second births, as shown in figure 3. Again, the 1936–40 cohorts had the largest number of second births in the early childbearing years, and again the 1941–45 cohorts began to compensate for their earlier low fertility rates in the 1970s.

The main question emerging from these comparisons is whether the cohorts of 1946–60 will catch up with the earlier cohorts after recording such low fertility rates in the late 1960s and 1970s. We do not yet have data to demonstrate conclusively whether a compensatory rise in fertility at the later childbearing ages is or is not occurring among the members of these cohorts, but such data will become available in the years immediately ahead. If annual birth statistics continue to show increases in rates for first and second births at ages 25–29 and 30–34, it will mean that the compensation for low fertility rates at the younger ages is proceeding. In fact, this may account for the slight rise in monthly

FIGURE 2

Cumulative Birth Rates and Additions to Cumulative Birth Rates up to Jan. 1, 1975, For First Births to Cohorts of 1931–35 to 1956–60.

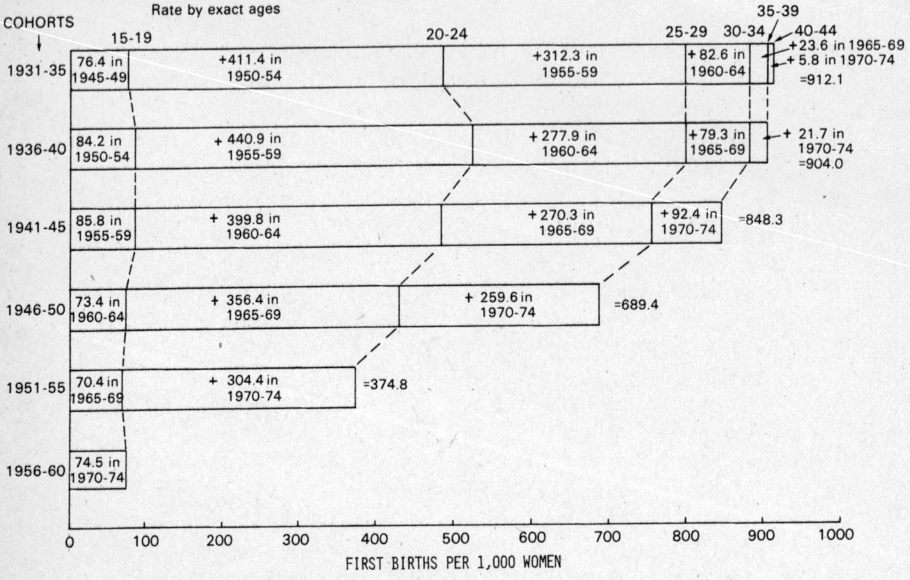

FIGURE 3

Cumulative Birth Rates and Additions to Cumulative Birth Rates up to Jan. 1, 1975, For Second Births to Cohorts of 1931–35 to 1956–60.

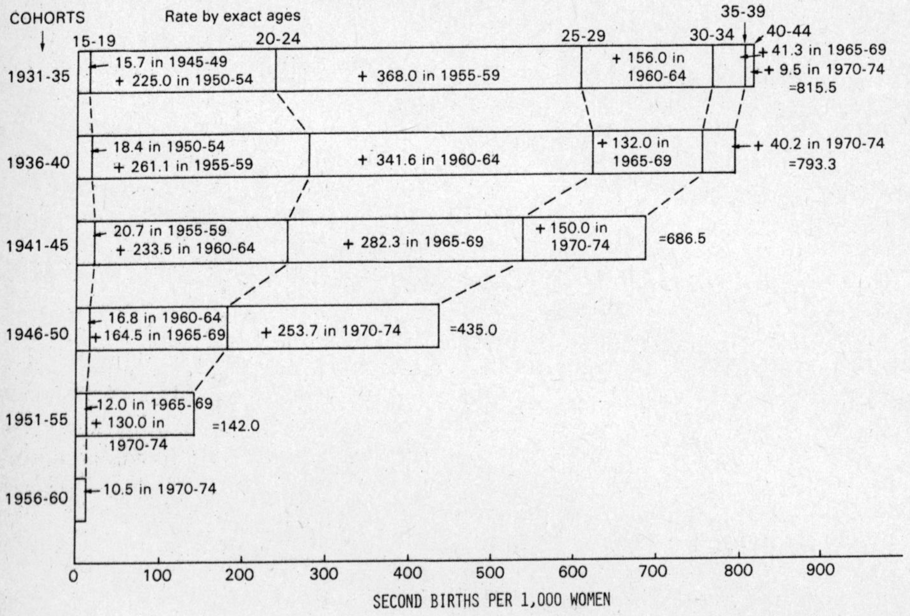

fertility rates that has been going on since the latter half of 1976. It is impossible to verify this interpretation because fertility rates by age and order of birth are not yet available for 1976.

THE IMMEDIATE FUTURE

If women do have more children at the later ages to make up for previously postponed births, how much will the total fertility rate rise? In 1975, the total fertility rate was 1,770. The component of this rate representing first and second births was 1,256 and the component representing third and higher order births was 514. If the completed fertility rate for first and second births rises to 1,700, in accordance with the stated expectations of young women, the total fertility rate for first and second births will also eventually rise to this level, resulting in an increase of over 400 in the total fertility rate. However, if young cohorts eventually have only 400 third and higher order births per 1,000 women, this will take away about 100 births from the total fertility rate. Therefore, if current expectations are achieved, the total fertility rate would rise about 300 points to a level near 2,100, bringing about an increase of 15 to 20 percent in the total fertility rate.

This outcome is approximately consistent with the "Series II" projections of the total fertility rate prepared by the U.S. Bureau of the Census, which assume that the total fertility rate will rise to approximately 2,100 by the end of this century.[3] It is possible that this change will occur more rapidly than assumed in Series II, but the Census Bureau projections provide a reasonable model of what might be expected to occur. Series II shows the annual number of births rising from a current level of around 3.2 million to 4 million by the 1980s. It also shows the birth rate rising from 15 births per 1,000 population to about 17 in the 1980s.

However, it is still entirely possible that young women of reproductive age will not meet their current goal of 1,700 first and second births per 1,000 women. If they return to the levels of childlessness and one-child families reported by the cohorts of the early 1900s, they may complete their fertility with as few as 1,300 or 1,400 first and second births per 1,000 women. If, in addition, they limit third and higher order births to the expected level of 400, the total fertility rate could remain at the low levels recorded in recent years.

THE LONG-TERM FUTURE

The preceding description of trends and projections shows that fertility patterns in the United States are structured in such a way as to bring about large fluctuations in annual and cohort rates. At no time in the past has either the completed fertility rate or the total fertility rate remained constant over a long series of cohorts or a long period of time. Furthermore, in the experience of the United States and of other countries, changes in the age distribution of fertility rates have tended to reinforce changes in completed fertility rates. That is, increases in completed fertility rates have been accompanied by high rates at both the younger and older reproductive ages and declining completed fertility rates

3. U.S. Bureau of the Census, "Projections of the Population of the United States: 1977–2050," in *Current Population Reports*, ser. P-25, no. 704 (Washington, D.C.: USGPO, 1977).

have been accompanied by relatively low rates at the younger and older reproductive ages. Hypothetically, rates could be constructed that would dampen, rather than intensify, trends in annual measures of fertility, but this is not what has happened in the real world. Therefore, it would seem reasonable to expect fairly substantial fluctuations to continue in the future.

For the following reasons it seems doubtful, however, that we will again witness as large a rise in the completed fertility rate as occurred between the cohorts of 1908 and 1933. First, any future rise cannot simulate the rise between the cohorts of the early 1900s and those of the early 1930s because these increases in completed fertility rates were brought about, in part, by the widespread rejection of childlessness. At the present time, it does not appear likely that cohorts now in the younger reproductive years of life will accept childlessness to the extent that the cohorts of 1906–15 did. Secondly, even during the rise in completed fertility in the United States, about one-third of third and higher order births were reported as unwanted.[4] With improvements in fertility control, such births need no longer occur. In fact, as of 1973, only one-sixth of third and higher order births were reported as unwanted.[5] Third, even during the rise in completed fertility rates, the probability of having sixth and higher order births continued to decline, signifying the continued drift away from large families. In summary, the only way to reverse the trend toward low completed fertility rates is for third and higher order births to rise, because the expected rates for first and second births are close to the highest levels ever recorded in the United States. At the present time the prospects for an increase in third and higher order births do not appear to be great.

SOCIAL AND ECONOMIC CAUSES OF CHANGES IN FERTILITY

A number of hypotheses have been developed to account for changes in levels of fertility in various societies. Perhaps the best known is associated with the "demographic transition," during which declines in birth rates followed declines in death rates as societies became industrialized. The declines in birth rates were thought to have been due, in part, to the fact that children lost their economic utility as societies became less rural-agricultural and more urban-industrial. It has also been hypothesized that as the mortality of children declined, with improvements in sanitation and living conditions, couples tended to reduce their fertility because it was not necessary to have as many births as previously to ensure the survival of a given number of children.

Such hypotheses applied only to the long-term decline in fertility that began over a century ago in developed countries. When fertility rose in the United States and other countries after World War II, new hypotheses were introduced to explain the rise. The most prominent of these was developed by Richard A. Easterlin

4. This estimate is based on unpublished tabulations from the 1960 Growth of American Families Study reported in: Pascal K. Whelpton, Arthur A. Campbell, and John E. Patterson, *Fertility and Family Planning in the United States* (Princeton, N.J.: Princeton University Press, 1966).

5. National Center for Health Statistics, "Wanted and Unwanted Births Reported by Mothers 15–44 Years of Age: United States, 1973," *Advance Data from Vital and Health Statistics*, no. 9, (August 10, 1977), p. 4.

who saw the postwar rise in fertility as the result of economic conditions and aspirations that made it possible for young couples to find relatively well-paying jobs, to marry, and to have children early in marriage.[6] Easterlin also points out that the cohorts that were in the younger portion of the labor force between 1945 and 1960 were born in the late 1920s and 1930s, when annual numbers of births were the lowest recorded in the United States since the nineteenth century. Because the members of these cohorts were so limited in number, there was relatively little competition for jobs among them, and they felt economically secure at an early stage in their marriages. Also, they were born during the Depression or spent their early childhood years in the 1930s, when they formed relatively modest material aspirations that did not interfere with their desire for children.[7]

Easterlin has also hypothesized that the low fertility of the cohorts of the 1940s and 1950s is related to their relatively large numbers, which increases competition for available jobs when they enter the labor force, and that since they developed their material aspirations during a period of economic expansion, they would not be as willing as earlier cohorts to forego the levels of living consistent with these aspirations simply to have children.[8]

Another hypothesis, developed by Larry Bumpass, relates specifically to the recent decline in fertility. He proposes that with improved methods of contraception, such as the pill, childbearing has become voluntary to an extent that it was not in the past, and that as a result decisions regarding when to have children and how many to have are becoming more deliberate.[9] In the process of arriving at such decisions, couples will count not only the benefits of having children but also the costs—in terms of the limitations imposed by parenthood as well as economic costs. These calculations will lead them to decide to have no children or very few.

If Easterlin is correct, the completed fertility rate, as well as the total fertility rate, will continue to rise and fall as cohort size and economic conditions vary, though perhaps the fluctuations will not be as great as those in the past. If Bumpass is right, the completed fertility rate will continue relatively unchanged at levels near or below replacement (that is, at 2,100 or below), and fluctuations in the total fertility rate will be limited to those arising from changes in the age distribution of childbearing.

Hypotheses linking changes in fertility with changes in economic and social conditions are necessarily tentative. We can only hope that further research will provide more substantial knowledge about the social and economic factors affecting trends in fertility.

6. Richard A. Easterlin, "The American Baby Boom in Historical Perspective" (Occasional paper no. 79, National Bureau of Economic Research, 1962).

7. Richard A. Easterlin, "Relative Economic Status and the American Fertility Swing," in *Social Structure, Family Life Styles, and Economic Behavior*, ed. Eleanor B. Sheldon (Philadelphia, Pa: Lippincott, 1972).

8. Richard A. Easterlin, "The Conflict Between Aspirations and Resources," *Population and Development Review*, vol. 2, nos. 3 and 4 (September/December 1972) pp. 417–26.

9. Larry L. Bumpass, "Is Low Fertility Here to Stay?," *Family Planning Perspectives*, vol. 5, no. 2 (Spring 1973) pp. 67–69.

Table 1/1
POPULATION GROWTH: 1790–2040

YEAR AND SERIES[1]	Population[2] (thousands)	Average annual rate of change (percent)	YEAR AND SERIES[1]	Population[2] (thousands)	Average annual rate of change (percent)
1790	3,929	(X)	1980 (Series I)	225,705	0.97
1800	5,297	2.99	1980 (Series II) ...	222,769	.84
1810	7,224	3.10	1980 (Series III) ...	220,356	.73
1820	9,618	2.86	1990 (Series I)	257,663	1.32
1830	12,901	2.94	1990 (Series II) ...	245,075	.95
			1990 (Series III) ...	235,581	.67
1840	17,120	2.83	2000 (Series I)	287,007	1.08
1850	23,261	3.07			
1860	31,513	3.04	2000 (Series II) ...	262,494	.69
1870	39,905	2.36	2000 (Series III) ...	245,098	.40
1880	50,262	2.31	2010 (Series I)	322,049	1.15
			2010 (Series II) ...	278,754	.60
1890	63,056	2.27	2010 (Series III) ...	250,193	.21
1900	76,094	1.88	2020 (Series I)	362,348	1.18
1910	92,407	1.94	2020 (Series II) ...	294,046	.53
1920	106,461	1.42			
1930	123,077	1.46	2020 (Series III) ...	251,884	.07
			2030 (Series I)	402,592	1.05
1940	132,594	.74	2030 (Series II) ...	304,328	.34
1950	152,271	1.38	2030 (Series III) ...	247,347	−.18
1960	180,671	1.71	2040 (Series I)	448,872	1.09
1970	204,879	1.26	2040 (Series II) ...	312,035	.25
			2040 (Series III) ...	237,926	−.39

Source: U.S. Department of Commerce, Bureau of the Census, *Historical Statistics of the United States, Colonial Times to 1970*, and *Current Population Reports*, Series P-25, No. 601.

X Not applicable.

[1] Series I presumes a fertility level of 2.7 children born per woman; Series II, 2.1 children; Series III, 1.7 children.

[2] Beginning in 1940, data include U.S. Armed Forces oversease. Data prior to 1940 exclude Alaska, Hawaii, and the Armed Forces overseas.

Chart 1/1A

Social Indicators, 1976

POPULATION GROWTH: 1790–2040

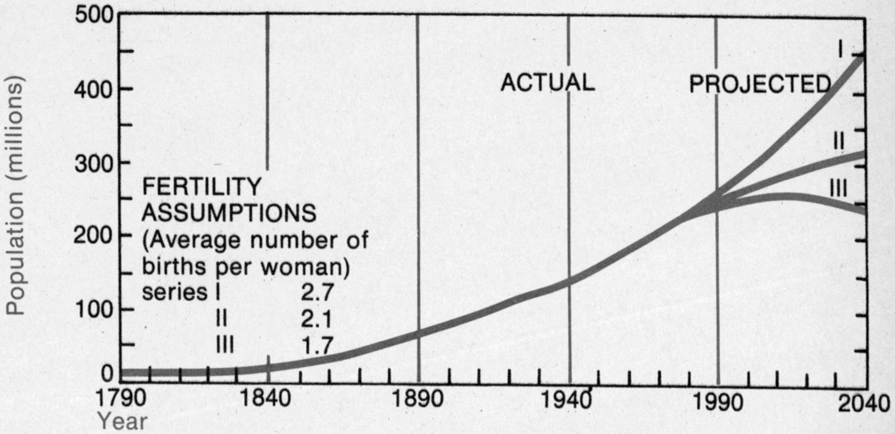

Chart 1/1B

AVERAGE ANNUAL RATE OF POPULATION CHANGE BETWEEN DECENNIAL CENSUS YEARS: 1790–2040

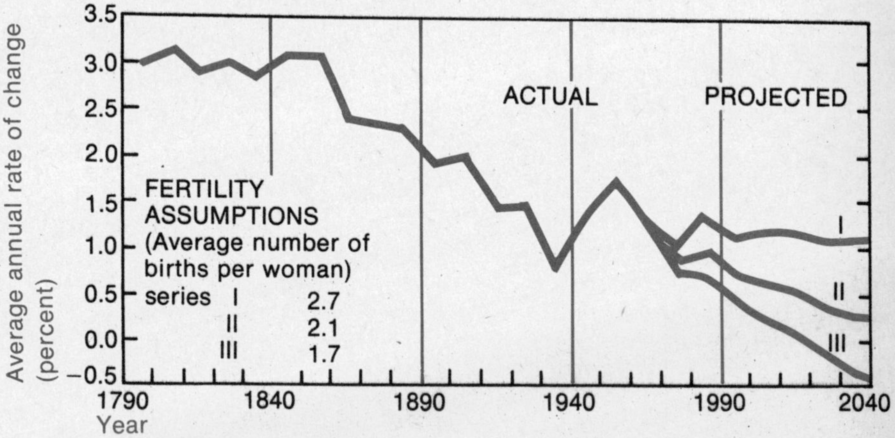

Source: see table 1/1

Table 1/5

COMPONENTS OF POPULATION CHANGE: 1930–2000

(Thousands)

CALENDAR YEAR	NET CHANGE[1]	BIRTHS[2]	DEATHS[3]	NET CIVILIAN IMMIGRATION
1930	1,128	2,618	1,419	113
1931	871	2,506	1,395	−16
1932	775	2,440	1,382	−62
1933	753	2,307	1,369	−34
1934	860	2,396	1,425	−7
1935	853	2,377	1,421	−2
1936	754	2,355	1,509	12
1937	864	2,413	1,480	33
1938	1,066	2,496	1,410	50
1939	1,039	2,466	1,416	53
1940	1,221	2,570	1,432	77
1941	1,382	2,716	1,415	60
1942	1,714	3,002	1,407	83
1943	1,799	3,118	1,503	148
1944	1,597	2,954	1,582	202
1945	1,462	2,873	1,549	162
1946	2,165	3,426	1,409	151
1947	2,653	3,834	1,455	238
1948	2,533	3,655	1,453	280
1949	2,556	3,667	1,452	323
1950	2,486	3,645	1,468	299
1951	2,588	3,845	1,501	335
1952	2,663	3,933	1,512	242
1953	2,717	3,989	1,531	261
1954	2,898	4,102	1,489	287
1955	2,925	4,128	1,537	337
1956	3,058	4,244	1,572	387
1957	2,961	4,332	1,641	272
1958	2,915	4,279	1,655	292
1959	2,939	4,313	1,663	292
1960	2,901	4,307	1,708	327
1961	2,955	4,317	1,703	373
1962	2,771	4,213	1,758	351
1963	2,655	4,142	1,815	361
1964	2,555	4,070	1,799	317
1965	2,315	3,801	1,830	373
1966	2,197	3,642	1,869	455
1967	2,072	3,555	1,861	414
1968	1,952	3,535	1,948	398
1969	2,089	3,630	1,934	453
1970	2,227	3,739	1,927	438
1971	2,012	3,556	1,930	387
1972	1,623	3,258	1,965	325
1973	1,494	3,137	1,974	331
1974	1,591	3,166	1,933	360

Table 1/5 (*Continued*)

CALENDAR YEAR	NET CHANGE[1]	BIRTHS[2]	DEATHS[3]	NET CIVILIAN IMMIGRATION
PROJECTIONS (Series II[4])[5]				
1975	1,582	3,232	2,050	400
1976	1,682	3,355	2,073	400
1977	1,802	3,500	2,098	400
1978	1,926	3,648	2,122	400
1979	2,045	3,792	2,147	400
1980	2,155	3,926	2,171	400
1981	2,220	4,014	2,194	400
1982	2,259	4,076	2,217	400
1983	2,284	4,124	2,240	400
1984	2,292	4,156	2,264	400
1985	2,284	4,172	2,288	400
1986	2,264	4,174	2,310	400
1987	2,232	4,164	2,332	400
1988	2,188	4,144	2,356	400
1989	2,134	4,114	2,380	400
1990	2,068	4,072	2,404	400
1991	1,996	4,025	2,429	400
1992	1,920	3,974	2,454	400
1993	1,844	3,922	2,478	400
1994	1,772	3,874	2,502	400
1995	1,706	3,832	2,526	400
1996	1,650	3,799	2,549	400
1997	1,606	3,778	2,572	400
1998	1,575	3,769	2,594	400
1999	1,556	3,774	2,618	400
2000	1,550	3,792	2,642	400

Source: U.S. Department of Commerce, Bureau of the Census, *Current Population Reports*, Series P-25, Nos. 521 and 541.

Note: Includes Alaska and Hawaii and Armed Forces abroad after 1939.

[1] Includes estimates of overseas admissions into and discharges from the Armed Forces and the error of closure between censuses.

[2] Adjusted for underregistration through March 1970.

[3] Deaths occurring in the United States plus estimated deaths occurring in the Armed Forces abroad except for 1930 through 1939 where the estimates are for the resident population of the conterminous United States only. Infant deaths adjusted for underregistration through March 1960.

[4] Series II presumes a fertility level of 2.1 children born per woman.

[5] Obtained by linear interpolation between successive fiscal year projections.

Chart 1/5

Social Indicators, 1976

COMPONENTS OF POPULATION CHANGE: 1930–2000

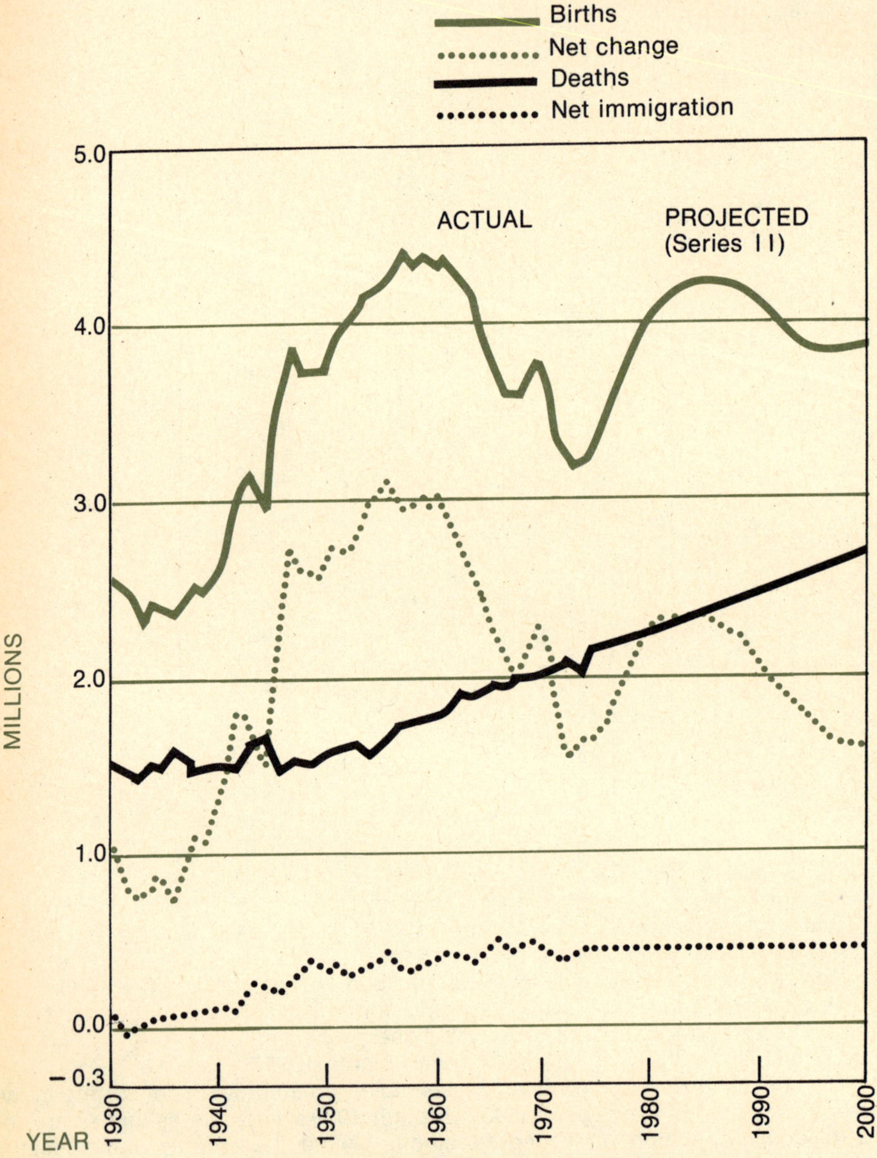

Source: see table 1/5

Table 1/6

FERTILITY RATES, BY RACE: 1940–1974

(Data relate to births adjusted for underregistration, 1940 to 1959; after 1959, data relate to registered births without further adjustment)

YEAR	TOTAL	WHITE	BLACK AND OTHER RACES	YEAR	TOTAL	WHITE	BLACK AND OTHER RACES
1940	2,301.3	2,229.1	2,870.2	1958	3,700.5	3,559.9	4,726.9
1941	2,399.1	2,328.0	2,956.3	1959	3,712.4	3,567.4	4,774.3
1942	2,628.3	2,577.3	3,022.1	1960	3,653.6	3,532.9	4,522.1
1943	2,718.3	2,664.3	3,128.2	1961	3,629.0	3,501.9	4,532.6
1944	2,567.6	2,500.5	3,075.0	1962	3,473.5	3,347.5	4,395.8
1945	2,491.2	2,421.2	3,016.7	1963	3,333.2	3,201.2	4,268.7
1946	2,942.7	2,900.9	3,238.3	1964	3,207.5	3,073.7	4,153.4
1947	3,273.5	3,229.5	3,575.3	1965	2,928.0	2,790.3	3,891.4
1948	3,108.5	3,021.7	3,742.1	1966	2,736.1	2,609.2	3,614.9
1949	3,110.1	3,008.7	3,854.8	1967	2,572.6	2,453.1	3,385.3
1950	3,090.5	2,976.8	3,928.3	1968	2,476.8	2,368.4	3,196.9
1951	3,269.3	3,156.9	4,091.2	1969	2,465.0	2,360.3	3,150.5
1952	3,358.4	3,249.9	4,146.9	1970	2,480.0	2,385.0	3,066.5
1953	3,424.1	3,306.4	4,283.4	1971	2,274.6	2,168.5	2,933.0
1954	3,542.6	3,415.1	4,473.9	1972	2,021.9	1,918.5	2,650.5
1955	3,579.7	3,446.0	4,549.7	1973	1,895.6	1,799.0	2,474.0
1956	3,689.0	3,545.5	4,729.9	1974	1,856.6	1,768.0	2,377.0
1957	3,767.0	3,625.2	4,797.8				

Source: U.S. Department of Health, Education, and Welfare, Public Health Service, National Center for Health Statistics, *Vital Statistics of the United States, 1968*, Vol. I; *Vital Statistics of the United States, 1969*, Vol. I; and *Monthly Vital Statistics Report*, Vol. 23, No. 11.

Chart 1/6

Social Indicators, 1976

FERTILITY RATES, BY RACE: 1940–1974

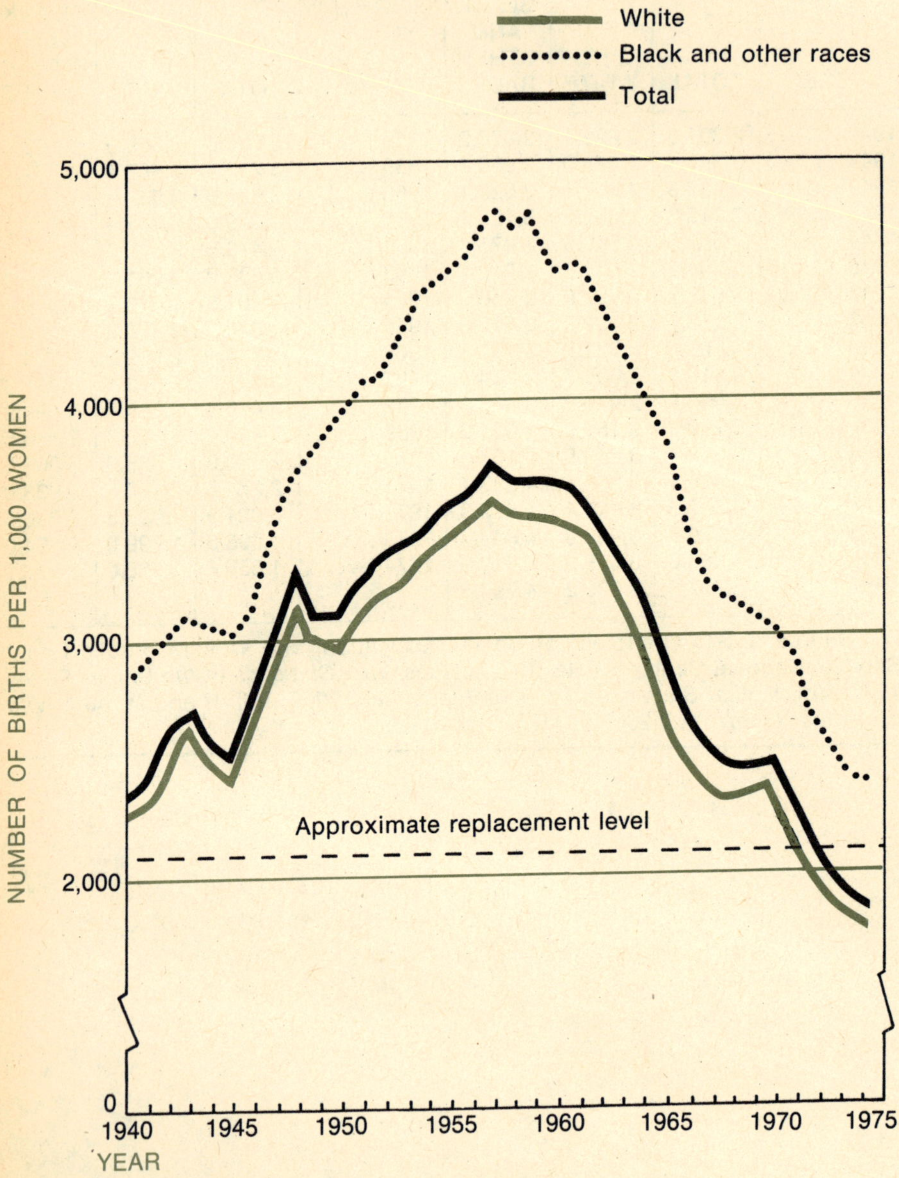

Source: see table 1/6

ANNALS, AAPSS, 435, Jan. 1978

Finally the Family

By MURRAY S. WEITZMAN

ABSTRACT: The family makes a belated but welcome appearance in *Social Indicators, 1976* after being all but ignored in *Social Indicators, 1973*. In recent years, statistics on the family have recorded a steady increase in the divorce rate, a decline in both the marriage and birth rates, and a rising proportion of premarital births to total births. These trends translate into family structures in which an increasing proportion of children are members of single-parent families. Although not inevitable, on balance some harmful spillover effects are probably generated such as less attractive human personal qualities, declining domestic tranquility in the community, and decreasing individual capability for educational achievement, work accomplishment, and earning power. After this second run through of social indicators, there seems to be sufficient evidence that, while the work was conducted by very competent people, the operational structure is far from optimal for achieving sustained progress in this field. Producing social indicators requires more than a process of searching and soliciting statistical tables from the statistical networks, assembling them in packages of charts, tables, and texts and marketing them in attractive publications. In the end it may come down to the fact that insufficient resources have been committed to these social indicator projects, precluding the formation of proper operational goals, rather than concluding that social indicator efforts are bereft of potential.

Murray S. Weitzman was Assistant Division Chief of the Population Division, U.S. Bureau of the Census in charge of Socioeconomic Statistics Programs from 1962 to 1977, and is now a Senior Researcher and Advisor on these subjects. He received a Doctorate in Economics from the University of Paris in 1950, and a masters degree from Columbia University in 1948. Prior research experience includes work on manpower and other economic aspects of the U.S.S.R. at the Bureau, participation in the U.S. Bureau of Labor Statistics' Interindustry Study of the American Economy for 1947 and its Long Range Economic Projections of the American Economy.

I am deeply grateful and indebted to two distinguished colleagues in the Population Division, U.S. Bureau of the Census, Dr. Paul C. Glick and Mr. Arthur J. Norton for their contributions to whatever measure of expertise I may have acquired with respect to the family and family statistics. Remaining shortcomings and personal perceptions in this paper are my own.

THE SECRET is out in *Social Indicators, 1976*. The family in this country continues to occupy a central and critical role in meeting many of the compelling needs of the young and not-so-young alike. Most would agree with this observation, including the people who assembled and issued *Social Indicators, 1973*. However, if there had been a request from this journal, or a similar one, for a set of interpretive papers in connection with the earlier social indicator report, a paper on the family would not have been required because the family was not of major significance in that volume. The family had become a noninstitution, deprived of its own proper identity, and was to be found only as a classification variable in *Social Indicators, 1973*, primarily in chapter 5 dealing with income.

INTRODUCTION

In recent years, statistics on the family have recorded a steady increase in the divorce rate, a decline in both the marriage and birth rates, and a rising proportion of premarital births to total births. These statistics translate into family structures in which an increasing proportion of children are members of single-parent families, primarily headed by women. Although not inevitable, on balance some harmful spillover effects and rising social and economic costs are probably generated; for example, less attractive human personal qualities and interpersonal relations, less domestic tranquility in the community and less individual capability for educational achievement, work accomplishment, and earning power. Whether the population's experiences involving marriage, divorce, births, and living arrangements tend to stabilize, turn around, or continue current trends is a matter of importance to all in every walk of life and endeavor. From stuff such as this, significant social indicators should emerge.

FAMILY INDICATORS

It should be pointed out that the census defines a family as all persons related by blood, marriage, or adoption who live in the same housing unit. This is a narrow definition which diminishes to some extent its value for purposes of social indicators. Working within its traditional operational framework of counting persons, assigning them to households, and identifying and combining them into families where appropriate, the Census Bureau has not been in a position to date to explore systematically more extensive and intricate family relationships, and the support and communication systems developed among kin networks. Ignoring behavioral patterns nurtured through affection, tradition, and family duty because of a lack of kinship information, not only removes a significant factor from consideration in the assessment of family life, but can affect the interpretation accorded family developments within a social indicator context. As an example of the limiting nature of the census definition of the family, part of a statement in *Social Indicators, 1976* seems to be unwarranted. The statement reads as follows:

> . . . the proportion of older men who are heads of their own households (either heads of primary families or primary individuals) has risen from 80 percent in 1955 to 95 percent in 1975—a clear indication of both growing independence and growing isolation of this population group.[1]

Although one can conjecture about the socioeconomic status of older men, it is not possible to infer solely from census data on living arrangements that there is a growing isolation of older men in the population—a negative social indicator in contrast to growing independence—a positive one.

Trends in family size and composition

The complement of charts and data in *Social Indicators, 1976* that serve to depict family size and composition catch many of the significant movements of the past decades and miss others. This is probably inevitable in the sort of statistical anthology that *Social Indicators, 1976* represents. The prose accompanying the statistical material is so calm and considered that the full impact of some of the profound developments changing the nature, characteristics, roles, and functions of the family and family members can go unrecognized. Although some enlightenment may be expected from review articles such as this one, further improvements may still be possible in Social Indicators' publications without the need to resort to editorializing. The reservations here expressed are well illustrated in the paragraph which begins the *Social Indicators, 1976* section on trends in family size and composition:

> The general trend during the past three decades in the growth of the number of families in the U.S. has been relatively stable. Projections of the number of families to the year 1990 reflect this stability and provide some insight into future demands in the area of family needs. While the husband-wife family group (over four-fifths of all families) remains the basic core of family types, the family headed by a female (with no husband present) will continue to be an important group affecting family and child care-related decisions.[2]

The distinct impression conveyed is that very little dynamic development has occured in the family during the past three decades. Although this impression is modified somewhat in the succeeding paragraphs, the tenor of the family conditions described in *Social Indicators, 1976* leads me to conclude that any overall summary would have to stress the thought that family composition, on balance, has been relatively stable during the past decades.

1. U.S. Department of Commerce, Office of Federal Statistical Policy and Standards and Bureau of the Census, *Social Indicators, 1976* (Washington, D.C.: USGPO, 1977), chap. 2, sec. II: "Living Arrangements."

2. *Social Indicators, 1976*, chap. 2, sec. I: "Trends in Family Size and Composition."

1. Family Growth and Composition

For the period 1960 to 1975, families as a group have been increasing more rapidly than husband/wife families with spouse present. All families increased from 45,149,000 in 1960 to 51,237,000 in 1970, an increase of 13.5 percent.[3] For the same period, the percent increase for husband/wife families was 12.1 percent, slightly lower than for all families. However, the disparity increased considerably from 1970 to 1975. Comparable estimates, which are multiplied by two to compare with those from 1960 to 1970, are 17.4 percent for all families and 11.4 percent for husband/wife families. Among black families, the 1970 to 1975 percent change on a decade basis is 30.4 percent for all families and 6.0 percent for husband/wife families.

All told, husband/wife families registered a sluggish increase of 2.2 million units between 1970 and 1975 on a 1970 base of 44.8 million families. In contrast, families headed by a female registered a strong 1.6 million gain from 5.6 million in 1970 to 7.2 million in 1975. Divorced women maintaining families were up 850 thousand from 1,260 thousand in 1970, while separated were up 400 thousand and single women heading families were up 300 thousand over 1970. Surely something more than relative stability has been occurring in family composition, something which can be extracted from the data included in *Social Indicators, 1976*.

The combination of sharp increases in the numbers and proportions of female heads of families, no spouse present, and wives in the paid labor force represent one of the most striking modifications in the composition of families. Not only is the traditional type of family, the husband/wife family, with wife not in the paid labor force, in decline, it may also be in disrepute among some members of the population. More than one wife has felt the need to defend and justify herself when, in responding to the question What do you do?, answers that she is a homemaker seeing to the welfare of her husband and children.

In 1960, 62 percent of all families in the United States consisted of husband/wife families with wife not in the paid labor force, 25 percent husband/wife families with wife in the paid labor force, and 10 percent female heads of families (figure 1). By 1970, the leading family group represented only 52 percent of all families as the other two family components under discussion increased their proportions of all families to 34 and 11 percent, respectively. Sometime between 1973 and 1974, husband/wife families with wife not in the labor force dipped below 50 percent. The reading for this group as of March 1975 was 48 percent of all families and by March 1976 it had further declined to 47 percent.

2. Marital Status

The text in *Social Indicators, 1976* that relates to marital status of the population 14 years old and over by sex, standardized on the basis of the age distribution in 1960, is a classic

3. Adjustments following revisions to 1970 census-based population controls result in the following revised estimates in parentheses, 13.5 percent (14.4 percent), 12.1 percent (13.8 per cent) 17.4 percent (16.0 percent) and 11.4 percent (10.0 percent). Estimates based on the Bureau of the Census, *Current Population Survey* are subject to sampling variability, nonresponse, and respondent bias. Therefore, it is possible that not all comparisons made in this paper, and based on the *Current Population Survey*, are statistically significant at designated standard errors of estimate.

FIGURE 1: TYPE OF FAMILY AS A PERCENT OF ALL FAMILIES: 1960, 1975

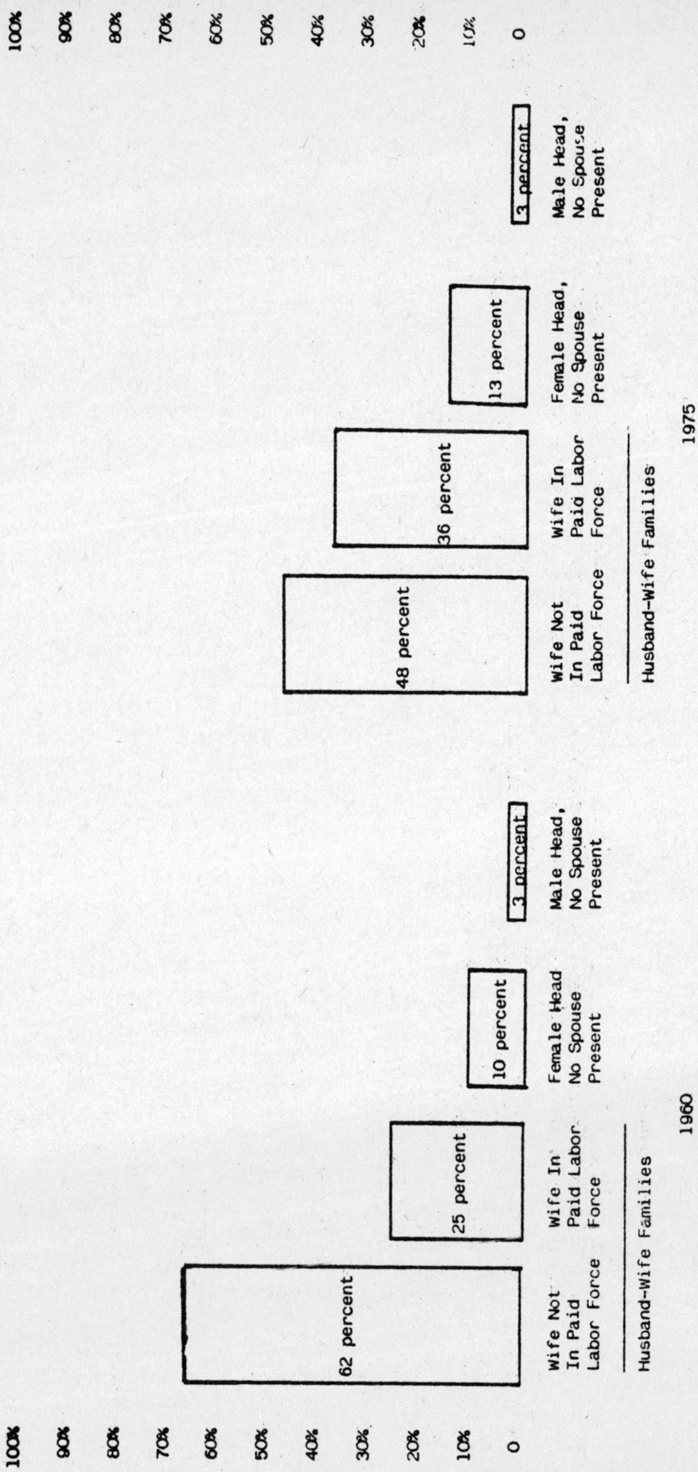

SOURCE: U.S. Bureau of the Census, *Current Population Survey*.

illustration of the danger of over looking the many significant changes taking place among the various components by presenting the data in terms of a general average. It states:

> Taking the changing age distribution of the adult population into account, it is evident that the proportion of married persons has remained remarkably stable over the 25-year span from 1950 to 1975. The only major changes in these proportions have occurred among the ("divorced") categories which have risen among both men and women.[4]

This "remarkably stable" proportion of married persons in the population, when standardized for age distribution, masks some significant developments. It is true that the percent of the married female population was 63.9 in 1950 and 63.5 in 1975, but the intermediate years include estimates of 65.6 percent in 1960 and 64.9 percent in 1970. In this instance, the stability referred to in the married component of the marital status of the population diverts attention from significant developments occurring among the different age groups at various stages of life. It tends to be the exception rather than the rule when many components of an aggregate or summary statistic move in the same direction and within a narrow range. It has been observed that prices in specific product markets do not move or mirror average price movements, but rather tend to adjust to specific supply and demand conditions, although general economic conditions undoubtedly do influence such markets.

Although those eligible for marriage can be drawn theoretically from the entire eligible population, generally, specific marriage markets neither encompass the entire age spectrum nor run the gamut of persons with widely varying backgrounds. But it should be possible, and such an effort is made in the following paragraphs to demonstrate that there is some merit in the criticisms raised with respect to the particular observation cited in *Social Indicators, 1976* about the "remarkable stability" in the proportion of married persons.

A bit of detective work into the basic marriage data for the years 1950, 1960, 1970, and 1975, and extending the review to some other years not shown in the report—1959, 1965, 1977—reveals different timing patterns of peaks and troughs with respect to the percent of women married by age groupings. If we consider marriage to be the preferred living arrangement for adults of the opposite sex, then we can formulate the following propositions with respect to the occurrences of peak and trough years for the percent of women married by age group:

1. The more recent the peak year, the more positive the social indicator;
2. The less recent the peak year, the less positive the social indicator;
3. The more recent the trough year, the less positive the social indicator; and
4. The less recent the trough year, the more positive the social indicator.

It is possible to limit the description of the changes that have occurred in the percent of married women by age group to the years cited in *Social Indicators, 1976* without distorting the basic trends. However, the addition of three years to the analysis, a compromise to showing consecutive years of annual data, lends a bit more

4. *Social Indicators, 1976*, chap. 2, sec. III: "Family Stability."

TABLE 1

PERCENT OF WOMEN MARRIED BY AGE GROUP: IDENTIFICATION OF PEAKS AND TROUGHS FOR SELECTED YEARS: 1950–77

	PEAK YEAR—PERCENT MARRIED							TROUGH YEAR—PERCENT MARRIED							
	POSITIVE TENDENCY IN TERMS OF A SOCIAL INDICATOR ← ; NEGATIVE TENDENCY IN TERMS OF A SOCIAL INDICATOR →							NEGATIVE TENDENCY IN TERMS OF A SOCIAL INDICATOR ← ; POSITIVE TENDENCY IN TERMS OF A SOCIAL INDICATOR →							
AGE OF WOMEN	MOST RECENT YEAR (1977)	1975	1970	(1965)	1960	(1959)	LEAST RECENT YEAR 1950	MOST RECENT YEAR (1977)	1975	1970	(1965)	1960	(1959)	LEAST RECENT YEAR 1950	AGE OF WOMEN
14–17							5.9	2.5 ←	———	2.7					14–17
18–19						33.7 ←	31.6	19.8 ←	21.6						18–19
20–24					69.3 →	69.7		51.3 ←	55.9						20–24
25–29					87.4 →	87.8		75.8 ←	79.3						25–29
30–34				90.5 ←	88.8			82.8 ←	84.8						30–34
35–44				87.9 ←	87.4			83.1 ←	———	———	———	———	———	83.7	35–44
45–54			82.2											77.3	45–54
55–64	70.1 ←	69.3												65.1	55–64
65–74	49.5 ←	49.0								45.1					65–74
75+		23.4									20.2 ←	21.0			75+

SOURCE: U.S. Bureau of the Census, *Current Population Survey* and table 2.
NOTE: Years in parentheses represent additional years not included in table and chart 2/3, *Social Indicators, 1976*.

currency to the data; it also suggests that data shown only for selected years may miss the actual peaks and troughs and, therefore, understate the degree of change that has actually taken place. In table 1, whenever the peak or trough year did not occur in the year cited in *Social Indicators, 1976*, there are two percents entered, one for the year cited in the report and the other for the year in which the peak or trough is indicated. The basic background data are presented in table 2 and show the variability and trends in percent married by age group.

From the data in table 1, it is apparent that for the selected years shown, marriage as a positive social indicator has had a checkered performance record when disaggregated by age. In contrast to the statement in *Social Indicators, 1976* noting the remarkable stability of the production of married persons, performance has tended to be negative for groups of women under 44 years of age, with poorer records for the younger women in this group. The latter tended to peak earlier and to trough later. For women 45 years and older, the trough years occurred at an earlier time than did the peak ones.

Marital status data in an age cohort format by race (black and white) and sex are intrinsically interesting in that they represent an historical tracing of people in the same chronological age group who have been exposed to generally common experiences under fairly comparable conditions. The effects of particular historical experiences tend to linger and influence current and future actions. Generally the analytic potential of the data is increased and the forecasting potential enhanced when it is feasible to combine a series of age cohorts into a single system and display it in tables and charts. The potential of this type of presentation is illustrated in table 2, in which se-

TABLE 2

PERCENT OF WOMEN MARRIED BY AGE GROUP: SELECTED YEARS 1950–77

<table>
<tr><th>AGE OF WOMEN</th><th>(1977)</th><th>1975</th><th>1970</th><th>(1965)</th><th>1960</th><th>(1959)</th><th>1950</th><th>AGE OF WOMEN</th></tr>
<tr><td>Total</td><td>59.3</td><td>60.4</td><td>61.9</td><td>63.9</td><td>65.6</td><td>66.3</td><td>66.1</td><td>Total</td></tr>
<tr><td>14–17</td><td>2.5</td><td>2.8</td><td>2.7</td><td>3.4</td><td>4.5</td><td>4.2</td><td>5.9</td><td>14–17</td></tr>
<tr><td>18–19</td><td>19.8</td><td>21.6</td><td>24.0</td><td>26.0</td><td>28.1</td><td>33.7</td><td>31.6</td><td>18–19</td></tr>
<tr><td>20–24</td><td>51.3</td><td>55.9</td><td>61.6</td><td>65.6</td><td>69.3</td><td>69.7</td><td>66.2</td><td>20–24</td></tr>
<tr><td>25–29</td><td>75.8</td><td>79.3</td><td>84.7</td><td>87.2</td><td>87.4</td><td>87.8</td><td rowspan="2">85.5</td><td>25–29</td></tr>
<tr><td>30–34</td><td>82.8</td><td>84.5</td><td>88.4</td><td>90.5</td><td>88.8</td><td>89.1</td><td>30–34</td></tr>
<tr><td>35–44</td><td>83.1</td><td>84.8</td><td>87.0</td><td>87.9</td><td>87.4</td><td>87.1</td><td>83.7</td><td>35–44</td></tr>
<tr><td>45–54</td><td>80.5</td><td>79.9</td><td>82.2</td><td>81.8</td><td>78.9</td><td>78.4</td><td>77.3</td><td>45–54</td></tr>
<tr><td>55–64</td><td>70.1</td><td>69.3</td><td>67.4</td><td>66.8</td><td>65.7</td><td>65.2</td><td>65.1</td><td>55–64</td></tr>
<tr><td>65–74</td><td>49.5</td><td>49.0</td><td>45.1</td><td>45.7</td><td>45.4</td><td>46.6</td><td rowspan="2">36.0</td><td>65–74</td></tr>
<tr><td>75 and over</td><td>21.5</td><td>23.4</td><td>21.0</td><td>20.2</td><td>21.0</td><td>20.8</td><td>75 and over</td></tr>
</table>

SOURCE: U.S. Bureau of the Census, *Current Population Survey*.

NOTE: Years in parentheses represent additional years not included in table and chart 2/3, *Social Indicators, 1976*

lected comparable age cohorts are linked by arrows from earlier years to later years.

Family stability

The section in *Social Indicators, 1976* dealing with family stability (Section III) concentrates on the formation and dissolution, via divorce, of husband/wife families and subsequent impact on the living arrangements of children. Although about 85 percent of all families are husband/wife families, a more apt title might be marital stability rather than family stability. There are, after all, many single-parent families headed by women or men that surely qualify as stable irrespective of the parents' martial status. In this context, the lead sentence in Section III seems less than precise: "Trends in the number of first marriages, divorces, and remarriages provide measures of family stability."[5]

Examining the information contained in the tables in this section and conceding that the term family stability is tantamount to husband/wife family stability, it is still questionable whether trends in marriage, divorces, and remarriages measure family stability. At best, it would seem that such trends and accompanying rates are suggestive of changes taking place in family stability and can possibly provide some intermediate inputs or corroborative information in estimating the duration of marriages and intervals between marriages.

As used in this section on family stability, data on marriages and divorces seem to be more appropriate in connection with husband-wife family growth and composition (Section I) than in connection with overall family stability. Data on marriages, divorces, and remarriages could be employed in preparing estimates of components of husband/wife family change paralleling estimates of components of population change for specific years, that is, the number of births, deaths, and net immigration. This latter series makes it possible to examine the amount that each element contributes to the change in population between two successive years. Similarly, for components of family change, it would be possible to estimate the major factors contributing to changes in husband/wife family numbers between successive periods, subject to errors of closure. In constructing this type of series, it would be necessary, in addition to marriage and divorce data, to introduce data on dissolution of marriage by the death of at least one marital partner. Also required would be adjustments for the net increase or decrease in husband/wife families arising from entries and exits from the country.

Because of the interrelationships between marital status and living arrangements of the population, estimates of component changes of husband/wife families during the period influence the number and average size of other family types and unrelatedness—the number, age, and sex of unrelated individuals. In effect the procedure would have many of the elements of a double entry system and would be geared to measure gross flows in reconciling and understanding net changes for specific family and unrelated individual groups. For example, families headed by a female are added during a period to the number of such families that were in existence at the beginning of the period as a result of the temporary absence of the husband, divorce, or the death of the husband which, of course, represent major attrition elements from the number of

5. Ibid.

husband/wife families in existence at the beginning of the period. Subtractions from the number of female heads of families during the course of the period arise for such reasons as the return of the husband, remarriages, death of the female head, or exit of all family members from the home resulting in the reclassification of the female head to that of an unrelated individual.

If in this instance the use of marriage and divorce data is less than satisfactory as a social indicator for measuring the stability of husband/wife families, are there any kinds of data available or on the horizon that can better meet this objective? One worthwhile approach may be the actuarial type of statistical statement that is used in life expectancy estimates: the number of children of given age cohort of women are likely to have by the end of their childbearing years, and length of working life.

Table 3 illustrates a probability approach to measure husband/wife family stability. The table displays the percent of ever-married persons by sex and year of birth whose first marriage had already ended in divorce in June 1975 and also the per-

TABLE 3

PERCENT OF EVER-MARRIED PERSONS WHOSE FIRST MARRIAGE MAY EVENTUALLY END IN DIVORCE AND WHOSE SECOND MARRIAGE MAY EVENTUALLY END IN REDIVORCE BY YEAR OF BIRTH AND SEX: JUNE 1975

Sex and Year of Birth	Percent of Ever-Married Persons Whose First Marriage—		Percent of Persons Married Twice Whose Second Marriage—	
	Had Ended in Divorce by 1975	May Eventually End in Divorce*	Had Ended in Redivorce by 1975	May Eventually End in Redivorce*
MALE				
1945–1949	13	34	5	35
1940–1944	17	31	6	32
1935–1939	20	29	5	28
1930–1934	18	24	8	24
1925–1929	18	22	7	20
1920–1924	18	20	9	18
1915–1919	17	18	9	13
1910–1914	17	17	7	9
1905–1909	15	15	7	8
1900–1904	13	13	6	6
FEMALE				
1945–1949	17	38	8	44
1940–1944	20	34	12	40
1935–1939	21	31	10	31
1930–1934	21	26	11	26
1925–1929	21	24	14	23
1920–1924	18	20	8	15
1915–1919	16	17	11	16
1910–1914	16	16	10	12
1905–1909	15	15	9	9
1900–1904	13	13	5	5

SOURCE: U.S. Bureau of the Census, *Current Population Reports*, ser. P–20, no. 297 (October 1976).

* If their future divorce experience is similar to that of persons in older age groups between 1969 and 1974.

cent of persons whose marriages may eventually end in divorce. This presentation is repeated in the table for persons married twice. As of June 1975, estimates indicate that the younger the ever-married person, the more likely the first marriage will eventually end in divorce. For those ever-married persons who were between 25 and 35 years old in 1975, about one-third will eventually have their first marriages terminated by divorce.

A variant of the estimates of marriages that may eventually end in divorce is table 4, recently prepared by Dr. Paul C. Glick. It is suggestive of what can be done periodically with the materials on hand regarding family dissolution (divorce and death) by skilled researchers on the family. The table approximates the estimated proportions of couples married only once, or more than once, reaching selected wedding anniversaries.

TABLE 4

ESTIMATED MARRIAGE SURVIVAL RATES TO SELECTED WEDDING ANNIVERSARIES BY FIRST MARRIAGE AND REMARRIAGE: CIRCA 1971

WEDDING ANNIVERSARY	FIRST MARRIAGE	REMARRIAGE
5th	5 of every 6	4 of every 5
10th	4 of every 5	3 of every 4
20th	3 of every 4	1 of every 2
30th	2 of every 3	1 of every 3
35th	1 of every 2	1 of every 5
40th	2 of every 5	1 of every 8
45th	1 of every 3	1 of every 15
50th	1 of every 5	1 of every 20
55th	1 of every 10	1 of every 50
60th	1 of every 20	1 of every 100
65th	1 of every 50	Very rare
70th	1 of every 100	Very rare

SOURCE: Unpublished estimates prepared by Dr. Paul C. Glick.

Marital history surveys yield data on the duration of current marriage, the interval between first marriage and divorce, and other marital and vital events. As social indicators for measuring husband/wife family stability, these statistical formulations may be more relevant than the mere presentation of data on marriages and divorces, numbers and rates found in *Social Indicators, 1976*.

Statistics on children in families (i.e., never married persons under 18 years of age) have interesting applications in a social indicator context. The living arrangements of children, obviously products of past events (marriages, births, divorces, deaths, premarital births), describe current child-parent relationships, and hint at future developments along a broad front of social and economic concerns. As employed in *Social Indicators, 1976*, children's living arrangements shown for both white and black children, are linked to family stability and reflect previous events associated with parental actions.

Indicative of the substantial decline in family stability in recent years is the sharp increase in the proportion of children in families living with single parents, primarily the mother. The percent of children living with only the mother increased from 8.1 percent in 1960 to 15.6 percent in 1975, and reached 15.9 percent in 1976. Only one-half of all black children in 1975 and 1976 lived with both parents, down from nearly 70 percent in 1960 and nearly 60 percent in 1970. Although the total number of children living in families declined from 68.7 million in 1970 to 65.7 million in 1975, the number in families living with mother only actually increased from 8 million in 1970 to 10 million in 1975.

Linkages also can be established between the living arrangements for children and the increasing socioeconomic phenomenon of wives in the paid labor force that was described previously. Among husband/wife families, the proportion of children with mothers in the labor force was 37.6 percent in 1970, 42.9 percent in 1975 and 44.3 percent in 1976. For children under 6 years of age, comparable percentages were 27.6 percent in 1970, 34.5 percent in 1975, and 35.1 percent in 1976. The generally noted development of the increasing participation of women in the labor force has also occurred for mothers who are the only parent rearing the children.

More than one-half of all children in 1970 (52.5 percent), lived with both parents and with the mother not in the labor force. By 1975, this percentage was down to 46.1 percent and in 1976 to 44.8 percent. Reflecting the strong pull of wives into the labor force, the percent of all children living with both parents, and with the mother in the labor force, has increased since 1970 (31.6 percent—1970; 34.7 percent—1975; and 35.7 percent—1976), notwithstanding the percent decline of all children living with both parents (84.1 percent—1970; 80.8 percent—1975; and 80.5 percent—1976).

As social indicators, the type of developments described here seem to be more open to normative interpretation than some types of economic indicators such as those relating to unemployment (low better than high), price change (small better than large), and gross national product (sustainable growth with low unemployment and relatively stable prices). In the case of working mothers there are many questions to be asked. What kind of care do children receive when the mother is working, and is it acceptable on the average as compared to that received from a mother who is not in the labor force? To what extent does the mother's income contribute to the welfare of the child and family structure? Is it worth it when all costs, both current and future, are considered?

Again focusing on the probability approach as a useful strategy in preparing social indicators, analytic estimates can be developed that are directed to answering the following type of question: What proportion of babies born in given years and surviving to age 18 will (or will not) experience growing up with both of their natural parents, or parents who adopted them very shortly after birth? Preparing such estimates for periodic intervals certainly can serve to summarize some of the major natural and social factors occurring in the population.

As an example of this probability approach, Arthur J. Norton recently performed a computational exercise to guesstimate an "expected" single-parent situation for a hypothetical 100 babies born in 1977. After making reasonable adjustments for statistics and conditions relating to premarital births, divorce, separation, and death of a parent, Norton found it conceivable that 45 percent of the babies born in 1977 will experience a single-parent situation before they reach 18. In order of descending contribution to the 45 percent guesstimate are divorces (27 percent), premarital births (10 percent), separations (5 percent), and death of a parent (3 percent). At about the turn of the century, the probability of a child experiencing a single-parent situation was less than it is now, with the death of a parent, rather than divorce, being the principal contributing factor. Norton speculates that children in the near future will be much younger when they experience a single-parent situation than was the case in the past.

Living arrangements

Changes in the living arrangements of persons since 1955 have been significantly affected by, and have had a significant effect on, changing social standards, expanding economic opportunities, and increasing government participation in all kinds of social programs. The text and some of the tables accompanying Section I of the family chapter of *Social Indicators, 1976* do capture and highlight the extraordinary changes that have occurred in living arrangements and in household composition in recent years, especially in the proportion of persons classified as primary individuals. In 20 years, from 1955 to 1975, this proportion increased from about 13 percent to 22 percent, corresponding to an increase in the number of primary individuals of from 6.1 to 15.6 million. There may be some doubt as to whether on balance the changing living arrangement patterns for a specific age and sex group represent positive or negative social phenomena. Undoubtedly, the developments are positive for persons engaged in construction, housing, and the other industries that benefit from household formations increasing at a much faster rate than the population. If one can infer that the evolving living arrangement patterns represent predominantly personal preferences, then the positive side of the equation comes out ahead. There have been some very positive factors supporting more independent living arrangements for the elderly population. These factors include increases in annual and lifetime income in a growing economy spurred on by productivity increases and wealth accumulations in the form of dollar savings, life insurance policies, home ownership, and private and public pensions. To these, it is necessary to add the supporting contributions from government programs such as social security, health care, housing subsidies, food stamps, and various other income supporting strategies.

CONCLUDING OBSERVATIONS

Social Indicators, 1976 represents the first effort in this program at organizing statistical material to describe family developments. It does not appear that a shotgun approach was used in the hope that some of the charts and tables would hit the target. At the same time the selection process should not be akin to shopping at the statistical supermarket and then trying to determine how many of the purchases were planned and how many the result of impulse selection. Choosing and presenting materials for the family chapter would benefit from establishing criteria that are explicit both in terms of placement of subject matter and the purpose of each chart and table. The suggestions made in the course of reviewing the family chapter can be modified or rejected outright, but stating them explicitly should give people the opportunity to examine the propositions without having to infer what was in the minds of the authors at the time the materials were brought together.

Producing social indicators requires more than a process of searching and soliciting statistical tables from the statistical network, assembling them in packages of charts, tables and texts, and marketing them in attractive publications. In the normal course of events, it is too much to expect that statistical suppliers, even with solid instruction on the purposes and uses of social indicators, will provide data that can be effectively employed as submitted in preparing social indicators. After this second runthrough of social indicators, there is proof positive that, while the work was conducted by very competent people, the operational structure is far from optimal for achieving sustained progress in the development of social indicators. Additional inspiration, expertise, and perspiration by a staff geared to a more structured effort of research and exploration, rather than to assembly and editing, seems to be required to produce a satisfactory product. In the end it may come down to the fact that insufficient resources have been committed to the projects, precluding the formation of proper operational goals.

The following questions have been asked before but should be asked again. (1) What is so new and different about social indicators and their potential usefulness, as compared with social statistics, that resources should be extended in their pursuit? (2) What kind of model or models can be constructed that give form to goals and at the same time are so structured that they facilitate the exploitation of ideas and relationships? (3) Are there any separate statistical series that already exist which are serviceable? (4) Which data can be modified to improve their relevance for future social indicators undertakings? and (5) What data are missing that should be collected or can be assembled from existing series?

Representing as it does, the primary social unit to which the vast majority of people are linked and on which they depend for so many human wants, the family and its members' positions and activities in it should occupy a central place in summarizing and describing individuals' experiences. Without constructing proper frames of reference for various social and economic phenomena that incorporate the family, and that hopefully can be extended to include information on kin networks, our heritage is many statistical sets of data that can impress users more than they can increase their perceptions of changes in social conditions and performance.

Table 2/1

FAMILIES, BY TYPE AND SIZE: 1950–1990

YEAR AND PROJECTION SERIES	TOTAL FAMILIES (THOUSANDS)	TYPE OF FAMILY						AVERAGE SIZE OF FAMILY		
		Husband-wife, husband head		Other male head, no wife present		Female head, no husband present				
		Number (thousands)	Percent	Number (thousands)	Percent	Number (thousands)	Percent	Total	Members under 18 years old	Members 18 years old and over
1950	39,303	34,440	87.6	1,184	3.0	3,679	9.4	3.54	1.17	2.37
1955	41,951	36,378	86.7	1,339	3.2	4,234	10.1	3.59	1.30	2.29
1960	45,111	39,329	87.2	1,275	2.8	4,507	10.0	3.67	1.41	2.26
1965	47,956	41,749	87.1	1,181	2.5	5,026	10.5	3.70	1.44	2.26
1970	51,586	44,755	86.8	1,239	2.4	5,591	10.8	3.59	1.34	2.25
1975										
Series A	56,231	47,783	85.0	1,449	2.6	6,901	12.3	3.39	1.17	2.23
Series B	56,219	47,784	85.0	1,449	2.6	6,888	12.3	3.39	1.17	2.23
Series C	56,197	47,785	85.0	1,447	2.6	6,863	12.2	3.40	1.17	2.23
Series K	56,185	47,786	85.1	1,446	2.6	6,851	12.2	(NA)	(NA)	(NA)
1980										
Series A	61,312	51,806	84.5	1,566	2.6	7,858	12.8	3.21	1.02	2.19
Series B	61,234	51,825	84.6	1,561	2.5	7,758	12.7	3.22	1.02	2.20
Series C	61,080	51,864	84.9	1,550	2.5	7,560	12.4	3.24	1.02	2.22
Series K	61,004	51,885	85.1	1,543	2.5	7,463	12.2	(NA)	(NA)	(NA)
1985										
Series A	66,440	55,715	83.9	1,723	2.6	8,942	13.5	3.09	.96	2.12
Series B	66,255	55,757	84.2	1,713	2.6	8,711	13.1	3.11	.96	2.14
Series C	65,894	55,845	84.8	1,686	2.6	8,260	12.5	3.15	.97	2.18
Series K	65,718	55,891	85.0	1,668	2.5	8,040	12.2	(NA)	(NA)	(NA)
1990										
Series A	70,943	59,033	83.2	1,893	2.7	9,983	14.1	3.00	.94	2.06
Series B	70,606	59,073	83.7	1,877	2.7	9,601	13.6	3.04	.95	2.09
Series C	69,947	59,163	84.6	1,830	2.6	8,857	12.7	3.10	.96	2.14
Series K	69,622	59,209	85.0	1,798	2.6	8,495	12.2	(NA)	(NA)	(NA)

Source: U.S. Department of Commerce, Bureau of the Census, *Current Population Reports*, Series P-20, Nos. 266 and 282, and Series P-25, No. 607.
NA Not available.

Chart 2/1

Social Indicators, 1976

NUMBER OF FAMILIES, BY TYPE, SELECTED YEARS, 1950 TO 1990 (SERIES B)

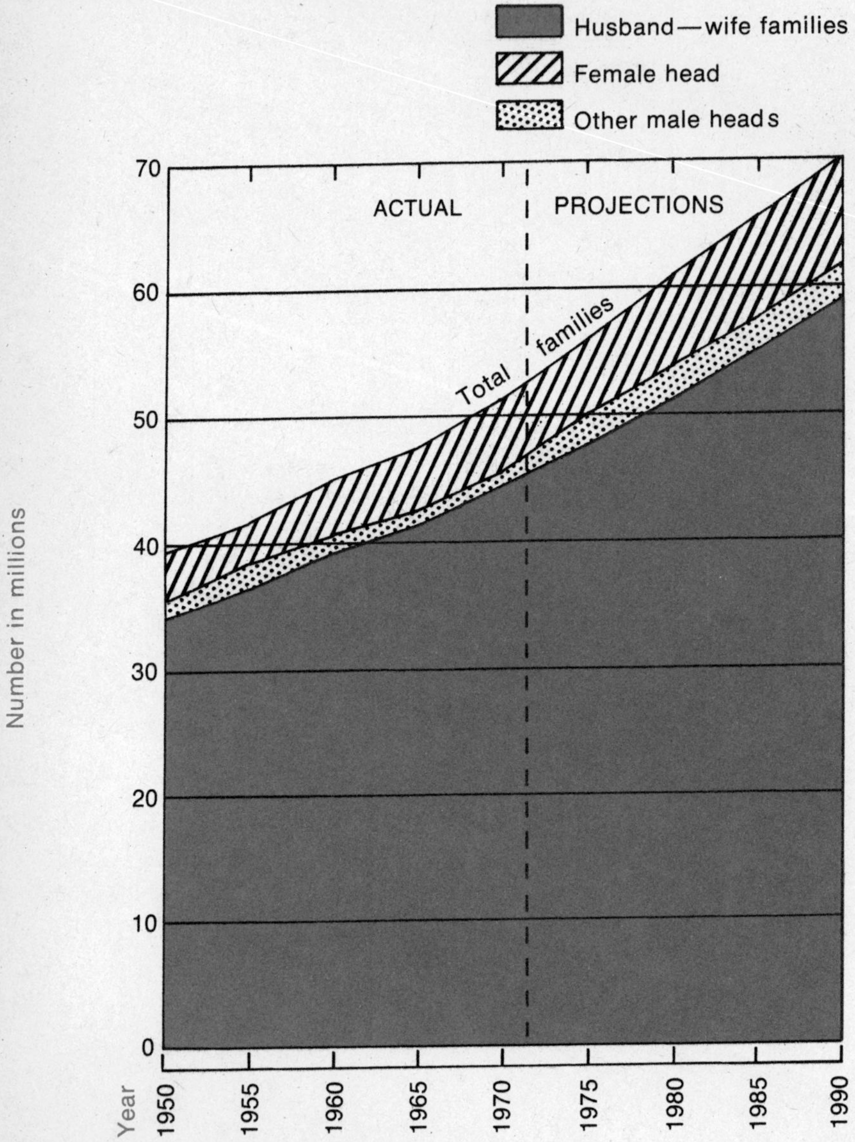

Source: see table 2/1

Table 2/2
SELECTED CHARACTERISTICS OF FAMILIES: 1960, 1970, AND 1975

SELECTED CHARACTERISTICS	1960			1970			1975		
	Total	White	Black[1]	Total	White	Black	Total	White	Black
All families. . .thous ...	45,149	40,887	4,262	51,237	46,022	4,774	55,712	49,451	5,498
Percent	100.0	100.0	100.0	100.0	100.0	100.0	100.0	100.0	100.0
Husband-wife	87.8	89.2	74.9	86.7	88.7	68.1	84.3	86.9	60.9
Other male head, no wife present	2.9	2.7	4.2	2.4	2.3	3.7	2.7	2.6	3.9
Female head, no husband present	9.3	8.1	20.9	10.9	9.1	28.3	13.0	10.5	35.3
Single, never married	1.1	1.0	2.3	1.2	.8	4.6	1.7	1.0	7.7
Widowed	4.6	4.2	8.4	4.7	4.3	8.4	4.6	4.2	8.7
Divorced	1.6	1.5	2.4	2.5	2.3	4.0	3.8	3.5	6.7
Married, husband absent	2.0	1.4	7.8	2.6	1.7	11.2	3.0	1.9	12.3
OWN CHILDREN UNDER 18									
None under 18	43.1	43.0	43.8	44.1	44.7	38.6	46.0	47.2	36.8
1 own child	18.4	18.7	15.6	18.2	18.2	17.9	19.7	19.4	22.0
2 own children	18.0	18.5	12.8	17.4	17.6	14.9	18.0	18.0	17.0
3 or more own children	20.5	19.7	27.9	20.3	19.4	28.7	16.2	15.4	24.2
Mean number per family	1.33	1.29	1.66	1.30	1.25	1.77	1.13	1.08	1.47
SIZE OF FAMILY									
2 persons	32.7	33.1	28.5	34.5	35.2	28.7	37.4	38.5	29.4
3 persons	21.6	21.9	19.1	20.9	20.9	19.9	21.8	21.6	22.7
4 persons	19.9	20.4	15.0	19.3	19.7	16.1	19.7	19.9	17.8
5 persons	12.8	12.9	11.6	12.5	12.6	11.7	11.3	11.3	11.3
6 or more persons	13.0	11.7	25.7	12.8	11.6	23.6	9.8	8.8	18.3

Source: U.S. Department of Commerce, Bureau of the Census, *1970 Census of Population*, Vol. II, Part 4A, and *Current Population Reports*, Series P-20, Nos. 218, 226, and 291.
[1] Black and other races in 1960.

Chart 2/2

Social Indicators, 1976

TYPES OF FAMILIES BY RACE OF HEAD, 1960, 1970 AND 1975

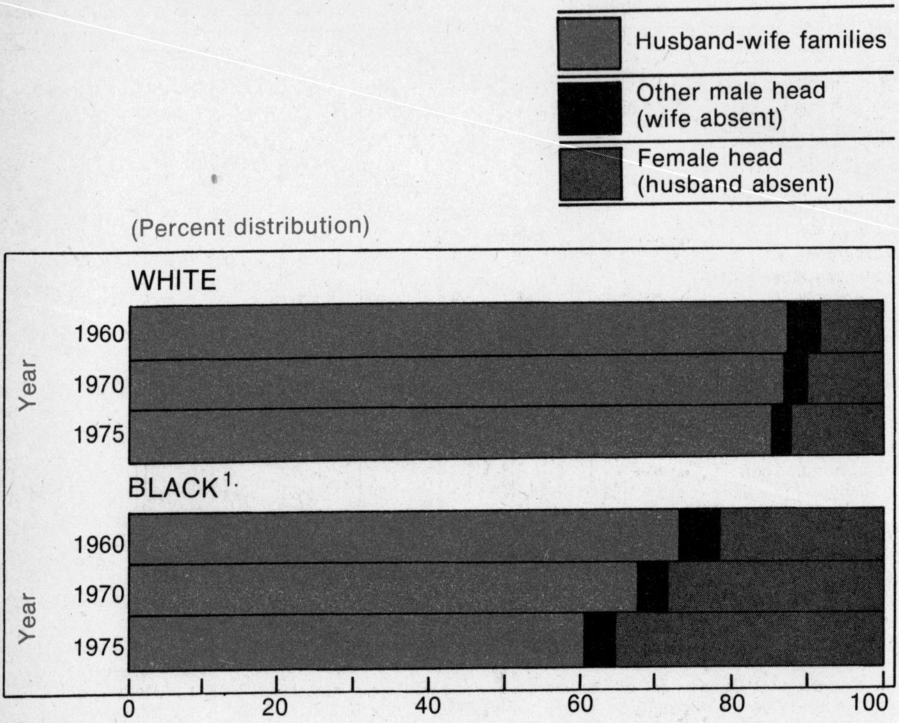

1. Black and other races in 1960

Source: see table 2/2

Table 2/4
MARITAL STATUS OF THE POPULATION, BY RACE AND SEX, FOR SELECTED COHORT GROUPS: 1950–1970
(Percent)

RACE, SEX, AND AGE	TOTAL	SINGLE	MARRIED	WIDOWED	DIVORCED
White male aged—					
25 to 34 in 1950	100.0	18.5	79.4	0.3	1.9
35 to 44 in 1960	100.0	7.7	89.3	.5	2.5
45 to 54 in 1970	100.0	6.1	88.8	1.4	3.6
White female aged—					
25 to 34 in 1950	100.0	11.3	85.1	1.0	2.6
35 to 44 in 1960	100.0	6.0	87.9	2.6	3.6
45 to 54 in 1970	100.0	5.4	82.2	7.2	5.2
Black male aged—					
25 to 34 in 1950	100.0	20.1	77.0	.9	2.0
35 to 44 in 1960	100.0	11.0	83.5	1.9	3.7
45 to 54 in 1970	100.0	8.9	81.1	4.3	5.7
Black female aged—					
25 to 34 in 1950	100.0	11.7	81.6	3.1	3.6
35 to 44 in 1960	100.0	7.0	79.9	7.1	5.8
45 to 54 in 1970	100.0	6.7	70.5	14.5	8.3

Source: U.S. Department of Commerce, Bureau of the Census, *1950 Census of Population*, Vol. II; *1960 Census of Population*, Vol. I; and *1970 Census of Population*, Vol. I.

Chart 2/4

Social Indicators, 1976

MARITAL STATUS OF THE POPULATION FOR SELECTED COHORTS, 1950, 1960 AND 1970, FOR WHITES AND BLACKS, BY SEX

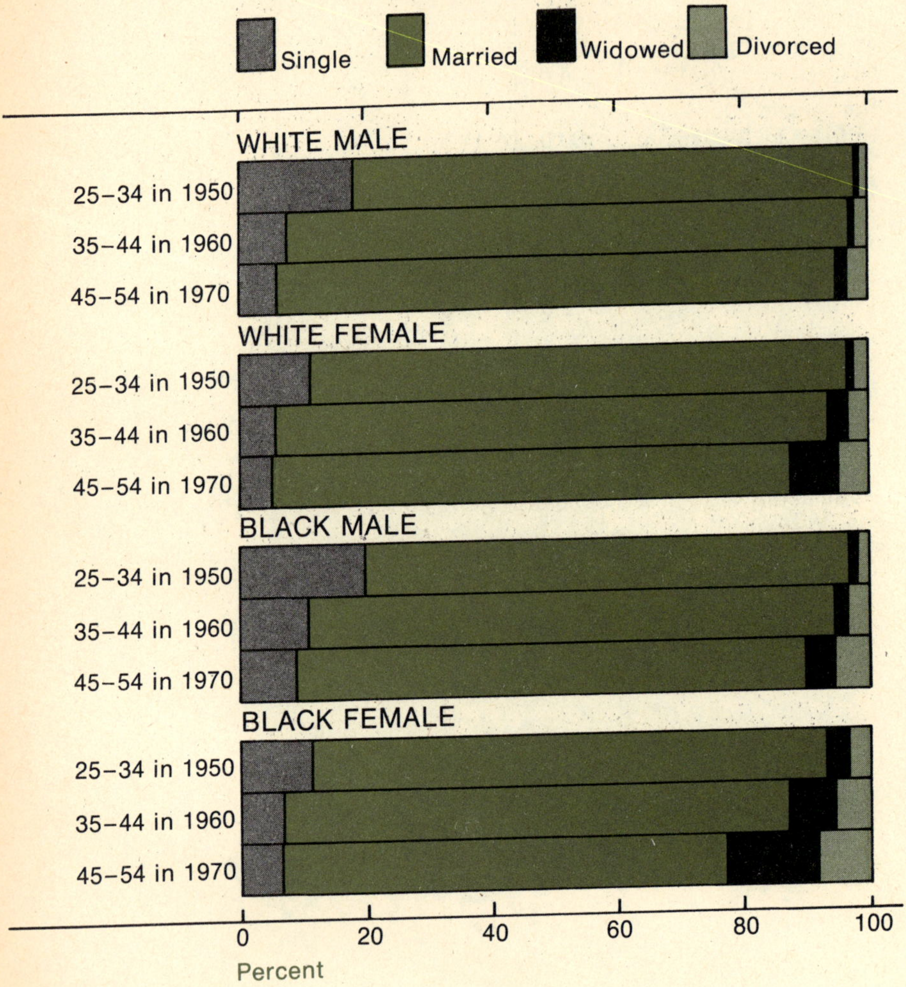

Source: see table 2/4

Table 2/7
PRIMARY INDIVIDUALS, BY SEX AND AGE: 1974–1990
(Thousands)

YEAR[1]	Male					Female				
	Under 25 years	25 to 54 years old	55 to 64 years old	65 to 74 years old	75 years and over	Under 25 years	25 to 54 years old	55 to 64 years old	65 to 74 years old	75 years and over
1974	905	2,703	715	709	622	749	2,073	1,799	2,578	2,089
1975	970	2,836	734	741	633	795	2,126	1,842	2,697	2,190
1976	1,022	2,958	749	765	639	836	2,172	1,879	2,792	2,271
1977	1,078	3,074	767	792	642	877	2,208	1,919	2,899	2,334
1978	1,130	3,204	782	818	649	916	2,250	1,954	3,001	2,412
1979	1,181	3,344	797	843	659	954	2,298	1,988	3,096	2,496
1980	1,228	3,498	812	867	671	989	2,348	2,021	3,187	2,590
1981	1,276	3,661	826	889	684	1,023	2,406	2,050	3,267	2,688
1982	1,313	3,832	841	910	697	1,048	2,467	2,075	3,341	2,793
1983	1,345	4,011	854	931	715	1,070	2,530	2,094	3,411	2,912
1984	1,372	4,200	864	955	733	1,088	2,592	2,102	3,492	3,036
1985	1,390	4,394	873	984	754	1,099	2,653	2,103	3,584	3,173
1986	(NA)	(NA)	(NA)	(NA)	(NA)	(NA)	(NA)	(NA)	(NA)	(NA)
1987	(NA)	(NA)	(NA)	(NA)	(NA)	(NA)	(NA)	(NA)	(NA)	(NA)
1988	(NA)	(NA)	(NA)	(NA)	(NA)	(NA)	(NA)	(NA)	(NA)	(NA)
1989	(NA)	(NA)	(NA)	(NA)	(NA)	(NA)	(NA)	(NA)	(NA)	(NA)
1990	1,430	5,415	882	1,123	838	1,129	2,996	2,034	4,053	3,820

Source: U.S. Department of Commerce, Bureau of the Census, *Current Population Reports*, Series P-25, No. 607.
NA Not available.
[1] Data for 1975 and later years are Series B projections.

Chart 2/7 Social Indicators, 1976

NUMBER OF PRIMARY INDIVIDUALS, BY AGE AND SEX, 1974 AND PROJECTED 1980, 1985 AND 1990 (SERIES B)

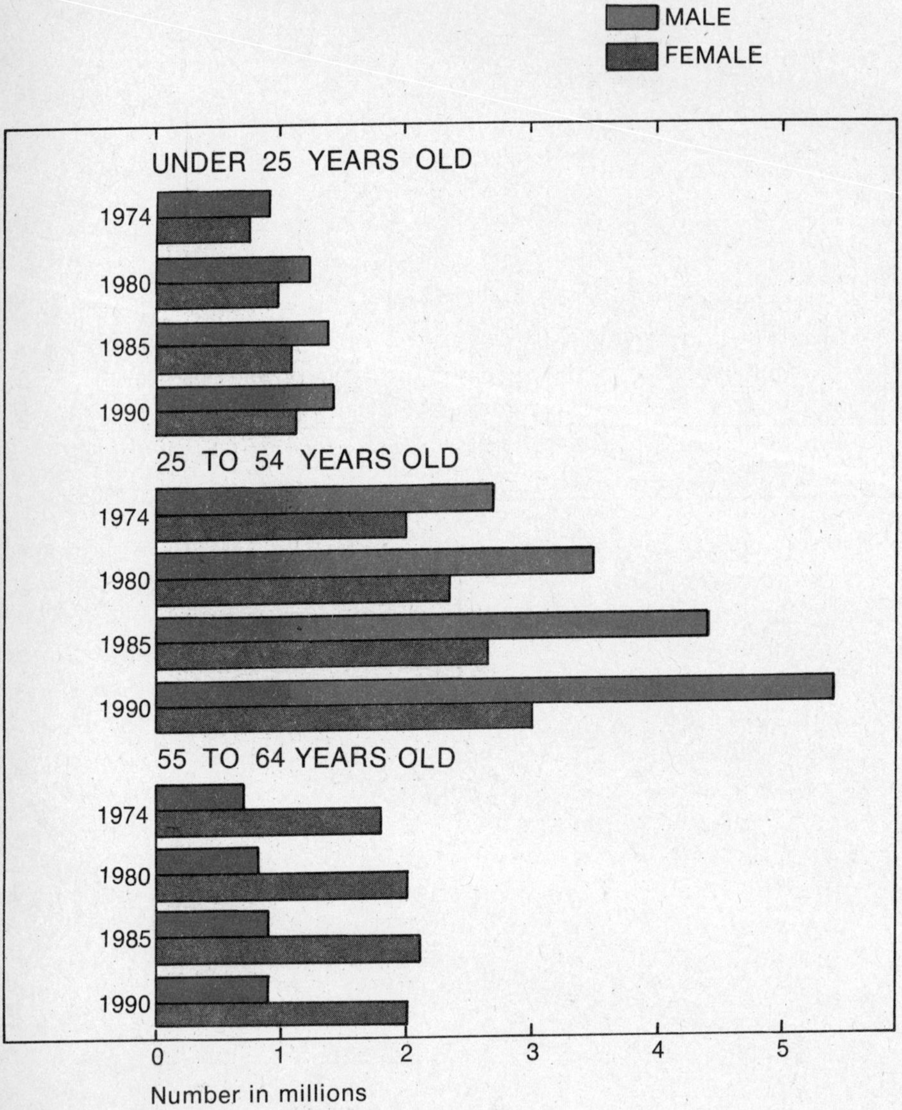

Source: see table 2/7

ANNALS, AAPSS, 435, Jan. 1978

Changing Work Life Patterns: A Twenty-five Year Review

By ANN R. MILLER

ABSTRACT: Over the past 25 years there have been substantial changes in the proportion of population engaged in market work and in the age and sex composition of the work force. The nonworker-worker ratio has fluctuated widely, primarily as a reflection of the dramatic fluctuations in birth rates, while the long-term trends of increasing participation by women and declining years of work by men have accelerated. Recent developments indicate that this acceleration of long-term trends has taken on certain new characteristics: young women appear to be returning to the labor market much more quickly after the birth of children, with a consequent reduction of time out of the work force; and the customary retirement age of men is falling. As a result, work life patterns are becoming increasingly similar for men and women and much higher proportions of the population in the age range 20–54 are working than has been true in the past. In a broader context, it is suggested that the rapid decline in average annual worker hours characteristic of the first part of the twentieth century may be transformed into a decline in average worker years in the last part.

Ann R. Miller is Associate Professor of Sociology at the University of Pennsylvania and Senior Research Associate in its Population Studies Center. She received her A.B. degree from Bryn Mawr College, her Ph.D. from the University of Pennsylvania. Over the past several years she has served on advisory committees to the U.S. Bureau of the Census and the National Institutes of Health and acted as consultant to the Statistical Policy Division of the Office of Management and Budget.

CHAPTER 8 of *Social Indicators, 1976* is concerned with work, the extent to which different groups in the population participate in this work, the kind of work done, and the rewards and satisfactions (or lack thereof) of work. It brings together a number of series, particularly in the section on "The Conditions and Quality of Work," that have not previously been assembled in one place and that provide the user with the opportunity to view the complexities of current issues in some perspective.

The present paper concentrates on the broad framework of the place of work in the life history of the individual. The availability of 25 years of data from the federal government's *Current Population Survey* enables us for the first time to monitor developments over a generation and it is this aspect of work that is preeminent as a social indicator, that is, that tells us most about the relation between work and the lives of people in this country.

LABOR FORCE AND POPULATION

It is a truism that, at any given time, the size and characteristics of the work force of a country are a joint product of its demographic history and of the probabilities that specific components of its population participate in market work. But it is only recently that the full significance of these two aspects of growth have emerged.

Table 1 presents summary indicators of the aggregate relation between population and labor force that reveal some of the long-term effects of our ability to control the basic demographic processes, that is, international migration, mortality, and fertility; less obvious, but also imbedded in the measures presented, are the effects of cumulative changes in the role of work in the individual's life.

The number of nonworkers per 100 workers rose sharply from 1950 to 1960, primarily as a result of the rapid increase in population below the working ages arising from the postwar "baby boom." Nonworkers in the older ages also increased in this period, but the rise was more than offset by the relative decline of nonworkers among those in the central ages, that is, 16–64. Since 1965, the ratio of nonworkers to workers has fallen precipitously, from 152 nonworkers for every 100 workers in 1965 to 125 in 1975; again the primary compositional factor has been the birth rate, which fell so sharply that in absolute terms there were almost 5,000,000 fewer persons below the age of 16 in 1975 than there had been in 1965.

If one makes the assumption that the nonworker-worker ratio is a crude approximation of a dependency ratio—and it is certainly only a crude approximation, since many nonworkers contribute essential services to the total national product—then the dependency burden is probably lower now than at any time in the previous history of the United States, and, as table 1 indicates, it is projected to fall to even lower levels. Its composition, however, is changing. Only slightly over 1 in 10 nonworkers was past 65 in 1950; by 1960 the proportion was 1 in 8; by 1975 it had risen to 1 to 6; and it is projected to reach 1 in 5 by 1990. This rising proportion does not occur because of a spurt in the growth of the older population. In terms of rates of increase, the major growth period for the population over 65 was the decade 1950–60, the years in which many of the large pre-World War I immigrant cohorts

TABLE 1

RATIO OF NONWORKERS TO WORKERS AND GROWTH RATES OF THE POPULATION AND LABOR FORCE, 1950–1990

	A. NONWORKERS PER 100 WORKERS				B. AVERAGE ANNUAL RATE OF CHANGE*			
		PROPORTION BY AGE				LABOR FORCE‡		
	TOTAL	UNDER 16	16–64	65 AND OVER	POPULATION†	TOTAL	MALE	FEMALE
1950	138	68	56	15	—	—	—	—
1955	144	75	52	16	1.72	1.28	.88	2.23
1960	150	82	50	19	1.70	1.16	.57	2.46
1965	152	81	50	20	1.46	1.35	.83	2.40
1970	138	72	47	20	1.06	2.14	1.29	3.70
1975	125	61	44	20	.84	1.97	1.20	3.23
1980	115	53	41	21	.84	1.81	1.43	2.38
1985	111	52	38	21	.99	1.29	.92	1.84
1990	111	53	36	22	.92	.92	.70	1.24

* Average over 5 previous years.
† All ages.
‡ 16 years of age and over.
SOURCE: *Social Indicators, 1976*, table 8/1.

attained this age. In the future, the growth rate for the population over 65 will be generally stable, or slightly downward, until well into the next century when the baby boom cohorts of 1947–62 reach this age. Although declines in mortality, and the concomitant increases in the average length of life, have obviously affected the size of the older population, their impact is gradual; the major determinants of rapid changes in this age group lie primarily in the previous migration and fertility history of the country. What accounts for the rising proportion of older persons in the nonworker group, then, is the relative decline in the other two components of nonworkers distinguished in table 1, that is, the population below working age and nonactive persons in the central ages.

The direct impact of the country's demographic history on the labor force is visible in another of the measures shown in table 1—the fluctuations in the average annual growth rate of the male labor force. Although many factors are associated with the changing size of the male labor force, fluctuations of the magnitude shown here are primarily reflecting fluctuations in past fertility levels. Most men enter the labor force between the ages of 18 and 24: the sharp fall in the growth rate in 1955–60 quinquennium (from 0.88 to 0.57 per annum) arises from the entry into these ages of the low birth cohorts of the Great Depression; the high growth rate starting in the 1965–70 period (1.29) and continuing through 1975–80 represents the coming of age of the baby boom cohorts; the rapid drops projected for the 1980s are the long-term effect of the very low levels of fertility prevalent during the past ten years. A considerable literature has developed on the effect of these fluctuations in the size of the entering cohort on the overall state of the labor market, and particularly on the rise in unemployment rates since 1970. But it is interesting to note in this connection that the period in which the annual growth rate of the total labor force was highest, 1965–70, was one in which unemployment was generally below 4 percent.

The size of the female population in any given age group is obviously affected by the same past fertility fluctuations that affect males. But it is clear from table 1 that the growth rate of the female labor force since 1950 has not been as sensitive to these variations in past birth rates as the growth of the male labor force has. The experience of the 1950s suggested to some that the opposite response, in fact, took place—that is, that the female labor force expanded rapidly precisely because of the slow growth rate for males, so that fluctuations in the overall growth rate for both sexes combined were minimized. Here again, however, the experience since 1965 raises questions on the general applicability of this hypothesis, since both male and female growth rates reached their highest postwar points during this period.

Although fertility and immigration history are the dominant demographic variables in short-term fluctuations of growth rates, the subtle effects of the increase in average length of life over the last 80 years may be associated with certain of the changes in work life history that have occurred. As more people reach the older ages with their health and resources sufficiently intact to permit them to enjoy leisure, the image of the retirement years has changed; and the prospect of retirement as a life cycle stage, characterized by freedom rather than fear, may be inducing many to hasten this step.

Such subtle associations cannot be measured directly by the indicators presently available. We can, however, look at trends in the relation between work and nonwork in the lifetime of the American people and it is to this that we turn now. Because both traditional patterns and current trends are quite different for men and women, we will initially deal with each sex separately; the concluding section will attempt to bring the two strands together in terms of their joint impact on the country's work force.

THE FEMALE LABOR FORCE

Probably the most dramatic, and certainly the most widely publicized change in the post-World War II labor force has been the rapid increase in the proportion of women engaged in market work. In fact, this has been the continuation of a gradual trend that can be observed over the past 100 years, but the pace accelerated after the War and has generally continued to accelerate over each succeeding decade. Two views of this development are presented in table 2. The upper panel indicates changes in the proportion of workers among women in each age group. In the immediate postwar period the increase was concentrated among older women, those past 40, while the proportions of younger women at work remained stable. Since 1965, however, the preponderance of the increase has shifted to younger women and rates for older women have stabilized and even declined slightly among those past 55. As a consequence, whereas in 1950 only among 18 and 19 year olds were a majority of women working, by 1975, well over half the women in every age group between 18 and 55 were in the labor force, and the differences among age groups within this range were much reduced.

The lower panel of table 2 follows

TABLE 2

TWO VIEWS OF THE RISING PROPORTION OF WORKING WOMEN

A. THE CROSS-SECTIONAL VIEW

AGE AT DATE OF SURVEY	PERCENT OF WOMEN IN THE LABOR FORCE, 1950	NET CHANGE IN PERCENT BETWEEN 1950–1960	1960–1965	1965–1975	PERCENT OF WOMEN IN THE LABOR FORCE, 1975
16 years and over	33.9	+3.9	+1.5	+7.1	46.4
16–17	30.1	−1.0	−1.4	+12.5	40.2
18–19	51.3	−0.2	−1.7	+8.9	58.3
20–24	46.1	+0.1	+3.8	+14.3	64.3
25–34	34.0	+2.0	+2.6	+16.0	54.6
35–44	39.1	+4.4	+2.6	+9.7	55.8
45–54	38.0	+11.8	+1.1	+3.7	54.6
55–64	27.0	+10.2	+3.9	−0.1	41.0
65 and over	9.7	+1.1	−0.8	−1.7	8.3

B. THE COHORT VIEW

YEAR OF BIRTH	PERCENT OF COHORT IN LABOR FORCE AT AGE 20–24	NET CHANGE IN PERCENT OVER 5 YEAR PERIOD BETWEEN AGES 20–24 TO 25–29	25–29 TO 30–34	30–34 TO 35–39	35–39 TO 40–44	40–44 TO 45–49	45–49 TO 50–54	50–54 TO 55–59	55–59 TO 60–64	60–64 TO 65–69	PERCENT OF COHORT IN LABOR FORCE AT AGE 65–69
1891–1895	*	*	*	*	*	*	*	*	*	−11.4	17.6
1896–1900	*	*	*	*	*	*	*	*	−4.2	−14.0	17.4
1901–1905	*	*	*	*	*	*	*	+0.7	−8.2	−16.7	17.3
1906–1910	*	*	*	*	*	*	+2.8	−1.6	−11.0	−21.6	14.5
1911–1915	*	*	*	*	*	+6.6	−0.6	−1.1	−15.7	(−18.7)	(14.6)
1916–1920	*	*	*	*	+7.1	+5.4	+2.1	−5.9	(−14.2)	(−19.4)	(14.3)
1921–1925	*	*	*	+6.1	+7.7	+6.5	−1.7	(−4.1)	(−15.5)	(−19.5)	(14.2)
1926–1930	46.1	−10.8	+1.0	+7.3	+9.3	+3.0	(+0.7)	(−6.2)	(−16.7)	(−)	(−)
1931–1935	46.0	−10.3	+2.5	+11.0	+7.6	(+0.8)	(+1.2)	(−7.8)	(−)	(−)	(−)
1936–1940	46.2	−7.3	+5.8	+10.2	(+3.8)	(+0.7)	(+0.9)	(−)	(−)	(−)	(−)
1941–1945	50.0	−4.8	+6.5	(+6.3)	(+3.2)	(−0.5)	(−)	(−)	(−)	(−)	(−)
1946–1950	57.8	−0.7	(−2.9)	(+6.9)	(+1.7)	(−)	(−)	(−)	(−)	(−)	(−)
1951–1956	64.3	(−3.9)	(−2.9)	(+5.7)	(−)	(−)	(−)	(−)	(−)	(−)	(−)

SOURCES: Panel A: *Department of Labor, Employment and Training Report of the President, 1976*. Panel B: *Social Indicators, 1976*, table 8/3.
NOTE: Figures in ( ) are projections; (−) projection not available (post 1990 dates).
* Comparable data not available.

each birth cohort of women over time, tracing changes in the proportion of workers as the group ages, the perspective presented in *Social Indicators, 1976*. Here it is clear that proportions are falling much less during the twenties for the younger cohorts than was previously true, and are rising more rapidly during the thirties.

For the central ages the net increase for successive cohorts is not changing much as they move from ages 35–39 to 45–49. Beyond age 45 there has been little increase in average participation for any of the cohorts, and each has shown a decline as its members entered their fifties. What appears as a major increase during these years in the cross-sectional picture in panel A is, of course, reflecting differences in the levels attained by successive cohorts when they reach the age of 45–54 rather than the behavior of specific cohorts.

The peak age of participation, then, for each of the cohorts is, roughly, 45–54. Beyond age 55 declines are clear, and clearly accelerating as we come forward in time. For the cohort entering the 55–59 age group most recently, there has already been a sharp drop. These declines parallel those for men and are substantial enough to indicate that they approach a "gross retirement" rate, that is, are unlikely to be a balancing of inflows and outflows to any considerable extent.

What the cohort view suggests is that young women are now less likely to leave the labor force in their twenties and, if they do leave, are returning at progressively younger ages. Since the age at which cohort rates reach their maximum has remained the same, the implication of such an inference is that working women will be spending a much higher proportion of their lifetimes in the labor force than has previously been the case. Unfortunately, however, cohort data cannot tell us the extent to which the net changes they show are a balance between substantial inflows and substantial outflows.

In general the *Social Indicators, 1976* projections, also included in panel B of table 2, take a quite conservative view of the behavior of cohorts whose future work life is estimated, with net declines postulated for the youngest cohorts as they move through their twenties and into their early thirties, and more modest increases as they enter the late thirties and forties. The basic assumption underlying these projected changes is that fertility levels for young women will increase and the consequent net effect will be to dampen their labor force participation.

Because marital status and child care responsibilities are so closely associated with women's labor force status and because the increase in the age at marriage and the precipitous decline in fertility after 1965 have obviously had their greatest impact on the age groups experiencing the sharpest labor force increases in the last decade, it is desireable to disaggregate the groups of women aged 20–24 and 25–34 by marital status and by the presence of children in their households. Clearly, if the striking increases in work rates for these young women are associated primarily with changes in the nature of their household commitments, the long-term significance of these increases is quite different from a situation in which the increases are occurring independently of these commitments. In the former case, a sharp reversal in the downward course of fertility, particularly, can

TABLE 3

CHANGES IN THE MARITAL STATUS AND CHILD CARE RESPONSIBILITIES AND IN THE PROPORTIONS WORKING FOR YOUNG WOMEN AGED 20–34 1965–75

MARITAL STATUS AND AGE OF YOUNGEST CHILD	A. DISTRIBUTION OF THE POPULATION				B. PERCENT IN THE LABOR FORCE					
	AGE 20–24		AGE 25–34		AGE 20–24		AGE 25–34		NET CHANGE 1965–1975	
	1965	1975	1965	1975	1965	1975	1965	1975	20–24	25–34
Total*	100.0	100.0	100.0	100.0	49.1	62.9	38.7	54.2	+13.8	+15.5
Never married	32.5	40.3	6.8	10.9	72.3	69.3	83.4	80.0	−3.0	−3.4
Previously married	6.9	8.7	10.0	12.9	58.6	67.6	62.8	67.4	+9.0	+4.6
Currently married	60.7	50.9	83.1	76.2	35.6	57.1	32.1	48.3	+21.5	+16.2
No child under 18	17.8† (No child under 18 and Youngest child 6–17 combined)	22.9† (No child under 18 and Youngest child 6–17 combined)	7.9	11.7	66.1† (No child under 18 and Youngest child 6–17 combined)	79.2† (No child under 18 and Youngest child 6–17 combined)	68.7	79.6	+13.1† (No child under 18 and Youngest child 6–17 combined)	+10.9
Youngest child 6–17			16.0	18.4			43.6	57.1		+13.5
Youngest child 3–5	5.1	6.5	22.2	21.0	33.8	52.0	31.5	42.1	+18.2	+10.6
Youngest child under 3	37.8	21.6	37.0	25.0	21.5	35.2	19.6	32.4	+13.7	+12.8

SOURCES: Bureau of Labor Statistics, *Special Labor Force Reports*, nos. 64 and 183.

* These data are for the month of March and therefore differ somewhat from the annual averages shown in table 2.

† Data for women aged 20–24 refer to those with no children under 18 plus those whose youngest child is 6–17; the latter group is very small for women of this age, so the combined figure essentially represents women with no children.

be expected to bring a concomitant fall in labor force activity; in the latter case, the effect of a rise in fertility will probably be much more muted.

Fortunately, *Current Population Survey* data allow us to examine the marital and child care status of these women more closely and to obtain some insight into the extent to which the cohort behavior shown in table 2 is independent of these factors. Table 3 presents the broad outline of the 1965–75 changes for selected components of the two groups. Panel A supports the statement that striking changes have occurred in the composition of both groups. Although noteworthy declines in the proportion who are currently married have occurred, by far the most impressive change is the decline in the proportion of young married women with preschool age children in their households. In 1965, 43 percent of all women aged 20–24 were in this category; by 1975, the figure is 28 percent. Among those in the 25–34 category, the percentage is 59 in 1965; 46, in 1975.

For purposes of the present review, however, it is the second panel of table 3 that is of most interest. Here it is clear that the major determinant (arithmetically) of the increase in economic activity among these women has been the rapid entrance of currently married women. Rates for widowed, divorced, and separated women, always higher than those for the currently married, have also risen but much more moderately; rates for single women, on the other hand, have fallen slightly and therefore, in view of their rising proportion of the total, have had a dampening effect on the aggregate increase.

Within the group of currently married women, those with no children in the household are now as likely to be working as are single women among those aged 25–34, and are considerably more likely to be in the labor market than the single among the younger group, presumably because young single women are more likely to be continuing their education than are the married. In effect, then, these data suggest that marital status per se no longer has any effect on the probability that a young woman is in the labor force; it is only the presence of children in the household that lowers the activity rate for currently married women.

That the presence of children and the age of the youngest child continue to affect labor force participation is obvious in table 3. What is more striking, however, is the rapid change in the impact of this effect. Viewed from the cohort perspective, what table 3 shows is that married women in the 1941–50 cohort (aged 25–34 in 1975) were about as likely to be working if their youngest child were aged 3–5 years (42.1 percent) as women with school age children in the previous (1931–40) cohort (43.6 percent); and women whose youngest child was under 3 were as likely to be in the labor force (32.4 percent) as those with children aged 3–5 were earlier (31.5 percent). Comparison of the younger cohorts shows a similar pattern—the proportion in the labor force among those with children under 3 in the 1951–55 cohort (35.2 percent) is as high as that for women with youngest child age 3–5 in the 1941–45 cohort (33.8 percent).

A crude indicator of the relative effects of composition versus participation rate changes can be obtained by standardization; that is, by looking at the effect on the general participation rate if one applies the labor force proportion for each component in 1975 to the distribution of population among the components shown for 1965 in panel A (or vice versa). This procedure indicates that about half of the 14.3 percentage point increase shown for women aged 20–24 in table 2 (panel A) can be attributed to changes in marital and child care status, and about half to the increase in labor force activity on the part of most components. For the 25–34 age group, roughly 60 percent of the 16 percentage point increase is attributable to activity rate changes, 40 percent to composition.

If one confines the standardization to currently married women, the category showing the greatest increase in labor force proportions for both age groups, the effect of changed activity rates is considerably greater: among women aged 20–24, 65 percent of the increase arises from increases in the rates for each category, only 35 percent from the decline in their child care responsibilities; and among those aged 25–34, 75 percent is associated with the rise in the rates, 25 percent with the lessening burden of preschool age children.

Beyond the age of 35, interdecade changes between 1965 and 1975 in the marital status and child care responsibilities of successive cohorts appear to play little part in the net changes in labor force proportions shown in table 2. Basically, the sharp upward shift in the cohort curves for women in the central working ages is accounted for by the increase in the proportions of currently married women, with children in their households, who are in the labor market.

The major factor differentiating the labor force behavior of recent cohorts, that is, those born after World War II, from that of those born before the War is the extent to which women with preschool children in the household are at work. This is an indicator of obvious importance in the structure of American family life. For the purpose of this paper, however, its significance lies in the suggestion that the average mother is returning to the labor market much sooner after the birth of her children than was true in the early postwar years. She is therefore more likely to have maintained contact with her previous work-life associates, her knowledge of the nature of the work world is fresher, and her work skills are not as likely to be obsolete. For these, and other reasons, the ease with which she reenters the labor market is likely to be improved over the experience of older cohorts.

MALE LABOR FORCE

Although there is growing evidence that neither entrance into nor exit from the labor force are simple one way processes for all men, on the whole the great majority have entered by their early twenties and remain in steadily for a number of years—that is, we do not have the problem of labor force turnover within the central and early working years that make both cohort and cross-sectional rates for women difficult to interpret. For the period covered by *Social Indicators, 1976* the pattern of delayed entrance associated with continued schooling is well established; cohort differences in labor force participation at ages 20–24 are generally abated by compensating differences in net entries for the succeeding five years, so that by ages 25–29, 95 percent or more of each cohort are in the labor force.

At the other end of the spectrum, however, the patterns of cohort change (shown in table 4) make it

TABLE 4

THE TREND TOWARD EARLY RETIREMENT FOR MEN 1955–1975

YEAR OF BIRTH	PERCENT OF COHORT IN LABOR FORCE AT AGE 45–49	NET CHANGE IN PERCENT OVER 5 YEAR PERIOD BETWEEN AGES				PERCENT OF COHORT IN LABOR FORCE AT AGE 65–69
		45–49 TO 50–54	50–54 TO 55–59	55–59 TO 60–64	60–64 TO 65–69	
1891–1895	*	*	*	*	−35.7	46.8
1896–1900	*	*	*	−11.3	−38.2	43.0
1901–1905	*	*	−4.1	−13.6	−36.4	41.6
1906–1910	97.1	−2.3	−4.6	−15.2	−43.3	31.7
1911–1915	96.6	−1.6	−5.5	−23.8	(−35.6)	(30.1)
1916–1920	96.1	−3.0	−8.7	(−21.3)	(−35.1)	(28.0)
1921–1925	95.4	−5.3	(−6.4)	(−23.8)	(−33.3)	(26.6)
1926–1930	94.1	(−4.7)	(−6.9)	(−24.8)	(−)	(−)
1931–1935	(93.3)	(−4.9)	(−6.8)	(−)	(−)	(−)
1936–1940	(92.7)	(−4.9)	(−)	(−)	(−)	(−)

SOURCE: *Social Indicators, 1976*, table 8/3.
NOTE: Figures in ( ) are projections; (−) projections not available (post 1990 dates).
* Comparable data not available.

clear that a significant and accelerating trend towards earlier retirement has been occurring: the 1911–15 cohort was twice as likely to leave the labor force between ages 55–59 and 60–64 as its predecessors born 15 years earlier (−23.8 versus −11.3 percent); the rate of decline for the 1916–20 cohort as it moved from 50–54 to 55–59 was also double that for the cohort 15 years older; even the 1921–25 cohort shows such a doubling of exit rates in the age range 45–49 to 50–54.

Is this acceleration a transitory phenomenon or does it represent emergence of the cumulative effect of long-term factors? These three cohorts are, of course, those which bore the brunt of World War II and perhaps a part of the rapid rise in their exit rates may represent the delayed impact of this experience. A second unique factor that may be associated with accelerated exits is the high unemployment rate prevailing in 1975. Although seniority rights usually protect older workers from the full immediate impact of a recession, once they lose their jobs they have more difficulty than younger persons in locating new employment, and it has often been suggested that they are therefore, in effect, "forced" into retirement. In the present case the acceleration of the gradual long-term trends in table 4 has been evident since 1970, and the general unemployment rate has been consistently higher during this period than in the late 1960s.

In this context, a demographic factor that may be relevant to the decision of older men to retire early is the rapid increase in the size of the male civilian labor force aged 20–34 over the last 15 years, and particularly among those aged 25–34, probably the group most competitive with older men for scarce jobs. Between 1970 and 1975, the number increased by 2.5 million, in contrast to a 1.4 million increase over 1965–70, and an absolute decrease of 350,000 between 1960 and 1965, the previous period of high unemployment rates (when the trend toward early retirement was much more moderate).

Such variations in the size of successive labor force cohorts among males are, as noted above, primarily a reflection of past fertility fluctuations. The effect of these fluctuations on the base populations from which the labor force is drawn will begin to be apparent for the population over 45 only after 1975 (men over 45 in 1975 were, of course, all born before the Depression decade). Whether, as these older men become a scarce resource their rates of retirement will level off or even decline, as the *Social Indicators, 1976,* projections imply, is a matter of conjecture.

Demographic factors may also be playing a part in the secular trend toward earlier retirement. The relation between fertility experience and women's labor force behavior has been extensively discussed in many studies; but the association between these two variables in men's life histories has been ignored. Nevertheless, one may expect that early completion of childbearing by wives has had the complementary effect of reducing the age for men at which the last dependent child becomes self-supporting. The trend towards higher levels of education for adult children—and therefore prolonged dependency—may have counterbalanced this development for some, and the aging of the baby-boom fathers may reduce the effect temporarily. But it is interesting to note that in 1975, 27 percent of husbands aged 45–54 had no children of any age in their households and 44 percent had none under 18. Such a situation may make early reduction in labor force participation a more feasible option than it was for earlier cohorts.

The adequacy of retirement income is, of course, a prime factor to be considered. Although Social Security benefits are often at or below the poverty level, recent beneficiaries probably do considerably better than previous cohorts; benefits, at a reduced level, are now available at age 62; and disability provisions permit earlier retirement for those who qualify. Moreover, the long-range effect of the rapid postwar increases in women's labor force participation probably means that, in an increasing proportion of families, both husband and wife are entitled to independent benefits, providing a larger total income than when the wife's benefit was tied to her dependent status.

The proportion of total employment in federal, state, and local governments increased substantially in the post-World War II period and most such employees are covered by pension schemes that provide more adequate benefits than Social Security; an increasing proportion of private employees are also covered by various pension arrangements which supplement Social Security benefits. Perhaps most important from the viewpoint of our present interest in early retirement, many government and private pension plans are tied to years of service, rather than to a specific retirement age; consequently, workers may become eligible for benefits long before what we have customarily thought of as retirement age. Such pensioners may not be prohibited from taking other employment, but they are certainly more able to make the decision to retire than were previous cohorts not covered by such schemes. What we may be seeing, then, is a first flowering of the cumulative effect of pension plan development over the last 30 years.

A less optimistic view of early retirement is raised by the possibility that it is a structural effect; that is, a change in the demand for labor that puts some workers at a disadvantage in the labor market because their skills are perceived to be less adequate (or obsolete) by employers in relation to current needs. The operation of this phenomenon is extraordinarily complex and its measurement in any precise manner is probably impossible. Nevertheless, one identifiable aspect of the recent trend toward early retirement suggests its impact, namely, the negative association between exit rates and levels of education shown in table 5. The cohort represented there, men aged 45–54 in 1965 and 55–64 in 1975, is the last of the cohorts reaching maturity before the second World War. About 50 percent had not completed high school and 16 percent had less than 8 years of schooling. As table 5 indicates, even at ages 45–54 some differential in labor force participation can be observed; but the substantial differences in retirement, particularly between those completing high school or higher levels and those with less than 12 years of school, exacerbates these differentials very considerably by ages 55–64.

Educational differences in retirement rates are undoubtedly associated with occupational differences, in particular with a white-collar–blue-collar dichotomy, and therefore may be very broadly associated with the long-term structural change in the labor market which has seen a continuing increase in the share of white-collar occupations in the total. Men whose work lives have been spent in the contracting blue-collar sector are perhaps more likely to be forced out through job loss and/or through greater difficulty in locating similar, scarce jobs than those whose experience is in the expanding white-collar sector.

The relation between these structural effects and the institutional effects, specifically, the availability of pensions at preretirement ages discussed above, raises some problems of reconciliation. A priori, one expects that the higher earner, higher education white-collar worker is more likely to be covered by such pensions than those who, as table 5 shows, are more likely to be retiring early. Recent studies by the Social Security Administration offer indirect evidence that this expectation is correct. So the question of whether the individual retiring early

TABLE 5

EARLY RETIREMENT AND EDUCATIONAL LEVEL AMONG MEN BORN 1911–1920

Years of School Completed	Percent in Labor Force at Age 45–54 (1965)	Percent in Labor Force at Age 55–64 (1975)	Net Change in Percent
Total	95.5	75.4	−20.1
Less than 5	86.0	52.0	−34.0
5–7	93.4	67.0	−26.4
8	94.8	71.6	−23.2
9–11	94.9	74.3	−20.6
12	97.2	79.3	−17.9
13–15	98.0	83.4	−14.6
16	98.2	83.3	−14.9
17 and over	99.4	88.1	−11.3

SOURCE: Bureau of Labor Statistics, *Special Labor Force Report* nos. 65 and 186.

TABLE 6

THE CONVERGING LIFE PATTERN: RATIO OF MALE TO FEMALE LABOR FORCE RATES

YEAR OF BIRTH	RATIO OF MALE TO FEMALE LABOR FORCE RATES AT AGE									
	20–24	25–29	30–34	35–39	40–44	45–49	50–54	55–59	60–64	65–69
1891–1895	*	*	*	*	*	*	*	*	284	266
1896–1900	*	*	*	*	*	*	*	260	259	247
1901–1905	*	*	*	*	*	*	231	217	229	240
1906–1910	*	*	*	*	*	212	195	192	208	219
1911–1915	*	*	*	*	222	191	190	183	197	(206)
1916–1920	*	*	*	251	211	186	173	176	(187)	(196)
1921–1925	*	*	283	240	200	173	169	(170)	(178)	(187)
1926–1930	193	275	271	225	182	168	(158)	(164)	(171)	(–)
1931–1935	197	272	257	198	168	(162)	(150)	(160)	(–)	(–)
1936–1940	195	249	218	175	(161)	(156)	(146)	(–)	(–)	(–)
1941–1945	176	212	186	(166)	(154)	(152)	(–)	(–)	(–)	(–)
1946–1950	150	166	(178)	(157)	(150)	(–)	(–)	(–)	(–)	(–)
1951–1955	134	(156)	(167)	(151)	(–)	(–)	(–)	(–)	(–)	(–)

SOURCE: *Social Indicators, 1976*, table 8/3; computed by dividing male activity rate by female activity rate and multiplying by 100.

NOTE: Figures in ( ) are projections; (–) projection not available (post 1990 date).

* Comparable data not available.

is choosing or being forced into this decision remains unanswered.

TOTAL LABOR FORCE

The previous discussion has focused on two of the most dramatic recent changes in labor force activity: the increased propensity among cohorts of young women to work even when young children are in the household; and the shift towards earlier retirement among men in their 50s.

One important social effect of these changes has been that the life history pattern of market work has apparently become much more similar for men and women in the United States. Whether viewed cross-sectionally or by cohort, it is clear from the ratios of male to female participation rates in table 6 that there has been a substantial convergence between the sexes over the last 20 years. In 1955, male rates were two to three times as great as female rates in every 5 year age group; by 1975, only past the age of 60 were men twice as likely to be in the labor force as women. The truncated cohort data suggest an increasing narrowing of the age range in which the ratio exceeds 200 and an increasing convergence of rates for each successive cohort.

By 1975, over 70 percent of the population in the age range 20–54 were engaged in market work, and there is every indication that this percentage will continue to increase. Beyond age 55 the trend appears to be downward. The aggregate effect of these developments constitutes what may be termed a "social revolution." For the trend is towards more equal participation by men and women in the economic work of the country and a concentration of this activity within about half the total life span. A substantial part of the economic growth of the country in the first years of the twentieth century went towards reduction of the annual hours of labor supplied by the average worker; perhaps a substantial part in the last years will go to the reduction of the total years of work.

Table 8/1

TOTAL POPULATION, WORKERS AND NONWORKERS, BY AGE: 1950–1990

AGE	1950	1955	1960	1965	1970	1975	1980[1]	1985[1]	1990[1]
Total population, all ages	152,271	165,931	180,671	194,303	204,878	213,631	222,769	234,068	245,075
Under 16 years	43,131	51,248	58,836	62,761	61,922	57,872	55,110	57,535	61,330
16 to 64 years	96,743	100,156	105,160	113,091	122,869	133,359	143,136	149,874	154,812
65 years and over	12,397	14,527	16,675	18,451	20,087	22,400	24,523	26,659	28,833
WORKERS[2]									
Total	63,858	68,072	72,142	77,178	85,903	94,793	103,761	110,690	115,927
Male	45,446	47,488	48,870	50,946	54,343	57,706	61,990	64,893	67,210
Female	18,412	20,584	23,272	26,232	31,560	37,087	41,771	45,797	48,717
16 to 64 years, both sexes	60,821	64,766	68,948	74,071	82,683	91,854	100,754	107,673	112,825
65 years and over, both sexes	3,037	3,306	3,194	3,107	3,220	2,939	3,007	3,017	3,102
NONWORKERS[3]									
Total	88,413	97,859	108,529	117,125	118,975	118,838	119,008	123,378	129,148
Under 16 years	43,131	51,248	58,836	62,761	61,922	57,872	55,110	57,535	61,330
16 to 64 years	35,922	35,390	36,212	39,020	40,186	41,505	42,382	42,201	41,987
65 years and over	9,360	11,221	13,481	15,344	16,867	19,461	21,516	23,642	25,831
NONWORKER/WORKER RATIO[4]									
Total	138	144	150	152	138	125	115	111	111
Under 16 years	68	75	82	81	72	61	53	52	53
16 to 64 years	56	52	50	50	47	44	41	38	36
65 years and over	15	16	19	20	20	20	21	21	22

	1950–55	1955–60	1960–65	1965–70	1970–75	1975–80	1980–85	1985–90
AVERAGE ANNUAL RATE OF CHANGE								
Total population, all ages	1.72	1.70	1.46	1.06	0.84	0.84	0.99	0.92
Total labor force, 16 years and over	1.28	1.16	1.35	2.14	1.97	1.81	1.29	.92
Male	.88	.57	.83	1.29	1.20	1.43	.92	.70
Female	2.23	2.46	2.40	3.70	3.23	2.38	1.84	1.24

Source: U.S. Department of Commerce, Bureau of the Census, *Current Population Reports*, Series P-25, Nos. 311, 321, 470, and 601; U.S. Department of Labor, *Employment and Training Report of the President*, 1976; and Bureau of Labor Statistics, "New Labor Force Projection to 1990," *Monthly Labor Review*, December 1976.

[1] Series II projections.

[2] Workers are persons 16 years old and over in the civilian labor force or Armed Forces.

[3] Nonworkers are persons under 16 years and persons 16 years and over not in the labor force.

[4] Number of nonworkers per 100 workers.

Chart 8/1B

Social Indicators, 1976

NONWORKER/WORKER RATIOS, 1950–1990

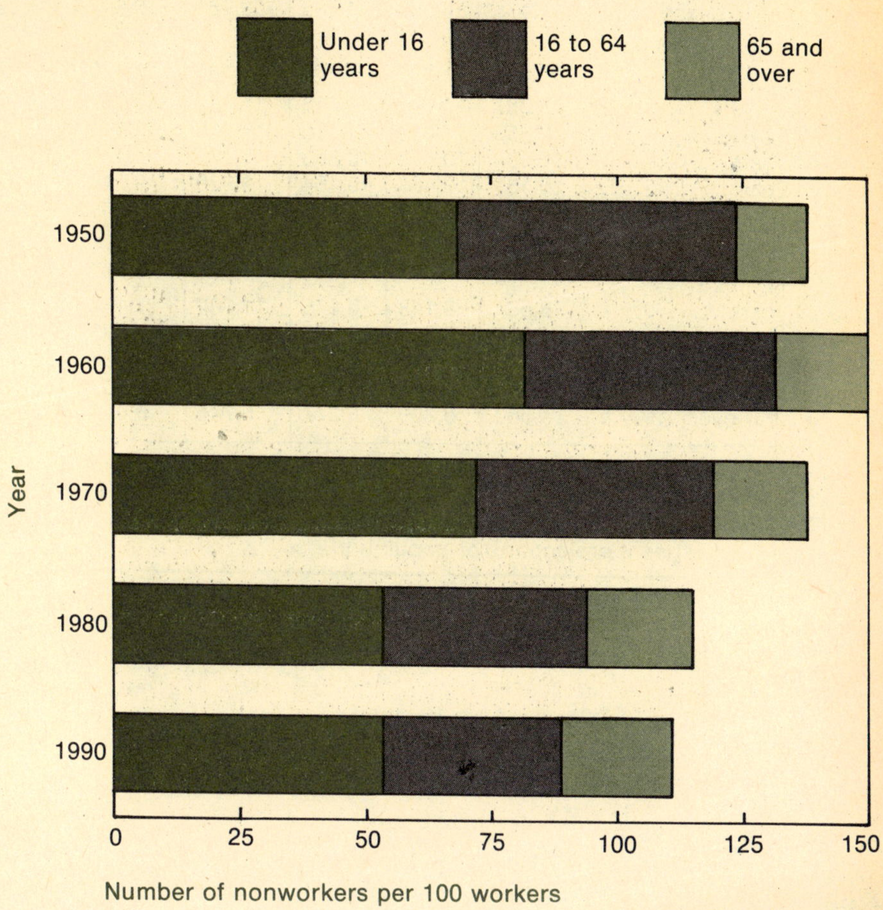

Source: see table 8/1

Table 8/2

TOTAL LABOR FORCE, BY AGE AND SEX: 1965–1990

(Annual averages, in thousands)

AGE GROUP AND SEX	1965	1970	1975	1980[1]	1985[1]	1990[1]
Total, both sexes	77,178	85,903	94,793	103,761	110,690	115,927
Total male, age 16 and over	50,946	54,343	57,706	61,990	64,893	67,210
16 to 24 years	9,757	11,773	13,313	14,092	13,094	11,765
25 to 34 years	10,653	11,974	14,456	16,926	18,578	19,102
35 to 44 years	11,504	10,818	10,583	11,878	14,470	16,849
45 to 54 years	10,131	10,487	10,464	9,929	9,746	10,938
55 years and over	8,899	9,291	8,890	9,165	9,005	8,556
Total female, age 16 and over	26,232	31,560	37,087	41,771	45,797	48,717
16 to 24 years	5,894	8,143	10,175	11,362	11,161	10,375
25 to 34 years	4,336	5,704	8,473	10,417	12,233	13,100
35 to 44 years	5,724	5,971	6,496	7,638	9,728	11,683
45 to 54 years	5,714	6,533	6,667	6,609	6,761	7,795
55 years and over	4,563	5,209	5,277	5,745	5,914	5,764

Source: U.S. Department of Labor, *Employment and Training Report of the President, 1976*; and Bureau of Labor Statistics, "New Labor Force Projections to 1990." *Monthly Labor Review*, December 1976.

[1] Based on Series II projections of population.

Chart 8/2 Social Indicators, 1976

TOTAL LABOR FORCE 16 YEARS OLD AND OVER, BY AGE AND SEX, 1965, 1970, 1975, 1980, 1985 AND 1990

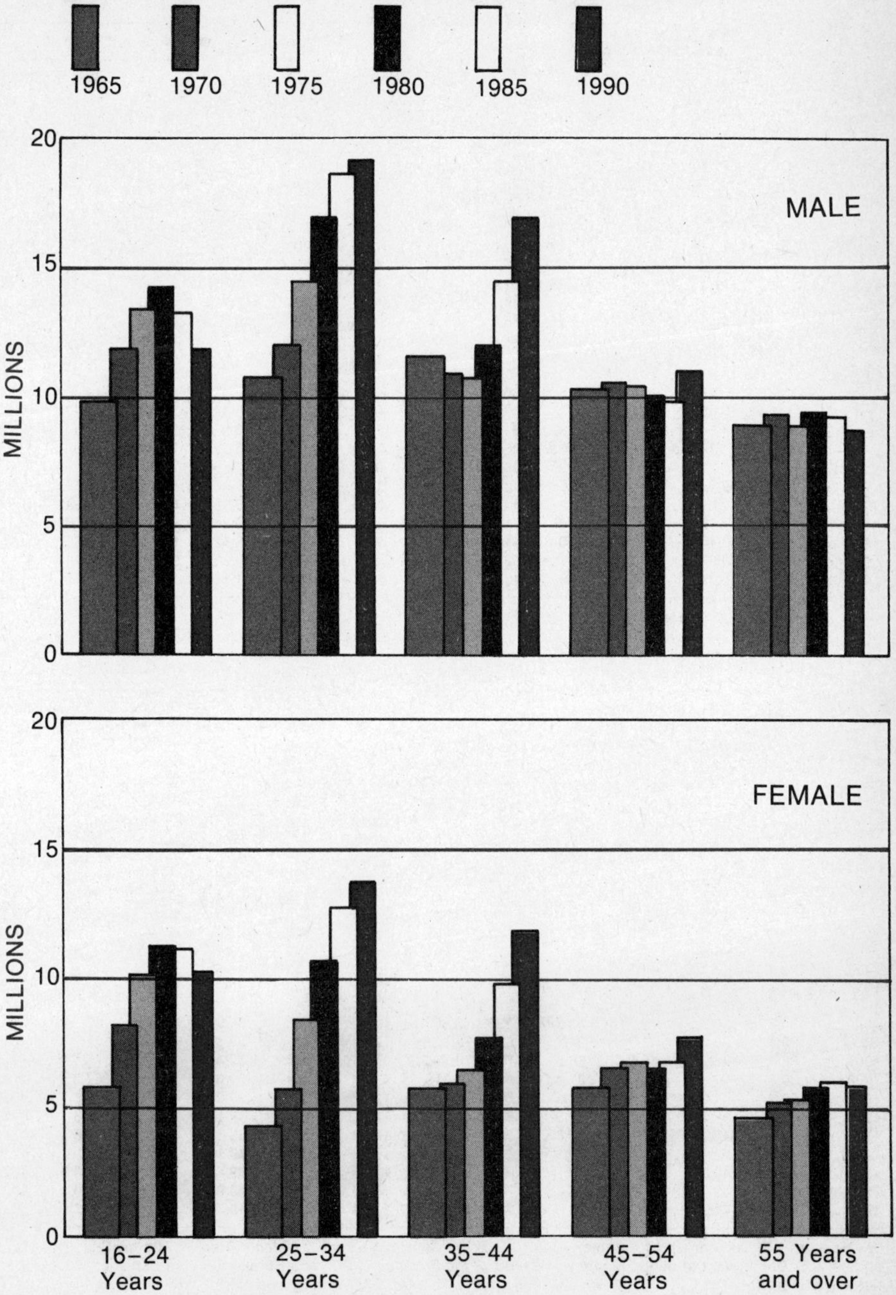

Source: see table 8/2

Table 8/7

LABOR FORCE PARTICIPATION OF EVER-MARRIED WOMEN, BY PRESENCE AND AGE OF CHILDREN: 1954–1975

(Civilian noninstitutional population in the civilian labor force)

	ALL EVER-MARRIED WOMEN[2]								MARRIED WOMEN, HUSBAND PRESENT			
	Number in labor force (thousands)				Labor force participation rates				Number in labor force (thousands)			
YEAR[1]	Total	No children under 18 years	Children 6 to 17 years old	Children under 6 years old	Total	No children under 18 years	Children 6 to 17 years old	Children under 6 years old	Total	No children under 18 years	Children 6 to 17 years old	Children under 6 years old
1954 ...	14,314	8,296	3,795	2,223	29.5	33.1	36.7	17.0	9,923	5,096	3,019	1,808
1955 ...	15,066	8,543	4,048	2,474	30.6	33.9	38.4	18.2	10,423	5,227	3,183	2,012
1956 ...	15,675	8,942	4,245	2,488	31.4	35.3	39.9	17.9	11,126	5,694	3,384	2,048
1957 ...	16,146	9,046	4,458	2,643	32.1	35.8	40.5	18.8	11,529	5,805	3,517	2,208
1958 ...	16,636	9,142	4,647	2,847	32.6	35.8	41.1	20.1	11,826	5,713	3,714	2,399
1959 ...	17,214	9,250	5,007	2,957	33.3	35.9	43.0	20.7	12,205	5,679	4,055	2,471
1960 ...	17,114	9,096	5,120	2,898	32.7	35.0	42.5	20.2	12,253	5,692	4,087	2,474
1961 ...	18,536	9,824	5,529	3,183	34.9	37.2	45.3	22.1	13,266	6,186	4,419	2,661
1962 ...	18,497	9,662	5,501	3,334	34.2	35.6	44.9	22.8	13,485	6,156	4,445	2,884
1963 ...	19,061	9,784	5,718	3,559	34.8	35.8	44.6	24.4	14,061	6,366	4,689	3,006
1964 ...	19,618	10,091	5,934	3,593	35.4	36.3	45.8	24.5	14,461	6,545	4,866	3,050
1965 ...	20,040	10,358	6,000	3,682	35.7	36.5	45.7	25.3	14,708	6,755	4,836	3,117
1966 ...	20,714	10,864	6,043	3,807	36.4	37.0	46.5	26.2	15,178	7,043	4,949	3,186
1967 ...	21,630	11,048	6,443	4,139	37.5	36.7	48.6	28.7	15,908	7,158	5,269	3,481
1968 ...	22,421	11,343	6,955	4,123	38.5	37.6	49.7	29.2	16,821	7,564	5,693	3,564
1969 ...	23,397	11,798	7,376	4,223	39.5	38.3	50.7	30.4	17,595	7,853	6,146	3,596
1970 ...	24,268	12,146	7,567	4,555	40.4	38.8	51.5	32.2	18,377	8,174	6,289	3,914
1971 ...	24,494	12,293	7,874	4,327	40.2	38.4	52.0	31.4	18,530	8,432	6,424	3,674
1972 ...	25,462	12,780	8,244	4,438	41.1	39.5	52.6	31.9	19,249	8,797	6,706	3,746
1973 ...	26,165	13,148	8,253	4,764	41.6	39.3	52.8	34.2	19,821	9,107	6,658	4,056
1974 ...	27,090	13,523	8,495	5,072	42.5	39.7	53.8	36.6	20,367	9,365	6,792	4,210
1975 ...	28,043	13,896	8,754	5,393	43.4	40.0	54.8	38.9	21,111	9,701	6,971	4,437

	MARRIED WOMEN, HUSBAND PRESENT—*CONTINUED*				OTHER EVER-MARRIED WOMEN[2]							
	Labor force participation rates				Number in labor force (thousands)				Labor force participation rates			
YEAR[1]	Total	No children under 18 years	Children 6 to 17 years old	Children under 6 years old	Total	No children under 18 years	Children 6 to 17 years old	Children under 6 years old	Total	No children under 18 years	Children 6 to 17 years old	Children under 6 years old
1954 ...	26.6	31.6	33.2	14.9	4,391	3,200	776	415	39.4	35.8	61.7	42.9
1955 ...	27.7	32.7	34.7	16.2	4,643	3,316	865	462	39.6	36.0	63.4	40.3
1956 ...	29.0	35.3	36.4	15.9	4,549	3,248	861	440	39.4	35.3	64.9	43.6
1957 ...	29.6	35.6	36.6	17.0	4,617	3,241	941	435	40.4	36.1	66.6	41.2
1958 ...	30.2	35.4	37.6	18.2	4,810	3,429	933	448	40.8	36.6	65.8	45.1
1959 ...	30.9	35.2	39.8	18.7	5,009	3,571	952	486	41.2	37.1	66.4	44.7
1960 ...	30.6	34.7	39.0	18.6	4,861	3,404	1,033	424	40.0	35.7	66.2	39.8
1961 ...	32.7	37.3	41.7	20.0	5,270	3,638	1,110	522	42.0	37.0	68.4	46.9
1962 ...	32.7	36.1	41.8	21.3	5,012	3,506	1,056	450	39.1	34.8	64.6	40.9
1963 ...	33.7	37.4	41.5	22.5	5,000	3,418	1,029	553	38.5	33.3	67.5	46.1
1964 ...	34.4	37.8	43.0	22.7	5,157	3,546	1,068	543	38.7	33.9	65.3	44.1
1965 ...	34.7	38.3	42.7	23.3	5,332	3,603	1,164	565	38.9	33.5	65.2	47.8
1966 ...	35.4	38.4	43.7	24.2	5,536	3,821	1,094	621	39.5	34.7	65.9	46.3
1967 ...	36.8	38.9	45.0	26.5	5,722	3,890	1,174	658	39.4	33.4	75.0	50.7
1968 ...	38.3	40.1	46.9	27.6	5,600	3,779	1,262	559	39.0	33.4	67.8	47.6
1969 ...	39.6	41.0	48.6	28.5	5,802	3,945	1,230	627	39.2	33.9	65.1	49.5
1970 ...	40.8	42.2	49.2	30.3	5,891	3,972	1,278	641	39.1	33.4	67.3	50.7
1971 ...	40.8	42.1	49.4	29.6	5,964	3,861	1,450	653	38.5	32.2	67.6	47.8
1972 ...	41.5	42.7	50.2	30.1	6,213	3,983	1,538	692	40.1	34.0	66.5	47.4
1973 ...	42.2	42.8	50.1	32.7	6,344	4,041	1,595	708	39.6	33.2	68.3	46.6
1974 ...	43.0	43.0	51.2	34.4	6,723	4,158	1,703	862	40.9	33.9	67.3	53.6
1975 ...	44.4	43.9	52.3	36.6	6,932	4,194	1,784	955	40.7	33.2	67.2	55.0

Source: U.S. Department of Commerce, Bureau of the Census, *Current Population Reports*, Series P-50, Nos. 11, 22, and 29; U.S. Department of Labor, *Manpower Report of the President, 1974*, and Bureau of Labor Statistics, *Special Labor Force Reports*, Nos. 7, 13, 20, 26, 40, 50, 64, 80, 94, 120, 130, 144, 153, 164, 173, and 183.

[1] Data for 1954–1966 include women 14 years old and over; data for 1967–1975 include women 16 years old and over.

[2] Includes women who are separated, widowed, or divorced.

Chart 8/7 Social Indicators, 1976

ECONOMIC ACTIVITY RATES OF WIVES ACCORDING TO THE PRESENCE AND AGE OF CHILDREN, 1954–1975

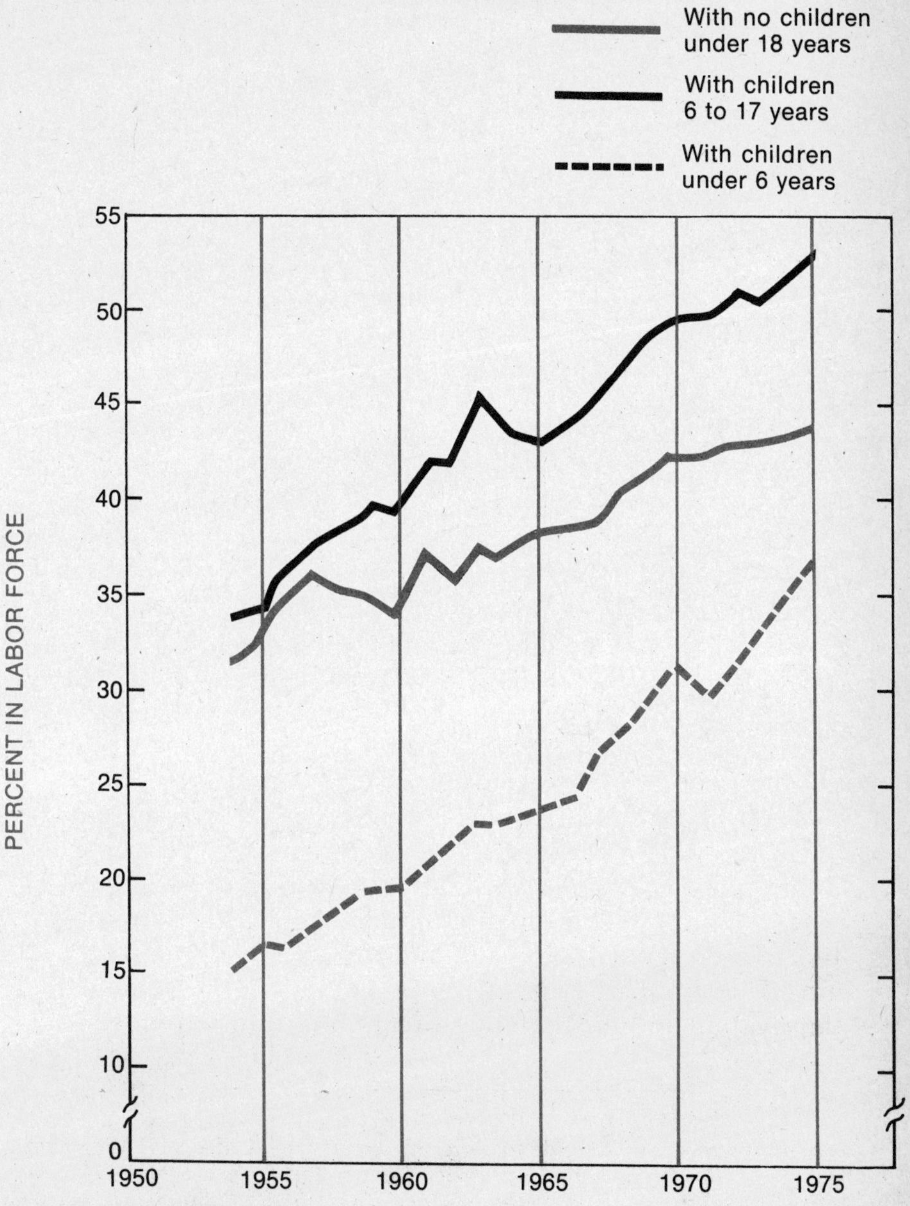

Source: see table 8/7

ANNALS, AAPSS, 435, Jan. 1978

A Decent Home and Suitable Living Environment

By DORIS B. HOLLEB

ABSTRACT: *Social Indicators, 1976* documents the success of the nation in solving the housing problems of the 1950s, in eliminating both a severe housing shortage and large numbers of substandard dwellings. Housing has improved greatly for all income classes, including the poor, for all races, and by all standards of measurement, but wide disparities remain. This suggests great relative deprivation in a society with such universally high standards.

A massive upsurge in housing construction, greater than rising demand, brought changes not only in the quality of the housing stock but in its location as well. The transformation of residential settlement patterns and the growth of extensive metropolitan cities have had profound effects on housing and community life. Because of racial and social barriers in local housing markets, polarities among metrpolitan neighborhoods have increased.

None of these pervasive changes emerge in the indicators. Nor do they address such contemporary concerns as rising housing costs, deteriorating neighborhood conditions in poverty areas, and the environmental and energy implications of emerging low density housing patterns. Thus, readers are likely to underestimate the scale and nature of housing deprivation and misread the direction of future trends.

Doris B. Holleb is Director of the University of Chicago's Metropolitan Institute and Research Associate at its Center for Urban Studies. She is a Commissioner and Secretary of the Northeastern Illinois Planning Commission. Economist and urban affairs specialist, she has served as a consultant to numerous public and private agencies, including HEW, HUD, and NSF. She is the author of Social and Economic Information for Urban Planning *and* Colleges and the Urban Poor *as well as many shorter works on urban issues.*

WHERE and how Americans live has changed dramatically since World War II. The metropolitan city with its downtown towers and ethnic neighborhoods, its suburban shopping centers, subdivisions, franchised food chains, and factories, tied together with ribbons of highways, is home to nearly three-fourths of all Americans. From the mountains to the prairies to the waving fields of grain, so universal a feature on the landscape is the low-slung, far-flung, multicentered regional metropolis that one can scarcely remember how new and distinctive it is.

Looking back at the last three decades, two sweeping changes have profoundly altered the quality and nature of housing and community life. First, residential settlement patterns have been transformed. Second, a massive increase in new housing construction and support systems facilitated the changes.

RESIDENTIAL SETTLEMENT PATTERNS

The urbanization of the nation and the growth of extensive clusters of regional cities is doubtless the single, most significant influence on housing and neighborhood life in the past quarter century. By 1974, 151.3 million persons lived in the 264 metropolitan areas (SMSAs) of the nation, approaching three-fourth (72.8 percent of the total population. Looking back to 1950, 84.5 million persons lived in 168 SMSAs, over half (56.1 percent) of the nation's population.[1] During this period, the territory within metropolitan boundaries doubled in size and densities of settlement declined sharply as highways and motor vehicles penetrated into open country.

Metropolitan cities are a mosaic of socially distinctive neighborhoods and local governments. They are separated, on the one hand, by increasing physical and social distances as the population and territory of metropolitan settlement has gradually enlarged. They are linked, on the other hand, by complex economic, communication, and transport networks. By 1975, suburbia, with its rows of single-family homes, was the dominant place of abode. In 1974, 39 percent of the nation's population lived in the suburbs of metropolitan areas, 29 percent in their central cities, and 32 percent in rural areas. In 1950, only 27 percent lived in suburbs, with 36 percent in central cities and 38 percent outside metropolitan areas.[2]

Even old suburban towns, from an historical standpoint, smack of newness. Half of the entire housing inventory of the United States in 1973 has been built since 1950. But two-thirds of all new dwellings built in metropolitan areas since 1950 have been constructed in suburbs.[3]

Low-density, single-family homes (attached and detached) are by far the most common type of housing in the nation, accounting for 68 percent of all year-round dwelling units. But single-family units comprise three-fourths of all housing in the suburbs. Multiunit structures account for only 28 percent of the total housing inventory. Yet they comprise half of all dwelling units in central cities. The remaining

1. U.S. Bureau of the Census, *Statistical Abstract of the United States: 1976.* (Washington, D.C.: USGPO, 1976), p. 15.

2. Ibid. p. 16.

3. U.S. Bureau of the Census, *Annual Housing Survey: 1973*, Current Housing Reports, ser. H–150–73A (Washington, D.C.: USGPO, 1975) p. xviii.

4 percent of the housing stock consists of occupied mobile homes and trailers, the low cost housing of the nation.[4]

The rise of the suburbs in the postwar years dealt a heavy blow to the compact cities of the northeastern and midwestern industrial belts and to their aging walk-ups and tenements. Then after 1970, the rapid growth of exurbs and rural centers and migrations South and West have further siphoned off demand for housing in old city and suburban neighborhoods. Meanwhile, other countervailing sources of urban growth, that in the past supported population increases, have also diminished since 1970. Birthrates were at historic low points; legal immigration was limited; and rural-to-urban migration was completed, in fact reversed, with a farm population reduced to only 4 percent of the nation's total. Further, new employment centers have also mushroomed most rapidly in outlying areas, particularly in the Sunbelt, to provide jobs for new settlers from old cities.[5]

Nowhere in *Social Indicators, 1976* is the transformation of national settlement patterns delineated. Nor are its neighborhood implications spelled out in the light of racially and socially segregated, local housing markets. On balance, more families, and families with higher incomes, both black and white, are leaving the cities than are moving in. Thus, the number and proportion of dependent households have increased in the backwater neighborhoods of central cities.[6]

No geographic points of reference are presented in the chapter devoted to housing (chapter 3), not even broad-brushed summaries of regional patterns or urban-suburban-rural differences. This is a grave lack in tracing trends in housing and community development since housing conditions can never be evaluated apart from a neighborhood setting. Without perspectives on urbanization, critical changes over the past three decades in the nation's highly segmented, yet interconnected, housing markets are lost. Nor can one think sensibly about the future since decentralized housing trends have not yet spent their force.[7] And trends toward urban deconcentration are common to the industrial democracies of the world.[8]

NEW HOUSING CONSTRUCTION

The driving force of the transformation, and the second key to housing trends after World War II, was the unprecedented expansion of new housing construction. As a result of the expansion, the nation's

4. Ibid. p. xvii.

5. For an analysis of these trends see: George Sternlieb and James W. Hughes, "New Regional and Metropolitan Realities of America," *Journal of the American Institute of Planners*, vol. 43, no. 3 (July 1977); Brian J. L. Berry and Donald C. Dahmann, *Population Redistribution in the United States in the 1970's* (Washington, D.C.: National Academy of Sciences, 1977); Doris B. Holleb, "The Direction of Urban Change," in *Agenda for the New Urban Era*, ed. Harvey S. Perloff (Chicago, American Society of Planning Officials, 1975).

6. Sternlieb and Hughes, "New Regional and Metropolitan Realities," pp. 238–39.

7. A recent Gallup Poll, for example indicates that only a small proportion (13 percent) of all Americans in 1976 would prefer to live in a "large city" than a small city or town and that the largest proportion (38 percent would prefer to live in a "rural area." *Los Angeles Times*, 21 November 1976, p. 8.

8. *Success Abroad: What Foreign Cities Can Teach American Cities: Hearings*, U.S. Congress, House, Subcomittee on the City, 95th Cong., 5 April 1977, pp. 2–11.

housing stock improved greatly over the years for all income classes, including the poor, for all races, and by all common standards of measurement.[9] Until the recent upward spiral in costs, housing, per se, was no longer among the first ranking issues of widespread national concern.

The level of new residential construction was escalated during the 1960s, reaching new peaks in the early 1970s. Then with recession, the bottom fell out of private housing markets; a moratorium was also imposed on federal subsidies for lower income housing. After the severe 1975 recession, the production of single-family homes and mobile homes once again picked up steam, but construction of multifamily units continued to lag below earlier levels.[10]

What matters most about the upsurge in housing production is that it more than surpassed rising demand, generated by rapid population growth and new household formations. By 1973, there were 75.9 million housing units in the United States, a net increase of 65 percent over the 46.1 million units in 1950. During the same period, the nation's population shot up 38.2 percent and the number of households 56.7 percent. Thus, during these years, for every two more persons in the nation, roughly three more new housing units were built.[11]

A rate of new housing construction, higher than growing demand, brought remarkable changes not only in the quantity of available housing, not only in its location, but in its overall quality as well. Abandonments and demolitions of the least desirable units, largely in central cities, were speeded up as the new supply filtered into the local housing markets.[12] These changes in the quality and location of housing altered the daily lives of millions of families.

In effect, the severe housing shortage left in the wake of the Great Depression and war years was wiped out. Furthermore, the number and proportion of substandard units, as variously defined by the Census Bureau, were also sharply and progressively reduced. Consequently there was demonstrable progress on two fronts, towards solving both the "too little housing problem" and the "bad housing problem," to borrow Henry J. Aaron's terminology.[13]

"Is this not the best of all possible worlds," Candide might ask, "with so few housing problems left in the United States?" Dr. Pangloss would then reply, "Yes, in only 25 years they have all but resolved the housing problems of the '50s."

HOUSING QUESTIONS

Social Indicators, 1976 documents the success of the nation in solving the housing problems of the 1950s. More than half the indicators in the chapter dealing with housing chart unwavering improvements in the nation's housing in-

9. Frank de Leeuw, Ann B. Schnare, and Raymond J. Struyk, "Housing," in *The Urban Predicament*, eds. William Gorham and Nathan Glazer (Washington, D.C.: The Urban Institute, 1976), pp. 119–73.

10. *Ninth Annual Report on the National Housing Goal*, (Washington, D.C., 19 January 1977), p. 11.

11. Based on data from the U.S. Bureau of the Census and the *Annual Housing Survey: 1973*.

12. For a good description of the "filtering process" in local housing markets, see Anthony Downs, *Opening Up the Suburbs* (New Haven, Conn.: Yale University Press, 1973), pp. 2–12.

13. Henry J. Aaron, *Shelter and Subsidies*, (Washington, D.C., The Brookings Institution, 1972), p. 2.

ventory and facilities, and exclusively in terms of decreasing numbers of persons per room in dwelling units and of units lacking complete plumbing facilities. The question is whether housing objectives and trends of the 1970s have much to do with these deficiencies. If not, what indicators would best depict the past sweep of change and provide yardsticks reflecting contemporary concerns and goals?

The selection of a few sturdy, valid "social indicators" of housing is extremely difficult. So many aspects of contemporary life come into focus in the home. Most of the other subjects in this volume bear on it: income and employment, social stratification, family structure, crime, education, health, welfare, recreation, and more. Furthermore, because of great variations among local housing markets, nationwide summary indicators should be built ideally from the bottom up.

Housing is also unique among durable consumer goods. It is by far the most durable, often lasting beyond the lifetimes of its original inhabitants. Housing and related expenditures usually absorb the single largest share of the family budget, always for lower income families. And a house is often a family's most valuable asset. Home ownership also has symbolic value, especially for working class families, and upward social mobility is frequently expressed in physical mobility, by moving to a better neighborhood. For families with higher incomes, there are tangible financial tax benefits as well.

Above all, housing is always rooted in a particular place, a neighborhood setting. As a building ages, the incomes, social characteristics and lifestyles of successive occupants will influence its maintenance and the fate of the neighborhood. Consequently, neighborhoods often reflect the age, ethnic, racial, and class differences in our society in clear geographic patterns.

The mini-neighborhood, in turn, is always part of a larger political entity in a specific area, state, and region. Its location greatly influences the cost and quality of public services, housing expenditures relative to income, and other neighborhood amenities or deficiencies, such as good schools, crime levels, or proximity to job opportunities. Since all these factors are critical to the quality of daily life, housing conditions must be appraised in a neighborhood context.

Thus, the term "housing" usually embraces at least four distinctive sets of questions, about which voluminous statistics are provided. These relate to: (1) the economic aspects of construction and investment in residential buildings; (2) the physical unit that provides shelter; (3) the characteristics of its occupants; (4) the location of the dwelling, both its immediate neighborhood and the larger geopolitical environs.

In attempting to fulfill the overarching goal of a "decent home and suitable living environment for every American family," federal housing and community development objectives have shifted over the years.[14] They have emphasized one or another of the above aspects of housing, and sometimes in conflicting ways. Federal and local transportation, education, criminal justice, environmental, banking, and fiscal policies are no less significant influences on housing patterns. But

14. This goal was first articulated by the Congress soon after World War II in the 1949 Housing Act and subsequently reaffirmed by Congress in the 1968 housing legislation.

the flow of private investment (and disinvestment) in residential buildings is doubtless the most powerful single determinant of changing housing conditions.

However important statistics might be about the housing industry, the balance wheel of the economy, or about shifting public policies, they are inappropriate "social indicators," which ostensibly reflect the effects of these forces. Of the three other dimensions of housing questions, what do the indicators in the chapter tell us and what do they omit?

HIGH NATIONAL STANDARDS

Social Indicators, 1976 provides broad-gauged information about four aspects of housing: (1) trends in the future demand for housing; (2) the condition and occupancy of the nation's housing stock; (3) international comparisons; and (4) public perceptions of neighborhoods. Information about future trends and international comparisons are both new and welcome additions, compared to the coverage of housing in the 1973 volume.

As for future trends, expected population changes that will most influence housing demand are presented. Projections of declining average household size, rising numbers of one-person households, largely females, and demand for single-family units are charted. Standing alone however, the demographic projections are of limited use in assessing future national housing and construction needs since other significant factors are uncharted, as for example, costs of interregional and intrametropolitan migrations.

The bulk of the chapter, as in 1973, documents the impressive past performance of the economy in providing basic shelter for a growing nation. Relying only on the chapter's charts, a reader might conclude that a decent home, if not always a suitable living environment, would seem within easy reach of all Americans, certainly by world standards.

International perspectives are offered in two series. For selected countries, *Social Indicators, 1976* measures the proportion of dwelling units with indoor piped water and toilet facilities and the number of persons per room occupying the units. International comparisons, are a particularly useful addition. They tell us how ample and spacious are the worst of the nation's dwellings. They remind us that housing standards are relative matters, time- and culture-bound, varying with lifestyles, general levels of living, and expectations.

Housing deprivation in the United States is no longer a simple question of physical shelter from the elements, sanitation or crowding, a giant step in 40 years when "one-third of a nation" was ill-fed, ill-clothed and ill-housed." Recent Census Bureau surveys of household appliances, not included in *Social Indicators, 1976,* confirm the extraordinarily high standards of living that for Americans "make a house a home." So high are our current standards that it is now assumed that all year-round housing units, even decrepit shacks and vermin ridden tenements, have running water, heating, cooking, sanitary facilities, and electricity. These basic, commonplace items are scarce luxuries in the shanty towns of developing nations, for hundreds of millions of the four billion people on earth.[15] In the People's Republic

15. No really poor nation was among the countries selected, perhaps in the spirit

of China, home to over a fifth of the world's population, for example, standard housing consists of two rooms for an average household of five persons, with shared toilet and cooking facilities. The prime objective is to provide all homes with electricity, cold piped water, sanitary facilities, and cooking fuels.[16]

Our censuses count other refinements in the housing stock, spelling out specific plumbing fixtures and living arrangements. After all, by 1975, more than 95 percent of all homes were equipped with TVs, radios, refrigerators, vacuum cleaners, electric coffee makers, irons, toasters, telephones and more. Over half of all households had air-conditioners, clothes washers and dryers, and 83 percent owned at least one automobile, the "second home" of many Americans.[17]

Social Indicators, 1976 tells us that in 1974 only 3.2 percent of all dwellings in the United States still were without complete, private plumbing facilities. In France, for example, almost half of all dwelling units lack inside toilets as do three-fourths of all Japanese homes. Further, in 1974, only 5.3 percent of all United States housing units were occupied by more than one person per room. Of these, only 1.1 percent were occupied by more than 1.5 persons per room, the density standard of the Census Bureau as recently as 1940. Few nations in the world would view this standard as crowded.

Additional charts fill out the picture of who lives in the nation's physically deficient dwellings. As might be expected, they are occupied principally by families with low incomes, a disproportionate number of which are black. Blacks are far more likely to live in crowded housing conditions than are whites. More than one person per room occupied 12.6 percent of all black households in 1974; the comparable proportion for whites was 4.5 percent. But improvements in living space have been dramatic for blacks as well as whites. In 1940, 40 percent of black households occupied dwelling units with more than one person per room as did 18.2 percent of white households.

A disproportionately high number of black households also occupy the few remaining housing units with incomplete, private plumbing facilities. Most of the latter are found in rural areas where rapid economic and population growth since 1970 suggest that deficient dwellings will soon be phased out. The speedy disappearance of substandard housing in core cities is far more problematic. At this juncture, poor maintenance and vandalism are decimating much of the formerly standard housing stock in urban poverty areas.

Apart from statistical problems of reliability, error and undercounting in black neighborhoods, how valid or useful are the two principal measures of housing quality (and, by inference, of housing deprivation) employed throughout the chapter? Granted, that as long as 3.2 percent of all dwellings lack complete plumbing facilities, and 5.3 per-

of noblesse oblige or because those nations with the poorest housing are also poor in statistics. Comparisons with a few developing nations would have highlighted our extraordinarily high housing standards.

16. Doris B. Holleb, "Regional Self-Sufficiency in China," *World Issues*, vol. 11, no. 1 (Santa Barbara, Calif.: Center for the Study of Democratic Institutions, March 1977), pp. 22–24.

17. *Statistical Abstract of the United States, 1976*, pp. 751 and 597.

cent are occupied by more than one person per room, these indicators are not irrelevant. These small proportions do stand for large numbers of people and homes. They mean that 2.3 million dwellings have incomplete plumbing facilities and that 3.8 million dwellings are rather densely occupied. The chief conclusion to be drawn from the tiny, dwindling percentages is that they suggest great *relative* deprivation in a society with such universally high housing standards.

Nonetheless, as the proportions decline over the years, so does the serviceability of the indicators. Not only are these measures becoming blunt as surrogates for housing quality, but above all, they are incomplete and therefore insensitive to other contemporary concerns.

CURRENT TRENDS

Missing from the chapter is information about three aspects of housing that have overshadowed the "too little housing problem" and the "bad housing problem." They revolve mostly around (1) disproportionately high housing expenses; (2) what might be called the "bad neighborhood problem;" and (3) environmental and energy conservation.

Housing costs, relative to other expenditures and incomes, skyrocketed midway in the decade, with two chief effects. First, an increasing number of families, more than the number living in physically substandard units, remain in adequate housing only by budgeting inordinate amounts for shelter. In 1975, for example, 44.8 percent of all renters spent more than a quarter of their incomes for housing. But for renters with incomes under $5,000, the comparable proportion was 84 percent.[18] Federal subsidy programs reach only a small fraction of eligible households.[19]

Second, homeowners are also devoting a rising proportion of their budgets to housing expenditures, and a growing number of families seeking to purchase homes for the first time are priced out of the market entirely.[20] Others sustain high housing costs only with the second income of a working wife. Soaring costs relative to incomes, after decades of stability, can have pervasive effects on family and community life, and relative cost information should be included.[21]

As for the "bad neighborhood problem," it is a hoary issue, limited mostly to poverty and older working class neighborhoods in central cities and industrial suburbs. Since 1970, conditions have deteriorated badly in these neighborhoods; and the outward trek from aging neighborhoods to newer, racially and socially selective, suburban and rural sites has accelerated. The slackening demand for housing in cities and towns with declining populations has resulted in increasing concentrations of the dependent poor, particularly female-headed households, in old central city neighborhoods. The lines of racial and socioeconomic separation

18. Based on data from the *Annual Housing Survey: 1975*. These surveys provide detailed data, heretofore lacking, not only about relative costs but about the actual condition of the housing stock and neighborhoods.

19. Arthur P. Solomon, *Housing the Urban Poor* (Cambridge, Mass.: The MIT Press, 1974), pp. 76–91.

20. U.S. Congressional Budget Office, *Homeownership: The Changing Relationship of Costs and Incomes, and Possible Federal Roles* (Washington, D.C., January 1977) pp. 7–22.

21. These data are now available in the *Annual Housing Survey*.

among metropolitan neighborhoods have hardened in the 1970s.

In declining poverty areas, it is impossible to maintain or restore housing by focusing exclusively on physical improvements; the social and economic problems of their inhabitants are far more overwhelming. Formerly standard housing has been ravaged by poor maintenance, abandonments, fire, and vandalism, and at a much faster rate than rehabilitations and additions. Some urban neighborhoods have become jungles, inhabited largely by predators and their victims. Neither their housing problem, nor its solution, is reflected in aggregate indicators measuring crowding or plumbing.

At the other end of the continuum, in growing, sprawling, suburban and exurban towns, emerging housing patterns give rise to quite different problems. As highways, sewer, water and utility lines reach out into open country, issues relating to preserving environmental quality and productive agricultural land, to rising automobile dependency and energy consumption are of foremost concern.[22] Although these issues may seem beyond the scope of a "housing" chapter, they are nonetheless high on the national agenda and are covered nowhere else in the volume.[23]

In short, because socioeconomic disparities among neighborhoods appear to be increasing and because these differences are essential to understanding changing housing issues and trends, insufficient information is provided about the characteristics of residents of neighborhoods in different national locales.

The only information about neighborhoods presented in the chapter is based on opinion polls. These subjective indicators record the attributes of neighborhoods as perceived by their inhabitants.[24] Most Americans are satisfied with their places of residence, rating their neighborhoods as good or excellent. Only 12.4 percent of all homeowners and 27.9 percent of renters view their neighborhoods as fair or poor. Even fewer wish to move, perhaps because the least satisfied recognize how limited are the alternatives within their means.

Since the chapter stops short with these subjective indicators, one can only surmise the actual situation of the neighborhoods in which, for instance, respondents are satisfied or dissatisfied with public transportation, shopping, or schools. One might guess, for example, that the high proportion of "satisfied" homeowners in 1974 who nonetheless rate public transportation in their neighborhoods as inadequate—some 47 percent of homeowners in contrast to 29.5 percent of renters—must live, by choice, in unserved suburban and rural communities.[25]

22. *The Annual Housing Survey* and the *1970 Census of Population and Housing* provided "journey to work" data indicating the progressive rise in the frequency and distance of automobile travel.

23. In a comparable volume for Japan, for example, indicators of environmental quality and housing are both provided and subsumed under the heading, "Material Environment." See: Research Committee, Council of National Living, *Social Indicators of Japan* (Tokyo, September 17, 1974). For a review of the "social reports" of other nations, see also Roxann A. Van Dusen, ed., *Social Indicators, 1973: A Review Symposium* (Washington, D.C.: Social Science Research Council, 1974), pp. 20–62.

24. For a discussion of the problems associated with relying on "subjective" indicators of "objective" conditions, see Leo A. Goodman and Stephen E. Fienberg, "Social Indicators, 1973: Statistical Considerations," in *Social Indicators, 1973: A Review Symposium*, pp. 74–76.

25. For another view, see statement by Harvey S. Perloff in *Public Policy Decision-Making and Social Indicators* (Santa Monica,

CONCLUSION

With such major omissions, readers are likely to grossly underestimate the scale and nature of housing problems. Nor can they easily discern the direction of future housing trends.

A recent study by Bernard J. Frieden and Authur P. Solomon, for example, estimates the extent of housing and neighborhood deprivation at nearly triple the amount implied in *Social Indicators, 1976* because it takes into account the full range of housing problems that may impinge on families.[26] In addition to the six million households living in crowded units with inadequate plumbing, highlighted in the *Social Indicators* chapter, those households whose plumbing, heating, or electrical equipment no longer works because of poor maintenance are included in the Frieden-Solomon estimate as are households living in neighborhoods with inadequate public services. Finally, Frieden and Solomon also consider those who pay excessive costs for housing according to conventional yardsticks. The grand total comes to 17 million households: roughly one out of four of all households in the nation experienced one kind of housing problem or another in 1973.

In sum, despite the modest intention in *Social Indicators, 1976* of providing only "the warp and woof into which a comprehensive picture can be woven," there are major missing threads. Because of them, readers are left with an incomplete canvas of "the direction in which we appear to be evolving." The dynamic relationship of the physical aspects of housing and the economic and social needs of its inhabitants remain confused, a confusion that has bedeviled federal housing policies from the beginning. Nor does the chapter illuminate the links among seemingly divergent national policy objectives of preserving urban neighborhoods and conserving environmental resources and energy.

Housing is a hydra-headed beast. After three decades, "a decent home and suitable living environment for every American family" is still an elusive goal.

Calif.: Urban and Regional Information Systems Association, 28 March 1974), pp. 87–94.

26. Bernard J. Frieden and Arthur P. Solomon, *The Nation's Housing: 1975 to 1985* (Cambridge, Mass.: Joint Center for Urban Studies, April 1977), pp. 131–41.

Table 3/6

HOUSING UNITS, BY AVAILABILITY OF PLUMBING FACILITIES: 1940–1974

Availability of plumbing facilities	1940	1950	1960	1970	1974
NUMBER (thousands)					
Total, occupied units	34,855	42,826	53,024	63,450	70,831
Lacking some or all plumbing facilities	15,547	14,575	7,785	3,773	2,274
With all plumbing	19,308	28,251	45,239	59,677	68,557
PERCENT					
Total, occupied units	100.0	100.0	100.0	100.0	100.0
Lacking some or all plumbing facilities	44.6	34.0	14.7	5.9	3.2
With all plumbing	55.4	66.0	85.3	94.1	96.8

Source: U.S. Department of Commerce, Bureau of the Census, *1940 Census of Housing*, Vol. II; *1950 Census of Housing*, Vol. I; *1960 Census of Housing*, Vol. I; *1970 Census of Housing*, Vol. I; and *1974 Annual Housing Survey*, Series H-150, Part A.

Chart 3/6 Social Indicators, 1976

HOUSING UNITS, BY AVAILABILITY OF PLUMBING FACILITIES: 1940–1974

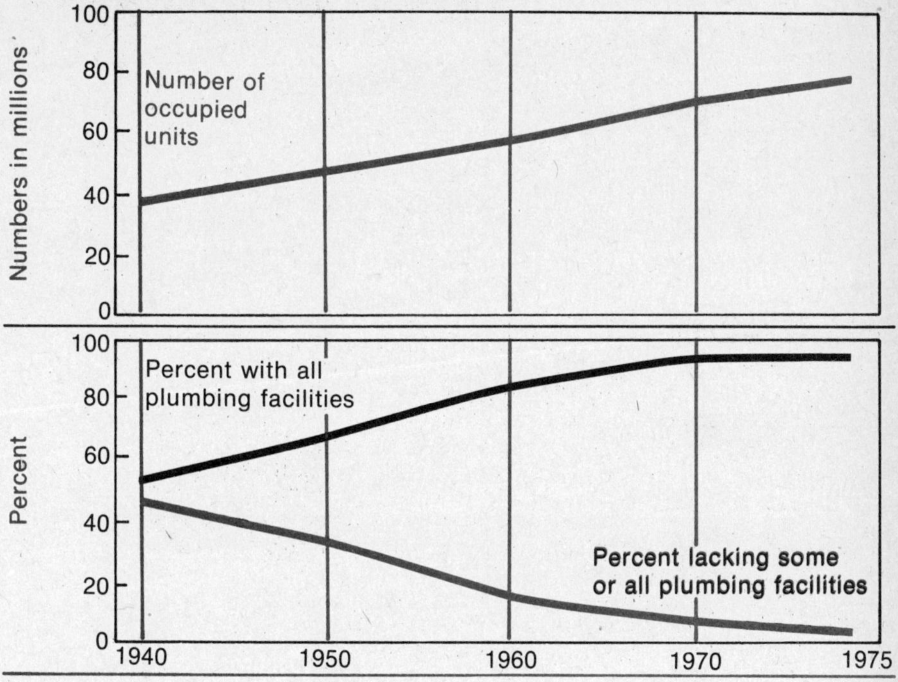

Chart 3/8 Social Indicators, 1976

PERCENT OF HOUSING UNITS LACKING SOME OR ALL PLUMBING FACILITIES, BY LOCATION: 1970 AND 1974

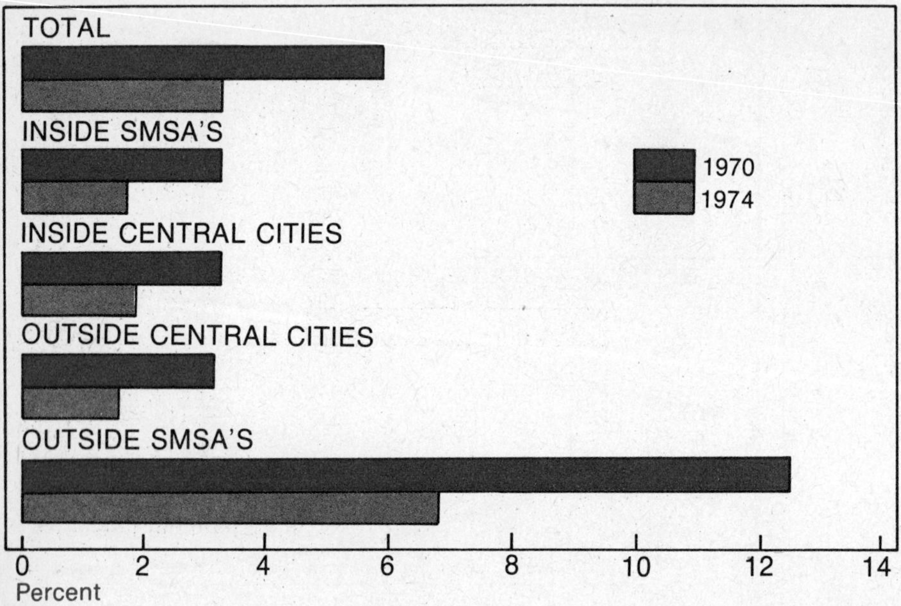

Table 3/8

HOUSING UNITS LACKING SOME OR ALL PLUMBING FACILITIES, BY LOCATION: 1970 AND 1974

Location	1970 Number (thousands)	1970 Percent of all housing units	1974 Number (thousands)	1974 Percent of all housing units
All housing units lacking some or all plumbing facilities	3,773	5.9	2,274	3.2
Inside SMSA's	1,387	3.2	807	1.7
Inside central cities	683	3.2	416	1.8
Outside central cities	704	3.1	392	1.5
Outside SMSA's	2,386	12.2	1,467	6.6

Source: U.S. Department of Commerce, Bureau of the Census, *1970 Census of Housing*, Vol. II, and *1974 Annual Housing Survey*, Series H-150, Part A.

Chart 3/10 Social Indicators, 1976

HOUSEHOLDS LIVING IN UNITS LACKING SOME OR ALL PLUMBING FACILITIES, BY RACE AND INCOME, 1974

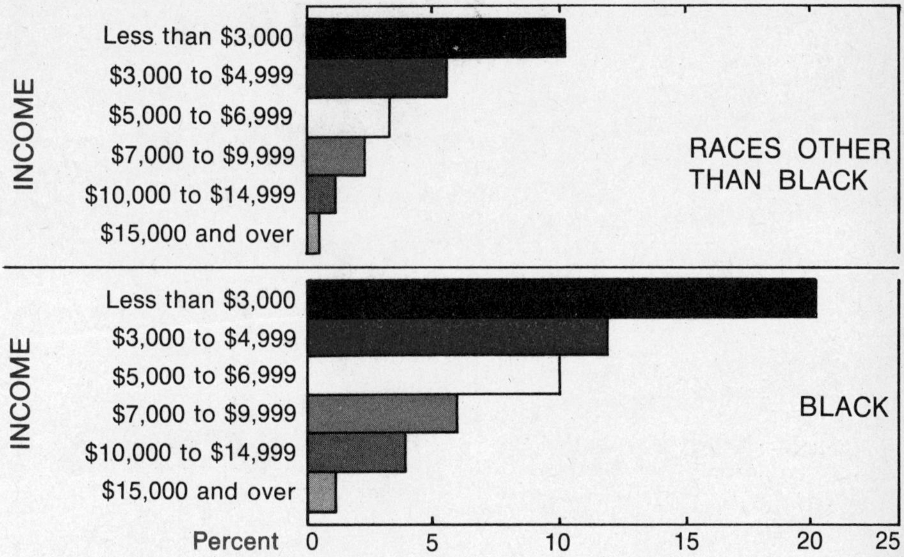

Table 3/10

HOUSEHOLDS LIVING IN UNITS LACKING SOME OR ALL PLUMBING FACILITIES, BY RACE AND INCOME: 1974

INCOME	ALL RACES		RACES OTHER THAN BLACK		BLACK	
	Number (thousands)	Percent of all households	Number (thousands)	Percent of all households	Number (thousands)	Percent of all households
All housing units lacking some or all plumbing facilities..	2,274	3.2	1,580	2.5	695	9.6
Less than $3,000	979	12.1	648	10.1	331	20.1
$3,000 to $4,999	493	6.5	349	5.5	144	12.0
$5,000 to $6,999	292	4.2	196	3.2	96	10.0
$7,000 to $9,999	254	2.6	189	2.2	65	5.9
$10,000 to $14,999 ...	173	1.1	128	.9	45	3.8
$15,000 and over	84	.4	70	.3	14	1.2

Source: U.S. Department of Commerce, Bureau of the Census, *1974 Annual Housing Survey*, Series H-150, Part B.

Chart 3/11 Social Indicators, 1976

PROJECTIONS OF THE NUMBER OF PRIMARY INDIVIDUALS, BY SEX: 1980, 1985, 1990

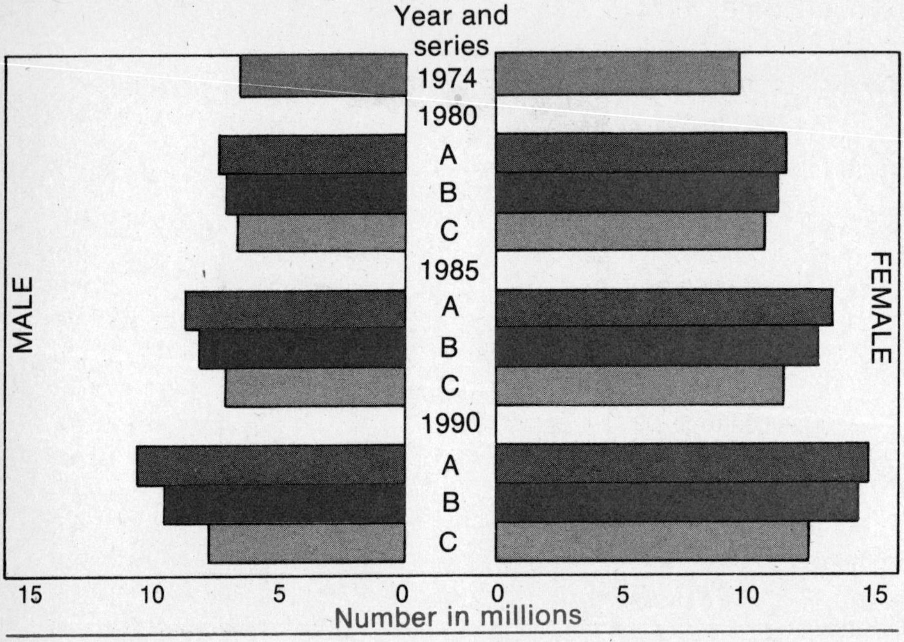

Table 3/11

PROJECTED NUMBER OF OCCUPIED HOUSING UNITS AND PRIMARY INDIVIDUALS: 1980, 1985, AND 1990

(Thousands) YEAR AND SERIES		Occupied housing units	PRIMARY INDIVIDUALS Male	Female
1974		69,859	5,654[1]	9,288[1]
1980	Series A	79,953	7,331	11,393
	Series B	79,356	7,076	11,135
	Series C	78,159	6,565	10,620
1985	Series A	88,456	8,932	13,144
	Series B	87,188	8,395	12,612
	Series C	84,655	7,320	11,545
1990	Series A	96,318	10,541	14,868
	Series B	94,270	9,688	14,032
	Series C	90,185	7,981	12,354

Source: U.S. Department of Commerce, Bureau of the Census, *Current Population Reports*, Series P-25, No. 607.

[1] Estimated.

ANNALS, AAPSS, 435, Jan. 1978

Social Security and Social Welfare Indicators

By IDA C. MERRIAM

ABSTRACT: The proportion of its total resources that a society devotes to social welfare is a useful general measure related to social policy. In fiscal 1976, the United States spent 21 percent of Gross National Product (GNP) for public social welfare programs, including health and education as well as social insurance (the largest segment) and assistance. Program developments, inflation, population growth, and the level of economic activity affect trends. The United States spends relatively less for social security than most industrial countries. Income maintenance programs now touch most families in the United States. More than 90 percent of all persons over age 65 get social security benefits. The extent of social security protection for survivors and disabled persons, the relative importance of private pensions, social security benefit replacement rates (the relation to previous earnings), and the income situation of aged persons are reviewed. There is brief reference to sickness insurance, unemployment insurance, and public assistance. Some possible directions of future change are noted. The interweaving of social welfare objectives and systems into the fabric of modern life cannot be undone. The attempt to develop clearer indicators of need and accomplishment is worth pursuing.

Ida C. Merriam was formerly an Assistant Commissioner and Director of Research in the Social Security Administration. She received a Ph.D. in economics from the Brookings Graduate School of Economics and Government in 1928. She has served as a technical advisor or consultant on social security with the International Labour Organization and the United Nations, and helped organize and served as the first chairman of an advisory committee on Social Security Research of the International Social Security Association.

LIKE most social indicators, statistics relating to social welfare are ambiguous. An increase in expenditures for unemployment insurance signals both a weakness in the economy that should disturb us and a strength in the protection for individuals and families that marks an effective social welfare system. Rising health costs attributable to price inflation are negative indicators; rising health costs due to better health care more equitably provided to all groups in the population are, up to some point, good. The questions "when is *more* useful" or "when is *little* wasted effort" are difficult to answer in relation to individual social programs. They probably cannot be answered at all in relation to the totality of social welfare measures.

Good program research has always provided, and effective planning has always used, a variety of indicators of both need and accomplishment. By their very nature, general social indicators give only gross and generalized information. They can clarify for us what have been the overall results of the multitude of decisions made in earlier years. Their ability to point directions for the future is more limited. It is easier to identify what is wrong in terms of general problems and needs than it is to visualize alternative patterns of change or to be sure about cause and effect relationships that would make the achievement of one or another pattern realistic. Nevertheless, the attempt to see and understand the general movement of social change is basic to efforts to achieve a more satisfactory social order.

SOCIAL WELFARE EXPENDITURES

One general measure which provides a useful framework for analysis is the proportion of its resources that a society devotes to social welfare. Broadly defined, social welfare programs include all programs directed specifically to the well-being of individuals and families, as distinct from expenditures for law and order or general community facilities and services. The range of such programs is much the same in all industrialized countries, although with significant variations in emphasis and priorities. Socially organized provision for income maintenance, health services, education, housing, and protective and personal services is an established and necessary feature of the modern world.

In fiscal 1976, the United States spent some $330 billion, or 20.6 percent of that year's gross national product (GNP) for public social welfare programs. (See table 1.) The largest amount, 44 percent of the total, went for social insurance—old age, survivors, disability and health insurance; railroad and public employee pension systems; unemployment insurance; temporary disability insurance; workmen's compensation.

Health and medical programs—public health activities, public hospitals, and other public civilian and military health services—accounted for only 6 percent of all public social welfare spending. This figure, however, gives a misleading impression of the extent of public expenditures for health services. A significant portion of such expenditures are made through other programs—social insurance (primarily Medicare and workmen's compensation), public assistance (Medicaid), and veterans' programs. In fiscal 1976 all expenditures from public funds for health and medical services were three times as large as those under programs specifically identified as health programs.

Public assistance for needy peo-

TABLE 1

SOCIAL WELFARE EXPENDITURES UNDER PUBLIC PROGRAMS AS A PERCENT OF GNP, SELECTED FISCAL YEARS 1929–1976

TYPE OF PROGRAM	1929	1935	1945	1950	1960	1970	1976
Total expenditures (millions)	$3,921	$6,548	$9,205	$23,508	$52,293	$145,856	$331,366
Percent of GNP							
Total	3.9	9.5	4.4	8.9	10.5	15.2	20.6
Social Insurance	.3	.6	.7	1.9	3.9	5.7	9.1
Medical benefits	(.07)	(.09)	(.06)	(.07)	(.09)	(.85)	(1.2)
Public Aid	.1	4.4	.5	.9	.8	1.7	3.0
Medical benefits				(.02)	(.10)	(.54)	(.95)
Health and medical programs	.3	.6	1.1	.8	.9	1.0	1.2
Veterans programs	.7	.9	.5	2.6	1.1	.9	1.2
Medical benefits	(.05)	(.07)	(.05)	(.28)	(.19)	(.19)	(.25)
Education	2.4	2.9	1.5	2.5	3.5	5.3	5.4
Other social welfare	.1	.1	.1	.2	.2	.4	.5
All health and medical expenditures	.5	.8	1.2	1.2	1.3	2.6	3.6
Federal funds as percent of total welfare expenditures	20.4	49.0	47.1	44.8	47.7	53.0	59.9
Social welfare expenditures as percent of all government expenditures	37.4	49.6	8.6	37.4	38.4	48.2	59.7

SOURCE: For years 1950–76, Alfred M. Skolnik and Sophie R. Dales, "Social Welfare Expenditures, Fiscal Year 1976," *Social Security Bulletin*, vol. 40, no. 1 (January 1977), pp. 3–19. For years 1929–45, Ida C. Merriam and Alfred M. Skolnik, "Social Welfare Expenditures Under Public Programs in the United States, 1929–66," DHEW, SSA ORA Research Report no. 25 (Washington, D.C.: USGPO, 1968).

ple, after an upsurge in the Depression of the 1930s and a decline in the war years, remained at a level of less than one percent of the GNP until 1965. By 1976, it amounted to three percent of GNP. Major factors in this increase were the very substantial rise of expenditures for medical care under Medicaid, and the introduction of the food stamp program, which by fiscal 1976 was paying subsidies of $5.7 billion, almost one-third as much as was paid in cash assistance in that year. The number of persons applying for cash assistance also increased under the impetus of the aggressive welfare rights movement and concern with poverty in the 1960s. It should be noted that all these figures relate to direct expenditures only. Public support through tax subsidies, important as it is, is not included in this method of accounting.

A number of factors in addition to program development underlie the growth of social welfare expenditures in the United States in recent years. A large part of the increase represents price inflation. Between 1950 and 1976, total social welfare expenditure in current dollars increased 1,312 percent, but in purchasing power (1976 dollars) the increase was 507 percent, less than half as much. When population growth also is taken into account, the increase in per capita expenditures in 1976 dollars was 327 percent. Demographic changes, such as the aging of the population, are also important, especially as they have been compounded by the lowering of the age (to 62) at which retirement benefits can be drawn under the basic social security system. The gradual maturing of that system, as well as the extension of the program to cover almost all employed persons and to provide disability benefits and health insurance for aged persons and disabled beneficiaries, was the major program expansion during these years.

The share of national output devoted to social welfare is affected not only by national priorities but also by the size of the national product at a particular time. Social programs have built-in stabilities—old age pensions continue to be paid, and indeed become more essential in recessions. Many programs—notably unemployment insurance, public assistance, food stamps—expand in bad times. While the statistic used in table 1—expenditure as a percent of GNP—is perhaps the best general measure of changes in welfare effort, there is still need for care in interpretation. The high totals in table 1 for 1935 and 1976, for example, reflect not only large expenditures for public aid and social insurance, but low (relatively) national output.[1]

It is useful to look also at the magnitude of private expenditures for social welfare purposes. Private pensions and other employee benefits, when added to cash social insurance and related public payments, brought total organized expenditures for income maintenance to 11 percent of GNP in fiscal 1976. (See chart 4/1A at the end of this article for earlier years.) Public programs have accounted for between 85 and 90 percent of all such direct expenditures since 1950. About 85 percent of all expenditures for education in the United States have also been from public funds, a larger proportion (93 percent) for elementary and secondary education, a smaller proportion (63 percent) for higher education. In the case of health and medical care, on the other hand, private expenditures still predominate. Public expenditures for health purposes (under all types of programs) amounted to 42 percent of all health expenditures in 1976. In this overall accounting, the costs of medical education are classified as educational, not health, expenditures. On this basis, total public and private health expenditures in the United States in fiscal 1976 amounted to 8.6 percent of GNP. This is a considerably larger proportion of GNP than other industrialized countries appear to spend in total for health, although many spend more than the United States on public health programs.

Some international comparisons

The social welfare expenditure series for the United States was first developed in response to an attempt at international comparisons of welfare spending. At a meeting of the United Nations Economic and Social Council (UNESCO) in the late summer of 1951, the United States was being attacked for its capitalist

1. Detailed data on individual program expenditures from federal, state, and local funds can be found in the sources cited in table 1. See those sources and tables 4/1 and 4/2 in *Social Indicators, 1976* for a regrouping of the data by major function (cash income maintenance, health, education, other welfare) and estimates of comparable private expenditures.

disregard of the welfare of its citizens, and figures that were cited in the debate did imply a very limited governmental commitment to welfare goals. A quick check showed that the figures in question had been accurately read from United States budget documents. The budget classifications, however, were not easily adjusted to reflect a broad definition of social welfare. Even more important, the large state and local government expenditures for welfare purposes ($14.5 billion compared with $9.6 billion from federal funds in fiscal 1950) had been completely forgotten.

The Research Office of the Social Security Administration provided data and analyses that proved illuminating in the U.N. debates.[2] The scope of the social welfare expenditure series that was published in the *Social Security Bulletin* first in 1951 (and annually since 1953) was very much influenced by this special use of the material, particularly in the inclusion of public education as a social welfare program.

There is no continuing statistical series for other countries with precisely the same scope, although occasional parallel compilations have been made. Social planning budgets or accounts in a number of countries cover the same general area. For a number of years the International Labor Office has compiled statistics obtained from its members on a uniform basis covering expenditures under social security programs, including social insurance, public assistance, health insurance and public health programs, and family or children's allowances. The most recent figures are for the year 1971.[3] Overall, the United States devotes a considerably smaller share of its GNP to social security, thus defined, than do most industrial countries: 11 percent in 1971, as compared with 18 or 19 percent in most of northern Europe and Canada and 22 percent in the Netherlands and Sweden. The difference results largely from the fact that we have neither family allowances nor a national health insurance or health service program covering the entire population. Even for old age, survivors, and disability insurance, however, United States expenditures as a percent of GNP (3.4 percent were about half those in the Federal Republic of Germany, the Netherlands, and Sweden (7.6 percent, 6.3 percent, and 6.0 percent).[4] The 1972 Social Security amendments substantially increased benefit levels in this country, and while benefits in other countries have also been liberalized and adjusted to price changes, the gap between us and other countries is certainly not as great in 1977 as it was in 1971.

A recent OECD study[5] analyzes trends in income maintenance in the member countries. The program def-

2. U.N. Economic and Social Council, 13th Session, E/L 186, "Report of the Social Commission," (9 August 1951). See also *Social Security Bulletin*, vol. 14, no. 10 (October 1951), pp. 14–16.

3. International Labor Office, "The Cost of Social Security—Bosie Tables, Eighth International Inquiry, 1967–1971," duplicated (Geneva: 1976).

4. Max Horlick, "National Expenditures on Social Security in Selected Countries, 1968 and 1971," DHEW, SSA Research and Statistics Note no. 29–1974 (Washington, D.C.: USGPO, 18 October 1974). The figures for total social security expenditures in the Note and in this article differ from those used in *Social Indicators, 1976* chart 4/21 because the *Social Indicators* report omits family allowances, cash sickness benefits, unemployment benefits, and public employee and veterans benefits.

5. "Public Expenditure on Income Maintenance Programs" (Organization for Economic Cooperation and Development Studies in Resource Allocation, no. 3, July 1976).

initions are slightly different than those used by the International Labor Office, but the general relationships found among countries are similar. One factor contributing to the differences among countries in the amounts spent on retirement benefits is the proportion of the population aged 65 and over—10 percent in the United States in 1972, as compared with 13 or 14 percent in most European countries. The length of time a pension plan has been in operation also is an important factor—the older and more mature the system, the larger the proportion of now aged persons will be who have had the opportunity to qualify for full benefits.

INCOME MAINTENANCE

With this background we can take a closer look at the income maintenance programs. Almost two-fifths of the social welfare expenditures under public programs in the United States in fiscal 1976 were for cash social insurance benefits. These benefits plus veterans compensation amounted to 10 percent of aggregate personal income. Cash public assistance plus the value of food stamp bonuses accounted for another 1.7 percent.

There are many ways of evaluating these programs and measuring their impact. Here the focus is on the extent of the protection against earnings loss afforded to individuals.

In an industrial society, most families depend on current earnings to cover their immediate consumption needs and an alternative source of continuing income is necessary when earnings cease or are interrupted. Long-term social insurance benefits for the aged, the permanently disabled, and for survivors account for the bulk of income maintenance payments.

Population with benefits

Retired Aged—Virtually all persons reaching age 65 in the United States now have a claim to a continuing income, under social security or another federal program. At the end of 1976, there were 15.4 million retired workers age 65 and over on the social security benefit rolls. Another 1.8 million persons aged 62–64 were drawing early retirement benefits. Women make up what has been an increasing proportion of retired workers (now 45 percent). Including persons receiving benefits as wives or husbands, widows or widowers, and a few aged parents, some 21.2 million persons age 65 and over, or more than 90 percent of that age group, were getting cash social security benefits. (Twenty years earlier, the proportion had been 40 percent.) Of the remainder of those over age 65, about half a million were working essentially full-time but could draw benefits if they retired; most of the others were drawing government employee pensions or veterans benefits.

In addition to social security benefits, a substantial number of aged persons have other sources of retirement income. Private pensions were paid to about 6.4 million persons (including some disabled and early retirees) at the end of 1976. Persons in military service and many state and local government employees are covered by social security and have both the basic social security benefit and their special pensions. Federal civilian employees are still not covered by social security but some former federal employees who have also worked elsewhere draw both civil service and social security benefits.

About 8 percent of Old Age, Survivors and Disability Insurance (OASDI) beneficiaries aged 65 and over (some 1.7 million persons) have incomes so low that they get cash income-tested assistance as well. Some 600,000 persons age 65 and over get only public assistance.

Survivors—More than 90 percent of all orphans or half orphans are now entitled to social security benefits based on the earnings of either the father or the mother. The surviving parent can also receive a benefit while caring for the child if he or she is not earning more than the amounts allowed under the retirement test. At the end of 1976, almost 3 million children were receiving survivor benefits. Including aged widows and widowers, the number of persons benefiting under the survivor provisions of the social security program was more than one third as large as the number of retired workers and their dependents. (See table 2.)

Disabled Workers—Some 2.7 million former workers with severe and long-continuing disabilities were drawing social security benefits at the end of 1976. Most workers injured in the course of their employment or in military service have long had recourse to workmen's compensation or military or veterans benefits. The increase in automobile accidents and in chronic disabilities linked to environmental pollution or other causes has given additional importance to the general disability benefits under the social security system.

The determination of inability to work or carry on one's usual occupation involves subjective factors not easy to measure. A special survey counted 8.6 million severely disabled adults aged 18–24 and not in institutions in 1972. Some 42 percent were receiving OASDI benefits; 22 percent were getting benefits under other long-term disability benefit programs—veterans, workmens compensation, railroad and public employee pension systems. A little less than 10 percent had income from private pensions.

The severely disabled include persons who are mentally retarded and others disabled at birth or in childhood who have never been able to work. Dependents or survivor benefits under OASDI are payable to such disabled "children" of any age when the parent is a beneficiary or dies, but there is no social insurance benefit for disabled children of working parents. One-fifth of all those counted as severely disabled in 1972 were getting public assistance.

Benefit levels and replacement rates under social security

Social security benefits reflect the range of incomes earned in the working years, with a floor in the form of a minimum benefit, a higher proportion of earnings replaced at lower earning levels and a ceiling on the maximum amount of earnings taxed and the maximum benefits paid. They also reflect the continuity of earnings.

The average monthly benefit amounts that were being paid in December 1976 under the OASDI program are shown in table 2. Benefit amounts are now automatically adjusted to increases in the cost of living. A 5.9 percent cost of living increase in benefits went into effect in July 1977. The minimum benefit then payable to a retired worker at age 65 (with no reduction for early retirement) was $114.30; the maximum for a retired worker was $437.10.

One of the most meaningful measures of the relative adequacy of benefits is the extent to which they replace previous earnings. The concept of the replacement rate is,

TABLE 2

OLD AGE, SURVIVORS AND DISABILITY INSURANCE: NUMBER OF BENEFICIARIES IN CURRENT PAYMENT STATUS AND AVERAGE MONTHLY BENEFIT AMOUNTS, DECEMBER, 1976

TYPE OF BENEFICIARY	NUMBER OF BENEFICIARIES (IN THOUSANDS)		AVERAGE MONTHLY BENEFIT AMOUNT
TOTAL*	33,024		—
Retired workers and their dependents	20,745		—
Retired workers		17,165	$225
Men		9,421	248
Benefits not reduced for early retirement		4,633	270
Benefits reduced for early retirement		4,788	226
Women		7,745	197
Benefits not reduced for early retirement		2,670	224
Benefits reduced for early retirement		5,075	183
Wives and husbands		2,896	114
Children		684	88
Disabled workers and their dependents	4,624		—
Disabled workers		2,670	245
Men		1,824	266
Women		846	200
Wives and husbands		474	73
Children		1,480	68
Survivors	7,446		—
Aged widows and widowers		3,995	207
Survivor children		2,872	152
Widowed mothers and fathers		579	160

SOURCE: *Social Security Bulletin*, vol. 40, no. 6 (June 1977), tables M10, M12, M13, M14, Q4 and Q8.
* Includes parents of workers and persons with special age 72 benefits not shown separately. Of the total number of beneficiaries, 21.2 million were aged 65 and over, 3.3 million were aged 62–64 (1.8 million drawing early retirement benefits, .6 million disability benefits and .9 million dependent or survivor benefits) and 8.5 million were under age 62 (5 million were children under age 18 or age 22 if fulltime students or of any age if disabled before age 18).

however, much more complicated than might at first appear. Should benefits be based on, and compared with, earnings in the year before retirement, which will be high relative to earlier years for most professionals and low for many low paid, irregularly employed workers? Or should the comparison be with earnings in the most recent five or ten year period—which, unless revalued, will be distorted by inflation as a measure of living standards? Or is the fairer measure earnings averaged over the individual's entire working career, a figure which generally will not only be much lower than either of the other measures but which will also change the relative position of different workers?

The formula in the United States is a modified career average, with the lowest five years of earnings omitted from the calculation. An analysis of the actual replacement ratio of benefits newly awarded in the period July–December 1974, showed a median replacement rate for men of 59 percent of career average taxable earnings (as defined in the law), but only 37 percent of taxable earnings in the three highest years of the preceding ten (1964–73). For women workers, because of their generally lower earnings and the weighted benefit formula, the replacement ratios based on these measures were 79 and 44 percent respectively. For persons who reached the taxable maximum in at least one of the three years of highest earnings (40 percent of the men, 11 percent of the women), total wages were estimated. Median replacement ratios in relation to total earnings in the three highest years were 29 percent for men and 31 percent for women.[6] Many of those with earnings above the taxable maximum were also receiving private pensions. An earlier study (in 1970) showed that for persons receiving private pensions the median replacement rate of social security benefits plus private pensions, based on estimated total earnings in the three best years, was about twice the replacement rate of social security benefits alone. The ten percent of newly-entitled beneficiaries who were also receiving railroad retirement or public employee pensions (civilian or military) similarly had combined replacement ratios about twice the rate for social security benefits alone.[7]

These replacement ratios are for individual workers. Private pension systems almost never pay benefits for wives. Under social security the wife's benefit is basically fifty percent of the husband's, unless reduced by his early retirement. The wife may, of course, qualify for a higher benefit as a retired worker. Unfortunately, the data are not yet available from which to compute actual replacement ratios for couples, relating the combined benefits to the combined preretirement earnings of both spouses.

One can evaluate benefit levels and replacement rates in several ways. Clearly some expenses are less in old age—most of the costs of childrearing and expenses in connection with going to work, for example. On the other hand, medical care costs increase—in the absence of really comprehensive health insurance or a national health service—and under inflationary conditions, housing costs (including property taxes, utilities, repairs, etc.) may rise significantly for the many old people who own their homes. Housing, medical care, and special homemaker services, or institutional care at later ages, may call for specific remedies or programs. For the ordinary expenses of living, pension benefits can be appropriately compared with previous earnings levels. Private pension plans frequently aim at a combined (social security and the private pension) replacement rate of 70–75 percent of previous earnings (meaning usually recent earnings). The fact that in the United States social security benefits are not taxable also has to be taken into account. This tax treatment of benefits is, of course, relatively much more valuable to those in the higher income brackets than it is to the many social security beneficiaries with low to moderate incomes.

6. Alan Fox, "Earnings Replacement from Social Security Benefits Newly Entitled Beneficiaries, 1974," SSA RS Note no. 13 (Washington, D.C.: USGPO, 15 June 1976).

7. "Reaching Retirement Age," USDHEW, SSA, ORA Research Report, no. 47 (Washington, D.C.: USGPO, 1976) pp. 145–49 and chapter 14.

Income of the aged

Judgments as to what would be the desirable replacement rate—however the rate is defined—reflect general assumptions about what other resources retired or disabled persons have in addition to their benefits. In order to find out, and to answer other questions relating to the characteristics and circumstances of persons who in any period were or were not drawing benefits, one has to turn to survey data. A large amount of such data is now available, most of it based on surveys undertaken by the Social Security Administration, with the Census Bureau usually responsible for data collection.[8]

Social Indicators, 1976 shows a few measures derived from these surveys. In the brief space of a general article it is impossible to do more than list some of the major conclusions that emerge from this growing mass of material. The analysis focuses on the aged, the largest group and the one for which most information is available. While certain relationships—and, of course, absolute numbers of persons or dollars—have changed since the 1950s, other relationships have remained remarkably stable.

1. For many in the age group 65–69, earnings remain an important source of income.

2. For those over 70, and for all who have fully retired, social security benefits constitute the major source of continuing income. A little more than half the married couples aged 65 and over and almost three-fourths of the nonmarried beneficiaries had less than $1,000 of other continuing retirement income in 1971. (See chart 4/10 at the end of this article.)

3. Private pensions provide an important supplement to social security benefits for an increasing number of beneficiaries but still a minority even of the men. Private pensions go disproportionately to workers with the higher benefits. They partially offset the effect of the weighted benefit formula in social security. Women and blacks and low paid workers generally are unlikely to have private pensions. Nor are such pensions usually available to survivors or dependents. Of the 6.3 million married couples in the 1971 survey, some 23 percent were receiving private pensions in addition to social security, while 6 percent were getting public assistance. In the case of nonmarried women beneficiaries (7.3 million, mostly widows) only 10 percent had additional income from private pensions, while 14 percent were on public assistance. In both cases, the median incomes of beneficiaries who were also receiving private pensions were more than twice as large as those of beneficiaries getting public assistance. (See chart 4/7 at the end of this article.)

4. Aged widows have been and remain the most disadvantaged group

8. The major survey reports published to date are: Lenore A. Epstein and Janet H Murray, "The Aged Population of the United States," USDHEW, SSA, ORS Research Report no. 19 (Washington, D.C.: USGPO, 1967); "Demographic and Economic Characteristics of the Aged. 1968 Social Security Survey," USDHEW, SSA, ORS Research Report no. 45 (Washington, D.C.: USGPO 1975); "Reaching Retirement Age: A Survey of Newly Entitled Workers 1968–70," USDHEW, SSA, ORS Research Report no. 47 (Washington, D.C.: USGPO, 1976); "Income of the Population Aged 60 and Older, 1971," DHEW, SSA, ORS, staff paper no 26 (Washington, D.C.: USGPO, April 1977). Findings from surveys of disabled persons, children living with widowed mothers, student beneficiaries, and a longitudinal survey of men and nonmarried women aged 58–63 in 1969 who will be reinterviewed at two year intervals for ten years, have been presented in preliminary reports and in articles in the *Social Security Bulletin*.

in the older population. This situation is changing somewhat as women who were too old to qualify for benefits as workers or dependents when the program started are replaced by younger cohorts, an increasing number of whom are entitled to benefits as former workers. The Social Security Act has also been amended (in 1972) to raise the level of widow's benefits to equal that of a worker. A disproportionately large number of widows and older, unmarried men and women are still getting public assistance, however.

5. Asset income is very unequally distributed. For most aged beneficiaries the only significant asset is an owned home. More than three-fourths of the married couples and more than one-third of the nonmarried beneficiaries aged 65 and over do own their homes, in about four-fifths of the cases, mortgage free. Few beneficiaries, however, have income-yielding assets of any consequence.

6. Early retirement poses increasing problems. Some persons retire before the age of 65 and take reduced social security benefits because they have adequate private pensions or other income. Many more are forced out of the labor market by ill health or continuing unemployment. They are not sufficiently disabled to qualify for disability benefits; unemployment insurance does not cover such long-continued inability to find a job, and public assistance is also available only for persons aged 65 and over or with severe disabilities. Early retirement benefits under social security rescue many, but at the price of continuing low benefits. The problem of assuring acceptable income support to those who cannot work, without discouraging those who can work from doing so, is far from resolved for this age group as well as for younger persons.

Income loss from short-term sickness

Protection against income loss from short-term illness presents somewhat different problems than long-term disabilities. The connection with the job may not be broken immediately and other adjustments in family living may not occur or be feasible (hence, sickness benefits are usually set at a higher level in relation to current earnings than are long-term disability benefits). On the other hand, it is not always possible to tell at the outset of an illness or injury how long it will last. Some countries combine short- and long-term disability protection in one system. In this country we have not. The OASDI program picks up only after an individual has been continuously disabled for five months. Sick leave or voluntary private insurance cover the early (but not always the first) weeks of wage loss due to illness for many workers, but the protection is, of course, uneven. Four states—California, New Jersey, New York, and Rhode Island—plus Puerto Rico and the railroad retirement system make statutory provisions for benefits during the first 26 weeks of disability. Overall, it is estimated that public and private insurance together replaced about 35 percent of the total wage loss from short-term (up to 26 weeks) disability in 1974. Excluding the relatively more generous sick leave payments and the corresponding earnings loss for government workers, the aggregate replacement for wage and salary workers was 25 percent. This was, nevertheless, almost double the protection that had been provided in 1950.[9]

9. Daniel N. Price, "Cash Benefits for Short-Term Sickness, 1948–74," *Social Security Bulletin*, vol. 39, no. 7 (July 1976), pp. 22–34.

Unemployment insurance

Unemployment insurance is more directly responsive to fluctuations in business and economic activity than any of the other social insurance programs. Since the early 1940s it has been—for workers with substantial attachment to the labor force—a source of continuing income between jobs and in bad times. The program has never covered all unemployment. Young persons without employment experience or older women or men trying to enter or re-enter the labor force, as well as workers who remain unemployed for very long periods, have been outside its scope.

Continuing high and pervasive unemployment in the past few years has led to a significant extension of benefit duration under most state laws and additional federal supplemental benefits for unemployed workers who had exhausted state benefits, thus providing a maximum of 65 weeks of benefit payments. During 1975, over four million persons exhausted their benefit rights while still remaining unemployed. Total expenditures for unemployment insurance in fiscal 1976 were just under $20 billion, or 16 percent of all cash social insurance benefits.

Public assistance

However adequate job opportunities may be, and however comprehensive and effective the social insurance program, there will probably always remain some persons who, at any given time, have less than enough to live on at accepted standards. Public assistance for aged and disabled persons became largely a federal responsibility beginning in 1974, although many states still find it necessary to supplement the federal payment. General assistance for persons in need, regardless of cause, is provided by most local governments, often with state financial aid, but at greatly varying levels of support. The largest assistance program is the federal-state program of aid to families with dependent children generally referred to as "the welfare program." A very few orphans and some children with disabled fathers or mothers are on the rolls, as are some children with unemployed parents in about half the states. The great majority of the 12 percent of all children under 18 who were receiving AFDC in 1975, however, lived in fatherless families. Analysis of the underlying social problems and of alternative methods of meeting society's responsibilities to such children and their parents could fill an entire issue of THE ANNALS. There is, as yet, no consensus on a preferred alternative or even on what would be the signs of improvement in the situation.

FOR THE FUTURE

Quite clearly, our social security system has largely achieved the goal of universal protection for income security in old age; but there remain both gaps and overlaps that could be corrected. Some liberalization of the permanent disability provisions for older workers under social security would ease the pressure for early retirement and provide protection for individuals now without real security. Social security benefit levels are now more than minimal, but still do not provide a level of living relative to that of the working population that is desirable for the large number of middle-income beneficiaries who have no other continuing income. Benefit levels and the maximum benefit amount could more justifiably be raised if benefit income were taxable. Judgments as to what is desirable will, of course, always be subject to change. Equity in the benefit structure for different groups —women who work for pay and women who do not, low wage and high income earners—is also a concept that will be redefined from time to time.

The low rate of wage loss replacement for temporary disability signals another area for potential improvement. The optimum mix of public job programs and unemployment insurance remains a matter of sharply differing opinions, as does the question of assistance to the working poor.

This analysis has not dealt with the economic impacts of the programs or with the question of alternative methods of financing social security. Current discussions of the future costs of OASDI invoke projections of the ratio of the retired to the working population in the next century that may be somewhat unrealistic. There is no doubt that the number and proportion of aged persons will increase. How many of them will continue working, how many women will be in the labor force for large parts of their lives, and whether the birth rate will remain at its present very low level are all matters about which there can be no assurance.

One factor that does stand out in the summary indicators is the critical importance of general economic conditions. The availability of jobs directly affects the number who need unemployment insurance or public assistance; it also determines how many older persons can continue to work and earn when they want to do so, and how many disabled will be successfully placed. The availability of enough jobs to go around also means fewer jobs at substandard wages and fewer workers with incomes below the poverty standard and in need of assistance. At the same time, a strong economy makes it easier to finance the cost of the income maintenance and income support that is provided.

Whatever the degree of success of general economic policy, the importance of social security as an institution will remain. The interweaving of social welfare objectives and systems into the fabric of modern life cannot be undone without a major breakdown of the whole society. Clearer general indicators of changing circumstances and potential areas of improvement can help promote public understanding and lay a basis for the detailed analysis of alternatives that is essential to the continuing achievement of social welfare objectives.

Table 4/1
PUBLIC AND PRIVATE EXPENDITURES FOR SOCIAL WELFARE PURPOSES: 1950–1975
(Fiscal years; in millions of current dollars)

Type of expenditure	1950	1955	1960	1965	1970	1975[1]
Total, net[2]	35,337	49,957	78,704	117,871	211,033	388,695
Public	23,508	32,640	52,293	77,175	145,761	286,547
Private	12,160	17,997	27,790	42,766	67,995	107,752
Income maintenance	10,723	17,304	29,827	42,530	72,399	152,794
Public	9,758	15,409	26,292	36,575	60,814	132,094
Private	965	1,895	3,535	5,955	11,585	20,700
Health	12,027	17,330	25,856	38,892	69,201	118,499
Public	3,065	4,421	6,395	9,535	25,237	49,947
Private	8,962	12,909	19,461	29,357	43,964	68,552
Education	10,914	14,206	21,742	34,228	62,368	98,359
Public	9,366	11,863	18,036	28,149	51,922	82,859
Private	1,548	2,343	3,706	6,079	10,446	15,500
Welfare and other services	2,004	1,797	2,658	4,291	9,788	24,647
Public	1,319	947	1,570	2,916	7,788	21,647
Private	685	850	1,088	1,375	2,000	3,000
PUBLIC EXPENDITURES AS A PERCENT OF ALL EXPENDITURES						
Total[3]	65.9	64.5	65.3	64.3	68.2	72.7
Income maintenance	91.0	89.0	88.1	86.0	84.0	86.5
Health	25.5	25.5	24.7	24.5	36.5	42.1
Education	85.8	83.5	83.0	82.2	83.3	84.2
Welfare and other services	65.8	52.7	59.1	68.0	79.6	87.8
ALL EXPENDITURES AS A PERCENT OF GROSS NATIONAL PRODUCT						
Total, net[2]	13.4	13.2	15.9	18.0	22.1	27.3
Income maintenance	4.1	4.6	6.0	6.5	7.6	10.7
Health	4.6	4.6	5.2	5.9	7.2	8.3
Education	4.1	3.7	4.4	5.2	6.5	6.9
Welfare and other services	.8	.5	.5	.7	1.0	1.7
PUBLIC EXPENDITURES						
Total	23,508	32,640	52,293	77,175	145,761	286,547
Percent	100.0	100.0	100.0	100.0	100.0	100.0
Income maintenance	41.5	47.2	50.3	47.4	41.7	46.1
Health	13.0	13.5	12.2	12.4	17.3	17.4
Education	39.8	36.3	34.5	36.5	35.6	28.9
Welfare	5.6	2.9	3.0	3.8	5.3	7.6

Table 4/1 (*Continued*)

Type of expenditure	1950	1955	1960	1965	1970	1975[1]
PRIVATE EXPENDITURES						
Total	12,160	17,997	27,790	42,766	67,995	107,752
Percent	100.0	100.0	100.0	100.0	100.0	100.0
Income maintenance	7.9	10.5	12.7	13.9	17.0	19.2
Health	73.7	71.7	70.0	68.6	64.7	63.6
Education	12.7	13.0	13.3	14.2	15.4	14.4
Welfare	5.6	4.7	3.9	3.2	2.9	2.8
PUBLIC AND PRIVATE EXPENDITURES IN CONSTANT (1975) DOLLARS						
Total, net[2]	73,772	91,833	130,955	185,332	283,266	388,695
Public	49,077	60,000	87,010	121,344	195,652	286,547
Private	25,386	33,082	46,240	67,242	91,268	107,752
Price deflators	47.9	54.4	60.1	63.6	74.5	100.0
	1950–75	1950–55	1955–60	1960–65	1965–70	1970–75
AVERAGE ANNUAL PERCENT CHANGE IN CONSTANT (1975) DOLLAR EXPENDITURES						
Total, net	6.64	4.38	7.10	6.95	8.48	6.33
Public	7.06	4.02	7.43	6.65	9.55	7.63
Private	5.78	5.30	6.70	7.49	6.11	3.12

Source: U.S. Department of Health, Education, and Welfare, Social Security Administration, *Social Security Bulletin*, January 1976.

[1] Preliminary data.

[2] Total expenditures adjusted to eliminate duplication resulting from use of cash payments received under public and private social welfare programs to purchase medical care and educational services.

[3] Before adjustment for elimination of duplication.

Chart 4/1A — Social Indicators, 1976

PUBLIC AND PRIVATE EXPENDITURES FOR SPECIFIED SOCIAL WELFARE PURPOSES AS A PERCENT OF GROSS NATIONAL PRODUCT: 1950–1975

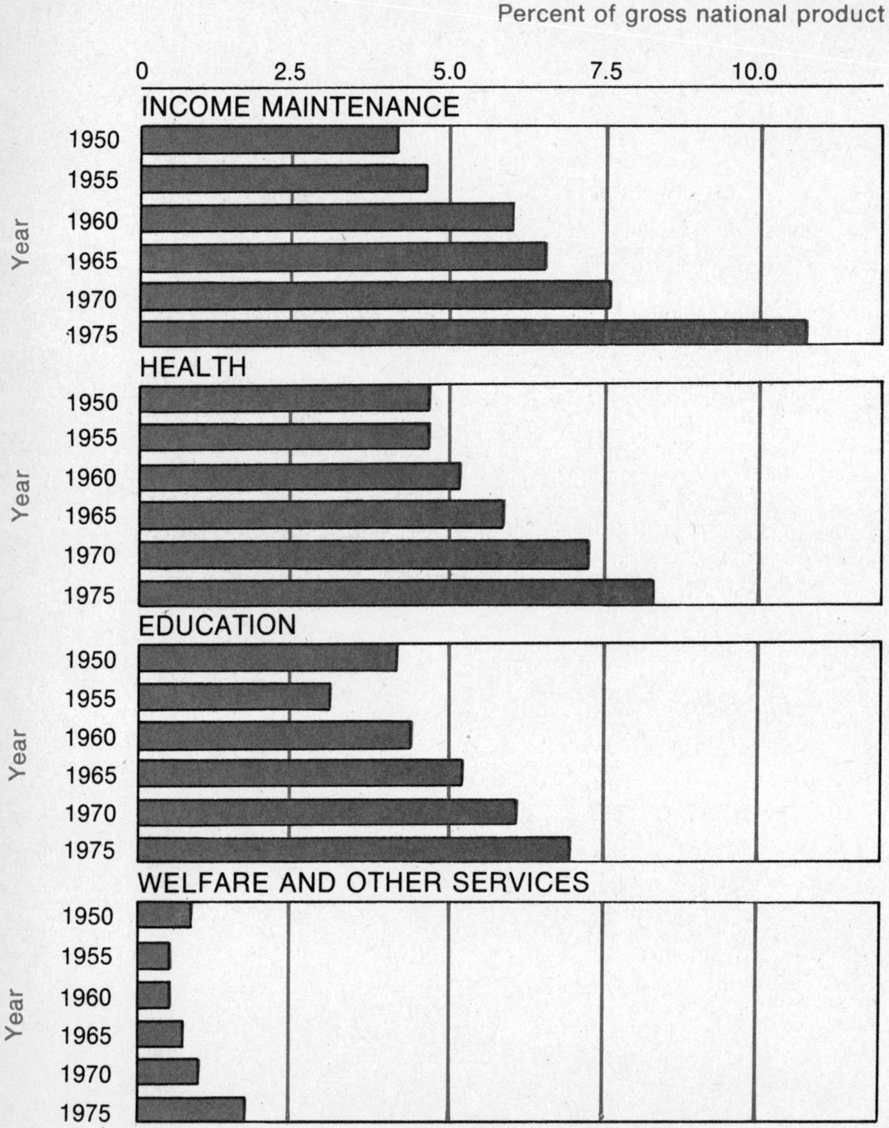

Source: see table 4/1

Chart 4/1B

Social Indicators, 1976

PERCENTAGE DISTRIBUTION OF PUBLIC AND PRIVATE EXPENDITURES FOR SOCIAL WELFARE PURPOSES: 1950–1975

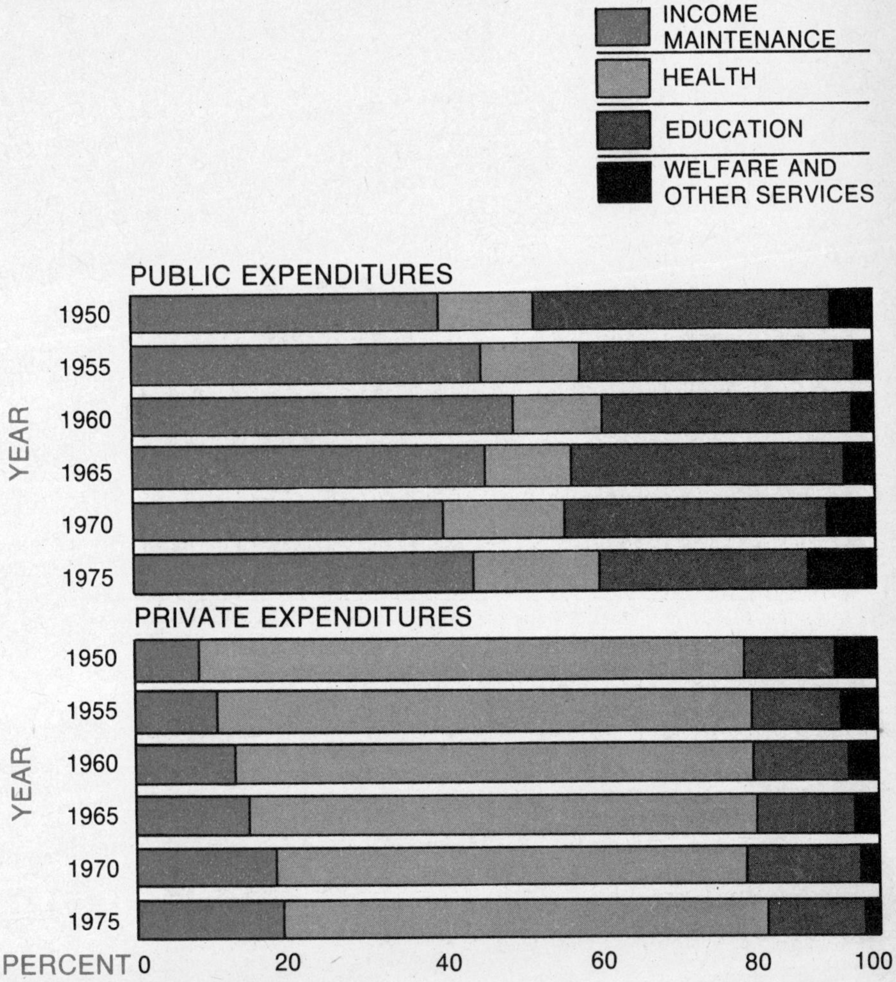

Source: see table 4/1

Table 4/2

TOTAL AND PER CAPITA SOCIAL WELFARE EXPENDITURES UNDER PUBLIC PROGRAMS: 1950–1975

FISCAL YEAR	Total social welfare expenditures[1] (millions of constant 1975 dollars)	Total[2]	Social insurance	Public aid	Health and medical programs	Veterans' programs	Education	Other social welfare[2]	All health and medical care (constant dollars)
		PER CAPITA SOCIAL WELFARE EXPENDITURES[3] (constant dollars)							
1950	48,895.3	318.50	67.20	33.95	28.06	92.23	90.75	6.10	41.69
1955	59,764.3	357.83	107.92	33.05	34.15	52.32	122.57	6.82	49.58
1960	86,699.3	474.91	175.29	37.37	40.68	49.12	160.45	10.38	58.29
1965	120,956.9	615.02	223.73	50.24	49.94	47.64	224.42	16.51	76.23
1970	195,153.4	940.70	352.31	106.68	63.10	58.08	329.17	26.82	163.29
1975[p]	285,819.1	1,319.42	567.32	187.13	76.80	76.23	361.95	36.36	230.57
		PERCENT DISTRIBUTION							Percent
1950	48,895.3	100.0	21.0	10.6	8.8	29.2	28.4	1.9	13.1
1955	59,764.8	100.0	30.1	9.2	9.5	14.8	34.2	1.9	13.9
1960	86,699.3	100.0	36.9	7.8	8.5	10.5	33.7	2.2	12.3
1965	120,956.9	100.0	36.4	8.1	8.1	7.8	36.4	2.7	12.4
1970	195,153.4	100.0	37.5	11.3	6.7	6.2	34.9	2.9	17.4
1975[p]	285,819.1	100.0	43.1	14.2	5.8	5.8	27.4	2.8	17.5
		FEDERAL FUNDING AS PERCENT OF TOTAL PUBLIC EXPENDITURES							
1950	44.8	(X)	42.5	44.2	29.2	93.0	2.4	40.8	(NA)
1955	44.8	(X)	64.9	50.1	37.1	98.7	4.4	46.1	(NA)
1960	47.7	(X)	74.1	51.6	38.9	98.0	4.9	42.6	(NA)
1965	48.9	(X)	77.5	57.2	44.5	99.7	8.8	44.1	(NA)
1970	53.1	(X)	82.7	58.5	49.0	98.6	11.5	58.6	(NA)
1975	57.9	(X)	80.4	65.7	50.5	99.1	11.0	60.2	(NA)

Source: U.S. Department of Health, Education, and Welfare, Social Security Administration, *Social Security Bulletin*, January 1976.

[p] Preliminary. X Not applicable. NA Not available.

[1] Excludes expenditures within foreign countries for education, veterans' payments, and OASDHI and civil service retirement benefits.

[2] Includes housing, not shown separately.

[3] Based on January 1 Bureau of the Census data for total U.S. population including Armed Forces and Federal civilian employees and their dependents overseas, and the civilian population of territories and possessions.

Chart 4/2A

Social Indicators, 1976

DISTRIBUTION OF SOCIAL WELFARE EXPENDITURES UNDER PUBLIC PROGRAMS: 1950–1975

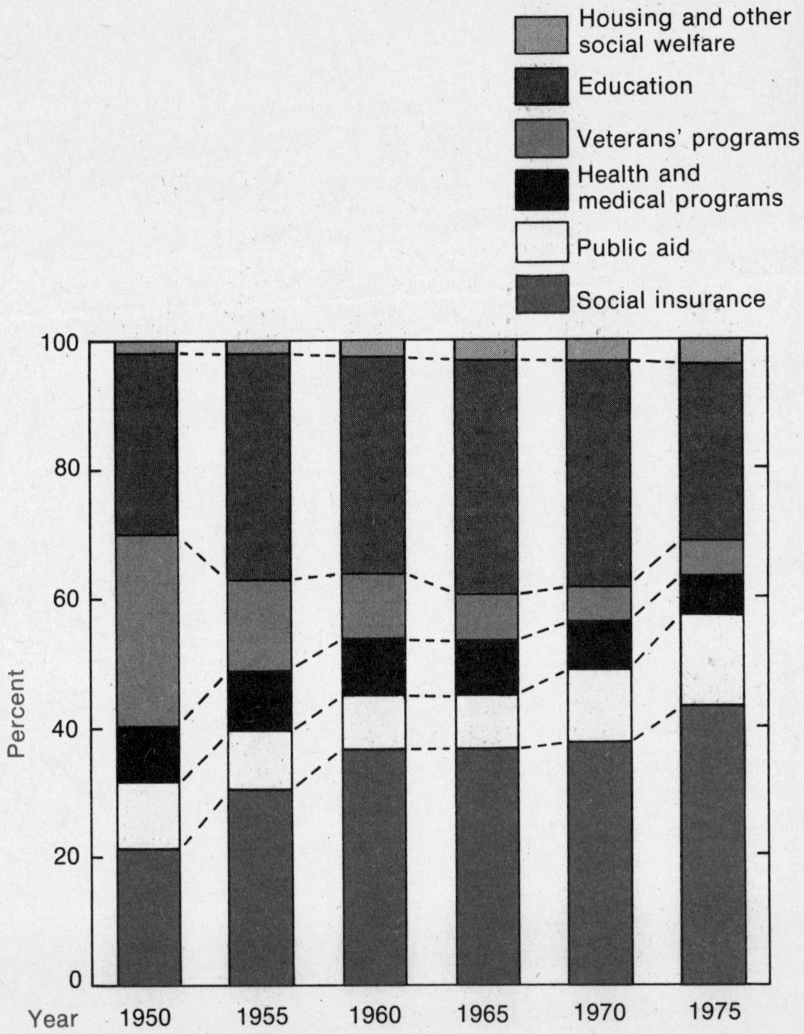

Source: see table 4/2

Table 4/7
MEDIAN INCOME OF SSI BENEFICIARIES AGE 65 AND OVER, BY TYPE OF INCOME: 1962, 1967, AND 1971

PERSONS AND INCOME	1962		1967		1971 current and constant dollars
	Current dollars	Constant 1971 dollars	Current dollars	Constant 1971 dollars	
Married couples—					
With private pensions ..	3,400	4,551	4,040	4,904	6,408
With public assistance ..	1,730	2,316	2,010	2,440	2,769
Nonmarried males—					
With private pensions ..	2,280	3,052	2,550	3,095	3,979
With public assistance ..	1,100	1,472	1,360	1,651	1,730
Nonmarried females—					
With private pensions ..	2,115	2,831	2,300	2,792	3,475
With public assistance ..	1,195	1,600	1,355	1,645	1,826

Source: U.S. Department of Health, Education and Welfare, Social Security Administration. For 1962, Research Report No. 19, *The Aged Population of the United States: The 1963 Social Security Survey of the Aged*, 1967. For 1967, Research Report No. 45, *Demographic and Economic Characteristics of the Aged: 1968 Social Security Survey*, 1968, and unpublished data on total income of beneficiaries receiving assistance. For 1971, Unpublished data from the 1972 Social Security Survey of the Status of the Elderly.

Note: See technical notes for explanation of current vs. constant dollars.

Chart 4/7

Social Indicators, 1976

MEDIAN INCOME OF SOCIAL SECURITY BENEFICIARIES AGED 65 AND OVER, BY TYPE OF INCOME: 1962–1971

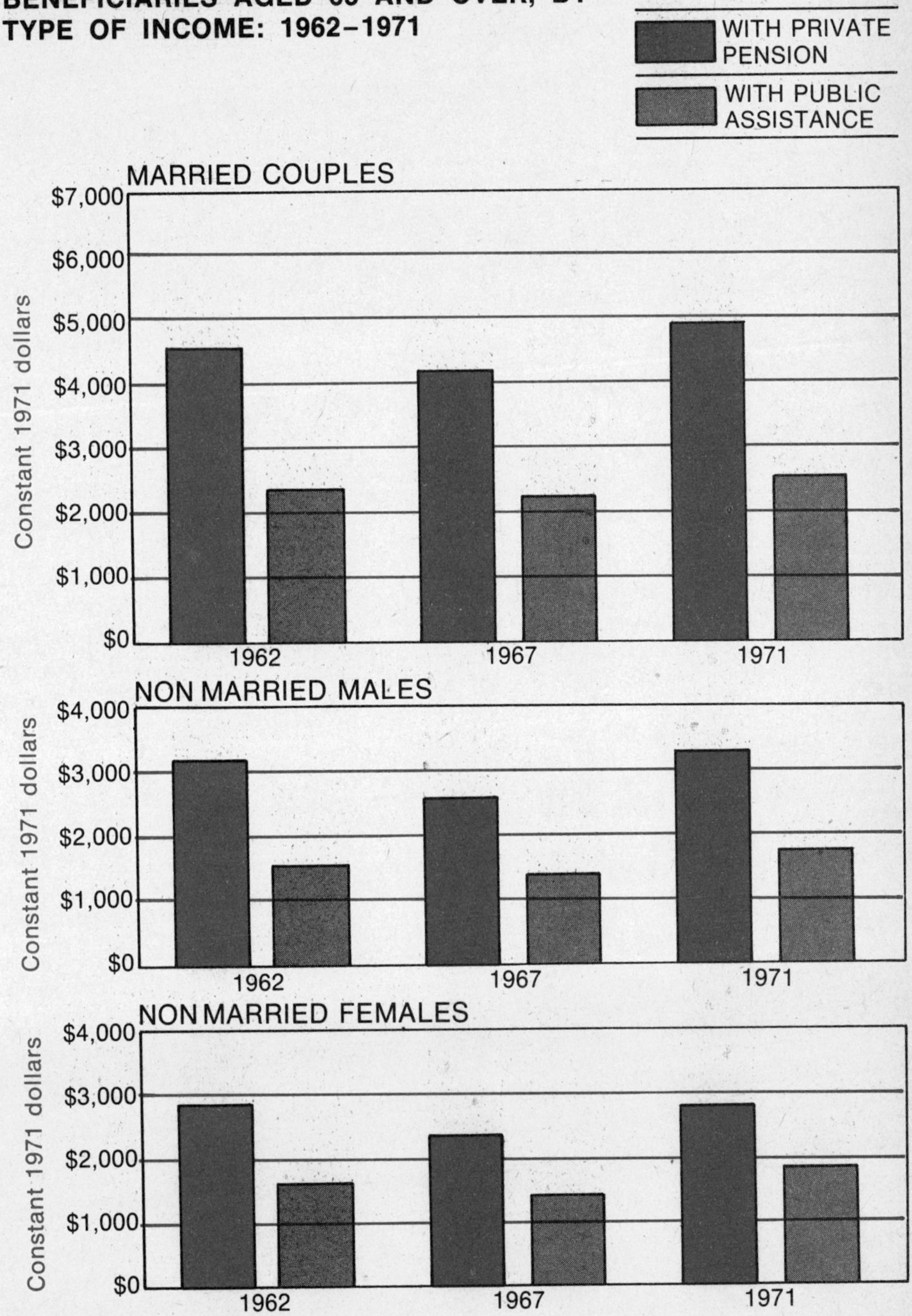

Source: see table 4/7

Table 4/10

RETIREMENT INCOME, OTHER THAN OASDHI BENEFITS, OF BENEFICIARIES AGE 65 AND OVER, BY MARITAL STATUS: 1962, 1967, AND 1971

Retirement income other than OASDHI benefits	1962 Married couples	1962 Non-married persons	1967 Married couples	1967 Non-married persons	1971 Married couples	1971 Non-married persons
Total percent	100	100	100	100	100	100
None	25	44	30	43	26	35
$1 to $149	14	19	12	14	8	14
$150 to $299	5	6	5	6	4	5
$300 to $499	7	6	5	6	4	5
$500 to $999	16	14	13	15	11	14
$1,000 to $1,499	9	6	11	7	9	8
$1,500 to $1,999	7	2	7	3	7	5
$2,000 to $2,499	5	1	4	2	6	3
$2,500 to $2,999	3	(2)	3	1	5	2
$3,000 to $3,999	3	1	4	1	6	3
$4,000 to $4,999	2	(2)	2	(2)	4	2
$5,000 or more	4	1	4	2	10	4

Source: U.S. Department of Health, Education, and Welfare, Social Security Administration. For 1962, Research Report No. 19, *The Aged Population of the United States: The 1963 Social Security Survey of the Aged*, 1967. For 1967, Research Report No. 45, *Demographic and Economic Characteristics of the Aged: 1968 Social Security Survey*, 1975. For 1971, *Income of the Population Age 60 and Older, 1971*, by Susan Grad and unpublished detail on type of pensions received.

[2] 0.5 percent or less.

Chart 4/10 Social Indicators, 1976

RETIREMENT INCOME, OTHER THAN OASDHI BENEFITS OF BENEFICIARIES, AGE 65 AND OVER, BY MARITAL STATUS: 1962, 1967 AND 1971

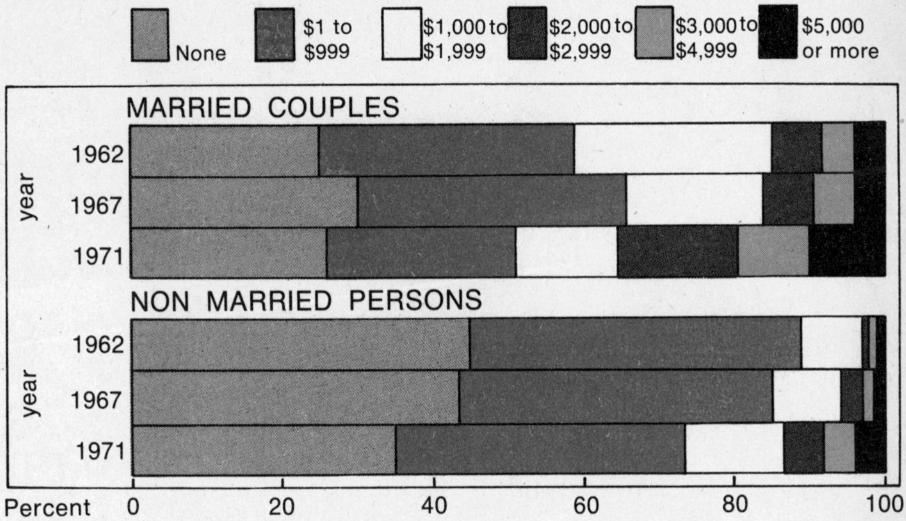

Source: see table 4/10

ANNALS, AAPSS, 435, Jan. 1978

Continuing Trends in Health and Health Care

By RONALD W. WILSON, JACOB J. FELDMAN, and MARY GRACE KOVAR

ABSTRACT: Current trends in health and health care that were identified in *Social Indicators, 1976* are discussed, including the recent and, in some cases, dramatic declines in mortality, increases in health expenditures, increases in health resources, and changes in health habits. These trends are compared with strikingly similar trends identified almost a half a century ago by The Research Committee on Social Trends established by President Hoover. The significance of the current data and some of their possible causes and implications for the future are addressed, as well as some of the potential pitfalls in interpreting the data.

Ronald W. Wilson is Chief of the Health Status and Demographic Analysis Branch of the Division of Analysis, National Center for Health Statistics, U.S. Department of Health, Education, and Welfare.

Jacob J. Feldman is the Associate Director for Analysis, National Center for Health Statistics, U.S. Department of Health, Education, and Welfare. Prior to coming to the Center in 1974, he was professor of Biostatistics, School of Public Health, Harvard University. He also served as Director of Research at the National Opinion Research Center, University of Chicago, where he received his Ph.D. in sociology.

Mary Grace Kovar is Chief of the Analytic Coordination Branch of the Division of Analysis, National Center for Health Statistics.

IT IS appropriate to begin the discussion of recent trends in the health sector by reviewing a similar, but more comprehensive, effort undertaken nearly a half century ago. In 1929 President Hoover established The Research Committee on Social Trends. The chapter, "Health and Medical Practice" by Harry H. Moore, in the final report addressed, among other things, the most noteworthy trends in the health area at that time.[1] There are striking similarities in what were then considered and are now considered as significant trends in health. Moore identified six trends: (1) growth in personnel and institutions; (2) militant advances in the control of specific diseases; (3) recent trends toward more effective organization; (4) growth of government participation; (5) development of methods of spreading the cost; and (6) the beginnings of coordination.

The trends presented in the health chapter of *Social Indicators, 1976* can be viewed as reflecting tendencies very similar to those identified almost a half a century earlier. Two phenomena that were not addressed by Moore as particularly characteristic of the early 1930s, but which are currently viewed as very important, are the proliferation of new technology and the rapid increase in the cost of health care. Only the latter is covered in *Social Indicators, 1976*.

MORTALITY

The first major set of trends presented in *Social Indicators, 1976* are those related to the continued decline in mortality. This trend is similar to the one identified by Moore as "militant advances in the control of specific diseases." While mortality rates have certainly been declining, there is less evidence of declines in the incidence or prevalence of many of the major diseases.

Life expectancy at birth, one of the more widely accepted indicators of health status, has increased dramatically since the turn of the century. A child born in 1975 could expect to live 72.5 years if the age-specific mortality rates prevailing in 1975 continued over his lifespan. However, the gap in life expectancy between males and females has increased over the period, while the difference between the life expectancy of the white population and all others has decreased. Given the 1975 mortality rates, white females born in 1975 could expect to live 4.9 years longer than females of all other races, 7.8 years longer than white males, and 13.6 years longer than all other males. Much of the increase in life expectancy can be attributed to the marked reduction in infant and childhood mortality. Increases in life expectancy at the older ages have not been as great. For example, a white male at age 60 in 1900 could have expected to live another 14.3 years, while a white male at age 60 in 1975 could expect to live 16.8 years, a gain of only 2.5 years. The greatest increase at the older years has occurred among nonwhite females, for whom approximately 7 years were added to life expectancy at age 60 between 1900 and 1975, that is, 13.6 years in 1900 and 20.7 in 1975. Recently, impressive increases in life expectancy at age 60 have begun to occur in both sex and color groups.

Heart disease is still the leading

1. Harry H. Moore, "Health and Medical Practice," in *Recent Social Trends in the United States: Report of the President's Research Committee on Social Trends* (New York: McGraw-Hill, 1933), pp. 1061–1113.

cause of death in the United States. However, the death rates from heart disease and cerebrovascular disease began to drop dramatically a decade ago. The explanation for this unforeseen drop has still not been determined, although reduced cigarette consumption, particularly among males, dietary changes, hypertension control, and improvements in life saving medical technologies have all been suggested. On the other hand, the cancer death rates, the second major cause of death, have continued to increase. The cancer mortality rate for males 45–64 years of age is almost 25 percent higher than it was 25 years ago. The rise in lung cancer mortality rates has been particularly great, having more than doubled since 1950 for this age group.

Another common indicator of a population's general health status is the infant mortality rate. The infant mortality rate had leveled off at about 26 deaths per 1,000 live births during the 1950s, but it has been declining every year since 1962, reaching 15.1 in 1976. The specific reasons for this decline are not clear, but factors that may be involved include: (1) more women receiving prenatal care in early pregnancy; (2) the declining proportion of births to older women, resulting in fewer higher risk births; (3) the establishment and use of regional perinatal centers; (4) increasing legal abortion rates; and (5) improved nutrition of pregnant women and infants. However, there are still marked differences between the white and black infant mortality rates, with the black rate 85 percent higher than the white in 1975. The declining infant mortality rate is not unique to the United States. The rates have been falling in many countries, even in countries which have had infant mortality rates considerably lower than the United States.

It has been suggested that the reduction in infant mortality and in deaths from certain diseases of childhood may result in more children surviving who will require relatively more intensive care, either in institutions or in the home. For example the life expectancy of a mongoloid child has increased to the point where many survive into adulthood and even old age.[2] These changes in survival patterns will have an impact on the immediate family as well as on the larger community.

More significantly, the declining mortality rates will have a major impact on the age distribution of the population. In 1975, there were 22.4 million Americans 65 years of age and older. Assuming the current mortality rates do not drop further, although there is no reason to assume they will not, by the year 2000, there will be almost 32 million elderly and by 2030, when the last of the post-World War II baby boom population reaches the age of 65, there will be 55 million elderly Americans. This increasing number of elderly persons in our population will present a challenge to the health care system, as the use of health services by this age group is considerably greater than by the younger segments of the population.

Furthermore, the application of new life-saving technology may result in increasing prevalence of highly impaired individuals. Resource requirements for the purposes of life maintenance and custoldial care can be expected to rise

2. Ernest M. Greenberg, "The Failures of Success," *The Milbank Memorial Fund Quarterly*, vol. 55, no. 1 (Winter 1977), pp. 3–24.

appreciably. Ethical issues, in terms of the rights of individuals to a dignified demise, and competing claims for scarce resources, are already being hotly debated.

HEALTH HABITS

Data presented in *Social Indicators, 1976* on changes in dietary habits show several marked shifts in consumption patterns, such as increases in meat consumption and decreases in fluid milk and cream consumption. However, these data reflect total consumption patterns but they do not indicate changes within specific age groups. For example, since the proportion of children in the population has been declining in recent years, and children drink considerably more milk than do adults, a part of this shift could be explained by changes in the population distribution. Also, the increase in the consumption of meat has been accompanied by a shift in the kinds of meat products eaten, with hamburger, with its generally higher fat content, accounting for an increasing proportion of total meat consumption. Traditionally there has been considerable concern about the possibility of undernutrition among certain segments of our population, but as more data become available from the National Health and Nutrition Examination Survey of the National Center for Health Statistics, much of the concern has shifted to dietary balance and overnutrition. There is also concern about the possible deleterious effects on health of various food additives, including the relation of salt intake to blood pressure.

There has been a growing interest in the overall role of health habits and their impact on personal health status as compared to the role of medical care. While there have been major decreases in the proportion of adults who smoke cigarettes, especially among middle-aged males, as well as a marked trend toward low tar and nicotine cigarettes, it is disturbing to see continued increases in the proportion of cigarette smokers among teenage females. As indicated earlier, the impact of the changes in dietary and other health habits on our falling mortality rates, particularly on the cardiovascular rates, is unclear.

HEALTH EXPENDITURES

The growth of government participation in the health field has continued to be a significant trend since it was identified by Moore almost a half a century ago. In 1929 the total national expenditures for health were $3.6 billion, of which less than one-half billion dollars, or 13 percent, were from public funds. In 1976 total national health expenditures for health had increased to $139.3 billion, of which $58.8 billion, or 42 percent, were from public funds. Public expenditures were predominantly from state and local government sources during much of the period but, at least since the Medicare and Medicaid programs went into effect in July 1966, this balance has shifted markedly to federal expenditures.

While efforts are underway in both the public and private sector to control the rapidly rising health care costs, it is almost certain that the governmental share of health care costs will continue to increase. How the impact of the drive to control rising health costs will affect quality of medical care and the accessibility of care is still unknown, but it is probably safe to assume that as the federal government provides a greater and greater proportion of the total dollars for health care, its impact on the system will also increase.

The increased share of health care costs paid by both the government and private health insurance (although the major increase in the proportion paid by health insurance occurred before 1970) illustrates another one of the six trends identified by Moore, that of developing methods of spreading the cost. Nearly 90 percent of personal health care expenditures were paid directly by the consumer in 1929. Twenty years ago, direct private payments still accounted for nearly 60 percent of personal health care expenditures, while by 1975 direct payments accounted for only 33 percent of all personal health care costs.

The data presented in *Social Indicators, 1976* regarding the public's attitude toward government expenditures for health care are consonant with the growth of government participation. In recent years about 65 percent of those polled indicated that the government was spending too little for health care and only about 5 percent said the government was spending too much. These figures must, of course, be considered in the context of attitudes towards spending on other federal programs. Respondents were also asked about spending priorities for such programs as space, environment, crime, education, big city problems, drug abuse, foreign aid, military, and welfare. For the three years 1973–75, the only other programs for which 60–70 percent said "too little" was spent were environment, crime and drugs abuse, with crime the only one that consistently ranked higher than health, about 70 percent.[3]

The same survey inquired about the public's confidence in the leadership of several institutional domains of our society—education, major companies, organized religion, executive branch of the federal government, organized labor, the press, medicine, Congress, the military and the Supreme Court. The health leaders scored considerably higher than any other sector. However, it should be remembered that these polls were taken during the Watergate Era when the public's confidence in a number of areas was badly shaken.

HEALTH CARE RESOURCES

Another one of the trends identified by Moore was the growth in health personnel and institutions. Although only one table in *Social Indicators, 1976* is devoted to examples of this trend, it is nevertheless an important issue today. In 1975 there were well over 5 million persons working in the health field. In the last 25 years the number of physicians in the United States increased by almost 70 percent and the ratio of physicians to population increased by 22 percent. There are projections that the number of physicians per 100,000 in 1990 could be as much as 50 percent higher than it was in 1975. There is now considerable concern over a surplus of physicians in the near future.

Some believe that there are excessive hospital bed population ratios in certain geographic areas. The number of hospitals providing specialized services, such as intensive coronary care and radioisotopic diag-

3. National Opinion Research Center, University of Chicago, *National Data Program for the Social Services, Codebook for the Spring 1973 General Social Survey*. Data was distributed by Roper Public Opinion Research Center, Williams College, July 1973. Also, 1974 and 1975 *Codebooks*, July 1974 and July 1975, respectively.

nosis, has been increasing rapidly resulting in excess capacity and inefficiency in the provision of such services. The number of nursing homes has been rising and the number of beds in nursing and personal care homes increased over 40 percent between 1969 and 1973. The aggregate numbers of beds in tuberculosis and psychiatric hospitals have been decreasing at a rapid rate during recent years. The decrease in tuberculosis beds reflects, in part, decreasing incidence and decreasing prevalence of active tuberculosis cases. The decrease in psychiatric beds is the result of advances in drug therapy, the transfer of psychiatric patients to nursing homes, and a great increase in the availability of out-patient services.

Maldistribution of health manpower and health facilities remains a major problem. Thus for example, in the core counties of the largest metropolitan areas there are over 200 physicians per 100,000 population, while in the most thinly populated counties outside metropolitan areas there are fewer than 40 physicians per 100,000 population. The problem of maldistribution points toward the two last trends identified by Moore in the late twenties, more effective organization and the beginning of coordination. Even after five decades these are, at best, goals rather than well-established tendencies. The concept of planning has become widely enough accepted to have permitted passage of the National Health Planning and Resources Development Act of 1974 (P.L. 93–641). The laissez faire principles of the earlier era are less frequently put forward as an argument against regulation of the health care system. However, the various interest groups involved in the health care domain remain in intense competition, and we do not as yet have effective mechanisms for resolving the many issues that confront us.

TECHNOLOGICAL INNOVATIONS

William F. Ogburn, the Director of The Research Committee on Social Trends, assigned a primary role to technological developments in accounting for change in a variety of social spheres. It is appropriate here to examine current views of the role of technology with respect to changes in the health area.

Ogburn assumed that technological innovations were at least technically efficacious: by using an automobile, one could transport people or goods from one place to another more rapidly than by using a horse. In the health and medical sphere, there are frequently serious doubts concerning the efficaciousness of newly adopted therapeutic procedures and organizational arrangements. While in Ogburn's day barriers and resistance to the adoption of new practices were seen as major problems, today there are many observers who see the premature adoption of new technology as being most problematic. The availability of public and private insurance financing, in combination with a driving desire to control disease and uncritical confidence in medical developments, has frequently led to the diffusion of new practices that increase the cost of medical care without concomitant benefit. Some of the new procedures are inefficacious, others may actually be harmful. On the other hand, with the growing concern over premature adoption, there is a danger that regulatory activities will retard for too long the availability of efficacious innovations.

In addition to problems related to the rapidity of diffusion, there are also those related to the extensiveness of diffusion. As was indicated above, there is a marked tendency for the redundant proliferation of specialized facilities and services. Regionalization, involving a referral network through which primary health centers feed patients with more complex conditions to secondary and tertiary centers for specialized diagnosis and treatment, has long been viewed as the rational model for the medical care system. However, few organizations and communities are willing to play the supporting roles. Nearly every unit sees the need for the availability of the newest, complex technology within its own purview. This tendency further contributes to the escalation of medical care costs and sometimes diminishes the quality of medical care.

Disability and Morbidity

A number of tables in *Social Indicators, 1976* are devoted to data on levels of illness, injury, and associated disability. While there are some marked differences between certain subgroups of the population with respect to illness and disability, it is difficult to detect significant trends. The general stability of these measures could well be the most important datum. The major exception to the general stability of measure of disability is an apparent rise in the proportion of males 45–64 years of age who are unable to carry on their major activity (usually gainful employment) because of a chronic condition. This rate has almost doubled over the past ten years. Some part of this increase may be due to improvements in survey techniques; however, it is possible that it is also related to the declining mortality rate. For example, a man who might have died from a heart attack in the past, is now surviving the initial incident, but with some degree of long-term disability. There is also some evidence that more liberal disability benefits, particularly those programs that facilitate earlier retirement for reasons of severe impairment, have resulted in an increasing number of workers leaving the labor force at earlier ages than in the past and reporting themselves as disabled.[4]

The text of *Social Indicators, 1976* comments on the downward trend of acute conditions over the past 20 years. This apparent trend is based on the observation of an unusually high level of acute illness in 1957–58 and very low levels in 1973–74. The 1957–58 rate resulted from the high rate of respiratory illness during that winter, primarily a reflection of the first Asian flu epidemic. On the other hand, the low rates in 1973–74 were the unanticipated consequences of technical changes in the questionnaires used during those two years. In 1975, the standard questionnaire was again used and the rate of acute illness returned to normal levels, obscuring the signs of any trend.

In the past, inferences regarding changes in the incidence and prevalence of mental disorders have been based on institutionalization rates. Given the previously discussed trend toward psychiatric deinstitutionalization, more direct measures of mental health status are very much needed. Data are presented in *Social Indicators, 1976* showing a decline, at least for females between the ages of 45 and 74, in the percent who claim to have had or to have felt near having a nervous breakdown. Whether this decline is due to

4. Lenore E. Bixby, "Retirement Patterns in the United States: Research and Policy Interactions," *Social Security Bulletin*, vol. 29, no. 8, (August 1976), pp. 3–19.

increased tolerance of adversity, a lower incidence of problematic situations, better supportive services, or changes in the use of the term "nervous breakdown" is not fully understood.

CONCEPTUAL PROBLEM OF HEALTH INDICATORS

The use of measures of disability and illness as indicators of health status presents a rather unique problem of interpretation, particularly if these measures are used to assess the impact of programs designed to improve health status. Under the usual concept of health, the existence of fewer conditions is "better" than more conditions, and minimum disability or impact, such as days in bed due to illness or days lost from work, is "better" than more disability. Thus health status is generally viewed as a continuum. One criterion of a good indicator measure is that changes in the indicator are consonant with changes in the phenomenon being measured. However, programs to improve health status, such as those designed to improve access to medical care, could have the opposite effect on many of the current "indicators" of health status, that is, health status as measured by those indicators would appear to have deteriorated rather than improved. For example, in a medically underserved area, data may be available from household surveys on the incidence and prevalence of certain illnesses and levels of disability. Improved accessibility to care tends to result in increased use of services. It is likely that a person who sees a doctor more frequently will be more likely to be diagnosed as having, for example, three specific conditions rather than one rather vague, ill-defined condition. Thus, the number of conditions people have, as reported in surveys, increases as health care becomes more readily available. At the same time the increased utilization and diagnosis can result in the physician telling the patient to stay home from school, work, or reduce other activities, therefore, causing the customary measures of disability to increase. The expanded and improved health care system in the area may have actually had a positive impact on health status, but this positive impact is not reflected in the usual indicators.

The levels of utilization of medical services are sometimes used as health indicators themselves, for example, the number of doctor visits per person per year, or levels of hospitalization. If utilization is used as a proxy measure for health status, it is assumed that sick people see a doctor more frequently than well people and therefore more visits mean poorer health status. However, measures of the use of health services may only be an indication of accessibility of services, and in no way reflect actual health status or need for medical care.

In the absence of more valid measures of health, or perhaps more importantly measures of "quality of life," it is not suggested that these old measures be discarded, but that caution be used in interpreting them. This is particularly true when interpreting trends in health indicators.

CONCLUSION

Social Indicators, 1976 has identified many of the current health trends, including (1) the recent and, in some cases, dramatic declines in the mortality rates; (2) increases in health expenditures; and (3) increases in health resources. Recent trends in illness and disability levels have been more difficult to identify. Even when these latter trends can be discerned, either from current or from future data, great caution must be exercised in interpreting them. The effects of changes in the provisions of social insurance programs and changes in accessibility to medical care are practically indistinguishable from changes in the more physiological aspects of health status. Henry Sigerist, the eminent medical historian, maintained that medicine is not so much a natural as a social science.[5] That view is particularly apposite to the development of indicators of the health status of populations.

Much of the health information in *Social Indicators, 1976* was derived from *Health: United States, 1975*[6]—the first of a legislatively mandated annual report from the Secretary of Health, Education, and Welfare to the President and the Congress. The reader is encouraged to refer to this and *Health: United States, 1976–77*[7] for a wealth of information on health status, health resources and their use and health expenditures.

5. Henry E. Sigerist, "The Social History of Medicine," *The Western Journal of Surgery, Obstetrics and Gynecology* 48 (December 1940), p. 715.

6. U.S. Dept. of Health Education and Welfare, Health Resources Administration, *Health—United States, 1975*, no. (HRA) 76–1232 (Washington, D. C.: USGPO, 1976).

7. U.S. Dept. of Health Education and Welfare, Health Resources Administration, *Health—United States, 1976–1977*, no. (HRA) 78–1232 (Washington, D. C.: USGPO, 1977).

Table 5/1
LIFE EXPECTANCY AT BIRTH, BY RACE AND SEX: 1900–1974
(Years)

YEAR	TOTAL			WHITE			BLACK AND OTHER RACES		
	Both sexes	Male	Female	Both sexes	Male	Female	Both sexes	Male	Female
DEATH REGISTRATION STATES									
1900	47.3	46.3	48.3	47.6	46.6	48.7	33.0	32.5	33.5
1901	49.1	47.6	50.6	49.4	48.0	51.0	33.7	32.2	35.3
1902	51.5	49.3	53.4	51.9	50.2	53.8	34.6	32.9	36.4
1903	50.5	49.1	52.0	50.9	49.5	52.5	33.1	31.7	34.6
1904	47.6	46.2	49.1	48.0	46.6	49.5	30.8	29.1	32.7
1905	48.7	47.3	50.2	49.1	47.6	50.6	31.3	29.6	33.1
1906	48.7	46.9	50.8	49.3	47.3	51.4	32.9	31.8	33.9
1907	47.6	45.6	49.9	48.1	46.0	50.4	32.5	31.1	34.0
1908	51.1	49.5	52.8	51.5	49.9	53.3	34.9	33.8	36.0
1909	52.1	50.5	53.8	52.5	50.9	54.2	35.7	34.2	37.3
1910	50.0	48.4	51.8	50.3	48.6	52.0	35.6	33.8	37.5
1911	52.6	50.9	54.4	53.0	51.3	54.9	36.4	34.6	38.2
1912	53.5	51.5	55.9	53.9	51.9	56.2	37.9	35.9	40.0
1913	52.5	50.3	55.0	53.0	50.8	55.7	38.4	36.7	40.3
1914	54.2	52.0	56.8	54.9	52.7	57.5	38.9	37.1	40.8
1915	54.5	52.5	56.8	55.1	53.1	57.5	38.9	37.5	40.5
1916	51.7	49.6	54.3	52.5	50.2	55.2	41.3	39.6	43.1
1917	50.9	48.4	54.0	52.0	49.3	55.3	38.8	37.0	40.8
1918	39.1	36.6	42.2	39.8	37.1	43.2	31.1	29.9	32.5
1919	54.7	53.5	56.0	55.8	54.5	57.4	44.5	44.5	44.4
1920	54.1	53.6	54.6	54.9	54.4	55.6	45.3	45.5	45.2
1921	60.8	60.0	61.8	61.8	60.8	62.9	51.5	51.6	51.3
1922	59.6	58.4	61.0	60.4	59.1	61.9	52.4	51.8	53.0
1923	57.2	56.1	58.5	58.3	57.1	59.6	48.3	47.7	48.9
1924	59.7	58.1	61.5	61.4	59.8	63.4	46.6	45.5	47.8
1925	59.0	57.6	60.6	60.7	59.3	62.4	45.7	44.9	46.7
1926	56.7	55.5	58.0	58.2	57.0	59.6	44.6	43.7	45.6
1927	60.4	59.0	62.1	62.0	60.5	63.9	48.2	47.6	48.9
1928	56.8	55.6	58.3	58.4	57.0	60.0	46.3	45.6	47.0
UNITED STATES									
1929	57.1	55.8	58.7	58.6	57.2	60.3	46.7	45.7	47.8
1930	59.7	58.1	61.6	61.4	59.7	63.5	48.1	47.3	49.2
1931	61.1	59.4	63.1	62.6	60.8	64.7	50.4	49.5	51.5
1932	62.1	61.0	63.5	63.2	62.0	64.5	53.7	52.8	54.6
1933	63.3	61.7	65.1	64.3	62.7	66.3	54.7	53.5	56.0
1934	61.1	59.3	63.3	62.4	60.5	64.6	51.8	50.2	53.7
1935	61.7	59.9	63.9	62.9	61.0	65.0	53.1	51.3	55.2

Table 5/1 (*Continued*)

YEAR	TOTAL			WHITE			BLACK AND OTHER RACES		
	Both sexes	Male	Female	Both sexes	Male	Female	Both sexes	Male	Female
1936	58.5	56.6	60.6	59.8	58.0	61.9	49.0	47.0	51.4
1937	60.0	58.0	62.4	61.4	59.3	63.8	50.3	48.3	52.5
1938	63.5	61.9	65.3	65.0	63.2	66.8	52.9	51.7	54.3
1939	63.7	62.1	65.4	64.9	63.3	66.6	54.5	53.2	56.0
1940	62.9	60.8	65.2	64.2	62.1	66.6	53.1	51.5	54.9
1941	64.8	63.1	66.8	66.2	64.4	68.5	53.8	52.5	55.3
1942	66.2	64.7	67.9	67.3	65.9	69.4	56.6	55.4	58.2
1943	63.3	62.4	64.4	64.2	63.2	65.7	55.6	55.4	56.1
1944	65.2	63.6	66.8	66.2	64.5	68.4	56.6	55.8	57.7
1945	65.9	63.6	67.9	66.8	64.4	69.5	57.7	56.1	59.6
1946	66.7	64.4	69.4	67.5	65.1	70.3	59.1	57.5	61.0
1947	66.8	64.4	69.7	67.6	65.2	70.5	59.7	57.9	61.9
1948	67.2	64.6	69.9	68.0	65.5	71.0	60.0	58.1	62.5
1949	68.0	65.2	70.7	68.8	66.2	71.9	60.6	58.9	62.7
1950	68.2	65.6	71.1	69.1	66.5	72.2	60.8	59.1	62.9
1951	68.4	65.6	71.4	69.3	66.5	72.4	61.2	59.2	63.4
1952	68.6	65.8	71.6	69.5	66.6	72.6	61.4	59.1	63.8
1953	68.8	66.0	72.0	69.7	66.8	73.0	62.0	59.7	64.5
1954	69.6	66.7	72.8	70.5	67.5	73.7	63.4	61.1	65.9
1955	69.6	66.7	72.8	70.5	67.4	73.7	63.7	61.4	66.1
1956	69.7	66.7	72.9	70.5	67.5	73.9	63.6	61.3	66.1
1957	69.5	66.4	72.7	70.3	67.2	73.7	63.0	60.7	65.5
1958	69.6	66.6	72.9	70.5	67.4	73.9	63.4	61.0	65.8
1959	69.9	66.8	73.2	70.7	67.5	74.2	63.9	61.3	66.5
1960	69.7	66.6	73.1	70.6	67.4	74.1	63.6	61.1	66.3
1961	70.2	67.0	73.6	71.0	67.8	74.5	64.4	61.9	67.0
1962	70.0	66.8	73.4	70.9	67.6	74.4	64.1	61.5	66.8
1963	69.9	66.6	73.4	70.8	67.5	74.4	63.6	60.9	66.5
1964	70.2	66.9	73.7	71.0	67.7	74.6	64.1	61.1	67.2
1965	70.2	66.8	73.7	71.0	67.6	74.7	64.1	61.1	67.4
1966	70.1	66.7	73.8	71.0	67.6	74.7	64.0	60.7	67.4
1967	70.5	67.0	74.2	71.3	67.8	75.1	64.6	61.1	68.2
1968	70.2	66.6	74.0	71.1	67.5	74.9	63.7	60.1	67.5
1969	70.4	66.8	74.3	71.3	67.8	75.1	64.3	60.5	68.4
1970	70.9	67.1	74.8	71.7	68.0	75.6	65.3	61.3	69.4
1971	71.1	67.4	75.0	72.0	68.3	75.8	65.6	61.0	69.7
1972	71.1	67.4	75.1	72.0	68.3	75.9	65.6	61.5	69.9
1973	71.3	67.5	75.3	72.2	68.4	76.1	65.9	61.9	70.1
1974	71.9	68.2	75.9	72.7	68.9	76.6	67.0	62.9	71.2

Source: U.S. Department of Health, Education, and Welfare, Public Health Service, National Center for Health Statistics, *Vital Statistics of the United States, 1973*, Vol. II, and *Monthly Statistical Report*, Vol. 24, No. 11, sup. 1.

Chart 5/1

Social Indicators, 1976

LIFE EXPECTANCY (YEARS) AT BIRTH, BY RACE AND SEX, 1929 TO 1974

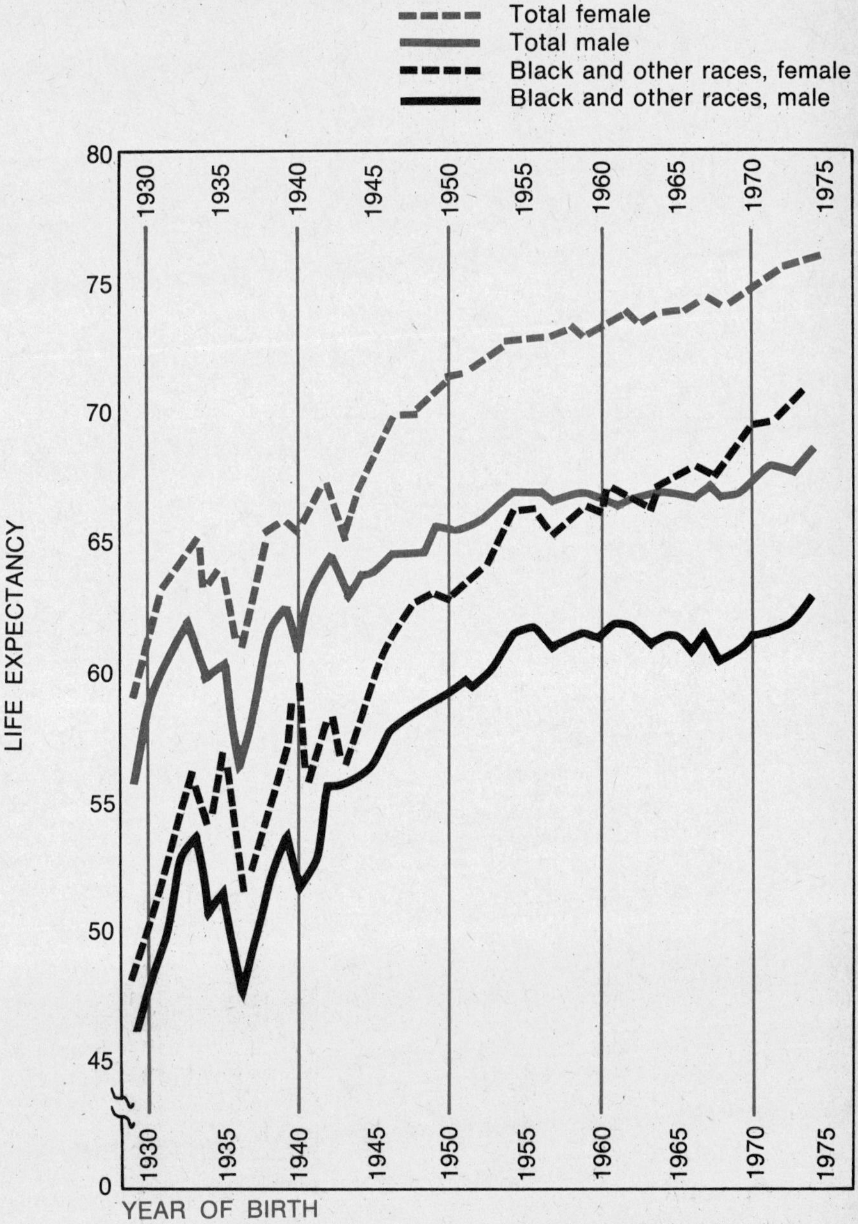

Source: see table 5/1

Table 5/5

INFANT AND NEONATAL MORTALITY RATES, BY RACE: 1940–1974

(Deaths per 1,000 live births in specified group)

	INFANT			NEONATAL		
YEAR	Total, all races	White	Black and other races	Total, all races	White	Black and other races
1940	47.0	43.2	73.8	28.8	27.2	39.7
1941	45.3	41.2	74.8	27.7	26.1	39.0
1942	40.4	37.3	64.6	25.7	24.5	34.6
1943	40.4	37.5	62.5	24.7	23.7	32.9
1944	39.8	36.9	60.3	24.7	23.6	32.5
1945	38.3	35.6	57.0	24.3	23.3	32.0
1946	33.8	31.8	49.5	24.0	23.1	31.5
1947	32.2	30.1	48.5	22.8	21.7	31.0
1948	32.0	29.9	46.5	22.2	21.2	29.1
1949	31.3	28.9	47.3	21.4	20.3	28.6
1950	29.2	26.8	44.5	20.5	19.4	27.5
1951	28.4	25.8	44.8	20.0	18.9	27.3
1952	28.4	25.5	47.0	19.8	18.5	28.0
1953	27.8	25.0	44.7	19.6	18.3	27.4
1954	26.6	23.9	42.9	19.1	17.8	27.0
1955	26.4	23.6	42.8	19.1	17.7	27.2
1956	26.0	23.2	42.1	18.9	17.5	27.0
1957	26.3	23.3	43.7	19.1	17.5	27.8
1958	27.1	23.8	45.7	19.5	17.8	29.0
1959	26.4	23.2	44.0	19.0	17.5	27.7
1960	26.0	22.9	43.2	18.7	17.2	26.9
1961	25.3	22.4	40.7	18.4	16.9	26.3
1962[1]	25.3	22.3	41.4	18.3	16.9	26.1
1963[1]	25.2	22.2	41.5	18.2	16.7	26.1
1964	24.8	21.6	41.1	17.9	16.2	26.5
1965	24.7	21.5	40.3	17.7	16.1	25.4
1966	23.7	20.6	38.8	17.2	15.6	24.8
1967	22.4	19.7	35.9	16.5	15.0	23.8
1968	21.8	19.2	34.5	16.1	14.7	23.0
1969	20.9	18.4	32.9	15.6	14.2	22.5
1970[2]	20.0	17.8	30.9	15.1	13.8	21.4
1971[2]	19.1	17.1	28.5	14.2	13.0	19.6
1972[2]	18.5	16.4	27.7	13.6	12.4	19.2
1973[2]	17.7	15.8	26.2	13.0	11.8	17.9
1974[2]	16.7	14.8	24.9	12.3	11.1	17.2

Source: U.S. Department of Health, Education, and Welfare, Public Health Service, National Center for Health Statistics, *Vital Statistics Rates in the United States, 1940–1960; Vital Statistics of the United States*, Vol. II, annual issues 1961 to 1970; *Monthly Vital Statistics Report*, Vol. 23, Nos. 3, 7, and 11, and Vol. 24, No. 11; and unpublished data.

[1] Excludes data for residents of New Jersey.

[2] Excludes deaths of nonresidents of the United States.

Infant mortality comprises deaths occurring to persons under 1 year of age; neonatal mortality comprises deaths occurring during the first 28 days of life.

Chart 5/5 Social Indicators, 1976

INFANT AND NEONATAL MORTALITY RATES, BY RACE, 1950 TO 1974

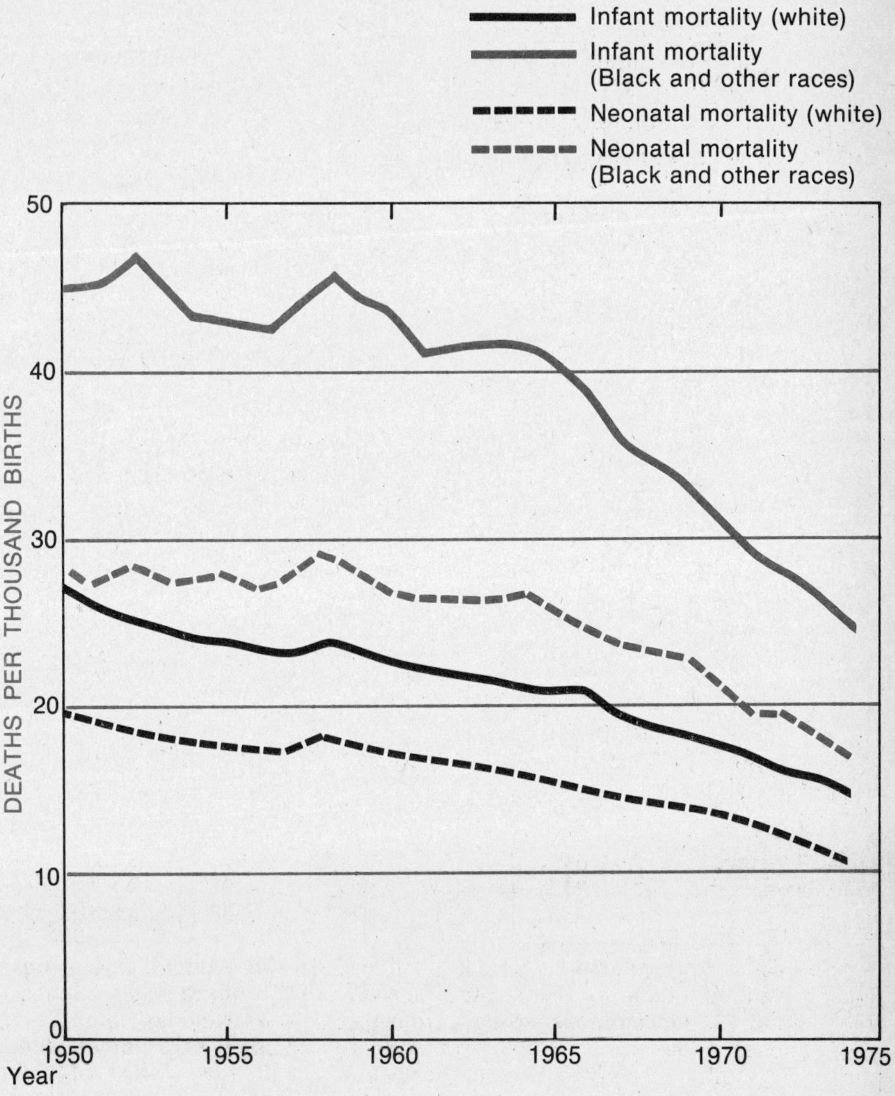

Source: see table 5/5

Table 5/22

PERSONS AGE 65 AND OVER IN NURSING HOMES, BY SEX, AGE, AND RACE: 1964, 1969, AND 1974

RACE AND AGE	MALE			FEMALE		
	Total population (thous.)	In nursing homes[1] Number	In nursing homes[1] Percent	Total population (thous.)	In nursing homes[1] Number	In nursing homes[1] Percent
1964						
Total, 65 years and over	7,855	157,600	2.0	10,001	330,100	3.3
65 to 74 years	5,146	40,400	0.8	6,259	64,000	1.0
75 to 84 years	2,311	74,100	3.2	3,105	156,800	5.0
85 years and over	398	43,100	10.8	637	109,300	17.2
1969						
Total, 65 years and over	8,216	207,100	2.5	11,114	515,200	4.6
65 to 74 years	5,232	52,200	1.0	6,624	86,300	1.3
75 to 84 years	2,498	90,800	3.6	3,694	231,100	6.3
85 years and over	486	64,100	13.2	796	197,800	24.8
Black, 65 years and over	614	10,700	1.7	793	16,500	2.1
65 to 74 years	372	4,800	1.3	459	4,100	0.9
75 to 84 years	185	4,100	2.2	257	6,800	2.6
85 years and over	57	1,800	3.2	77	5,600	7.3
1973–74						
Total, 65 years and over	8,801	265,500	3.0	12,528	694,800	5.5
65 to 74 years	5,750	65,100	1.1	7,467	97,900	1.3
75 to 84 years	2,506	102,300	4.1	3,976	282,100	7.1
85 years and over	545	98,100	18.0	1,085	314,800	29.0
Black, 65 years and over	815	20,100	2.5	1,056	30,200	2.9
65 to 74 years	549	7,700	1.4	676	8,300	1.2
75 to 84 years	213	6,700	3.1	292	12,100	4.1
85 years and over	53	5,700	10.8	88	9,800	11.1

Source: U.S. Department of Health, Education, and Welfare, Public Health Service, National Center for Health Statistics, *Vital and Health Statistics*, Series 12, Nos. 12 and 19, and unpublished data from the 1973–74 Nursing Home Survey.

[1] Includes personal care homes with nursing, personal care homes without nursing, and domiciliary care homes except for 1974 data which do not include personal care homes.

Chart 5/22 Social Indicators, 1976

PERCENT OF POPULATION 65 AND OVER IN NURSING HOMES, BY SEX, AGE AND RACE, 1964, 1969, AND 1974

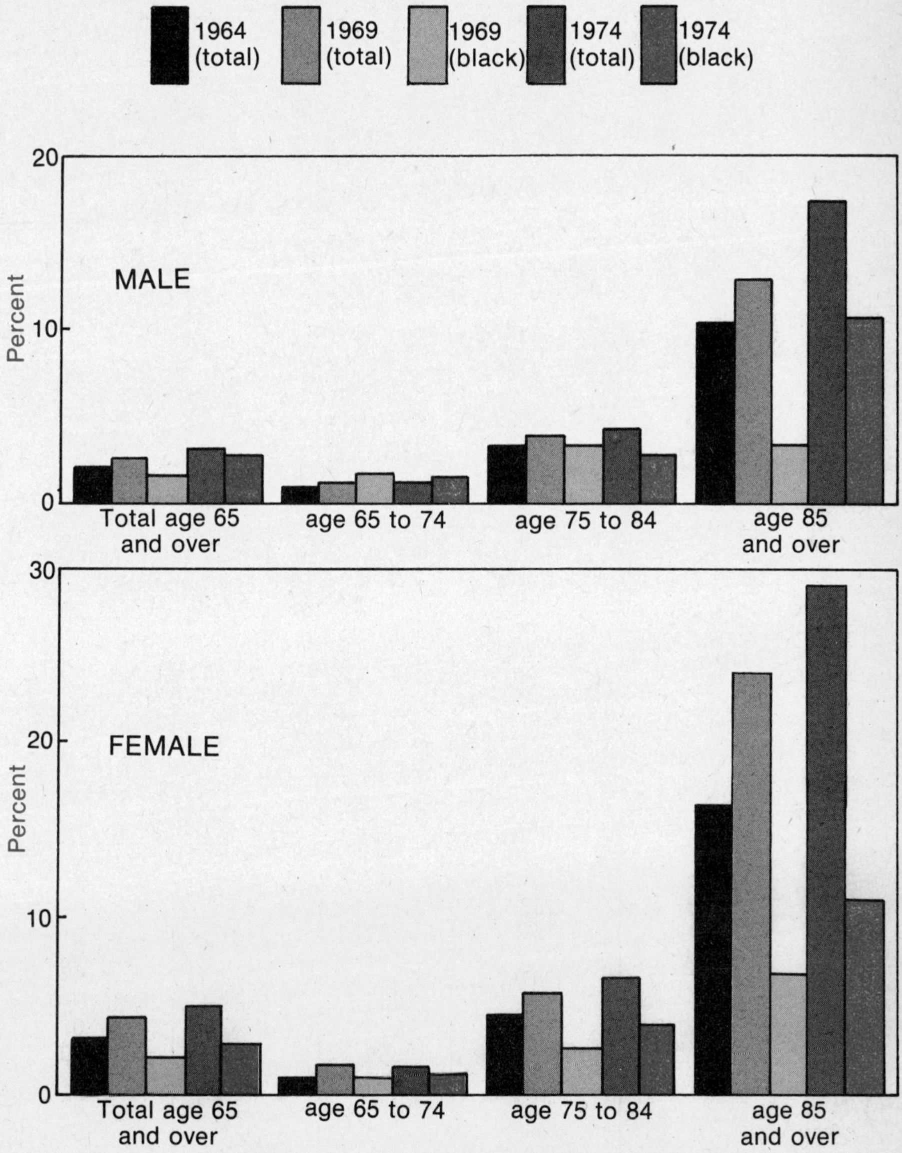

Source: see table 5/22

Chart 5/26

Social Indicators, 1976

NUMBER OF PHYSICIANS, NURSES, DENTISTS AND PHARMACISTS PER 100,000 POPULATION, SELECTED YEARS, 1960–1973

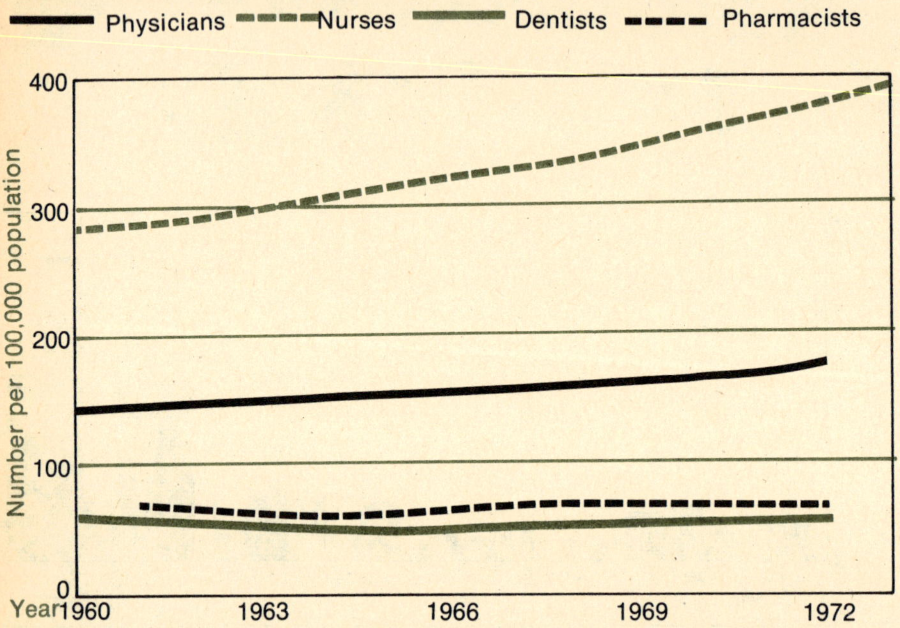

Table 5/26

PHYSICIANS, NURSES, DENTISTS, AND PHARMACISTS: 1960–1973

(Number per 100,000 population)

YEAR	PHYSICIANS	NURSES	DENTISTS	PHARMACISTS
1960	148	282	56	(NA)
1961	(NA)	(NA)	(NA)	65
1962	(NA)	298	(NA)	(NA)
1963	(NA)	(NA)	(NA)	64
1964	(NA)	306	(NA)	(NA)
1965	153	(NA)	(NA)	61
1966	(NA)	319	(NA)	(NA)
1967	(NA)	327	(NA)	62
1968	161	335	(NA)	(NA)
1969	163	345	(NA)	62
1970	166	356	56	63
1971	170	366	(NA)	63
1972	174	376	57	63
1973	(NA)	390	(NA)	63

Source: U.S. Department of Health, Education, and Welfare, Public Health Service, National Center for Health Statistics, *Health Resources Statistics*, 1974.

NA Not available.

ANNALS, AAPSS, 435, Jan. 1978

Trends in Education and Training

By ABBOTT L. FERRISS

ABSTRACT: Because of changes in the magnitude of cohorts to be educated, the elementary school population will fluctuate by a decrease of some 7 million pupils and more than a quarter of a million teachers, followed by increases of the same magnitude over the 14 years following 1982. Such variation will impose traumatic adjustments upon the educational system. The increasing enrollment in prekindergarten schools pushes new responsibilities on the school system and promises to accelerate progress in primary grades. A number of unmet needs of school children, which require attention, correction of speech deficiencies and the special problems of the emotionally disturbed, for example, are identified. The record of retention in school is satisfactory up to high school ages, but drop-outs and decreasing enrollment of youth 17 years and over are unmistakable. Educational lag is apparent in both dropping out and in falling behind the modal grade of the school age group. Females are beginning to surpass males in college going. The continuation from high school to college appears to have peaked and now is decreasing, but the college attendance of youth in the top half of the ability spectrum may be superior to the record two decades ago. As to learning, particularly in the secondary schools, the evidence of improvement is scant while there are extensive indicators of decreasing test performance at the end of high school. Models of processes of education are needed to identify appropriate educational statistics to improve social indicators of education in the United States.

Abbott L. Ferriss is Professor of Sociology at Emory University. He has been Research Sociologist with the Russell Sage Foundation, Study Director with the National Science Foundation, Statistician with the Outdoor Recreation Resources Review Commission, Chief of the Health Statistics Branch of the U. S. Bureau of the Census and Chief of various human relations research units of the United States

Air Force. He is the author of Indicators of Trends in the Status of American Women (1971), Indicators of Change in the American Family (1970), Indicators of Trends in American Education (1969), The National Recreation Survey (1962), *and others. In 1971, Dr. Ferriss edited the volume* Research and the 1970 Census.

Parts of this paper were developed under National Science Grant SOC 76-17387—"A Test of Demographic Accounting Methods with U.S. Data on Education"—to Emory University. Appreciation is expressd for the bibliographic and computational assistance of Charles Warren and Hugh Spitler.

THE EDUCATIONAL system in the United States, when compared with that of other industrial societies shows marked superiority in some respects and notable weaknesses in others. When compared with its own ideals, or even with its own recent past record, American education reveals many areas for improvement. This is the picture one reads in the graphs and statistical tables of chapter 7, "Education and Training," in *Social Indicators, 1976 (S. I. '76).*

This paper is not a critical review of the selection of data by the editors of *S. I. '76*, nor a catalogue of ways to improve educational data were resources available. It does not offer a framework nor conceptual model for the collection and analysis of educational indicators. Rather, it is a commentary on "Education and Training" for the general public and the molders of public policies affecting education. It seeks to interpret the trends revealed by the statistics. Where are we falling down in educating future generations? What trends foretell changes which call for planning? In what ways may educational indicators contribute to the more rational ordering of our society? A comprehensive interpretation of the educational data in *S. I. '76* is prevented by the limits on available space; consequently, this review is selective.

THE DEMOGRAPHIC MOVER

Above all, population change pervades the educational system. Changes in the size of the cohort to be educated, either through increases or decreases in the birth rate, or through migration or the demands of war, alter the supply of students and require adjustments in educational institutions. Following the 1969 peak of 36.8 million children aged 5–13, a population decline occurred, creating many adjustment problems for the schools. Decreases in the school population of 500,000 to 1.2 million will continue to be experienced each year until 1982. What does this mean for our elementary schools?

If a school is closed and the building locked up, a functioning service institution has been removed from the community. "Our school" is no longer there, even though the building remains. This lacuna may be avoided by constructive educational planning. Educational alternatives include adult education, noncredit courses in arts, crafts, and the performing arts, and vocational education to serve the requirements of industries in the community.[1] How-

1. A number of suggestions have been advanced to further these objectives. See, for example, "Declining Enrollment: Current Trends in School Policies and Programs," (Arlington, Va.: National School Public Relations Association, 1976).

ever, if the school population is sufficiently large for the school to remain open, adjustments in the program are needed to decrease the number of pupils per teacher, to add new academic programs, and to devote attention to persistent educational problems, such as lagging performance in reading or mathematics.

Series II Census projections predict a decline of 7 million pupils between the ages of 5 to 13 in the years from 1969 to 1982. Assuming we retain a student-teacher ratio of about one teacher for each 25 students, this implies a loss of 280,000 teachers or about one-fourth the teachers in fall 1969. In the 14 years following 1982 an equal number of new teachers must be added. Colleges must assume responsibility for alerting students to the ebb and flow of teacher demand.

The demographic waves of fluctuating cohort size will impose traumatic adjustment problems on the school system, its buildings and equipment, its patrons, and its students. The maximum demand for high school education occurs between 1974 and 1978; its nadir, in 1990. The college population peaks in 1981 after which it bottoms out in 1997. Local and state planning should adjust programs to these stresses and shocks so as to improve the quality of education, to conserve the educational resources of the community, to meet needs for adult and vocational education, and to anticipate the eventual revival of demand for elementary and high schools.

PREKINDERGARTEN ENROLLMENT

Enrollment of 3- and 4-year-olds in nursery school has increased from 5 percent of this population to approximately 25 percent between 1964 and 1975. The increase, a continuing trend, is shared by white, black, Spanish-speaking and Mexican segments of the population.

The preprimary enrollment rate (nursery school and kindergarten) is directly associated with the child's family income, increasing as income increases ($r = .75$, approximately), and is as strongly associated among whites as among blacks and other "races." The family income of enrollees in private preprimary schools ($14,130, median, 1974) is approximately 30 percent greater than the family income of enrollees in public preprimary schools ($10,861, median), and the heads of households of preprimary enrollees are slightly better educated than other heads of households who have children enrolled in school.

The enrollment rate (1974) was considerably lower in nonmetropolitan areas (20 percent) than in the suburbs (34 percent) or central city (32 percent). Only about one-third of the preprimary school children remain a full day in school.[2] This increasing enrollment represents a revolution in child care and in shifting responsibility from the family to public and private agencies. If learning experiences in nursery school are more enriching than in the isolated family, it could significantly improve future learning capability, accelerating the transmission of skills and competencies.[3]

2. "Social and Economic Characteristics of Students, October 1974," *Current Population Reports*, ser. P–20, no. 286 (Washington, D.C.: USGPO, November 1975), pp. 12 and 19.

3. Cycle II study, the National Health Examination Survey of children 6–11 years old showed that the intelligence of children who had some preschool educational experience, when educational attainment of parent was held constant, "generally showed some advantage" over children who had not attended kindergarten or nursery

The shift also weakens the ties of the family to the child. The quality of the nursery school becomes quite important. A study (1971–72) estimated that less than 20 percent of children under 6 years of age were cared for in licensed or approved day care centers.[4] If unlicensed centers provide less effective learning experiences, communities need to improve the quality of preprimary schools.

UNMET NEEDS OF SCHOOL CHILDREN

In Cycle II, for children 6–11 years of age, and Cycle III, for those 12–17 years, the National Health Examination Survey requested teachers of children in the samples to complete a questionnaire on the needs of the children.[5] Table 1 translates the rates into population estimates for 1976, assuming the teachers' evaluations and the students' needs remain the same as when the rates were current. Table 1 estimates only the perceived needs for which no resources are available.

There are unmet needs among both talented and slow learners. Table 1 shows that a large population of slow learners needs remedial and special instruction and that many of the gifted require additional resources to develop their capacities. What priority on the allocation of resources should be made for these two groups? Many of the slow, with appropriate stimulation and motivation, can improve, and the gifted, if not cultivated, become a talent loss to the nation's potential creativity.

While most of these deficiencies can be relieved by the school program, the emotionally disturbed require something more than special classes and devices. They require resources capable of adjusting the social and emotional climate of the home and neighborhood, resources normally beyond the capacity of the school to provide.

All but one—mental retardation—are perceived by teachers as less acute for older than younger children. Perhaps many of the retardees have been institutionalized in special schools, as have the deaf and the blind. The mental retardee, distinguished from slow learner, begins to be recognized by the teacher among 9 year olds. The slow learner is recognized by age 7 and the label persists to age 12. The rate of slow learners after age 11 is less than half the rate of those 11 and younger. Has the problem been "corrected?" Is the teacher of older children less sensitive to the problem? Or, has the problem disappeared with maturity?

Except for those requiring orthopedic corrective devices and for the gifted, more boys invariably are per-

---

school. Jean Roberts and Arnold Engel, "Family Background, Early Development, and Intelligence of Children 6–11 Years, United States," ser. 11, no. 142, DHEW Publication no. HRA 75-1624 (Rockville, Md.: National Center for Health Statistics, Health Resources Administration, August 1974).

4. Kurt J. Snapper et al., *The Status of Children, 1975* (Washington, D.C.: Social Research Group, George Washington University, 1975), p. 18.

5. Jean Roberts and James T. Baird, Jr., "Behavior Patterns of Children in School, United States," ser. 11, no. 113, DHEW Pub. no. HSM 72-1042 (Rockville, Md.: National Center for Health Statistics, Health Services and Mental Health Administration, February 1972); Lincoln I. Oliver, "Behavior Patterns in School of Youths 12–17 Years, United States," ser. 11, no. 139, DHEW Pub. no. NRA 74-1621 (Rockville, Md.: National Center for Health Statistics, Health Resources Administration, May 1974). For a review of the extensive literature in this area, see Nicholas Hobbs, general editor, *Issues in the Classification of Children*, vols. 1 and 2 (San Francisco: Jossey-Bass, 1975).

TABLE 1

NUMBER OF CHILDREN FOR WHOM TEACHER RECOMMENDS SPECIAL RESOURCES ARE NEEDED BUT UNAVAILABLE, BY TYPE OF PROBLEM, 1976 (ESTIMATED)

TYPE OF PROBLEM	AGE OF CHILDREN		
	6–11 YEARS	12–17 YEARS (THOUSANDS OF CHILDREN)	TOTAL
Hard of hearing	110.3	20.1	130.4
Sight-saving	150.6	5.5	156.1
Speech therapy	442.0	71.3	513.3
Orthopedic handicap	21.1	4.5	25.6
Gifted	556.7	51.7	608.4
Slow learner	1,590.9	282.8	1,873.7
Mentally retarded	48.4	32.4	80.8
Emotionally disturbed	399.8	88.3	488.1
Other	434.6	152.9	—
Remedial reading		270.5	—
English for youths from non-English speaking environments		76.8	—
Remedial training		229.5	—

SOURCE: For 1963–65: NCHS Series 11–113, p. 27. For 1966–70: NCHS Series 11–139, p. 20. Data for both groups are applied to estimates of the population of youth in the Census Bureau's 1976 *Current Population Reports*, ser. P–20, no. 307, p. 12. See also footnote 5.

NOTE: The rates prevailing between 1963 and 1965 for 6–11 year-olds and between 1966 and 1970 for 12–17 year-olds were multiplied by the 1976 population to produce the above estimates. It is possible that the needs of children, as perceived by teachers, have changed and that the resources for meeting those needs have also changed during the intervening years. The estimates should be considered only gross approximations.

ceived as having needs requiring attention than girls. A larger proportion of girls than boys are thought to be gifted, and smaller proportions of girls are perceived as slow learners, as mentally retarded, as emotionally disturbed, as needing speech therapy, as being hard of hearing, etc., than boys.

The acuteness of the "remedial reading" problem among 12–17-year-old youth may be further explored through a special study of illiteracy. Inversely associated with parental education and income, illiteracy is greater among males than females, among black than white youths, among residents of rural and small urban places than residents of larger places, and is more prevalent in the South and less in the Midwest, even when race and sex are controlled, than other regions. The illiteracy rate declines slightly with age: from 9.4 per 100 male youths 12 years of age to 6.5 for 17-year-olds, and from 4.3 per 100 females 12 years of age to 2.3 for those 17.[6] These results indict the educational system and parents for failure to provide a skill essential for adjustment in a complex society. In terms of the 1976 population, 140,000 17-year-old young men and 47,000 17-year-old young women enter adult life unable to read!

ARE THEY STAYING IN SCHOOL?

A central value of American culture, reinforced by history, holds that education is a good thing, the more the better. It is the avenue to

6. Dorothee K. Vogt, "Literacy Among Youths 12–17 Years, United States," ser. 11, no. 131, DHEW Pub. no. HRA 74–1613 (Rockville, Md.: National Center for Health Statistics, Health Resources Administration, December 1973).

upward occupational and social mobility and a primary means for advancing social justice.[7] Social policy to maximize opportunity emphasizes keeping youth in school, preventing dropouts and opening educational opportunities to otherwise disadvantaged youth. Recent international comparisons show that United States enrollment rates among 15–18-year-olds and the full-time enrollment of 19–25-year-olds exceed other modern Western nations.

School enrollment and retention rates must be regularly monitored to detect evidence of weakening.[8] In recent years considerable weakness has developed. The enrollment record through age 13 years is satisfactory. A trend toward lower attendance is developing among youth 14 to 17 years—the high school years—and attendance rates are undeniably turning downward among males, 18–19 and 20–21, while enrollment rates of females in these older age categories have reached a peak and levelled off. Is there a declining interest in attending school and college among older youth? Enrollment rates for males are as low now as they were in the early 1960s.

In a study of dropouts and other youth in two Louisiana parishes, Bertrand found higher dropout rates among families of lower occupational and social status.[9] He hypothesized that school retention was dependent both upon the family reinforcing educational aspirations and upon a school environment where the student found rewarding relationships with peers and teachers through athletic and club participation, and through successful classwork. Other studies have shown that dropping out of school among older youth may accompany expansions of military forces or periods of high employment, luring youth away to jobs.[10]

The lower enrollment in the high school ages may be partly attributed to compulsory school attendance laws, which in most states do not require attendance of the 17-year-olds (only 11 states require attendance of 17- or 18-year-olds). Enrollment rates of 18-19 year-old males, which had increased over the long term during the post-World War II years, turned downward after 1968 and have declined with some consistency since then. None of the explanations for a decline in enrollment proves satisfactory in this case. Neither high employment nor the expansion of manpower in the military explains the downturn in the enrollment rate. Males evidently turned their backs on school enrollment when deferments from Selective Service were reduced after 1968, and shortly thereafter, when the lottery system was

7. In the context of public goals in this country, see Carnegie Commission on Higher Education, *Priorities for Action: Final Report of the Carnegie Commission on Higher Education* (New York: McGraw-Hill, 1973), pp. 33–41. See also footnote 25.

8. Abbott L. Ferriss, "Monitoring and Interpreting Turning Points in Educational Indicators," *Social Indicators Research* 1 (1974), pp. 73–84.

9. Alvin L. Bertrand, "School Attendance and Attainment: Function and Dysfunction of School and Family Social System," *Social Forces* 40 (March 1962), pp. 228–33.

10. Beverly Duncan, "Trends in Output and Distribution of Schooling," in *Indicators of Social Change: Concepts and Measurements*, eds. Eleanor Bernert Sheldon and Wilbert E. Moore (New York: Russell Sage Foundation, 1968), pp. 601–74; Abbott L. Ferriss, *Indicators of Trends in American Education* (New York: Russell Sage Foundation, 1969), pp. 36–49; Marcus Felson and Kenneth C. Land, "A Dynamic Macro Social Indicator Model of Changes in Educational Enrollments, Attainments, and Organizations in the United States: 1947–74," Working Paper 7610, mimeographed (Urbana, Ill.: University of Illinois, October 1976).

introduced in the draft, making for an earlier decision on induction or noninduction. Finally, the draft was discontinued entirely. About the same time the dampening influence of negativism among youth toward the achievement oriented values of the "Establishment" was felt and an alternate youth counterculture arose.[11] Both the 18–19 and the 20–21 year-old males were influenced. The consequence was a reduction in the educational level of the labor force, a reduction already evident in the average educational attainment of the cohorts affected.

In contrast, the long-term increase in enrollment of females 18–21 years of age has merely levelled off; by 1976 it had actually inched up 4 or 5 percentage points over 1969. Current emphases upon changes in the role of women have brought about this result, attesting to the potency of peer social influences. Meanwhile, the labor force participation rates of these ages, both male and female, continue to increase, even though the unemployment rates are about double that of the total labor force among these ages.

Another means for detecting changes in school enrollment are school retention rates. The most recent tracing of the experience of the 1966 5th grade cohort (graduating 1974) presents a high school graduation rate slightly less than that of the graduating class of 1973; the 1975 class graduated at an even lower rate.

The evidence of lower rate of high school graduation and a lower enrollment rate among older youth is sufficient to call for a national program to stimulate school retention, beginning with 17-year-olds. Adequate numbers of junior colleges, community colleges, and technical institutes now are organized to provide additional years of education. A sophisticated industrial, commercial, and artistic society requires well trained personnel. The program should seek to make the home and school environments more supportive of educational achievement. "Stay in School" bumper stickers are not enough.

11. Ferris, "Monitoring and Interpreting Turning Points," pp. 77–80.

Educational lag

A useful indicator of relative lag in school progress is based on the percent of enrolled population in the modal grade for selected ages and the percent below the modal grade by sex and color. The record for 1974 is not as good as the record for 1970, larger percentages being below the modal grade among all youth 17 years of age and older, with the one exception of 21-year-old females. As age increases there is an increasing percentage below the modal grade. The percent enrolled below the modal grade among blacks is greater than the percent below among whites of the same sex, some comparisions being twice greater. Unsettling as this may be, it is not the entire picture. For the whole story, the population not enrolled at all must be added. To illustrate, in 1975, 34 percent of white males age 18 enrolled in school were below the modal first year of college. However, only 56 percent of 18 year-olds were enrolled. Actually, 63 percent of the 18 year-olds were either not enrolled or enrolled below the modal grade. This index for the age reveals the true dimension of educational lag.

Educational lag has been slowly edging up for 17-year-old white males, but it has been increasing even more rapidly among 18 year-olds. Educational lag is clearly more severe among black than among white males. Among white 17 year-old males the average over the past seven years has been 35 percent; among black males it has been 57 percent. Among white 18 year-old males, the average over the past seven years has been 52 percent; among black males it has been 82 percent. If additional schooling is important to the national interest in developing its human resources, then the national interest clearly is not being served.

Among white females slight increases in educational lag are evident, but the total percent lag is less. Black 17-year-old females are more likely than white 17-year-old females to be below the modal grade by a factor of 2, and the same is generally true for black 18 year-olds. In general, black and white females show slightly better school progress than their male counterparts of the same age.

What level of educational lag among 17 and 18 year-olds can the nation tolerate? One-third? One-half? When more than one-third of the 17 year-olds and one-half the 18 year-olds are lagging or not progressing at all, a flag of warning should be raised to alert parents, school, and public policy officials to a generation of youth which is bypassing the opportunity to formally develop its talents.[12]

COLLEGE GOING

Often before high school graduation the student decides whether to go on to college, to enter vocational school, or to try for a job. Several studies have identified the characteristics of students who plan to continue school. Clearly high school seniors with definite plans to attend college are decreasing. Studies show that future plans for additional education influence eventual college enrollment.

In 1974 females (44.7 percent) were more likely to plan to attend college than males (39.4 percent). High school seniors who had a relative living in the household who was already attending college (61.2 percent) were more likely to plan to attend than seniors with no other relative in the household attending college (38.9 percent). This is an unexpected result, for one might expect that the prospect of two attending college from the same household might exceed the family's educational budget. That the opposite obtains testifies to the importance of the family orientation toward educational achievement.

Seniors living outside the central city of metropolitan areas were more likely (47.4 percent) to plan to attend than those living in the central city (40.7 percent) or those living in nonmetropolitan areas (36.9 percent). Seniors living in the West were more likely to plan to attend (56.3 percent), than those in the Northeast (40.8 percent), the South (38.8 percent), or the North Central (38.1 percent). Seniors of Spanish origin were more likely to plan to attend college (47.1 percent) than other white (43.4 percent) or black (33.5 percent) seniors.

The higher the socioeconomic status, the more probable is college attendance. For example, the percent of seniors planning to attend increases from the lowest income category (under $5,000 family in-

12. A table of the percent of 17 and 18 year-olds not enrolled or below the modal grade for the age, by color and sex, will be provided upon request. Write: Department of Sociology and Anthropology, Emory University, Atlanta Ga., 30322.

come) (25.8 percent) to the highest ($25,000 and over) (67.6 percent). Indicators of education and occupation underscore this same relationship. This pinpoints precisely the population not inspired to attend college. Progression up the educational ladder provides the means of upward social mobility. School enrollment by socioeconomic status supplies a critical social indicator criterion for monitoring how effectively educational opportunity is being achieved. If the nation aims to maximize the opportunities to youth to realize its potentialities, the educational aspirations of lower socioeconomic groups must be influenced.

Based upon aggregate high school graduation and college entrance ratios, college going by males reached a peak in 1969 (70.3 percent), declined through 1973, and since has increased very slightly. The continuation ratio still is 5.7 percentage points below the 1969 record. Among females, the continuation ratio leveled off between 1969 and 1973, and since 1974 has been inching up, now standing (1976) at its highest point (58.2 percent). Thus, the social influences that are retarding the progress of male youth are not similarly affecting females.

Ratio of college degrees to high school graduates

The ratio of bachelor's degrees to high school graduates four years earlier shows females making marked progress but males making no improvement in the past seven years.

This ratio is a remarkable indicator, reflecting changes in the educational system as it has responded to social, economic, and industrial-commercial needs for trained personnel. During the period 1885–95 secondary schools and colleges were primarily for the male elite, and the indicator showed that approximately half the high school graduates completed college four years later. Then the expansion of secondary schools took place.[13] The declining ratio reached a low point during World War I of less than .2. The industrial-commercial system needed college-trained personnel; in response, higher education expanded after 1920, as did the ratio of college completions. The ratio declined with the Great Depression and when youth went away to World War II, reaching its lowest point (.1) at the end of the War. The revival of college enrollments in the late 1940s brought the indicator back up, peaking at an artificial high in 1950 when many veterans obtained bachelors degrees. Since the late 1950s the indicator has been close to .3. Now, a high school education is nearly universal and postsecondary vocational-technical training is viewed by many as being sufficient preparation. Youth today, particularly men, view college attendance as less compelling than formerly. There is little likelihood that this indicator soon again will reach the peak it attained in the 1890s.[14]

Are the most capable high school graduates entering college?

The answer to this question is strongly in the affirmative. Con-

13. Martin Trow, "The Second Transformation of American Secondary Education," *International Journal of Comparative Sociology* II (September 1961), pp. 144–66.

14. Ferris, *Indicators of Trends in American Education*, pp. 107–12 and idem, "Monitoring and Interpreting Turning Points," pp. 140–51.

TABLE 2

ESTIMATES OF THE PERCENT OF THE TOP HALF IN ABILITY OF HIGH SCHOOL GRADUATING CLASSES WHICH ENTERED COLLEGE, VARIOUS STUDIES, 1950–1972, UNITED STATES

YEAR	TEST CRITERION	PERCENT OF HIGH SCHOOL GRADUATING CLASS ENTERING COLLEGE: WITHIN 1 YEAR	WITHIN 5 YEARS
Circa 1950	Above the mean AGCT score of high school graduating class[1]	54.4	
1960	1960 high school graduates in top 50% in ability (I.Q.) enrolled in college in the fall, 1960[2]	52.3	
1960–65	Top 50% in ability of 1960 high school graduates enrolled in college within five years of graduation[3]		63.9
1965	October 1965 high school seniors who graduated with high school grade point average of A or B (51.4% of the class), enrolled by February, 1967[4]	55.1	
1972	High school graduates in the top 50% in ability, enrolled in October, 1972[5]	61.0	

1. Dael Wolfle, *America's Resources of Specialized Talent* (New York: Harper and Bros., 1954), calculated from Appendix G, pp. 311–14.

2. Charles B. Nam and James D. Cowhig, "Factors Related to College Attendance of Farm and Nonfarm High School Graduates, 1960," *Farm Population*, Census–ERA P–27, no. 32 (Washington, D.C.: U. S. Bureau of the Census, 15 June 1962), pp. 14 and 16.

3. Department of Health, Education, and Welfare, *Toward a Social Report* (Washington, D.C.: USGPO, 1969), p. 21. Probabilities from the 1960 11th and 12th grade classes follow-up study by Project TALENT.

4. "Factors Related to High School Graduation and College Attendance: 1967," *Current Population Reports*, ser. P–20, no. 185 (Washington, D.C.: USGPO, 11 July 1969), p. 7.

5. Kenneth A. Tabler, *National Longitudinal Study of the High School Class of 1972, Tabular Summary of the First Followup Questionnaire Data*, NCES 76–212 (Washington, D.C.: USGPO, 1976). Ability is a composite index. The 50th percentile is estimated as middle position of the two middle quartiles from data presented pp. 290 and 28. The estimate excludes vocational-technical and "other" enrollment.

sidering the upper quartile in ability as the "most capable," the 1972 high school graduating class registers 80 percent in college or vocational-technical school. There is reason to believe that this record is superior to previous high school graduation classes, but the many variations in method, definition of "college," period of time when the graduate entered college, and definition of "ability," renders any direct comparison impossible. The authors of *S. I. '76* enforced more rigorous conditions of comparability for an examination of trends than seem necessary. Table 2 draws together the best comparisons over time of samples representing American high school graduating classes.[15] Be-

15. Other studies have used different cutting points for identification of high-ability youth, such as the 10th, 25th, and 30th percentile. See Donald S. Bridgman, *The Duration of Formal Education for High-Ability Youth*, NSF 61-36 (Washington, D.C.: National Science Foundation, 1961); Christopher Jencks, "Social Stratification and Higher Education," *Harvard Educational Review* 38 (Spring 1968), p. 277; Glen Stice, William G. Mollenkopf, and Warren S. Torgerson, *Background Factors and College-Going Plans Among High-Aptitude Public High School Seniors* (Princeton, N.J.: Educational Testing Service, August 1956). One of the most intensively studied cohorts,

cause of differences in the sources of variation just mentioned, one cannot rely too heavily upon the evidence, but the data suggest that there has been only slight improvement in the rate of entering college by high school graduates in the top half of ability. In a 20-year span, from the early 1950s to the early 1970s, there may have been an increase of 6 percentage points in the continuation ratio of the upper half in ability, if vocational-technical enrollment is excluded. If all types of institutions are counted, the current picture is brighter.

ARE THEY LEARNING MORE?

Toward a Social Report, the initial federal attempt to summarize social indicators of change, answered this question affirmatively in 1969: ". . . American children in the sixties are learning more than their older brothers and sisters learned in the fifties."[16] Since then, a National Assessment of Educational Progress (NAEP) has been launched to periodically administer achievement tests to 9, 13, and 17 year-olds and to adults 26 to 35 years of age. The sample, sufficiently large to represent segments of the population, produces test scores in eight subject matter areas, but each administration does not include all subjects; consequently, the change over time in achievement scores cannot be assessed each year. With this more definitive testing program, can it be said that students are learning more? The answer: in some subjects, among some ages, yes; in others, no.

The 1974 17 year-olds did slightly better on reading than the 1971 17 year-olds, improvement showing up in all categories of learners. Nine year-olds were tested in reading in 1970 and 1974. The more recent 9 year-olds responded correctly to 1.2 percent more of the questions than did the 1970 9 year-olds.[17]

Tests of writing were administered in 1970 and 1974. The 9 year-olds in 1974 did slightly better than the 9 year-olds in 1970, but both the 13 and 17 year-olds in 1974 did not perform as well as comparable ages in 1970.

Science tests were administered to 17 year-olds in 1969–70 and 1972–73. The more recent scores in all categories of the 17-year-old population were lower, except for those living in small places and rural areas.

Tests given in various years between 1969 and 1973 enable comparisons of 17 year-olds with young adults 26 to 35 years of age. The 17 year-olds performed better than adults did on tests of social studies, citizenship, writing, and music, but the older group was superior on literature, reading, science, and mathematics.

This more definitive testing program gives us no comfort. In reporting the drop of nearly 2 percent in the national level of performance in science, the NAEP labelled the decline "disturb-

---

the Wisconsin high school graduating class of 1957, was followed up in 1964–65 to determine its educational progress. Some 53.4 percent of the high school graduates entered college and, after 7–8 years, 30 percent had completed college. William H. Sewell and Vimal P. Shah, "Socioeconomic Status, Intelligence and the Attainment of Higher Education," *Sociology of Education* 40 (Winter 1967), pp. 1–23.

16. *Toward a Social Report* (Washington, D.C.: USGPO, 1969), p. 67.

17. Mary A. Golladay, *The Condition of Education*, 1977 edition, vol. 3, pt. 1 (Washington, D.C.: USGPO, 1977), p. 108.

ing."[18] With gratitude for the slight gains that have been registered, the public can find little solace that student learning has increased comparable to the increase in expenditures for education. The latter increased from 6.6 percent of the Gross National Product in 1965 to 7.9 percent in 1975, the total expenditure in 1975 being in excess of 120 billion dollars (a figure more than half the public thinks is "too little."[19] Reverting to our knowledge of what makes Sammy learn, however, the public must acknowledge that the family must assume equal responsibility with the school for the sluggish trend in pupil achievement.

More definitive conclusions of the decline in test performance were reached by Harnischfeger and Wiley after they reviewed trends in all the major mass test results.[20] They found lower test scores in the last ten years on "English, writing, literature, vocabulary, reading, social studies, mathematics, and natural sciences"[21]—the traditional academic learning areas. In many test series the decline began after 1963. As one important cause, the authors attribute changes in the secondary school curriculum: lower enrollments in academic courses. Over time, also, a lower pupil dropout rate has been experienced, perhaps retaining in school pupils of less potential.

The decline in achievement test scores, however, was not evident below grade 5 and it was more pronounced in the higher grades. Harnischfeger and Wiley suggest that this may have resulted from "a differential effect of television viewing of different age groups,"[22] even though conclusive proof of this point is lacking. They see a need to reconsider the school curriculum in relation to the skills needed in our society for adjustment in employment, leisure, consumption behavior, political life, etc. If changes in the curriculum are indicated they would lead naturally to changing the content of the tests. Opposing this view, of course, is the "back to basics" movement in education.

Finally, the authors attribute to the school, rather than to the social background of the students, the primary source of academic achievement.[23] The question certainly deserves more definitive research. Until such results are available, however, a model of pupil academic

18. *The National Assessment of Educational Progress* (Washington, D.C.: USGPO, 1975), p. 10.

19. W. Vance Grant and C. George Lind, *Digest of Educational Statistics*, 1976 edition, NCES 77–401 (Washington, D.C.: USGPO, 1977), p. 25.

20. These included the Scholastic Aptitude Test, The American College Testing Program, the Preliminary Scholastic Aptitude Test, the Minnesota Scholastic Aptitude Test, the Iowa Test of Educational Development, the Iowa Tests of Basic Skills, Comprehensive Tests of Basic Skills, as well as the National Assessment of Educational Progress. Annegret Harnischfeger and David E. Wiley, *Achievement Test Score Decline: Do We Need To Worry?* (Chicago: CEMREL, Inc., 1975).

21. Ibid., p. 118.

22. Ibid., p. 116.

23. Reference is to the results of studies which have found the social background of the students to account for more variance in achievement than the characteristics of the schools, as reported by J. S. Coleman, *et al.*, *Equality of Educational Opportunity* (Washington, D.C.: USGPO, 1966) and C. S. Jencks *et al.*, *Inequality: A Reassessment of the Effect of Family and Schooling in America* (New York: Basic Books, 1972). An intensive study of the decline in SAT scores was completed by a panel headed by Willard Wirtz: *Report of the Advisory Panel on the Scholastic Aptitude Test Score Decline* (Princeton, N.J.: College Entrance Examination Board, Educational Testing Service, 1977). The Wirtz study was discussed in *The Chronicle of Higher Education* XV (6 September 1977), pp. 1–13.

achievement is suggested which would attribute weight both to the school and the family for the academic attainment of youth. The primary basis for motivation and reward rests in the social and cultural influences of family and school. Where the home or the school fails to stimulate maximum personal development by youth, techniques of intervention, politically feasible or not, are needed. Social and educational research should show the way.

MODELS ARE NEEDED

This commentary on the Education and Training chapter of *Social Indicators, 1976* has not considered many time series on education in the volume: the public's perception of aspects of education, adult and vocational education, international comparisons, and others. Neither has it discussed the many relationships presented in the volume between education and many important indicators of societal functions: fertility, occupational attainment, educational differences between ethnic groups, attitudes and opinions toward several important social issues, the distribution of income and consumer expenditures by educational level, trends in knowledge-producing and -disseminating occupations, trends in the subject matter of books published, intergenerational shifts (father to son) in years of school completed, and others.

These extensive data on education attest to the richness of the United States social accounting system and to continuing efforts to improve the quality and usefulness of the data, particularly in the last decade.[24] Despite these accretions a persistent cry for more and more data is heard. The need arises from attempts to understand more fully the structures and processes of society. This laudable objective can be aided by more educational data only if the data would serve to explicate models of processes within and affecting the educational system.

Models are needed to interpret social indicators of education. Models are conceptual schemes of interacting variables which account for variation in a criterion indicator. Many such models have been, and are being, developed.[25] Many, for example, predict the manpower output of the educational system while others predict the manpower requirements of education.[26] Im-

24. See chapter 5 on education by Ezra Glaser in *Social Statistics in Use*, ed. Philip M. Hauser (New York: Russell Sage Foundation, 1975).

25. The Organization for Economic Cooperation and Development has released several publications on modeling in education. Two of these are: Richard Stone, *Demographic Accounting and Model-Building* (Paris: OECD, 1971) and idem, *Mathematical Models for the Education Sector* (Paris: OECD, 1973). Status and educational attainment have been favored criteria in sociological models. Some recent studies: James G. Anderson, "Causal Models and Social Indicators: Toward the Development of Social Systems Models," *American Sociological Review* 38 (June 1973), pp. 285–301; Kenneth L. Wilson and Alejandro Portes, "The Educational Attainment Process: Results from a National Sample," *American Journal of Sociology* 81 (September 1975), pp. 343–63; Karl L. Alexander, Bruce K. Eckland, and Larry J. Griffin, "The Wisconsin Model of Socioeconomic Achievement: A Replication," *American Journal of Sociology* 81 (September, 1975), pp. 324–42.

26. Four models have been the subjects of National Science Foundation and the Department of Health, Education, and Welfare support: Thomas Wallace, "An Empirical Investigation of Expenditures and Time Spent on Formal Schooling," (Raleigh: North Carolina State University); Saul J. Gass, "Enrollment and Financial Aid Model for Higher Education," (Bethesda, Md.: Mathematics Inc.); Vaughn Huckfeldt, "National Planning Model," (Boulder Colo.: National Center for Higher Education Manage-

proving them and extending them to encompass the major significant criteria is necessary. Specifying the model is the first step toward identifying needed indicators of education. Until such models are developed and tested by social science, improvement in the quality and utility of educational indicators is likely to be piecemeal.

Social indicators of education are statistical time series that reflect the condition of some aspect of the system.[27] Indicators of normative interest may be taken as criteria indicators which are dependent upon the independent predictors in an interactive system. When arranged in a time series, singly or in combination, the independent predictors herald changes in the criterion indicator. Educational indicators of this kind are needed to monitor the system, to anticipate future changes, to plan, to facilitate adjustment, and to understand the social forces at work.

The need for models of numerous processes in the educational system is crucial. Analytical models are needed to facilitate the interpretation of the successive stages of growth and learning upon the basis of longitudinal observations of a cohort. Models are needed that predict the growth function in learning skills and competencies upon the basis of personal traits and situational influences of home and school. Models are needed of classroom activity, teacher behavior, and peer influences on learning. Models are needed which more clearly identify the effect of the numerous inputs to the educational system on learning. Improved models of manpower requirements are needed for more deliberate educational planning. Models of the broader social consequences of education, viewed as generational change, as occupational achievement, as increments to the quality of life, and, broadly, as social and cultural change are also of critical importance.

---

ment Systems); James F. McNamara, "Mathematical Progression Models in Educational Planning," (Eugene, Ore.: Center for Advanced Studies in Educational Administration, University of Oregon). The latter study is cited in Gary Fromm, William L. Hamilton, and Diane E. Hamilton, *Federally Supported Mathematical Models: Survey and Analysis*, NSF–RA–S–74-029 (Washington, D.C.: USGPO, 1975).

27. Ferriss, *Indicators of Trends*, pp. 2–6. Broad societal relationships to education have been modeled by Felson and Land, *A Dynamic Macro Social Indicator Model*.

Table 7/1
POPULATION UNDER 25 YEARS OF AGE, BY SELECTED AGE GROUPINGS: 1940–2000
(Thousands)

Year	Total	Under 5 years	5 to 13 years	14 to 17 years	18 to 24 years	Year	Total	Under 5 years	5 to 13 years	14 to 17 years	18 to 24 years
1940	132,122	10,579	19,936	9,844	16,616	1970	204,879	17,156	36,636	15,910	24,683
1941	133,402	10,850	19,674	9,742	16,747	1971	207,045	17,174	36,104	16,281	25,776
1942	134,860	11,301	19,427	9,643	16,845	1972	208,842	17,006	35,456	16,556	25,901
1943	136,739	12,016	19,319	9,568	16,878	1973	210,404	16,714	34,739	16,746	26,381
1944	138,397	12,524	19,246	9,474	16,852	1974	211,909	16,304	34,082	16,878	26,908
1945	139,928	12,979	19,326	9,251	16,728	1975	213,450	15,910	33,441	16,923	27,597
1946	141,389	13,244	19,625	9,019	16,583	1976	215,074	15,545	32,957	16,879	28,161
1947	144,126	14,406	20,118	8,878	16,382	1977	216,814	15,589	32,252	16,774	28,616
1948	146,631	14,919	20,990	8,656	16,309	1978	218,678	15,988	31,413	16,632	28,967
1949	149,188	15,607	21,634	8,502	16,024	1979	220,663	16,589	30,682	16,259	29,282
1950	152,271	16,410	22,424	8,444	16,075	1980	222,769	17,259	30,246	15,753	29,441
1951	154,878	17,333	22,998	8,499	15,781	1981	224,963	17,935	30,009	15,211	29,488
1952	157,553	17,312	24,501	8,684	15,472	1982	227,207	18,546	29,979	14,650	29,332
1953	160,184	17,638	25,701	8,792	15,257	1983	229,484	19,066	30,051	14,305	28,998
1954	163,026	18,057	26,887	8,959	15,103	1984	231,776	19,484	30,181	14,259	28,458
1955	165,931	18,566	27,925	9,248	14,968	1985	234,068	19,785	30,380	14,388	27,834
1956	168,903	19,003	28,929	9,617	14,980	1986	236,345	19,984	30,974	14,311	27,069
1957	171,984	19,494	29,672	10,303	15,094	1987	238,596	20,110	31,842	13,980	26,435
1958	174,882	19,887	30,651	10,786	15,308	1988	240,809	20,167	32,827	13,502	25,960
1959	177,830	20,175	31,767	11,108	15,677	1989	242,973	20,161	33,774	13,027	25,621

Table 7/1 (*Continued*)

Year	Total	Under 5 years	5 to 13 years	14 to 17 years	18 to 24 years	Year	Total	Under 5 years	5 to 13 years	14 to 17 years	18 to 24 years
1960	180,671	20,341	32,965	11,219	16,128	1990	245,075	20,096	34,643	12,941	25,162
1961	183,691	20,522	33,217	12,052	17,004	1991	247,109	19,978	35,382	13,199	24,700
1962	186,538	20,469	33,897	12,759	17,688	1992	249,068	19,817	35,974	13,669	24,261
1963	189,242	20,342	34,578	13,500	18,268	1993	250,950	19,619	36,410	14,203	23,984
1964	191,889	20,165	35,244	14,274	18,783	1994	252,758	19,395	36,678	14,773	23,780
1965	194,303	19,824	35,754	14,153	20,293	1995	254,495	19,161	36,799	15,317	23,641
1966	196,560	19,208	36,283	14,405	21,376	1996	256,170	18,934	36,808	15,784	23,576
1967	198,712	18,563	36,629	14,735	22,327	1997	257,795	18,728	36,714	16,162	23,927
1968	200,706	17,913	36,804	15,173	22,883	1998	259,381	18,557	36,530	16,437	24,617
1969	202,677	17,376	36,836	15,560	23,723	1999	260,943	18,432	36,273	16,625	25,478
						2000	262,494	18,364	35,963	16,752	26,328

Source: U.S. Department of Commerce, Bureau of the Census, *Current Population Reports*, Series P-25, Nos. 311 (1940 to 1959), 519 (1960 to 1973), and 541 (1974 to 2000).

Chart 7/1 — Social Indicators, 1976

U.S. POPULATION UNDER 25 YEARS OF AGE BY SELECTED AGE GROUPINGS, 1940 TO 2,000 (Series II projections)

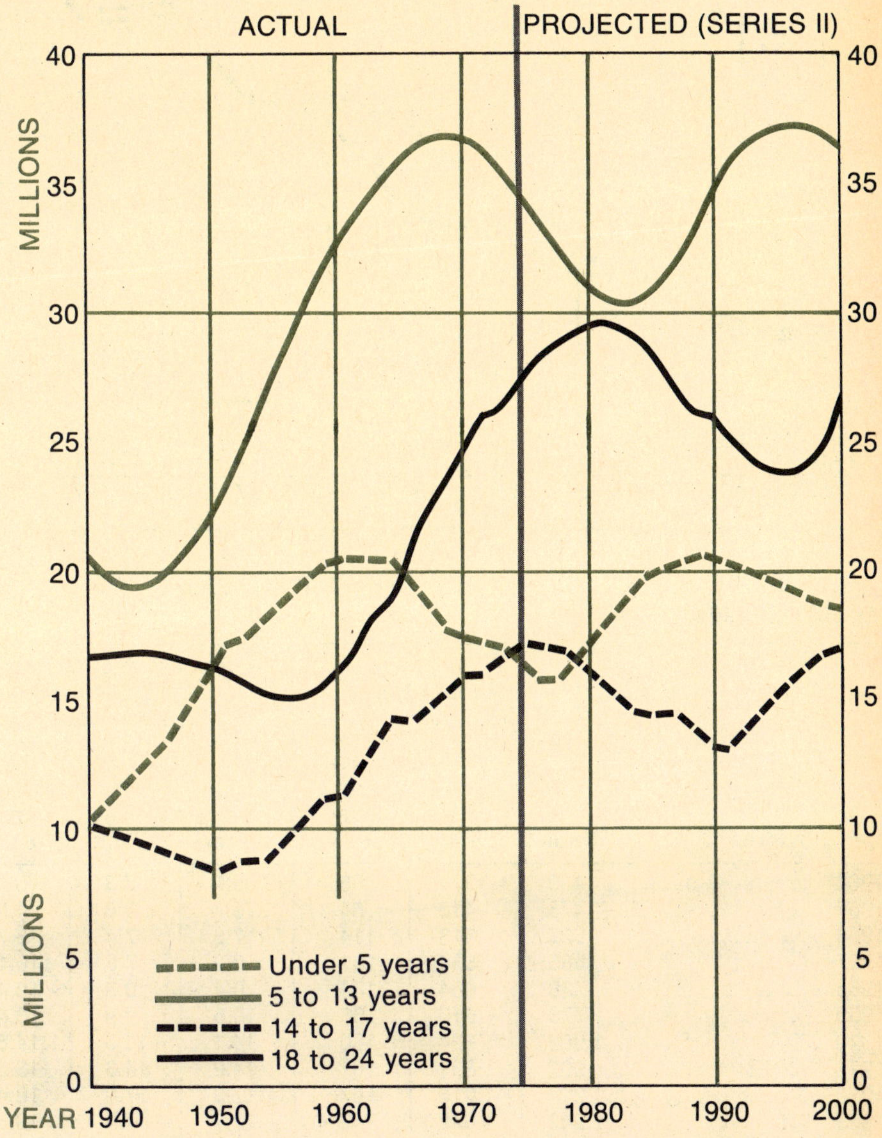

Source: see table 7/1

Chart 7/2 Social Indicators, 1976

PREKINDERGARTEN ENROLLMENT OF 3- AND 4-YEAR-OLDS, BY RACE: 1964–1974

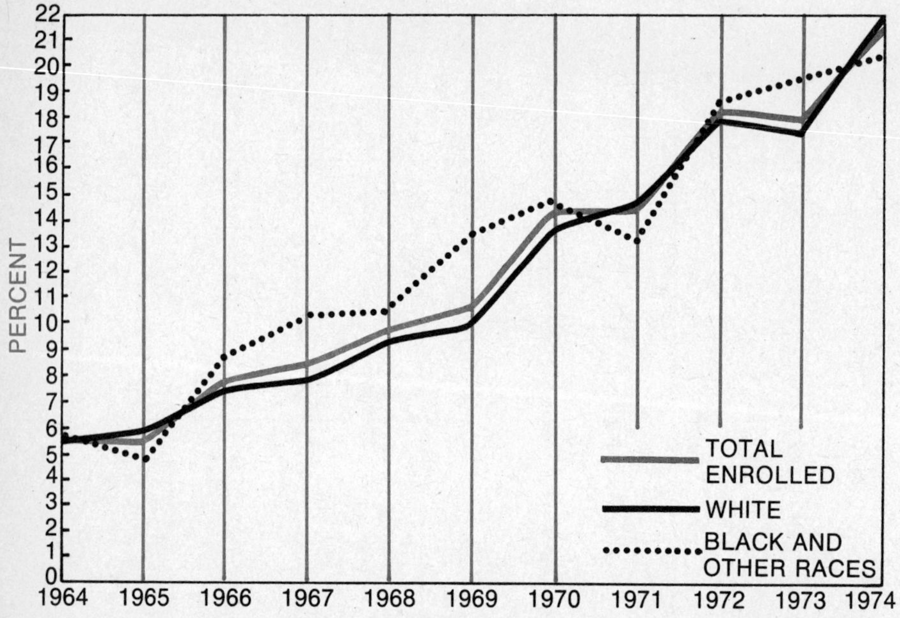

Table 7/2

PREKINDERGARTEN ENROLLMENT OF 3- AND 4-YEAR-OLDS, BY RACE: 1964–1974

Year	Number enrolled (thousands)			Percent of 3- and 4-year-old population enrolled		
	Total	White	Black and other races	Total	White	Black and other races
1964	439	374	65	5.2	5.3	5.1
1965	475	413	64	5.7	5.8	4.9
1966	627	513	114	7.6	7.4	8.7
1967	665	534	131	8.2	7.9	10.1
1968	738	604	134	9.4	9.3	10.4
1969	778	610	168	10.5	9.9	13.4
1970	1,003	824	180	14.1	13.9	14.8
1971	992	831	161	14.2	14.3	13.5
1972	1,213	1,015	197	17.9	17.8	18.4
1973	1,242	1,022	219	17.7	17.4	19.6
1974[1]	1,515	1,273	243	21.7	21.9	20.9

Source: U.S. Department of Health, Education, and Welfare, National Center for Education Statistics, *The Condition of Education, 1976.*

[1] Estimated.

Table 7/7

SCHOOL RETENTION RATES: 1924–1974

(Retention rates per 1,000 students who entered 5th grade)

School year pupils entered 5th grade	5th grade	6th grade	7th grade	8th grade	9th grade	10th grade	11th grade	12th grade	High school graduation	
									Number	Year
1924	1,000	911	798	741	612	470	384	344	302	1932
1934	1,000	953	892	842	803	711	610	512	467	1942
1944	1,000	952	929	858	848	748	650	549	522	1952
1954	1,000	980	979	948	915	855	759	684	642	1962
1960	1,000	980	973	967	952	913	858	787	749	1968
1965	1,000	996	983	980	980	947	874	786	749	1973
1966	1,000	989	986	985	985	959	871	783	744	1974

Source: U.S. Department of Health, Education, and Welfare, National Center for Education Statistics, *Digest of Educational Statistics, 1975.*

Chart 7/7 Social Indicators, 1976

SCHOOL RETENTION RATES FROM FIFTH GRADE TO HIGH SCHOOL GRADUATION: 1924–1974

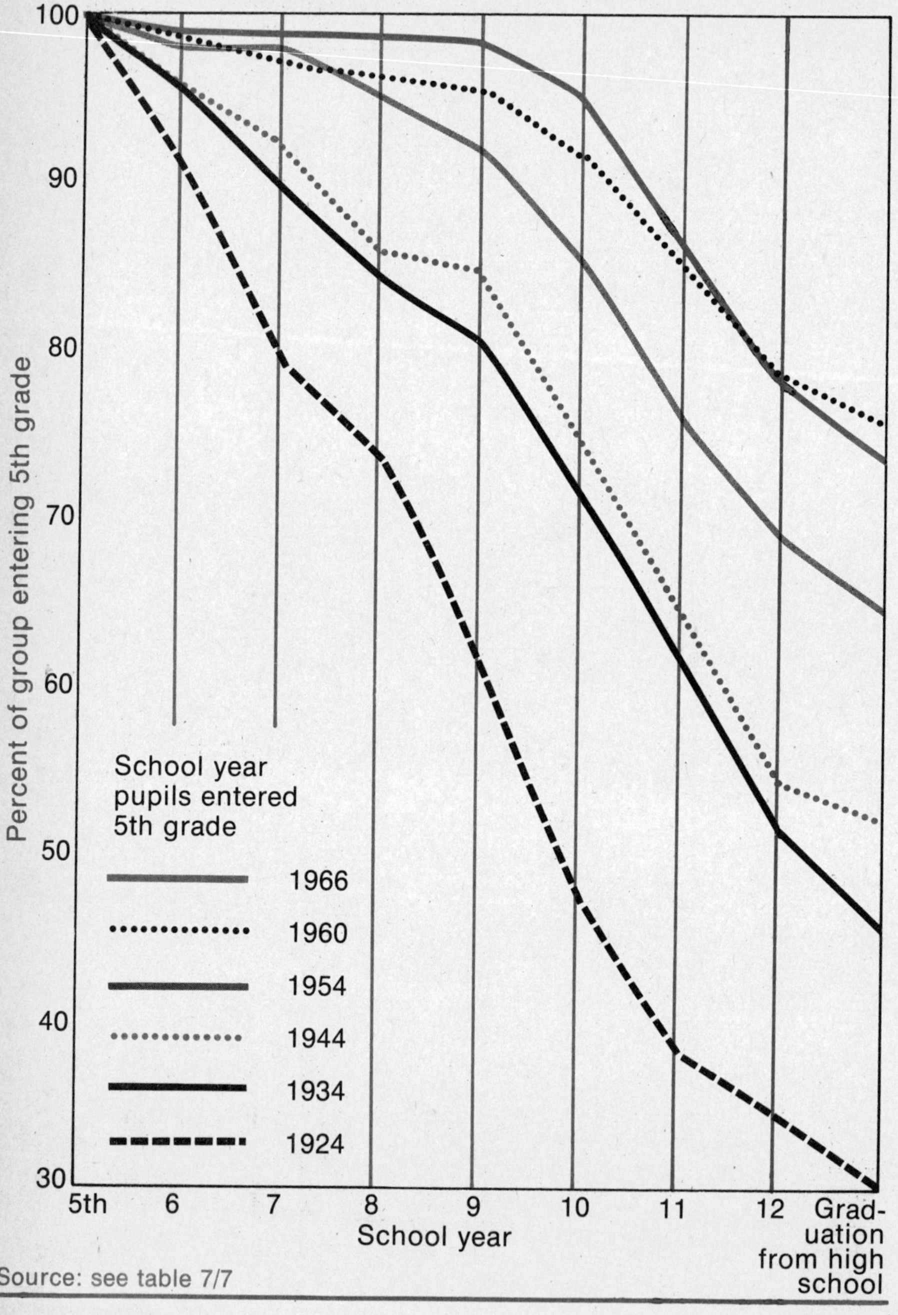

Source: see table 7/7

Table 7/19
PERFORMANCE IN SUBJECT AREAS, BY AGE LEVEL AND SEX: EARLY 1970'S
(Percent)

Subject area, year of assessment, and sex[1]	9-year-olds	13-year-olds	17-year-olds	26- to 35-year-olds
MATHEMATICS, 1972–73				
National norm	36.7	51.3	57.1	59.3
Male	.7	.4	2.3	5.4
Female	–.7	–.4	–2.2	–5.0
SCIENCE, 1972–73				
National norm	68.2	58.3	47.0	51.2
Male	.8	1.5	2.8	5.2
Female	–1.0	–1.4	–2.4	–4.7
SOCIAL STUDIES, 1971–72				
National norm	72.2	66.2	73.8	72.4
Male	.4	.1	.6	2.3
Female	–.4	–.1	–.6	–2.2
CITIZENSHIP, 1969–70				
National norm	64.1	63.1	61.8	60.4
Male	.1	.3	.4	1.4
Female	–.2	–.4	–.4	–1.3
WRITING, 1969–70				
National norm	28.3	55.4	62.5	58.4
Male	–4.0	–3.4	–3.4	–2.3
Female	4.1	3.2	3.0	2.1
READING, 1970–71				
National norm	70.4	68.1	77.5	83.5
Male	–2.4	–2.5	–2.0	.2
Female	2.3	2.3	1.9	–.3
LITERATURE, 1970–71				
National norm	43.9	53.4	61.3	64.0
Male	–.7	–1.6	–1.1	—
Female	.6	1.6	1.0	–.1
MUSIC, 1971–72				
National norm	53.8	48.9	49.2	41.5
Male	–.3	–.9	–.9	–.9
Female	.3	.9	.8	.9

Source: U.S. Department of Health, Education, and Welfare, National Center for Education Statistics, *The Condition of Education, 1976*, and National Assessment of Educational Progress, Education Commission of the States, Newsletter VIII, No. 5 (Denver, Colorado: October 1975).

— Represents zero.

[1] Figures for sex indicate median difference in percentage points from the national norm.

Chart 7/19

Social Indicators, 1976

PERFORMANCE IN SUBJECT AREAS FOR SELECTED YEARS

males perform better than females in mathematics, science, social studies and citizenship at all age levels

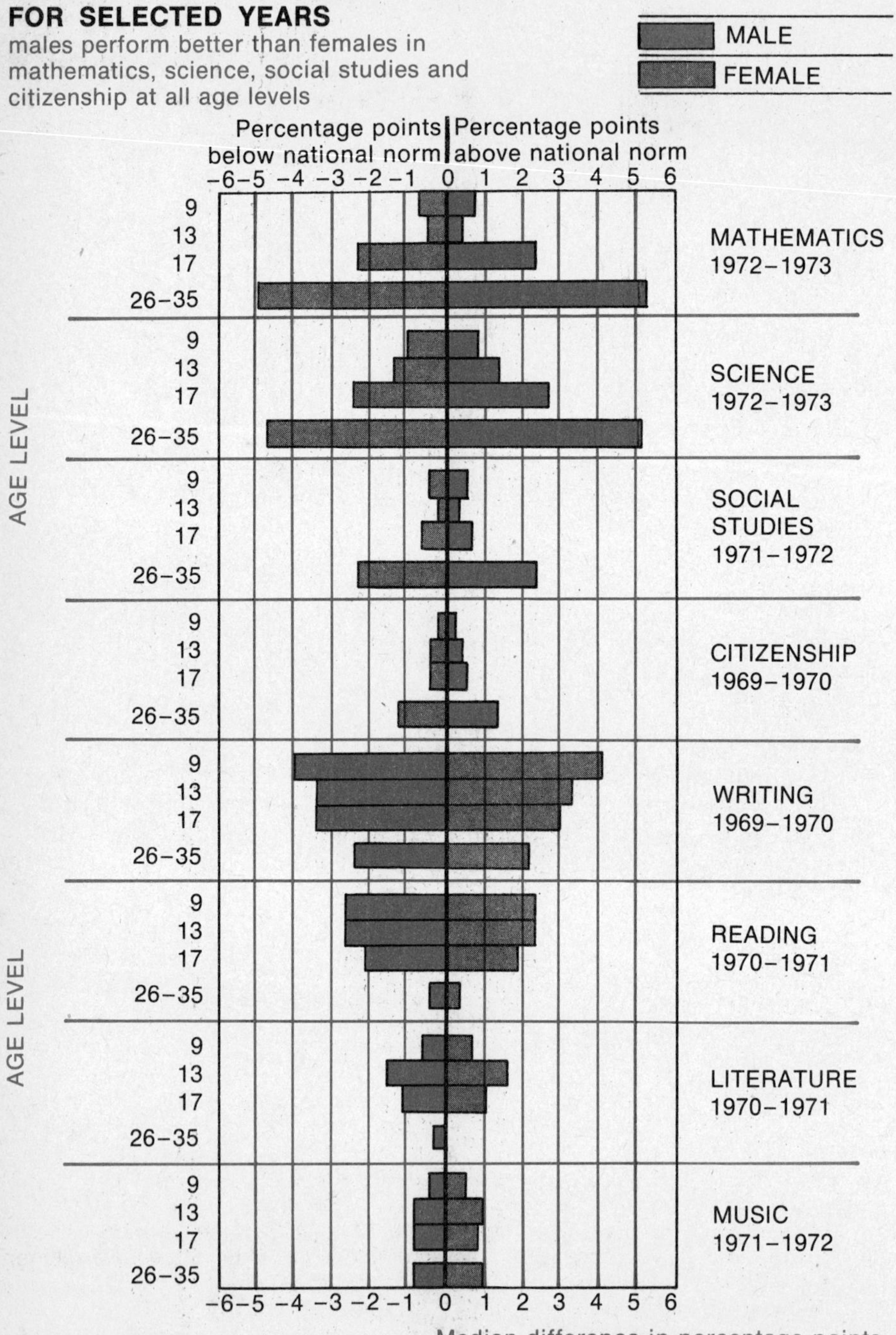

Source: see table 7/19

ANNALS, AAPSS, 435, Jan. 1978

Perceptions About Black Americans

By BARBARA L. CARTER AND DOROTHY K. NEWMAN

ABSTRACT: The data sources used in *Social Indicators, 1976* are more restricted and interpretation more restrained than in earlier reports by the Census or the Bureau of Labor Statistics. Available data that measure how institutions established for dealing with racial injustice are working have not been incorporated in the report.

Black Americans continue to have less of the society's most valued characteristics and conditions and more of those that are disvalued and stigmatized, or are evidence of discrimination and neglect. At the root of blacks' disfavored position is a combination of interacting forces. These include the cumulative effects on American institutions of generations of blatantly overt racial discrimination in every area of life; the continuing subtle practices of racial and economic discrimination; and the absence of a national will or commitment to undertake those pragmatic political, social, and economic policies necessary to erase discrimination, and to enforce those policies forthrightly.

Barbara L. Carter holds a doctorate in sociology from Brandeis University. She is a co-author of Protest, Politics and Prosperity: Black Americans and White Institutions, 1940–75, *and has done research on the experiences of women in prison. She is Associate Provost and Associate Professor of Sociology at the University of the District of Columbia.*

Dorothy K. Newman, who received her doctorate in sociology from Yale, is senior author of Protest, Politics and Prosperity *and of* The American Energy Consumer. *She has directed many socioeconomic studies for the Bureau of Labor Statistics and has written extensively about minorities, the consumer, housing, and employment. She founded the National Urban League Research Department in Washington, where she was the Director from 1968 to 1972.*

THE SOCIAL indicators movement blossomed in the 1960s when all eyes were focused on the social changes taking place in American race relations. The civil rights movement, and especially black initiatives, were aimed at destroying a centuries old caste system, reinforced by the sanction of law, that kept blacks at the back of the bus, at the bottom of the economic ladder, in the poorest health, in the worst housing, disenfranchised in many places, and often as fearful of law enforcers as of lawless offenders. Through their active and highly visible protest in the 1960s, black Americans called national attention to their second-class citizenship and set in motion policies to reduce overt discrimination to a minimum, and to improve their social and economic conditions and opportunities.[1]

SOCIAL INDICATORS—BLACK HISTORY

A by-product of this struggle and the national spotlight that it achieved was a growing concern among social policy professionals with the measurement and publicizing of the extent to which changes were actually occuring. One of the results was a White Paper entitled "To Fulfill These Rights" prepared for President Johnson's White House Planning Conference on economic security held in Washington in November 1965. The conference was called following serious disorders in Birmingham, Cambridge, Maryland, Chicago, Harlem, Hough in Cleveland, and Watts in Los Angeles, among others. The issue paper prepared in the Bureau of Labor Statistics (BLS)[2] had a number of precursors in much earlier years, which reflected substantial effort to glean and analyze whatever hard data existed about black Americans. They were published in 1952, 1957, 1958, 1959, 1960, and 1962.[3] The title of the 1962 report, like that of the others, featured only the economic condition of blacks. But the titles are misleading, since in addition to information about work and wages, the BLS studies investigated voting rights, educational segregation, segregation in public accommodations, as well as demographic questions such as population trends, birth and death rates, mobility, and life expectancy. Interspersed with statistics are informative analyses of trends, and outspoken discussion of discrimination as reflected in data from sources both in and out of the federal government. In fact, the sources are not as restricted and the interpretation as restrained in these early reports as they are in *Social Indicators, 1976*. Yet the 1970s abound with a huge volume of government and nongovernment data upon which to draw for studying the conditions, pace of change, and the extent of equality of black Americans with

1. For analysis of the significance of black protest in bringing about political and legal action, see *Protest, Politics, and Prosperity: Black Americans and White Institutions* by the authors of this article, with Nancy J. Amidei, Dawn Day, William J. Kruvant, and Jack S. Russell (New York: Pantheon Books, forthcoming, 1978).

2. Dorothy K. Newman prepared the paper and attended the conferences as a resource person for the panel sessions that dealt with economic security and housing.

3. U.S. Dept. of Labor, Bureau of Labor Statistics, *Negroes in the United States, Their Employment and Economic Status*, BLS Bulletin no. 1119 (Washington, D.C.: USGPO, 1952); idem, *Notes on the Economic Situation of Negroes in the United States* (Washington, D.C.: USGPO, 1957 and revised and repeated in 1958 and 1959); idem, *The Economic Situation of Negroes in the United States*, BLS Bulletin no. S-2 (Washington, D.C.: USGPO, 1960); BLS Bulletin S-3, 1962.

others in our society. Data are available also that can measure how institutions established for dealing with racial injustice are working. The 1965 White House Conference issue paper, and its charts and tables, evolved into the BLS 1966 publication, *Social and Economic Conditions of Negro American*,[4] and gave rise to an annual series of reports about American blacks by the Census Bureau, beginning with the joint BLS-Census bulletin *Social and Economic Conditions of Negroes in the United States*,[5] published in October 1967. The analytic thrust in the latter report began the effort to present a minimum of large and confusing numbers and yet cover a wide range of readily interpretable data. Its simplicity of presentation for ready understanding depended on substantial knowledge of the subject beforehand, thoroughly digested data, and the use of several sets of data within tables in an analytical frame to shed light on significant issues.

The statistics about blacks in *Social Indicators, 1976*, while numerous, are scattered throughout the chapters. Since they are not drawn together and interpreted in one place, they leave a vague, diffused impression. Those responsible for the *Indicators* publication as a whole may well have reasoned that the undertaking was ambitious enough without a chapter devoted entirely to blacks. After all, they could refer readers to the Census Bureau's annual series, *The Social and Economic Status of the Black Population in the United States*. But a social indicators report was an opportunity to use creativity and depth of interpretation about race in our country during the mid-1970s when malaise was increasing, and when the indicators that did exist showed a gulf between black and white, and lagging enforcement both of the letter and the spirit of the law. One of the main reasons for a race classification as a social indicator is to provide a way of discerning causes for the trends as well as insights into positive changes and continuing disparities between the races. But, as the report itself tells the reader, the question is not "Why?" but "What?" Even without considering the "why," the significance of the fact never surfaces that in America being black is a social indicator. What happens to black people describes progress made and successes or failures of American society.

THE "WHAT?" AND SOME OF THE "WHY?"

In virtually all areas for which race data are shown in *Social Indicators, 1976* trends for black Americans are identical to those for the white majority. This is a simple, but often overlooked, point. It is as true for changes in population growth, marriage and divorce, fertility, health, and family arrangements as for employment and unemployment, for instance. When the society as a whole, and the white majority in particular, gains or loses, so do blacks. But the rub is, that although going in the same direction, blacks are on a different track. They continue to have

4. U.S. Dept. of Labor, Bureau of Labor Statistics, *Social and Economic Conditions of Negro Americans*, BLS Bulletin 1511 (Washington, D.C.: USGPO, 1966). The Bulletin was prepared by Dorothy K. Newman.

5. U.S. Dept. of Labor, Bureau of Labor Statistics, *Social and Economic Conditions of Negroes in the United States*, BLS Report no. 332 (Washington, D.C.: USGPO, 1967) and *Current Population Reports*, ser. P–23, no. 24. Herman P. Miller of the Bureau of the Census and Dorothy K. Newman of the Bureau of Labor Statistics developed the latter Report.

less of the most valued characteristics and conditions and more of those that are disvalued and stigmatized or are evidence of discrimination and neglect.

Health

Using health as an example, while the proportion of those healthy enough to live to or beyond 65 has increased for everyone over the past few decades and is expected to continue to rise, blacks' shorter life expectancy has persisted, so that proportionately fewer blacks experience those "golden years." Similarly, as we place increasing value on smaller, planned families, the fertility rate has declined among blacks and whites, but it remains higher among blacks. Black women, like white women of childbearing age, want fewer children than they used to, so family size for both races has dropped sharply. By 1975, average family size was 2.5 for white and 2.9 for blacks. Infant and neonatal mortality rates also have fallen, but they remain substantially higher for blacks than whites.

High blood pressure is substantially more prevalent among blacks than whites. If stress is a factor in high blood pressure, that may be why the highest incidence is among black women, who disproportionately suffer from the double burdens of being black and women in our society.[6] And blacks, who average less income than whites, are less able to pay for increasingly expensive health care, and they tend not to be covered by group health insurance. The tensions of daily living under varying levels and patterns of discrimination have been associated with higher incidence of mental illness among blacks.[7] Blacks, more than whites, cannot afford private psychiatric care and show much higher admission rates to psychiatric inpatient and outpatient services of mental hospitals.

Ironically, when illness would interfere with getting a full pay check, health "indicators" appear to be better for blacks than whites. Blacks between 45 and 65 have fewer days of work loss. Black children under 16 have fewer days of restricted activity, school days loss, and bed disability days than white children. This is linked, no doubt, to the larger proportion of black than white mothers who work outside the home, are unable to afford household help, or are without the paid annual leave that makes it possible for them to stay home with their ill children.

Housing

The quality of housing has improved dramatically for all Americans during the past several decades, but blacks continue more often to live in overcrowded and substandard housing. Especially significant is the fact that the races live almost entirely apart. Blacks reside mostly in the central cities of metropolitan areas; whites, in the suburban ring or the open country. The extent of housing segregation has not changed since 1940; not even the most active period of civil rights protest in this

6. See Jermiah Stamler *et al.*, *Hypertension In The Inner City* (Minneapolis, Minn.: Modern Medicine Publications, 1974), pp. 11–30 for a discussion of social, psychological, and economic factors related to hypertension.

7. Thomas F. Pettigrew, *A Profile of The Negro American* (Princeton, N.J.: D. Van Nostrand, 1964), pp. 73–82; Morton Kramer *et al.*, Definitions and Distributions of Mental Disorders In A Racist Society" in *Racism and Mental Health*, eds., Charles V. Willie, *et al.*, (Pittsburgh: University of Pittsburgh Press, 1973), pp. 353–459.

century, the 1960s, has affected the pattern of segregated housing. The intensity of both hidden and overt discrimination is especially demonstrated in the housing arena.[8] Data are abundantly available that afford good measures of this, but they do not appear in *Social Indicators, 1976.*

Work

Earnings and incomes are unequal between the races as is the acquisition of those components of income that create wealth. Unemployment rates are shockingly higher among blacks than whites and a larger proportion of black people live in poverty. Even comparable years of schooling and a college degree do not bridge the gap. Some of it narrows when incomes are similar, but the basic pattern of inequality does not disappear.

It is said often that blacks' economic difficulties are affected to a large degree by an unusual mix of demographic groups in their labor force, with blacks having a larger proportion of those most vulnerable to unemployment. Regardless of the merits of this argument, which describes, but does not deny the problem, a close look at data, not all of which are in the *Indicators* report, shows that however well or poorly the economy is doing and whatever the high-risk group—whether high school dropouts, teenagers, women, or persons in unskilled occupations —the black unemployment rate is invariably much higher than the white. In the best of times, when employers are in great need of labor, the preference is for whites whatever the qualifications. In the worst of times, white high school dropouts are kept on or hired in preference to blacks with substantially more schooling.[9]

Quality of schooling or scholarship standings also are often cited for discrepancies in hiring, promotion, and occupational achievement between black and other workers. But just a casual look at the figures shows that white applicants and workers who have not finished high school are much more numerous than all black applicants or workers, whatever their qualifications. One of the truly analytical tables in the report concisely illustrates that blacks tend to have even more schooling than whites in jobs for which education could be presumed most necessary—professional and managerial work. Further analysis, using well-known studies about the gap between black and white occupational achievement relative to education, shows that a sizable gap in job levels remains over three decades between blacks and whites of the same age group as well as between blacks and whites in the same educational group.[10]

Yet most jobs can be performed without the schooling American employers require of American applicants, according both to the United States Employment Service's *Training and Reference Manual for Job Analysis* and its *Dictionary of Occupational Titles*, and the BLS *Occupational Outlook Handbook.* The overwhelming majority of the American work force—black and white alike—has had as much or more schooling than successful job perform-

8. See Newman and Carter, *Protest, Politics, and Prosperity*, chap. 5 for a full development of housing segregation, its extent and courses.

9. For a more complete development of this point and associated documentation, see Newman and Carter, *Protest, Politics, and Prosperity,* chap. 2.

10. See Newman and Carter, *Protest, Politics, and Prosperity,* end of chap. 3.

ance requires. Most jobs are learned by doing, and in a short time. A large component of the white labor force has long held such jobs without much formal schooling, whereas blacks have been called unqualified for lack of school credentials. In 1950 half of the **total** experienced labor force, including two-thirds of all clerical and sales workers, were whites with less than a high school education. In 1970 white workers without a high school diploma still were half of all production workers, one-fifth of the police, and about one-fourth of clerical and sales workers.[11]

That it is hyprocrisy and discrimination that downgrades black Americans' capabilities for the work that has to be done in the United States is revealed by the hiring practices of multinational American firms abroad. In industrialized Western Europe migrant Southern European workers, who were untrained and illiterate in any language, were hired to produce the same commodities for which black Americans are required to have a high school education, experience, or special training here[12] —black Americans, who grew up knowing the language and customs of their native land.

The occupational distributions in *Social Indicators, 1976* show that a large shift has occurred over several decades among women, especially among black women, into low paying clerical and sales jobs requiring the least education, and also and especially, in the health services. They are not flocking into such professions as doctors, lawyers, dentists, college professors, physicists, and social scientists. These are the most advantaged in professional work in terms of security, status, and earnings, and white men still dominate them. White men, followed by black men, also dominate industrial jobs, which are not just better paid than are the usual clerical and sales work women do, but carry with them more security in the form of collective bargaining agreements, seniority lines, and coverage by private pension and health plans. Some of these facts are present among the tables and charts in the report, but some are missing. It would be difficult to sort out viable conclusions without the missing pieces, and without prior knowledge, and an analytical frame of reference. Especially misleading is the dichotomy between "white collar" and "blue collar," leaving the often made assumption that jobs in the former are "better" than those in the latter.[13]

11. Ibid.
12. Ibid.

Wages and wealth

Americans, black and white, tend to earn most of their income by working for someone else, as the *Social Indicators* report clearly shows. After this, the facts are not so clear. For instance, some of the income that is unearned and is not from self-employment in a business or profession is presented in economic terminology as a "transfer payment." So-called transfer payments are principally from social security programs (Old Age and Survivors and Disability and Health Insurance [OASDHI] unemployment insurance, and public assistance). Looked at by many as a way of bilking Uncle Sam, such payments show up as being more prevalent among black than white

13. For more data documentation about the relative position of black workers by occupation and education, and the deceiving nature of white-collar and blue-collar designations, see Newman and Carter *Protest, Politics, and Prosperity*, chaps. 2 and 3.

families. Analyses are needed from data that reflect other parts of the picture. For instance, in the largest program with most status—OASDHI—black families get less per recipient than white families.[14] Also, the nation's security programs as a whole are more effective in bringing white families out of poverty than black families.[15] In addition, taxes foregone or forgiven, so that they do not reach the nation's coffers at all—called tax preferences or loopholes, as you will—benefit white families far more than black.[16]

The tables and charts in *Social Indicators, 1976* plainly show that blacks have substantially less wealth and less means of creating it. They show that, counting income alone, the ratio of black to white family income has hovered around the same figure for almost a decade—about 60 percent. When the concept of wealth is used, the gap is far greater.[17] And, as we all know, money makes money. The emphasis in *Social Indicators, 1976* is on vast improvements in income among black families. Money income has risen sharply for us all, but the true measure of economic status is in wealth, and it is relative. The ratio of black to white family income alone edged up only about 10 points in almost 30 years, with most of that rise occurring in the 1960s. Relatively, very few black families are wealthy or receive large incomes from property.[18]

Further exaggeration about income results from including other races, mostly Chinese Americans and Japanese Americans, with black Americans. Data are available from 1968 on that exclude the other races, who are so affluent, on the average, that their median family income is well above that of white Americans and almost twice that of black Americans. Misinterpretation is especially great when using the whole group of "Negroes and Other Races" in presenting comparative data for the West. These show deceptively high black to white income ratios. But in the West, blacks are only half the total of "Negroes and Other Races." Chinese, Japanese, and Filipinos are almost all the rest,[19] with substantially higher median family income than blacks. Blacks' median income nationally is just a shade higher than that of American Indians, the most oppressed of us all.

The family

Because the family is so central in importance in the society, its treatment in a report called Social Indicators is a clue to the nature of the treatise as a social document. An acquaintance with the process of social change and with variations in kinship bonds and social networks is a necessary background for selecting the data and lines of analysis. The report gives trends in divorce rates, the number of children who live in husband-wife households, and the number of households in which women have been enumerated as the "head." These are slim reeds on which to base the analysis of differences between groups in family life and affectional ties.

As with all gross assumptions about the causes of social malaise, those

14. *Protest, Politics, and Prosperity*, chap. 7, table 7.

15. *Protest, Politics, and Prosperity*, chap. 7, table 1.

16. *Protest, Politics and Prosperity*, chap. 7, analysis and footnote references.

17. *Ibid.*

18. *Ibid.*

19. U.S. Bureau of the Census, *1970 Census of Population, General Population Characteristics, U.S. Summary*, PC(1)–B1, (Washington, D.C.: USGPO, 1972), table 55, pp. 1–281.

about problems associated with divorce, children in fatherless homes, and in homes in which women are the principal breadwinner or manager have the merit of some truth in fact. The monolithic nature of the data selected, however, and the moralistic tone in them, create a false impression. It is true, of course, that black families are well in the lead in the decreasing proportion of husband-wife families, and in the proportion of children in homes without two parental *guardians* present,[20] (not all two-parent households include both the *natural* parents of the children).[21] The differences between black and white are very wide, with the white well above the black in being "together." These differences are the result of dissimilarities in nurturing and family adaptation, stemming from a combination of social and economic conditions, social attitudes, and pragmatic adjustment to life situations in an often hostile and discriminatory environment. Almost insuperable problems have generated great strengths. The strengths of black families have been documented in several studies using many sources of statistical data. One of the most significant works cites the strengths of black families as "adaptability of family roles, strong kinship bonds, strong work orientation, strong religious orientation, and strong achievement orientation."[22]

Some of the differences in family arrangements between the races have to do with demographic matters, for instance, differences in the number of persons living or available to marry. Thus, for example, higher black than white death rates among men in the prime of life result in twice as large a proportion of black widows to white widows. Also, even talking into consideration at least a 10 percent undercount of young black men by census or *Current Population Survey* interviewers, black Americans' sex ratio (males per 100 females) has been substantially lower than whites' in the ages when people are seeking mates to marry.[23] This leaves more women single.

Economic hardship is stressful, taking its toll on the individual, and, in turn, on the family.[24] Blacks, much more than whites, are likely to endure unemployment, low wages, and dead-end jobs. Their divorce and separation rates are higher, adding to the discrepancy between black and white women managing alone in their own household. Black households' acceptance of others' children to love and nuture, and close bonds among relatives increases the extent to which they include children, with or without a man in the home. A white mother will, more often, place illegitimate children for adoption while she remains under the parental roof, or will choose the route of an abortion, or will marry after pregnancy

20. For a comprehensive review of social understanding on this topic, see Elizabeth Herzog and Cecelia E. Sudia, "Family Structure and Composition," in *Race, Research and Reason: Social Work Perspective* (New York: National Association of Social Workers, 1967), pp. 145–164. See also, by the same authors, "Children in Fatherless Families," *Review of Child Development Research*, vol. 3 (1973), pp. 141–232.

21. U.S. Bureau of the Census, *Current Population Reports, Population Characteristics, Marriage, Divorce, Widowhood, and Remarriage by Family Characteristics*, Ser. P–20, no. 312 (Washington, D.C.: USGPO, 1977) pp. 16–17.

22. Robert B. Hill, *The Strengths of Black Families* (New York: Emerson Hall, 1971), p. 4.

23. U.S. Bureau of the Census, *1970 Census of Population, General Population Characteristics*, table 52.

24. Sar A. Levitan, William B. Johnston, Robert Taggart, *Still A Dream* (Cambridge, Mass.: Harvard University Press, 1975), pp. 121–24.

has occurred. Abortions have increased among blacks, but are still less common among blacks than whites. Black women are less likely to have the funds necessary for an abortion or access to an attending physician. But, on the other hand, they are much more likely to want their babies and to keep them even when they do not want to marry the father. The black family has a place for them in its extended nurturing system.[25] In March 1970, for example, families with a woman as household manager and with no children of her own, were six times as likely to occur in black families than in similar white families.[26] Grandmothers, aunts, cousins, and neighbors help. Many help to bring up related and unrelated children, sometimes because educational facilities are deemed better in the "adopted" home, sometimes because the child's family was having financial or health difficulties, and for many other reasons. This difference between the races in nurturing is great even in husband-wife families, which, while declining, continue to be dominant in black as well as white households.

The phenomenon of the declining husband-wife family among whites as well as blacks, and the women's movement, is creating general acceptance of the woman as household manager, or as "head" of household. Such acceptance has long been true among blacks. Besides, dramatic changes have occurred during this generation in attitudes toward cohabitation without or before marriage, toward permitting unmarried women to adopt children legally, and toward the woman partner assuming an equal managerial position in the husband-wife home. The Bureau of the Census and the Bureau of Labor Statistics have recognized this trend and are preparing new approaches to collecting and presenting family data that reflect it. Janet L. Norwood, Deputy Commissioner of Labor Statistics, recently wrote that "Attitudes toward marriage, childbearing, and toward the position of women in the family have been changing all over the world. . . ," that "The past few decades have seen an upheaval in social patterns," and that "Government statistical agencies have an obligation to ensure that the data they produce reflect the conditions of the times and that the analyses they publish are relevant to contemporary issues."[27]

If some steps had been taken in this direction in *Social Indicators, 1976*, the black family would have looked much more like the white family. Today only 16 percent of all families are the stereotypical model consisting of a husband, a wife who is not in the labor force, and one or more children under 18 years of age.[28] If the reason for not taking such steps was to preserve the consistency of trends over time, anyone reading the report can point to numerous instances in other spheres in which only one or two recent years were used for analysis. Recognition of a change in social attitudes was especially important in this sensitive area in view of the hue and cry in the 1960s about the "crumbling"

25. For a discussion of these points see Hill, *Strengths of Black Families;* idem, *Informal Adoption Among Black Families,* (Washington, D.C.: National Urban League, 1977); Carol B. Stack, *All Our Kin* (New York: Harper & Row), 1974.

26. Hill, *Strengths of Black Families,* table 1, p. 41.

27. Janet L. Norwood, "New Approaches to Statistics On the Family," *Monthly Labor Review,* vol. 100, (July 1977), pp. 31, 33, and 34.

28. *Ibid,* p. 31.

black family.[29] The cries of alarm then were a classic example of cultural lag. They were taking place at the very time coed dorms, "living together", bachelor apartments, and the safety-first of "the pill", among other developments, were prominent in middle-class, white male-female relations.

Ethnicity

The Introduction to *Social Indicators, 1976* is a welcome attempt to address special social issues. It is in the same genre as the editorial, social commentary, and special articles in the United Kingdom's *Social Trends.*[30] The ethnic diversity of immigrants is one of the issues discussed in the Introduction to *Social Indicators, 1976*. It is a subject of great importance in our country which consists of people of many national origins, and commentary on it is a welcome departure from its usual treatment. However, the result is disappointingly narrow in scope and fragmentary. The only blacks involved are those migrating from the Caribbean in this century. The rich source of disaggregated data from censuses since 1820 on the number of blacks, slave and free, are not given,[31] nor are data about blacks coming voluntarily from countries outside the Caribbean, for example, from other parts of the Antilles and from Africa.[32]

The white immigrant groups—those of Spanish origin and the Germans, Irish, Italians, plus the English, Scots, and Welsh—are discussed in terms of immigration streams only since 1891. This ignores not just the heavy immigration of blacks before Emancipation, but the large numbers of Irish and Germans who migrated from the mid-nineteenth century until 1891—especially the Irish from 1847–54 and the Germans from 1852–54 and 1881–88.[33] Except for the first decade of the twentieth century, the rate of United States immigration has never been greater than in the half century 1841–90.[34] The European late comers are compared with "Spanish," meaning—to name a few—those of Mexican, Puerto Rican, Panamanian, Chilean, and Argentinian origin. Few Americans of Spanish origin have come directly from Spain.[35] Asian Americans and native Americans are scarcely discussed in the section on ethnic diversity. The main immigration of

29. The badge of social science was placed on this conception with the release of the report by Daniel P. Moynihan, *The Negro Family: The Case for National Action* (Washington, D.C.: U.S. Department of Labor, Office of Planning Policy and Research, March 1965).

30. United Kingdom, Central Statistical Office, *Social Trends* (London, Her Majesty's Stationery Office, 1975).

31. See especially, U.S. Bureau of the Census, with the cooperation of the Social Science Research Council, *Historical Statistics of the United States: Colonial Times to 1957*, Ser. A95–122 (Washington, D.C.: USGPO Office, 1961), p. 11.

32. Idem, Ser. C88–114, pp. 56–59. See also *Annual Reports of the Immigration and Naturalization Service* and U.S. Bureau of the Census, *Statistical Abstract of the United States, 1975* (Washington, D.C.: USGPO, 1975), table 160, p. 101.

33. U.S. Bureau of the Census, *Historical Statistics*, Ser. C88–114, pp. 56–59.

34. U.S. Bureau of the Census, *Statistical Abstract 1975*, Table 157, p. 99.

35. See chart on cover of U.S. Bureau of the Census, *Current Population Reports, Population Characteristics, Persons of Spanish Origin in the United States: March 1975*, Ser. P–20, no. 290 (Washington, D.C.: USGPO February 1976). The chart shows between six and seven million Mexican-Americans, between one and two million Puerto Ricans, about half a million each of Cubans and Central and South Americans as a group, plus about one million other Americans of Spanish origin.

Japanese and Chinese, the largest of the Asian groups, was in the late nineteenth century and early in the twentieth.[36]

A fascinating set of comparative analyses could be made quite easily using appropriate segments of the Spanish origin population, the European groups, the Asian peoples, native Americans, and black Americans. It would show, referring only to a few available facts, that the Asians are the best educated, have achieved most in job levels and income, and native Americans the least in all these categories. It would show that blacks have more schooling than Mexican-Americans and those of Puerto Rican origin, and that, despite the fact that most blacks have been in the United States over more generations than most people of Mexican or Puerto Rican stock, blacks have not achieved as much occupationally, or in earnings and income. The groups of European origin are in between the Asians and the Mexican, Puerto Rican, blacks, and native Americans. Their occupational distribution, for instance, is very like the average for the nation, whereas the Japanese and Chinese show the largest proportion as professionals and managers and the lowest in unskilled low paid work. Blacks are close to the other end of the spectrum.[37]

36. U.S. Bureau of the Census, *Historical Statistics*, Ser. C88–114, pp. 56–59.

37. U.S. Bureau of the Census, *1970 Census of Population, Subject Reports, Negro Population*: PC(2)–1B; *American Indians*: PC(2)–1F; and *Japanese, Chinese, and Filipinos*: PC(2)–1C (Washington, D.C.: USGPO, 1973). See also U.S. Bureau of the Census, *Current Population Reports, Population Characteristics, Characteristics of the Population by Ethnic Origin: March 1972 and 1971*, Ser. P–20, no. 24g (Washington, D.C.: USGPO, 1973). See also Newman and Carter, *Protest, Politics, and Prosperity*, Chap. 3, figure 1.

Blacks are the largest group after those originating in the British Isles and Germany. They are almost three times as numerous as Italians, comprise four times the number of Mexican Americans, and twenty times the number of Puerto Ricans. Blacks were counted in all the population censuses, in some of them, even to the point of describing their complexions—mulatto or octaroon.[38] But blacks could not be naturalized Americans until passage of the 14th and 15th Amendments. As one authority wrote "In 1870 in consequence of the changed status of Negroes, eligibility to naturalization was extended to aliens of African nativity or persons of African descent."[39] Here was a unique opportunity to add a stimulating dimension to the Social Indicators and an unusual analysis to the status of black Americans in the context of our ethnic diversity.

ASSESSMENT

In part because *Social Indicators, 1976* does not include a chapter on blacks, a publication devoted to indicators of social change fails to address one of the most crisis-laden issues of our times. The authors could argue that enough is included with which to formulate conclusions and analyze a number of issues in the broad area of race relations. The data are many and varied, but the traditional manner in which they are structured has left them well behind current knowledge.

What is of even greater concern is the dearth of information about discrimination and efforts to reduce it. There is nothing that reveals

38. See, for example, the 1860 census of population.

39. Maurice R. Davie, *World Immigration* (New York: Macmillan, 1936), p. 80.

prejudice in the housing market, including redlining, blockbusting, and the differential price and cost of housing for blacks and whites; about the changing extent of school desegregation and the significance of school resegregation; about the pace of civil rights enforcement in employment, in financial institutions, and in educational organizations. These are indicators of "system performance," which are said to have been included among the broad types of indicators considered for the report. Many can be derived from administrative statistics like those used in presenting information about social security and unemployment insurance.

The tables and charts in *Social Indicators, 1976* reveal the often told story about "how far they have come." They quantify the most usually presented gaps between black and white. They do not fulfill, in the field of social indicators about black Americans, the hope expressed by Natalie Rogoff Ramsøy, in her critique of *Social Indicators, 1973*, that the next report might "give a . . . more connected picture of the way things work in American society."[40] Even though interpretation was to be left to others, value judgments had to be made in selecting and combining the data that appear. It is impossible to approach an undertaking such as a social indicators report without such judgments. In the sphere of race relations the judgments are old fashioned, peripheral to many of the main issues, and lacking in courage and commitment. They are not sufficient for a social document for our country in our time.

At the root of blacks' disfavored position is a combination of interacting forces in the society. These include the cumulative effects on American institutions of generations of blatantly overt racial discrimination in every area of life; the continuing subtle practices of racial and economic discrimination; and the absence of a national will or commitment to undertake those pragmatic political, social, and economic policies necessary to erase discrimination, and to enforce those policies forthrightly.[41] The necessary policies include ensuring the franchise, the right to a home of one's choice, a full employment program, and equal educational and job opportunity.[42] Such policies and the commitment to enforce them are necessary if blacks are not to continue to be unduly disadvantaged by our traditional systems of privilege. Affirmative action is one of those pragmatic policies needed to erase subtle forms of discrimination, but, still in the late 1970s, it has been the subject of wide-ranging attacks to discredit it.[43]

The most vocal and influential thrust against affirmative action has come from colleges and universities—our institutions of higher

40. Natalie Rogoff Ramsøy, "Social Indicators in the United States and Europe: Comments on Five Country Reports," in *Social Indicators, 1973: A Review Symposium*, ed. Roxann A. Van Dusen (Washington, D.C.: Social Science Research Council, 1974), p. 48.

41. U.S. Commission on Civil Rights, *The Federal Civil Rights Enforcement Effort, 1974: Volume VII: To Preserve, Protect and Defend the Constitution* (1977) and Newman and Carter, *Protest, Politics and Prosperity*.

42. U.S. Commission On Civil Rights, *The Unfinished Business Twenty Years Later* (September, 1977). This report summarizes civil rights issues in each of the 50 states and the District of Columbia. Also see *Protest, Politics and Prosperity*.

43. *The Urban League Review*, vol. 2, no. 2 (Summer 1977). This was a special issue devoted to affirmative action.

learning. These institutions have long perpetuated more "acceptable" and traditional forms of affirmative action such as the "old buddy" system of hiring and recruitment; maintaining geographic distribution of the student body by waiving certain scholastic requirements for students coming from underrepresented areas; admitting athletes without the usual scholastic qualifications, and favoring the sons and daughters of alumni. But efforts made to incorporate race and sex within the traditionally accepted systems of privilege have been met with outrage and charges of reverse discrimination. And because the university elite, with its special power of the pen and access to wide segments of the population is so influential, the issue has generated controversy and debate out of all proportion to the reaction when private industry was the special target. Of great significance is the pending United States Supreme Court case of Allan Bakke, a University of California medical school applicant who, white and male, has charged reverse discrimination on the grounds that although he presented high grades and test scores, he was denied admission while 16 of 100 openings were filled by minorities. The Court's decision will have a great impact on efforts to implement policies and practices to ensure equal opportunities and life chances for minorities and women.

Now that most widespread practices of overt racial discrimination have been eliminated as a result of the 1960s protest actions that generated greater protection of the rights of all minorities and disadvantaged groups, it has become increasingly difficult for the white majority to accept the reality that racial discrimination exists and influences American society. The situation is exacerbated by the different way minorities and the white majority define the presence or absence of discrimination. Minorities define discrimination in terms of its consequences or effects. The white majority perceives it largely in terms of the intent of both our institutional practices and consequences. This crucial difference in definition is evident in a recent Supreme Court ruling on job seniority systems. In the spring of 1977 the court ruled that seniority systems that perpetuate the effect of past discrimination in hiring or promotion are not unconstitutional unless the systems were created for discriminatory purposes.[44] While the full impact of this decision is still being debated by attorneys, civil rights advocates, and policymakers, the ruling itself reflects a serious dilemma. Until we accept and act upon the fact that racial discrimination exists and is not likely to disappear voluntarily, the opportunities and life chances will continue to be less for blacks and those others who are likewise disadvantaged, than for the privileged in the society.

Those who have the personal power to discriminate, however subtly, or by whatever outside institutional means, are not easily persuaded to alter the practices that have prejudicial results. It is essential that we the people become aware of the negative consequences of policies that are presumably neutral, but disproportionately harm black Americans. These are policies, for instance, that perpetuate less than full employment as a national goal, that call for the armed forces

44. *International Brotherhood of Teamsters*, v. *U.S. et al.*, 97 S. Ct. 1843 (1977).

to reduce recruitment efforts in central cities, or that effectively kill legal and administrative efforts to make our educational institutions more accessible to blacks. To advocate and support ostensibly neutral policies that have clearly negative racial consequences is discriminatory; it insures blacks' continued disadvantaged status. And so the trends that identify blacks' social and economic status will be repeated year after year, not because blacks cannot achieve more, but because we as a people are geared to thwarting that achievement. Hopefully we are maturing as a nation, so that *Social Indicators, 1979* will analyze what is going on in race relations in the society—how and why. Hopefully, also, that maturity will yield more salutory results.

Table 8/5
CIVILIAN LABOR FORCE PARTICIPATION OF PERSONS 16 YEARS OLD AND OVER, BY AGE, SEX, AND RACE: 1948–1976
(Percent of the civilian noninstitutional population in the civilian labor force; annual averages)

Race, sex, and year	Total, 16 years and over	16 and 17 years	18 and 19 years	20 to 24 years	25 to 34 years	35 to 44 years	45 to 54 years	55 to 64 years	65 years and over	14 and 15 years
WHITE										
Male										
1948	86.5	51.2	76.2	84.4	96.0	98.0	95.9	89.6	46.5	26.1
1949	86.4	50.1	74.8	86.5	95.9	98.0	95.6	87.6	46.6	26.3
1950	86.4	50.5	75.6	87.5	96.4	97.7	95.9	87.3	45.8	27.6
1951	86.5	52.7	74.2	88.4	97.0	97.6	96.0	87.4	44.5	26.9
1952	86.2	51.9	72.7	87.6	97.6	97.9	96.3	87.7	42.5	25.3
1953	86.1	49.8	72.8	87.4	97.5	97.9	96.4	87.7	41.3	23.6
1954	85.6	47.1	70.4	86.4	97.5	98.2	96.8	89.2	40.4	24.5
1955	85.4	48.0	71.7	85.6	97.8	98.3	96.7	88.4	39.5	23.5
1956	85.6	51.3	71.9	87.6	97.4	98.1	96.8	88.9	40.0	26.7
1957	84.8	49.6	71.6	86.7	97.2	98.0	96.6	88.0	37.7	25.1
1958	84.3	46.8	69.4	86.7	97.2	98.0	96.6	88.2	35.7	24.1
1959	83.8	45.4	70.3	87.3	97.5	98.0	96.3	87.9	34.3	24.2
1960	83.4	46.0	69.0	87.8	97.7	97.9	96.1	87.2	33.3	22.2
1961	83.0	44.3	66.2	87.6	97.7	97.9	95.9	87.8	31.9	22.2
1962	82.1	42.9	66.4	86.5	97.4	97.9	96.0	86.7	30.6	22.3
1963	81.5	42.4	67.8	85.8	97.4	97.8	96.2	86.6	28.4	21.4
1964	81.1	43.5	66.6	85.7	97.5	97.6	96.1	86.1	27.9	21.2
1965	80.8	44.6	65.8	85.3	97.4	97.7	95.9	85.2	27.9	21.7
1966	80.6	47.1	65.4	84.4	97.5	97.6	95.8	84.9	27.2	22.3
1967	80.7	47.9	66.1	84.0	97.5	97.7	95.6	84.9	27.1	22.6
1968	80.4	47.7	65.7	82.4	97.2	97.6	95.4	84.7	27.3	22.7
1969	80.2	48.8	66.3	82.6	97.0	97.4	95.1	83.9	27.3	23.0
1970	80.0	48.9	67.4	83.3	96.7	97.3	94.9	83.3	26.7	23.0
1971	79.6	49.2	67.8	83.2	96.3	97.0	94.7	82.6	25.6	23.7
1972	79.6	50.2	71.1	84.3	96.0	97.0	94.0	81.2	24.4	23.5
1973	79.5	52.7	72.3	85.8	96.3	96.8	93.5	79.0	22.8	24.4
1974	79.4	53.3	73.6	86.5	96.3	96.7	93.0	78.1	22.5	24.4
1975	78.7	51.8	72.8	85.5	95.8	96.4	92.9	76.5	21.8	23.1
1976	78.4	51.8	73.5	86.2	95.9	96.0	92.5	75.4	20.3	(NA)
Female										
1948	31.3	31.7	53.5	45.1	31.3	35.1	33.3	23.3	8.6	11.1
1949	31.8	31.4	54.0	44.4	31.7	36.1	34.3	24.2	9.1	10.3
1950	32.6	30.1	52.6	45.9	32.1	37.2	36.3	26.0	9.2	11.5
1951	33.4	32.4	54.1	46.7	33.6	38.0	38.0	26.5	8.5	11.2
1952	33.6	34.1	52.0	44.8	33.8	38.9	38.8	27.6	8.7	10.2
1953	33.4	31.2	51.9	44.1	31.7	38.8	38.7	28.5	9.4	9.9
1954	33.3	29.3	52.1	44.4	32.5	39.4	39.8	29.1	9.1	10.5
1955	34.5	29.9	52.0	45.8	32.8	39.9	42.7	31.8	10.5	11.2
1956	35.7	33.5	53.0	46.5	33.2	41.5	44.4	34.0	10.6	12.7
1957	35.7	32.1	52.6	45.8	33.6	41.5	45.4	33.7	10.2	12.5
1958	35.8	28.8	52.3	46.1	33.6	41.4	46.5	34.5	10.1	12.2
1959	36.0	29.9	50.8	44.5	33.4	41.4	47.8	35.7	10.2	13.0
1960	36.5	30.0	51.9	45.7	34.1	41.5	48.6	36.2	10.6	12.5
1961	36.9	29.4	51.9	46.9	34.3	41.8	48.9	37.2	10.5	13.5
1962	36.7	27.9	51.6	47.1	34.1	42.2	48.9	38.0	9.8	13.7

Table 8/5 (*Continued*)

CIVILIAN LABOR FORCE PARTICIPATION OF PERSONS 16 YEARS OLD AND OVER, BY AGE, SEX, AND RACE: 1948–1976—*Continued*

(Percent of the civilian noninstitutional population in the civilian labor force; annual averages)

Race, sex, and year	Total, 16 years and over	16 and 17 years	18 and 19 years	20 to 24 years	25 to 34 years	35 to 44 years	45 to 54 years	55 to 64 years	65 years and over	14 and 15 years
1963	37.2	27.9	51.3	47.3	34.8	43.1	49.5	38.9	9.4	12.2
1964	37.5	28.5	49.6	48.8	35.0	43.3	50.2	39.4	9.9	12.7
1965	38.1	28.7	50.6	49.2	36.3	44.3	49.9	40.3	9.7	12.9
1966	39.2	31.8	53.1	51.0	37.7	45.0	50.6	41.1	9.4	14.5
1967	40.1	32.3	52.7	53.1	39.7	46.4	50.9	41.9	9.3	15.4
1968	40.7	33.0	53.3	54.0	40.6	47.5	51.5	42.0	9.4	16.0
1969	41.8	35.2	54.6	56.4	41.7	48.6	53.0	42.6	9.7	16.1
1970	42.6	36.6	55.0	57.7	43.2	49.9	53.7	42.6	9.5	17.3
1971	42.6	36.4	55.0	57.9	43.6	50.2	53.7	42.5	9.3	17.2
1972	43.2	39.3	57.4	59.4	45.8	50.7	53.4	42.0	9.0	17.7
1973	44.1	41.7	58.9	61.6	48.5	52.2	53.4	40.8	8.7	18.9
1974	45.2	43.3	60.4	63.8	51.1	53.7	54.3	40.4	8.0	18.9
1975	45.9	42.7	60.4	65.4	53.5	54.9	54.3	40.7	8.0	18.4
1976	46.9	43.8	61.8	66.2	55.8	57.1	54.7	40.8	8.0	(NA)
BLACK AND OTHER RACES										
Male										
1948	87.3	59.8	77.8	85.6	95.3	97.2	94.7	88.6	50.3	39.3
1949	87.0	60.4	80.8	89.7	94.1	97.3	95.6	86.0	51.4	36.6
1950	85.9	57.4	78.2	91.4	92.6	96.2	95.1	81.9	45.5	37.7
1951	86.3	54.7	80.8	88.7	95.7	96.4	95.1	84.6	49.5	34.6
1952	86.8	52.3	79.1	92.8	96.2	97.2	95.0	85.7	43.3	30.5
1953	86.2	53.0	76.7	92.3	96.7	97.3	93.9	86.7	41.1	27.8
1954	85.2	46.7	78.4	91.1	96.2	96.6	93.2	83.0	41.2	27.2
1955	85.0	48.2	75.7	89.7	95.8	96.2	94.2	83.1	40.0	27.1
1956	85.1	49.6	76.4	88.9	96.2	96.2	94.4	83.9	39.8	25.5
1957	84.3	47.5	72.0	89.6	96.1	96.5	93.5	82.4	35.9	24.7
1958	84.0	45.1	71.7	88.7	96.3	96.4	93.9	83.3	34.5	21.3
1959	83.4	41.7	72.0	90.8	96.3	95.8	92.8	82.5	33.5	23.9
1960	83.0	45.6	71.2	90.4	96.2	95.5	92.3	82.5	31.2	23.3
1961	82.2	42.5	70.5	89.7	95.9	94.8	92.3	81.6	29.4	19.2
1962	80.8	40.2	68.8	89.3	95.3	94.5	92.2	81.5	27.2	16.5
1963	80.2	37.2	69.1	88.6	94.9	94.9	91.1	82.5	27.6	17.2
1964	80.0	37.3	67.2	89.4	95.9	94.4	91.6	80.6	29.6	18.7
1965	79.6	39.3	66.7	89.8	95.7	94.2	92.0	78.8	27.9	18.9
1966	79.0	41.1	63.7	89.9	95.5	91.1	90.7	81.1	25.6	17.3
1967	78.5	41.2	62.7	87.2	95.5	93.6	91.3	79.3	27.2	18.3
1968	77.6	37.9	63.3	85.0	95.0	93.4	90.1	79.6	26.6	18.1
1969	76.9	37.7	63.2	84.4	94.4	92.7	89.5	77.9	26.1	15.8
1970	76.5	34.8	61.8	83.5	93.7	93.2	88.2	79.2	27.4	16.6
1971	74.9	32.4	58.9	81.5	92.9	92.0	86.9	77.8	24.5	15.2
1972	73.7	34.1	60.1	81.5	92.7	91.4	86.1	73.6	23.6	14.7
1973	73.8	33.4	61.4	81.8	91.7	91.3	88.0	70.7	22.6	13.5
1974	73.3	34.6	62.4	82.1	92.3	90.9	84.7	70.2	21.7	14.8
1975	71.5	30.1	57.5	78.4	91.4	90.0	84.6	68.7	20.9	12.8
1976	70.7	30.2	55.6	78.4	90.6	90.6	83.4	65.7	19.7	(NA)

Table 8/5 (*Continued*)

CIVILIAN LABOR FORCE PARTICIPATION OF PERSONS 16 YEARS OLD AND OVER, BY AGE, SEX, AND RACE: 1948–1976—*Continued*

(Percent of the civilian noninstitutional population in the civilian labor force; annual averages)

Race, sex, and year	Total, 16 years and over	16 and 17 years	18 and 19 years	20 to 24 years	25 to 34 years	35 to 44 years	45 to 54 years	55 to 64 years	65 years and over	14 and 15 years
Female										
1948	45.6	29.1	41.2	47.1	50.6	53.3	51.1	37.6	17.5	21.0
1949	46.9	30.1	44.8	49.8	50.9	56.1	52.7	39.6	15.6	23.5
1950	46.9	30.2	40.6	46.9	51.6	55.7	54.3	40.9	16.5	22.0
1951	46.3	30.4	40.2	45.4	51.1	55.8	55.5	39.8	14.0	17.3
1952	45.5	27.4	44.7	43.9	50.1	54.0	52.7	42.3	14.3	18.5
1953	43.6	24.2	37.8	45.1	48.1	54.9	51.0	35.9	11.4	14.9
1954	46.1	24.5	37.7	49.6	49.7	57.5	53.4	41.2	12.2	16.2
1955	46.1	22.7	43.2	46.7	51.3	56.0	54.8	40.7	12.1	11.4
1956	47.3	28.3	44.6	44.9	52.1	57.0	55.3	44.5	14.5	14.4
1957	47.2	24.1	42.8	46.6	50.4	58.7	56.8	44.3	13.6	12.6
1958	48.0	23.2	41.2	48.3	50.8	60.8	59.8	42.8	13.3	11.6
1959	47.7	20.7	36.1	48.8	50.0	60.0	60.0	46.4	12.6	12.6
1960	48.2	22.1	44.3	48.8	49.7	59.8	60.5	47.3	12.8	13.2
1961	48.3	21.6	44.6	47.7	51.2	60.5	61.1	45.2	13.1	11.0
1962	48.0	21.0	45.5	48.6	52.0	59.7	60.5	46.1	12.2	9.7
1963	48.1	21.5	44.9	49.2	53.3	59.4	60.6	47.3	11.8	8.7
1964	48.5	19.5	46.5	53.6	52.8	58.4	62.3	48.4	12.7	8.0
1965	48.6	20.5	40.0	55.2	54.0	59.9	60.2	48.9	12.9	8.1
1966	49.3	23.6	44.0	54.5	54.9	60.9	61.0	49.1	13.0	7.5
1967	49.5	22.8	48.7	54.9	57.5	60.8	59.6	47.1	13.0	9.4
1968	49.3	23.3	46.9	58.4	56.6	59.3	59.8	47.0	11.9	7.2
1969	49.8	24.4	45.4	58.6	57.8	59.5	60.8	47.5	11.9	7.1
1970	49.5	24.3	44.7	57.7	57.6	59.9	60.2	47.1	12.2	9.7
1971	49.2	21.9	41.4	56.0	59.2	61.0	59.4	47.1	11.5	8.3
1972	48.7	21.4	43.9	56.7	60.1	60.7	57.3	43.9	12.8	9.3
1973	49.1	24.3	45.1	57.5	61.0	60.7	56.4	44.7	11.1	7.4
1974	49.1	24.2	44.6	58.2	60.8	61.5	56.9	43.5	10.0	9.1
1975	49.2	26.5	45.1	56.2	61.4	61.7	56.8	43.8	10.5	8.5
1976	50.2	23.9	43.3	57.9	65.3	62.2	57.3	43.4	11.2	(NA)

Source: U.S. Department of Labor, *Employment and Training Report of the President, 1976*.

NA Not available.

Chart 8/5 Social Indicators, 1976

RATES OF ECONOMIC ACTIVITY FOR PERSONS 16 YEARS AND OVER, BY COLOR AND SEX: ANNUAL AVERAGES, 1948–1975

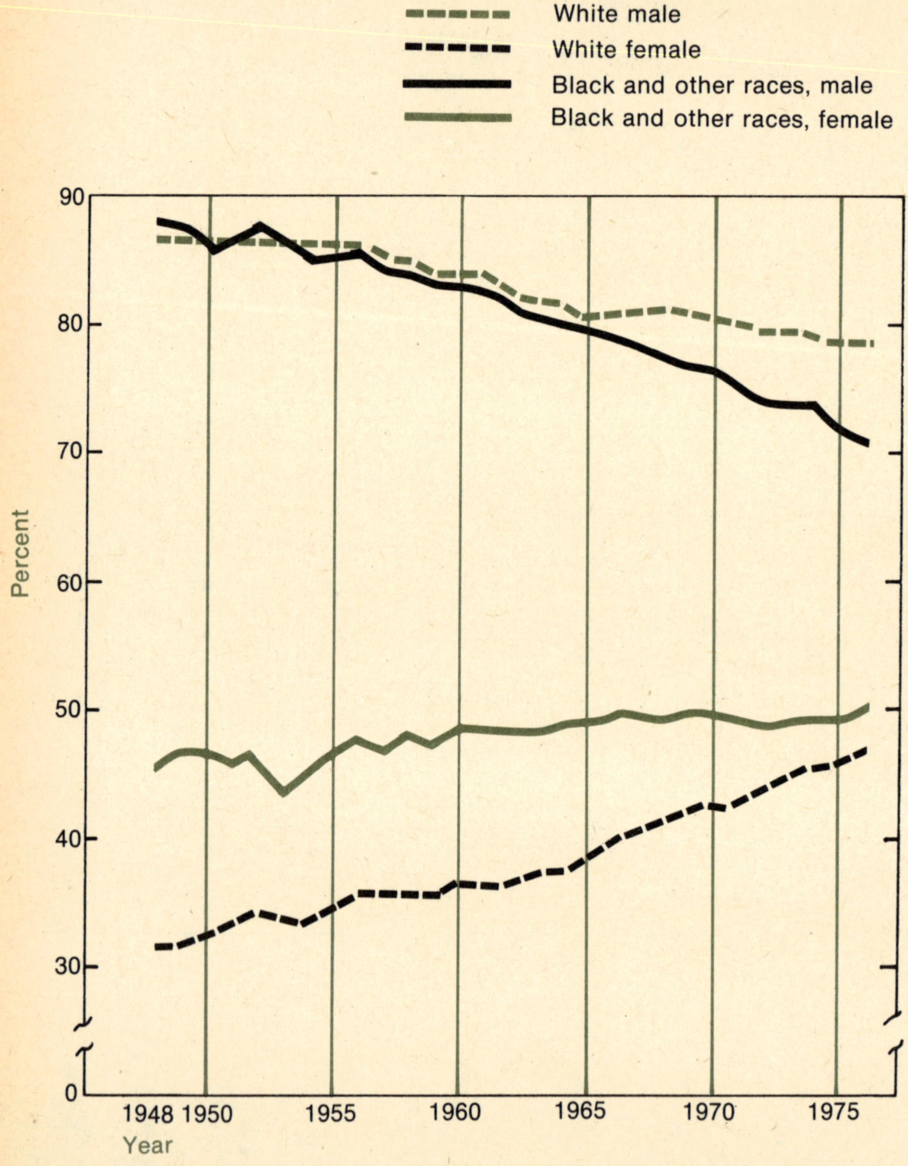

Source: see table 8/5

Table 9/6

TOTAL FAMILY INCOME, BY RACE OF FAMILY HEAD: 1947–1974

(1974 constant dollars)

Family income and race of family head	1947	1950	1955	1960	1964	1965
ALL RACES						
Number of families. . . .thous.	37,237	39,929	42,889	[r]45,539	[r]47,956	[r]48,509
Percent	100.0	100.0	100.0	100.0	100.0	100.0
Under $3,000	16.7	17.4	14.1	11.5	8.8	8.4
$3,000 to $4,999	17.1	15.4	11.5	10.3	10.1	9.3
$5,000 to $6,999	22.8	19.8	14.9	12.0	10.9	10.1
$7,000 to $9,999	19.6	23.1	24.5	21.2	17.9	17.3
$10,000 to $11,999			13.5	14.6	12.2	12.3
$12,000 to $14,999	23.7	24.4	9.7	11.6	14.4	15.0
$15,000 and over			11.9	18.8	25.8	27.6
Median income	6,691	6,800	8,137	9,358	10,444	10,874
WHITE						
Number of families. . . .thous.	34,120	(NA)	38,982	41,123	43,081	43,497
Percent	100.0	100.0	100.0	100.0	100.0	100.0
Under $3,000	14.2	15.3	12.1	9.6	7.5	7.2
$3,000 to $4,999	16.3	14.5	10.7	9.5	9.0	8.2
$5,000 to $6,999	23.6	19.8	14.5	11.6	10.2	9.3
$7,000 to $9,999	20.6	24.3	25.3	21.6	17.9	17.2
$10,000 to $11,999			14.2	15.4	12.6	12.7
$12,000 to $14,999	25.2	26.1	10.3	12.2	15.2	15.8
$15,000 and over			12.9	20.1	27.6	29.5
Median income	6,970	7,057	8,495	9,716	10,903	11,334
BLACK AND OTHER RACES						
Number of families. . . .thous.	3,117	(NA)	3,907	4,333	4,754	4,782
Percent	100.0	100.0	100.0	100.0	100.0	100.0
Under $3,000	42.5	39.8	33.5	28.9	20.5	19.7
$3,000 to $4,999	26.0	25.4	19.6	17.7	19.6	18.9
$5,000 to $6,999	14.8	19.4	19.0	16.3	17.1	17.3
$7,000 to $9,999	8.8	9.7	16.6	16.9	17.5	17.6
$10,000 to $11,999			6.5	8.1	8.1	8.5
$12,000 to $14,999	7.9	5.7	3.1	5.6	7.4	7.9
$15,000 and over			1.7	6.6	9.8	10.2
Median income	3,563	3,828	4,685	5,379	6,102	6,242

Table 9/6 (*Continued*)

1966	1967	1968	1969	1970	1971	1972	1973	1974
[r]49,214	[r]50,111	[r]50,823	[r]51,586	[r]52,227	53,296	54,373	55,053	55,712
100.0	100.0	100.0	100.0	100.0	100.0	100.0	100.0	100.0
7.0	6.7	5.9	5.9	6.1	5.9	5.4	5.1	5.3
8.7	8.4	7.7	7.3	7.5	7.8	7.7	7.5	7.8
9.2	8.8	8.5	8.2	8.7	9.1	8.3	8.3	8.9
16.6	16.0	15.3	14.4	14.3	14.5	13.8	13.3	13.8
12.0	11.8	11.6	10.8	10.8	10.1	9.7	9.7	10.2
15.3	15.5	15.7	15.8	15.2	15.4	14.7	14.4	14.1
31.1	32.7	35.4	37.7	37.4	37.2	40.5	41.7	39.8
11,445	11,717	12,236	12,689	12,531	12,523	13,013	13,375	12,836
44,110	44,814	45,437	46,022	46,535	47,641	48,477	48,919	49,451
100.0	100.0	100.0	100.0	100.0	100.0	100.0	100.0	100.0
5.8	5.8	5.0	5.0	5.1	4.9	4.4	4.1	4.3
7.7	7.4	6.9	6.5	6.7	6.9	6.7	6.6	6.8
8.5	8.2	7.8	7.5	8.1	8.6	7.7	7.7	8.4
16.4	15.7	15.0	13.9	13.9	14.1	13.5	12.9	13.5
12.3	12.1	11.8	10.9	11.0	10.3	9.8	9.8	10.5
16.0	16.1	16.2	16.3	15.7	16.0	15.2	14.8	14.6
33.2	34.7	37.3	39.9	39.4	39.2	42.7	44.2	42.0
11,890	12,162	12,668	13,175	13,000	12,995	13,614	13,977	13,356
4,954	5,020	5,074	5,215	5,413	5,655	5,896	6,134	6,262
100.0	100.0	100.0	100.0	100.0	100.0	100.0	100.0	100.0
16.9	15.0	14.0	13.9	14.5	14.2	13.5	13.3	13.5
17.4	17.6	15.7	14.1	14.0	14.9	15.7	15.1	16.0
15.3	14.2	14.7	13.7	13.6	14.1	13.2	13.2	13.1
18.5	18.5	17.4	18.5	17.6	17.6	16.1	16.5	16.1
9.5	9.5	9.6	9.6	9.3	8.6	8.8	9.2	8.3
9.6	9.9	10.6	11.6	11.0	10.9	10.5	10.8	10.7
12.9	15.3	18.1	18.6	19.9	19.9	22.2	22.0	22.3
7,128	7,524	7,924	8,328	8,275	8,175	8,376	8,429	8,265

Source: U.S. Department of Commerce, Bureau of the Census, *Current Population Reports*, Series P-60, No. 101.

[r] Revised from earlier published data to reflect population controls based on the 1970 census. Population controls based on the 1970 census not available by race.

NA Not available.

Chart 9/6

Social Indicators, 1976

PERCENT OF FAMILIES WITH TOTAL MONEY INCOME UNDER $3,000 AND OVER $15,000, BY RACE OF HEAD, 1960–1974

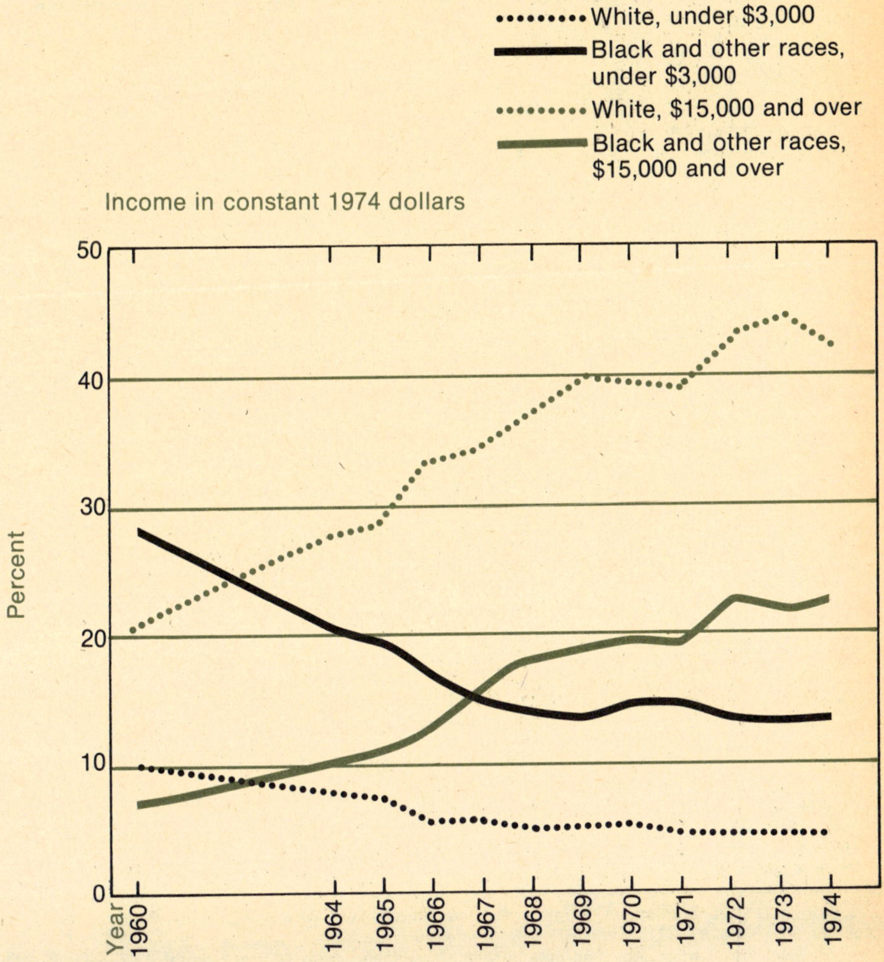

Source: see table 9/6

Table 9/9
FAMILIES RECEIVING INCOME, BY SOURCE AND BY RACE OF FAMILY HEAD: 1967–1974
(Current dollars)

Source of income and race of family head	1967	1968	1969	1970	1971	1972	1973	1974
ALL RACES								
Number of familes, thousands	r50,111	r50,823	r51,586	r52,227	53,296	54,373	55,053	55,712
Percent[1]	100.0	100.0	100.0	100.0	100.0	100.0	100.0	100.0
Wage or salary income	85.6	85.9	85.8	85.3	85.4	85.1	84.9	84.4
Nonfarm self-employment income	11.8	12.2	12.1	12.2	12.1	12.1	11.9	11.7
Farm self-employment income	5.9	5.9	5.5	5.2	5.1	5.1	5.0	4.6
Income other than earnings[1]	53.6	59.3	61.4	64.1	64.6	66.1	66.6	71.8
Social Security	19.4	19.2	19.3	19.8	19.9	20.6	21.6	21.8
Dividends	32.4	39.2	41.4	41.6	41.4	43.9	44.1	48.9
Public assistance	4.2	4.9	5.0	6.0	6.6	6.7	16.5	7.8
Unemployment	11.3	12.7	13.8	16.3	17.0	16.2	15.4	18.5
Private pensions	6.8	8.9	9.9	9.4	9.6	10.4	10.7	11.8
WHITE								
Number of familes, thousands	44,814	45,437	46,022	46,535	47,641	48,477	48,919	49,451
Percent[1]	100.0	100.0	100.0	100.0	100.0	100.0	100.0	100.0
Wage or salary income	85.9	86.3	86.2	85.7	85.5	85.3	85.1	84.6
Nonfarm self-employment income	12.5	12.8	12.8	13.0	12.7	12.8	12.6	12.6
Farm self-employment income	6.2	6.3	5.9	5.6	5.4	5.5	5.4	5.0
Income other than earnings[1]	54.8	60.9	62.9	65.5	65.6	67.1	67.5	73.2
Social Security income	19.7	19.6	19.7	20.0	20.1	20.8	21.7	22.0
Dividends	35.0	42.2	44.7	45.1	44.8	47.4	47.7	52.8
Public assistance	3.0	3.4	3.6	4.3	4.5	4.6	4.4	5.7
Unemployment	11.5	13.0	14.0	16.6	17.4	16.7	15.8	19.0
Private pensions	7.0	9.2	10.2	9.8	9.9	10.7	11.2	12.3
BLACK AND OTHER RACES								
Number of families, thousands	5,020	5,074	5,215	5,413	5,655	5,896	6,134	6,262
Percent[1]	100.0	100.0	100.0	100.0	100.0	100.0	100.0	100.0
Wage or salary income	87.4	87.5	88.1	86.3	84.6	83.1	83.7	83.0
Nonfarm self-employment income	6.9	6.8	6.6	6.3	6.7	6.0	15.3	5.3
Farm self-employment income	3.3	3.2	2.2	2.0	1.9	1.5	1.7	1.5
Income other than earnings[1]	45.5	49.1	51.6	55.0	56.1	57.6	58.8	61.2
Social Security income	17.0	16.9	17.2	18.9	17.9	18.8	20.5	20.2
Dividends	11.1	14.2	14.7	14.0	13.1	15.4	15.1	18.4
Public assistance	15.8	18.4	18.1	20.6	23.9	23.8	23.4	24.8
Unemployment	10.0	10.4	12.4	14.5	13.8	12.6	12.4	14.5
Private pensions	5.5	7.2	8.4	6.7	7.5	7.6	7.1	8.2

Source: U.S. Department of Commerce, Bureau of the Census, *Current Population Reports*, Series P-60, Nos. 59, 66, 75, 80, 85, 90, 97, and 101.

r Revised from earlier published data to reflect population controls based on the 1970 census. Population controls based on 1970 census not available by race.

[1] Detail does not add to total because some families have more than one of the types of income specified and some families have no income.

Chart 9/9 Social Indicators, 1976

PERCENT OF FAMILIES RECEIVING INCOME OF SPECIFIED TYPE BY RACE OF HEAD: 1967 AND 1974

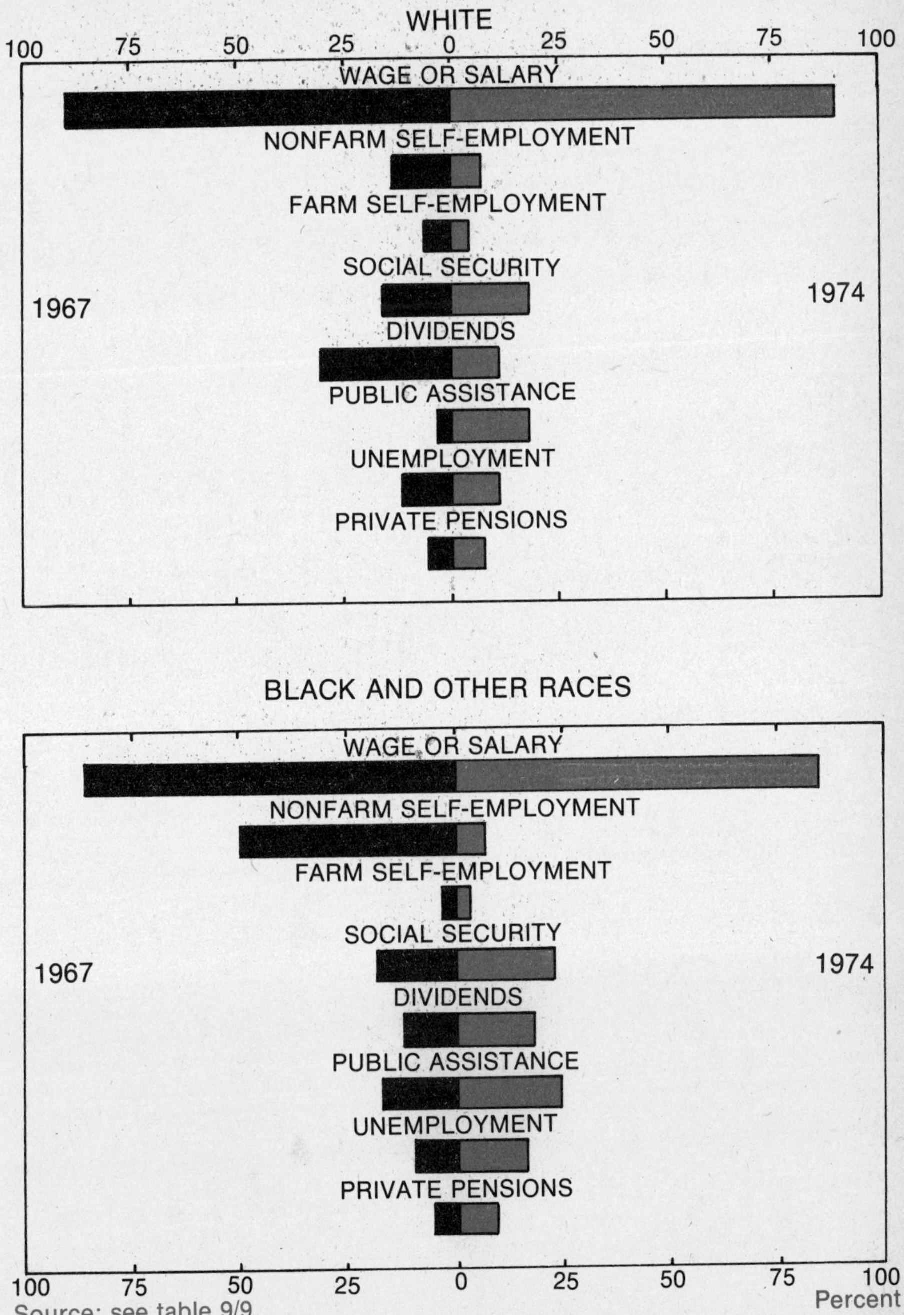

Source: see table 9/9

Table 9/10
AGGREGATE FAMILY INCOME, BY SOURCE: 1967–1974
(Current dollars)

TYPE OF INCOME AND RACE OF HEAD	1967	1968	1969	1970	1971	1972	1973	1974
ALL RACES								
Aggregate income. . .mil. dol.	438,575	488,411	541,915	576,915	617,339	686,442	749,922	807,935
Percent	100.0	100.0	100.0	100.0	100.0	100.0	100.0	100.0
Earnings	90.4	89.5	89.1	88.6	87.9	87.6	87.1	86.1
Wage or salary income	80.8	79.7	80.2	80.1	79.1	78.8	78.3	78.2
Nonfarm self-employment income	8.0	8.3	7.5	7.2	7.5	7.4	6.9	6.4
Farm self-employment income	1.7	1.5	1.5	1.3	1.3	1.5	1.9	1.4
Income other than earnings	9.6	10.5	10.9	11.4	12.1	12.4	12.9	13.9
Social Security income	3.3	3.2	3.0	3.3	3.7	3.9	4.3	4.6
Public assistance income	.6	.7	.7	.9	.9	.9	.9	1.0
All other unearned income	5.7	6.5	7.2	7.2	7.5	7.6	7.7	8.3
WHITE								
Aggregate income. . .mil. dol.	408,528	454,472	504,080	534,914	571,529	635,335	692,838	744,089
Percent	100.0	100.0	100.0	100.0	100.0	100.0	100.0	100.0
Earnings	90.5	89.6	89.1	88.7	88.1	87.7	87.2	86.2
Wage or salary income	80.5	79.4	79.8	79.8	78.9	78.5	77.9	78.0
Nonfarm self-employment income	8.2	8.6	7.8	7.5	7.8	7.7	7.2	6.7
Farm self-employment income	1.7	1.6	1.5	1.4	1.4	1.6	2.0	1.5
Income other than earnings	9.5	10.4	10.9	11.3	11.9	12.3	12.8	13.8
Social Security income	3.2	3.2	3.0	3.3	3.7	3.9	4.3	4.5
Public assistance income	.4	.4	.5	.6	.6	.6	.5	.7
All other unearned income	5.9	6.7	7.4	7.4	7.7	7.8	8.0	8.6
BLACK AND OTHER RACES								
Aggregate income. . .mil. dol.	30,047	33,939	37,835	42,001	45,810	51,107	57,084	63,822
Percent	100.0	100.0	100.0	100.0	100.0	100.0	100.0	100.0
Earnings	89.3	88.6	88.9	87.8	86.2	86.3	86.0	85.0
Wage or salary income	84.4	83.9	84.8	84.1	81.9	82.5	82.9	81.4
Nonfarm self-employment income	4.2	4.0	3.6	3.5	4.1	3.7	2.8	3.3
Farm self-employment income	.7	.6	.5	.2	.3	.2	.2	.3
Income other than earnings	10.7	11.4	11.1	12.2	13.8	13.7	14.0	15.0
Social Security income	3.5	3.4	3.0	3.6	3.9	4.3	4.7	4.9
Public assistance income	3.7	4.2	3.9	4.4	5.3	5.2	5.0	5.1
All other unearned income	3.6	3.8	4.2	4.3	4.6	4.2	4.3	5.0

Source: U.S. Department of Commerce, Bureau of the Census, *Current Population Reports*, Series P-60, Nos. 59, 66, 75, 80, 85, 90, 97, and 101.

Chart 9/10B

Social Indicators, 1976

PERCENT OF AGGREGATE INCOME OF FAMILIES, BY RACE, FROM SOURCES OTHER THAN WAGES AND SALARIES, 1967–1974

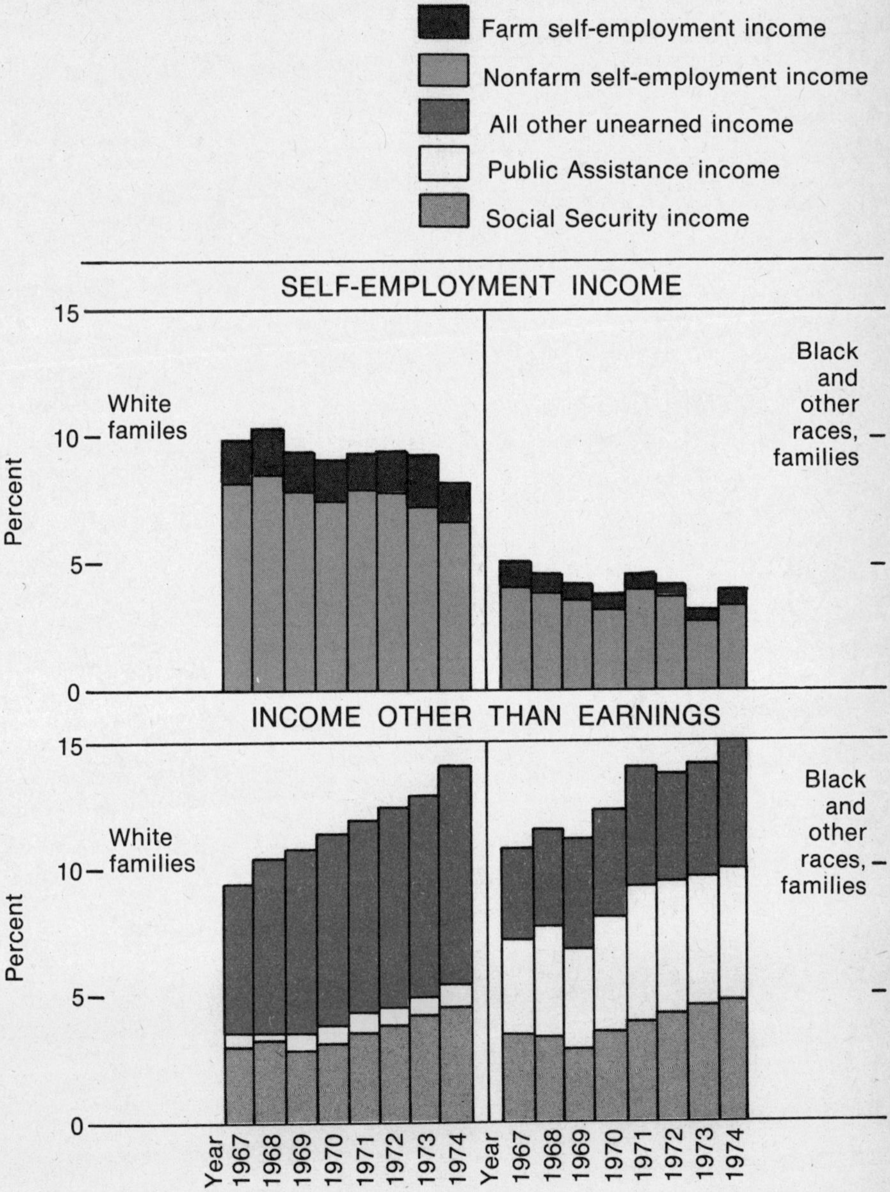

Source: see table 9/10

Table 9/11
MEDIAN FAMILY INCOME, BY RACE OF FAMILY HEAD AND BY REGION: 1953–1974
(Median income in 1974 constant dollars)

YEAR	Northeast			North Central			South			West		
	Median income		Ratio of black and other races to white	Median income		Ratio of black and other races to white	Median income		Ratio of black and other races to white	Median income		Ratio of black and other races to white
	White	Black and other races		White	Black and other races		White	Black and other races		White	Black and other races	
1953.....	8,590	6,201	0.72	8,575	6,539	0.76	6,856	3,353	0.49	8,560	7,001	0.82
1954.....	8,578	6,010	.70	8,155	5,971	.73	6,859	3,369	.49	8,306	5,912	.71
1955.....	8,916	6,129	.69	8,845	6,804	.77	7,509	3,456	.46	9,077	6,691	.74
1956.....	9,769	6,729	.69	9,412	7,182	.76	7,645	3,590	.47	9,650	6,555	.68
1957.....	9,717	6,946	.71	9,194	6,556	.71	7,650	3,540	.46	9,749	7,048	.72
1958.....	9,684	6,734	.70	8,953	6,473	.72	7,786	3,435	.44	9,833	6,984	.71
1959.....	10,147	7,130	.70	9,540	6,647	.70	8,294	3,264	.39	10,645	7,540	.71
1960.....	10,359	7,040	.68	9,788	7,175	.73	8,169	3,527	.43	11,041	8,988	.81
1961.....	10,589	7,180	.68	9,828	7,038	.72	8,152	3,482	.43	11,458	9,936	.87
1962.....	10,989	7,205	.66	10,408	7,067	.68	8,500	4,004	.47	11,177	8,137	.73
1963.....	11,407	7,426	.65	10,810	7,916	.73	8,964	4,057	.45	11,521	8,725	.76
1964.....	11,795	7,877	.67	11,129	8,023	.72	9,364	4,614	.49	11,777	9,199	.78
1965.....	12,110	7,822	.65	11,642	8,611	.74	9,717	4,730	.49	12,205	9,810	.80
1966.....	12,424	8,529	.69	12,374	9,218	.74	10,459	5,250	.50	12,624	9,828	.78
1967.....	12,789	8,592	.67	12,333	9,568	.78	10,869	5,880	.54	13,009	10,930	.84
1968.....	13,211	9,307	.70	13,127	9,878	.75	11,286	6,088	.54	13,412	11,646	.87
1969.....	13,808	9,471	.69	13,713	10,401	.76	11,789	6,741	.57	13,717	11,138	.81
1970.....	13,892	10,042	.72	13,345	9,928	.74	11,735	6,681	.57	13,185	11,223	.85
1971.....	13,748	9,416	.68	13,417	9,359	.70	11,818	6,629	.56	13,154	11,250	.86
1972.....	14,507	9,411	.65	14,083	10,107	.72	12,336	6,754	.55	13,820	11,121	.80
1973.....	14,681	8,908	.61	14,568	10,072	.69	12,770	7,207	.56	14,050	11,328	.81
1974.....	14,164	9,399	.66	14,017	9,901	.71	12,050	6,805	.56	13,339	11,107	.83

Source: U.S. Department of Commerce, Bureau of the Census, unpublished data.

Chart 9/11A

Social Indicators, 1976

MEDIAN FAMILY INCOME, BY RACE OF HEAD, FOR REGIONS: 1954, 1964 AND 1974 (in 1974 dollars)

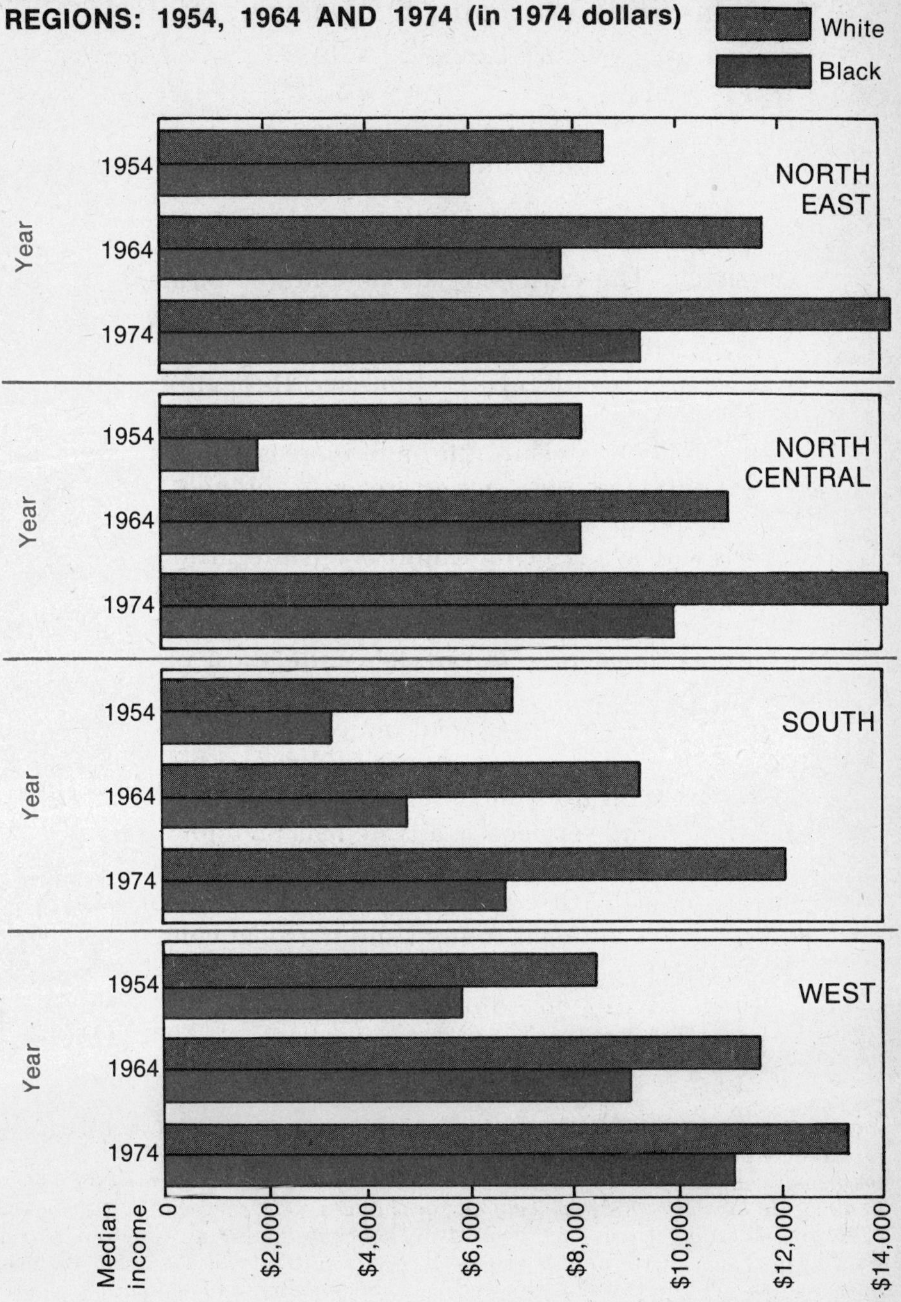

Source: see table 9/11

ANNALS, AAPSS, **435**, Jan. 1978

"Massification" and Democratization of the Leisure Class

By JOHN P. ROBINSON

ABSTRACT: The enriched data on culture and leisure presented in chapter 10 of *Social Indicators, 1976* support both the hypotheses of massification of leisure (through increasing availability of free time and through greater use of this time for the mass culture of television) and of democratization of leisure (through increasing attendance at sports events and performing arts and through increasing dissemination of knowledge and books on the arts). Many problems with available indicators of leisure participation and spectatorship are identified from the perspective of time diaries of how Americans spend the full 24 hours of their day. The lack of trend data on the arts to parallel those presented in chapter 10 on the humanities and sciences is noted, along with the need to present social indicator data in some form of input-output context. Possible candidates for future leisure and culture indicators include: monetary expenditures for leisure goods and services, available data on television viewing habits and program content, the satisfactions and pressures associated with time uses, accessibility of leisure facilities, conversational content and personal contemplation about leisure, and an inventory of "experiences" to which individuals have been exposed.

John P. Robinson is Director of the Communication Research Center and Professor of Communication at Cleveland State University. His Ph.D. degree in mathematical and social psychology was received from The University of Michigan in 1965. He has written extensively on survey data concerned with attitudes and behavior, including How Americans Use Time, *the* Statistical Appendix *to* The Use of Time, *and* Measures of Social Psychological Attitudes. *He is on the editorial boards of the* Public Opinion Quarterly *and* Sociometry, *and served as research coordinator for the U.S. Surgeon General's study of Television and Social Behavior. He is currently on leave at the Audience Research Branch of the British Broadcasting Corporation.*

NOT A week goes by, it seems, without a magazine or newspaper article about the "culture boom" or the latest adventure to be enjoyed in our "expanding leisure" time. Such articles invariably support their arguments with statistics on the increased spending for this or that recreational activity or on the decreasing importance of the workweek as more vacations and early retirement become realities. Increases in the mass availability of leisure and culture are usually assumed to be a good thing, allowing individuals greater freedom of expression, enjoyment and appreciation of the finer things in life than they can find in increasingly bureaucratized work settings. This greater use of discretionary time for cultural pursuits, formerly only the province of the rich, has been referred to as a "democratization of leisure".[1]

The democratization has occurred at the same time as a concern has developed about the "massification" of leisure, that is the availability of abundant leisure time to a pubic unprepared to use it for anything more than the consumption of frivolous and undemanding mass culture, particularly television. Assumptions about increasing free time also pervade academic literature and policy discussion of the world of leisure and culture. The arguments of those who have drawn different conclusions from the data —such as those who see in government figures little drop in the length of the workweek,[2] or who see little change in recreation expenditures once inflation and gains in disposable income are taken into account,[3] or who wonder whether our "harried leisure class" has become the servant and not the master of its leisure technology[4]—tend to get less attention in these speculations and beliefs about leisure.

Chapter 10 of *Social Indicators, 1976* presents vivid evidence that the apparently divergent phenomena of massification and democratization may coinhabit the world of culture and leisure. The charts and tables in chapter 10 provide an opportunity to see what has happened in this world over the last decade, a period during which increased value has been placed on self-expression or hedonism, depending on whom you read. Has massification or democratization prevailed across what one observer has called the "Me decade?"

A DIGEST OF MATERIAL COVERED

As seems true of other chapters in *Social Indicators, 1976*, chapter 10 on culture and leisure contains a far richer and more ambitious set of data than was available in the pioneering 1973 volume. Only two data sources in the 1973 edition are employed again: data from Michigan's Survey Research Center on how people spend time, and data collected by the U.S. Bureau of Outdoor Recreation on participation in selected outdoor recreation activities. The only

1. Rolf Meyersohn, "Is There Life After Work?" *Saturday Review*, 4 May 1974, p. 14–16.

2. Examples may be found in Sebastian DeGrazia, *Of Time, Work and Leisure* (New York: Twentieth Century Fund, 1962); John Robinson and Philip Converse, "Social Change as Reflected in the Use of Time," in *The Human Meaning of Social Change*, eds. A. Campbell and P. Converse (New York: Russell Sage Foundation, 1972); John Owen, "Workweeks and Leisure: An Analysis of Trends 1948–75," *Monthly Labor Review* (August 1976), p. 3–8.

3. Sylvia Porter, "Spending Patterns—Here are Some Surprises," *Detroit Free Press*, 15 July 1977, p. 6B.

4. Staffan Linder, *The Harried Leisure Class* (New York: Columbia University Press, 1970), for example.

other data source used in the 1973 edition—TV ratings data from the A. C. Nielsen Company—is not utilized.

Several new indicators make a welcome appearance. To this reviewer, somewhat of a "subjective indicator" advocate (as will become apparent) the Gallup data which stretch back to 1938 on favorite leisure activities and the categories of new book titles provided the most novel insights. Attendance figures for the performing arts and sports events are particularly appropriate additions, even though these have long been available in the *U.S. Statistical Abstract* and pose severe interpretative problems as described below; much the same characterizes the data presented on employment trends in "knowledge industries." Subjective indicators of the "output" from leisure (which could be argued is a contradiction in terms) are presented on the satisfaction levels that the public reports about its friendships and nonwork activities, their confidence in the mass media, and the daily frequency with which television is behaviorally boycotted "because there weren't any programs worth watching." The chapter closes with 1965 comparisons of how time was used in the United States compared to nine other countries, with particular reference to work and media usage and emphasizing parallel "hard" data on the production of books in each country.

It is difficult to judge which findings in the rich collection would most intrigue readers unfamiliar with recent literature in culture and leisure, but this reviewer was struck by the following:

1. *The 10 to 20 percent increase in free time available to members of the labor force households between 1965 and 1975.* This increase, made possible by decreased time devoted to family care and work activities, represents the first evidence of an increase of leisure in periods outside of holiday and vacation days—the major source of increased free time in the work force in previous periods. Some increase in sleep and resting was also noted over this period, a further indicator of a possible general movement of daily life in a more relaxed or passive direction in this country.

2. *The close match between free time expenditures as measured by time-diaries and the frequency with which activities Gallup independently reports are chosen as favorite leisure activities.* Television leads both lists (which also share a common pattern of demographic correlates), taking up 35 percent of free time in diaries and being cited by 46 percent of national samples as the favorite leisure activity. Visiting with family and friends and reading are mentioned with next most frequency in time-diaries as favorite activities.

3. *A slight increase (from 10 to 12 percent)—higher among blacks, younger adults, and the college educated—in the frequency with which people say they turned off their television sets on a particular day because of poor programming.* This increase is far less dramatic than the increase noted in actual viewing time between 1965 and 1975, but parallels a recent decrease in the confidence the public expresses in the personnel responsible for television.

4. *The 50 to 300 percent upsurge between the early 1960s and 1970s in attendance counts at sports events and the performing arts.* That horse racing annually outdraws

baseball by a 2½ to 1 margin continues to boggle the mind, but the almost 300 percent increase in the number of professional boxers over the decade may be the most counterintuitive trend to be found in the chapter.

5. *The 78 percent increase in knowledge producers (researchers and professors) between 1960 and 1970 and the 55 percent increase in knowledge disseminators (teachers and media specialists).* The gap between the two may possibly explain why those of us in research feel frustrated in not reaching audiences with the results of our research. Alternatively, it may say something uncomplimentary about the quality of our output and diffusability of the research. Research professionals may be more encouraged to find that research and publications have kept pace with the three-fold increase in awards made by the National Endowment for the Humanities between 1969 and 1974; or that titles in economics and sociology have shown the greatest increase (almost 12-fold) in book title trends between 1955 and 1975.

6. *Compared to workers in other countries, Americans spend neither more time nor less time at work or in commuting to work*—nor in front of their television sets, given set ownership, nor in reading, given our higher educational levels. While the United States and the U.S.S.R. lead the world in book production, most other European countries outproduce both in book publication on a per capital basis.

In brief, this evidence tends to favor the first answer to Zuzanek's question,[5] "Society of leisure or the harried leisure class?" If one defines "the leisure class" by the amounts of free time it has, then the size of this class has certainly increased over time—that is, become massified—and the mass cultural use of television has grown at an even greater pace than increase in free time.

SOME PROBLEMS WITH THE DATA PRESENTED

Since the perfect social indicator for any topic area has yet to be developed, each of the indicators employed in this chapter shares its own weaknesses and ambiguities in the methodology of data collection and interpretability. This section describes some of the major problems with each data source, quite apart from the problems of small sample size and representativeness that usually plague these and other social indicators.

This examination proceeds in large part from biases ingrained by the reviewer's intimate involvement in the Americans' Use of Time project over the last 12 years. Time is a commodity that is increasingly thought about and planned for in a postindustrial society.[6] Time planning not only consciously enters the leisure world of individuals, but of those in the leisure industries who cater to them in convenient time packages, e.g. book digests and amusement park day passes. Time-diaries of how people spend the 24 hours of a particular day then provide an opportunity to operationalize a quantitative measure of that most elusive concept, free time. As Meyersohn has cogently pointed out, however, not all free

5. Jiri Zuzanek, "Society of Leisure or the 'Harried Leisure-Class,'" *Journal of Leisure Research* 6 (Fall 1974), pp. 293–304.

6. Daniel Bell, *The Coming of Post-Industrial Society*, 2nd edition (New York: Basic Books, 1976).

time is leisure.[7] The valuable feature of the time-diary method is that investigators with alternative definitions of what activities comprise leisure or free time can apply them to generate their own measures.

Because time-diaries are something like a "census" of free time activity in society, their examination puts the world of culture and leisure in clear perspective and also alerts one to its understudied or forgotten aspects. From time-diaries, the pervasive and increasing role of the mass media during free time becomes quickly obvious. No other class of activities has taken as large a share of the increased free time available over the last ten years as the mass media, with television being practically the sole overall beneficiary. Television's gains are found in all sex, race, age, education, and employment groups. Visiting and related social life, the second most prevalent use of free time, have shown some modest decline over the same period. The "semi-leisure" activities of adult education and organizational participation show some modest gains.

In terms of time use, then, time-diary data suggest only about 5 to 10 percent of free time is devoted to such activities as participation in outdoor recreation and attendance at sports and cultural events. In fairness, this is a bias shared by most of the academic literature and policy discussion of leisure and culture, and these activities could be argued to be the most uplifting and engaging uses of free time (even though they do not appear on Gallup's list of favorite free time activities). Nonetheless, aggregate attendance data from institutions miss the more time consuming spectatorship of local sports and cultural events for which no admission may be charged or counts tallied—high school football games or neighborhood art exhibits, for example. In fact, concert and museum attendance is noted less often in time-diaries than personal participation in cultural activities—pottery, painting, practicing music, or literature.

The indexing of sports and recreation is possibly even more hazardous. Like museum attendance, a substantial number of children attend sports events. Multiple attendance for sports events is also likely and the tabulation of the possibly sporadic attendance of season ticket holders is uncertain. The repeat visits of horse race fans, and the greater number of racing days, must have something to do with these astronomical attendance figures (horse racing was reported in only two of the over 1,500 time-diaries in 1975). How else is it possible for attendance at greyhound races to outnumber attendance at professional football games? How much of this attendance is accounted for by people out of the "mainstream" of society; i.e. the retired or the unemployed?

How does the National Golf Foundation estimate that there were almost 12 million persons who had played more than 15 rounds of golf in the last year? The Bowlers Association estimates there are only 9 million bowlers,[8] yet in time-diaries bowling was mentioned more often than all other sports activities combined—making it, incidentally, Americans' favorite

7. Rolf Meyersohn, "Leisure," in *Human Meaning of Social Change*, eds. Campbell and Converse.

8. U.S. Bureau of the Census, *Statistical Abstract of the United States 1976* (Washington, D.C.: USGPO, 1977).

participation sport.[9] Yet the American Softball Association estimates there were over 25 million softball players in 1975 (*U.S. Statistical Abstract, 1976*), more than the number of bowlers and golfers combined. Quite aside from any possible vested interests that may be served by these estimates, their value as social indicators is highly ambiguous unless they are collected on a systematic, periodic basis by a single data collection method or agency.

Even this step will not necessarily ensure that usable social indicator data will become available, if the record of the U.S. Bureau of Outdoor Recreation (BOR) affords any example. The Bureau has conducted five national surveys (in 1960, 1965, 1970, 1971, 1972) of participation in outdoor recreation, and is now embarking on a sixth. None (including the sixth) has used common survey questions so that we might know about trends in participation across this transitional time period.[10] The BOR trend figures presented in chapter 10 represent extrapolations from the 1975 data; differential participation in activities by income and by situs of the activity are shown for the 1972 data only. Some figures are for the entire year; others, for the summer only. Popular indoor sports, like bowling, racquet ball, and basketball, are not examined.

Moreover, it is not obvious that participation based on direct respondent estimates for a lengthy time period, such as a season or a year, provide data that are suitably accurate or reliable. Compared to time-diary estimates, whose aggregate accuracy seems quite satisfactory, respondents estimate very generous amounts of weekly or yearly time on housework, volunteer work, television and several other activities.[11] If one asks people to estimate the hours per week they spend on various activities, the total will likely far exceed the 168 hours a week that are available, and the discrepancy cannot be readily resolved by distinguishing between primary and secondary activities. There is the more basic and subtle matter of activity definition: does the respondent consider shuffleboard or chess a "sport;" is a walk for the dog or to the store counted as "walking for pleasure;" has one gone "swimming" if not even the ankles get wet? Such problems are not likely to be solved soon, and BOR has wisely shifted its survey attention to gauging availability and unmet needs for recreation facilities and to gathering public opinion data on the same dilemmas that policymakers face: to improve existing facilities or to build new ones; to concentrate on land- or water-based facilities, for example.

The time-diary data have been cited as a basis for criticizing other data sources, but they, too, suffer from severe limitations. Only one day's activities are collected from each respondent and participation in active leisure activities is rare on a particular day. Thus far, only sporadic sampling of summer days, vacations, and holidays has been

9. John Robinson, *How Americans Use Time: A Social-Psychological Analysis of Everyday Behavior* (New York: Praeger, 1977), p. 108.

10. Carol Stowell, *Evaluation of Five Previous Nationwide Citizen Surveys* (Washington, D.C.: Kirschner Associates, Inc. November 1975).

11. John Robinson, "Methodological Studies into the Reliability and Validity of the Time Diary," in *Studies in the Measurement of Time Allocation*, ed. T. Juster (Ann Arbor, Mich.: Institute for Social Research, forthcoming).

undertaken, and these are the peak periods of outdoor recreation and spectator activities. No national time-diary data are available for children. And the behavioral context or psychological consequences of participation are seldom revealed.[12]

Some subjective indicator data related to participation presented in chapter 10 concern overall satisfaction with nonwork activities and with friendships. On the four occasions the question has been asked by the National Opinion Research Center, satisfaction with spare time activities (58 percent satisfied "a great deal" in 1976) is reported at a lower level than satisfaction with friendships (69 percent satisfied "a great deal"), consistent with the higher satisfaction with visiting noted in footnote 12. The less-educated claim less satisfaction from spare time activities, and it becomes interesting to know whether there are distinctive patterns of free time activity among the less-educated that make this the case, particularly since satisfaction with spare time activities has shown some general decline in recent surveys. Are less-educated people watching more TV than they should, for example?

Satisfaction with friendships has also declined recently, and again the less-educated, along with younger people and men, are less satisfied. It would be useful here, as well, to know what objective factors—number of close friends or relatives; frequency of interaction; marital status—accompany these lower levels of satisfaction with friendships. Is it possible that some people are dissatisfied because they have too many acquaintances, or that wives and/or relatives dominate the social circles of men and the less educated, or that men in our society are socialized to be so isolated or mobile that they are unable to form permanent friendships? Similar interesting, but unanswered, questions arise in connection with why the public has more confidence in people running the press than in people running television.[13] How directly do these ratings relate to the product for which these people are responsible? How do these ratings compare to other professions, particularly the products of those professions with which the public comes into daily contact?

On the other hand, the indicators of cultural activity seem unduly narrow for this multivaried concept. For example, number of people in cultural occupations is a natural indicator, but scientific researchers and teachers would seem more

12. Subsequent to compilations of *Social Indicators, 1976*, data are now becoming available on the "psychological meaning" of various activities in which people participate, particularly the satisfactions or "consumption benefits" they derive from various free time activities (Robinson, *How Americans Use Time*, pp. 116–32). There is a marked tendency for people to engage more in activities from which they claim to derive greater satisfaction, that is; people who get more satisfaction from television watch more than those who are not satisfied and vice versa. However, there is little carryover at the aggregate level, in the sense that visiting and social life rank near the top of satisfying activities overall, and well above television, but television takes up much more of peoples' free time—and is taking up more of it vis-a-vis the more satisfying activity of visiting since 1965. Television is also reported as a highly elastic activity, being the first people say they would give up if some urgent matter arose on a particular day. (See Robinson and Converse, "Social Change as Reflected in Use of Time.")

13. Ratings of press performance show an interesting divergence starting with 1974, perhaps indicating the polarization caused by Watergate—more people now say they have a good deal of confidence in the press and more people also say they have hardly any confidence.

appropriately considered as knowledge producers than as culture producers when compared to artists, writers, composers, musicians, sculptors, dancers, jugglers, and actors. While it is instructive to find a three-fold increase in the number of awards by the National Endowment for the Humanities between 1969 and 1974, one assumes that the increase was achieved without the offsetting decrease in the monetary value of the awards. Apart from this consideration is the question of output from these awards. How many outstanding essays or exchanges of ideas were stimulated that would not have occurred without the awards? Less abstractly, how many recipients were satisfied that the awards enriched their lives or careers in some significant way and how did the awards aid in this personal growth? How would awards from the National Endowment for the Arts, again more directly tied to culture than to knowledge, compare with these outputs?

The trends in book topics between 1955 and 1975 were fascinating,[14] but prompted this reviewer to wonder about parallel trends in the topics covered in the other mass media—movies, records, television, magazines, radio, and newspaper—for which there are probably few data. Media researchers know that the most significant trends over this period came as a result of competition with the more pervasive medium of television—the decline of fiction, the rise in specialty magazines, the growth of specialized FM stations, and the appearance of pornographic and spectacular movies. It would be fascinating to be able to document the subtle changes that media observers claim are taking place in media content over the last two decades, e.g., the shorter and simpler stories reported in newspapers, the movement of interest from local stories to national stories in the news (a trend possibly now being reversed), and the increasing sophistication of popular television scripts or television advertising.

Finally, the international comparisons might have better focused on differences in total free time across countries, rather than in time spent working, commuting, and using media. Americans in the 1965 study were distinctive in terms of the greater free time they had available compared with people in European countries. Moreover, while the total time spent reading in the United States and the U.S.S.R. was almost equivalent, as was book production in the two countries, a closer examination of the sources of these time-use data reveals that reading times in the Soviet Union are preponderantly devoted to books while those in the United States are preponderantly spent with newspapers.[15]

This last observation illustrates the major problem in this chapter, as perhaps with the social indicator movement in general—namely, that of relating inputs to outputs, or

14. After book titles on social science, those dealing with recreation and with art experienced most growth between 1955 and 1975. With regard to cultural production (see comments on these occupations above), art books experienced far more growth than those dealing with music, literature, and poetry-drama, all of which experienced average or slightly below average growth compared to other publications. The lowest growth rates were noted for children's books and for fiction, again reflecting the spectre of television. It should be remembered that these figures are for books published and may not necessarily reflect their public diffusion through sales.

15. John Robinson, Philip Converse, and Alexander Szalai, "Everyday Life in Twelve Countries," in *The Use of Time*, eds. A. Szalai *et al.*, (The Hague: Mouton, 1972).

input-output at one level, for example, production of books, with input-output at another level, for example, time spent reading books and individual gains in information or cultural awareness. To be sure, indicators are only supposed to draw our attention to something, an early warning system of the appearance or continuation of a trend or social condition. But unless we are able to invest them with further meaning, or match them with related indicators of input-output, their use for policymaking and understanding will be too severely restricted.

These remarks are not meant to detract from the rich compilation of information assembled in this chapter. As the authors note in the introduction to *Social Indicators, 1976*, the data "are also likely to raise additional questions and may provide contradictory interpretations." The authors' zeal and creativity in overcoming monumental obstacles in data availability, comparability, and interpretability with limited resources is obvious and commendable. The collecting of social indicators is still in its infancy, and most of the problems and criticisms raised by this reviewer are hardly insoluble.

POSSIBLE FUTURE DIRECTIONS

As one looks forward to future editions of this invaluable and insightful reference work, it might be hoped that material on culture and leisure would be as enhanced as this one was over its predecessor. Sources of enrichment come both from data already available and data not now available.

In the first category, one might like to include available data on monetary expenditures for leisure and culture. These figures should be suitably corrected for spurious economic factors so that we might know if leisure and culture are sharing disproportionately in our economic growth. While these are not likely to dovetail closely with time expenditure data,[16] the discrepancies between time and money investment might themselves be provocative indicators. Some attempt should also be made to distinguish data that refer to the entire population and data that exclude particular demographic groups, such as children, the unemployed, or the retired.

Some reference ought to be made to other data available on that most prominent facility for leisure and culture—television. Whatever criticisms one may have about the validity of the Nielsen data,[17] their annual yearbook contains a wealth of historical information on programming trends and highlights gathered in a consistent and systematic fashion. The same holds true for the survey data collected periodically since 1959 by Roper for the Television Information Office and the yearly content analysis of television violence conducted by the Annenberg School of Communications at the University of Pennsylvania.[18] C.B.S. may soon sponsor another replication of Steiner's classic study of public perceptions of television; a 1970 replication found trends consistent with those in the chapter 10 data, that is, toward longer but more selective viewing, and more

16. Robinson, "Methodological Studies."

17. Robinson, *How Americans Use Time*, p. 175.

18. Burns Roper, *Changing Public Attitudes Toward Television and Other Mass Media, 1959–1976* (New York: Television Information Office, 1977); George Gerbner and Larry Gross, "Living with Television: The Violence Profile," *Journal of Communication* 26 (Spring 1976), pp. 172–99.

criticisms of television in general terms but more opportunity to find programs that satisfied particular interests.[19]

Research into time use and leisure may soon begin to generate time series data on the leisure activities that people find most enjoyable or satisfying.[20] Given the greater concern with time in a postindustrial society, data on whether people feel they have enough, or too much, free time would seem an essential complement to feelings about satisfaction with free-time activities.[21] The incidence of "secondary activities" in time-diaries may be taken as a further indicator of the hectic pace of modern life and "time deepening," the ability to squeeze more experience out of the same amount of leisure time available.

Of course, availability of time and money comprise only two of the many resource factors that constrain participation in leisure and culture. One of the new measurement areas that policymakers, as well as indicator researchers, will have to face is the accessibility of leisure facilities in terms of distance and economic cost. Some promising work in this area is already underway in Europe[22] and in the latest survey conducted by the Bureau of Outdoor Recreation. Accessibility becomes especially important in light of the severe energy shortages forecast for the future; if fuel for transportation becomes more scarce, the less energy-consuming activity of TV viewing may become an even more popular alternative.

Moving to the output side of the ledger, data on information processing that takes place during leisure would seem a natural type of indicator, although measurement issues abound. Katz has proposed a scheme for systematically monitoring the content of people's conversations.[23] Some national survey data on the most interesting conversations and most pressing personal concerns people reported on a particular day are already available,[24] although these are in need of extensive refinement before they can serve as viable social indicators. One researcher has begun to monitor what people think about on a time sampling basis; an intriguing indicator from this research is the frequency with which leisure activities are contemplated while at work.

19. Gary Steiner, *The People Look at Television* (New York: Knopf, 1963); Robert Bower, *Television and the Public* (New York: Holt, 1972).

20. One of the more intriguing features of these activity satisfaction ratings is that they show relatively little difference between the reported satisfaction of free-time activities and work activities (Robinson, *How Americans Use Time*), bringing into question the common assumption that leisure has replaced work as a central life interest. Perhaps work is being underrated as a relative source of gratification, or perhaps leisure itself affords little opportunity to satisfy central life interests of workers.

21. In the 1965 time use study, about a quarter of the respondents said they "always feel rushed" to do the things that had to be done. While people who felt always rushed also reported lower than average satisfaction with their lives, people who "hardly ever feel rushed" reported even lower life satisfaction (Robinson and Converse, "Social Change as Reflected in Use of Time"). This curvilinearity between life satisfaction and perceived time also appears for actual time (Robinson, *How Americans Use Time*) and indicates that too much free time may be more of a burden than too little. Teenagers in particular complained about having too much free time.

22. I.N.S.E.E., *Les Comportments de Loisir des Francais* (Paris: I.N.S.E.E., 1967), pp. 16–19. The Central Bureau of Statistics in Norway has relevant data for 1971–72.

23. Elihu Katz, *Social Research on Broadcasting* (London: British Broadcasting Corporation, 1977), pp. 46–47.

24. Robinson, *How Americans Use Time*, pp. 138–46.

Finally there ought to be a way to index a shift that some observers suggest has accompanied more democratized leisure,[25] namely from collections of things and technology to collections of "experiences"—the trips to faraway places and natural wonders, the participation in mystical or exotic events, such as the Boston Marathon or the King Tut exhibit, the endless search for peak experiences or offbeat thrills, and the attempts to make one's way somehow into the Guinness Book of Records. If such a shift in societal emphasis is taking place—"You only go around once in life . . ." as the ad says—then cultural deprivation could challenge economic and educational deprivation as a major social concern in the years ahead. Perhaps a "poor" person in the year 2000 will be defined as an individual who, by a certain year in life, has never had a "peak experience," been fascinated by some work of art, won a sports award beyond his or her supposed athletic ability, become "famous" for some accomplishment during leisure time, lived in another culture, or worked through a personal definition of the meaning of life.

25. Geoffrey Godbey, "Time Deepening and the Future of Leisure," *Leisure Today* (October 1976), pp. 9–11; Alvin Toffler, *Future Shock* (New York: Bantam Books, 1970).

Table 10/1

AVERAGE HOURS PER WEEK SPENT IN MAJOR TYPES OF ACTIVITY BY SELECTED URBAN POPULATION GROUPS, 1965 AND 1975

TYPE OF ACTIVITY	Race		Total sample	Employed men		Employed women		Married housewives
	White	Black and other races		Married	Single	Married	Single	
1965 URBAN SAMPLE								
Size of sample (number)	1,030	103	1,218	448	73	190	152	341
Total time (hours)	168	168	168	168	168	168	168	168
Sleep	53.4	50.9	53.3	53.1	50.6	53.8	52.6	53.9
Work for pay	31.9	36.6	33.0	51.3	51.4	38.4	39.8	.5
Family care	26.0	23.6	25.4	9.0	7.7	28.8	20.6	50.0
Personal care	21.8	19.9	21.5	20.9	22.2	20.3	21.7	22.6
Leisure time (total)	34.9	36.9	34.8	33.7	36.1	26.7	33.3	41.0
Organizations	2.8	3.0	2.8	2.6	3.6	1.4	3.7	3.4
Media	14.8	15.7	14.7	17.1	13.9	10.7	11.1	15.3
Social life	9.3	9.1	9.4	7.2	10.4	7.9	9.6	12.6
Recreation	1.1	.6	.9	1.4	1.3	.6	.5	.6
Other leisure	6.9	8.4	7.0	5.4	6.9	6.1	8.4	9.1
1975 URBAN SAMPLE								
Size of sample (number)	680	77	726	245	87	117	108	141
Total time (hours)	168	168	168	168	168	168	168	168
Sleep	54.5	54.8	54.7	53.4	54.1	55.1	54.3	56.8
Work for pay	30.0	30.0	32.5	47.4	40.0	30.1	38.8	1.1
Family care	21.1	17.6	20.5	9.7	9.0	24.9	16.6	44.3
Personal care	22.1	21.0	21.8	21.4	20.0	26.2	21.9	21.4
Leisure time (total)	40.3	44.6	38.5	36.1	44.9	31.7	36.4	44.4
Organizations	4.4	4.9	3.8	3.7	4.8	2.2	4.4	4.8
Media	18.7	19.6	18.2	18.9	18.5	15.6	14.5	20.4
Social life	8.2	9.8	7.8	6.4	8.9	6.6	8.9	10.1
Recreation	1.5	.4	1.3	1.3	4.1	.8	.5	.7
Other leisure	7.5	9.9	7.4	5.8	8.6	6.5	8.1	8.4

Source: John P. Robinson, "Changes in America's Use of Time, 1965–1975," *Report of the Communication Research Center*, Cleveland State University, 1976. Used by permission.

Chart 10/1A

Social Indicators, 1976

AVERAGE HOURS PER WEEK SPENT IN MAJOR TYPES OF ACTIVITY FOR SELECTED URBAN POPULATION GROUPS, 1965 AND 1975

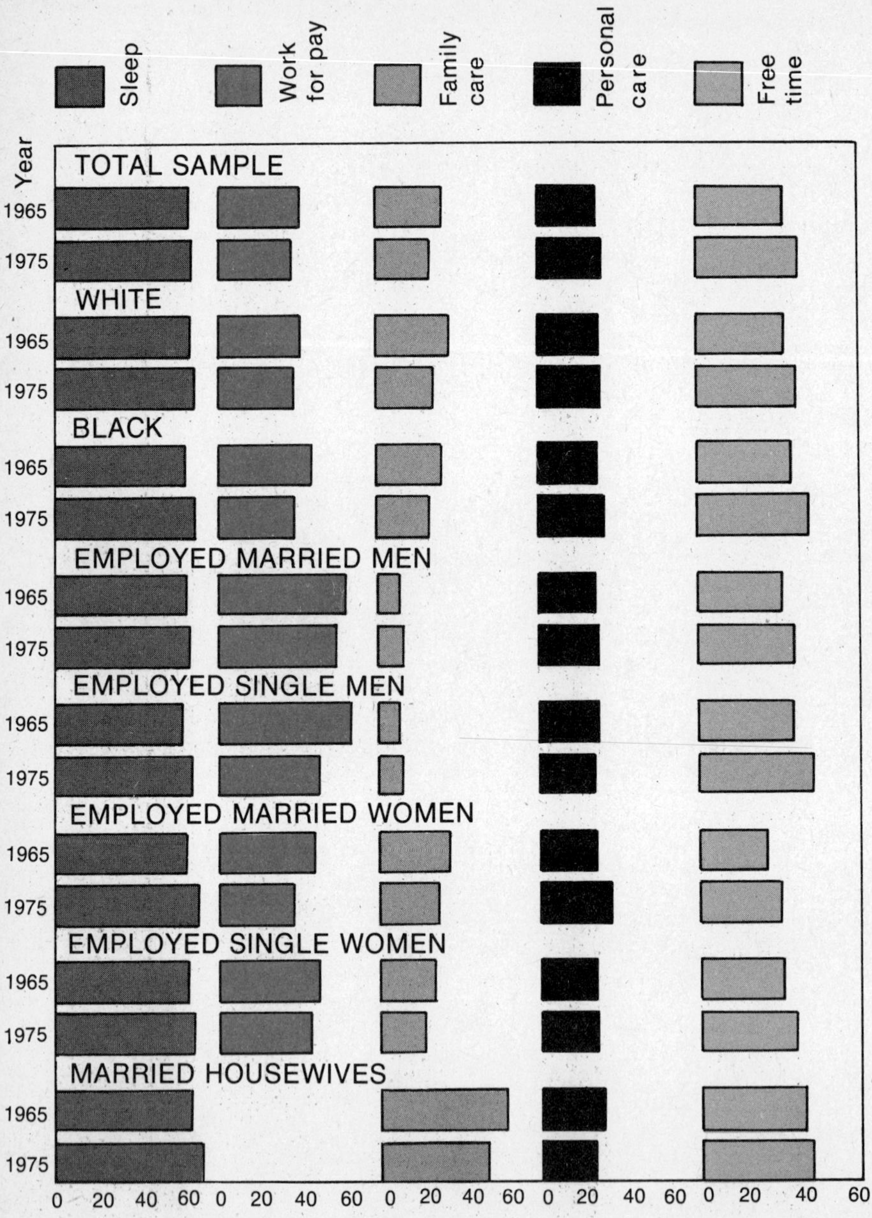

Source: see table 10/1

Chart 10/1B Social Indicators, 1976

TIME USE: AVERAGE HOURS PER WEEK OF "FREE TIME" BY TYPE OF ACTIVITY FOR SELECTED URBAN POPULATION GROUPS, 1965 AND 1975

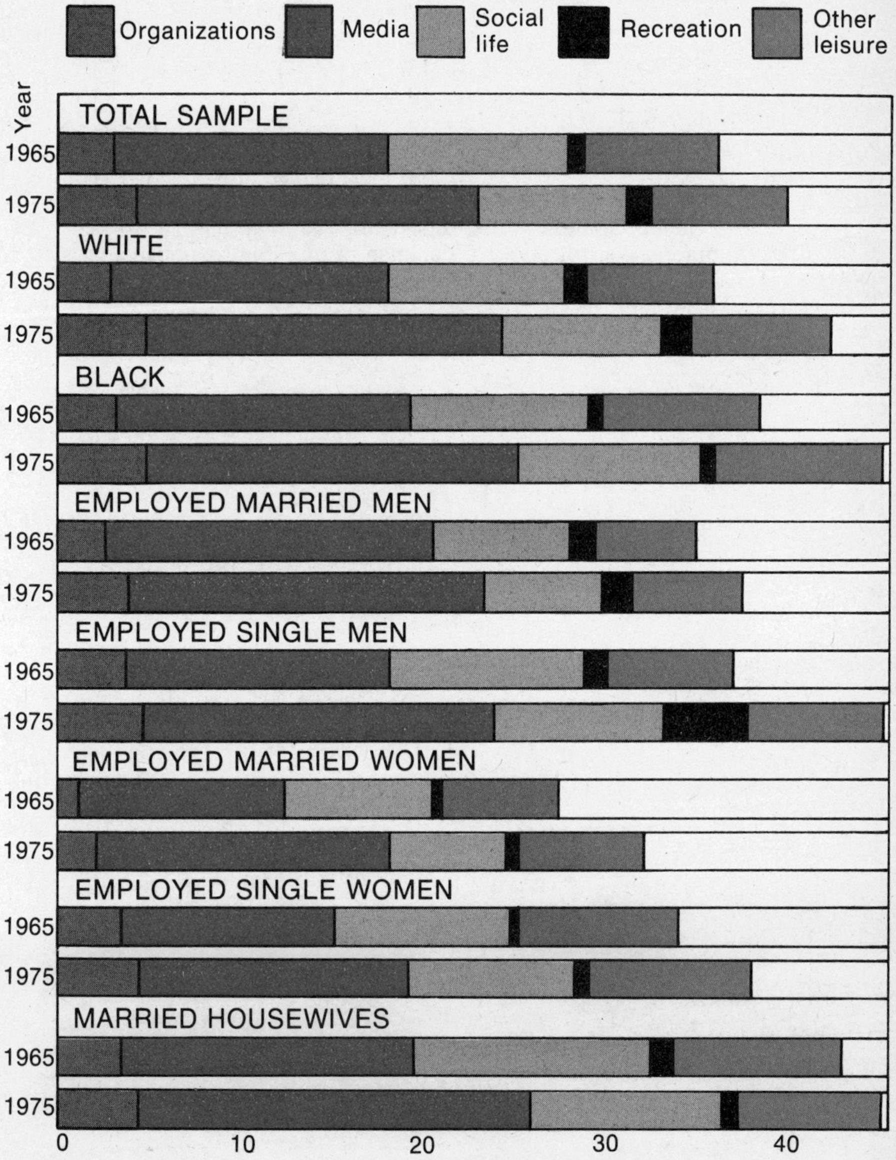

Source: see table 10/1

Table 10/4

FAVORITE LEISURE ACTIVITIES, BY SELECTED YEARS: 1938–1974

(Percent reporting)

Type of activity	1938	1960	1966	1974
Reading	21	10	15	14
Movies and theater	17	6	5	9
Watching television	(NA)	28	46	46
Dancing	12	3	2	4
Radio	9	([1])	2	5
Playing cards and games	9	6	5	8
Staying home with family	7	17	5	10
Visiting friends	4	10	5	8

Source: The Gallup Opinion Index, report No. 105, March 1974.
Note: Percentages are not additive because of multiple responses.
NA, Not available.
[1] Less than 1 percent.

Chart 10/4 Social Indicators, 1976

SELECTED FAVORITE LEISURE ACTIVITIES BY TYPE OF ACTIVITY 1938–1974

(Percent responding)

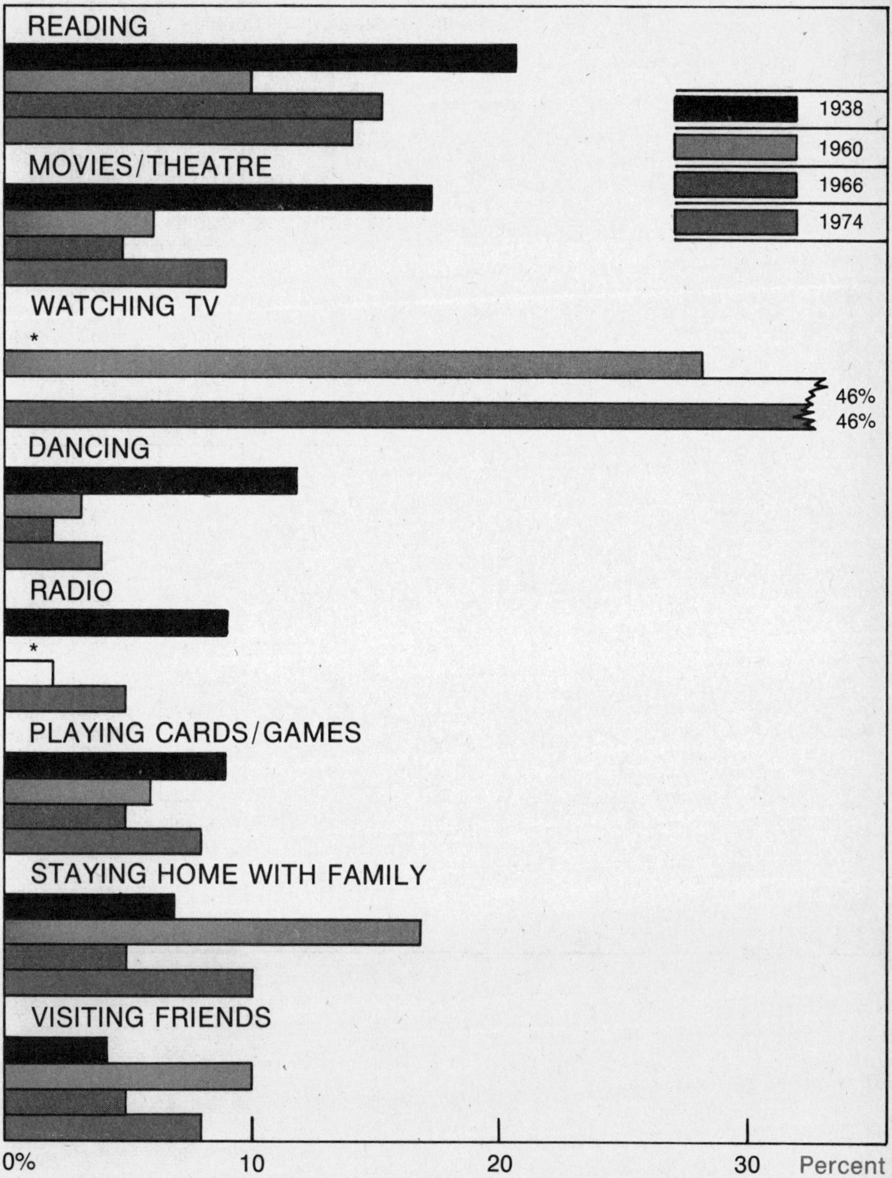

* Less than 1 percent or not available.

Source: See table 10/4

Table 10/16

SATISFACTION WITH FRIENDSHIPS AND LEISURE-TIME ACTIVITIES AND CONFIDENCE IN TELEVISION AND THE PRESS: 1973–1976

RESPONSE	1973 Number	1973 Percent	1974 Number	1974 Percent	1975 Number	1975 Percent	1976 Number	1976 Percent
SATISFACTION WITH FRIENDSHIPS								
TOTAL NUMBER RESPONDING	1,495	100.0	1,484	100.0	1,484	100.0	1,492	100.0
A great deal[1]	1,044	69.8	1,073	72.3	1,050	70.8	1,035	69.4
Quite a bit[2]	405	27.1	376	25.3	393	26.5	383	25.7
A little or none	46	3.1	35	2.4	41	2.8	74	5.0
Total sample size ...	1,504	(X)	1,484	(X)	1,490	(X)	1,499	(X)
SATISFACTION WITH NONWORK ACTIVITIES, HOBBIES, AND THE LIKE								
TOTAL NUMBER RESPONDING	1,487	100.0	1,479	100.0	1,477	100.0	1,489	100.0
A great deal[1]	813	54.7	811	54.8	841	56.9	856	57.5
Quite a bit[2]	521	35.0	523	35.4	505	34.2	430	28.9
A little or none	153	10.3	145	9.8	131	8.9	203	13.6
Total sample size ...	1,504	(X)	1,484	(X)	1,490	(X)	1,499	(X)
CONFIDENCE IN PEOPLE RUNNING TELEVISION								
TOTAL NUMBER RESPONDING	1,480	100.0	1,464	100.0	1,451	100.0	1,464	100.0
A great deal	278	18.8	347	23.7	265	18.3	279	19.1
Only some	875	59.1	861	58.8	853	58.7	779	53.2
Hardly any	327	22.1	256	17.5	333	23.0	406	27.7
Total sample size ...	1,504	(X)	1,484	(X)	1,490	(X)	1,499	(X)
CONFIDENCE IN PEOPLE RUNNING THE PRESS								
TOTAL NUMBER RESPONDING	1,477	100.0	1,463	100.0	1,442	100.0	1,463	100.0
A great deal	346	23.4	383	26.2	354	24.6	424	29.0
Only some	911	61.7	821	56.1	823	57.0	776	53.0
Hardly any	220	14.9	259	17.7	265	18.4	263	18.0
Total sample size ...	1,504	(X)	1,484	(X)	1,490	(X)	1,499	(X)

Source: National Opinion Research Center (NORC), University of Chicago, *National Data Program for the Social Sciences, Code Book for the Spring 19--, General Social Survey* (1973, 1974, 1975, and 1976). Copyright by NORC. Used by permission.

X Not applicable.

[1] Includes the response category "a very great deal."

[2] Includes the response categories "a fair amount" and "some."

Chart 10/16A

Social Indicators, 1976

SATISFACTION WITH FRIENDSHIPS AND LEISURE-TIME ACTIVITIES AND CONFIDENCE IN TELEVISION AND THE PRESS: 1973–1976

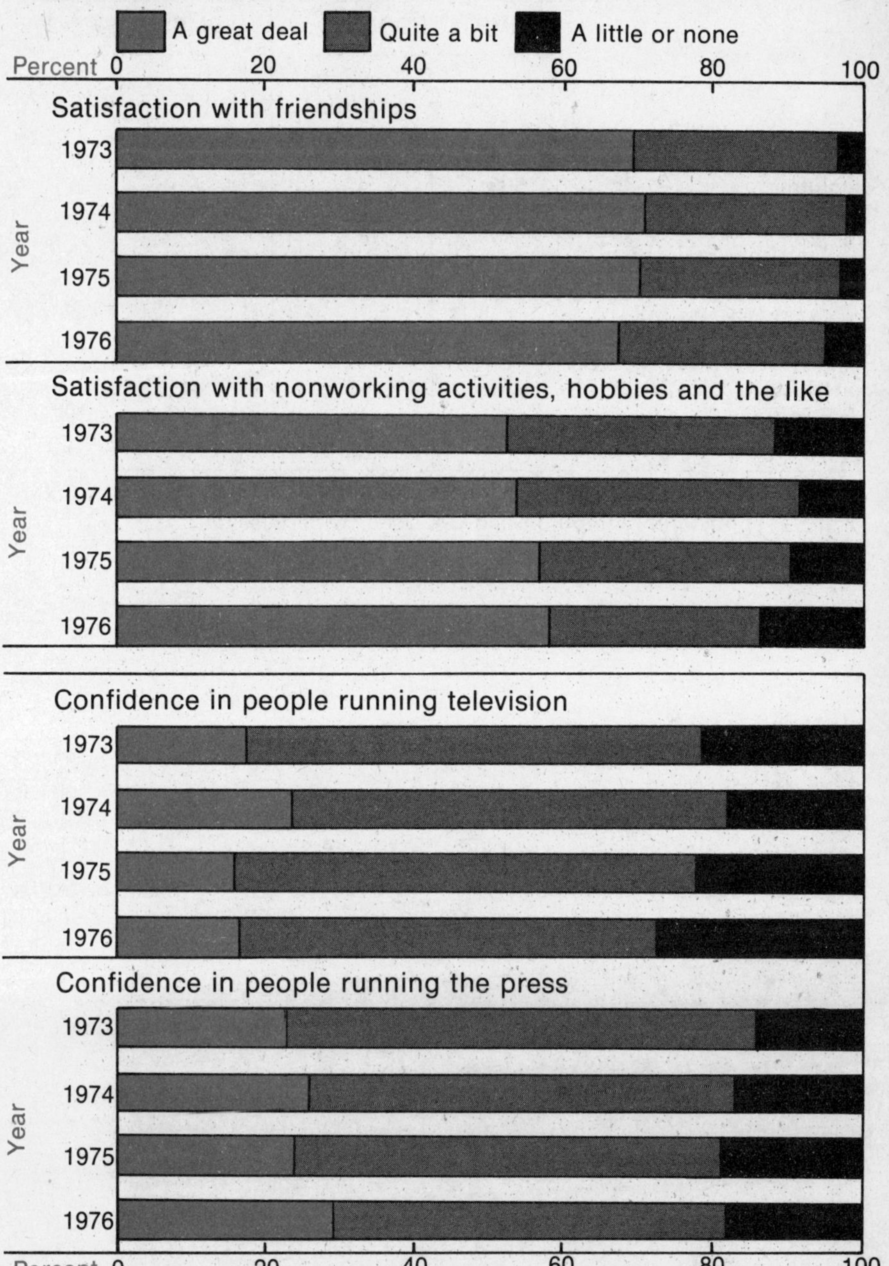

Source: see table 10/16

Table 10/17

TIME SPENT AT MAIN JOB AND TRAVEL TO AND FROM JOB, BY SEX, SELECTED COUNTRIES: 1965–66

(Average minutes per workday)

COUNTRY	EMPLOYED MEN		EMPLOYED WOMEN	
	Main job	Travel to and from job	Main job	Travel to and from job
Belgium	503	47	412	34
Czechoslovakia	477	53	390	39
France	517	47	439	38
Germany (Fed. Republic)	538	45	387	29
Hungary	503	69	454	50
Peru	445	84	361	63
Poland	482	61	427	52
United States	480	52	411	42
U.S.S.R.	444	48	429	42
Yugoslavia	465	52	428	46

Source: Alexander Szalai (ed.), The Use of Time, (The Hague: Mouton and Co., 1972). Copyright by Mouton and Co. Used by permission.

Chart 10/17

Social Indicators, 1976

TIME SPENT AT MAIN JOB AND TRAVEL TIME TO AND FROM JOB: 1965–1966

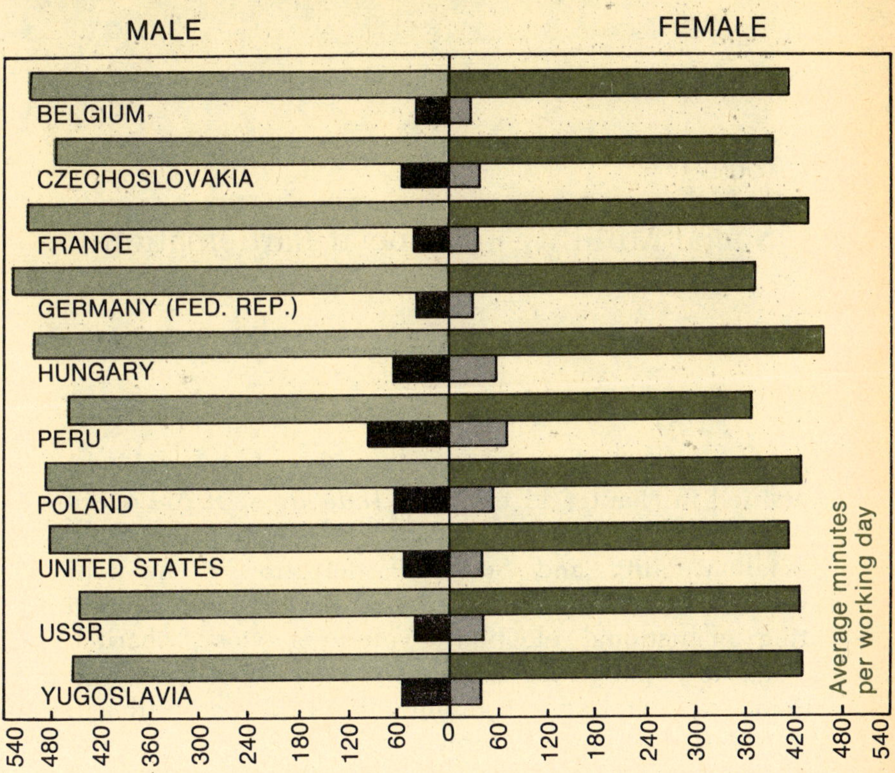

Source: see table 10/17

ANNALS, AAPSS, 435, Jan. 1978

Social Mobility and Social Participation

By WILLIAM H. SEWELL

ABSTRACT: This article examines the charts and tables contained in chapter 11 of *Social Indicators, 1976* covering a wide range of social behavior under the general topic "Social Mobility and Social Participation." The topics covered include educational and occupational mobility, voting in national elections, volunteer work, charitable giving, participation in community organizations, views on religion, and feelings of anomie. Most readers will agree that this is a potpourri of topics but that all have bearing on the well-being of citizens. There would be less agreement on the significance of most of the indicators for public policy. The factual conclusions that can be drawn from the tables and charts are discussed and additional information from recent research on some of the topics is presented—particularly on educational and occupational mobility, voting and political behavior, and participation in community organizations.

William H. Sewell is Vilas Research Professor of Sociology at the University of Wisconsin. He has published extensively on social stratification. His recent books include: The Uses of Sociology (1969) *(coedited with Lazarsfeld and Wilensky)*; Attitudes and Facilitation in the Attainment of Status (1972) *(coauthored with Gasson and Haller)*; Education, Occupation, and Earnings: Achievement in the Early Career (1975) *(coauthored with Hauser); and* Schooling and Achievement in American Society (1976) *(coedited with Hauser and Featherman).*

CHAPTER 11 of *Social Indicators, 1976*, is devoted to the topic "Social Mobility and Social Participation." It includes 22 charts and the tables on which these charts are based. The sources of this information are numerous, but all come from sample surveys made by various governmental and private-not-for-profit research agencies. Unlike indicators based on census data, the time dimensions involved are usually limited to recent years; consequently, it is difficult in some instances to detect a trend. The indicators selected for inclusion actually cover a very wide range of social behavior that presumably provide a basis for gauging the well-being of citizens in the United States, which is the stated purpose of the chapter. They are educational and occupational mobility, voting in national elections, volunteer work, charitable giving, participation in voluntary associations, views on the importance of religion, and feelings of anomie. This is indeed a potpourri of topics, but most readers would agree that all of them have a bearing on the well-being of citizens. On the particular indicators selected for presentation and their importance for social well-being, there will be much less general agreement. Finally, there would be great disagreement about the significance of most of the indicators for public policy. I am not convinced that my opinions on these matters are of any great interest, nor are any more informed than those of the reader. Consequently, little space will be devoted to these matters. Rather, the factual conclusions that can be drawn from the information contained in the indicators will be discussed. If I consider the topic to be of great importance and if I know something about it from my own research and reading, additional information will be presented. Greatest attention will be given to social mobility because this is my area of specialization. Somewhat less attention will be given to voting and political behavior because I have not done original research in this area, but an attempt will be made to supplement the information reflected in the indicators by providing a brief and selective summary of pertinent findings from recent research on the topic. I have no special knowledge or interest in the other topics contained under the rubric social participation. Consequently, my handling of these matters admittedly will be perfunctory.

SOCIAL MOBILITY

Sociologists have long been fascinated with the amount and nature of social mobility in a given society. American sociologists have been particularly concerned with this subject, perhaps because the American value system places great emphasis not only on socioeconomic achievement but also on equality of opportunity for social and economic advancement. Much of the research on social stratification in American society has been involved with the extent to which the members of our society, at a particular point in time, have been able to take advantage of opportunities to improve their social status over that of their parents and with the trends in social mobility over time. Most of the studies have been of adult, white males, and have been concerned with comparing the attainments of a sample of sons with those of their fathers. Much of this research has been done using a mobility table in which the son's current status (education, occupation, earnings, etc.) is cross-tabulated with his father's status at some point in the father's working career. Such a table provides the basis for estimating the extent to which adult sons have moved up or down or remained in the same status category as their fathers. The marginals of the mobility table also provide information on the status distributions of the father's and the son's generations. However, only limited inferences about earlier periods may be drawn from these comparisons because the fathers tend to be a biased sample of men in the parental generation—obviously males without male children could not possibly be in the sample. For that matter, there are a number of technical problems, which need not be gone into here, in the computation of mobility statistics from mobility matrices.[1]

The two status achievements that have been the subject of greatest analysis are educational and occupational attainments—the two on which charts and tables have been presented in Chapter 11 of *Social Indicators, 1976.*

Educational mobility

Data are available to show the changes in the mean levels of education completed by five-year birth cohorts of American men in the civilian, noninstitutionalized population in March 1962 and March 1973, and to indicate the intergenerational—father to son—shifts in educational attainment at the two time periods. The 1962 data are from the Blau and Duncan Occupational Changes in a Generation (OCG) survey[2] and the 1973 data are from replicate surveys conducted by Featherman and Hauser.[3,4]

Levels of education of cohorts of men born since 1900 have been increasing substantially and regularly over a period of 50 years. The evidence for this is that both in the 1962 and in the 1973 samples, men in each successively younger birth cohort had obtained more education than those born earlier in the century. Thus, in the 1962 sample the range in mean educational attainment was from 8.9 for men aged 60–65 (born 1897–1901) to 11.8 for men aged 20–25 (born 1937–41). In the 1973 sample, the means for the same age groups were 9.9 (born 1907–11) and 12.8 (born 1937–51), respectively. If we compare the oldest age group, those who were 60–65 in 1962, with the youngest, those who were 20–25 in 1973, the mean increase in schooling is 3.7 years, which probably is an underestimate of the true increase because many of those in the youngest cohort were still in school or would return for more schooling in the future.

Another important trend is that there has been a great decrease in the variability of schooling across age cohorts. Because of this trend and the general trend toward higher levels of educational attainment, inequality in the distribution of schooling has fallen rapidly from one

1. For a discussion of these problems, see Robert M. Hauser, "A Structural Model of the Mobility Table," *Social Forces*, vol. 56 (March 1978).

2. Peter M. Blau and Otis D. Duncan, *The American Occupational Structure* (New York: Wiley, 1967).

3. David L. Featherman and Robert M. Hauser, "Design for A Replicate Study of Social Mobility in the United States," in *Social Indicator Models*, eds. Kenneth C. Land and Seymour Spilerman (New York: Russell Sage Foundation, 1975) pp. 219–52.

4. Robert M. Hauser and David L. Featherman, "Equality of Schooling: Trends and Prospects," *Sociology of Education*, vol. 49 (April 1976) pp. 99–120.

cohort to the next. Thus, schooling has become more equally distributed during the twentieth century.[5]

In March 1962 sons reported that they have had from two to three years more education than their fathers. For the 1973 survey, the sons reported from two to almost four years more schooling than their fathers. The intergenerational differences were greatest in the ten year period 1917–27 and have since declined. Thus, the trend would appear to be for the educational gap between fathers and their sons to be narrowing over time. It is possible that this gap will continue to lessen because of the increasingly high proportion of men in each cohort who are graduating from high school and obtaining postsecondary education. Unless a trend toward greater college retention occurs in the future, it seems quite likely that we will soon be reaching a mean educational level that will not be greatly exceeded by future generations.

Hauser and Featherman have done further analysis of the data from the OCG surveys. Their regression analysis of factors associated with educational achievement indicates that the disadvantages which in the past have been associated with farm background, broken families, southern birth, black skin, and Spanish origin seem to be declining but that those associated with large families and poorly educated fathers have persisted. Finally, their analysis of similarities in the correlations between the educational attainments of their sample members and their eldest brothers indicates that at least 50 percent of the variance in schooling which they have observed in their analysis can be explained by the global effects of family background.[6]

Race and schooling

Unfortunately, there is no information on mean years of schooling completed nor on intergenerational shifts in educational attainment for blacks. However, we may again turn to the research of Hauser and Featherman for information on trends in schooling by race.[7] Their evidence, comparing the educational achievements of white and black men in the 1962 and 1973 OCG samples, shows that there were large and regular increases in the educational attainments of both races. The mean years of schooling of the total sample of black males was 8.1 years in 1962 and 10.1 years in 1973; the comparable figures for white males were 11.0 years in 1962 and 12.0 years in 1973. In 1962, the oldest cohort of black workers (aged 60–65) averaged 5.4 years of schooling, but by 1973 the youngest cohort (aged 20–25) averaged 11.6 years; for whites the comparable means were 9.6 and 12.7. Also, there was a decline in educational inequality, as indicated by lower standard deviations, for both black and white males. This decline was brought about by the combined effects of the reduced importance of social background and by increased equality among men with the same social backgrounds. Specific comparisons of the mean educational attainments of black and white males by birth cohorts reveals that among young males (aged 25–34) the gap between the races narrowed from 2.3 in 1962 to 1.2 years in 1973. Actually, when differences in the socioeconomic backgrounds of black and white young men are

5. Ibid., pp. 102–104.

6. Ibid., pp. 104–18.

7. Ibid., pp. 111–16.

taken into account, their educational attainments are now virtually identical. Hauser and Featherman did not have similar information on the educational attainments of either black or white females, so parallel comparisons were not made for women.

The fact that comparable tables covering women's educational achievements by race are not available from the OCG surveys, and that no attempt has been made to present the data from Census and other sources on trends in women's educational mobility, must be counted as a major shortcoming of Chapter 11 of *Social Indicators, 1976.*

Occupational mobility

There have been important changes in social stratification and, more particularly, in occupational mobility in the United States in the period 1962–73.[8] A comparison of the data for 1962 with the same data for 1973 for all employed men, mainly white, shows a trend away from farming and manual occupations into white-collar occupations. The percentage of all employed men who were in each of the white-collar occupational categories was somewhat larger in 1973 than in 1962, whereas the percentage in each manual occupational category declined slightly and the percentage in farming declined markedly during the period. This overall trend out of farming and manual occupations into the white-collar occupations has been going on in the United States throughout this century.

8. Based on tables contained in Robert M. Hauser and David L. Featherman, "Occupations and Social Mobility in the United States" (Discussion Paper no. 36, Institute for Research on Poverty, University of Wisconsin, Madison, 1976).

On the whole, blacks have made a rather striking shift from lower status occupations to higher status occupations during the period. Just under 6 percent of all employed black men were in upper white-collar jobs in 1962, but in 1973 almost 12 percent were so employed. Likewise, only 6 percent of the blacks were in lower white-collar occupations in 1962 in comparison with just over 11 percent in 1973. Moreover, black gains were not limited to the white-collar occupations; blacks were also considerably more likely to be in upper manual occupations in 1973 than in 1962 (15 percent versus 9 percent, respectively). These upward trends in the occupational distribution of black workers resulted from shifts out of lower manual work and farming into higher status occupations. However, it should be noted that despite the marked gains by blacks, inferrable from the occupational distributions in 1962 and 1973, blacks in 1973 were still noticeably concentrated in the lower manual occupational status category; 68 percent of all black workers were lower manual in 1962 and in 1973 the figure was 59 percent.

There was a marked tendency toward occupational status inheritance for the total male civilian labor force, both in 1962 and in 1973. Sons in a given occupational status category were more likely to have been recruited from their father's occupational category than from any other occupational category. There was also a great deal of occupational mobility among male workers, both in the 1962 and in the 1973 samples. In both years, well over one-fourth of the sons of upper white-collar workers were in manual occupations; for sons of lower white-collar workers the movement into the manual occupations was still greater. However, there was even more upward mobility: in both of the years, from 30 to 40 percent of the sons of manual workers were engaged in white-collar work. A comparison of the occupational distributions of sons and their fathers indicates that approximately one-half of the sons were upwardly mobile in 1962 and in 1973. What is striking, however, is that there are no important differences in the patterns of father-son mobility in 1962 and 1973.

The pattern of occupational inheritance, indicated by the fact that sons were most likely to be in the same occupational status category as their fathers, does not hold for blacks in either 1962 or 1973. The most striking fact is that black fathers are less able to pass on their higher status occupations to their sons than are higher status fathers generally. Thus, in both 1962 and 1973, but especially in 1962, the most likely destination for sons of blacks whose fathers were white-collar workers was lower manual occupations. In fact, this was the most likely occupation for black males, in both 1962 and 1973, regardless of their origins. Upward movement, from the manual to the white-collar occupations, although sizeable, was considerably less marked in both years. The movement out of farming, especially into the manual occupations, was impressive in both years. Still there was a rather dramatic shift in 1973 in the occupational mobility of black men toward the pattern which characterized all men in the labor force in 1962 and 1973. Thus, in 1973 there was a strong tendency for black sons of white-collar fathers to become white-collar workers, and there was an increased likelihood that sons of farmers and manual workers would enter the white-collar occupations. Even with these changes, black men in 1973 experienced less occupational inheritance and less upward mobility than all employed men.

What has been said above is true only in a gross sense and more precise conclusions about occupational mobility in the period can come only from more complete analysis of the data. It is obvious that one would wish to know more accurately the extent to which upward mobility during the period is due to increases in the relative mobility chances of men whose fathers held different occupations, rather than to changes in the occupational structure over the period. One would wish also to know the extent to which any gains in upward occupational mobility, for either whites or blacks, were distributed among various age cohorts of employed men. Finally, to the extent possible, one would wish to know more about the complex process by which sons attain their current occupational status, taking into account at least their socioeconomic origins, including their fathers' occupation and their fathers' education, their own educational attainments, and their initial jobs. These are the variables used by Blau and Duncan in their now classic causal model of occupational attainment.[9] If possible, one would wish also to know the effects of measured ability and other social-psychological variables such as school grades, the encouragement of significant others, and educational and occupational aspirations in the attainment process. These are the variables that Sewell and his associates have introduced into the Blau and Duncan model to

9. Blau and Duncan, *American Occupational Structure*, pp. 163–204.

further explain the process of socioeconomic achievement.[10]

Fortunately, in the past ten years a great deal of analyses of the kinds noted above have been completed. Although many scholars have been involved in this research, the most pertinent and extensive recent work has been carried out by Featherman and Hauser, using data from the OCG surveys and the Census. While it would be impossible in the space available to adequately summarize their analyses, several of their major conclusions should be presented to round out our discussion of occupational mobility.[11]

First, using much finer grained categories of occupational status, they have shown that the shift in the occupational structure, toward the ranks of upper white-collar and lower white-collar occupations and away from farming and manual occupations, has been going on for several decades in the United States.[12]

Second, the long-time trend in occupational mobility in the United States is neither uniform nor inevitable. In the period 1962–73 there was more mobility than in the previous decade but less than in 1942–52. Future occupational mobility is greatly limited by the rapid depletion of such occupational groups as service workers, laborers, and farmers, which in the past have served as sources for recruitment into the higher status occupations.

Third, no changes have taken place in the rates of intergenerational occupational mobility in the American male labor force in the last half-century that cannot be accounted for by the changing occupational distribution.[13] The evidence

10. William H. Sewell, Archibald O. Haller, and Alejandro Portes, "The Educational and Early Occupational Attainment Process," *American Sociological Review*, vol. 34 (February 1969) pp. 82–92; and William H. Sewell, Archibald O. Haller, and George W. Ohlendorf, "The Educational and Early Occupational Attainment Process: Replication and Revisions," *American Sociological Review*, vol. 35 (December 1970) pp. 1014–27.

11. For further detail and for consideration of aspects of their work not covered by references in this article, the reader may wish to consult Robert M. Hauser and David L. Featherman, *The Process of Stratification: Trends and Analysis* (New York: Academic Press, 1977); and David L. Featherman and Robert M. Hauser, *Opportunity and Change* (forthcoming, Academic Press).

Important recent work on stratification and social mobility not cited in this article would include at least the following: James S. Coleman *et al.*, *Equality of Educational Opportunity* (Washington, D.C.: USGPO, 1966); Otis D. Duncan, David L. Featherman, and Beverly Duncan, *Socioeconomic Background and Achievement* (New York: Seminar Press, 1972); R. W. Hodge and D. J. Treiman, "Class Identification in the United States," *American Journal of Sociology*, vol. 73 (March 1968), pp. 535–42; Leo A. Goodman, "How to Ransack Social Mobility Tables and Other Kinds of Cross-Classification Tables," *American Journal of Sociology*, vol. 75 (July 1969) pp. 1–40; Otis D. Duncan, "Social Stratification and Social Mobility: Problems in the Measurement of Trend," in *Indicators of Social Change*, eds. Eleanor B. Sheldon and Wilbert E. Moore (New York: Russell Sage Foundation, 1968); Natale R. Ramsøy, "Changes in the Rates and Forms of Mobility," in *Social Structure and Mobility in Economic Development*, eds. Neil J. Smelser and Seymour M. Lipset (Chicago: Aldine, 1966); Lawrence E. Hazelrigg and Maurice A. Garnier, "Occupational Mobility In Industrial Societies: A Comparative Analysis of Differential Access to Occupational Ranks in Seventeen Countries," *American Sociological Review*, vol. 41 (June 1976) pp. 498–510); and Joan Huber and William H. Form, *Income and Ideology* (New York: Free Press, 1973).

12. Robert M. Hauser and David L. Featherman, "Trends in the Occupational Mobility of U.S. Men, 1962–1970," *American Sociological Review*, vol. 38 (June 1973) pp. 302–10.

13. See especially Robert M. Hauser *et al.*, "Temporal Change in Occupational Mobility: Evidence for Men in the United States,"

indicates that although successive cohorts have had more opportunities to enter high status occupations, regardless of their social origins, the dependence of son's occupation upon father's has been remarkably stable for more than 50 years in the United States.

Fourth, turning more specifically to the findings regarding occupational mobility by race, it is clear that although the average occupational status of men in the experienced civilian labor force rose between 1962 and 1973, blacks gained more than whites but black men were still considerably behind white men in occupational status in 1973. In fact, blacks in 1973 had not yet reached the average occupational status held by white men in 1962.[14] In examining the reasons behind the shifts, Featherman and Hauser note that among white men family factors were less important in occupational allocation in 1973 than they were in 1962, but that schooling had increased in importance; whereas, among black men the effects of family background have become more closely linked with occupational attainment over the period and black men with the same socioeconomic background and educational attainment were in higher status jobs in 1973 than in 1962.[15] Moreover, in younger cohorts of workers, patterns of occupational stratification by race were less in 1973 than in 1962, but socioeconomic discrimination by race was still marked in the older cohorts of workers. Featherman and Hauser in summarizing their findings say ". . . race and class have become less important in the processes that allocate men from families to schooling and subsequently to positions in the occupational hierarchy."[16]

Economic attainments

The distribution of income and wealth have not been discussed in this paper, even though many consider this to be the ultimate stratification issue, because these matters are covered in another chapter of *Social Indicators, 1976*, and in another essay in this issue of THE ANNALS. We should summarize briefly, however, the results of recent attempts to use the Blau and Duncan[17] and the Wisconsin causal models[18] to explain economic achievements. The two best-known studies, by Jencks[19] and Sewell and Hauser[20] have shown that although the status attainment models explain educational and occupa-

American Sociological Review, vol. 40 (June 1975), pp. 279–97; and Robert M. Hauser *et al.*, "Structural Changes in Social Mobility Among Men in the United States," *American Sociological Review*, vol. 40 (October 1975), pp. 585–98.

14. Robert M. Hauser and David L. Featherman, "White-Nonwhite Differentials in Social Mobility Among Men in the United States, 1962–1972," *Demography*, vol. 11 (May 1974) pp. 247–65.

15. David L. Featherman and Robert M. Hauser, "Changes in the Socioeconomic Stratification of the Races," *American Journal of Sociology*, vol. 82 (November 1976) pp. 621–51.

16. Ibid., p. 621.

17. Blau and Duncan, *American Occupational Structure*.

18. Sewell, Haller, and Portes, "Educational and Early Occupation Attainment Process."

19. Christopher Jencks, *et al.*, *Inequality: A Reassessment of the Effects of Family and Schooling in America* (New York: Basic Books, 1972).

20. William H. Sewell and Robert M. Hauser, "Causes and Consequences of Higher Education: Models of the Status Attainment Process," *American Journal of Agricultural Economics*, vol. 54 (December 1972) pp. 851–61 and Idem, *Education, Occupation, and Earnings: Achievement in the Early Career* (New York: Academic Press, 1975).

tional attainments quite effectively (as being largely dependent on socioeconomic background and ability), they are much less efficient in explaining economic attainments, accounting for 8 to 20 percent of the variance in earnings or income, depending on the model and the sample used.

This finding has resulted in a great deal of controversy, especially among those who have thought that programs designed to reduce educational inequality would greatly reduce economic inequality. While neither Jencks nor Sewell and Hauser deny that education influences earnings or income, their results indicate that factors not included in their models must be taken into account in explaining inequality in economic attainment. Jencks has said that the principal factor may be luck. Sewell and Hauser place less emphasis on luck, although not denying its importance, and suggest that factors having to do with more recent experiences such as family formation, marital stability, migration, job markets, on-the-job training, and job satisfaction may help to explain economic success. They and other researchers, including Jencks, have undertaken research to test these suppositions. The search for causal explanations of differences in economic attainments is likely to continue to engage the attention of social scientists during the next decade as new data accumulate and as better multivariate techniques become available for data analysis.

Sexual stratification

Although the tables on social mobility presented in *Social Indicators, 1976*, do not contain information on sexual inequalities in socioeconomic achievements, our exposition would be incomplete without a summary of the most important findings of the recent research on the occupational mobility of women. The major studies have been those of Tyree and Treas, Treiman and Terrell, McClendon, Featherman and Hauser, and Sewell, Hauser and Wolf.[21] Because the Featherman and Hauser analysis is based on the OCG–I and –II surveys, and because their results do not differ greatly from those of most of the other studies, we may summarize their findings, supplementing them with information from other research where appropriate.[22]

The Featherman and Hauser

21. Andrea Tyree and Judith Treas, "The Occupation and Marital Mobility of Women," *American Sociological Review*, vol. 39 (June 1974), pp. 293–302; Donald J. Treiman and Kermit Terrell, "Sex and the Process of Status Attainment: A Comparison of Working Women and Men," *American Sociological Review*, vol. 40 (April 1975) pp. 194–200; McKee J. McClendon, "The Occupational Status Attainment of Males and Females," *American Sociological Review*, vol. 41 (February 1976), pp. 52–64; David L. Featherman and Robert M. Hauser, "Sexual Inequalities and Socioeconomic Achievement in the U.S., 1962–73," *American Sociological Review*, vol. 41 (June 1976) pp. 462–83; and William H. Sewell, Robert M. Hauser, and Wendy C. Wolf, "New Findings in Sex Similarities and Differences in the Occupational Attainment Process," (Paper for the Center for Demography and Ecology, University of Wisconsin, Madison, 1977).

22. The analysis reported by Featherman and Hauser is based on married persons in the experienced labor force in 1962 and 1973 and therefore their findings for women (the wives of the men in the OCG samples) may not hold for all employed women. However, evidence from a recent study indicates that this sampling limitation probably does not bias their results appreciably. Wendy C. Wolf, "How Biased are Sex Comparisons of Occupational Attainment when Wives of Male Respondents are Utilized as the Sample of Women?" (Paper no. 17 for the Center for Demography and Ecology, University of Wisconsin, Madison, 1977).

analysis of intercohort shifts in educational attainment, occupational status, and earnings, indicates that there were socioeconomic improvements for both men and women during the period 1962–73. Improvements in the educational and occupational attainments of women somewhat exceed those for men, on the average, but the ratios of female to male average earnings were slightly lower in 1973 than in 1962, 0.38 and 0.39, respectively. Thus, greater equality of educational and occupational opportunity has not yet produced anything approaching equality of economic opportunity for women. Causal models show that men and women tend to be allocated to educational and occupational statuses in much the same way. Women's socioeconomic achievements are less related to family origins, especially farm origins, than are men's and the net effect of educational attainment on occupational status is greater for women than for men.[23]

These findings are in general agreement with the earlier studies cited above. However, the most recent study, by Sewell, Hauser, and Wolf, in which attainment models are based on large independent samples of men and women, and which contain additional important variables not available in the OCG data sets, such as parental income, measured intelligence, and first job, reports interesting differences in the occupational attainment processes of males and females that have not been noted before.[24] The most important finding from the standpoint of the current discussion is that, although women obtain first jobs that on the average are of considerably higher status than those of men, by mid-life men are in higher status occupations than women. Their discussion of the way men and women are sorted into occupations suggests a complicated allocation process. Apparently both men and women rely heavily on their educational attainments for their first jobs but for later occupational placement men rely increasingly on experience and less on educational attainments. Women, on the other hand, because they have less continuous occupational histories and because the occupations they enter provide fewer opportunities for promotion to higher status jobs, must continue to depend mainly on their educational qualifications for later occupational placement. Men clearly profit by their experience in the labor market and tend to be upwardly mobile over their working lives, whereas women tend to remain essentially at the same occupational status level throughout their working careers.

Subjective class placement

American scholars have long been interested in subjective class placement; essentially the question is "how do people place themselves in the class structure?" Subjective class placement may be viewed as the psychological dimension of class, based on self-attribution and identification with others perceived to have similar attitudes, values, and interests. Centers's classic studies showed that over half (51 percent of all American adult male workers in 1945 considered themselves to be in the working class and well over two-fifths (43 percent) placed themselves in the middle class.[25] Only 3 percent

23. Featherman and Hauser, "Sexual Inequalities and Socioeconomic Achievement."

24. Sewell, Hauser, and Wolf, "New Findings in Sex Similarities."

25. Richard Centers, *The Psychology of Social Class* (Princeton, N. J.: Princeton University Press, 1949) and Idem, "Social

placed themselves in the upper class and only 1 percent said they were lower class. One of the most interesting findings was that, regardless of occupation, most men placed themselves in either the middle or the working class category. Even the owners of large businesses and professional men were quite unlikely to place themselves in the upper class, and manual workers were even more unlikely to place themselves in the lower class.

Centers's questions have been repeated in the National Opinion Research Center's General Social Survey in each successive year since 1972. The interesting fact is not that so little change has taken place in subjective class placement over the four-year period covered by the NORC surveys, but that contemporary men's subjective placements do not differ in any substantial way from those reported by Centers over 30 years ago. Thus, it would appear that, for whatever reasons, American men hold tenaciously to the view that they are members of a society in which almost everyone is concentrated into two main classes at the middle of a hierarchy in which few persons are in either the upper or the lower classes.

SOCIAL PARTICIPATION

This section of the social report has little if anything to do with social mobility but is included in the same chapter because social participation and social mobility are assumed to have a central role in the well-being of the citizens of the United States. The section is concerned with the extent to which citizens are involved in different forms of personal and community activities, including voting in national elections, volunteer work, philanthropy, and group and association membership. Also included are selected indicators of religiosity and anomie.

Voting behavior

Perhaps the most generally interesting set of indicators in this section have to do with voting behavior. This is a topic to which social scientists have devoted great attention over the years.[26] These indicators are designed to call attention to trends in voting in national elections and to the reasons given for not participating in elections by various categories of persons of voting age. Voting in national elections has varied a good deal between 1930 and 1976, reaching a peak in 1960 when 63 percent of the voting aged population voted in the presidential election. Since 1960 the percentage voting in presidential elections

Class, Occupation, and Reputed Belief," *American Journal of Sociology*, vol. 58 (May 1953), pp. 543–55. See also, Mary R. Jackman and Robert W. Jackman, "An Interpretation of the Relationship Between Objective and Subjective Social Status," *American Sociological Review*, vol. 38 (October 1973) pp. 569–82.

26. In addition to those studies directly cited in this article, at least the following should be mentioned: Paul F. Lazarsfeld, Bernard R. Berelson, and Helen Gaudet, *The People's Choice* (New York: Duell, Sloan, and Pierce, 1944); Bernard R. Berelson, Paul F. Lazarsfeld, and William N. McPhee, *Voting* (Chicago: University of Chicago Press, 1954); Gabriel Almond and Sidney Verba, *The Civic Culture* (Princeton, N.J.: Princeton University Press, 1963); V. O. Key, *Public Opinion and American Democracy* (New York: Knopf, 1961); Sidney Verba and Norman H. Nye, *Participation in America: Political Democracy and Social Equality* (New York: Harper and Row, 1972); James D. Wright, *The Dissent of the Governed* (New York: Academic Press, 1976); Walter D. Burnham, *Critical Elections and the Mainsprings of American Politics* (New York: Norton, 1970).

has declined steadily, reaching a low of 53 percent in the 1976 elections. The trend in voting in congressional elections is exactly the same, but the percentage voting is always smaller than in presidential elections. Voting is still less in congressional contests in which there is no presidential election. This oldest of political democracies had the lowest voting participation rate of any of the seven major democratic countries for which such data are available.

Comparisons of voting behavior by race and ethnic origin categories over the period 1964–76 show quite clearly that whites are more likely to vote in national elections than are blacks; persons of Spanish origin are least likely to vote of any of the three racial-ethnic categories. There has been a downward trend in voting in presidential and congressional elections by blacks and persons of Spanish origin, just as by white voters, since 1964.

The reason respondents to a national survey, who were registered to vote in the 1974 elections, gave for not voting indicates differences by race and sex.[27] Women, regardless of race, gave illness or family emergencies as their main reasons for not voting. Men were much more likely than women to claim that they could not leave work or get to the voting place—this was particularly true for black men. Lack of interest was given as the reason for not voting by almost one-fifth of all voters and the differences between the races and sexes were small. Very few persons (less than 2 percent) indicated that they did not vote because they felt that their vote would not count.

Two-fifths of the respondents to the survey question asking people why they did not register to vote in the November 1974 election gave as their reason lack of interest.[28] There were no marked sex differences in responses to this question, but blacks gave this response more frequently than whites. Other analysis of the data from these surveys reveals that there were striking differences between major social categories in both registration and voting. The social categories with the highest participation were older persons (aged 45 to 74), those who resided outside of the South, the highly educated (college graduates), those with high annual incomes (over $25,000), and professional and technical workers. Those least likely to register and vote were young persons (aged 18 to 24), residents of the South, those with less than eight years of schooling, those with low annual incomes (less than $5,000), and blue-collar laborers.

The decline in political participation during the past 20 years has occupied the attention of many students of political behavior. Much of the research seeking to explain voter apathy has been done using data from periodic surveys of the public conducted by the Survey Research Center of the University of Michigan, beginning with the 1944 presidential election and continuing to the present.[29] Data from these surveys have been supplemented by

27. U.S. Department of Commerce, Bureau of the Census, "Voting and Registration in the Election of November 1974," *Current Population Reports*, ser. P–20, no. 293 (Washington, D.C., April 1976).

28. U.S. Department of Commerce, Bureau of the Census, "Voting in November 1976" (Advanced Report), ser. P–20, no. 204 (Washington, D.C., December 1976).

29. Angus Campbell and Robert L. Kohn, *The People Elect A President* (Ann Arbor, Michigan: University of Michigan Survey Research Center, ser. no. 9, 1952); and Angus Campbell *et al.*, *The American Voter* (New York: Wiley, 1960).

less comprehensive information on the political activities of Americans from the Gallup poll, since 1935,[30] and from the National Opinion Research Center study of the 1944 presidential election.[31]

It is neither possible nor necessary to go into detail about the results of the many studies of political behavior in the past 20 years, but a recent comprehensive analysis of changing political behavior, based largely on the Survey Research Center files, by Nye, Verba, and Petrocik (*The Changing American Voter*) may be paraphrased and summarized.[32] They find that politics in the United States has changed markedly since the 1950s and that the public has responded in ways that differ fundamentally from political behavior typical of earlier periods. In the 1950s the vast majority of citizens were satisfied with the political process and, although they were only mildly involved in politics, were aligned with one or the other of the two major political parties. In contrast, in the 1960s and early 1970s, citizens were politically aroused by specific issues, identified less with political parties, had less faith in political leaders, and tended to be dissatisfied with the political process.

Nye, Verba, and Petrocik suggest that the political malaise of recent years can perhaps be attributed to the failure of government to solve the major crises of the period: race conflict, the war in Viet Nam, urban decay, Watergate, unemployment, and inflation. All of these issues cut across traditional political party lines and have resulted in a weakening in party loyalty on the part of both voters and candidates. The percentage of citizens who consider themselves to be independent voters has grown substantially and now is approximately the same as the proportion who say they are Democrats and is twice the size of the percentage who say they are Republicans. Issue voting has increased greatly over the period and there has been greater emphasis on the personality of the candidates, with increasing dependence on television in political campaigns. Issue orientation, lack of party identification, distrust of the political process, and a tendency not to register to vote unless the issues or candidates engage their attention, all tend to characterize the younger voters—especially those who have recently obtained the franchise.[33]

What these changes portend for the future of party politics in the United States is not presently apparent. Nye, Verba, and Petrocik suggest that what may evolve is a politics of issue-based factions, with parties and candidates becoming more responsive to citizens' concerns. This does not mean that party politics is likely to fade out of the picture. There are still many more citizens who identify with one of the two major parties than who consider themselves to be independents. Moreover, there is no evidence suggesting the emergence of any signifi-

30. George Gallup, *The Gallup Poll, 1935–1971* (New York: Random House, 1972).

31. Sheldon J. Korchin, "Psychological Variables in the Behavior of Voters" (Ph.D. diss., Harvard University, 1946).

32. Norman H. Nye, Sidney Verba, and John Petrocik, *The Changing American Voter* (Cambridge, Mass.: Harvard University Press, 1976).

33. Participation in elections is lower for citizens 18 to 20 than for any age category. The next least likely group to register or to vote is the 21 to 24 age category. (See the previously cited *Current Population Reports*, ser. P–20, no. 293). Thus has the extension of the franchise to citizens aged 18 to 20 contributed to the downward trend in voting in national elections since 1972.

cant new party. Pomper, in his preliminary analysis of the 1976 presidential election, finds party loyalty to be on the upsurge for the first time in a generation and suggests that the existing parties may be in the process of creating new alliances along regional, class, and issue lines.[34] Miller and Levitan argue that lasting political partisan realignment will depend on the ability of leaders to mobilize the electorate around issues.[35] Crucial in any realignment will be the young voters, about half of whom are independents and thus are open to persuasion, rather than older voters, most of whom tend to be identified with and loyal to their political party.[36]

Other indicators

Just under 24 percent of all persons over 14 years of age did volunteer work of one kind or another in 1974. There appears to have been an increase in the percentage engaged in volunteer work since 1965. Volunteer workers tend to be employed, married, and in the age group 25–44. Whites are much more likely than blacks to do volunteer work. Unfortunately, nothing in the *Social Indicators, 1976* is given on the sex composition of volunteers. The principal reasons given for doing volunteer work are the desire to help people, a sense of duty, and enjoyment of the work.

Households with incomes of over $20,000 in 1973 accounted for almost half (46 percent) of all charitable giving in the United States. The estimated funds spent on private philanthropy rose from just under $9,000,000 in 1960 to over $25,000,000 in 1974. The largest allocations throughout the period were for religion, followed by health, education, and welfare.

National associations are also considered in chapter 11 of *Social Indicators, 1976*. Apparently educational and cultural organizations have grown most rapidly during the period (1968–73), followed by health and medical associations, with scientific, engineering, and technical organizations also prominent. All the types of organizations studied seem to have grown over the period with the single exception of the fraternal, nationality, and ethnic category. The chapter also shows that membership is greatest in church affiliated organizations, followed by membership in school-related groups, sports associations, labor unions, and fraternal associations. There has been a general increase in participation in Red Cross and in scouting organizations through 1970, with some decline in 1974.

Religious beliefs

A huge majority of those responding in 1975–76 to a question on the relative importance of religious beliefs to them said that religious beliefs are very important. Likewise, the preponderant majority expressed a great deal of confidence in or-

34. Gerald M. Pomper, "The Presidential Election" in *The Election of 1976*, eds. Gerald M. Pomper *et al.* (New York: McKay, 1976).

35. Warren E. Miller and Teresa E. Levitan, *Leadership and Change: The New Politics and The American Electorate* (Cambridge, Mass.: Winthrop Publishers, 1976).

36. Converse has demonstrated the importance of new entrance into the voting electorate in producing enduring shifts in political alignments as far back as the elections of 1932 and 1936. See especially, Philip E. Converse, "Public Opinion and Voting Behavior" in *Handbook of Political Science*, vol. 4, eds. Fred Greenstein and Nelson Polsby, (Reading, Mass.: Addison-Wesley, 1975), pp. 75–171; also Kristi Andersen, "Generations, Partisan Shifts and Realignment" in Nye, Verba, and Petrocik, *The Changing American Voter*, chap. 5, pp. 74–95.

ganized religion. Although the majority of those in all social categories shared this view, it was held most strongly by nonwhites, housewives, those with no more than eight grades of schooling, and persons over 50 years of age. A comparison between respondents to this question from selected countries indicates that Americans are outstanding in their confidence in organized religion. The percentage believing that religion is increasing its influence declined drastically between 1957 and 1970, but rose appreciably in 1975 for both males and females and for Protestants and Catholics.

Alienation

From the responses of national samples of adults to specific statements in the Srole Anomie Scale, it is apparent that the majority subscribe to the view that most people do not really know on whom they can count these days, think that public officials are not interested in the common man, and don't care what happens to the next guy. On the other hand, most people disagree with the view that a person has to live for today, that nothing is worthwhile anymore, that it is unfair to bring a child into the world anymore, and that money is the most important thing in life. Between 1974 and 1976 there was a slight trend toward agreement with the latter set of responses. The answers reflecting the more anomic positions are much more likely to be held by those with little schooling. There is no striking response pattern by age. No comparisons are made by sex, race-ethnicity, or socioeconomic categories.[37]

An Additional Note on Social Participation

Social scientists have long been interested in the study of citizen participation in the formal and informal activities of the community. Numerous articles and books have been devoted to this general subject. Unfortunately, there have been very few national surveys of the extent and nature of social participation in the United States at different points in our history. Hyman and Wright have succeeded in providing us with the best available information on trends in voluntary association membership by means of secondary analysis of replications of national surveys made over the period 1955–69 by the National Opinion Research Center.[38] Voluntary association membership is not, and has not been, characteristic of the majority of American adults. Relatively few belong to as many as two organizations. However, there has been a small, but noteworthy, increase in memberships over the period studied. Membership is directly related to current socioeconomic status, measured in a variety of ways, including income, occupation, and education. The trend toward in-

37. There is a vast literature on alienation in the United States, much of which deals with political alienation. Even a summary review of this literature is beyond the scope of this paper. Fortunately for the interested reader recent reviews are available. For an authoritative summary and critique of writings on the general topic, see Melvin Seeman, "Alienation Studies," in *Annual Review of Sociology*, ed. Alex Inkeles (Palo Alto, Calif.: Annual Reviews, Inc., 1975), pp. 91–124. Robert R. Alford and Roger Friedland, "Political Participation and Public Policy," in Ibid., pp. 429–79, provide and equally comprehensive and authoritative review of the literature on political alienation.

38. Herbert H. Hyman and Charles R. Wright, "Trends in Voluntary Association Memberships of American Adults: Replication Based on Secondary Analysis of National Sample Surveys," *American Sociological Review*, vol. 36 (April 1971), pp. 191–206.

creased associational membership occurs in each socioeconomic category, especially among those of lower socioeconomic status. The trend toward increased membership applies to both black and white adults, but is greater for blacks. A recent comprehensive review of the literature on voluntarism by Smith adds to the above the following facts: males have higher membership rates in voluntary associations than females, persons in the age range 35–55 are more likely to participate than those in older or younger age groups, and married people are more likely to participate than single people.[39] Smith also presents evidence from a small number of studies which suggests that higher participation in voluntary associations is associated with more favorable test scores on such personality traits as social conformity, efficacy (internal control), self-confidence, sociability, assertiveness, need for affiliations, and general personality adjustment. Hyman and Wright and Smith point to the great need for national panel studies on social participation and suggest the need for more sophisticated research on the causes and consequences of participation in voluntary associations.[40]

SUMMARY AND CONCLUSIONS

The level of education in the United States has increased substantially for both black and white men over the past 50 years. Blacks still lag behind white men in schooling but the gap is closing. Among young men racial differences in educational achievement are least because of increased educational opportunities for blacks in recent years.

There has been a marked change in the occupational structure in the United States in the last half century, with a great shift out of farming and manual occupations into white-collar occupations and professions. Blacks have shared in this shift but still continue to be concentrated in the lower status manual occupations.

Occupational status inheritance continues to characterize the employed male population in the United States; sons in a given occupational status category are more likely to have been recruited from their fathers' occupational status category than from any other category. But occupational mobility also continues in the United States. Clearly there is more upward mobility, sons of farmers and manual workers becoming white-collar workers, than downward mobility, sons of white-collar workers becoming blue-collar workers and farmers. However, no changes in occupational mobility have taken place in the last half century that cannot be accounted for by the changing occupational distribution.

National surveys show that black men have made greater gains in occupational status than white men during the period 1962–73, but still in 1973 had not reached the average occupational status held by white men in 1962.

Analysis of intercohort shifts in educational attainment, occupational status, and earnings indicates that there were socioeconomic improvements for both men and women in the period 1962–73. Improvements in the educational and

39. David H. Smith, "Voluntary Action Groups and Voluntary Groups" in *Annual Review of Sociology*, vol. 1, ed. Inkeles (Palo Alto, Calif.: Annual Review, Inc., 1975), pp. 247–70.

40. For examples of the use of causal models in the explanation of participation, see Richard F. Curtis and Elton F. Jackson, *Inequality in American Communities* (New York: Academic Press, 1977).

occupational status of women exceeded those for men but these gains had not yet resulted in anything approaching equal economic opportunity for women.

Recent surveys indicate that Americans hold tenaciously to the view that our society consists of two main classes, positioned in the middle of a status hierarchy, in which relatively few persons are in either the lower or the upper class.

Voting in national elections in the United States has varied considerably from 1930 to 1976, reaching a high of 63 percent in 1960 and steadily declining to 53 percent in 1976. Those least likely to register to vote are young persons (18–24), residents of the South, those with eight years of schooling, blue-collar workers, and blacks.

Recent studies of elections and political participation have noted marked changes in political beliefs and behavior in the past 20 years. In comparison with the 1950s, citizens of the 1960s and 1970s tend to be much less identified with political parties, have less faith in political leaders, are more dissatisfied with the political process, and are more likely to be aroused by specific issues. Young people, particularly those who have recently gained the franchise, are most likely to exhibit these characteristics and are least likely to register to vote.

What these changes portend for the future of party politics in the United States is not clear at present. Possibly a new politics will emerge based on issue-based factions with parties and candidates becoming more responsive to citizens' concerns. Possibly the existing parties will be able to create new alliances along regional, class, age, and issue lines. To date there is little evidence suggesting the emergence of any significant new party.

It is difficult to make any broad generalization on the basis of the evidence contained in *Social Indicators, 1976* concerning social participation in the United States. Participation in voluntary organizations does not appear to have changed greatly in recent years. Most Americans participate in fewer than two voluntary associations. Answers to questions regarding the importance of religion and religious beliefs indicate a higher level of religiosity in the United States than in other industrialized countries for which comparisons are possible. From survey information there is evidence that the majority of adults subscribe to statements which indicate lack of trust in others—especially public officials—but most seem to think that life is still worthwhile and say that money is not the most important thing in life. How this would compare with what citizens would have said a generation or two ago or how these responses would differ from country to country is not known. Without such comparisons it is difficult to gauge the significance of these responses as indicators of the well-being of the citizens of the United States.

Table 11/1
EDUCATIONAL ATTAINMENT AND INTERGENERATIONAL SHIFTS IN EDUCATIONAL ATTAINMENT OF MALES, BY YEAR BORN: 1962 AND 1973
(As of March of each year: civilian noninstitutional population)

Year of birth	Mean years of school completed		Intergenerational shifts (father to son)	
	1962	1973	1962	1973
1947–1951	(1)	12.81	(1)	2.13
1942–1946	(1)	12.76	(1)	2.87
1937–1941	11.78	12.40	2.14	3.22
1932–1936	11.75	12.02	2.93	3.56
1927–1931	11.57	11.72	3.16	3.72
1922–1926	11.19	11.46	3.28	3.77
1917–1921	10.80	11.03	3.07	3.68
1912–1916	10.40	10.55	3.03	3.44
1907–1911	9.86	9.87	2.47	2.97
1902–1906	9.22	(1)	2.06	(1)
1897–1901	8.91	(1)	1.98	(1)

Source: Robert M. Hauser and David L. Featherman, *Equality of Access to Schooling: Trends and Prospects*, (Madison, Wis.: University of Wisconsin). Used by permission.

[1] Not covered in survey.

Chart 11/1B

Social Indicators, 1976

INTERGENERATIONAL SHIFTS IN MEAN YEARS OF SCHOOL COMPLETED (FATHER TO SON): U.S. MALE CIVILIAN NONINSTITUTIONAL POPULATION IN 1962 AND 1973 BY YEAR OF BIRTH

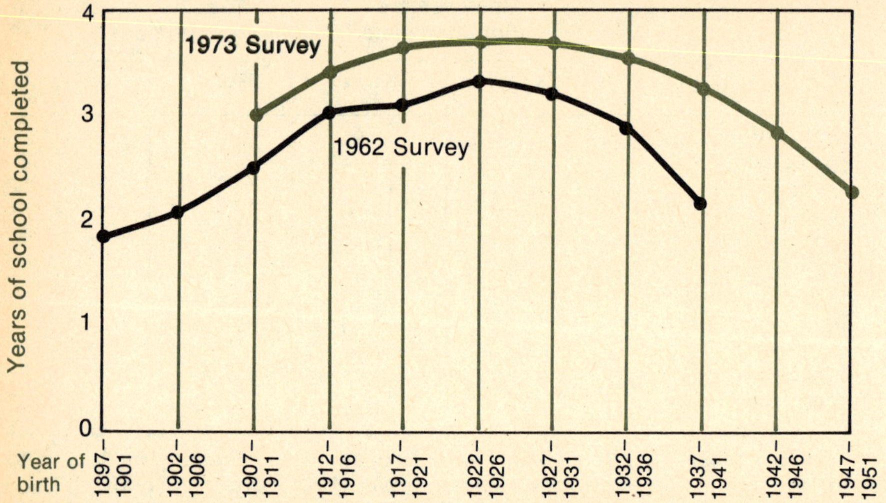

Source: see table 11/2

Table 11/2

OCCUPATIONAL MOBILITY OF MALES, BY RACE: 1962 and 1973

(Percent of the experienced civilian labor force aged 20 to 64)

Year of survey and father's occupation	Total	Son's current occupation: Upper white collar	Lower white collar	Upper manual	Lower manual	Farm	Distribution of fathers by occupation
ALL MALES							
1962							
Total	100.0	27.8	12.4	20.0	32.1	7.7	100.0
Upper white collar	100.0	53.8	17.6	12.5	14.8	1.3	16.5
Lower white collar	100.0	45.6	20.0	14.4	18.3	1.7	7.6
Upper manual	100.0	28.1	13.4	27.8	29.5	1.2	19.0
Lower manual	100.0	20.3	12.3	21.6	43.8	2.0	27.5
Farm	100.0	15.6	7.0	19.2	36.1	22.2	29.4
1973							
Total	100.0	29.9	12.7	21.7	31.5	4.1	100.0
Upper white collar	100.0	52.0	16.0	13.8	17.1	1.1	18.2
Lower white collar	100.0	42.3	19.7	15.3	21.9	.8	9.0
Upper manual	100.0	29.4	13.0	27.4	29.0	1.1	20.5
Lower manual	100.0	22.5	12.0	23.7	40.8	1.0	29.7
Farm	100.0	17.5	7.8	22.7	37.2	14.8	22.6
BLACK MALES							
1962							
Total	100.0	5.9	6.1	9.1	68.3	10.6	100.0
Upper white collar	100.0	10.4	10.3	19.7	59.6	—	4.5
Lower white collar	100.0	14.4	13.5	—	72.1	—	1.9
Upper manual	100.0	8.5	9.7	10.4	67.9	3.6	9.0
Lower manual	100.0	7.6	8.0	10.8	71.4	2.3	37.2
Farm	100.0	3.2	3.3	7.0	66.7	19.8	47.4
1973							
Total	100.0	11.8	10.6	14.8	59.4	3.6	100.0
Upper white collar	100.0	33.2	21.8	10.1	34.8	—	5.0
Lower white collar	100.0	23.8	17.2	12.3	45.8	.9	3.5
Upper manual	100.0	15.2	14.7	15.0	54.9	.2	10.2
Lower manual	100.0	12.4	11.2	13.9	61.4	1.1	46.1
Farm	100.0	5.6	6.2	16.8	62.9	8.5	35.1

Source: Robert M. Hauser and David L. Featherman, *Occupations and Social Mobility in the U.S.* (Madison, Wis.: University of Wisconsin). Used by permission.

— Represents zero.

Chart 11/2 Social Indicators, 1976

MOBILITY FROM FATHER'S (OR OTHER FAMILY HEAD'S) OCCUPATION TO CURRENT OCCUPATION, BY RACE: U.S. MEN IN THE EXPERIENCED CIVILIAN LABOR FORCE AGED 20 TO 64 IN 1962 AND 1973

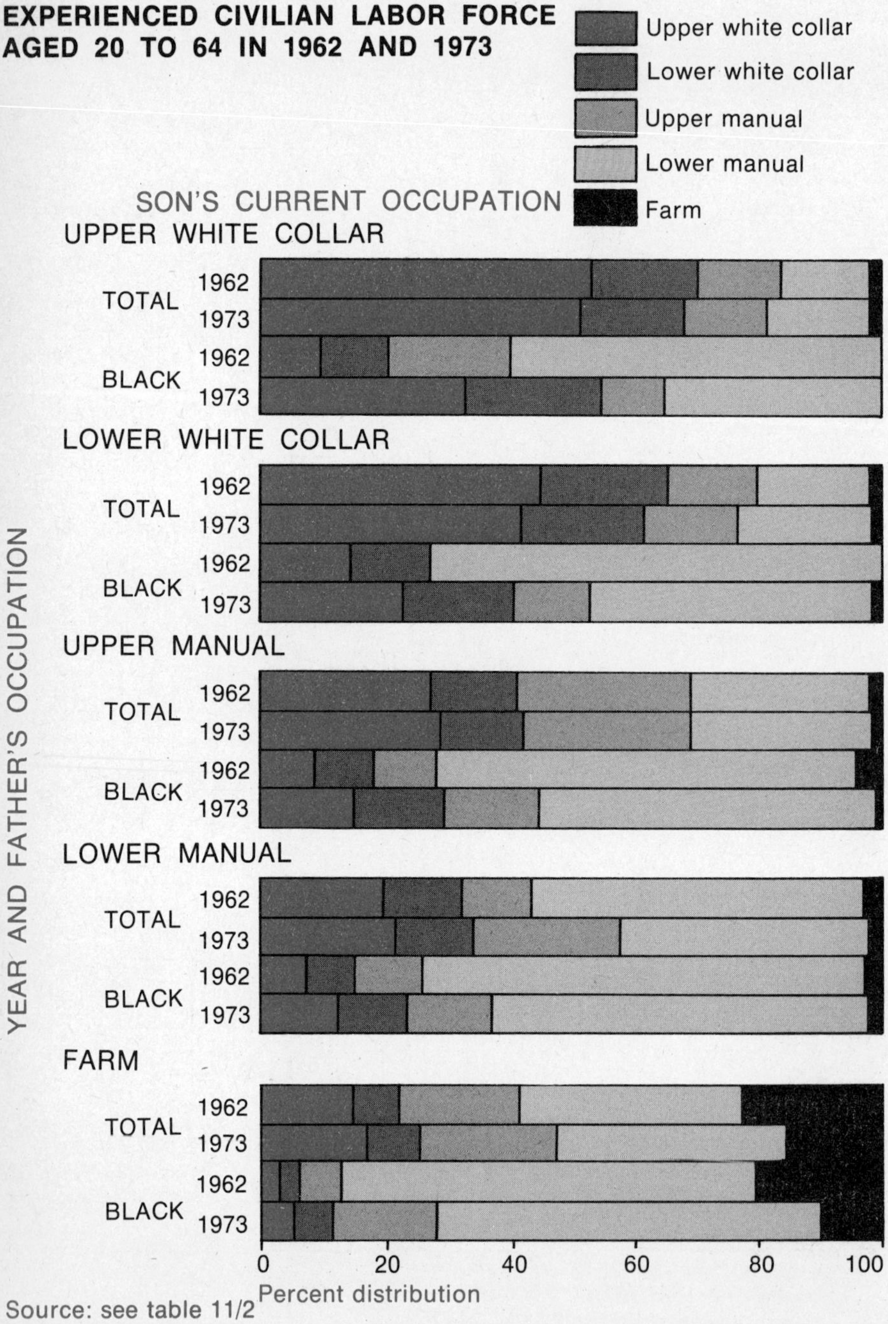

Source: see table 11/2

Chart 11/4 Social Indicators, 1976

REPORTED VOTERS AS A PERCENT OF POPULATION OF VOTING AGE, 1964 TO 1976

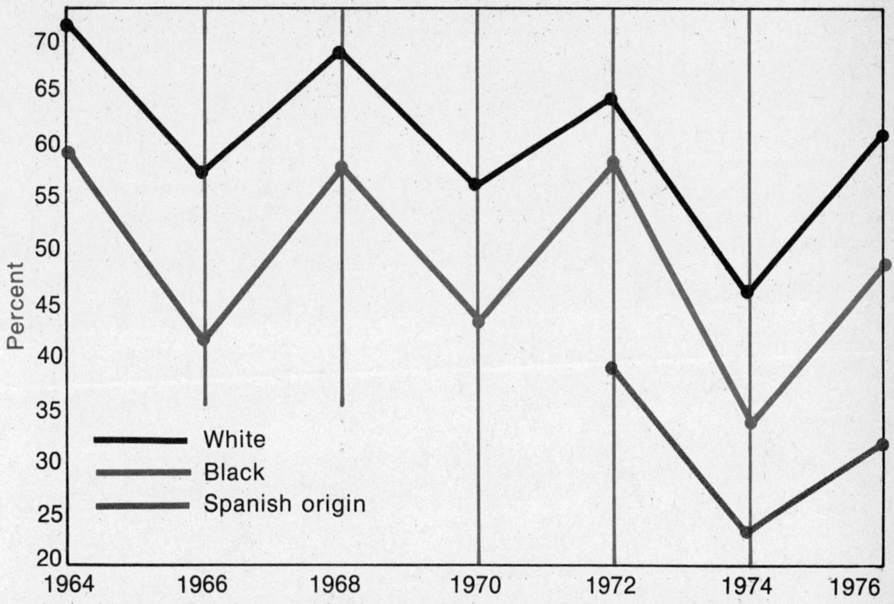

Table 11/4

REPORTED VOTERS AS A PERCENT OF THE VOTING-AGE POPULATION, BY RACE AND SPANISH ORIGIN: 1964–1976

Race and Spanish Origin	1964[1]	1966[2]	1968[1]	1970[2]	1972[1]	1974[2]	1976[1]
Total voting age population, thous. .	110,604	112,800	116,535	120,701	136,203	141,299	146,548
PERCENT REPORTING THAT THEY VOTED							
Total	69.3	55.4	67.8	54.6	63.0	44.7	59.2
White	70.7	57.0	69.1	56.0	64.5	46.3	60.9
Black	58.5	41.7	57.6	43.5	52.1	33.8	48.7
Spanish origin[3]	(NA)	(NA)	(NA)	(NA)	37.5	22.9	31.8

Source: U.S. Department of Commerce, Bureau of the Census, *Current Population Reports,* Series P-20, No. 304.

Note: In 1964, 1966, 1968, and 1970, data include persons 18 years old and over in Georgia and Kentucky, 19 years old and over in Alaska, 20 years old and over in Hawaii, and 21 years old and over in the remaining states. Includes all persons 18 years old and over in 1972, 1974, and 1976. Data relate to the civilian noninstitutional population, excluding inmates of institutions and members of the Armed Forces.

NA Not available.

[1] Presidential election years (including congressional elections).

[2] Congressional election years only.

[3] Persons of Spanish origin may be of any race.

ANNALS, AAPSS, 435, Jan. 1978

Public Safety: Crime Is Up, But What About Punishment?

By DAVID SEIDMAN

ABSTRACT: Reported crime rates have risen, and arrest rates have too, particularly among the young. Men have higher victimization rates than women, and blacks have higher victimization rates for crimes of violence than whites. *Social Indicators, 1976* tells us this and a bit more about crime and responses to it, but overall the picture presented is at once insufficiently informative and inappropriately precise. The shortcomings of major data sources are acknowledged, but questionable findings are presented as near certain. Uniform Crime Reports trends for 1960–75 are presented without the important context of earlier trends. Important data from the National Crime Survey are presented without mention of probable artifacts.

Data on system response to crime could have been presented so as to provide insight into the probable cause of the increases shown in trends in reported offenses. Important data, particularly those showing a declining rate of imprisonment, have been omitted, and the interrelations of crime and response have not been highlighted. The major shortcomings of the chapter seem to result not from inadequacies in execution of the design, but rather from limitations in available data and from the apparent assumption that data presented in chart form speak for themselves.

David Seidman, Ph.D., Washington, D.C., is a Staff Associate of the Social Science Research Council's Center for Coordination of Research on Social Indicators. A political scientist, he taught at Princeton University and has published articles on social indicators, crime statistics, administrative structure, statistical methodology, and the regulation of pharmaceuticals.

The members of the Social Science Research Council's Subcommittee on Criminal Justice Statistics (Albert J. Reiss, Jr., Albert D. Biderman, Alfred Blumstein, Stephen Fienberg, Don Gottfredson, and Leslie Wilkins) provided, over the past three years, most of the useful ideas in this paper. Albert J. Reiss, Jr., offered important advice on an earlier draft. The views expressed in this article are those of the author, and not necessarily those of the Social Science Research Council. Preparation of this article was supported by Grant No. SOC 74-07148 from the National Science Foundation.

"PUBLIC Safety and Legal Justice," not just "Public Safety," was the title of chapter 6 of *Social Indicators, 1976* when I first saw an outline of the proposed volume. The reason for the deletion is plain: there is very little national data concerning legal justice, and even less that is good. Data on the federal courts, prisons, and parole system exist, and if we knew how to measure "justice," legal or otherwise, these would be useful indicators. But the business of justice in the United States is predominantly the business of state and local governments. Since the early 1930s, the federal government has assiduously amassed state and local data on crimes, but it has done far less with possible measures of justice—here, perhaps, is an indicator of our national preoccupations. Ambitious plans are now afoot to generate and amass such data,[1] but their realization is a long way off, and far from certain. In 1931, the Wickersham Commission noted the same lack of national statistics and urged that something be done. From 1932 through 1946, the Census Bureau collected court statistics from the states on a voluntary basis.[2] No one has done so since then.

"Public Safety" is a misleading title for what is left. Except for one table, only the "International Comparisons" section deals with noncriminal hazards. Fires, floods, earthquakes, hurricanes, tornadoes, industrial accidents, and dangerous products are peripheral to this chapter when they appear at all.[3] As the text explains, "the overriding public concern in this broad area, at least in the United States, is with crime . . ." That may be, though no data are presented to prove it. Publications such as *Social Indicators, 1976* could, of course, attempt public education and the shaping of public concerns. That choice was not made, and it might be more appropriate to call this chapter "Crime and Response." Even that is too broad. American society has not organized itself to generate reliable information about more than a small number of the many different types of crime. The text itself comments on the absence of information about white-collar crime. There are also no data on extortion, kidnapping, arson, and any number of other crimes. A chapter which began as "Public Safety and Legal Justice" emerges as one about murder, rape, robbery, assault, burglary, larceny, motor vehicle theft, and some of the responses to these crimes. The content is, in short, the usual.

SOME ORGANIZING QUESTIONS

What ought we to learn about crime and response from a report of this kind on "current social conditions and trends"? I suggest the report should tell us about the direction of trends in crime events, the reasons for these trends, the distribution of criminal victimization in society, changes in the nature of offending, the effect of crime on

1. U.S. Department of Justice, Law Enforcement Assistance Administration, National Criminal Justice Information and Statistics Service, *Program Plan for Statistics 1977–81* (Washington, D.C.: USGPO, n.d.).

2. For a review of the history of national criminal justice statistics, see President's Commission on Law Enforcement and Administration of Justice, Task Force on Assessment, Task Force Report: *Crime and Its Impact—An Assessment* (Washington, D.C.: USGPO, 1967), chap. 10.

3. A useful compilation on such matters is the annual *Insurance Facts*, published by the Insurance Information Institute. The data, like much crime data, are of uncertain reliability.

our lives, the nature and extent of public and private response to crime, and the effect of that response on crime and on other aspects of our lives. A minimum set of questions is, what is happening? who is doing it? to whom is it happening? with what response? and why? I will examine the chapter for the light it sheds upon these questions, occasionally drawing upon other data.[4]

TRENDS IN CRIME

The Uniform Crime Reporting (UCR) Program, administered by the Federal Bureau of Investigation, is the only source of national trend data on crime before 1973, and *Social Indicators, 1976* quite naturally uses these data. They show that, from 1960 to 1975, the trend for seven crimes, murder, rape, robbery, aggravated assault, burglary, larceny, and motor vehicle theft, is upward, more or less unrelievedly so. The seven trends are quite similar, though robbery, sometimes considered particularly significant because it involves predatory violence, or the threat of it, rises a bit faster than the others, and the rise in motor vehicle theft tapers off a bit at the end.[5]

The data suggest, rather dismally, that the rise in recorded crime rates is inexorable and inevitable. It is not. The series presented in *Social Indicators, 1976* begin in 1960, and therefore cannot show that the period from 1960 to 1975 is unusual. Peculiarities in the way estimates of national reported crime rates have been constructed make extended comparisons over time highly questionable.[6] However, *Social Indicators, 1973* published trend data extending back to 1933. The trends generally appear U-shaped, falling from a peak in 1933 to a trough in the mid-1940s, generally flat until the late 1950s or early 1960s, and rising thereafter. Murder, for example, does not regain its 1933 peak until 1970; robbery, until 1967; burglary, 1954; and motor vehicle theft, 1965. The trends for the remaining three categories have less pronounced U-shapes, with aggrevated assault and larceny regaining their early peaks in the mid-1940s, while rape shows a gradual increase over the entire period. Perhaps the most important point about the time covered by *Social Indicators, 1976* is that it is an exceptional period and, unfortunately, the reader is not shown that.

These are trends in offenses recorded by the police, and what they tell us about trends in crime events is unclear. A crime comes to the attention of the police if they observe it or if another observer reports it to them. In recent years, surveys

4. Much information on these questions is available in small scale studies. I accept the same restrictions that apply to *SI '76* and use only national data.

5. The calculated "annual average rates of change" in the chapter manage to suggest the similarity of trends in spite of a somewhat eccentric method of calculation. The endpoints of the five-year intervals have been used to calculate an exponential growth curve, which ignores what happened in the intervening years. The reader is advised to pass over these calculations and to simply observe the logarithmic plots.

6. The technical notes explain that "the time-series of these data, which extends back to 1933, has undergone numerous adjustments from year to year, reflecting changes in the reporting units and in the concepts and definitions employed in classifying criminal events. Thus, the data shown in this report cover only the period 1960 to 1975, for which an internally consistent set of definitions and classifications has been utilized." This explanation is certainly correct in suggesting enormous difficulties for comparison over time, and almost surely overoptimistic in suggesting that the problems have been solved for the period since 1960.

of the population have asked people about their experiences as victims of crime. Many of the victims of crime do not report the event to the police, so a large proportion of all crimes cannot be recorded by the police. We do not know whether an increasing proportion of the crimes which occur have been reported to the police over the last 15 years or so, but it has been suggested that "as larger proportions of the population become integrated into the dominant society and come to share its normative conceptions, more people mobilize the police to enforce private deportment," and that "the professionalization and bureaucratization of police forces with centralized command and control leads to improved recordkeeping and greater use of formal, as opposed to informal, police procedures, with consequent increases in figures of offenses. . . ."[7] It would be ironic if the great increase in recorded crime over the period were explained by increasing police professionalism and racial integration, which both lead minority populations increasingly to report crimes which once went unreported. As Albert Biderman has written,

> As people who once felt they were outside of the society feel more and more that they are a part of it, and as our law enforcement officials come to judge them by the same standards and give them the same protections as the middle class, we shall go through a period of decreasing crime but of increasing crime statistics. There will not be more crimes, but more *recorded* crimes.[8]

That is a comforting thought, but unlikely to be the full explanation of the recent rise in recorded crime.

Once reported to the police, events must be recorded, classified in the appropriate crime category, and reported to the FBI. Many reports do not survive the trip. Administrative practices within police departments explain much of the loss in transit,[9] and administrative practices have changed over time. Some of the increase in UCR figures may be explained by these changes.

The FBI attempts to estimate the amount of crime which would be recorded by those police departments which do not actually report to it. Over the years, the proportion of the population covered by reporting agencies has grown, so the published figures rely less and less on estimates for missing areas. Then, each year the FBI reestimates the totals and rates for previous years to take into account new knowledge about trends in areas newly reporting and to reduce the effects of changes in administrative practices. Thus the 1963 aggravated assault rate as reported in *Crime in the United States 1975* is 17.8 percent higher than the rate as reported in *Crime in the United States 1963*. Robbery is 16.4 percent higher; burglary, 11.4 percent; rape, 8 percent; while murder is only 2.2 percent higher and motor vehicle theft, 2.4 percent.[10] The price of better data is unstable history.

7. Albert D. Biderman and Albert J. Reiss, Jr., "On Exploring the 'Dark Figure' of Crime," *The Annals*, vol. 374 (November 1967), p. 7.

8. Albert D. Biderman, "Social Indicators and Goals," in *Social Indicators*, ed. Raymond A. Bauer (Cambridge, Mass.: M.I.T. Press, 1966), p. 125.

9. David Seidman and Michael Couzens, "Getting the Crime Rate Down: Political Pressure and Crime Reporting," *Law and Society Review*, vol. 8 (Spring 1974), pp. 457–93.

10. The FBI does not publish reestimates for years before 1960, which in large measures explains why *SI '76* did not use earlier data. It is perhaps significant that murder and motor vehicle theft show the smallest adjustments. Both bodies and automobiles are large, valuable, uniquely identified, enmeshed in govern-

It is possible, then, that crime rates have been decreasing, while recorded crime rates have been increasing. But it is not likely. We have all seen too much of the changing character of life in our cities to believe the increase in crime is all a paper increase. And there is other hard evidence to confirm this impression: murder statistics are assembled by the Public Health Service as well as the FBI, and the two sources report much the same picture,[11] even though definitions vary slightly.

Dissatisfaction with both the reliability and the scope of UCR has led to the development of a new system for measuring crime rates. It grows from a simple, seemingly obvious, insight: if a major problem with UCR is that individuals frequently do not report their victimizations to the police, that problem could be avoided by asking scientifically selected samples of individuals about their experiences as victims of certain kinds of crimes. The interviews could also produce other information about crimes and victims not now available through UCR and, by preserving records organized in terms of individuals, allow more sophisticated analyses of relationships than is possible with UCR. From this insight has grown the National Crime Survey (NCS), a continuing national sample survey program (with additional surveys of a number of urban areas) of substantial cost and complexity.[12] Unlike UCR, NCS counts victimizations, not offenses.

In a perfect world, NCS would provide the "true" crime rate as a way of checking on the UCR rate. In the real world, NCS, like any other data system, provides only another probe into reality, and not reality itself. Furthermore, NCS does not use the same definitions as UCR and purports to describe a different universe. It relies on the fallible memories of victims, who differ in their propensities to report events to interviewers. And because NCS is new, it has unresolved methodological and conceptual problems.

In any event, UCR trends cannot be checked against NCS data simply because there are no NCS data before 1973. While differences in definitions, universes, and the like make comparison between the two data sources treacherous, a brief comment on trends from 1973 to 1975 may be useful. I compared the victimization rates of individuals or households for rape, robbery, aggravated assault, burglary, and motor vehicle theft with the UCR offense rates for similar categories. None of the 1973–74 changes in victimization rates was statistically significant,[13] though all but one had the same sign as the corresponding UCR changes. One of the 1974–75 NCS changes—aggravated assault—was statistically significant (at the 90 percent level), but it was a decrease

ment paper chains, and likely to be insured. It is hard to ignore a dead body or the loss of a car.

11. The homicide rates in *SI '76* chart 6/3A are age adjusted: they reflect what the homicide rate would be with current age-specific rates and the age structure of the 1940 population. The adjustment is designed, in effect, to control for the relationship between homicide rate and the age of the victim. The figures before adjustment are different, but the trend is quite similar.

12. The most complete discussion of NCS available is National Research Council, Panel for the Evaluation of Crime Surveys, *Surveying Crime* (Washington, D.C.: National Academy of Sciences, 1976).

13. Because NCS is based on sampling techniques, variability in estimates is to be expected. Therefore, statistical tests of hypotheses such as no change are appropriate. UCR is not based on sampling, so tests of this kind are not appropriate for UCR data.

while the corresponding UCR change was an increase. Indeed, while all of the UCR categories showed increases, four of the five NCS categories (motor vehicle theft is the exception) showed decreases. Percentage changes from 1973 to 1975 were small. The largest was a decrease of 4.3 percent in aggravated assault. Two were increases, two were decreases, and one was approximately zero. UCR offense rates for these five crimes increased by from 6 percent to 24 percent. Very different pictures emerge from the two sources of data.

NCS provides estimates of the proportion of victimizations reported to the police. Since changes in that proportion might account for the different pictures, I multiplied the victimization rates by the appropriate proportions and then recomputed the percentage changes. For the one year changes, there is one additional instance of agreement in sign between UCR and NCS. The two-year NCS changes now all agree in sign with the UCR changes, but differ substantially in magnitude. Major discrepancies between the two data systems remain, and they are unexplained.

The unfortunate conclusion is that we do not have very much information about trends in crime. The data suggest a sustained increase in crime rates over a 15-year period and that our experience in the 30 years before that was quite different. But while it is implausible that there was no substantial increase in crime between, say, 1960 and 1975, we simply do not know how much of the increase in measured crime rates is due to increases in real crime rates and how much is due to other factors. *SI '76* recites the appropriate caveats, but I suspect they carry little weight when the pictured trends are so striking and when it is baldly stated that "the rates of both violent and property crimes have risen substantially and dramatically." The art form *SI '76* represents has difficulty coping with such peculiar data.

THE VICTIMS

The chances of being a victim are not evenly distributed throughout the society. UCR data are published disaggregated by size of reporting jurisdiction, though without many of the refinements and adjustments used for the national data. They show, roughly, that crime rates increase with the size of the reporting jurisdiction, and that rates of increase have been roughly the same for all size categories over the 1960–75 period. Since the data are worse than the national data, it was perhaps wise not to include them in *SI '76*.

UCR data are available by jurisdiction, so it is also possible to examine the statistical relationships between various characteristics of jurisdictions and crime rates. This kind of analysis has long been a staple of criminology,[14] but none of the findings are included in *SI '76*. Reasons for the omission may include the unreliability of the crime rates, the unenlightening character of the findings, and the lack of time series studies.

Vital Statistics has long reported homicide rates by age, sex, and color of the victim. As displayed in *SI '76*, the disparities in rates when sex and color are considered are enormous and relatively stable, though the rates themselves are rising. The reasons for the disparities

14. The state of the art, as of a decade ago, is reviewed by Judith A. Wilks, "Ecological Correlates of Crime and Delinquency," in President's Commission on Law Enforcement and the Administration of Justice, *Crime and its Impact*, appendix A.

are suggested by nothing in *SI '76*. Indeed, other data in the chapter suggest mainly the extraordinary character of the disparities. Undoubtedly the apparent importance of color here and elsewhere would diminish substantially if such variables as education, income, and employment status were simultaneously considered. Color bears a heavy weight when other variables are ignored.

NCS allows much more detailed analysis of the distribution of victimization in society. The chapter text summarizes much of the information nicely:

> In general, males are about twice as likely as females to fall victim to crimes of violence and are also more likely to fall victim to personal crimes of theft . . . Blacks and persons of Spanish origin are somewhat more likely than whites to be victimized by personal crimes of violence and theft. [But the data show whites have higher victimization rates for crimes of theft.] The rate of victimization for personal crimes of violence tends to decline with increased income of the victim, while that of victimization for personal crimes of theft rises with increased income of the victim.

These findings are hardly surprising, but the details raise some questions. The victimization rate for crimes of violence for black males is 23.6 percent higher than the rate for white males,[15] a remarkably small difference in light of the difference in age-adjusted death rates from homicide: the rate for "other" males (mainly black) in 1973 was 786.2 percent higher than that for white males. Disaggregating "crimes of violence," we find that white males have a higher victimization rate for combined aggravated and simple assault than black males (35.0 versus 31.9). This is composed of a lower white rate for aggravated assault (15.5 versus 19.2) and a higher one for simple assault (19.5 versus 12.7). Similarly, white males have a lower robbery victimization rate (8.9 versus 22.6), but a higher proportion of that rate is "without injury" for whites (70 percent) than for blacks (64 percent). Thus the data show that black males are relatively and for simple assault absolutely, infrequently victimized by the less serious crimes of violence. This does not seem reasonable, and suggests artifacts in the data. Blacks appear less likely than whites to report minor incidents to interviewers. Educational attainment may explain some of the difference. Then, undercoverage and nonresponse in NCS "vary by demographic categories, and it is a fair presumption that undercoverage is greatest for persons with no usual place of residence and for some classes of persons who have higher-than-average exposure to victimization."[16] Black males are especially likely to be both victimized and undercounted. NCS findings here may be misleading.

Victimization rates show little variation by place of residence, and most of the variation is between central cities and other places. UCR shows much larger variations by size of place, but the categorization is by size of the jurisdiction where the

15. The rates do not include "series victimizations (i.e., those cases in which the respondent says he was victimized three or more times but cannot give certain details of the individual incidents.)" National Research Council, *Surveying Crime*, p. 77. NCS methodology depends upon descriptions of details, so these are set aside. Obviously, including them would increase the victimization rates by an unknown quantity, and not necessarily by the same quantity for different population groups or different types of victimizations.

16. National Research Council, *Surveying Crime*, p. 28.

crime occurred, not, as in NCS, by size of central city in the metropolitan area where the victim resides. NCS would probably show more variation by size of place if UCR categories were used, and tallying victimizations by place of occurrence rather than by place of residence would surely sharpen the differences between central cities and other places. With these adjustments, NCS data might or might not show variation by size of place as large as that found in UCR. As they stand, they suggest that location matters less to victimization than other data have indicated.

Sharp differences do appear in the rates of victimization for different age groups—and these are not mentioned in *SI '76*. Considerable public attention has been given to the victimization of the aged, but NCS data consistently show that victimization rates for the elderly are substantially lower than those for the young: rates peak in either the 12–15 age group or the 16–19 age group and taper off sharply after that. For crimes of violence and personal larceny, the victimization rate of those 65 and over in 1974 was about 13 percent of the rate for those 16–19.[17] Youth is the time for victimization.

Why do the elderly appear less threatened than others? Perhaps because they avoid threatening places, situations, and associates. If so, victimization rates are limited as a means of identifying social problems, because they take no direct account of exposure. Street crime must be low when no one uses the streets. More useful rates would relate victimization to the activities in which people engage and the places they frequent. The logic here is more general, and is occasionally followed by NCS: the rates for crimes against households use number of households, not individuals, as the base. And *SI '73* recomputed UCR motor vehicle theft and burglary rates, using registered vehicles as the base for motor vehicle theft and households and business establishments for burglary. Choice of base for rates is an unresolved problem, and that choice matters.

The victimization data in *SI '76* reflect insufficient analysis. We learn from *SI '76* and published reports of the NCS that victimization by violent crimes is relatively high among blacks, the poor, those in central cities, and the young. But blacks are disproportionately poor, young, and located in central cities (though those who live elsewhere may be victimized in central cities). Neither the independent effects of these factors nor their patterns of interaction are revealed in *SI '76*. Since *SI '76* is based on data analysis done elsewhere, the problem lies elsewhere: the tabulations produced by the Law Enforcement Assistance Administration and the Census Bureau do not allow the requisite multivariate analysis. Producing these tabulations is a needed step towards answering some important questions.[18]

VICTIMS AND OFFENDERS

Common wisdom among criminologists has long held that in a large proportion of violent crime, victim and offender know each other—

17. U.S. Department of Justice, Law Enforcement Assistance Administration, National Criminal Justice Information and Statistics Service, *Criminal Victimization in the United States: A Comparison of 1974 and 1975 Findings* (A National Crime Survey Report, no. SD–NCP–N–5, February 1977), table 4.

18. This is difficult, because crime is a rare event. It may be necessary to aggregate data over a considerable period of time in order to find enough victimizations of, say, wealthy old suburban blacks to allow analysis.

indeed, they are often relatives or spouses. This wisdom has been based on fragmentary information. The point is an important one, because the social character of violent crime depends in large measure upon whether it consists of friends and relatives brutalizing each other or of anonymous attacks by strangers. NCS, which asked victims about the offender, provides the first detailed national look at this question, and *SI '76* reports the results. They do not support the common wisdom: according to NCS data, the victims of violent crime are more often the victims of strangers.

While important, the finding is also questionable. There is good evidence that victimizations by strangers are more likely to be reported to survey interviewers than victimizations by nonstrangers, and the effect of this differential reporting may be substantial:

> We are not concerned that there might exist a small bias in this stranger-violence quotient; we are not quibbling over whether 60 or 70 percent of violent crimes reported to NCS interviewers are attributed to strangers. Rather, we are concerned that a more appropriate figure, adjusted for differential reporting of victimizations according to relationship between victim and offender, could be less than one-half; if so, the policy implications would appear to be quite different.[19]

The adjustment will not be an easy one.

While murder is undoubtedly an atypical crime, comparison with UCR statistics on the circumstances of murder may be instructive. UCR classifies murders according to whether they are "spouse killing spouse, parent killing child, other relative killings, romantic triangle and lovers' quarrels, known felony-type, and suspected felony-type." Felony-type murders are "those killings resulting from robbery, burglary, sex motive, gangland and institutional slaying, and all other felonious activities."[20] In 1974, only 27.8 percent of the murders were counted as known or suspected felony-type, but the proportion has been rising. (See table 1.) If these statistics reflect the circumstances of other violent crimes, the common wisdom on the relationship between victims and offenders is correct, but is becoming less valid. Since the NCS finding was known to be subject to question, *SI '76* might well have omitted it.

TABLE 1

PERCENTAGE OF UCR MURDERS WHICH ARE KNOWN OR SUSPECTED FELONY TYPE

YEAR	PERCENT FELONY TYPE
1963	17
1964	20
1965	21
1966	22
1967	21
1968	25
1969	26
1970	29
1971	28
1972	27
1973	29
1974	28
1975	32

SOURCE: *Uniform Crime Reports—Crime in the United States*, annual issues.

SYSTEM RESPONSE AND THE CAUSES OF CHANGE

It is difficult to separate the question of the criminal justice system's response to the (presumed) increase in crime from that of the explanation of the increase, in part because system response provides much of the data upon which explanation rests,

19. National Research Council, *Surveying Crime*, p. 120.

20. U.S. Department of Justice, Federal Bureau of Investigation, *Uniform Crime Reports: Crime in the United States 1973* (Washington, D.C.: USGPO, 1974), p. 9.

and in part because system response may itself be a large part of that explanation. As the system arrests and further processes individuals, records are created. By telling us about individuals identified by the system as having committed offenses, these records help explain the increase. But the criminal justice system does not identify all offenders, and in any event is permeated by administrative discretion. Police, for example, arrest on the basis of both discretionary judgments and the information they are able to obtain. Arrest statistics, therefore, are partly determined by the number of offenders, partly by the skill of offenders in avoiding arrest, and partly by the habits and patterns of the police in the use of their discretion.[21] Data from later stages of the criminal process are probably even less likely to reflect the offender population accurately, so it is perhaps fortunate that such data were not available for *SI '76*: they might suggest inappropriate conclusions.

It is unlikely that estimates of arrest rates for different age groups for urban places were included in *SI '76* merely to provide information about the changing behavior of the police. For better or for worse, they must be considered as saying something about offenders as well. The message is striking: arrest rates increased rapidly over the period, and, particularly for crimes of violence, the increase was even more rapid for youths, who began the period with rates already higher than those for the older population.[22]

These changes in rates obscure the change in age composition of arrestees, because over the period the age distribution of the population shifted. For example, between 1960 and 1973, the proportion of the total United States population aged 14–24 grew from 15.1 percent to 20.5 percent. Thus, those under 25 accounted for 46 percent of arrests in 1960, but for 61 percent in 1974. For crimes of theft, the proportion rose from 75 percent to 80 percent.

If age-specific arrest rates reflect age-specific offense rates (and of course they may not), some of the increase in total offense rates can be attributed simply to the changing age distribution. If the age-specific 1960 arrest rates applied to the 1974 population distribution, the total arrest rate for violent crimes would be about 54 percent of the actual total arrest rate in 1974, and the same is true for crimes of theft.[23] So the age distribution may directly account for about half the increase.

The rest of the increase in offense rates is, under the assumption linking arrests and offenses, due to rising age-specific rates. Convincing ex-

21. See, for example, Jerome H. Skolnick, *Justice Without Trial* (New York: Wiley, 1966). UCR collects arrest data, but from fewer jurisdictions than report offenses.

22. The choice of an arithmetic scale for these charts obscures the rates of increase. For both crimes of violence and crimes of theft, the percentage increase was highest for the youngest age group and lowest for the oldest. The most extreme difference, between 11–14 year olds and those 25 and older for crimes of violence, is the difference between a 1960–74 increase of 177.8 percent and one of 52.2 percent. The pattern is not the same for each of the separate crimes. For example, arrest rates for motor vehicle theft did not increase much at all, and those for 15–17-year-olds were lower at the end of the period than at the beginning.

23. The figure varies for the separate crimes. These computations are not very reliable: the population figures, those used to compute the rates in *SI '76*, are derived by assuming the age distribution for the jurisdictions reporting arrests to UCR is the same as that for the United States as a whole. If UCR published lists of the reporting jurisdictions, the age distribution for at least Census years could be examined, but the lists are not published. The results might also differ somewhat if finer age categories were used.

planations of these increases are not easy to find. The high arrest rate increases among the young provide a clue. A major function of social institutions is the socialization of the young. It has been argued that as the moving wave of the baby boom passed through adolescence, these social institutions—schools and employment markets, for example—were swamped, and the result was rising crime rates.[24] This is hard to demonstrate with available data, but Irving Leveson has found a relationship between crime rates and that part of the youth unemployment rate which is not related to the adult unemployment rate; this is at least consistent with the socialization argument. Leveson also found that adult unemployment rates over the period were not significantly related to crime rates.[25]

UCR publishes arrest data by sex and race, as well as by age, but simultaneous classifications by these three variables are not published or even collected. Analysis is therefore limited in sophistication. The separate tabulations by sex and race include a single age break, at age 18. Some of the increase in arrest rates can be attributed to more rapid increases for females than for males. For crimes of theft, about 11 percent of all arrests were of women in 1960, but by 1974, the proportion had grown to about 22 percent. The increase was about the same for the two age groups, under 18 and 18 and over. For crimes of violence, excluding rape, the proportion changed almost not at all (from 12 percent to 11 percent), but among those under 18, there was an increase from 7 percent to 10 percent, while for the older age group, there was a decrease from 13 percent to 11 percent. Increases may be due to either, or both, increased offense rates among women, or an increased willingness to arrest women.[26] In any event, these data do not suggest that women played any great role in the large increases in offense rates. Perhaps no damage was done by excluding these data from *SI '76*, though there may be substantial public curiosity about them.

The link between race and crime is a sensitive subject, which may explain why no equivalent of the *SI '73* chart showing arrest rates by race is included in *SI '76*. Blacks have higher arrest rates. Some of the difference may well be attributable to differential police treatment of whites and blacks, but not all: blacks have higher victimization rates as well. Differences between blacks and whites in age distribution, income, and so forth might account for the rest, but the data to test the hypothesis do not exist. While arrest rates for both blacks and whites increased over the period, the rate of increase for whites has in general been greater.[27] Be-

24. James Q. Wilson makes roughly this argument in *Thinking About Crime* (New York: Basic Books, 1975), chap. 1.

25. Irving Leveson, "The Growth of Crime," (Hudson Institute HI-2444/2-D, July 1976), chap. III.

26. The data here differ from those analyzed by Rita James Simon, *The Contemporary Woman and Crime*, Crime and Delinquency Issues: A Monograph Series, National Institute of Mental Health, Center for Studies of Crime and Delinquency (Washington, D.C.: USGPO, 1975), because Simon did not use the age classification. To use it, I had to rely on a different set of tables in the annual issues of Uniform Crime Reports. Further, there are slight differences in categories of crime examined. The results for the total population, however, are essentially identical. Simon points out that increased willingness to arrest does not explain the differences between crimes of violence and crimes of theft. Thus she sees the explanation largely in terms of changes in women's opportunities to commit certain types of crimes. See Simon, p. 48.

27. Leveson has examined this in some detail in *The Growth of Crime*, chap. II. The outcome of the comparison depends upon

cause black arrest rates are so much higher, arrest rates for the total population may have increased because of an increasing black proportion of the population in the reporting jurisdictions, particularly in the high arrest age groups. But UCR does not tell us which are the reporting jurisdictions. Leveson, using crude data, concludes that the effect here was small.[28]

Considered as indicators of system response, the key fact about the arrest rates—which *SI '76* does not point out—is that they grew less rapidly than reported offense rates.[29] UCR provides data on the proportion of arrests which result in criminal charges, the proportion of charges which result in conviction—by trial or plea—and the disposition of those convicted, but they are of very poor quality. For what it is worth, Leveson has assembled and examined the data, finding that, in general, the dropoff at each stage in the criminal process has increased over time.[30]

The classic form of punishment for crime is imprisonment. Since the rise in arrests has not kept pace with the rise in reported offenses, and since arrests have become less likely to lead to conviction, it would not be surprising to find that the proportion of the population imprisoned has not increased as rapidly as the reported offense rate. In fact, the imprisonment rate has declined since 1961. Since 1926, the National Prisoner Statistics (NPS) program has assembled data on the year-end population of state and federal prisons. Figure 1 presents these data as rates per 100,000 along with UCR offense rates for crimes of violence.[31] The number of prisoners has also declined since 1961. The increase in recorded offense rates has evidently been accompanied by a decline in punishment.[32] This is important for at least two reasons: First, incarceration undoubtedly affects the quality of life of those incarcerated, and the size of the institutionalized population may say something about the character of a society. Second, imprisonment may affect the crime rate through deterrence of potential offenders and incapacitation of those in prison.[33] It may be that the decline

both the precise crimes considered and the exact time period. Thus, between 1963 and 1973, the percentage increase in arrest rates for crimes of violence taken together and for crimes of theft taken together was greater among whites, but the reverse is true between 1963 and 1969. And for 1963–73, blacks had the larger percentage increase in arrest rates for murder and robbery.

28. Ibid., pp. IV–11 and pp. IV–12.

29. The relation between arrests and offenses is tangled. One offense, with multiple offenders, may lead to many arrests. One arrest, of a multiple offender, may "clear" many offenses. And, of course, some arrests are of individuals who have committed no offense. UCR data do not permit untangling. UCR data on the proportion of offenses "cleared by arrest" exist, but they are generally considered highly unreliable.

30. Leveson, *The Growth of Crime*, chap. VI. There is variation by crime type.

31. NPS is a voluntary reporting program which has been modified over the years. The data should be taken as only roughly approximating the trend. NPS also provides a series on prisoners received by state and federal prisons, but it is less reliable than the series used here.

32. For a discussion of the long-term stability of the prison population, see Alfred Blumstein and Jacqueline Cohen, "A Theory of the Stability of Punishment," *Journal of Criminal Law and Criminology*, vol. 64 (June 1973), pp. 198–207, and Alfred Blumstein, Jacqueline Cohen, and Daniel Nagin, "The Dynamics of a Homeostatic Punishment Process," *Journal of Criminal Law and Criminology*, vol. 67 (Sept. 1976), pp. 317–34.

33. The literature on deterrence is immense, and that on incapacitation is growing. For a recent discussion of both, see National Academy of Sciences, Panel on Research on Deterrent and Incapacitative Effects, *Deterrence and Incapacitation: Estimating the Effects of Criminal Sanctions on Crime Rates* (Washington, D.C.: National Academy of Sciences, forthcoming).

FIGURE 1

POPULATION OF STATE AND FEDERAL PRISONS AT END OF YEAR; CRIMES OF VIOLENCE, 1940–1973 (RATES)

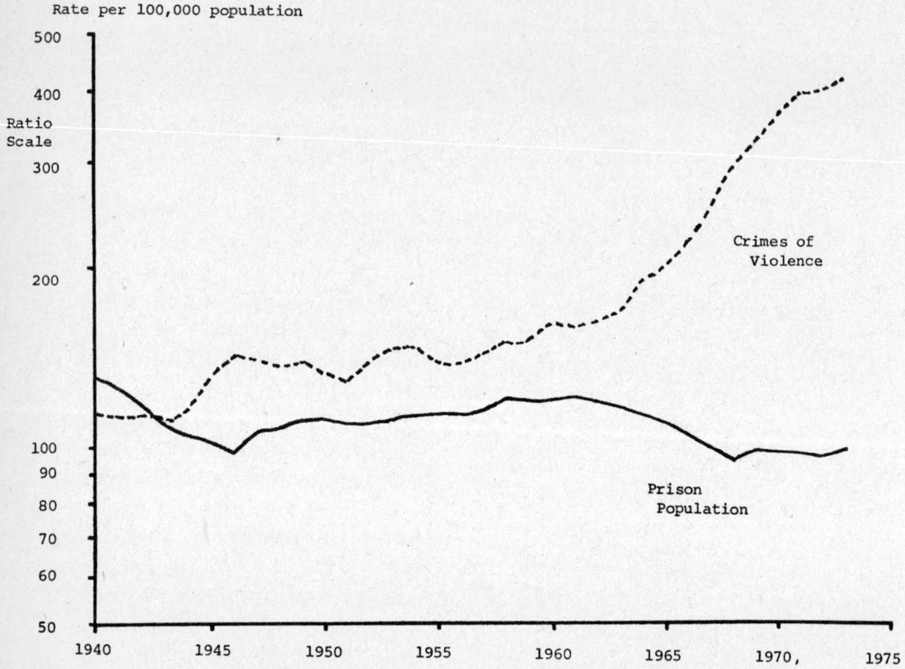

SOURCE: *Imprisonment Rate.*
1940–1970: U.S. Department of Justice, Bureau of Prisons, "National Prisoner Statistics: Prisoners in State and Federal Institutions for Adult Felons, 1968, 1969, 1970," table 2.
1971–1973: U.S. Department of Justice, Law Enforcement Assistance Administration, National Criminal Justice Information and Statistics Service, "Prisoners in State and Federal Institutions on December 31, 1974," table 4.
Crimes of Violence.
Social Indicators, 1973.

in punishment, reflected in both the prison and the arrest statistics, provides not merely information about the performance of the criminal justice system, but also a partial explanation of the rise in the recorded offense rate.

It is difficult to understand why *SI '76* did not include the NPS data.[34] The omission is just one of the weaknesses of the "Social Responses" section of the chapter, which tells us very little about explanations of the presumed increase in crime, the response of the system to that increase, or the consequences of system response. Part of the weakness can be attributed to the difficulty of providing explanation in a chartbook, part to the weaknesses of the available data. But there were readily avail-

34. It provides instead data on the jail population in 1970 and on juveniles in detention and correctional facilities in 1971 and 1973. The data are of interest, but they say nothing about trends or system response to serious crime.

able data which could and should have been used.

PRIVATE RESPONSE

The consequences of a rapid increase in crime rates might best be understood through an examination of the responses of individuals to perceived threats to their own safety. Unfortunately, data concerning such responses are hard to find. *SI '76* includes only a series on production and importation of firearms for private sale and some opinion poll responses covering very little of the period in which the increase occurred. The firearms data are striking—and the absence of such data for 1971–73 illustrates the failure of the system to monitor private responses. Reading into the series perhaps more than is there, the fear of crime seems to have led many individuals to resort to self-defense measures, indicating their lack of faith in the ability of the system to provide protection.[35] The consequences are perhaps shown in the rising proportion of murders which are committed with firearms. Some argue that the rising murder rate is in part attributable to the increased availability of firearms,[36] but a linkage between firearms purchases induced by the fear of crime and firearms murders has not been clearly established.

The opinion data, covering at best the period 1972–75, are not very revealing: the period is too short for substantial changes in opinion to be found, and the major increase in recorded crime rates preceded the earliest data point. The restricted range appears to reflect a decision to take all the data from the General Social Survey (GSS) of the National Opinion Research Center. GSS, however, was designed to repeat questions asked earlier in other surveys, so longer time series were available for *SI '76*. For example, a series on the question "Are you in favor of the death penalty for persons convicted of murder?" can be constructed from Gallup Polls beginning in 1936.[37] The percentage favoring the death penalty reached its low point in 1966, and has risen rather steadily since then. The period of the rise corresponds to a period of noticeably rising recorded crime rates, which suggests that support for capital punishment is a response to rising crime rates. However, it also corresponds to a period in which there were no executions.[38] Support may decline again if executions become frequent.

The data on private response are exceedingly sketchy, but *SI '76* concludes that, taken together with the data on system response, "they provide ample evidence that concern with the impact of crime on public safety is perhaps second only to concern with health in our society." Perhaps not. The 1974 *Annual Housing Survey* asked occupants of a sample of housing units in the United States about the adequacy of neighborhood services. The proportion responding that the service was inadequate was higher for public transportion, shopping, and hospitals and health clinics than for police protection. Of those saying the service was inade-

35. I have explored this question extensively elsewhere. See David Seidman, "The Urban Arms Race: A Quantitative Analysis of Private Arming" (Ph.D. diss., Yale University, 1975).

36. See, for example, Richard Block, "Homicide in Chicago: A Nine-year Study (1965–1973)," *Journal of Criminal Law and Criminology*, vol. 66 (Sept. 1975), pp. 496–510.

37. There are minor variations in question wording. The data can be found in Michael J. Hindelang *et al.*, *Sourcebook of Criminal Justice Statistics—1976* (Washington, D.C.: USGPO, 1977), table 2.59.

38. The number fell from 56 in 1960 to 1 in 1966, rising to 2 in 1967. Then there were none until 1976. Ibid., table 6.124.

quate, there were more respondents who said that public transportation was so inadequate they would like to move from the neighborhood than there were who said this about police protection. When asked about undesirable conditions in the neighborhood, more people cited noise and heavy traffic than cited crime.[39] These data, of course, are not precisely to the point, but neither are the data in *SI '76*. In any case, they begin to suggest that concern about crime may have less to do with its impact on public safety than with something else, perhaps a generalized concern about the character of the society.[40] This seems to be one of the rare instances in which *SI '76* drew an incautious inference. The effort could better have been made elsewhere.

CONCLUSION

Having abandoned the aim of reporting on "Public Safety and Legal Justice," *SI '76* was still faced with an extremely difficult problem. The major source of data on trends (UCR) is unreliable, while the other major data source (NCS) is new and insufficiently analyzed and understood. The variables which would allow description and understanding of social conditions are often not measured at all. Crucial relationships are difficult to show in graphical form. Mainly for these reasons, though in part because of choices made in the design of the chapter, "Public Safety" is a weak report on "social conditions and trends."

Early in this paper, I identified a minimum set of questions. How well does *SI '76* do in answering them? First, in answer to "what is happening?," it suggests that crime is increasing, but the time period chosen removes the data from their context. Less information is provided on why there has been such an increase, though some can be teased out of the data. The distribution of criminal victimization is haphazardly presented, though, since the data are less familiar than the UCR trends, this presentation is particularly important. Questions about the nature of offending and offenders are hardly addressed at all, and in at least one instance addressed with highly questionable data. Response to increases in reported crime is presented only in very sketchy form, with the data on imprisonment the most striking omission. The interaction of response and trend, never mentioned in *SI '76*, is particularly difficult to address because the imprisonment data are missing. In short, the minimum set of questions is not well answered. Neither is it well answered here. *SI '76* can be no better than the available data base.

39. U.S. Department of Commerce, Bureau of the Census, *Current Housing Reports*, Final Report H-150074, Annual Housing Survey; 1974, part B; "Indicators of Housing and Neighborhood Quality for the United States and Regions" (Washington, D.C.: USGPO, 1976), table A-4.

40. See Frank F. Furstenberg, Jr., "Public Reaction to Crime in the Streets," *American Scholar*, vol. 40 (Autumn 1971), pp. 601-10.

Chart 6/11 Social Indicators, 1976

PERCENT OF VICTIMIZATIONS REPORTED TO THE POLICE, BY RACE OF VICTIMS AND TYPE OF CRIME, 1974

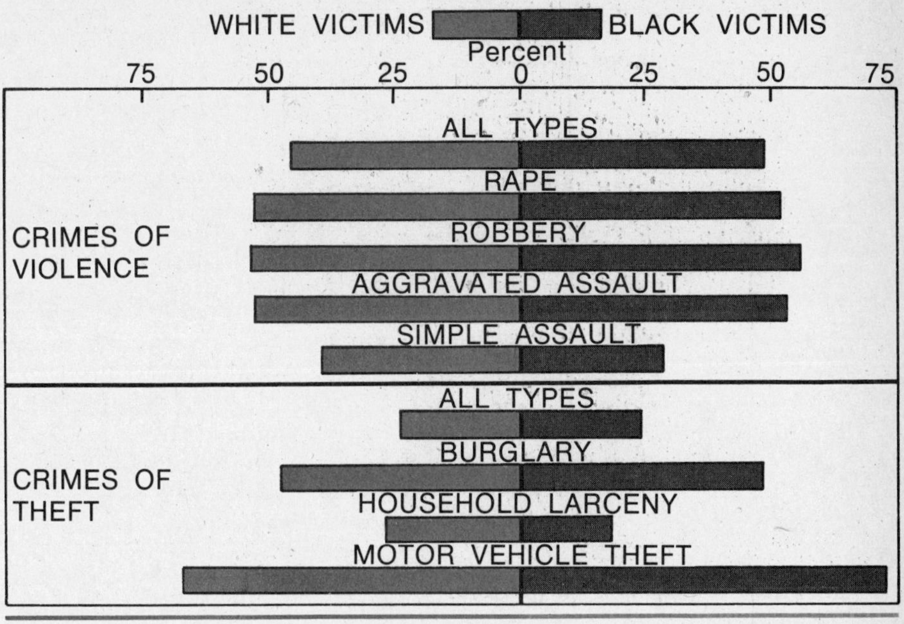

Table 6/11

VICTIMIZATIONS REPORTED TO POLICE, BY RACE OF VICTIMS AND TYPE OF CRIME: 1974

(Percent)

Type of crime	White victims	Black victims
All crimes of violence . . .	46.7	48.0
Rape	52.5	52.2
Robbery	53.1	55.3
Aggravated assault	52.9	54.4
Simple assault	39.6	28.5
All crimes of theft	24.7	24.0
Burglary	47.7	48.6
Household larceny	26.1	17.9
Motor vehicle theft	66.6	72.8

Source: U.S. Department of Justice, Law Enforcement Assistance Administration, *Criminal Victimization in the United States, A Comparison of 1973 and 1974 Findings*, Report No. SD-NCP-N-3, 1976.

Table 6/12
URBAN POLICE ARRESTS OF SUSPECTED OFFENDERS FOR CRIMES OF VIOLENCE, BY AGE OF SUSPECTS: 1960–1974
(Rate per 100,000 urban population)

Year	Total, all ages	11 to 14 years old	15 to 17 years old	18 to 24 years old	25 years old and over
1960	144.1	70.3	273.0	357.6	111.3
1961	150.5	69.1	287.5	386.5	114.1
1962	144.0	76.3	272.4	360.9	109.6
1963	145.3	73.7	272.9	356.9	108.0
1964	151.6	79.1	279.9	368.5	111.8
1965	162.8	99.3	323.0	379.9	115.7
1966	176.2	110.9	362.4	400.5	123.7
1967	189.2	122.9	408.3	436.1	127.3
1968	200.0	146.0	437.3	473.3	125.4
1969	215.9	153.1	476.5	526.0	130.6
1970	232.1	163.9	523.5	550.3	140.0
1971	201.0	180.3	574.6	599.4	150.3
1972	270.6	194.9	601.2	634.3	163.0
1973	262.6	186.7	595.3	607.7	158.0
1974	291.5	195.3	674.7	703.4	169.4

Source: National Commission on the Causes and Prevention of Violence, Staff Report, *Crimes of Violence*, Vol. II, 1969; U.S. Department of Justice, Federal Bureau of Investigation, *Uniform Crime Reports for the United States*, annual issues, 1960–1974; and U.S. Department of Commerce, Bureau of the Census, *Current Population Reports*, Series P-25, Nos. 519 and 529.

Chart 6/12 Social Indicators, 1976

URBAN POLICE ARREST RATES OF SUSPECTED OFFENDERS FOR CRIMES OF VIOLENCE, BY AGE OF SUSPECTS, 1960–1974

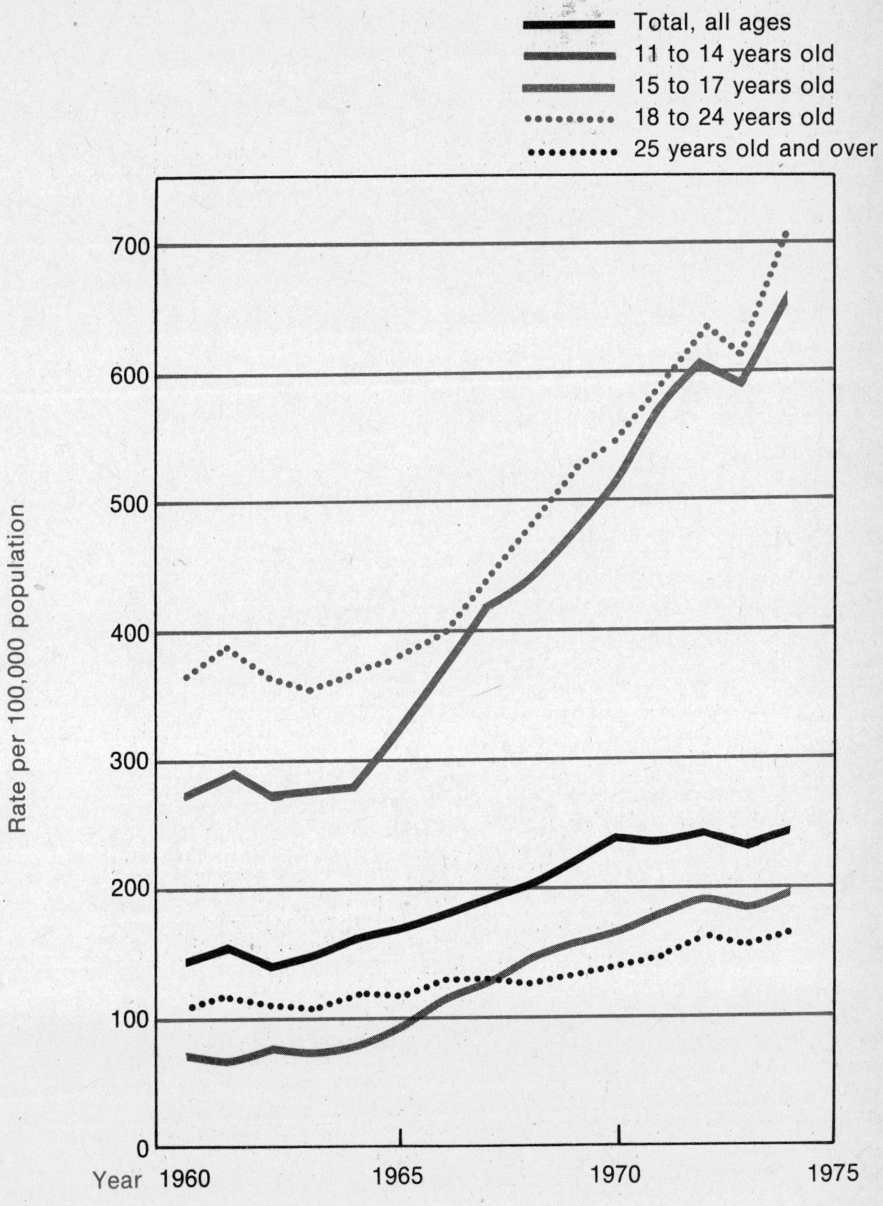

Source: see table 6/12

Table 6/13

URBAN POLICE ARRESTS OF SUSPECTED OFFENDERS FOR CRIMES OF THEFT, BY AGE OF SUSPECTS: 1960–1974

(Rate per 100,000 urban population)

Year	Total, all ages	11 to 14 years old	15 to 17 years old	18 to 24 years old	25 years old and over
1960	581.0[1]	1,212.3[1]	2,596.1	1,181.1	206.9
1961	618.9[1]	1,261.6[1]	2,790.0	1,240.3	223.2
1962	617.2[1]	1,339.1[1]	2,679.2	1,153.8	210.6
1963	662.4[1]	1,410.6[1]	2,830.3	1,224.1	222.4
1964	692.5	1,636.4	2,930.3	1,278.9	217.2
1965	718.3	1,744.8	3,087.8	1,258.6	226.9
1966	722.2	1,831.5	3,113.0	1,218.8	217.5
1967	773.3	1,912.5	3,288.6	1,323.2	232.8
1968	815.3	1,944.8	3,448.7	1,448.0	239.1
1969	861.4	2,007.0	3,557.1	1,571.6	250.9
1970	968.1	2,080.2	3,905.9	1,826.7	295.4
1971	1,003.7	2,126.8	4,049.5	1,933.3	307.9
1972	984.9	2,097.9	3,871.4	1,877.0	305.9
1973	954.6	2,013.2	3,820.2	1,807.4	294.4
1974	1,164.1	2,470.0	4,734.9	2,260.1	344.6

Source: U.S. Department of Justice, Federal Bureau of Investigation, *Uniform Crime Reports for the United States*, annual issues, 1960–1974; and U.S. Department of Commerce, Bureau of the Census, *Current Population Reports*, Series P-25, Nos. 519 and 529.

[1] Arrest data include persons under 11 years of age; population base includes persons 10 years old but not under 10.

Chart 6/13

Social Indicators, 1976

URBAN POLICE ARREST RATES OF SUSPECTED OFFENDERS FOR CRIMES OF THEFT, BY AGE OF SUSPECTS, 1960–1974

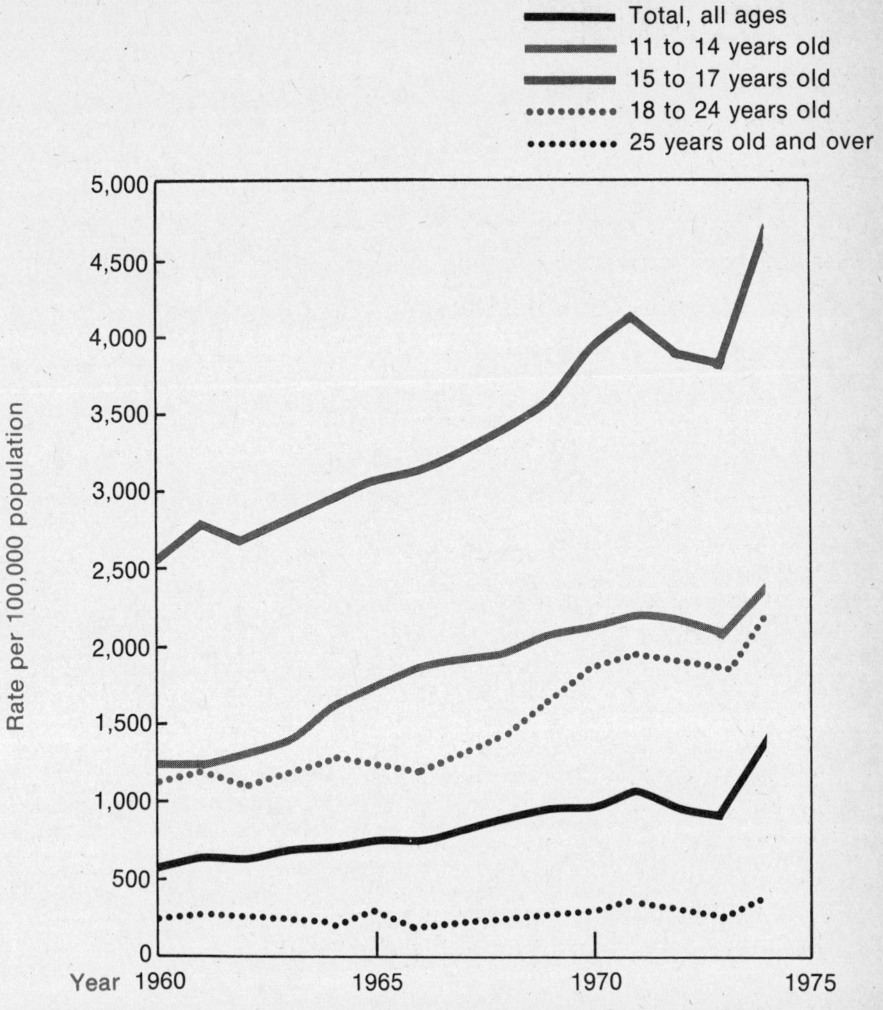

Source: see table 6/13

ANNALS, AAPSS, 435, Jan. 1978

Social Indicators, 1976 and *Perspective Canada II*: Elixirs of Reason or of Sleep?

By DAVID A. BRUSEGARD

ABSTRACT: Both *Social Indicators, 1976* and its Canadian counterpart, *Perspective Canada II*, are produced by government organizations with the intent to develop social indicators and provide a social report on the condition and progress of their respective nations. Having examined both publications, the author suggests that neither goal has been accomplished or properly dealt with. It is argued that to accomplish either objective in a satisfactory manner, both *Social Indicators, 1976* and *Perspective Canada II* must change their organization, commentary, authorship, and intended audience. Among other things, such publications must seek authors outside of government and actively draw them to the attention of education and public audiences.

David A. Brusegard is the Chief of the Social Indicator Unit of Statistics Canada. He formerly headed the Social Statistics unit of the province of Alberta. The author of articles on the development of social indicators and social reporting, Dr. Brusegard is the associate editor of and a contributor to the Perspective Canada *series. A major monograph on national level social reporting for the Organization for Economic Cooperation and Development is in press.*

Perspective Canada II is available from: Publications Distribution, Statistics Canada, Ottawa, Ontario, Canada K1A 0T6 (Order catalogue number 11-508/1977). It may be purchased for $9.25 ($11.00 for orders outside Canada).

If ever the reasonable musings of men were to submit to the shackles of censorship, the standard four letter words would not be the target of the outlawing knife. By far the most disreputable and myth-conjuring expression to creep into rational discussion is the innocuous but prostitutional, "quality of life." Mere utterance of the words can seduce research grants, father promiscuous social surveys, and breed varied reports, books, and papers, all seeking recognition as the true and rightful offspring. This is the most bogus concept ever to have been embraced by seemingly intelligent men and women.

Concern with this elusive element of our existence has resulted in a situation in which almost every piece of social research, government program, and statistical measurement is reputed to be in some way prompted by or related to our quality of life. Those concerned with monitoring or measuring social conditions and trends, and who took both their work and a humanistic concern seriously, saw it as only fair to erect a terminological barrier to protect themselves. "Social indicator" is still an attempt to keep out the vulgate.

The problem in moving emphasis from concern with the quality of life to the development of social indicators is that the defense is almost too good. Few if any serious researchers in government and the academic community will admit to having come across a bona fide member of the species. While the publication *Social Indicators, 1976* offers great hopes, it slips in the escape rider that its data are not really ideal social indicators, only a step in the appropriate direction. The Canadian contemporary, *Perspective Canada II*, makes no pretense at backbone. For the original authors, social indicators were to be those data series that people ended up calling "social indicators"—hardly an indefensible position even if no data were so named.

Social Reporting in Canada and the United States

In attempting to contrast *Social Indicators, 1976* with *Perspective Canada II* I found myself continually drawn to more fundamental questions that lay at the existence and character of both. It is clear that both publications are up to the same thing, but there is a distinct flavor to the introductions of both that would indicate that neither is aware of exactly what they are up to. We should wonder then, what in the world is being delivered to us in these relatively lush government publications, and what should be delivered. Public funds and hard work have generated these publications, but are they examples of the trivia buff's delight, statistical digests for a select few, or something beyond this?

The original intentions of the masterminds of social reporting were somewhat diverse, but in general their publications were to provide a decisionmaking tool for high-level policymakers. The audience for social reports were the policymakers themselves and the planning establishments who served the usually elected policymakers. Depending upon the perspective, such tools were to help in the management of social phenomena in the same way that economic indicators permitted control of and reaction to economic phenomena,[1] or to provide an information system for social plan-

1. See for example, Bertram N. Gross, *The State of the Nation: Social Systems Accounting* (New York: Tavistock Publications, 1966).

ning,[2] or place social issues into a cost/benefit context so that they could be dealt with in those terms.[3] All this was to provide a value-introducing, politically-motivating, and problem-solving force, the vehicles of which were to be publications like *Social Indicators, 1976* and *Perspective Canada II*, which in some way applied social and socio-economic statistics to common concerns.

What has happened is that neither *Social Indicators, 1976* nor *Perspective Canada II* have become the Bible of the planning elite or the embodiment of early hopes. The early hopes were too lofty and significant strides toward a comprehensive set or system of social indicators require much more work than the original proponents might have imagined. Thus there may be a tendency for some critics to set these statistical pachyderms aside as monuments to an impractical idealism that preached concern with the well-being of the individual and consideration for human benefit. I suggest, however, that such a dismissal would constitute a tragic error, for what is at present correctly perceived to be a low-to-moderate-use reference item for planning agencies and researchers, is in fact the embryo of what could become a widely used and valuable vehicle for social communication and understanding for elected officials, socially aware citizens, and their future counterparts—the high school and university student.

2. See Raymond A. Bauer, *Social Indicators* (Cambridge, Mass.: The MIT Press, 1966); and "Societal Feedback," *The Annals*, vol. 373 (Sept. 1967), pp. 180–92.

3. See Daniel Bell, "The Idea of a Social Report," *The Public Interest* 15 (Spring 1969), pp. 72–84; and "The Adequacy of Our Concepts," in *A Great Society?*, ed. Bertram N. Gross (New York: Basic Books, 1966), pp. 127–61.

THE NEED FOR CHANGE

To discover how this might happen, and how social reports must change, one must see the other premises in the argument:

1.) Both *Social Indicators, 1976* and *Perspective Canada II* conflate the presentation of social indicators with the different, but related, task of providing national level social commentary and explanations of social changes. At the root of the problem is a preoccupation with social indicators. Social indicator strategies focus upon standardized areas of concern and attempt to provide a few series that permit inferences regarding the attainment of national or obvious social goals; but there is a natural tendency and need in publications like *Social Indicators, 1976* and *Perspective Canada II* to detail and make clear the social changes and trends taking place in our society. To do the second job using the strategies of the first results in half-way products like the documents just mentioned.

Social Indicators, 1976 divides its chapters into three sections, the basic "hard" measures, public perceptions, and international comparisons. This very structure lends itself to continued regimentation over time and the logical product of such work, given progress in the development of social indicators, is an even more defined publication that would provide us with the same statistical series year after year. It thus becomes an increasingly less useful publication, much on the model of major economic indicator summaries.

2.) A second premise is that the really important debates on social planning and alternatives take place in various direct or indirect forms between politician and politician, or politician and the public or special interest groups. Neither politicians nor the public are overly sophisticated with respect to the use of statistics for decisionmaking or problem solving. Both must be approached in a way that is not only comprehensible but intuitive in its use of concepts and treatment of the interrelations of social phenomena. In the simplest terms social reports must address the issues of what is happening, what are the likely reasons for its happening, and what does this mean for us as a group or segment of the population five or ten years down the road. There is little of this integrated approach in either *Social Indicators, 1976* or *Perspective Canada II.*

3.) The last premise is that interesting and topical national level social policy and social problem issues are not easily organized under the national goals model presently used by *Social Indicators, 1976* or *Perspective Canada II.* Treatment of issues such as children's rights, women's rights, immigration policies, and drug abuse do not fall neatly into chapters standardly titled "Family," "Population," or "Health." It is perhaps noteworthy that *Social Indicators, 1976* has considered immigration in its introduction rather than in a specific chapter. One can only guess whether this is a consequence of the rigidity of the book's structure or the intentions of the authors.

If these three fundamental premises are accepted, then we can come closer to a conception of what such publications can do best and what they should be doing. It is evident from what I have said so far that I take the real goals of government-sponsored documents like *Social Indicators, 1976* and *Perspective Canada II* to be separable into two components: (1) the provision of social indicators relating to the attainment of national goals, and (2) the provision of social intelligence to the public, who pays for the production, in a form that relates to processes, changes, and trends, and deals with reasons and consequences.

The first goal can be attained by separating the indicator sections of publications from interesting, supporting, and thematically organized data. If we are serious about social indicators then let us see a few series offered as and argued for as indicators, and commence the debate from there. The second goal cannot be accomplished by simply paying attention to topical issues like children's rights or the consequences of our immigration policies. Since most of the audience for social reports are interested citizens and students, we cannot simply assume that this audience has a clear conception of the questions and problems involved in any issue, let alone the understanding of how existing social institutions and programs which deal with those problems work. This would imply a burdensome, but necessary, educative role for social reports, including the numerical detailing of such things as, for example, how the justice system works, with its charging, reduction of charges, diversion, possibilities for disposition, to mention only some of its components. Again, apart from providing statistical data on criminal activities, the detailing of information on matters like clearance rates can only be interpreted in the context of an understanding of how the system that generates those rates works. Since the

FIGURE 1

INCIDENTS, VICTIMS AND LEGAL STATUS OF MURDER SUSPECTS, 1961–1974

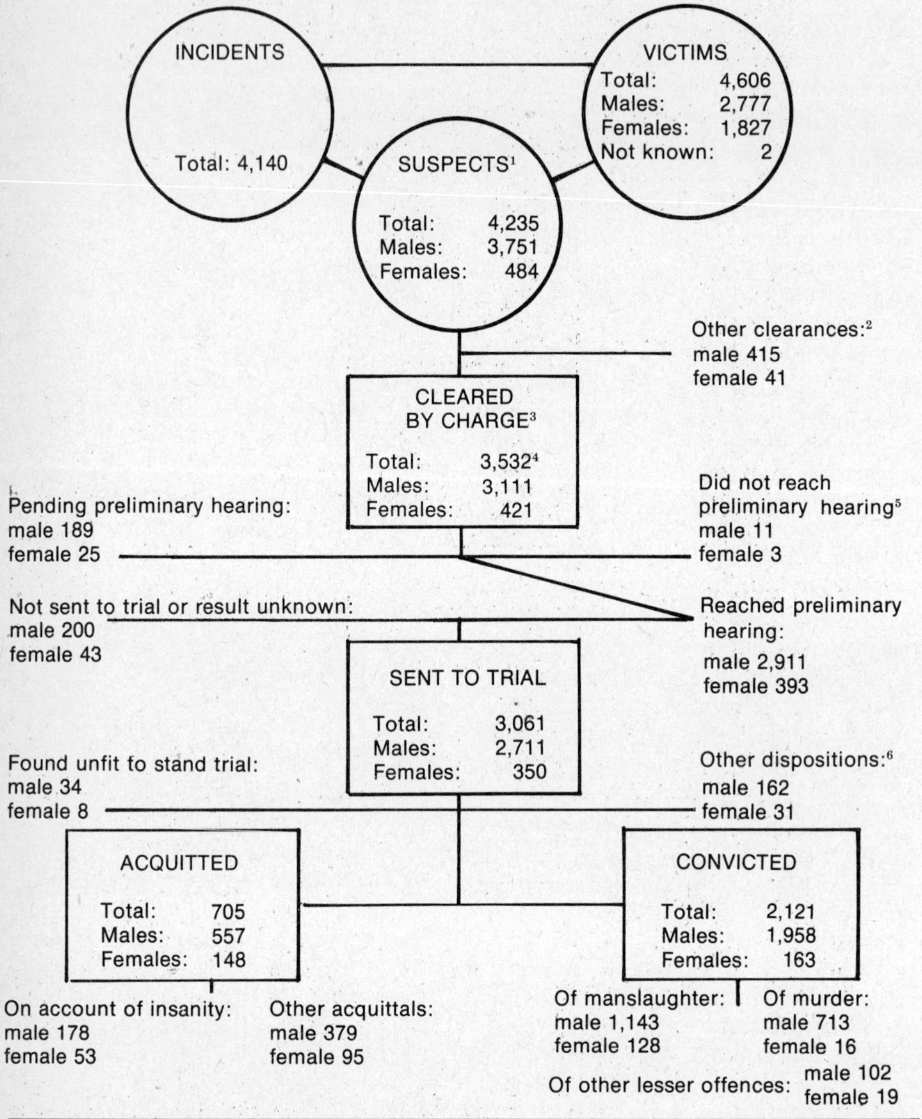

SOURCE *Perspective Canada II*, 1977, p. 306.

1. *Includes 3,988 adult and 247 juvenile suspects.*
2. *Includes only adult suspects who were cleared otherwise.*
3. *Cleared by charge in this case means that charges were laid against a suspect.*
4. *These and subsequent figures pertain only to adult suspects.*
5. *Includes those suspects who committed suicide or died of natural causes after being charged, as well as those who had their charge(s) withdrawn before preliminary hearing.*
6. *Includes those suspects who were awaiting trial, who had a stay of proceedings or had their charge(s) withdrawn, who died before conviction or acquittal, who received an absolute discharge, and those for whom the status or disposition at trial was not known.*

authors of chapters on public safety or crime and punishment must be aware of how things work in order to rationalize their choice of material, it is not excessive to demand that such crucial understanding be communicated to the readers for whom it is produced.

In looking at both *Social Indicators, 1976* and *Perspective Canada II* the single example I can find of an attempt to show a process in operation is a chart in the latter that outlines the flow of murder suspects through the criminal justice system and down its various alleys and pathways during a 14-year period. This is clearly not an attempt at providing a social indicator but rather an extremely informative look at what we, as a society, are doing to a certain group via the institutional reaction to the offense. (See figure 1.)

In presenting social data such publications are also obliged to inform us about how these processes may affect our lives. For example, while *Perspective Canada II* provides some interesting information (see tables 1 and 2) within its sometimes overwhelming tables and charts on the elderly, little is made of the data as a harbinger of possible future social conditions. Yet, it is possible to notice that the rates of hospitalization for the elderly are extremely high while the number of hospitals and the number of hospital beds per 1,000 persons have been stable since the mid-1960s. Couple this with the increasing growth rate for the elderly population, and it can at least be conjectured that either more hospitals or hospital beds will be needed in the future or that some other form of care for the elderly, now normally placed in hospitals, will have to be found. In another chapter the rather eclectically presented education data indicates that the unit costs of university education

TABLE 1

PERCENTAGE OF CANADIAN POPULATION 65 AND OVER, 1881–2001

Year	Percent
1881	4.1
1891	4.5
1901	5.0
1911	5.4
1921	4.8
1931	5.5
1941	6.7
1951	7.8
1961	7.6
1971	8.1
Projections	
1981	9.0
2001	9.8

SOURCE: *Perspective Canada II*, 1977, p. 39.

TABLE 2

NUMBER OF OPERATING HOSPITALS AND RATED BED CAPACITY, BY TYPE OF INSTITUTION (1958–1974)

Year	Number of Operating Hospitals	Rated Bed Capacity per 1,000 Population
Public General Hospitals		
1958	955	5.5
1963	976	5.9
1968	1,043	6.3
1973	1,049	6.4
1974	1,043	6.6
Public mental institutions (3):		
1958	71	3.5
1963	83	3.5
1968	105	3.3
1973	110	2.6
1974	108	2.1
Public tuberculosis sanatoria:		
1958	51	0.7
1963	39	0.4
1968	36	0.2
1973	11	—
1974	6	—

SOURCE: *Perspective Canada II*, 1977, p. 82.

will no doubt rise as a consequence of declining enrollments and a low average age of university professors. The young teachers will rise through the ranks, drawing increasingly large salaries, and driving up the per student costs.

While these examples are not particularly ominous or earth-shattering from the point of view of consequences for our future, they are the minimal kinds of things that can be said about even the most eclectically organized chapters in *Social Indicators, 1976* or *Perspective Canada II*. The point to be made is that not only do these publications avoid telling us what their data might mean or suggest, they seem oblivious to the fact that this is what social reporting is all about—the provision of a tool that will assist in planning our future, not simply provide us with random snapshots of our past. Unless some concern is given to the communication and reporting aspects of social reports, including the addressing of both problems and prospects, they will indeed become little more than statistical digests of passing interest.

THE PROBLEM OF GOVERNMENT SPONSORSHIP

Social Indicators, 1976 and *Perspective Canada II* have not fulfilled their potential as funnels of social communication and intelligence, and if they utilize their own extant resources and staff it is likely that they will be unable to do so. The task is too great and too diverse. The only method that will permit the realization of their potential is the bringing together of external authors in a publication framework espousing definite goals of social description and education. At present the situation will permit such expansion. Both the American and Canadian publications have established reputations, markets, and wide ranging staff contacts. This combination should be sufficient to lure capable people, both inside and outside government, to write and publish in a national social report in return for little more than author credit and possibly a modest honorarium.

Even if social reports were what they could be, they are produced by governments, and governments are notorious for hiding lights under bushels; and the sales of these reports to date indicate that this is exactly what is happening. These are public documents, supposedly produced to open debate between the public and the political processes, but the public, especially teachers, seems unaware of the existence of either *Social Indicators, 1976* or *Perspective Canada II*. This is especially ironic for these publications are produced in countries which have a national pride in the efficiency and effectiveness of their marketing and advertising skills. At the very least, social reports should be advertised to teachers of high school and university courses. Teachers teach people, not students, and it is in the school setting that strategies for problem solving and problem understanding are formed. If we are ever to have a socially astute electorate, our educational institutions must encourage the exposure of social concerns.

In this regard it is worth noting that *Social Indicators, 1976* does contain a section explaining how to read and come to grips with various types of charts and graphs, and, *Perspective Canada II* will be supported by a teacher's guide and a supplementary booklet on delineating social problems and issues by using social statistics.

The Problem of Limited Readership

There is an old chestnut that old news is no news. Since social reports present data that are usually at least two years out of date, there is a tendency among some groups, the media especially, to regard them as having the same informative level as history texts. Such data, however, are not only the most recent that reports can call upon, but the trends and changes they signal have implications for the present, and ten or twenty years hence. The fact that newspapers and other commentators fail to notice these reports attests to the point I have been making here that social reports are not carrying through with their mandate and responsibility. Neither *Social Indicators, 1976* nor *Perspective Canada II* have made the best seller list for nonfiction or the *New York Review of Books*. This should have been because of poor advertising and not because the publications were perceived of as not relevant to their focus or concerns. I fear, however that it is the latter, but I would contend that the interested reader has as much to learn from *Social Indicators, 1976* or *Perspective Canada II* as from *The Joy of Sex*.

Inclusion of Attitudinal Data

One of the major shifts in emphasis in the second American social report has been the inclusion of data on public perceptions in every chapter. The measurement of public attitudes and opinions is very much in vogue and including these measures, particularly those on overall life satisfaction, seems to be more out of concession to this present interest than out of their relevance for interpretation of other data. However, this is not always the case: attitudes on priorities are generally relevant to underscoring differences between population groups, and the data on attitudes toward abortion, for example, may signal a decline in birth rates and possibly marriage rates. Both of these possibilities have consequences for our national future. Similarly, consideration of the attitudes of grown children toward sharing their home with their aged parents may be extremely relevant in the context of planning future out-of-home housing for the elderly. Negative attitudes towards home-sharing on the part of grown children could foretell a large exodus from shared homes if other housing facilities for the aged were available. While this is conjectural at best such data at least permit the question to be raised and aired, and this is the essence of social reporting.

Some attitudinal data are extremely difficult to interpret. *Social Indicators, 1976* includes data on satisfaction with neighborhoods and neighborhood facilities, yet one is hard pressed to see what is at issue in cases where satisfaction differed even as much as 30 to 40 percent. I do not know whether this is a national issue, a social problem, or municipal mismanagement. The context in which the table on satisfaction with neighborhood appears sheds no light on how to interpret its inclusion. It seems that, so far as public attitudes toward housing are concerned, the authors have put in what attitudinal data were available rather than noting that which would have been most relevant.

Conclusion

In sum, I have been trying to argue that social reports like *Social*

Indicators, 1976 and *Perspective Canada II* have the choice of sinking together or picking up the challenge of organizing and distributing what I have chosen to call social intelligence, as opposed to social data. We have not been taught to, and we may not have the inclination to work hard at, understanding and using social data. This process must be started for us through increased commentary and explanatory material in social reports, and the vehicle for the process must literally be placed in front of us through educational institutions and advertising.

I do not mean to underplay work on social indicators and consideration of the attainment of national goals. Publications cannot ignore these important measures, but neither can they present them to us out of context. Trends and changes, forecasts and estimates, and reasoned possibilities give us one of the few accurate pictures of where we are, or seem to be going, and our national goals themselves are formulated against this background. The planning elite will unearth the information they require with or without *Social Indicators, 1976* or *Perspective Canada II*, but the people who pay their salaries need all the help they can get.

ANNALS, AAPSS, 435, Jan. 1978

Social Indicators and Congressional Needs for Information

By ELMER B. STAATS

ABSTRACT: The second edition of *Social Indicators* again presents valuable information on the social well-being of the nation. The Congress of the United States, in its appropriation, authorization, budgeting, and oversight functions, has a growing need for social statistics. These statistics are increasingly being used in program operations—in some cases triggering the beginning and end of programs and in other cases targeting funds under allocation formulas.

Congressional needs also exist for social indicator information in the oversight functions. Social indicators can provide a data base for program evaluation and policy analysis of social programs, however they are only a part of the federal statistical system. The Congress is taking a closer look at that highly decentralized system in an attempt to specify statistical needs of government better, to establish priorities for statistics, and to consider improvements to the current system.

Elmer B. Staats became Comptroller General of the United States in March 1966, after 26 years of service in the federal government. Before this appointment, Mr. Staats had served as Deputy Director of the Bureau of the Budget under Presidents Johnson, Kennedy, Eisenhower, and Truman. He is a graduate of McPherson College in Kansas, holds the M.A. from the University of Kansas and the Ph.D. from the University of Minnesota. He received the Rockefeller Public Service Award in 1961.

AMERICANS began realizing in the mid-sixties that economic prosperity and growth had components and complications which our national economic accounts could not reveal. At the same time we were finding that efforts to assess non-economic problems and accomplishments were frequently blocked by limited theoretical understanding and limited descriptive measures. It was in this context that the need for social indicators was proposed. Questions then followed: What are social indicators? How should we define them? How should we use them? With the appearance of *Social Indicators, 1976*, these questions will be asked again.

There have been many definitions and many proposed uses for social indicators since the mid-sixties. The social indicator movement drew together numerous groups interested in the fuller development of social statistics and social theory and, in most cases, in the fuller and more significant use of social statistics and social theory in public management and decisionmaking. The movement, however, never reached a consensus on the definition of social indicators, which statistics were social indicators, or how to use social indicators. Much of this lack of consensus still exists.

The definitions and uses proposed in the past decade have ranged from the very pragmatic and particular to the highly theoretical and mathematical. For example, *Social Indicators, 1976* defines its contents as "selected descriptive statistics or statistical measures . . . which indicate the general status of the population with respect to certain aspects of each concern."[1] A well-known definition for social indicators comes from the 1969 publication *Toward a Social Report:*

> A social indicator . . . may be defined to be a statistic of direct normative interest which . . . is in all cases a direct measure of welfare and is subject to the interpretation that if it changes in the right direction, while other things remain equal, things have gotten better. . . .[2]

By this definition, a social indicator is a social statistic that measures, for example, the health of the population directly; it is not a count of doctors. Increased numbers of doctors are only one input to health and may or may not change the health of the population. There is no legal definition or mandated use of social indicators. The Congress, however, has tried to use social statistics in public management and decisionmaking. Congressional interest is part of the demand for information relevant to the Congress's multiple responsibilities:

—authorization of new and renewable legislation;
—appropriation of funds;
—oversight of the executive's implementation of laws and programs.

Congress would like social statistics for program operation, program evaluation, and policy and program development. The use of social statistics in these processes is consistent with several definitions of social indicators. The Congress has made direct efforts to incorporate social statistics into program operation and program evaluation but does not have

1. U.S. Department of Commerce, Office of Federal Statistical Policy and Standards and Bureau of the Census, *Social Indicators, 1976* (Washington, D.C.: USGPO, 1977), "Introduction."

2. U.S. Department of Health, Education, and Welfare, *Toward a Social Report* (Washington, D.C.: USGPO, January 1969), p. 97.

direct methods to use social statistics in policy and program development.

As a result of attempting to obtain relevant statistics for these uses, and having some experience with the available statistics, Congress has increased the attention given the federal statistical agencies and their products.

PROGRAM OPERATION

Congress has used several statistical series in powerful roles in program operation. Social statistics have been used in public programs as eligibility criteria, automatic program triggers, and in distributional formulas. Values of the statistical series are associated with individuals, communities, or states experiencing degrees of distress or change that require or recommend public action. For example, the Comprehensive Employment and Training Act of 1973 and Public Works Employment Act of 1976 both use unemployment rates for states and local areas to determine eligibility for funds. Also, both Acts use unemployment counts as weights in the distribution of funds among areas. The Economic Development Administration, under the Public Works and Economic Development Act, uses unemployment rates to establish eligibility for area assistance programs.[3]

Income figures are used directly to allocate funds in revenue sharing programs and indirectly in public works programs. Several programs aimed at helping older Americans—for example, providing part-time jobs—use an income figure as an eligibility standard. Poverty indexes help determine who is eligible for food stamps, job corps training, and summer youth employment.[4] Population figures are an important factor in the revenue sharing formulas. In fiscal year 1975, there were 75 population-based grants-in-aid to states and local governments which used Census Bureau population data. These grants represented about $34 billion in federal funds for states and local governments.[5]

Because of these program operation uses by the Congress, social statistics have become extremely significant to states, localities, and individuals. Their prospects for receiving public funds are directly affected by whether series values are changing, are above or below a normative value, or are different from a given value by some relative or absolute amount.[6]

The significance of these numbers has resulted in public attention to their definitions and accuracy. The series have been criticized as

3. For uses of the unemployment rates, see U.S. Department of Labor and the U.S. Department of Health, Education, and Welfare, *Employment and Training Report of the President* (Washington, D.C.: USGPO, 1977), p. 29.

4. For uses of income and poverty figures, see U.S. Department of Health, Education, and Welfare, *The Measure of Poverty: A Report to Congress as Mandated by the Education Amendments of 1974* (Washington, D.C.: USGPO, April 1976), pp. 14–17.

5. Charles A. Ellett, "A Study of Data Requirements of Population Based Formula Grants," *Statistical Reporter* (November 1976), p. 49.

6. Most bloc and revenue sharing grant formulas use more than one social statistic. The array of statistics used includes: Population data—total population, population in urbanized places, population 16 and 17 years old, population 18–64 years old, Indian population; Income data—per capita income, extent of poverty, adults in families with annual income less than $7,000; Housing data—housing overcrowding, housing vacancies, substandard housing; Labor force—number of unemployed in state and unemployment rate. See Ellett, "A Study of Data Requirements," pp. 51–53.

inaccurate because of poor technique or because they are not appropriate for representing the concerns described in the legislation. Population counts, income measures, and, most recently, unemployment statistics have been criticized in one or both of these ways. Thousands of challenges were made to revenue sharing data elements by state and local governments in the early years of that fiscal assistance program. In some cases, local governments went to court to prove that a social statistic was not correct and should be changed. In 1976, the Congress authorized the creation of the National Commission on Employment and Unemployment Statistics to examine both conceptual and technical issues of employment statistics.[7]

Many of the statistics which are used in program operation are included in *Social Indicators, 1976*. However, the frequencies and levels of aggregation of the statistics are different from their use in the formulas. Because of the focus of the report—an overview—program operators will continue to rely on other documents for current and detailed information. However, in setting or amending normative values for operational series, Congress and others should find the time series format and the international comparisons in *Social Indicators, 1976* helpful.

PROGRAM EVALUATION

Because of the increasing number and size of social programs in the federal government and a desire to determine whether these programs are effective, Congress has stated that it shall receive noneconomic as well as economic information for program evaluation. It has legislated important changes in the functions of both the General Accounting Office and the Congressional Research Service, and has added new support offices—the Office of Technology Assessment and the Congressional Budget Office—to create, collect, and make accessible the program evaluation information it requests.

When the General Accounting Office was created by the 1921 Budget and Accounting Act, we looked at the application of public funds in a narrow sense, relying almost entirely on the accountant's most common information—the information records of the operation being audited. This limited application, however, has long since changed. Today, with the expanded responsibilities assigned by Congress, we are looking at programs to see whether the application of funds has any effect. And as government moves more and more into social programs, we are looking more and more into social measurement. Thus, our increased responsibility, along with the increasing use of social statistics as indicators by the Congress, has made the criticisms leveled at these statistics an important concern of the General Accounting Office.

We have broadened our base of resources by hiring economists, actuaries, systems analysts, doctors, psychologists, and many other experts. By using representatives from these disciplines, we can often get a better fix on changes in social indicators and whether they have been affected by government programs.

In 1970, Congress gave new responsibilities to both GAO and the Congressional Research Service.[8]

7. Emergency Jobs Program Extension Act of 1976, Public Law 444, 94th Cong., Sec. 13.

8. Legislative Reorganization Act of 1970, Public Law 510, 91st Cong.

The Congress extended the role of GAO beyond determining whether programs were being administered efficiently, effectively, and in conformity with the letter and spirit of the law, to include performing program evaluations and assisting Members and Committees to interpret program evaluation information. The Congressional Research Service was called on to produce briefs and bibliographies on expected issue areas and to keep computerized records of proposed and expiring legislation. In addition, because the House adopted Committee amendments in 1974 that required standing Committees to "undertake futures research and forecasting in matters within the jurisdiction of that Committee," the Congressional Research Service has established a futures research group.[9] In 1972 Congress created the Office of Technology Assessment to identify existing and probable impacts of technology and ascertain cause and effect relationships.[10] The Office's duties include identifying the social effects of technology.

One of the more significant changes in the kind of information Congress has indicated it needs came as a result of the Congressional Budget and Impoundment Control Act of 1974. The Act created the House and Senate Budget Committees and directed that they study ways of "developing techniques of human resource accounting and other means of providing noneconomic as well as economic evaluation measures."[11] The Act also revised and restated GAO's mandate to review and evaluate government programs and activities. It required that GAO develop and recommend to Congress methods for reviewing and evaluating government activities and perform certain functions regarding collecting and disseminating fiscal, budgetary, and program-related information. Because these kinds of data are so varied and large, organization and categorization of information were stressed. The inventories of information sources and systems, recurring reports, and evaluations which GAO has created since then are indeed evidence that organization and categorization are of prime importance.[12]

Although these laws do not specifically require social data, they do require program evaluation. Program evaluators seek to discover whether a program has achieved its stated objectives in a legal and efficient manner. They compare measures of program concerns before a program is undertaken and after it has been in operation. They also compare the outcome and costs of one program with other programs or uses of resources. The social impact of a program is conveyed through analysis of many statistics, especially since programs often have multiple objectives and outcomes. However, the statistics alone have not been sufficient to measure whether programs are causing substantive changes.

Program evaluation requires data to evaluate program performance and not general indicators of system

9. House Committee Reform Amendments of 1974, H.R. 988.

10. Technology Assessment Act of 1972, Public Law 484, 92nd Cong.

11. Congressional Budget and Impoundment Control Act of 1974, Public Law 344, 93rd Cong., Sec. 703 (a)(4).

12. U.S. General Accounting Office, *Federal Information Sources and Systems* (Washington, D.C.: USGPO, 1976), OPA-76-23; U.S. General Accounting Office, *Federal Program Evaluations* (Washington, D.C.: USGPO, 1976), PAD-77-5; U.S. General Accounting Office, *Requirements for Recurring Reports to the Congress* (Washington, D.C.: USGPO, 1977), PAD-77-61.

performance. The indicators in *Social Indicators, 1976* are not program specific. As the General Introduction states, the report contains indicators of system performance, indicators of well-being, and indicators of public perceptions.[13] To use them alone as program evaluators is to make heroic simplifying assumptions.

POLICY AND PROGRAM DEVELOPMENT

Policy and program development in today's world are complex processes. To develop national policies and programs, the Congress requires information to assess present situations, knowledge of what will change these situations, and administrative procedures to accomplish policy intents.

Social Indicators, 1976 presents a collection of measures of individual or family well-being. It gives a broad overview of social conditions in the United States, but reflects results or outcomes rather than inputs of resources. The report differs from another well-known statistical compendium, the *U.S. Statistical Abstract*, by omitting most administrative and program data, including information about public attitudes from nongovernment sources, and making international comparisons. It differs from a statistical agency report because the data it publishes are highly aggregated. It is unlike *Toward a Social Report* because it does not try to make a written interpretation of the statistics and status of a social concern.

In recent years, Congress has considered requiring a social report from the executive branch to assess the social well-being of the nation and to suggest new and different directions for social programs and policy. In each legislative session from 1967 through 1973, Senator Walter F. Mondale and others proposed The Full Opportunity and Social Accounting Act, also called The Full Opportunity and National Goals and Priorities Act. The Act would have created a Council of Social Advisors in the executive branch and would have required a social report from the President to the Congress. The bill passed in the Senate in 1970 and 1972, but not in the House.[14]

In deciding whether *Social Indicators, 1976* will serve policy and program development purposes, experiences with *Social Indicators, 1973*—the first volume in this series—need to be considered. A 1975 sample survey of upper level executive branch policymakers conducted by Nathan Caplan and Eugenia Barton found fewer than four percent of the sample made use of *Social Indicators, 1973* in their work.[15] Although Caplan and Barton had learned in an earlier study that the officials expected social indicator data to be valuable, the few reported uses involved speech and report writing. Those interviewed attributed the low level of use to the availability of better, more specific, or more up-to-date

13. *Social Indicators, 1976*, "Introduction."

14. The bill was introduced in 1973 as S.5, "Full Opportunity and National Goals and Priorities Act," and was reported by the Senate Committee on Labor and Public Welfare but tabled in 1974.

15. Nathan Caplan and Eugenia Barton, "Social Indicators, 1973: A Study of the Relationship between the Power of Information and Utilization by Federal Executives," *Program in Social Research and Public Policy* (Ann Arbor, Mich.: The University of Michigan, Institute for Social Research, Center for Research on Utilization of Scientific Knowledge, 1976).

information and the report's lack of interpretation and subjective data. It is probably true that a good number of the policymakers were more concerned with the program development and implementation stages of policy development than with the planning stages. They needed more demographic and geographic disaggregations in the data, more timely data, and more data about behavior than *Social Indicators, 1973* provided.

Caplan and Barton argued, however, that the minimal use was explained by the fact that the data were not linked to policymaking in a "system of national evaluation of progress toward more clearly defined goals"[16] and because an assessment did not emerge from the facts alone but needed to appear within a framework of goals. They deplored the tendency "toward a widespread and often desultory collection of data conducted with the implicit hope that somehow, from this pragmatic but goalless effort, some notions would evolve about what is the good life and how responsible governments may help achieve it."[17]

Other explanations of the use of *Social Indicators, 1973* deemphasize goals. Goals are made concurrently with an assessment of the present and an assessment of the ability to cause change. What are present conditions; does the society want to change them; does it know how to create change; does it know and accept the changes in behavior and costs in resources required to accomplish change? Social science theory and empirical research cannot always answer these questions.

Because policymakers are aware of the shortage of this kind of information, they have actively supported social measurement research in social experiments, demonstrations, and evaluations. The General Accounting Office has recently criticized the management of federally-supported and federally-performed social research and suggested that national policymakers could make greater use of social research and information about program development if there were more planning and coordination of the various research programs and if the findings were more accessible.[18]

FOCUSING ON THE SYSTEM

The Congress, in its attempts to gather and use social statistics for the purposes of program operation, program evaluation, and policy and program development, has become increasingly aware of limitations in federal statistical outputs and of the complications, expense, and burden of collecting these statistics. Fifty-four agencies have all or a part of their budgets designated for statistical activities, and there are over 100 recognized collectors of statistical data. In fiscal year 1977, over half a billion dollars will be spent on federal statistical activities.[19]

The agencies within the federal statistical system can be grouped into four categories according to their principal activities.

16. Ibid., p. 37.
17. Ibid., p. 38.

18. U.S. General Accounting Office, *Social Research and Development of Limited Use to National Policymakers* (Washington, D.C.: USGPO 1977), HRD–77–34.

19. Executive Office of the President, Office of Management and Budget, "Special Analysis G: Principal Federal Statistical Programs," in *Special Analyses: Budget of the United States Government, Fiscal Year 1978* (Washington, D.C.: USGPO, 1977), pp. 143–58.

1. A central coordinating office, now the Office of Federal Statistical Policy and Standards, Department of Commerce (where this report was prepared), to prevent duplication, achieve balance, and develop procedures for an integrated system of governmental statistics;
2. Five general purpose statistical collection agencies, whose primary function is the collection, compilation, and publication of statistics: the Bureau of the Census, Department of Commerce; the Bureau of Labor the Statistical Reporting Service, Department of Agriculture; and the National Center for Health Statistics and National Center for Education Statistics, Department of Health, Education, and Welfare;
3. Analytic and research agencies which use statistics collected by other agencies for interpretive purposes including preparation of composite measures; and
4. Administrative and regulatory agencies which collect statistics primarily as a by-product of their administrative and operation responsibilities.

Because of the way it developed and the diversity of agencies producing statistics, the system provides data in different timeframes, geographic detail, demographic breakdowns, and definitions. The nature of the federal system makes it difficult to determine both the worth of many of the statistics that are gathered and the real demand for social statistics. In many cases, the agencies that collect the information are not aware of the extensive uses that are made of the data.

In the opinion of some, the available data would be easier to use for social measurement, social research, and causal analysis if the system were more centralized or somehow more planned and coordinated. In the opinion of others, the decentralized system acts as a system of checks and balances on the perceptions we have of ourselves and allows more responsiveness in the system to special needs.[20] In either case, based on the way statistical gathering techniques grew in government, systematic attempts to set priorities on the gathered data, to evaluate their usefulness, or to determine whether the data collection process could be more efficient and effective are faced with a difficult challenge.[21]

Questions about organization and priorities have been raised in both Congress and the executive branch. Congressional studies have been made of the subject and the Office of Federal Statistical Policy and Standards, U.S. Department of Commerce, is drafting a report entitled "Framework for Planning U.S. Federal Statistics 1978–1989."[22] The im-

20. Executive Office of the President, Office of Management and Budget, *Issues '78—Perspectives on Fiscal Year 1978 Budget* (Washington, D.C.: USGPO, 1977), pp. 271–72.

21. For further discussion of the problems, especially with reference to education statistics, see the report of the Panel on Methodology for Statistical Priorities of the Committee on National Statistics, *Setting Statistical Priorities* (Washington, D.C.: National Academy of Sciences, 1976).

22. See for example, U.S. Congress, House, Committee on Post Office and Civil Service, *Coordination in Federal Statistics Gathering Programs* (Washington, D.C.: USGPO, 1977). Also selected issues from May 1976 through 1977 of Office of Management and Budget, *Statistical Reporter* (Washington, D.C.:

portance of priorities developed also from a concern about information-gathering burdens. The Federal Commission on Paperwork, which just recently completed its task of evaluating federal data collection, focused on much more than social statistics, but the congressionally-established Commission did recommend improved ways for the government to obtain data.[23] It recognized that obtaining information imposes a reporting burden which should not exceed the value of the information obtained.

In 1976, Congress passed a bill to provide for a mid-decade census. The first such census will be conducted in 1985. The mid-decade efforts will provide an opportunity for a periodic updating of significant national, social, and demographic characteristics. This should reduce the concerns about adjusting data series over the ten years between population censuses and limit the number of special surveys needed. GAO has undertaken a systematic review of the accuracy and use of statistical series which eventually will include social indicators. This effort is being undertaken not only to see if we can offer suggestions relating to the improvement of this information but also to learn about appropriate and inappropriate uses of the information.

CONCLUSION

In looking at *Social Indicators 1976*, I think it is necessary to understand the size, complexity, and multiple purposes of the total federal statistical system. *Social Indicators, 1976* has made full use of the system. Its relatively consistent viewpoint and data levels are an accomplishment, given the decentralized statistical system. The authors of *S.I., 1976* have selected carefully from statistics whose original purposes were more specific than reporting on social well-being, and have integrated both international and nongovernmental data. While this document may have insufficient detail for program operation and too little sophistication for program evaluation, it can be a source for those general assessments which are the first step in policy development. *Social Indicators, 1976* is not designed with the expert in mind anyway. It is for the nonexpert, but interested, citizen. It will be these individuals who will give it the relevant review.

USGPO) contain portions of the "Framework." Forthcoming issues of the *Statistical Reporter*, now to be issued by the U.S. Department of Commerce, will contain additional portions of the "Framework."

23. Commission on Federal Paperwork, *A Report of the Commission on Federal Paperwork* (Washington, D.C.: USGPO, 1977).

ANNALS, AAPSS, 435, Jan. 1978

Postlude: Past, Present and Future*

By DENIS F. JOHNSTON

ABSTRACT: Recent federal efforts to produce social indicator reports are a partial response to the growing perception that economic indicators alone cannot provide an adequate informational basis for developing viable public policies and programs. That perception stems in part from the rise in public concern regarding the nonmaterial ingredients of the good life and in part from the emergence of a bewildering variety of problem areas whose components include a complex of social, economic, political, and ecological factors. Significant improvements in the state of the art of social reporting await the establishment of an improved data base that would permit more sophisticated analysis of the interplay of environmental and socioeconomic factors, but even if our analytic capabilities are increased, the essential task remains: that of effectively communicating these findings and interpretations to as wide an audience as possible. Such communication will promote informed public consideration of the issues we face and will thereby encourage the development of both public and private policies that reflect a realistic appraisal of our present condition and an appreciation of our goals and aspirations. *Social Indicators, 1976*, together with this issue of THE ANNALS, represents a modest effort in that direction.

Denis F. Johnston assumed responsibility for the preparation of Social Indicators, 1976 *in July 1974, when he joined the staff of the Statistical Policy Division, Office of Management and Budget (since reorganized as the Office of Federal Statistical Policy and Standards, U.S. Department of Commerce). He also serves as United States representative to the Working Party on Social Indicators of the Organization for Economic Cooperation and Development (OECD) in Paris. He holds the Ph.D. degree in sociology and is the author of numerous articles on such topics as labor force projections, manpower development, social forecasting methods, and social indicators.*

* The views and interpretations expressed in this article are the author's and do not necessarily reflect the positions or policies of the agencies with which he is affiliated.

FEDERAL efforts to produce national social indicator reports (as distinct from compendia of social statistics) were begun in 1929, when President Hoover commissioned a four-year research project under the direction of William F. Ogburn.[1] However, that pioneering effort at comprehensive societal assessment was not sustained, except in the more narrowly defined area of economic indicators. Not until the early 1960s were social indicator reports again issued, albeit on a much smaller scale.[2]

The resurgence of interest in societal assessment that accompanied the Great Society programs of the mid-1960s prompted the establishment, in 1966, of an advisory group of social scientists to advise Wilbur J. Cohen (then Secretary of the Department of Health, Education, and Welfare) on the measurement of social change and the preparation of a social report. The brief report (101 pages) that resulted from this group's work was entitled *Toward a Social Report*. That publication is an important prototype in providing assessments of our current status in selected areas of social concern.[3]

An independent but conceptually related undertaking, oriented toward future goals and policy initiatives, was begun in July 1969, when President Nixon established a National Goals Research Staff within the White House, under the direction of Leonard Garment.[4] Its research culminated in the issuance of a report in July 1970 entitled *Toward Balanced Growth: Quantity with Quality*.[5]

Taken together, these two reports illustrate both the potential and the limitations of social reports as produced under federal auspices. *Toward a Social Report* was intended to serve as a prototype for annual assessments of social well-being that would, in turn, "facilitate informed decisions about priorities and directions in this Nation's social programs."[6] The analysis it contained was deliberately normative and the criteria employed in selecting the few social indicators it contained emphasized their normative significance. *Toward Balanced Growth* had a different focus. It

1. President's Research Committee on Social Trends, *Recent Social Trends in the United States* (New York: McGraw-Hill, 1933). For brief accounts of the origins of social reporting efforts and current thinking on the subject, see Philip M. Hauser, *Social Statistics in Use* (New York: Russell Sage Foundation, 1975) pp. 339–56 and articles by Daniel Bell, "The Idea of a Social Report," and Mancur Olson, Jr., "The Plan and Purpose of a Social Report," *The Public Interest*, no. 15 (Spring 1969) pp. 72–84 and 85–97, respectively.

2. Beginning in 1961, the Department of Health, Education, and Welfare issued a monthly report entitled *Indicators*, supplemented by an annual compilation of time-series entitled *Trends*. Both reports presented selected statistics relating to program developments and pertinent population characteristics in the above subject areas, together with brief articles. Both series were discontinued in 1968.

3. U.S. Department of Health, Education, and Welfare, *Toward a Social Report* (Washington, D.C.: USGPO, 1969).

4. An earlier effort of this kind was the report of the President's Commission on National Goals, *Goals for Americans* (New York: The American Assembly, 1960). A more recent effort in a similar vein has been the work of the Commission on Critical Choices for Americans established by Nelson A. Rockefeller. The reports issued by this Commission are published by Lexington Books (D C. Heath and Company) is a series entitled *Critical Choices for Americans*.

5. National Goals Research Staff, *Toward Balanced Growth: Quantity with Quality* (Washington, D.C.: USGPO, 1970).

6. As stated in the Letter of Transmittal from Wilbur J. Cohen to the President, in *Toward a Social Report*, p. iv.

was designed to explore possible alternatives for future societal development by proposing a number of "debates of emerging issues" for public consideration. Thus the former report offered an assessment of our current status; the latter, a discussion of options to be considered in our future development. The authors of these reports were keenly aware of the limited value of available statistical data for the purposes envisaged. Statistics describe facts, but the deeper concern in both reports was with values.[7]

THE CURRENT FEDERAL EFFORT

Shortly after publication of *Toward a Social Report*, work was begun within the Statistical Policy Division of the Office of Management and Budget on the first comprehensive national social indicator report. *Social Indicators, 1973* was finally issued in February 1974, after more than four years of development. Its basic format and orientation were quite different. First, it was not designed to be a social report; it did not provide any interpretations of the data presented. Second, it placed far greater emphasis upon comprehensive coverage of major areas of social concern, using descriptive statistics presented in graphic as well as tabular form. Finally, it tried to select and organize the data it contained so as to facilitate independent assessments of emerging social trends and current conditions by the interested reader. It was assumed, perhaps optimistically, that such data, if presented in graphic form, would provide a coherent picture of trends and conditions without the need for extensive interpretation. It was also assumed that, in any case, detailed interpretations could not be provided with the resources available.[8]

The preparation of the second report, *Social Indicators, 1976*, was begun shortly after the first one was issued. Like its predecessor, the second report is basically a chart book. Its principal distinctive features are its expanded coverage of major areas of social concern and the inclusion in each chapter of separate sections on public perceptions and international comparisons.[9]

The strengths and limitations of a report like *Social Indicators, 1976* should be recognized by those who peruse it. For readers with general interests in the topics covered, a chart book is an effective means of presenting summary information in compact form. Presented in this manner, the highlights of the data can be quickly seen and grasped. A further advantage is its compre-

7. The need to distinguish between "facts" and "values" without losing sight of either realm continues to prompt much philosophical discussion. For recent examples, see Mario Bunge, "What is a Quality of Life Indicator?", *Social Indicators Research* 2, no. 1 (June 1975), pp. 65–80 and Ian Miles, *The Poverty of Prediction* (Lexington, Mass.: Lexington Books, 1975) pp. 19–89.

8. The principal motivation for this issue of *The Annals* is to meet the need for interpretive essays based on the contents (and omissions) of *Social Indicators, 1976*. It is hoped that future social indicator reports can be designed to incorporate independent interpretive essays of this kind.

9. Daniel B. Tunstall, who was responsible for the preparation of *Social Indicators, 1973*, was most helpful in guiding the initial development of its successor report, although he cannot share the blame for its defects. For his views on future reports of this kind, see his "Social Indicators and Social Reporting" (Paper presented at the Joint American Marketing Association and British Marketing Research Society Conference: Changing Values and Social Trends: How do Organizations React?, Oxford, England, June 6, 1974).

hensive coverage, affording an overview of the several areas of social concern from a uniform perspective. But the data presented, insofar as they reflect a variety of complex social conditions, are self-explanatory only superficially. They tell us "what" but not "why" or "how." A further limitation relates to the criteria employed in selecting and organizing the data shown. No matter how large such a report is, its preparation requires the rejection of far more data than are finally included. The editorial judgment that must be exercised in making this selection should certainly be scrutinized, particularly in view of the fact that the most important single factor governing the inclusion or omission or any given body of information was whether or not it was available in a form suitable for graphic presentation. The resources available did not permit extensive analysis or reworking of data. It must also be recognized, especially with regard to the time-series of data, that today's rich fund of information did not spring forth in full bloom with the birth of the nation. The principal factor limiting the coverage and detail of these time-series is simply the absence of comparable information for the earlier periods.[10]

A final limitation is the paucity of "explanatory" measures—statistical measures that represent inferences drawn from the analysis of relationships among groups of variables selected to test hypotheses concerning some phenomenon of interest. Stated simply, that is not the primary aim of the report; its objective is to provide a body of comprehensive statistical information from which individual readers may develop independent assessments of the condition and trends in our society. Readers seeking authoritative interpretations of these data will find them in the preceding essays of this issue; those seeking analytical studies of social phenomena will find them in the academic journals and in some of the references to further reading provided in the report itself.[11]

In summary, *Social Indicators, 1976* places a heavy burden upon its readers. It provides a rich diversity of statistical data, but of variable quality. The available data do not permit equal coverage of each area of social concern. Proxy measures have often been shown in the absence of the indicators that might be preferred. Descriptive statistics that reveal differences among population groups may invite facile interpretations or unwarranted conclusions. Finally, the report may contain both good measures of the wrong things and poor measures of the right things. It is evident, therefore, that much remains to be done

10. Data limitations also explain the paucity of detailed information for different ethnic or racial groups for earlier periods, except for recent decennial censuses. For further discussion of these and other limitations, see the Introduction to *Social Indicators, 1976*.

11. A growing number of annual federal publications provide more detailed coverage of some of the areas of social concern included in *Social Indicators, 1976*. Examples include the U.S. Department of Health, Education, and Welfare, *Health, United States* (first issued in 1976), *The Condition of Education* (first issued in 1975), the *Annual Statistical Supplement* to the Social Security Bulletin (first issued as a separate publication in 1955) and the U.S. Department of Labor, *Employment and Training Report of the President* (first issued in 1964). In general, the essays included in these reports are more descriptive than analytic, in keeping with the decriptive nature of the data they contain.

in this challenging area; that is the subject of the concluding section.

PROSPECTS FOR THE FUTURE

Cooperative international efforts

The concern of national governments with the need to supplement their reports of national economic accounts with assessments of national welfare or the well-being of their citizens is reflected in the growing number of national "social indicator" reports that have been issued during the past decade.[12] These reporting efforts have both stimulated and been strongly influenced by the research and development activities of the Organization for Economic Cooperation and Development (OECD) and the United Nations Statistical Office (UNSO) in the area of social indicators, social accounts, and related conceptual development.[13]

The OECD effort, with a small professional staff within the OECD Secretariat and a Working Party on Social Indicators composed of representatives from the member countries, has been focused on a three-phase development project. In Phase I, a basic list of areas of social concern was agreed upon. Phase II, still in process, is aimed at specifying statistical measures (social indicators) that would reflect conditions and trends in each of the areas of social concern with acceptable reliability and validity. Phase III, now being planned, will seek to establish a common reporting framework for presenting available indicators from member countries for purposes of policy analysis and development. It will also provide recommendations for the development of such indicators for concerns not adequately represented by available measures.[14]

The work of the United Nations Statistical Office and affiliated agencies is designed to provide more fundamental improvements in the underlying data systems on which all measures in the socioeconomic realm must rely. The centerpiece

12. The Introduction to *Social Indicators, 1976* lists such reports as already published or in preparation in 24 countries. Exemplary in this reporting effort are the annual *Social Trends* reports of the United Kingdom, issued annually since 1970. For some of the thinking behind this effort, see Sir Claus Moser, "Social Indicators—Systems, Methods and Problems," *The Review of Income and Wealth*, ser. 19, no. 2 (June 1973) pp. 133–41 and Muriel Nissel, "Government Social Statistics," *HMSO Statistical News*, no. 25 (May 1974) pp. 25.1–25.6.

13. For an account of the origins and purpose of the OECD effort, see David E. Christian, *Social Indicators: The OECD Experience* (Paris: OECD, June 1974) and his expanded treatment, "International Social Indicators: The OECD Experience," *Social Indicators Research* 1, no. 2 (September 1974), pp. 169–86. For critical examinations of these national reporting efforts, see Bernard Cazes, "The Development of Social Indicators: A Survey," in *Social Indicators and Social Policy*, eds. Andrew Shonfield and Stella Shaw (London: Heinemann Educational Books, 1972), pp. 9–22; Abbott L. Ferriss, "National Approaches to Developing Social Indicators," *Social Indicators Research* 2, no. 1 (June 1975), pp. 81–92; Wolfgang Zapf, "Social Indicators 1973: Comparisons with Social Reports of Other Nations," and Natalie Rogoff Ramsøy, "Social Indicators in the United States and Europe: Comments on Five Country Reports." The latter two articles were published in Roxann A. Van Dusen (ed.), *Social Indicators 1973: A Review Symposium* (Washington, D.C.: Social Science Research Council, Center for Coordination of Research on Social Indicators, 1974), pp. 20–40 and 41–62, respectively.

14. Progress on the first two phases of this effort is reported in OECD, *List of Social Concerns Common to Most OECD Countries* (Paris: OECD, 1973) and OECD, *Measuring Social Well-Being: A Progress Report on the Development of Social Indicators* (Paris: OECD, 1976).

of the UNSO effort is the "system of social and demographic statistics" (SSDS).[15] Full implementation of the SSDS framework would require fundamental transformation of existing procedures for collecting and tabulating much of the statistical information in these subject areas. The principal objective of the SSDS and similar proposals is to establish a comprehensive, integrated body of statistical data whereby information on both the characteristics of given units of observation (stocks) and their movements across subsystem boundaries (flows) could be recorded. With such a system, observations tracing the movement of population groups could be linked with corresponding data from national economic accounts so that economic and social transactions could be analyzed in comparative perspective. Even limited implementation of such a system promises to yield a number of useful social indicators.

Improving the data base

The recent passage of legislation authorizing a mid-decade census in 1985 provides federal statistical agencies with a valuable opportunity to develop and introduce a set of common concepts, classifications, and coverage specifications whereby information from a number of sample surveys could be linked with census data for purposes of comparative analysis. By means of this developmental effort, the SSDS concept can be tested and adapted to meet our particular information needs.[16]

Two additional research needs may be mentioned here. First is the need for replicative studies—studies designed to repeat selected base-line studies at appropriate intervals so as to yield information on emerging trends and changes over time.[17] Second, there is a need for continued research in the general area of perceptual indicators. If social indicators purport to reflect significant aspects of the quality of life, they cannot be limited to objective measures of our social conditions. Inasmuch as our perceptions of or attitudes toward these conditions are the only direct indicators of their impact on the quality of our lives, they must be included together with objective measures. It must be admitted that the bulk of the subjective measures now available represent "poor measures of the right things." But there is little reason to believe that further experience and experimentation with such measures will fail to produce

15. United Nations Statistical Office, *Towards a System of Social and Demographic Statistics* (New York: United Nations, ST/ESA/ STAT/SER.F/18, 1975). On the development of social indicators within an SSDS framework, see the United Nations Secretariat, *System of Social and Demographic Statistics (SSDS)—Draft Guidelines on Social Indicators* (New York: United Nations, ST/ESA/STAT.76/24, April 1975). Also pertinent in this regard is D. W. Henderson, *Social Indicators: A Rationale and Research Framework* (Ottawa: Economic Council of Canada, 1974).

16. For details, see Joseph W. Duncan, "Priority Setting in the Coming Decade—Survey Linkage and Integration" (Paper presented at the Economic Commission of Europe Seminar on Statistics in the Coming Decade, Washington, D.C., March 21–25, 1977, reprinted in the *Statistical Reporter*, no. 77–7 [April 1977] pp. 221–28) and Denis F. Johnston, "Social Indicators and Social Accounts—A Developmental Strategy," *Statistical Reporter*, no. 77–8 (May 1977) pp. 346–57.

17. On this point and related approaches, see Otis Dudley Duncan, *Toward Social Reporting: Next Steps* (New York: Russell Sage Foundation, 1969) and Eleanor Bernert Sheldon and Robert Parke, "Social Indicators," *Science*, vol. 188 (16 May 1975), pp. 693–99.

significant improvements in our ability to glean useful information from such data.[18]

The need for "counter indicators"

A number of social analysts have expressed the concern that social indicator reports, particularly those developed within government agencies, could readily evolve into instruments of propaganda. The data they present could be carefully selected in a way to justify or elicit popular support for established policies. Indicators would thus become "vindicators."[19] No amount of evidence concerning the methods employed in developing statistical concepts and definitions is likely to overcome the suspicions of the more extreme skeptics. But by marshalling a variety of statistics relating to a given subject area, it is at least possible to reveal different aspects and thus discourage premature fixation on any single measure. It is also possible (as shown by some of the preceding essays in this issue) to develop reasonable but different interpretations of the same data, so that no single, "official" view need be accepted as definitive. In short, the need for "counter indicators" might be interpreted more realistically as a need for "counter interpretations" of the available data. Such interpretations can and should include criticisms of the underlying concepts and definitions, so that needed improvements can be brought to light.[20]

The need for projections

To differentiate social indicators from the much larger body of social and economic statistics from which they are selected, it is often asserted that indicators possess normative significance. This means, of course, that the phenomena they reflect are widely perceived in normative terms, that is, as "good" or "bad." The statistics are themselves neutral: murder statistics are not murderous. It is precisely these normatively significant statistics that are especially important in assessing our condition, inasmuch as they pertain to those aspects of our lives that either reflect or affect our values. But the significance of values, in turn, lies in the sphere of human action; values determine our goals and priorities. Facts can only tell us what we have done or what we have become. Values can tell

18. For insight into both the problems and potentialities of this area of social indicator development, see Frank M. Andrews and Stephen B. Withey, *Social Indicators of Well-Being: Americans' Perceptions of Their Life Quality* (New York: Plenum Press, 1976); Angus Campbell, Philip E. Converse, and Willard L. Rodgers, *The Quality of American Life: Perceptions, Evaluations, and Satisfactions* (New York: Russell Sage Foundation, 1976); and Burkhard Strumpel, ed., *Subjective Elements of Well-Being* (Paris: OECD, 1974).

19. On this sensitive issue, see Albert D. Biderman, "Social Indicators and Goals," in *Social Indicators*, ed. Raymond A. Bauer (Cambridge, Mass.: The M.I.T. Press, 1966) pp. 68–153; Bertram M. Gross and Jeffrey D. Straussman, "The Social Indicators Movement," *Social Policy* 5, no. 3 (Sept./Oct. 1974), pp. 43–54; and Peter J. Henriot, *Political Aspects of Social Indicators: Implications for Research* (New York: Russell Sage Foundation, 1972).

20. In this regard, see the remarks of Bertram M. Gross, "A Historical Note on Social Indicators," in Bauer, ed., *Social Indicators*, pp. ix– xviii; Dennis L. Little, "Social Indicators and Public Policy," *Futures* 7, no. 1 (February 1975), pp. 41–51; Judith Innes de Neufville, *Social Indicators and Public Policy* (Amsterdam: Elsevier Scientific Publishing Company, 1975), pp. 225–47; and Genevieve J. Knezo, "The Potential for Using Social Indicators in the Congress" (Paper presented at the annual meeting of the American Association for the Advancement of Science, February 24, 1977).

us what we should aspire to become in the future. Thus social indicators, from this perspective, are essentially future oriented.[21]

When they are available in time-series form, social indicators can readily be projected on the basis of specified assumptions to yield plausible estimates of their future values at a given future time. But even when social indicators consist only of single-time observations, they can suggest fruitful directions for future actions. For example, current measures of the prevalence of physical defects or disabilities offer advance warnings of potential future demand for health care services. Furthermore, observed differences among population groups with respect to such characteristics as health status, educational achievement, and the like can be employed in developing normative projections that suggest the path of improvement to be followed in bringing the less favored groups to the level enjoyed by the more favored. The objective of such exercises is not to predict the future but rather to explore the possibilities that exist in the present. It is hoped that the few illustrative projections included in *Social Indicators, 1976* will prompt greater interest in such exercises.[22]

The need for explanatory measures

Social scientists engaged in research seek to deepen our understanding of human behavior by exploring the determinants and consequences of delimited areas of behavior. For the areas under study, they try to identify those factors (variables) that exert a significant impact. From this perspective, social indicators are those variables that can "explain" significant amounts of the change in the phenomenon under study. The identification of such indicators depends upon the accumulation of research findings in the different areas of social concern. But it must be stressed that descriptive indicators, particularly when available as time-series or in disaggregated form, are highly informative in their own right. They cannot provide rigorous cause and effect explanations, but they can reveal the realities against which such explanations must be compared and verified. In addition, they offer clues as to what needs explaining and thus guide research efforts in more fruitful directions. Given the present state of the art, social indicator reports must continue to rely upon descriptive indicators for the bulk of the information they present. But as explanatory measures are developed, they, too, can be incorporated in such reports.[23]

21. Argument is detailed in Denis F. Johnston, "Social Forecasting Methods and Social Indicators," in *Handbook of Futures Research*, ed. Jib Fowles (Westport, Conn.: Greenwood Press, forthcoming). Also pertinent are Jib Fowles, "The Problem of Values in Futures Research," *Futures* 9, no. 4 (August 1977), pp. 303–14; Richard L. Henshel, *On the Future of Social Prediction* (Indianapolis: The Bobbs-Merrill Company, 1976); and Irene Taviss, "Futurology and the Problem of Values," *International Social Science Journal* XXI, no. 4 (1969), pp. 574–84.

22. For contrasting views on approaches to social forecasting, see Daniel Bell, "Twelve Modes of Prediction—A Preliminary Sorting of Approaches in the Social Sciences," *Daedalus*, (Summer 1964) pp. 845–80, reprinted in Albert Somit, ed., *Political Science and the Study of the Future* (Hinsdale, Ill.: The Dryden Press, 1974), pp. 40–67 and Seymour Spilerman, "Forecasting Social Events," in *Social Indicator Models*, eds. Kenneth C. Land and Seymour Spilerman (New York: Russell Sage Foundation, 1975), pp. 381–403.

23. For numerous examples of current research efforts related to social indicator development, see Eleanor Bernert Sheldon and Wilbert E. Moore, eds., *Indicators of Social Change—Concepts and Measurements* (New

The issue of policy relevance

From its inception, the social indicators movement has been oriented toward meeting the information needs of policymakers in assessing social conditions, monitoring social change, and evaluating social programs. But no single social indicator report, however comprehensive, can hope to satisfy these requirements. Such a report can only provide general background information; it cannot address the specific information requirements of policymakers who must cope, on a daily basis, with an ever-changing variety of issues. Therefore, it is not policymakers in situ but policymakers in training that may be expected to find such reports useful. It follows that such reports, if they are to find their greatest potential usefulness, should be directed primarily toward the staffs of government training institutes, to teachers of college courses in public administration and contemporary society, and above all to the nation's librarians.[24]

CONCLUSION

It is perhaps appropriate to close with a word of caution. Social reality has many dimensions and can be appraised from many viewpoints. Social indicators are conceptual constructs that guide our perceptions of that reality. In revealing certain aspects, they obscure or remove attention from other aspects. There is a danger that policymakers and the general public alike may have their attention captivated by a few officially or professionally sanctioned measures and thus become ignorant of or insensitive to other perspectives. Exclusive reliance upon a rigid set of indicators or a prescribed mode of interpretation could threaten our ability to perceive or adapt to changing conditions. Agreement on the use and meaning of certain basic indicators is of course essential; without such agreement, meaningful dialogue becomes impossible. But in moving toward such agreement, we must exercise care to ensure that our perceptions of social reality give us both an adequate grasp of our current condition and an adequate awareness of the possibilities open to us in our pusuit of our goals and aspirations.[25]

York: Russell Sage Foundation, 1968) and Land and Spilerman, eds., *Social Indicator Models*. For approaches that place less emphasis upon quantitative methods and the metaphors of physical science, see Bertrand de Jouvenel, *The Art of Conjecture* (New York: Basic Books, 1967) and Richard H. Brown, *A Poetic for Sociology* (Cambridge, Eng.: Cambridge University Press, 1977).

24. Evidence indicating the limited usefulness of *Social Indicators, 1973* for direct policymaking is reported by Nathan Caplan and Eugenia Barton, "Social Indicators 1973: A Study of the Relationship Between the Power of Information and Utilization by Federal Executives" (Paper published by the Center for Research on Utilization of Scientific Knowledge, Institute for Social Research, University of Michigan, September 1976). For additional criticisms, see Walton J. Francis, "A Report on Measurement and the Quality of Life" (Staff paper of the U.S. Department of Health, Education, and Welfare, January 1973) and Michael Springer, "Social Indicators, Reports, and Accounts: Toward the Management of Society," THE ANNALS, vol. 388 (March 1970), pp. 1–13.

25. For pertinent arguments, see Bruce L. Gates, "Knowledge Management in the Technological Society: Government by Indicator," *Public Administration Review* 35, no. 6 (Nov./Dec. 1975), pp. 589–93 and Fred A. Kramer, "Policy Analysis as Ideology," *Public Administration Review* 35, no. 5 (Sept./Oct. 1975) pp. 509–17.

American Politics: Playing the Game

Susan Rouder, City College of San Francisco
518 pages / paper / Instructor's Manual / 1977

In an eminently practical introduction to American politics, Rouder teaches students how to "budge the system" at all levels of government. Covers American political culture and institutions with a pragmatic approach.

> "A wholly original approach . . . presents the case for citizen action with zest and thoroughness. The author's style is easy and her command of her material is excellent."
> John W. Gardner, Common Cause

Foreign Policy for a New Age

Robert G. Wesson, Stanford University
462 pages / Instructor's Manual / 1977

In addition to matters of security, Wesson explores the economic, cultural-psychological, and Third World aspects of foreign policy, noting the new direction policy decisions must take. The text's problem-solving orientation involves students in appraising the policy-making process.

The Comparative Study of Politics

David F. Roth and
Frank L. Wilson, both of Purdue University
507 pages / 1976

American Government: Policy and Process, Second Edition

Robert L. Morlan, University of Redlands
450 pages / paper / Instructor's Evaluation and Project Guide by Arlene Saretsky and Stanley Moore / 1975

Political Research Methods: Foundations and Techniques

Barbara Leigh Smith, University of Nebraska
Karl F. Johnson, University of Missouri
David W. Paulsen, University of Nebraska
Frances Shocket
332 pages / 1976

Politics and Government: How People Decide Their Fate, Second Edition

Karl W. Deutsch, Harvard University
650 pages / Instructor's Manual / 1974

Conflict and Order: An Introduction to International Relations

Forest L. Grieves, University of Montana
409 pages / Instructor's Manual / 1977

Structured around the impetus toward conflict and the search for order, Grieves examines a range of issues in international relations, with case studies to stimulate interest in selected problem areas.

The Mexican Political System Second Edition

L. Vincent Padgett, San Diego State University
332 pages / paper / 1976

Public Administration: Concepts and Cases

Richard J. Stillman, II, California State College, Bakersfield
372 pages / paper / 1976

Victims of Groupthink: A Psychological Study of Foreign-Policy Decisions and Fiascoes

Irving Janis, Yale University
277 pages / paper / 1972

Form and Style: Theses, Reports, Term Papers, Fifth Edition

William Giles Campbell
Stephen Vaughan Ballou, California State University, Fresno
About 192 pages / paper / spiralbound
Now available

For adoption consideration, request examination copies from your Houghton Mifflin regional office.

Houghton Mifflin

Dallas, TX 75235 Geneva, IL 60134
Hopewell, NJ 08525 Palo Alto, CA 94304
Boston, MA 02107

Book Department

INTERNATIONAL RELATIONS AND POLITICS

FRED L. BLOCK. *The Origins of International Economic Disorder: A Study of United States International Monetary Policy from World War II to the Present*. Pp. 294. Berkeley: University of California Press, 1977. $14.00.

The theme of this work is that the Bretton Woods international monetary system can be more readily understood if its growth and development is perceived as an attempt by the United States to control the economic growth of Western Europe following World War II. Although not denying the importance of security issues and Cold War ideological disputes, Professor Block argues that a primary objective of United States foreign policy was to discourage the emergence of nationalist capitalism within the countries of Western Europe.

The book is divided into two parts. Part 1 focuses on the evolution of the Bretton Woods system. Because of the author's painstaking attention to historical detail, it would be difficult for the reader to finish this section without acquiring some appreciation of the way in which the building of the international monetary order was interwoven with the political fabric of the Cold War. Block does an excellent job in illustrating how the British loan, the Marshall Plan, and the decision to rearm Europe were equally as important in the assault on the growth of national capitalism as they were in containing communism. Such an analysis is valuable because it demonstrates how fruitless it is to search for a primary explanatory factor, whether it be economic or political. The only reservation that can be offered concerning this part of the work is that the thrust of the author's argument forces him to diminish the idea that the leaders of Western Europe had similar views on rebuilding a capitalistic world. The context provided by postWorld War requirements for reconstruction and the need for Cold War leadership did allow the United States to assume a hegemonial position, but the vision of a capitalist world economy was already well formed in the minds of British, French, and German leaders by their own historical experience. Block's argument based on American fears of emerging national capitalism in Western Europe is important, but it unduly obscures the common historical background and basic economic and political ties between the actors involved in building the Bretton Woods system.

Part 2 of the work is devoted to an

examination of the various factors that led to the dismantling of the Bretton Woods monetary system. Professor Block contends that unilateral United States efforts to: first, confront a persistent balance-of-payments deficit; and second, to deal with the more recent enigma of growing inflation are critical in explaining the breakdown of the old order. The author's analysis, however, might have been more complete if he had adequately linked attempts at adjustment and inflation control with the growing importance of displaced domestic groups; for example, labor, and the influence of government cartels, agricultural trade.

Overall, this volume is a valuable addition to the burgeoning literature on international political economy. Most significantly, it emphasizes how various systems of interaction (in this case, the international monetary order) can be utilized to control or structure relationships among nations.

LAWRENCE V. GOULD, JR.
Purdue University
West Lafayette
Indiana

T. A. COULOUMBIS, J. A. PETROPULOS, and H. J. PSOMIADES. *Foreign Interference in Greek Politics: An Historical Perspective.* Pp. 171. New York: Pella Publishing Co., 1976. $6.00.

Usually on account of their location, some countries seem destined to be a focus of foreign attention. Greece is a case in point. Those with a strategic interest in the eastern Mediterranean, notably Britain (latterly succeeded by the United States) and Russia, could hardly fail to take an interest in her affairs. Additionally, history gave this particular pot an influential stir. From the Crusades until recent times, France sought prominence in the area. And for 100 years Greece encouraged intervention by her large irredentist claims and concerns, only a quarter of the nation being gathered within the state which came to birth in 1832.

This study deals with the effect of foreign interference on Greece's foreign policy and its internal scene. The first half discusses the nineteenth century, suggesting that while the Powers obstructed Greek territorial ambitions, so far as domestic politics were concerned, they simply nourished existing tendencies. During the interwar period Greece was, for the first time, left very much to herself and, having put irredentism to one side, did not attract attention. But beginning with the Second World War, this pattern was drastically reversed. A harsh German occupation was followed by a "covert form of [British] colonialism" (p. 115), with Churchill as "Greece's arch-penetrator" (p. 107). It is argued that whether Britain is seen as defending Greece against Communism or engaged in an antiliberal conspiracy, she polarized Greek politics and so prepared the way for the civil war of the late 40s. Britain's successor from 1947, the United States, is charged with tilting Greek politics towards conservatism, bolstering the military, and bearing much indirect responsibility for both the 1967 colonels' coup and the 1974 crisis over Cyprus. However, while the authors' views regarding these matters are clear, they do not ascribe blame. Instead they see Greece's experience as almost inevitable, given the way in which the international system works. And they look forward to the possibility that Greece will be able to build up her West European connections and so diffuse American influence.

It is regrettable that the book does not include any maps. But it is clearly written and, though brief, has wide implications. It should be of value not only to those interested in Greece but also to analysts of foreign policy and of the relations of great and small states, especially those concerned with the idea and practice of intervention.

ALAN JAMES
University of Keele
England

RICHARD COX, ed., *Operation Sealion.* Pp. 190. San Raefel, Calif.: Presidio Press, 1977. $8.95.

Unlike most military accounts of World War II, Richard Cox's, *Operation Sealion* provides the military historian with a unique war game narrative of Operation Sealion, the planned German invasion of England which was postponed by Hitler on September 16, 1940. The war game was organized jointly by London's *Daily Telegraph* and the Royal Military Academy at Sandhurst. The gamers, players, and umpires were evenly divided in numbers between former German and British military officers, some of whom had actually participated in the planning and preinvasion activities of Sealion. As it may surprise no one, the game concludes in a German defeat, within three days after 90,000 troops had landed, on September 22, 1940, on the Dover coast between Folkestone and Seaford. Only 15,000 managed to escape to Dover.

While the tactical analyses of armies locked in battle are an important part of *Operation Sealion*, the major portion of the book is devoted to examining what factors determined the war game defeat of the Germans. On this account alone, the 190 page book is well worth its price.

The gamers found that only two of Hitler's four preconditions for Sealion's success were attained. While the sea lanes from France to the English coast for landing and resupply may have been partially cleared and the north/south channel flanks protected, the inability of the Germans to neutralize the Royal Navy and the failure of the Luftwaffe to gain air superiority over the RAF, and therein the Channel, proved disasterous for the German invaders. In addition, there was a lack of any plan for a combined operations headquarters, a situation quite different in Operation Overlord; German failure to recognize the complexity of an amphibious operation, whereby Sealion found all cross-channel resupply efforts thwarted by bad weather, inadequate landing craft, and British air and naval harassment; and possibly most important, Hitler's deflection, in the middle of Sealion, to the planning for Operation Barbarossa, the invasion of Russia, and Hitler's paramount objective in World War II.

One distracting feature of the book is that Mr. Cox can't seem to make up his mind on whether to write a war novel or report the results of a war game. However, any criticism of this informative and very readable book may be overshadowed by the research problem all World War II military historians may now face in light of the publication of *The Ultra Secret* by F. W. Winterbotham in 1974. Cox does not mention or allude to ultra, the codeword for the intercepted top secret messages between Hitler and his generals, and Winterbotham contends that the intelligence gained by the British in breaking the German code early in the war proved decisive, not only in Sealion, but in many other allied victories in the European theatre of operations. If one believes Winterbotham's account, the rewriting of the military history of World War II, including Operation Sealion, should keep revisionist historians busy for decades.

RICHARD E. JOHE
Department of State
Washington, D.C.

ROBERT E. HUDEC. *The GATT Legal System and World Trade Diplomacy*. Pp. vi, 339. New York: Praeger, 1975. $23.50.

This is a detailed and sometimes enthusiastic survey of the origins of the General Agreement on Trade and Tariffs, and of its structure and procedure up to 1974. In his preface, the author says that GATT "Law" is a unique blend of legal and diplomatic strategies, and in subsequent chapters he describes its rules and procedures as legal, but recognizes that "it is impossible to make any meaningful appraisal of how much legal rulings contribute to results." The book will be of special value to students of the history and significance of modern international organizations. Six of the early cases brought to GATT are discussed in detail, and an appendix lists the 77 complaints made up to 1974.

Before the end of his book, however, Professor Hudec writes of GATT'S "current legal malaise" and even of its "delegalization." The formation of the EEC was a serious blow to the organization's original concept of global reciprocity, and the consensus necessary to its effectiveness disappeared as member countries increased from 34 to 100 between 1955 and 1973. This increase consisted almost entirely of Third World countries, and "by the latter part of the 1960s most developed countries had come to view the developing country bloc as nonpaying participants who had lost their standing to enforce legal claims." At the same time, domestic and regional issues had become more important for most members than the global principles of GATT, and after the 1950s, the number of cases brought to it declined substantially. However, the organization has shown a strong survival capacity in accepting these new conditions, and it is not surprising that the "skeletal organizational structure of the early GATT blossomed into a full-time institution with an intricate bureaucracy." It is unfortunate not to find in the book the names of member countries at significant stages of GATT'S career, for readers should be informed not only of those who joined the organization, but of those who did not.

IDA GREAVES
Royal Bank of Canada
London

RICHARD LOWENTHAL. *Model or Ally? The Communist Powers and the Developing Countries*. Pp. vi, 400. New York: Oxford University Press, 1977. $12.95.

The Third World has loomed ever larger in the thinking of Soviet and Chinese leaders. Both Communist powers court key Afro-Asian and Latin American countries for combinations of ideological, political, strategic, and economic reasons that vary over time and with the target country. Both commit considerable resources to this aspect of their foreign policy.

This collection of updated essays was written over a period of more than a decade. It examines Soviet and Chinese efforts "to win imitation for their system as a model, and [their] efforts to win support for their overall international policies from existing governments." In the process, one becomes familiar with the difficulties and dilemmas facing Moscow and Peking, the limits of ideology as a motivating factor, the prominence of strategic considerations, and the emergence of long-term economic needs in shaping political ties.

Professor Richard Lowenthal's versatility, originality, deep understanding of the arcane byways of Communist ideology and in-fighting and his facility for integrating analysis make each essay, which is an entity unto itself, a rewarding experience. The essays cover a wide range of topics: the role of the state in the transformation of Third World countries, with an overview of the Communist, Western, and nationalist dictatorship models of development; the Soviet system of one party rule and its impact on the political-economic policies of noncommunist Kemalist Turkey, Kuomintang China, Mexico, and some of the African and Arab states that have attempted "selective imitation" (more than one-third of the book is devoted to this selection); "the background of the evolution of Soviet ideas from Lenin's vision of the colonial revolution through the Chinese experience of the 1920s to Stalin's dogmatic hostility toward the ex-colonial states and its revision by Khrushchev"; the background of Khrushchev's strategy of "licensed infiltration" of noncommunist single party systems and the reasons for its failure; the contrasting Maoist and Soviet approaches to economic development; the domestic and international determinants that led Moscow and Peking increasingly to follow divergent policies in the Third World; the reasons for the transformation of Marxism as it has taken root in different countries; and the economic motivation behind present-day Soviet policies in the Third World.

The essays deal more with doctrinal formulations and perceptions than with the opportunism underlying the quest of Moscow and Peking for tangible political and strategic advantages; and they do not devote much attention to the complex diplomacy of the 1970s. However, Professor Lowenthal has provided us with valuable information and rich insights on a subject of growing importance.

ALVIN Z. RUBINSTEIN
University of Pennsylvania
Philadelphia

MICHAEL S. SHERRY. *Preparing for the Next War: American Plans for Postwar Defense, 1941–45.* Pp. x, 260. New Haven, Conn.: Yale University Press, 1977. $12.50.

This book provides a splendid introduction to postwar defense planning during World War II. Author Michael Sherry has thoroughly canvassed the pertinent source materials, particularly the labyrinthine army files, and has written a convincing account that should remain standard on the subject for years to come. His clear prose style has resulted also in a readability rare in books utilizing such heavy archival materials.

A member of the postwar generation, Sherry writes from "a need, personal and intellectual, to understand better the origins of the Cold War." He reflects some of the bewilderment of his generation over Cold War issues and particularly the tendency to seek military solutions to political problems. He believes that the Cold War mentality was attributable in part to wartime defense planning. These plans generated an "ideology of national preparedness," that abetted the growth of Cold War policies.

The author's chief contribution is in recounting the army side of postwar planning. Others have provided similarly excellent accounts of navy and air force planning. Serious army planning began with the creation of the Special Planning Division of the Special Staff. Sherry makes the first scholarly study of the work of SPD. Its powers, he claims, were insufficient to accomplish its purposes. It lacked adequate staff, prestige, or authority to achieve success in planning. The core of SPD plans was universal military training, designed to build a large postwar reserve force. UMT, however, was already anachronistic and different opinions within the Army General Staff prevented the development of a completed plan capable of winning approval either from the military establishment or Congress.

Special coverage is also given to other topics that shed much light on the postwar services, such as the intense interservice rivalries for funds and force levels, the changing attitudes within the military services toward scientific research and development, and the gradual recognition of Russia as the chief potential antagonist of the postwar era. Sherry also evaluates the impact of the atomic bomb on military thought and planning, pointing to an early trend to rely on nuclear weapons as instruments of deterrence and massive retaliation.

Despite a tendency to criticize the military and its plans for the postwar period, the book is not overly tendentious, and provides a good factual account of postwar military planning. Perhaps the chief defect is a failure to indicate the author's view of a more reasonable defense program and to show how it might have moderated the Cold War.

FRANK D. CUNNINGHAM
Southwest Baptist College
Bolivar
Missouri

AFRICA, ASIA, AND LATIN AMERICA

HOLDEN FURBER. *Rival Empires of Trade in the Orient, 1600–1800.* Vol. II of *Europe and the World in the Age of Expansion.* Pp. ix, 408. Minneapolis: University of Minnesota Press, 1976. No price.

This is one of a ten-volume series on Europe and the World in the Age of Expansion. It is divided into two parts. The first deals with European commercial activity in the East (principally south and southeast Asia), the analytical framework being the three main commodities that successively formed the basis of trade between Asia and Europe: spices, calicoes, and tea. The second part is concerned with the structure of empire in Asia and deals with the organization of the various European trading companies, with the commodities they trade in, both with Europe and within Asia (the latter being the country trade), and with the personal contacts between Europeans and Asians.

Holden Furber brings to the subject of European expansion in Asia a lifetime's research and writing in this field and a thorough familiarity with the English and Dutch sources, at least of the eighteenth century, as well as a sound knowledge of the secondary literature. The main outlines of the story are familiar enough but Furber fleshes out his account with a wealth of interesting detail written in a felicitous style that makes the book a pleasure to read. The most important theme is the significance of the country trade between Asian ports as the factor explaining the building of European empires of trade and subsequently of the conquest in Asia. The key commodities were tea, for which a wholly unexpected European demand developed, and opium; the upsurge in the country trade and the trade with Europe which took place as a result led to the eventual British supremacy over the other European companies. On the Asian side, the power of local European rulers was lessened by the European desire to monopolize a commodity, combined with the desire to exclude other Europeans from the dominions of an Asian prince, their powerlessness at sea, and the weakness of their political authority, especially in India and the Malay archipelago.

Furber shows that it is too facile to view the seventeenth and eighteenth centuries as simply a period of exploitation of Asia by Europe, though there were pockets of exploitation, both as to particular regions and periods of time. Nor, he argues, was Europe progressively enriched chiefly by its trade with Asia, though individual entrepreneurs made large fortunes. He rightly warns against transferring back into earlier eras modern criteria for determining economic growth which present Asia today as underdeveloped in contrast to highly developed Europe. Equally, he shows that there was a rough similarity of economic conditions between Europe and Asia at the beginning of the seventeenth century. This is a work both of synthesis and of original scholarship which provides an excellent survey of European expansion in southern Asia in the early modern era.

PETER HARNETTY
University of British Columbia
Vancouver
Canada

JOHN G. GURLEY. *China's Economy and the Maoist Strategy*. Pp. ix, 325. New York: Monthly Review Press, 1976. $15.00.

The deaths of Mao Tse-tung, Chou En-lai and other veteran leaders of the Chinese Communist Party (CCP), the purge of the Gang of Four, and the complicated leadership succession, (including Teng Hsiao-p'ing's return from political oblivion) mark a watershed in the Chinese struggle to reach revolutionary modernization along Marxist streams. Reviewing the long period during which Chairman Mao's charismatic guidance left an indelible imprint on Chinese society calls for a clear view of the strategy which has yielded such impressive results in human and material terms. Unfortunately, even in the postNixon visit period, when interest is high and reports on China and Mao now abound, valid and meaningful insights into the Chinese process of economic development are few. Two major barriers help explain this situation: Mao and other leaders have not set forth their strategy in readily identifiable, complete form, and most outside economic analysts have viewed China's development process in a narrow economic context, applying bourgeois economic canons, and either ignoring or minimizing important social and political linkages.

Professor John Gurley of Stanford University and Monthly Review Press deserve our thanks for the publication of *China's Economy and the Maoist Strategy*, for it helps greatly to put China's development process in a meaningful context and to set forth precisely the evolution and specifics of the Maoist model for Chinese revolutionary modernization. The author's eight essays on the political economy of China's development, written for a broad audience, fulfills a need to deal with the background, strategy, programs, and outcomes through which the CCP has steered the Chinese people for half a century. His is a sympathetic, though not uncritical, analysis of the Chinese experience written from a Marxian viewpoint. His synthesis of the emergence and development of the Chinese economy derives from two contradictory sources: the Chinese-Marxist version and the work and analyses of tens of outside bourgeois economic specialists on China.

Gurley's eight essays integrate the Chinese development experience within the framework of an evolving Maoist strategy. Four of the essays had been published separately earlier and the remaining four are presented afresh. First, the Maoist strategic overview with its rejection of a trickle-down development approach and its building on the worst, that is; depending on the masses, rather than elites, to mount sustained economic development is described. The second essay sketches the formation of Mao's economic strategy in the crucible of revolutionary struggle from 1927 to the eve of the takeover. Next, Gurley takes the measure of China's economic performance by reviewing, critically but fairly, the data and analyses of over two dozen books on the economy. The fourth and fifth essays trace the economic background and history of the building of socialism in China: the Russian experience and contribution, the Chinese development strategy, the Maoist vision of Communism, and rural development problems and policies—the heart of China's modernization question. The remainder of the book covers the financial system, prices, profits, and the question on the diffusibility of the Chinese model.

This fine book helps specialists and generalists to fathom the strategy and meaning of one of the world's great happenings, the Chinese Revolution. Given the great confusion that results both from the rapid, far-reaching changes in China and the often feeble or well-intentioned but incomplete interpretations of these changes outside China, Professor Gurley's volume contributes in many ways to a better understanding of what the Chinese are about, why, and how well they have done.

CHARLES HOFFMAN

State University of New York
Stony Brook

BENEDICT J. KERKVLIET. *The Huk Rebellion: A Study of Peasant Revolt in the Philippines*. Pp. xviii, 305. Berkeley: University of California Press, 1977. $16.00.

DENNIS MORROW ROTH. *The Friar Estates of the Philippines*. Pp. xi, 1970. Albuquerque: University of New Mexico Press, 1977. $12.00.

In 1950—my first visit to Manila—I vividly remember my apprehension when I saw the major highways leading to central Luzon with barbed wire barricades manned by armed soldiers. It was rumored (falsely) that the Huk rebels ("Most of them are Commies") were planning to invade Manila. *The Huk Rebellion* is a splendid investigation of this agrarian uprising, "perhaps the most important and certainly the largest" in Philippine history. Kerkvliet analyzes his impressive data with keen insight and elegance. He states:

> My purpose in this book is to understand the Huk movement from the point of view of its participants and sympathizers. This is a perspective other social scientists have ignored when writing about the Huks and one frequently absent in studies of peasant movements in general [xi].

The author's scholarship for the preparation of this important book included 17 months in the Philippines researching his subject (with residence in rural central Luzon), interviews with major Huk leaders (some then in prison), and the examination of records in Manila archives. An additional year in Washington, D.C., was devoted to the study of pertinent American materials related to the rebellion and writing the book.

To obtain the desired peasant perspective, Kerkvliet lived in a village in central Luzon for four months. "In San Ricardo and other villages, I talked to people wherever I found them—inside their homes, working in the fields, standing on the roadsides, resting under shade trees, chatting at village hang-outs" [xvi]. Each chapter begins with what he learned about the Huk rebellion from his tenant informants in San Ricardo and then analytically moves to its broader setting of central Luzon and Manila. This approach gives the book an unusual warmth and poignancy, for the usually muted voices of the peasants are heard.

The limited space available for this review is best used by briefly summarizing some of the author's major conclusions. First, "A major cause for the unrest was the dramatic deterioration of traditional ties between local elites and peasants." The traditional patron-client bonds between landlord and tenant had been cruelly weakened by a growing population, an increasing scarcity of agricultural land, and expanding commercial markets. New markets, for example, increased the prosperity of the landlords, while the tenant's subsistence way of life became more miserable and uncertain. In their efforts to organize (eventually militantly) to regain their waning rights (not new privileges), the peasants were brutally evicted by many of their former patrons, grossly abused by armed guards and Filipino soldiers, and largely abandoned by an insensitive landlord-centric bureaucracy.

Second, "Peasants' demands were moderate, not radical." They rose, in their slowly accumulated wrath, not to overthrow the government or illegally seize their former fields, but only to regain traditional rights essential for a humble existence. They were Rizalian in their demands: they wanted reform not the establishment of a new revolutionary government. In this regard, *The Huk Rebellion* is a corrective to earlier accounts (e.g. Baclagon, *Lessons from the Huk Campaign in the Philippines*, Scaff, *The Philippine Answer to Communism.*) that "portrayed the Huk movement as being more radical than my findings would allow."

Third, the "peasants tried a variety of ways to cope with the drastically changing agrarian conditions and to demand reform" before they revolted. Kerkvliet disputes the conclusions of earlier books on the Huk rebellion that "describe unrest in central Luzon prior to the revolt . . . as if it were a sudden explosion of discontent. . . . Finally, neither the Huk rebellion itself nor the peasant unrest preceding it resulted from outsiders coming into the villages to start trouble." Fourth, the book documents in detail that the "PKP [Philippine Communist Party] did not inspire or control the peasant movement in central Luzon during the 1930s and 1940s, the Hukbalahaps, or the Huk rebellion itself." These are specious conclusions of Filipino elite, American military leaders, and Filipino government officials many writers uncritically embraced.

Finally, Kerkvliet reports the rebellion "hastened the decline of the old order, which peasants had set out to restore." The ancient patron-client relationships were fractured beyond repair. Increasing mechanization of agriculture enhanced the value of nameless, *compadre*-less salaried workers. Unlike some Filipinos today, the peasants were agitating for a just, not a new, society. They have found in Kerkvliet an able chronicler of their struggles.

The Friar Estates of the Philippines is a carefully researched account of these once vast fiefs, their religious, political, and economic administration, internal labor conditions, and the socioeconomic changes that occurred during the late eighteenth and nineteenth centuries that led to their crucial role in the 1896 revolt of the Filipinos against the Spaniards. These estates, (that often included towns), owned by the Dominicians, Jesuits, Augustinians, and Recollects, included nearly one-half of the total land area of the four provinces surrounding Manila, Bulacan, Rizal, Cavite, and Laguna. At this time this region was the most developed heartland of the nation. The disputes that swirled around them, their subsequent purchase by the new American colonial government for reallotment to tenant farmers (who quickly lost them to the elite) are central topics in modern Philippine history.

Roth reports that the friars' involvement in the economy of the Philippines was facilitated by the small Spanish commercial group in Manila, largely explained by the distance of the colony from Spain and the archipelago's lack of precious metals that discouraged outlanders from rushing to the new Asian colony. Hence, there was little competition or conflict between the businessmen in Manila and the friars. During the seventeenth century, many Spanish landowners (for religious and economic reasons) donated or sold their estates to the friars. Roth then skillfully compares the religious, political, and economic administration of these estates with those in Latin America. This is a book, therefore, that Latin Americanists should not overlook.

Another chapter deals with the techniques the friars used to obtain workers for the estates that frequently involved defrauding the state and exploiting the Filipino peasant. He discusses the marketing of estate produce, largely rice, for the cattle ranches developed in Latin America were a failure in the Philippines. He concludes that the estates did not become significant sources of profit to the monastic orders until the nineteenth century.

By the nineteenth century, conditions on the estates had changed drastically. The workers rents accelerated while crop declines left them with smaller shares of the harvest. A class of noncultivating tenants (including the family of José Rizal) was created who engaged subtenants to till their leased fields. The social structure of the haciendas was modified and the paternalistic aspects of their administration decreased. "In the Weberian vocabulary . . . power, rather than authority, had become the more fragile basis on which rested the relationships between landlord and tenant." Conditions became unbearable so that "agrarian unrest on the friar estates was one of the main causes of the Revolution of 1896." This theme is a tragically familiar one in Philippine history as the review of Kerkvliet's book demonstrates.

Roth made extensive use of neglected materials in the Archivo de la Universidad de Santo Tomás and the Archivo de la Provincia de Santisimo Rosario in the Philippines. He also used the Newberry and Lilly holdings on the Philippines and the Vatican Collection of Saint Louis University. He notes various gaps in the archival materials for his investigation of the friar estates. For example, there is a dearth of descriptions of life on the haciendas—a vexing hiatus for an anthropologist. However, he tries to overcome these limitations "through a process of ethnohistorical reasoning and some educated guesswork." I see no reason to dispute his facts, reasoning or guesswork.

DONN V. HART

Northern Illinois University
DeKalb

IRVING LEONARD MARKOVITZ. *Power and Class in Africa.* Pp. xii, 398. Englewood Cliffs, N.J.: Prentice-Hall, 1977. $12.95.

Power and Class in Africa offers a unique perspective on contemporary African states. Professor Markovitz departs from the "currently fashionable political positions that masquerade under an academic facade . . . ," which focus on instability and malaise in African states and which also assume African societies to be classless.

For Markovitz, the key to understanding contemporary Africa is to appreciate the continuity of modern Africa from its antiquity and to see African evolution as similar to the evolution of other societies at comparable stages of social development. The chief characteristic of African society, especially of African kingdoms, has been, Markovitz tells us, its class character. Since independence, African traditional elites have continued their roles as elite social classes in the modernizing state.

This thesis is sustained by a survey of African history which focuses on the Great Kingdoms of the past two thousand years and by presenting evidence that the slave trade and the era of imperialism served to reinforce the positions of ruling classes. In contemporary Africa, the author reviews the roles of the bureaucracy, business, labor, military, peasantry and farmers to assess the nature of classes in Africa today. From the ruling classes of earlier times has emerged a contemporary bourgeoisie which rules. Throughout black Africa an organizational bourgeoisie, ". . . distinguishable by their strategic locations in society, from which they make major decisions that affect the life chances of thousands of their compatriots . . ." exercises power invariably for their class advantage.

For those who look upon African societies as essentially classless, Markovitz's case to the contrary must be considered. His argument might be either enhanced or refuted by statistical data. The author's approach is largely anecdotal, but the case he makes has weighty evidence in its support.

Yet, should we grant that African societies have been class stratified, what has been the consequences of class divisions? One might expect, as a matter of course, that class divided societies are inevitably class conflict societies. Markovitz has little to report of evidence of such class conflict. Indeed, only when class lines and ethnic identities are one, for example, as between the Tutsi and Hutu, is class conflict demonstrably present.

While classes are described and discussed fully, the other theme of this work, the evolution of African society along trends similar to those of Europe, is treated too briefly. It deserves a fuller discussion and one might suspect, in additional chapters, for an adequate explication. If the case can be sustained, then could it be expected that nationalism and the industrial revolution would turn African politics toward democratic/capitalist structures?

Markovitz decries African class systems because they lead to economic growth rather than development. His distinction defines growth as a greater output and ascribes to development a more equitable sharing of the country's wealth by the people. The Western model suggests that only after productive forces develop can one expect a more equalitarian distribution of a country's resources, but this approach was barely considered.

What emerges then is a worthwhile discussion of forces molding contemporary Africa, but an inconclusive case that classes provide the master key for understanding Africa and for predicting its destiny.

J. LEO CEFKIN

Colorado State University
Fort Collins

THOMAS A. METZGER. *Escape from Predicament: Neo-Confucianism and China's Evolving Political Culture.* Pp. vii, 303. New York: Columbia University Press, 1977. $15.00.

This highly complex work is, among other things, a re-evaluation of traditional China's response to being brought into the modern world. Utilizing cross-cultural and interdisciplinary perspectives, Metzger focuses on late Imperial China and its neo-Confucian structure and elite, and asserts that the confrontation between the neo-Confucian ethic and the West led not to the widely accepted politics of despair, but rather to a welcome escape from predicament and a new optimism. While not attempting, certainly, to slay any giants among the pioneers in his field of inquiry, he nevertheless casts a very critical eye on many of the conclusions of his predecessors, ranging from Weber through Levenson to Solomon.

Rejecting standard interpretations of Chinese attitudes toward dependence and individuality, Metzger argues that the neo-Confucian elite was the product of an ethos of interdependence which allowed considerable inner personal autonomy. Self-assertion was possible, praiseworthy, and even common, although it was not the sort the West knew or understood. The Confucian, imbued with a sense of the possibility of achieving within himself a godlike sort of moral power, nevertheless faced most anxiously the probability that his society would ultimately ensure that he did not. His internalized sense of worth and potential morality was inhibited by the externals of his society. Escape from this frustrating predicament began to seem possible only when the West pushed in and offered an alternative, not to the individual's perception of his own worth and perfectability, but to the nature of external and inhibiting society. Far from despair, sustained contact with the West brought optimism and hope. Internal moral power might still be achieved, if nurtured in a new milieu. Metzger sees a large degree of continuity into the Maoist present.

This is an important piece of revision, broad-ranging in scope and yet careful in detailed evidence. Its many aspects should occupy scholars for some time, for it demands response. It is a major and exciting work.

R. KENT LANCASTER

Goucher College
Baltimore
Maryland

JANICE E. PERLMAN. *The Myth of Marginality: Urban Poverty and Politics in Rio de Janeiro*. Pp. xxiv, 341. Berkeley: University of California Press, 1976. $14.95.

In 1968–69, the author, now an assistant professor of city and regional planning at the University of California, Berkeley, went to Brazil to do field work for her doctoral dissertation. (She had already visited the country briefly, during the wild days of João Goulart, and shared his enthusiasm for "structural reforms.") She studied three types of squatter settlements in Rio de Janeiro, "a favela on a hillside in the midst of an upper-class residential and commercial area," "a favela in the industrial periphery of the city," and "a subúrbio—a group of neighborhoods in an outlying satellite, or dormitory city."

She lived in each for "a few weeks to several months," and used "a mixture of informal and formal research techniques." There were interviews with a random selection of residents and a group of community leaders. She returned to Rio in 1973 "to update my study for this book," but the earlier data forms its backbone.

Dr. Perlman concludes that the favelados "are not politically and economically marginal, but are instead repressed and exploited." She was a witness to "the poverty, the exploitation, and the systematic repression which, although affecting the entire social pyramid, are most visible in the favelas." Fernando Henrique Cardoso calls the book "a major contribution to our theoretical understanding of marginality and urban poverty in developing nations. . . ." Her analysis "illuminates the dialectical relationship between the world of the disinherited and the poles of dynamism and economic growth of the system."

Under the circumstances, the approach could hardly have been moralistic or theological, only doggedly and determinedly social scientific. Dr. Perlman is not interested in poverty as such, and would surely scoff at the traditional view, that poverty is part of man's condition. Without telling us exactly what poverty is, she is convinced that it can be eliminated. It is a serious "problem" of modern society, but like all problems identified or posed by social scientists, capable of being "solved." (She assumes that the resources of the earth are enough to make everybody rich, and is unaware that human "problems" are filled with mystery.)

The book paints the life of the favelas in dark and somber colors, and no basic changes are possible so long as the status quo continues. Only by changing the structures of society will the "evil" be eliminated. (I am at a loss to know what kind of ideal society she has in mind, what system intended to supersede the existing one would insure the abolition of poverty and favelas. She does not say that she shares the Marxist view of capitalism, as does D. Helder Câmara, the revolutionary antipoverty archbishop of Olinda-Recife.)

This type of research is not my dish of tea, and I put the book down with the feeling that a poet let loose in the favelas of Rio de Janeiro would have come up with the same conclusions, but less tediously, less repetitiously, and at less cost to the foundations. The author is of course very objective (if one assumes the validity of her premises). Her dedication to methodology is impeccable but it tied her down: her refusal to leap unaided by others or trust her own intuitions led her to prove many obvious things. It is an intense book, one that reflects the author's emotional involvement with her subjects, and there are autobiographical insights of a prissy irrelevance. She takes social scientists to task for their earlier, fuzzier studies, and castigates the "capitalist" establishment. Her most clearly humanistic concept is that favelas ought to be left alone.

These strictures to the contrary notwithstanding, the book is an impressive contribution to the study of urban poverty. It pinpoints, at a moment in time, what the situation was and what the feelings were. Granted that change is of the nature of man, will the author have to return periodically to update her findings? Will her personal involvement, the friendships that she forged, be lost and forgotten now that the book has seen the light of day? The dangers and limitations of the subject are, I think, apparent enough. What remains to be said is that she proves her thesis, that marginality in her Rio sampling is a myth.

MANOEL CARDOZO
The Catholic University of America
Washington, D.C.

G. WILLIAM SKINNER, ed. *The City in Late Imperial China*. Pp. xvii, 820. Stanford, Calif.: Stanford University Press, 1977. $35.00.

Although for the past 3000 years many of the major cities of the world have been located in China, it is only recently that scholars have begun serious study of the institutional framework and ecology of Chinese cities. There is no lack of descriptive material concerning the physical makeup of these cities or documentary evidence concerning their institutions, but Chinese political and intellectual elites, wedded to an agrarian ideal, never regarded the city as a primary social entity or a crucial element in the expansion of Chinese society. Traditional Chinese scholars seemed to feel that the basic cosmological significance and physical form of Chinese capital cities had been set by the beginning of the first millenium and subsequently sanctified by tradition, while lesser cities were primarily political extensions of the capital, reproducing its form and significance in microcosm. Thus they paid little attention to further development of urban theory. Later Western scholars basically followed their Chinese teachers in their approach to understanding Chinese cities.

The City in Late Imperial China, represents the most recent and most comprehensive break with this traditional approach and is the last of three studies emanating from two conferences in 1968–69 sponsored by the Subcommittee on Research on Chinese Society under the Social Science Research Council and American Council of Learned Societies' Joint Committee on Contemporary China. The two previous works: *The City in Communist China*, edited by John Wilson Lewis (1971), and *The Chinese City Between Two Worlds*, edited by Mark Elvin and G. William Skinner (1974), dealt with the transformation of the Chinese city from about 1850 on. The present work, consisting of some 16 essays by 15 different writers, primarily deals with the city from the fourteenth to the nineteenth centuries. It is divided into three parts, each preceded by an introduction by William Skinner. In these introductions, Skinner not only summarizes the main points of the individual essays, but attempts to provide a common theoretical framework for the whole, thus tying together what would otherwise often appear as disparate and unrelated studies.

While the work as a whole is primarily concerned with Chinese cities of late imperial times, part one on "The City in History" also contains discussions of general development since earliest times in two articles by the late Arthur Wright on "The Cosmology of Chinese Cities" and Sen-dou Chang on "The Morphology of Walled Capitals." Specific examples of urban development in later times are then provided by two articles of F. W. Mote, "The Transformation Nanking 1350–1400" and Harry J. Lamley, "The Formation of Cities: Initiative and Motivation in Building Three Walled Cities in Taiwan." Skinner himself contributes a major article on "Regional Urbanization in Nineteenth-Century China," which further enhances our understanding of the importance of regional studies when dealing with socioeconomic and political problems in Chinese history.

Part two on the "City in Space" deals with the relationship between the city and countryside. In many respects this is the most valuable section of the book. Skinner again provides a major interpretive study on "The Cities and the Hierarchy of Local Systems," which expands on the article mentioned above and shows that: "the formal administrative attributes of capital cities stemmed in large part from their place in the relevant regional system of economic central places," and that "the size and strength of informal political systems varied inversely with the intensity of bureaucratic government—a covariation that expressed the structure of 'natural' economic regions at least as much as the arrangement of provinces" (p. 254). On p. 345, he concludes that: "Ch'ing field administration was marvelously adapted to the realities of regional structure within the empire. On the one hand, the revenue potential of different localities was largely a function of their place in the hierarchy of nodal economic systems that culminated in eight regional economies, each with a core-periphery structure. On the other hand, defense requirements varied in conformity with the structure of physiographic regions; critical defense perimeters were closely associated with regional frontiers, and other strategic sites guarded the major approaches to the heartland of physiographic regions, whose rich resources and great cities constituted the ultimate military objectives."

Skinner's article is followed by John R. Watt's discussion of "The Yamen and Urban Administration," which treats with the relationship between the magistrate and his yamen, representing the central administration and local interests. Two fascinating articles, showing the specific workings of this regional system, are then provided by Yoshinobu Shiba dealing with "Ningpo and its Hinterland" and Mark Elvin on "Market Towns and Waterways: The County of Shanghai from 1480 to 1910." They, in turn, are supplemented by two studies on "The Academies and Urban Systems in Kwangtung" by Tilemann Grimm and "Extended Kinship in the Traditional City" by Hugh D. R. Baker. Both of these articles show the interlocking nature of the educational and kinship systems within the regions dominated by urban centers.

Finally, part three attempts to deal with "The City as a Social System." Skinner's introduction provides a particularly valuable overview of the social composition, spatial arrangement, and administration within the city. Peter J. Golas, Stephan Feuchtwang and Sybille van der Sprenkel contribute interesting articles on "Early Ch'ing Guilds," School-Temple and City God," and "Urban Social Control," and the work concludes with two studies on Taiwan cities by Donald R. DeGlopper and Kristofer M. Schipper, "Social Structure in a Nineteenth-Century Taiwanese Port City" and "Neighborhood Cult Associations in Traditional Tainan." To me this was the least satisfactory part of the book, not because of any deficiency on the part of the individual articles, but because they seemed to raise more questions than the limited space allotted could answer. In discussing "The City as a Social System" the writers were constantly skirting the questions of "how things worked" and "how people lived." This is where the analytical approach of the social historian breaks down, and the reader begins to wonder where all the people were.

In spite of the inevitable unevenness among the articles, this is clearly the most important volume on Chinese social history to be produced in the past ten years, and special thanks are due to William Skinner, who not only performed a masterful feat in tying it all together, but produced some of the most insightful writing on the structure of Chinese society in many years. The work is further enhanced by some thirty-six maps and twenty-two illustrations. In addition there is a comprehensive "character list" and index.

W. ALLYN RICKETT
University of Pennsylvania
Philadelphia

ALEXANDER STEWARD. *The World, the West and Pretoria.* Pp. ix, 299. New York: David McKay, 1977. $14.95.

Part one of the book covers the years 1945 to 1960, and is entitled "World Context: *Idealism*."

In the first four chapters, Steward talks about the five years he spent in North America (Canada). He sets the political stage by describing how apartheid contradicted and challenged the hopes and ideals of the postwar Western world; Pretoria's race superiority was to be countered by the Western belief that all men were to be regarded as the same politically and socially. Since the United States had become the world reformer and missionary, leading the revolution for liberty and human rights, Steward felt that Pretoria's case could not get a fair hearing. While the rest of the world was proclaiming the sameness of men, Pretoria was implementing a policy of apartheid based on the essential difference between them.

The author defines the pseudo liberal, and claims that his pernicious influence was apparent everywhere in America. He argues that all men are not created equal. "Except in obedience to authority there is no liberty; and the pursuit of happiness is, in itself the chase of the wild goose."

Steward next examines the national and international policies of Britain which he traced to their historical origins. He discusses the utilization doctrine of Jeremy Bentham, the greatest happiness of the greatest number. This doctrine, he claims, was implemented by the Fabian society, whose goal it was to establish a socialist society where equality of opportunity would be assured. Classes were to be abolished and wealth was to be distributed equally. These ends were to be achieved by evolution rather than revolution. Steward contends that these socialist policies have caused Britain to lose her leadership in the world. He then argues that Britain's governmental policies against apartheid incited the agitations against Pretoria's policy of separatism.

Steward turns to the world movements and discusses the United Nations and its charter. He reminds the reader of the article of non-intervention in the affairs of any state, and argues that other states of the West and the world have continuously violated it. He also examines the pros and cons of membership for Pretoria in the world body. He takes another world body to task—the Church—because of its continued attack on the apartheid policies of South Africa.

The writer moves on to black Africa, where he describes the tribal societies of South Africa. He said that they survive, but do not progress. "It was in the areas of technology that the black man is so utterly dependent on Western culture. . . ." He claims the African is not equipped to participate in a materialistic, competitive, technological, Western-oriented world.

Steward, in part one/section one, sets against the proposition of World Context: Idealism, the Pretoria Theme, which is separatism. He gives a brief history of the origin of the white Africaners. Then he discusses the important crossroads. Should Pretoria's policies go to the left (the direction of the West and the world) and adopt integration, or go to the right where the sign post is marked domination? Pretoria, he said, chose to live in peace along side the black man.

The author traces the origin of the policy of the apartheid. He sets forth the land legislation; the laws on influx control; and the new concept of separate development of the territories established by Pretoria.

In part two/section one, Steward examines the World Context: Disillusion.

His theme is that the West, during the 1960s, had become disillusioned and moved toward a breakdown. The United States' civil rights commitment to blacks had failed. Our relations with black Africa professed to be for equality, and this incited Africans to overthrow the government of South Africa.

He takes Britain to task by arguing that it had lost its leadership in the world because it adopted socialism. He pointed out that Britain had the same kind of race problem as the United States; now they are trying to contain it by passing legislation.

The author again looks at world movements and reviews the attacks by the Third World on Pretoria's policies. The toleration of these attacks by the West brought about a decline of the reputation of the world body. Steward discusses the effect of Britain's decolonization of black Africa. He then returns to the Pretoria Theme: Engagement.

Steward tells why the influx control law (pass law) is necessary. He also considers Pretoria as the custodian of the black man's heritage, and would not abandon its role to the (black) African National Congress. He also states that separatism reached its fruition in the Bantu Authorities Acts, purporting to grant self-government to the black nations within its borders.

Part three: section one is about Now. The World Context: Balance. Steward approaches the subject of balance by again examining the policies of the United States, the United Kingdom and the United Nations.

He says the United States suffered a loss of authority and leadership in its war with Viet Nam; its appeasement of Russia with Detente; and its failure to act decisively in the Angola conflict. His solution was that the United States must strike a balance between discipline and intuition, reason and imagination. He asks: Can Britain forget Bentham and Marx and strike a balance between capital and exploitation and labor blackmail?

In his discussion of the United Nations, he argues that this is not a democratic world and never will be, and international affairs cannot be properly handled through majority vote in the world organization. He thinks that regional grouping of states with commonality would be better. He feels confederation is best for the black nations and that separatism is the proper direction. There are no crossroads. Integration would mean a disaster for the people of South Africa.

Steward saves the last piece of the puzzle to the world picture until the end—The Need for God. He states that Western society with its cultural anarchy, cannot live by reason alone, but must return to God. If not, then Western civilization will perish from the earth. "Even Separatism."

Using the point-counterpoint method of presentation, Steward sets up the West versus Pretoria; The World versus Pretoria, and the Black Nationalists versus Pretoria. He then argues for the rightness of his conclusions based upon his own premises. He argues against those nations that strive for morality among their fellow men, stating that they are wrong for offering equality to blacks. Then he argues that the only way to save Western civilization is to return to the principles of God. Morality seems to be all right for the whites in South Africa and their allies, but not for blacks in South Africa and elsewhere in the world.

Such an intransigent position is certain to precipitate an international race war. This will be the second war, because in the first war, the Africans lost the Roman Empire and the world to the present German race. This, the author failed to mention as a part of his historical background.

EDWARD L. JONES
University of Washington
Seattle

PIERRE L. VAN DEN BERGHE and GEORGE P. PRIMOV. *Inequality in the Peruvian Andes: Class and Ethnicity in Cuzco*. Pp. iii, 324. Columbia: University of Missouri Press, 1977. $17.50.

WILLIAM FOOTE WHYTE and GIORGIO ALBERTI. *Power, Politics and Progress: Social Change in Rural Peru*. pp. iii, 307. New York: Elsevier Scientific Publishing Company, 1976. $15.00.

Two books of interest to scholars of social structure, power relations, and modernization or development are *Inequality in the Peruvian Andes: Class and Ethnicity in Cuzco* by Pierre L. van den Berghe and George P. Primov and *Power, Politics and Progress: Social Change in Rural Peru* by William Foote Whyte and Giorgio Alberti. The authors of these two studies start with the same basic preoccupation: the organization and distribution of power. They ask the same basic question: what determines unequal development or progress? Both books are written by specialists trained in the same field, using comparable methods of data collection and analysis.

Despite these initial and underlying similarities, the studies differ significantly in focus, format, and findings. Van den Berghe and Primov present a very readable and well-organized study of the determinants of relations of inequality in one region of highland Peru—the department of Cuzco, based on almost a year and a half in the field. After a general introduction to the geography and history of the area, they proceed to discuss the political and economic structures which define relations of inequality, the cultural and linguistic dynamics of class and ethnic relations, and the institutional framework within which these relations are played out. Following this theoretical discussion, they report their empirical findings in three locations: rural areas, market towns, and the regional metropolis of Cuzco. They conclude with a model of class and ethnic relations.

Focusing on the individual, van den Berghe and Primov ascribe intraregional disparities in social position to class (which they do not explicitly define, but equate with occupation) and ethnicity (which they index by fluency in Spanish, dress, and customs). They maintain that although these two factors greatly overlap and are essentially synonymous in some localities, they are sufficiently different to reject the class-based, radical definition of Indian. Stratification in the Cuzco area is a result of both class and ethnicity, the latter magnifying the clear inequalities of the former. They assert that although class structure is rigid and changes slowly, ethnic lines are fluid and social mobility is considerable. When the authors analyze interregional relations, they criticize both the so-called radical models of dependency and internal colonialism and the conservative model of plural societies. They argue that the subordinate position of the Cuzco region vis à vis the coast, and particularly Lima, is more the consequence of economic marginality than overt, calculated exploitation, except for the lowland tropical fruit and cash crop sector and the wool-producing industry. They adopt a middle position, concluding that reality lies somewhere between the two models.

Whyte and Alberti report the results of a ten-year collaborative research effort between sociologists and anthropologists at Cornell University and the Lima-based Instituto de Estudios Peruanos. Their book consists of a short introductory section; a series of brief reports on twelve communities in three regions—Cuzco, Junin and Chancay—and a section on theory, methodology and practice. Although somewhat disjointed, pieced-together, and therefore difficult to read, their monograph is a valuable manual for students who are contemplating field work because the authors candidly and systematically outline the successive changes in their thinking and hypotheses as their project progressed. They began to study modernization in rural Peru expecting personality traits (values, attitudes, beliefs and perceptions) to be the important variables explaining change, but such factors proved inadequate explanations of the process. In the course of their study, the authors accept and use Marx's formulations of economic interests and class conflict and conclude that structure accounts for more of the variance in rate and success of community development than personality. They formulate a typology of communities based on scores on two scales of conflict and cooperation which together indicate a community's potential for modernization. They reject on the basis of their field experience several accepted premises, such as the passive peasant. They also find that individual social mobility is difficult, albeit increasing.

In short, Van den Berghe and Primov stress marginality, not dependency, and ethnicity, not class. Whyte and Alberti, in contrast, start with sociocultural leanings and end stressing economic factors. What are the explanations for these two interpretations of Peruvian reality? One factor is philosophical orientation. Van den Berghe and Primov, on the one hand, avoid radical interpretations of regional disparities in development and power in favor of a more neutral stance, based on economic isolation. Their basis for dismissing the theories of dependency and internal colonialism in the nineteenth century, however, seems unconvincing because their explicit exceptions—the cash crop and wool industries—directly or indirectly affected almost everyone in the region from omnipotent landowner to tenant farmer, merchant, and bureaucrat. The fact that nearly everyone was integrated to some degree into the larger export-oriented system seems a sufficient basis on which to negate marginality in favor of integration and, by extension, dependency. Likewise, on the individual level, they emphasize sociocultural factors instead of economic ones. Whyte and Alberti, on the other hand, move away from their preconceived notions on personal attributes and adopt as explanations structural determinants of change, asserting that the latter define the context which limits individual behavior and interaction. Second, van den Berghe and Primov limit their investigation to one selected region, where ethnic differences are as marked as anywhere else in the country. Ethnicity, as they define, it is not as evident on the coast or in the northern highlands, where, according to their criteria, the percentage of Indians would be insignificant. On a national scale, sociocultural differences are less important than economic ones; hence, Whyte and Alberti's emphasis on structure.

These disparities in philosophical underpinnings and scope, in turn, affect the authors' respective findings on social mobility. Van den Berghe and Primov's conclusion that there is a great deal of mobility is based on the fact that many individuals made relatively small moves up the hierarchical social structure, essentially changing their ethnic designation from that of Indian to mestizo, although their class position remained the same. Whyte and Alberti, in contrast, base their assessment on economic criteria. They assert that relatively few individuals were upwardly mobile, by which they mean that few persons made the move between lower class and middle or upper class. The difference is one of categorization and magnitude of moves. Whether or not you agree with one set of authors or the other depends on your own world view and philosophical leanings and the definitions you are willing to accept.

SUSAN RAMÍREZ-HORTON
Ohio University
Athens

EUROPE

CLYDE BINFIELD. *So Down to Prayers, Studies in English Nonconformity 1780–1920*. Pp. xiv, 296. Totowa, N.J.: Rowman & Littlefield, 1977. $15.00.

This volume of essays on different aspects of the life of the English Protestants who dissented from the Church of England professedly aims to evoke the atmosphere of this significant element of English social and religious life during the nineteenth century, with some chronological overlapping at either end of that century. In a series of independent, but not unrelated, studies of important Nonconformist leaders, including Edward Baines, Edward Miall, Baldwin Brown and Silvester Horne, and of such topics as church architecture, English foreign missions, and reactions to British involvement in World War I, insofar as they relate to Protestant Nonconformity, the author achieves his goal. In the course of his discussions, many illuminating remarks about the character of English Nonconformity are made, and if any consistent impression results from all of the essays together, it is that these Protestant dissenters had an important and influential role in English life, which increased, rather than decreased, in the nineteenth century. The author is especially concerned with the relationship of his subject to English politics and to literary and artistic culture; with reference to the second of these there runs throughout the book a gentle but effective argument against the famous strictures of Matthew Arnold concerning the Philistinism of Protestant dissent. The suburban and middle-class character of Nonconformity is another recurrent theme. In painting his picture of the Nonconformists, Binfield draws heavily from such sources as letters, diaries and local church records. His focus is somewhat more on the laity than the clergy, and more on Evangelical Nonconformity, especially the Congregationalists, than on the Quakers or Unitarians.

Binfield, a Lecturer in History at the University of Sheffield, writes as an insider, though certainly not as an uncritical one, a fact which is perhaps helpful in a book which seeks to evoke atmosphere. But whether because of this, or because he writes as an essayist, with an almost casual and certainly very literate style, these studies are skillfully crafted, impressionistic reflections upon events and persons, rather than attempts to establish precise points by marshalling evidence. Accordingly, these essays leave the reader with various impressions about English Protestant Nonconformity in the nineteenth century without convincing him or her that really important (and perhaps significantly revisionist) conclusions have been proved or even reached. The essays also assume a certain familiarity with the subject on the part of the reader, making them unsuitable as an introduction to Protestant Nonconformity from 1780 to 1920.

DEWEY D. WALLACE, JR.
The George Washington University
Washington
D.C.

NORMAN MACKENZIE and JEANNE MACKENZIE. *The Fabians*. Pp. 446. New York: Simon & Schuster, 1977. $30.00.

The Fabians will be more appreciated by the general reader than by the scholar. As the title indicates, the emphasis is not on the Fabian Society itself, that is, its relation to social change in general and to political reform movements in particular during the late Victorian period and the Edwardian years. One would hardly guess from an examination of this book alone that the actual contribution of the Fabian Society has been a matter of considerable controversy among historians in recent years, with works such as A. M. McBriar's *Fabian Socialism and English Politics, 1884–1918* (1962) and Paul Thompson's *Socialists, Liberals and Labour: The Struggle for London, 1885–1914* (1967), heavily discounting the role claimed for so many years by the Fabians themselves. Indeed, the student thoroughly grounded in the period will find little of significance, particularly in matters of interpretation, that he doesn't already know. In this respect this book is hardly in the same class with the excellent biography of H. G. Wells, published by the same authors in 1973.

But "contribution to knowledge" aside, *The Fabians* is an absorbing narrative of the roles of the leading Fabians themselves, especially those of Sidney and Beatrice Webb, George Bernard Shaw, Graham Wallas, Annie Besant, James Ramsay MacDonald, Hubert Bland, Sydney Olivier, William Clarke, and H. G. Wells. It holds close attention from the initial gathering of 15 at the home of Edward Pease in London in 1883 until World War I, when the energy of the founding Fabians flagged. The authors, for the most part, write directly from manuscript material, particularly the Passfield Papers and the Shaw Papers, and often provide detail beyond other historians who have used the same material. Indeed, it is the detail which gives this book distinction, even when it seems to wander somewhat in elaborating such matters as Sidney Webb's courtship of Beatrice Potter, the marriage of Bernard Shaw and Charlotte Payne-Townshend, Shaw's plays, and the origins and early history of the London School of Economics.

The history of the Fabian Society, it should be emphasized, is there as well—its organization, activities, controversies within and without—but this is overshadowed by the story of the careers of its leaders. The work as a whole suggests, perhaps without the authors so intending, that the Fabians as individuals contributed far more to the English experience in these years than did the Fabian Society itself.

ALFRED F. HAVIGHURST
Amherst College
Massachusetts

FERGUS MILLAR. *The Emperor in the Roman World*. Pp. xiii, 656. Ithaca, N.Y.: Cornell University Press, 1977. $27.50

"The emperor 'was' what he did," according to Fergus Millar and in government "the most significant form of action is communication between persons." Thus, with these assumptions as its basis, *The Emperor in the Roman*

World is considered by its author as "a guide whose aim is to map out certain essential elements in the structure and functioning of the Roman Empire," or as he reiterates, "this book is largely a map of who said or wrote what to whom." This communications map is arrived at without the benefit of sociological jargon or systems analysis and leads Millar to maintain that what the emperor did was the fusion of what the Roman senator did and what the Hellenistic king did. Thus Millar argues "the role and function of an emperor present us, if examined closely, with the most complete exemplification of the predominance of rhetoric in the culture of the Graeco-Roman world." The object of Millar's "essay in historical interpretation" is "to suggest that these patterns are of fundamental importance in understanding what the Roman empire was."

For more than 600 pages, Millar demonstrates the breadth and depth of his erudition over a highly selective landscape that includes among many other topics imperial residences, provincial councils, athletes, and bishops. Scores of pages are devoted to detailed discussions of instruments of communication such a *libelli*, *mandata*, *epistulae*, *codicilli* and other equally specialized materials. Much of this detailed technical argument, which wanders far from the author's purpose, might well have been omitted since Millar eschews presenting "the bibliography of the question" and "does not set out to provide the complete evidence on any point." Rather, the many pages devoted to technical discussions of various classes of documents or of legal status, and an even greater amount of space wasted on superfluous examples illustrating the same point, might well have been used to cover important areas that the author neglected such as client kings, diplomatic contacts with kings and peoples beyond the empire, the role of the emperor as general and his relations with his soldiers and allies, the imperial secret service, *delatores*, and propaganda—especially as developed on coinage. Millar might even have been drawn to examine the evidence for the western half of the empire in the detail it deserves; he might thus perhaps have been less seduced by communication and have seen the emperor more as a soldier and a builder and less as a *rhetor*. A less arbitrary choice of topics and evidence might well have led Millar to see that form is not substance and there is more to the man than style.

BERNARD S. BACHRACH
University of Minnesota
Minneapolis

DENNISON RUSINOW. *The Yugoslav Experiment 1948–1974*. Pp. xxi, 410. Berkeley: University of California Press, 1977. $16.50.

Dennison Rusinow, author of *Italy's Austrian Heritage, 1919–1946*, now turns his hand to Tito's Yugoslavia. Mr. Rusinow, an executive of the American University's field staff, has lived in Yugoslavia for many years. The work relies principally upon published Serbo-Croatian and English sources. The author has also interviewed numerous personages important in the new Yugoslavia.

The study actually antedates 1948, going back to the days of defeat during World War II, the Chetniks, and the beginnings of the Communist-led Partisan movement. The cruelties and mutual hatreds, political and ethnic, of these times stand out.

The author treats events and policy-making in postwar Yugoslavia in analytic detail. He ranges widely: the concept of Tito and his associates as to what the new Yugoslavia would be; the setting up of the put-together state and reconstruction; the break with Stalin; the attempts to create laissez faire socialism; the price of pluralism; the 1974 constitution, with its emphasis upon "impressive further development of plural institutions" plus "a blatantly increased role for the Party as the one ring to bind them all. . . ."

What emerges from all of this is rather perplexing. On the one hand, Tito's Yugoslavia, unlike Czechoslovakia, managed to defy the USSR and maintain its independence. The new Yugoslavia, it is further claimed, has also sometimes managed to produce goods superior to those of the East European bloc, and hence these are coveted by the latter.

On the other hand, the reconciliation of freedom with socialism (one of the slogans, incidentally, of the June 1968 strike of the Belgrade university students) has never really occurred. No freedom of political dissent is to be found during these years, except in the most patchy way. As for the goal of brotherhood and unity among the south Slavs, this has no more been achieved under the present federation than in the Serb-dominated Yugoslavia of the interwar years.

Mr. Rusinow strives to be critical, even though his enthusiasm for the new Yugoslavia and its leaders is visible throughout the presentation. Hence his conclusions are somewhat startling.

"As the State and the regime began their fourth decade . . . it seemed more likely that Yugoslavia would become merely another slovenly, moderately oppressive, semi-efficient; semi-authoritarian State run by an oligarchy of contending élites, a society in which many people are free and participant and many are not. Like most States."

Apart from the probably justified evaluation of Yugoslav socialism, the cynical generalization, "Like most States" is certainly questionable. This monograph deserves serious study. But a turgid style will deter even a determined and sympathetic reader. An unfortunate misprint on the very fist page of the preface reads "Yugoslave" instead of "Yugoslav".

DAVID HECHT

Pace University
Westchester
New York

BRADLEY F. SMITH. *Reaching Judgment at Nuremberg: The Untold Story of How the Nazi War Criminals Were Judged.* Pp. xviii, 349. New York: Basic Books, 1977. $15.00.

For more than 30 years, the German city of Nuremberg has been synonymous with the International Military Tribunal that judged major figures of the Nazi regime. Countless articles and books have been written on the subject. This latest work by Bradley Smith, author of two important studies on the early years of Hitler and Himmler, is by no means just another book on the subject. Making use of recently released British and American documents on the trial, Smith has probed deeply into the negotiations leading to the establishment of the Tribunal, selection of defendants, indictments, legal aspects of the trial and the secret deliberations on the verdicts. This is, indeed, a significant book that deals with issues largely ignored in earlier accounts.

Among the problems the author grappled with are the conspiracy to commit aggressive war and the criminal organizations of the Nazi movement. Conspiracy is a common, but often controversial, aspect of Anglo-American law; however, it is virtually unknown to continental law. Most of the German defense lawyers, and the defendants, failed to comprehend fully this complex legal concept. Moreover, neither the Russian nor the French members of the Tribunal had experienced legal cases involving conspiracy. In the author's opinion, the crimes of the Nazis had so inflamed world opinion that failure to condemn the SS and the Gestapo would have brought about serious political consequences. The situation was a delicate one, but the Tribunal by declaring several lesser groups not criminal, avoided political repercussions and possible miscarriages of justice. Lurking behind everything at Nuremberg was the ever-present question: was this ex post facto law?

In a fascinating and compelling section, Smith carefully describes the reaching of individual verdicts, from the easy ones to the acquittals. Through the use of unpublished sources, particularly Biddle's papers, he has reconstructed brilliantly and meticulously the controversies and compromises leading to final judgment. Here the role of biases, national policies, personalities, and differing approaches to law can readily be seen.

This book has great value for students of European affairs as well as for specialists in the Nazi era. Smith also views the Nuremberg trial as contemporary history. He convincingly shows how the changes that accompanied the transition from war to peace became evident in American values and policies. Those concerned with efforts to make leaders accountable for unleasing war and causing mass atrocities will also profit from this superb study.

CHARLES J. HERBER
The George Washington University
Washington
D.C.

SIDNEY TARROW. *Between Center and Periphery. Grassroots Politicians in Italy and France*. Pp. xv, 272. New Haven, Conn.: Yale University Press, 1977. $15.00.

Following his studies on communism in south Italy, and another book on communism in Italy and France, Sidney Tarrow of Cornell University now presents his 1969–72 investigation of 117 French and 131 Italian mayors in four regions of France and Italy, where the populations of the cities varied from 500 to 50,000.

The book first reviews some political science and sociological studies, and refers, among others, to the work of Edward Shils and especially to Michel Crozier and his co-workers, Jean-Claude Thoenig and Jean-Pierre Worms. Let me immediately make a critical observation here by saying that usually Max Weber is not classified as a functionalist. Moreover, there is an absence of reference to any human ecological studies that have been developed—especially in the United States—that deal with problems of centralization and decentralization of urban communities.

Referring to interview data and chapters describing citizens and mayors and their governmental structure which links them to major capital centers, the author calls the French type dirigiste and the Italian clientelistic. Not only in the French case does the role of the state governmental structure become more important, with the mayors playing a more active role, but, also, the French mayors frequently do not stress their party allegiance, professing, rather, to being apolitical, and serving the whole community. The Italian mayor, on the other hand, was more politically involved. He was usually a party member and he spent most of his time trying to obtain favors for his clients. He frequently contacted different political centers in the capital, exploring and experimenting with different channels, both formal and informal. In other words, grassroots democracy was practiced more in Italy than in the more administratively organized French arrangement. An Italian mayor felt that meetings with citizens were helpful to reach decisions, while his French counterpart used meetings mostly to explain something to the voters. Italians appeared more competitive, while rationality tended to prevail in France.

Reflecting on his data, Professor Tarrow feels that in the Italian case an increase of bureaucracy makes a desirable improvement difficult, while in France, the state is impermeable and less likely to enhance local responsibilities. But it appears that in the small community of Italy, there was relatively quite a lot of cooperation between different political groups in spite of an absence of such cooperation at the national level. In France, there was less cooperation at the local level and more at the national level. In France there was also, of course, local sentiment which showed in terms of anti-party attitudes, or perhaps we could say in apolitical attitudes.

This analysis has provided us with good insights corroborating that a comparison of the same category of phenomena opens new perspectives that replace our usual inability to experiment. Critically considered, I have two questions: Italian mayors did not aspire to continue in their jobs, and they disliked being asked to intervene personally in matters. However, the majority of French mayors felt gratified with their jobs. Why? This should be further explored. Maybe the state also functions somewhat differently in the

Napoleonic France, as it was frequently described by the author, than in the state of Italy. Secondly, Tarrow almost apologetically uses the term system. It appears that this attitude is unnecessary since the concept of social system and other systems has been critically and usefully accepted into sociology.

JIRI KOLAJA
University of West Virginia
Morgantown

HOWARD J. WIARDA. *Corporatism and Development: The Portuguese Experience.* Pp. x, 447. Amherst: University of Massachusetts Press, 1977. $20.00.

Professor Wiarda's study is a major contribution to the English language literature on Portuguese politics. Indeed, there is no other book length analysis which covers twentieth century Portugal so thoroughly.

The principal thesis of the book may be stated simply. It is that "corporatism"—a form of political and social organization through which, in effect, the central government controls the structures of interest representation—is more or less natural to the Iberic-Latin tradition. How is such a system different from outright totalitarianism? Although Wiarda does not stress the point, the hallmark of Portuguese authoritarianism during the Salazar-Caetano era (from the early thirties to the early seventies) was mass demobilization. Widespread popular participation in politics was not encouraged, not even symbolically, as in certain totalitarian systems; the apolitical nature of the Portuguese political system set severe limits to the implementation from above of corporate organizations and activities.

Wiarda recognizes that there are at least two problems with the Ibero-Latin thesis. One is that it tends to degenerate into an explanation of authoritarian rule based on national character or a vaguely defined political culture. After all, modern authoritarianism is not peculiarly Latin. The second difficulty concerns the reality of the corporatist organizations, which, in theory, were supposed to thrive during the renaissance of Ibero-Latin authoritarianism in Portugal. In fact, these organizations existed for the most part on paper. The workers' syndicates had almost no real power. For that matter, the employers' associations were largely window dressing. Salazar himself did not take corporatist theory, such as it was, very seriously. The actual system of power appears to have been highly personalistic and based, as well, on rather clearcut differences between classes.

Thus, Wiarda's central hypothesis does not seem to go far in explaining Portuguese politics. To be sure, he is aware of competing theories, and he does not press his own to the exclusion of others. The trouble with this approach is that it entails much "on the one hand, on the other hand" discussion, with the result that the book begins to lose focus and a definite point of view.

Nevertheless, despite the conceptual uncertainty, Wiarda's presentation of the ins-and-outs of Portuguese politics during the Salazar-Caetano years is impressively rich. His book constitutes a baseline on which subsequent studies of Portuguese authoritarianism can build. The defects of Wiarda's study are real, but they do not outweigh the value of his pioneering effort.

PETER J. MCDONOUGH
The University of Michigan
Ann Arbor

UNITED STATES

HERMAN BEITZ. *A New Birth of Freedom: The Republican Party and Freedman's Rights, 1861–1866.* Pp. xv, 199. Westport, Conn.: Greenwood Press, 1977. $16.95.

Some historians, sympathetic with the civil rights movement of the 1960s, have berated Republicans for failing to legislate complete equality a century ago. The failure, these writers explain, was due to the Republicans' racial prejudices or their laissez faire convictions.

Other historians, equally devoted to civil rights for Negroes, have credited the Republicans with going to unexpected lengths to establish such rights. According to this view, the Congress of the 1860s fully intended in the fourteenth amendment to give the federal government the power—which it now exercises—of intervening against private groups as well as state officials.

In *A New Birth of Freedom* Professor Belz of the University of Maryland takes issue with both schools of thought. Belz concludes, on the one hand, that the fourteenth amendment was designed to limit only public, not private, action. Thus he implies that the Supreme Court followed legislative intent in the civil rights cases of 1883. He concludes, on the other hand, that Congress went as far as could be reasonably expected, considering the spirit of the times. "The really significant fact is that Republicans asserted equality before the law as the foundation of national policy toward the freedmen, in conscious despite of the contemporary belief in inherent racial differences and Negro inferiority" (p. 177). This was, in itself, a tremendous gain for blacks, and it provided a basis for further gains in the future.

Belz arrives at this conclusion after reviewing the steps that led up to the fourteenth amendment and discussing contemporary opinions of the significance that each step had for the legal status of blacks. The "revolution in personal status" advanced through black military service, the confiscation acts, the Emancipation Proclamation, Lincoln's plan of reconstruction, the Wade-Davis Bill, the Freedmen's Bureau, the thirteenth amendment, and the 1866 Civil Rights Act. On Lincoln's stand, Belz involves himself in some confusion. He is quite incorrect when he says (p. 35) Lincoln "abandoned his border state policy" of gradual, compensated emancipation after the passage of the Second Confiscation Act. He is on dubious ground when he indicates (pp. 41–2) that Lincoln made complete abolition a sine qua non for reconstruction under the ten-percent plan. Belz himself later (p. 62) contradicts this impression.

Despite these few lapses and a number of clumsily constructed sentences, he succeeds in making a convincing case. The book is a worthy successor to his *Reconstructing the Union* (1969), which it parallels and elaborates.

RICHARD N. CURRENT
University of North Carolina
Greensboro

WILLARD W. COCHRANE and MARY E. RYAN. *American Farm Policy, 1948–1973.* Pp. vii, 431. Minneapolis: University of Minnesota Press, 1976. $18.50.

GARIN BURBANK. *When Farmers Voted Red: The Gospel of Socialism in the Oklahoma Countryside.* Pp. xvi, 225. Westport, Conn.: Greenwood Press, 1976. $13.95.

Professor Cochrane of the University of Minnesota, as one of the most prominent agricultural economists of the contemporary period, played a significant role in the Kennedy-Johnson administrations as an advisor to Orville Freeman, Secretary of Agriculture. Therefore, his historical and analytical study of the origins and development of the agroeconomic programs of the federal government since the 1920s certainly must be considered as a serious and authoritative account.

Beginning with the initial lobbying for federal aid to agriculture during the Harding administration (the so-called McNary-Haugen Movement), he traces the gradual transition of American agriculture from a laissez faire economy to one managed by the government. This process then expanded with the growth of the Welfare State until a series of highly complex farm programs were in operation. The basic farm act was the Agricultural Adjustment Act of 1938. Its modification, revision, and amendment produced the modern program, a process to which Cochrane personally contributed as a leading Democratic advisor. He is thus well equipped to explain the meaning and significance of such concepts as: parity, domestic allotment, price supports, marketing agreements, P.L. 480, Soil Bank, set asides, reserves, etc.

In addition to this overall survey, Cochrane and his co-author Mary Ryan also made a detailed study of each commodity and how it prospered or declined under each successive program. Their final conclusion was that the federal price support program has been salutary because it stabilizes the agricultural sector of the economy and successfully has reconciled the conflicting interests of producers and consumers. Likewise, despite its complexity, the program has remained democratic, pragmatic and flexible.

In contrast to the broad national scope of Cochrane and Ryan's study, Gorin Burbank has investigated only one small aspect of the total agricultural picture. As a Berkeley graduate student during the turbulent 1960s, he became imbued with the desire to explore alternatives to capitalism, and hence focused on Socialist efforts to proselytize tenant farmers in Oklahoma during the early twentieth century. Whereas Cochrane dealt with the successful innovation of today's farm programs, Burbank relates the failure of the Socialists to make any real impact upon the farmbelt. Although plagued with many internal doctrinal disputes, the Socialists did receive a modicum of protest votes in support of their agitation for federal aid to agriculture; but essentially their failure was an inability to promote such concepts as class struggle, cooperative farming and collective ownership. The traditional Puritan ethic was too deeply ingrained in the dirt farmers of the Sooner state to be enticed by a collectivist ethic. The mixed economy of free enterprise and governmental aid offered to them by the Progressives and New Dealers was much easier to assimilate into their traditional agrarian value system. The Socialists erroneously tried to impose a doctrinaire solution upon farm problems rather than to seek a grass roots consensus of farm organizations, the way Henry A. Wallace and other New Dealers did.

Socialism, as Populism, served a role as a vehicle for protest; but neither possessed the political and economic acumen to formulate realistic farm programs that could gain widespread support.

Cochrane has utilized a vast storehouse of statistical and economic data from governmental sources, as well as private institutes and academic studies. His work is extremely well documented and also reflects his own personal knowledge and experience. This expertise provides insights and judgments that are invaluable. Burbank, on the other hand, has based his dissertation primarily upon newspapers of the period; and while capturing the emotional fervor of the times, it cannot overcome this one dimensional handicap. The author decries the fact that Socialist leaders did not preserve their records, and if they did, their families chose not to make them accessible for research. This forced him occasionally to quote Debs or Berger, although they were not directly involved in the Oklahoma activities.

The Cochrane and Ryan book would be of great value to any political or social scientist seeking a better understanding of our past and present farm policies and programs. It would serve as a fundamental primer for novices and an interesting stimulant to those well acquainted with the subject. Burbank's book has a more restricted value in the field of agriculture, but as a part of the Contributions in American History series, it would interest those studying the American radical or socialist movement.

FREDERICK H. SCHAPSMEIER
University of Wisconsin
Oshkosh

ROGER H. DAVIDSON and WALTER J. OLESZEK. *Congress Against Itself.* Pp. ix, 306. Bloomington: Indiana University Press, 1977. $15.00.

Can the House of Representatives be kept safe from the ambitions of its members? This book is a lucid and fascinating study of the House and its

Select Committee on Committees of the 93rd Congress (1973–74) which will prompt most readers to answer, "probably not."

Congress Against Itself is a case study of House committee reorganization. The authors, seasoned political scientists, were professional staff members to the Select Committee. The book is an excellent journalistic account tracing the creation of the Standing Committee, its proceedings, and final action by the House on its recommendations. It records the evolving views of the members, as they wrestled with advocates and opponents of change. However, the authors go beyond reporting by reviewing reformism in the House, by the history of its organizational development, and by explaining the behavior of House members when a majority adopted the milder Hanson Committee substitute reorganization plan.

The book has many strengths and few deficiencies. All who are interested in American governmental processes, whether as a citizen, agent of change, defender of tradition, spokesperson for a special interest, novice student, or distinguished scholar, should read it. (1) It shows that Congress is a changing institution. Too many people remember the strong committees and strong chairmen of the past. Today's House is marked by scatteration of responsibility over nearly 150 subcommittees. (2) It shows that no one is in charge of the House—not party leaders, committee chairmen, or any establishment elite. Influence is notable for its diffusion. (3) It sets the specific actions of the Select Committee in the larger context of House behavior. How do members of a committee "mark up" a bill? The process is well illustrated by a description of fine tuning the Committee's resolution. (4) It illustrates that member ambitions, and perceptions of them by others, powerfully affect behavior. House decentralization is a response to member aspirations to really take part in policymaking. Majority Leader O'Neill's ambitions for the Speakership discouraged his support for Bolling's reforms. Both members and staff of threatened committees mobilized opposition to structural changes.

Some readers will desire a more balanced analysis. Have the authors given short shrift to good reasons for defeating the Select Committee's proposal? Does their regard for Bolling color their explanation of ranking minority member Martin's late substitute proposal? The caveats are worth mentioning, but I do not ascribe them much force. This case study is important for understanding the House today and in the future.

JACK VAN DER SLICK

Southern Illinois University
Carbondale

ANDREW M. GREELEY. *The American Catholic: A Social Portrait*. Pp. vii, 280. New York: Basic Books, 1977. $15.00.

On the basis of popular social commentary and mass media coverage of busing demonstrations in Boston, most social scientists and laymen alike "know" that urban working class Catholics comprise an important part of the new conservatism emerging in the United States. Two characteristics customarily attributed to Catholics are racial intolerance and a lack of education, so that the only feature that distinguishes Archie Bunker from the average Catholic in the American weltanschauung is ownership of a crucifix. Correspondingly, the church hierarchy is typically viewed as initiating inept and/or reactionary measures when confronted with rapidly changing social conditions. The conservation of the church is purportedly intensifying the estrangement of young clerics from Catholicism. Professor Greeley's new monograph disputes this popular characterization of the congregation, while merely clarifying what could be deemed as minor misconceptions regarding the church hierarchy. Consequently, Greeley at least implicitly shifts the blame for the negative light in which Catholics are currently viewed in America from parishioners to higher-level clergy.

The American Catholic is from the outset a self-proclaimed marriage of social science and polemics. Regrettably, this wedlock occasionally assumes the appearance of a mismatch. As a social scientist, Greeley better succeeds when defending the image of the congregation against the popular stereotype. As he repeatedly asserts, contemporary American Catholics are more liberal, less racist, and equally well-educated, when they are compared under controlled conditions with their Protestant counterparts. Culled from numerous articles published over the past decade, the empirical evidence Greeley amasses in support of this argument is absolutely conclusive.

As a polemicist, however, Greeley reaches his zenith when chastising the church hierarchy. Owing to the "decrepit institutional structure of the church," the changing needs of the congregation are no longer adequately fulfilled by contemporary Catholicism. Unfortunately, the staid hierarchy of the church has misinterpreted declining parishioner participation as backlash against the Second Vatican Council (which resulted in an English spoken liturgy) rather than as disenchantment with the Vatican's recent *Humanae Vitae* statement on birth control. While Greeley adequately demonstrates the fallacy of church policy based on misinterpretation of congregational sentiments, his subsequent characterizations of bishops as incompetent conservatives, chosen for their prudent rather than charismatic temperaments, maybe difficult for non-Catholic social scientists to fathom.

It is apparent that Greeley wrote this book for two divergent audiences—liberal Catholic laymen who disagree with current church policy and social scientists. Unfortunately, social scientists, while finding Greeley's efforts to discredit prevailing Catholic stereotypes most laudable, may be offended by his polemical characterizations of the church hierarchy (just as liberal Catholics, while applauding Greeley's polemics, may find his social science boring and tedious). To have best accommodated both audiences, Greeley perhaps should have written two books—one polemical and the other scientific. Indeed, as the reception of this monograph among academicians may substantiate, even talented social scientists who have large polemical axes to grind sometimes end up with their own heads on the chopping block.

RICHARD A. WRIGHT

Indiana University
Bloomington

KIRSTEN A. GRØNBJERG. *Mass Society and the Extension of Welfare, 1960–1970*. Pp. xiii, 266. Chicago: The University of Chicago Press, 1977. $16.00.

Concerned with what she calls "the crisis of explanation surrounding the rising welfare rolls" (p. 35), the author of this sociological monograph describes her primary purpose as restating "the problem of the welfare crisis so as to place it in a larger perspective" (p. 2). Along the way she rebuts some of the pet hypotheses of such welfare theorists as Banfield, Moynihan, Piven, and Cloward.

After a short, but adequate, survey of the welfare crisis that distinguishes the popular and sociological conceptions of poverty, Professor Grønbjerg outlines her framework of analysis and study design. Briefly, her study is restricted to the AFDC program (ADC before 1961) for the years 1960 and 1970, and her principal tool of analysis is stepwise regression analysis. Throughout the book the author views the welfare explosion of the 1960s, which occurred in a time of increasing personal income and decreasing poverty, in the larger perspective of sociological theory about mass society. Morris Janowitz, in a foreword, only slightly exaggerates when he depicts the work as "sociology in the grand manner," resting on "a fusion of theoretical concerns with detailed empirical research" (p. x).

The chief findings of Professor Grønbjerg's quantitative analysis can be briefly summarized. The welfare growth of the 1960s was greatest in the largest, most industrialized, and wealthiest states—though not because poor blacks and whites fled the South to seek the more generous welfare benefits of the North. Since that decade, there has been an increasing separation of property and dependency and a corresponding closer association between affluence and dependence; from this flows the crisis of our understanding of welfare. More important, for some time now the United States has been moving away from a pattern where poverty alone was the occasion for the distribution of public aid. Formal requirements of AFDC eligibility, somewhat surprisingly, have little, if any direct relationship to the size of AFDC rolls, the largest and most rapidly growing of all the public aid programs. Finally, "the United States has been gradually and haltingly moving toward a mass society in which the definition of citizenship is being extended to include economic rights and duties" (p. 153). This trend, the author thinks, may eventually end with some form of guaranteed annual income or a universal flat grant system, but not for some time to come.

Since this book is so thoroughly committed to a quantitative methodology, it is scarcely surprising that the conclusions are less than world shaking. The conclusions, modest as they are, typify the author's judicious and restrained approach to one of the most complicated issues of public policy. Though she is to be highly commended for having surveyed such an amazing amount of welfare literature in a relatively brief space, the general reader will be happy to know that much of the statistical and methodological materials have been confined to 25 pages of appendices in the back of the book. In addition to these, the author has wisely included voluminous notes for each chapter, an author index, a subject index, and an extensive bibliography.

The deficiencies of the book are relatively minor. Many of the laboriously derived findings actually do little more than confirm common sense. Perhaps somewhat more should have been made of the politics and economics of welfare. The explanatory concepts, "social stratification approach" and "mass society approach," though central to the book's analysis, are somewhat ambiguous. Much repetition occurs in the later chapters, not all of it necessary. There is a surplus in the writing of such conjunctive adverbs as yet, however, and nevertheless. Not nearly enough was said about the fundamental dilemma of all welfare statist democracies: the problem of simultaneously maximizing equality and freedom, given an economy of scarce resources. Finally the writing, though commendably objective, lacks even a hint of verve or literary panache. But that, alas, seems the inevitable price one must pay for quantitative sophistication in an age that views scholarship and readability as antithetical.

In spite of these reservations, it is impossible not to be impressed by the performance of an industrious scholar who has plowed deeper than most of her colleagues into the raw materials of the welfare crisis. This book, therefore, definitely belongs on the shelf of all serious students of poverty, public policy, social change, and federalism. It is, to be sure, only a monograph; but until a comprehensive synthesis comes along, it remains a wide-ranging study that will leave the defenders of right-wing orthodoxy unhappy, the readers who crave pat answers hungry, and those eager for the stimulation of quantitative scholarship satiated.

FRANCIS M. WILHOIT

Drake University
Des Moines
Iowa

ALBRO MARTIN. *James J. Hill and the Opening of the Northwest.* Pp. xii, 676. New York: Oxford University Press, 1976. $19.50.

The last quarter of the nineteenth century witnessed a period of great change in the United States. Developments in industry, transportation, and finance, were dominated by the efforts of an unusually large number of giants—men who not only made large fortunes, but who transformed the American economic scene and made possible the industrial machine that was to win two world wars and dominate the entire world during the first half of the next century. Among these giants, a man possessed of unusual talents, tremendous drive, and impressive skill, was James J. Hill, the subject of this biography.

Son of immigrants from northern Ireland, James Jerome Hill was born on a farm in the back country of Ontario Province, Canada, in 1838. Provided with limited, but unusually effective education, young Hill came to the United States at the age of 17. Within ten years, he had established himself as a young man of integrity, ambition, and ability, and was ready to enter business on his own. A dozen years later, at the age of 40, Hill and four associates took over the management of the St. Paul & Pacific Railroad. They established a connecting link with Winnipeg, and by 1893 had extended their railroad to Seattle. These were the formative years of the man who was, in the next decades to dominate the transportation of the American Northwest.

Hill's Great Northern was the only northern transcontinental railroad to avoid bankruptcy during the hard years of the 1890s. Hill acquired the bankrupt Northern Pacific and, with the assistance of J. P. Morgan, gained control of the Burlington, overthrowing Edward Harriman in the process. From then until his death on May 29, 1916, James J. Hill dominated the transportation of the Northwest. The man who had been successful in selling coal to the early railroads, the marketing specialist who had labored long hours and established himself as a young man with great business acumen, became one of the nation's wealthiest and most successful businessmen.

Hill was an articulate man; he preserved his voluminous correspondence, and the files of the James J. Hill papers not only reveal much of the man and his business methods, but also tell of many of his associates, his competitors, and the business practices and problems of his era. These sources have been examined, thoroughly and with great care, by Professor Martin, who teaches in the Harvard University Graduate School of Business Administration and also edits *The Business History Review*. The author has not only been thorough in his research, he has been insightful in his analysis of Hill and his era. Avoiding a weakness found in many comparable biographies, Professor Martin reveals the human being as well as the business tycoon. Mrs. Hill, the large family of children, their home life, are all given sympathetic and understanding treatment. Professor Martin writes with sureness and feeling; his text is carefully documented; the result is certainly one of the great biographies of the decade, a study that will long remain the definitive analysis of Hill and the Northwest railroads.

RALPH ADAMS BROWN
State University of New York
Cortland

JACK NEWFIELD and PAUL DUBRUL. *Abuse of Power: The Permanent Government and the Fall of New York*. Pp. ix, 368. New York: Viking Press, 1977. $12.50.

This book is difficult to review for a social science journal. It is basically a newspaper editorial centered about the assumptions that New York City's woes, past and present, were and are caused by the bankers and their political henchmen. Messrs. Newfield and DuBrul list a series of alleged actions by Nelson and David Rockefeller and their proteges and attempt to relate these actions to successive financial crises confronting the city. Nothing is said about banking activities that precede the subsidence of crises.

The authors lay out the "true history" of the fiscal crisis, stating that the investment sector's refusal to buy municipal paper and the redlining of neighborhoods by the bankers and realtors are the causes of the city's financial decline.

Could it be that the decline caused the banks and realtors to react? The federal government is charged with diverting "New York money" to the Sun Belt, with consequent dire results to the whole Northeast. No statement is made that federal taxes are levied on firms and individuals who may have made their income over an extended area, national as well as international. The permanent government of New York, alleged to consist of the banks, the "Feds", and the metropolitan authorities, such as the New York Port Authority, is the chief culprit in milking the city and its citizens. Had the temporary government of Lindsay, Beame and company stood up to the permanent government all would have been well. How they should have stood up is never quite spelled out. It is at this point that the authors fail to do any political science. Cause and effect relationships, tenuous at best, get very murky. Names and events are listed with reckless abandon, but the reader searches in vain for any high degree of correlation between events and personal activities of the presumed decisionmakers. As a treatise in political decisionmaking, the work would have extreme difficulty in any accredited graduate seminar.

At the end the authors make recommendations for saving the city, one of which is to establish a federal urban bank with power to fix interest rates and the duty to create a municipal bond market. How long would such a bank stay in business if it did not reflect the going interest rate and the current price of municipal bonds generally?

There is little discussion of the roles played by municipal unions, street gangs, or overpopulation of certain minorities, in the city's financial situation. Rather the blame is laid squarely on the bankers in typical devil theory fashion. Perhaps, if the authors had started with Plato's concept of metabole and stasis, an operational hypothesis concerning New York City's fiscal problems would be forthcoming. As it stands, this book is nothing more than questionable journalism.

PAUL DOLAN

University of Delaware
Newark

FRANK S. ROBINSON. *Machine Politics: A Study of Albany's O'Connells.* Pp. ii, 249. New Brunswick, New Jersey: Transaction Books, 1977. $12.95.

American political machines perpetually fascinate novelists, political parties professors, journalists, reformers, and indeed most folks. Their classical escapades could be fun, and the muckrakers gained attention as much for the amusement as for the evil doing they uncovered. Functionalists have had a field day with urban political machines, many contemporary observers study quantitatively and qualitatively presumed virtues of machine corruption in developing nations and the problem of lack of political system balance between bureaucratic and representative institutions when party machines are weak, and historians would find difficulties explaining melting pots without reference to bosses and ward leaders.

Albany, which for over half this century has been dominated by one political machine, presents numerous excellent perspectives for urban politics students. It is an old school organization with a constituent service-oriented ward leader structure, tax assessments and delinquencies manipulations, low paying though numerous patronage positions, power partly gained through justice administration control from police to grand juries, local Catholic church public policy linkages, wealth garnered by political leaders through municipal business dealings. It is a Democratic machine which at times controlled local Republican, Liberal and Conservative parties. And it is a personal story of the O'Connell family, particularly of longtime boss Daniel P. O'Connell, and of long-time mayor Erastus Corning.

Frank S. Robinson's *Machine Politics: A Study of Albany's O'Connells* provides wide-ranging details concerning Albany's machine, from its evolution as a youthful reformist group throwing Republican rascals out, through an epoch of unquestioned supremacy to its first serious electoral challenges in the early 1970s Robinson uses primarily files of local newspapers detailing that history and certainly aiding understanding specific machine procedures. Yet, that history never comes alive. Perhaps not interviewing Daniel P. O'Connell and many of his cohorts contributed to omission of the spirit of what kept the machine going for so long; indeed, long after Robinson shows its vitality dissipating, its hierarchy aging, its failure to induce new and committed precinct recruits, its failing to keep pace with Albany's drastic demographic changes, and its becoming increasingly status quo oriented. It somehow escaped the last hurrah theme of replacement by New Deal bureaucracy and then lingered. Analysis of why this happened, not given by Robinson, would have presented a provocative critique. Capturing the spirit of the pols who kept the machine going so long also could have been a great deal of fun.

CHARLES A. JOINER
Temple University
Philadelphia
Pennsylvania

ELLIOT A. ROSEN. *Hoover, Roosevelt, and The Brains Trust: From Depression to New Deal.* Pp. x, 446. New York: Columbia University Press, 1977. $16.95.

The main themes running through this scholarly monograph are as follows: (1) Hoover's failure to swerve from the course set in his *American Individualism* (1922) in the struggle to preserve America's decentralist past and to rely on individual, community, and voluntary solutions. In Rosen's opinion Hoover's program "promoted the Depression" and was no forerunner of the New Deal, contrary to some revisionists' views.

(2) Roosevelt's candidacy. The Albany group of Jim Farley, Louis Howe, and Colonel House almost botched his nomination, but the conservative coalition (Raskob, Smith, Baruch, etc.) was unable to hold its forces together. At the Chicago convention McAdoo and California, not Texas, played the decisive role on the crucial fourth ballot. During the campaign FDR was caught between a crossfire of Democratic conservatives, who favored an international approach to the problems of the Depression, and the liberal intranationalists, who wished to concentrate on domestic solutions. His campaign speeches reflected political reality.

(3) In March 1932 FDR became convinced of the need of a group of academic advisers; hence, the "Brains Trust" of Raymond Moley, Rexford Tugwell, and Adolf Berle, Jr. was recruited. During the next 12 months they constantly studied, consulted others, and advised FDR. Most of the later New Deal legislation was formulated during that time by the Brains Trust (not the Albany group) in collaboration with Roosevelt. These men believed in expansion of government functions at the national level. Planning and regulation, not ownership, was their goal.

Rosen notes that Roosevelt had a keen mind, was receptive to ideas, was not doctrinaire, but ever the politician. He rejected some proposals out of hand, some because of poor timing, and some as not politically feasible. Until his inauguration, conservatives of both parties tried to influence FDR to follow their policies. Momentarily he wavered, but in the end followed the line he and the Brains Trust had projected.

Rosen spent 13 years on this book, which includes 50 pages of footnotes, many from primary sources. The author interviewed and corresponded with many of the principals. Moreover, he notes that often recollections published in later memoirs are at odds with letters and memos written in 1932. He is particularly indebted to Moley, whose papers have received scant use, and he believes Moley deserves a larger share of credit for the New Deal than Moley himself claimed.

The author furnishes excellent background chapters on the political and economic philosophy of each of the Brains Trusters, and his chapter "Disharmony of International Cooperation" is a severe indictment of American shortsightedness toward the world economic crisis of 1931–32. Finally, Rosen contends that the conservative forces suffered only temporary defeat with the advent of the New Deal. Some critics, however, will note his bias against Hoover and will dispute his view that there were not "two" New Deals. Nevertheless, this is a fine study which will be particularly rewarding to specialists.

ERNEST M. LANDER, JR.
Clemson University
South Carolina

UPTON SINCLAIR. *The Coal War*. Pp. xcii, 417. Boulder: Colorado Associated University Press, 1976. $12.50.

Social scientists can learn much from the sociological novel, where concrete examples of the processes of conflict, change, and other areas of human interaction are portrayed by the writer of fiction. Upton Sinclair, whose centenary will be celebrated in September 1978, was a great journalist, whose sociological novels were both propaganda tracts and economic reports.

A socialist, the last of the muckrakers, a symbol of a strand of American idealism, founder of the American Civil Liberties Union and the League of Industrial Democracy, he was for a long time the best read American author abroad. About 800 translations of his books were made, in 47 languages and almost as many countries. His early work, *The Jungle*, published in 1906 when he was a young man of 28, brought to light conditions in the Chicago stockyards and made him famous.

The Coal War, until now an unpublished novel, is significant from several perspectives. It is, in effect, a documentary account of a vicious labor-capital battle in the Colorado coal fields in 1913–14. It also portrays, in a most graphic way, the bitter struggle of the labor movement in the United States at a time when the laissez faire social Darwinism of Herbert Spencer and William Graham Sumner was the dominant and fashionable ideology of American industry. A 92-page Introduction by John Graham of the University of Colorado provides a succinct history of the times and the background to the strike in the coal fields that culminated in the 1914 Ludlow Massacre.

Sinclair was actively involved in the strike, made an unsuccessful effort to interview John D. Rockefeller, Jr., met with protestors, picketed, was arrested and imprisoned. He later wrote *King Coal*, to which this novel is a documentary follow-up. The manuscript was rejected by Macmillan in 1917 and Sinclair refused to revise it. To him, any book was important insofar as it was influential as a force for change. Here is a valuable historical novel, but one based upon actual historical events, which the author not only observed, but also participated in.

Both John Graham's Introduction and the novel are a genuine contribution to social history. This book can be read with profit not only by literary scholars but by all interested in United States social and economic developments in the early 1900s, political processes, and the role of individuals in protests against injustice.

JOHN E. OWEN
Arizona State University
Tempe

SOCIOLOGY

CHARLES F. DELZELL, ed. *The Future of History: Essays in the Vanderbilt University Centennial Symposium*. Pp. xi, 263. Nashville, Tenn.: Vanderbilt University Press, 1977. $13.95.

During the 1975–76 academic year the history department of Vanderbilt University, celebrating the beginnings of that University's second century of classroom teaching, offered a series of public lectures by prominent historians. The department did not overly structure the series; rather, it asked the lecturers to "address themselves to the problem of 'the future of history' as they perceive it in their own fields of inquiry, fields which embrace some of the new as well as more traditional approaches to the discipline." Each guest was particularly encouraged "to engage in cautious speculation about the paths that Clio may be inclined to pursue in the years that lie just ahead" (p. vi). The participants represented 11 of the most distinguished historians in the discipline today, including Lawrence Stone, Stephan Thernstrom, Kenneth A. Lockridge, I. Bernard Cohen, Paul K. Conkin, C. Vann Woodward, Woodrow Borah, John Whitney Hall, Lewis W. Spitz, Gordon Wright, and Richard W. Leopold.

Based on the symposium's published results, the Vanderbilt history department not only served its university well but did also for the profession as a whole. The published lectures sparkle as historiographical pieces. They will become standard reading fare for practicing historians and graduate students alike, indeed important reading for all those seeking to know more about the current state of research and writing among the guild of academic historians.

The topics of inquiry are as diverse as the special fields of the contributors. The essays touch upon subjects such as historical demography, the history of science, Latin America, periodization as related to the Renaissance and Reformation, and contemporary history. The breadth of topics normally would make substantive generalizations difficult for reviewers, were it not for the attention that some of the authors pay to the maturing relationship between history and the social sciences.

Lawrence Stone's opening essay sets the tone for much of the volume. Stone stresses the decline of the narrative form and the rise of new analytical modes. Others consider the same issue in more than passing commentary, discussing new research strategies, methodologies, and techniques (especially quantification) now being employed for conquering the past. Each author varies in his appraisal of the possible beneficent effects. Stone issues a full list of warning signals about the pursuit of value-free social sciencism through history. That topic clearly reverberates through the essays by Thernstrom, Lockridge, Conkin, and Vann Woodward. Lockridge enthusiastically endorses the new history by chiding those who deny that the bits and pieces of accumulated data on human existence can become the basis for a more fully developed understanding of dynamic social change through time. Yet the others warn that new methodologies and techniques may be as dehumanizing to Clio's subject as they are envigorating. The exchange epitomizes the collection's high point, in that it puts critical methodological issues in perspective, without falling prey to the tiresome debate over the so-called sciences-humanities dichotomy.

What also emerges from the volume is the impression that historians are not particularly comfortable about probing the future. Some contributors frankly admit that confronting the crystal ball wrenches them too much from their natural character. As a result, the essays, while illuminating as historiography, are fuzzy as predictive explorations. The collection might have been served better with a title emphasizing recent important trends. Then again, the Vanderbilt series might have been served better had the participants been more willing to look ahead boldly, especially when the profession is under increasing attack in today's academic world for reputedly pursuing a nonutilitarian and, worse yet, uninformative subject. If the recent trends and subjects are as pathbreathing as some of the authors suggest, then why all the din and fuss about history as a declining field? Is it possible that the new techniques have already stripped history of its humanizing vitality, leaving behind a residue of scholarship that fascinates only a few initiated specialists? Such questions should have had meaning in a centennial celebration, especially when many who pick up this volume will be wondering whether Clio can hold on in the next century as a subject worthy of the uninitiated's attention. More concern about the future might have made this important collection even more valuable.

JAMES KIRBY MARTIN
Rutgers University
New Brunswick
New Jersey

H. WENTWORTH ELDREDGE, ed. *World Capitals: Toward Guided Urbanization.* Pp. xiii, 642. Garden City, New York: Doubleday, 1975. $19.95.

The process of urbanization has positive and negative aspects. First, it involves the physical concentration of people which makes possible more efficient exchanges of goods and services in an industrial economy with concurrent increases of wealth and well-being. Second, it brings intensification of buildings and pollution, beauty and ugliness, affluence and poverty, social change and stress, giving rise to appalling problems which threaten to break down civilization and destroy our natural environment. The process is occurring everywhere in the world, and at accelerating rates, so that by the year 2000 A.D., it is expected there will be three billion urban dwellers—half of the projected world total population. City and regional planners look with dismay upon the results of urbanization, the negative aspects of which they endeavor to control and rationalize. The tasks set by urban planners for themselves are outlined in the introductory chapter and three concluding chapters by H. Wentworth Eldredge, the editor of this massive volume.

The contents comprise largely the substantive chapters on 11 metropolises, written by 11 authors drawn from varied backgrounds in universities and planning agencies. Nine of the metropolises are national capitals (Brasilia, Caracas, Dakar, London, Moscow, Paris, Stockholm, Tokyo, and Washington), while two are state or provincial capitals (Chandigarh and Toronto). These places represent a broad range of historical growth, economic and cultural development, and degrees of effectiveness in planning policy. The selection of capital cities is intended to focus attention on such places as the symbols of political power and the problems arising from either too little control with conflicting goals, as observed in Western Europe, certain of the countries of the Americas, Japan, and newly-independent Africa and India, or in a planned society, under powerful centralized authority, as in the Soviet Union. The descriptions and interpretations, however, are as varied as the viewpoints of the authors, six of whom are professional planners (Bozarth, Dakin, Feiss, Honjo, and Sidenbladh), three, geographers (Bastie, Shepherd, and Sommer), two, political scientists (Frolic and Violich), and one, an architectural historian (Evenson).

In the opinion of this reveiwer, the editor is not successful in deriving integrating principles or programs for the future from these contributions. One does not conclude this volume with a sense of how urbanization may be guided, especially in free democratic political systems and free market economies.

The book has value for reading in courses on comparative urbanism and planning as a reference for the treatment given to particular cities. On the basis of personal experience and classroom use, this reviewer recommends the chapters on Stockholm, Toronto, Moscow, Tokyo and Chandigarh. The chapters on Washington, prepared by two authors, is particularly disappointing. It would be impossible in a volume of this size to exclude all errors and correct all typography. However, it should be mentioned that the map of Tokyo's urbanized area in 1965, appearing on page 112, has been transposed from the chapter on Tokyo (pp. 340 ff.) to the chapter on London. The grouping of the cities into four parts (I—Western: Old World; II—Western: New World; III—Non-Western; and IV—Developing Nations) does not seem cogent and can be regarded only as historically valid.

JOHN E. BRUSH

Rutgers University
New Brunswick
New Jersey

WILLIAM B. GOULD. *Black Workers in White Unions:* Job Discrimination in the United States. Pp. 506. Ithaca, N.Y.: Cornell University Press, 1977. $20.00.

This is a comprehensive study of the scope and effectiveness of our national laws prohibiting racial discrimination in employment. The study reveals the long road we have yet to travel to remove discrimination in the work place, despite the existence of a plethora of laws prohibiting racial discrimination. The media frequently feature the most prominent discrimination suits which reach the courts, but most Americans are scarcely aware of the widespread racial discrimination in labor unions, offices, factories, government, and, of all places, among institutions of higher learning.

Despite the statements of George Meany and other labor leaders to the contrary, trade unions, more than any other institutions, are, according to the author, "the focal point of racial discord in our society." "Unions," he says, "often constitute roadblocks to the achievement of nondiscriminatory employment practices."

It comes as no surprise that the business community in general lacks sympathy for the nondiscrimination laws. Business too often accepts, or participates with unions, in discrimination in apprenticeship placements, in hiring, promotion, layoff and related job actions. Although the book details much of the extensive litigation relating to discrimination in the lily-white construction industry and the building trades, racial issues in the industrial unions—autos, rubber, meat cutting, trucking, to cite some of the larger ones—carry a different emphasis. The issues here are more those of the type of jobs, promotion, and union leadership posts made available to minorities. Blacks, as a percent of their numbers in the mass production industries, attain few skilled jobs, supervisory posts or union offices.

Gould, while giving credit for progress made toward eliminating discrimination in employment, cites other reasons for our stumbling progress: inadequate enforcement of the laws due to insufficient funding by Congress, "the absence of political will and competence . . . to crack down on offenders," and the poor performance of the Equal Employment Opportunity Commission.

The extensive research which went into this work is evident in the scores of cases cited and documented. It is at once a record of where we stand regarding antidiscrimination legislation, how we got to where we are, what remedies are available to the aggrieved, and what improvements can be made in law and enforcement. The author's dissatisfaction with the record to date points however at more than discrimination in employment. He sees employment as "the key to the colorblind society that must remain this country's objective. Resistance in other areas should decline to the extent that blacks progress up the economic ladder."

JAMES R. BELL
California State University
Sacramento

DAVID KIPNIS. *The Powerholders*. Pp. ix, 230. Chicago: University of Chicago Press, 1976. $12.50.

In an effort to better understand the dimensions of the exercise of power in society, Kipnis concentrates on various methods, procedures and previous studies to be utilized in understanding the roles and functions of the powerholder or the powerwielder. Emphasis is placed on an examination of strategies used by powerholders because it is felt that "psychology has had surprisingly little to say about the use of power" which leads the author to lament "we find comparatively few mentions of the topic 'social power' in reference periodicals that list topics studied in psychology." (p. 4) The expectation is thereby created early on that Kipnis will concentrate on making up for these deficiencies by providing new studies, in depth analyses and thought provoking insights about powerholders and "target persons," the phrase used by the author to describe those who are subject to the orders, whims, slings(?) of powerwielders, evidently considered to be almost always to be hit or harmed in the process. These new analytic studies never appear in the two hundred some pages of the text. What does materialize is a recitation of the discourses of philosophers, the recording of results of studies on power exercised in work relationships, in the context of marriage and "among employers of housemaids," with a few quotations from the plays of Sophocles, Shakespeare, and *My Fair Lady* thrown in for good measure.

In attempting to support a developing orientation which Kipnis calls "the metamorphic effects of power;" i.e., that any exercise of successful power on the part of the powerholder will influence both the perception of the powerholder's own sense of self and self-esteem, as well as the powerholder's perception of the "target person" who has been, evidently, suitably demeaned and defeated in the encounter. Several hypotheses are posited for consideration, but not tested, as part of this metamorphic effect. Indeed, one tentative statement, "To the extent that powerholders believe that they have caused a target's behavior, powerholders are likely to devalue the target's worth" (p. 196), is alleged to be true based on 1) a study of marriage customs in the Victorian age and 2) from the work of "Undergraduate students in several of my classes [who] distributed the questionnaire to all the married persons they knew, most of whom were living in the Philadelphia area." (p. 189) With these kinds of sampling methods, who needs rigorous scientific procedures?

Briefly, in summary, one could ask if the author has ever given thought to the possibility of considering the findings in the field of social psychology. There is an abundance of studies on community power structures, personality and power, strategies of wielding power from presidents to mayors, and (sadly) the poor as target persons in urban renewal programs across the country. The various hypotheses relating to the metamorphic effects of power would be suitably tested and might conceivably fill in for "the lack of a broad empirical base for my ideas" (p. 214). A very helpful start would be an analysis of *The Power Broker: Robert Moses and The Fall of New York* by Robert A. Caro. Mr. Moses was a consummate powerholder and when he wielded his power, everybody became target persons.

JOHN J. LENNON

University of Arkansas
Little Rock

ELLIOT A. KRAUSE, *Power and Illness: The Political Sociology of Health and Medical Care.* Pp. vii, 383. New York: Elsevier Scientific Publishing Company, 1977. $12.95.

The author employs a Marxist perspective to account for the failure of the health and medical institutions in the United States to provide adequate care. The introduction surveys the historical development of health systems in Western society followed, in Part I, by an analysis of the occupational structure of health care. The profit motive and the legal basis for physicians' control of medical practice is used to explain the persistent dominance of medical doctors as loci of power on which other health practitioners depend and for the limitations observed on the type, amount, and location of delivery of health services.

The focus of the analysis, in Part II, expands from the structure of hospital-based medical occupations to the social context of health care. The author asserts that it is the capitalist system of political economy, with it's accompanying profit motive, which mandates a two-class system—a private system for the rich; and a public system for the poor.

Part III discusses the politics of national health planning as a system in which producer and consumer compete for control of health resources. But the producer, aided by the sanctions of a capitalist bureaucratic government, dominates and therefore is unresponsive to consumers. The final chapter predicts the future health care system in the United States will result from the outcome of the conflict between the many interest groups with a stake in the health care field; but that the creation of a consumer-based system requires the abolition of corporate power. Only in this way can the distribution of power between producers and consumers be equalized.

The book is well written and conceptually interesting. The limitations are inherent in what the author has chosen to do. Once having selected a macrosociological approach, the scope becomes enormously broad, and much is oversimplified. The emphasis on a single factor explanation means that the analysis overlooks other factors in the system which affect the outcome. Only one among the questions which might be raised is the extent to which it is the nature of the political economy or the structure of complex organizations which are detrimental to consumers' interests. Nevertheless, it is an enlightening book which presents an enlarged picture of medical sociology. It would be useful for courses in social problems and social issues, as well in courses in the sociology of medicine and health care.

CAROLYN R. DEXTER
The Pennsylvania State University
Middletown

LEON RADZINOWICZ and JOAN KING. *The Growth of Crime: The International Experience*. Pp. v, 342. New York: Basic Books, 1977. $11.95.

This book is clearly written for a lay audience, and there is, one suspects, an important reason for this. The data on crime and criminal justice from many countries of the world are simply too scant and unreliable to allow anything more than impressionistic comparisons to be made from one country to another. Furthermore, there are many serious methodological difficulties in making international comparison of crime rates, prison rates, and criminal justice practices.

Sir Leon has, therefore, wisely chosen to share with us his international experiences, making clear, when necessary, that his observations are impressionistic, and tempering his interpretations of the research and practice with his vast knowledge and experience in criminology. The result is an immensely readable book, full of interesting details (Iceland has only one prisoner in its prison; Sir Leon was shot by a psychotic in a Viennese cafe) and a great deal of information concerning every aspect of crime and criminal justice.

The authors have tried assiduously to present a balanced account of the current state-of-the-art in criminology (concerning research and practice and policy) and by and large they achieve their goal. They have also shown considerable restraint in not assigning to any particular country the label of being the worst in its level of crime or treatment of criminals. This is indeed a worthy achievement since the temptation is always there these days to point the accusing finger at the United States (and conversely to feel smug about one's own country). But the authors point the finger at issues and problems rather than countries.

Another positive feature of the book is its clear awareness of the history of criminology and of criminal justice, so that when we reach the final chapter, which deals with various aspects of prison and alternative penal measures, Sir Leon and Ms King are well aware of the trap that lies for overzealous reformers. They do not offer pop solutions; rather they make clear the incredible complexity of the issues, both from a theoretical and practical point of view. Yet they are also able to assert that some programs have been successful in some parts of the world, and it is on these that we should build.

Two important issues are raised by this book. The first is Sir Leon's constant observation that different countries are at different stages of "penal development." The authors never elaborate upon this concept, and one wonders what is meant by this term, when so much time is spent these days arguing that things today are no better than they were 200 years ago. (As the authors point out, in 1975, 200 years after Beccaria's treatise, the U.N. was very proud of its achievement in passing a resolution denouncing the use of torture on prisoners). Is there an implication that the United States or Britain, or some other Western country is "better" penally developed than other "backward" countries? If so, which are these countries, and what is the yardstick of "progress?" These are tremendously complicated problems which have yet to be addressed in the field of comparative criminology.

The second important issue is raised by default. This is the only criminology book that I have read that has ventured a comment regarding the comparative level of crime or treatment of criminals in Communist areas such as the U.S.S.R., East Europe and China. But the authors' references to these cover no more than a few lines. In comparison, the failures in penal measures, the constant increase in crime are catalogued in great detail for the Western countries. The clear reason for this is what everyone knows but is inclined to forget: the Communist countries continue to be extremely secretive about even the most basic information (such as crime rates, prison rates, etc.), so that the illusion is created that crime is somehow the responsibility and sole problem of the West.

This is an excellent book, delightfully written and informative to sophisticates and laymen alike.

GRAEME R. NEWMAN
State University of New York
Albany

SEYMOUR B. SARASON. *Work, Aging, and Social Change: Professionals and the One Life-One Career Imperative.* Pp. xiii, 298. New York: The Free Press, 1977. $14.95.

There is a need for a comprehensive treatment of work values and experiences of professionals. Seymour Sarason's *Work, Aging and Social Change* is an attempt to fill this need. The book is a treatment of "emergent values" especially authenticity, autonomy, search for novelty and personal growth, which arose during and after World War II (the "Age of Psychology"), and had spread extensively by the sixties. It focuses on the notion of "one life-one career" imperative as it applies to professionals. Because of these emergent values, the imperative is breaking down.

The book has some qualities. For example, it focuses on an often unexpressed sentiment (job dissatisfaction) among many professionals. It discusses several major post World War II phenomena, such as the effects of the atomic bomb and Vatican II. And it integrates dramatic works, such as *Death of a Salesman* into the discussion.

Nonetheless, it is seriously flawed. To begin with the title is misleading. "Aging" is not a focus, as it is rarely mentioned, except in one brief chapter. There are errors in grammar; e.g., "is to indulge presumption" (p. 117). There are a number of small errors in facts or interpretation; for example, whether Betty Ford "explicitly sanctioned premarital sex" (p. 48) is questionable. Sarason uses himself as an example of a "changed career;" yet, he has been a psychologist (admittedly in several settings) throughout his career. In fact, he (over) uses his own experiences (and cites his own work) much too heavily to be credible. He refuses to define most of his central concepts, including what constitutes career change, and especially "values, ideas and attitudes—call them what you will" (p. 53). There are many unsupported impressions and sweeping generalizations. For example, he states "to talk candidly about one's relationship to one's work is as difficult as talking about one's sex life" (p. 57). Finally, the book is replete with stylistic flaws. There are too many exclamatory statements and overused metaphors, especially of the sewn seeds, ballgame, and stage acting varieties. The most serious defect is that the book has scores of clichés; e.g., "old hat" (p. 55), "Lady Luck" (p. 85), "eat his cake . . . and have it" (p. 135).

It is tempting to review the book with clichés, sweeping generalizations and personal experiences. However, it is enough to say that it is a poor effort and is not recommended.

WILLIAM BRIDGELAND
Michigan State University
East Lansing

DOUGLAS E. SCHOEN. *Enoch Powell and the Powellites.* Pp. xviii, 317. New York: St. Martin's Press, 1977. $18.95.

Enoch Powell was born to lower middle class parents, both school teachers; as a young boy he won scholarships to grammar school and developed a special interest in the classics; he won a classics scholarship to Trinity College, Cambridge, and soon was recognized as a brilliant scholar, especially in Greek, totally uninterested in social or other activities; at age 25, he became Professor of Greek at Sydney University, the youngest professor in the British Commonwealth. This academic career was, however, interrupted by the World War II. He joined the British army in 1939 as a private and left it six and one-half years later as a Brigadier, having again performed brilliantly.

Finally, in 1947, Powell entered politics as a right wing Conservative and imperialist; he fought a hopeless battle for a parliamentary seat in a safe Labour constituency, but in the general election of 1950 he won the marginal Wolverhampton seat by a small majority, even though the Tories lost the country. Thereafter, he held that seat with increasing majorities until he withdrew his candidacy in 1974; he was then adopted by an Ulster constituency and continues to serve a somewhat anomalous role as an Ulsterite M.P. During those years Powell soon distinguished himself as the most intellectual, principled, and independent of the Tory leaders, and always as a rigid Conservative. For some time he was generally considered to be among the top three or four leaders of the party, serving in several ministries, in the Shadow Cabinet, and in the Cabinet, and was even thought of as a possible Prime Minister. But his rigid Tory principles made him a critic, and an increasingly bitter critic, of the chosen party leaders, especially of Mr. Heath and Mr. Maudling, and they, in turn, resented Powell's attitude and blocked his ambitions. He was eventually ousted from the Shadow Cabinet, denied further appointments to the Cabinet or other high posts, and lost the support of the Tory backbenchers as well as of the leadership. Although he insisted that he remained a Tory and that his quarrel was only with the party leaders, he went so far as to support Labour in the 1974 election, and has become a lonely and somewhat tragic figure.

All this, and much more, is told in detail and closely analyzed in this book. The eleven chapters are divided into two parts, Part one (7 chapters) being a detailed account of Enoch Powell's career as a British politician, while Part two (4 chapters) is an attempt to explain him, the theories or issues for which he fought (Powellism), the nature of his following (Powellites), the reasons for his high standing with the electorate, but consistent failure as a leader. Mr. Schoon, an American, who was introduced to the fascinations of British politics by his professors at Harvard and Oxford, seems particularly well prepared to make this study; and he made it without the cooperation of his subject, Enoch Powell, who not only refused to be interviewed and objected to interviews with other M.P.'s about himself, but even submitted a bill for the few speeches that he did provide. In addition to the usual sources of information, Mr. Schoon relied heavily on public opinion polls, the data from which is represented by 111 tables and 31 figures scattered throughout the book. These are, however, intelligible to any reader, and are interpreted in pages of clear, well-written English text, for which the author should be complimented. The book has all the other paraphernalia of good scholarship—a bibliography of more than seven pages, 21½ pages of notes, and an index. Altogether, it is a useful addition to the literature of British politics.

CLARENCE A. BERDAHL
University of Illinois
Urbana

J. THORSTEN SELLIN. *Slavery and the Penal System.* Pp. viii, 202. New York: Elsevier Scientific Publishing Company, 1976. $12.50.

Professor Sellin's latest contribution to the criminological literature is a brief volume which traces the influence of chattel slavery on the evolution of the penal system from ancient times to the present. The author's historiography provides a concise, eloquent, and compelling argument to the effect that the social institution of slavery has had a direct and pronounced effect on the criminal law of all Western nations.

In the early chapters of the book, Sellin focuses on ancient Greece and Rome, where slavery was regarded as a natural and legitimate social institution. In Greece, slaves were regarded as articles of property and were thus subject to the whims of their owners. Slaves were regarded as things and, as such, they could be bought, sold, traded, and even killed. The history of ancient Greece reveals two penal systems, one for citizens and one for noncitizens (including slaves). When slaves were brought to public trial, they, as well as other noncitizens, could be subject to judicial torture. If convicted, they could be punished by flogging, and for gross offenses the slave might be put to death. Sellin finds no evidence that in Greece the two systems ever merged to make slave punishments applicable to all law violators. However, conclusive evidence that punishments applicable only to slaves became proper punishment for certain classes of citizens is found in the history of ancient Rome. The evolutionary process leading to the merger of the two systems reveals an abandonment of the traditional principle of equity before the law as Rome evolved from a primitive small city-state to a multiple-nation world-state. Although the traditional punishments of exile, deportation, fines, and so on were retained for criminals of the upper classes, judicial torture and various slave punishments (e.g., hanging, crucifixion, burning at the stake) were introduced for the lower classes. Moreover, the lower classes, which comprised the majority of the population, were subjected to penal slavery in mines and various forms of public work. Thus it was during this period that hard labor or penal servitude developed into a favored punishment for lower class criminals. The penal system that Rome left as a legacy to the Middle Ages was one which oppressed the lower classes and favored the powerful upper classes.

The notion that domestic punishment for slaves and, in particular, penal servitude, was made applicable to all offenders over the centuries is developed further by Sellin in subsequent chapters dealing with the following: Germanic nations of the Middle Ages; galley slavery in maritime countries; the rise of slavery on public works; the radical changes leading to houses of correction; the naval arsenal prisons (bagnes) operated in France, Spain, and Italy; penal slavery in Russia; and penal slavery in the antebellum South, including the convict lease system, chain gangs, and penal farms and plantations. For example, according to Sellin, galley slavery, as one form of penal servitude for crime, was never intended to reform offenders and restore them to the community as better citizens. Its aim was to remove undesirable or dangerous persons from the community and to put them to work for the profit of the state. Sellin notes that "penal slavery in other guises was to become a feature of the treatment of serious offenders down to our times" (p. 55). Thus Sellin argues, that while houses of correction signified a radical innovation in penal practice, they were in reality also important for making prison labor profitable to the state. This premise is further elaborated upon in his discussion of the convict lease system in southern states following the Emancipation Proclamation of 1863, where convict labor became a windfall for politically powerful lessees, who profited from a form of chattel slavery often worse than that from which blacks had been freed. That some fixtures of penal servitude survive to the present day is amply documented in the chapter dealing with chain gangs and prison farms (e.g., Cummins Farm and Tucker Farm in Arkansas).

Sellin synthesizes a mass of literature and data to support the contention that the penal systems of Western nations reflect slavish origins. Some may not agree with a perspective which portrays the evolution of penal systems as being unaffected by other forces, such as the theories of punishment in vogue at a given time. Nevertheless, the book is an important contribution to the literature questioning the forces that shape punitive practices and systems of punishment. The author's scholarship and his impressive list of sources provide ample support for the thesis of the book.

DAVID M. PETERSEN
Georgia State University
Atlanta

OLIVER THOMSON. *Mass Persuasion in History: An Historical Analysis of the Development of Propaganda Techniques.* Pp. vi, 142. New York: Crane, Russak & Co., 1977. $13.50.

The promise of historical perspective in media studies is always welcome. The genre suffers traditionally from too little diachronicity. The credentials of the writer in this instance also raise our expectations: a multinational graduate (from the college of J. Walter Thompson) who now heads a Scottish advertising agency and lectures on mass persuasion at Glasgow University. Alas, the high cost and low quality of the illustrations make this reader question the value of the book, intellectually and financially. But it does turn over the soil for the first time (in my reading) in a way that reveals a crucial turf that needs to be plowed by deeper, more controlled minds.

The book is divided into two parts of very divergent size: The Vocabulary of Leadership deals with an introduction, discussion of sources, a typology (objectives, media, message, inhibiting factors, intensifying factors, side effects), criteria of penetration, audience analysis, response analysis, access to media, and media development); and Historical Case Studies, including the Roman Empire, the Papacy, the Reformation, the Revolutionary Period, Nineteenth Century Propaganda, Lenin and Communism, Hitler and Fascism, Modern China, Democracy and the Western World, and Epilogue (which basically is sensible talk about how not to give into apocalyptical interpretations of what he bizarrely calls the "octopoidal media"). The second section is by far the more entertaining. The first is mainly "potted" media sociology, probably in both the British and American senses of that adjective. The second is a tasty plum pudding, cultural history seen through the narrow perspective of a movieola, as if H. G. Wells were a student of Marshall McLuhan's.

One original idea of Thomson's deserves a very careful analysis. He argues very plausibly that political rhetoric, which he somewhat capriciously keeps calling "social cybernetics", must include the study of things as well as the traditional study of words.

> Architecture should be included within the umbrella of graphic communication media. Traditionally, it has been given little attention from the standpoint of its use as a medium of propaganda. It is, nevertheless, of great importance. Buildings are capable of communicating awe, size, assurance, power, or dynamism, and if in a central or imposing position, can do this to a fairly large audience over a long period. Inevitably, in political terms, it tends to be a medium for the establishment, not the revolution, although a rebel hideout or catacomb can become a symbol by contrast (p. 41).

Indeed, they can—as the public demolition of the Pruitt-Igoe project in St. Louis announced the end of an era of complacency about welfare culture. But the same architect, Minoru Yamasaki, gave Manhattan the twin-towered World Trade Center. The folk here who climbed it—"because it was there"—sends us one message; more likely, it will become in history the tallest mausoleum ever—to the memory of Robert Moses. I was amused in Cairo recently to read in the Egyptian Museum that Rameses I had his name carved covertly on the unseeable bottom of his granite likeness—to discourage Rameses II from converting it to *his* image! And when you read line markers in the apse of St. Peter's in Rome bragging that this is as far as St. Paul's comes, you know that the Counter Reformation at least was using its buildings to bully its congregations.

Thomson is right about the rhetoric of things. We need to become sophisticated in "reading" the man-made environments—as well as its degradations. Norman Mailer's touting the defaced New York subway cars as great art is condescending, ignoble savagery. And the blackout looting in New York is a classic text we are only now trying to learn how to decipher. What is missing from most of that analysis and what is missing from this book is a sense of dynamics. The media are the sum total of their contradictory messages. When Thomson says cinema proper had only a 50-year reign (p. 49), I wonder where that leaves Joan Micklin Silver, Fred Wiseman, and Judy Peiser of the Center for Southern Folklore—not to mention my own introduction to film course, which only a few of the students find dead! Atmospheric level generalizations about media are worse than no generalities at all, I guess.

And while I really enjoyed the anecdotes about media and propaganda over time (that Vergil's *Aeneid* was commissioned by the Emperor, for example), I would always want to check Thompson's stories out with standard histories, especially when I find allusions to Senator Jo Macarthy (p. 21)—does this new firm have no American proofreaders? Or see Dr. Johnson's famous aphorism come out 180 degrees from where he left it: "Patriotism may be the last refuge of a gentleman" (p. 22). No matter, maybe it is just one Scotsperson's way of getting even with another one who said mean things about the country he fled for London. Thomson has identified an important terrain, no small contribution to a field that sprawls and yawns erratically, leaving much of the past unconnected with contemporary media sociology.

PATRICK D. HAZARD

Beaver College
Glenside
Pennsylvania

HARRIET ZUCKERMAN. *Scientific Elite: Nobel Laureates in the United States.* Pg. XV, 335. New York: The Free Press, 1977. $14.95.

The major focus of this study is ninety-two Nobel laureates who worked in the United States on the research that was to bring them their rewards. The data include interviews with forty-one of them, as well as other scientists, and autobiographical and biographical accounts of scientists. An array of comparative data on the productivity and career patterns of laureates, members of the National Academy of Sciences, and a sample of scientists matched with the laureates on age, field of specialization, and type of organizational affiliation is also included.

After a brief introductory chapter, in which Pareto's conception of an elite is discussed, the author traces the process through which Nobel Prizes became preeminent symbols of scientific excellence. Their rapid early rise to eminence appeared, in part, to result from a backlog of highly prestigious scientific figures who were the earliest laureates. Their later stature was further enhanced by the symbolic value that various organizations, universities, research institutes, and other sectors of society have bestowed upon these particular awards. Chapter three, which compares the social and educational origins of future laureates with those of their eminent colleagues, traces the processes involved in the accumulation of advantages which characterize the laureate's career. Such processes, which result in the rich becoming richer and the poor poorer, help create and maintain the structure of stratification in science. Compared to other scientists, future laureates came from families of somewhat higher socioeconomic status, more frequently attended elite colleges, and did their graduate work at the top ranked universities. A striking feature of their graduate training is that over half of the ninety-two laureates worked with older Nobel laureates either as students, recipients of post doctorates, or as junior collaborators. Chapter four traces these relationships between apprentice and masters and touches on their dynamics. In the following chapter, the careers of these laureates are traced, and their rates of productivity are compared to members of the larger elite of the National Academy as well as a sample of other scientists. In chapter six, the personal and social context of the research that led to their award is examined. In this chapter, the author brings her data to bear on the widespread belief that important scientific breakthroughs are made primarily by the young. The data suggests that this conclusion has been much overdrawn. While it is true that slightly over a third did their prize-winning work before the age of 35, it is the middle-aged scientists who turn up disproportionately among the laureates.

Chapter seven examines the consequences for them for having won the prize, including their later rate of productivity, their relations with other scientists, and their roles outside the scientifiic community. The prize, as could be expected, is not an unmixed blessing. With it comes a host of demands that sharply reduce the laureate's productivity, particularly for those thrust suddenly into emminence; yet, it should be added that their productivity on the average remains above that of the matched sample of scientists. The final chapter sums up the author's observations concerning scientific elites, stratification in the sciences, and the effects of the Nobel Prize as the ultimate award in Science. As the author recognizes, her study raises more questions than it answers, but this does not detract from an excellent first step in the study of the reward system in the scientific community.

CARL W. BACKMAN
University of Nevada
Reno

ECONOMICS

JOHN A. BRITTAIN. *The Inheritance of Economic Status*. Pp. ix, 185. Washington, D.C.: The Brookings Institution, 1977. $9.95.

This book, by an economist, is a recent addition to the debate over education, educational policy, and the persistence of economic inequality. The author touches upon the historical roots of the debate involving the American belief in the importance of equal opportunity, as well as the more recent implications of human capital theory and education as a tool in the war on poverty. His analysis and findings are contrasted with those of Jencks et al. Family background, according to Brittain, exerts a strong effect upon later economic success; in addition, there is a strong independent effect of educational attainment upon economic success.

The advantage which Brittain's analysis has over Jencks's lies in the nature of the sample, a sample of actual brothers. Family background, therefore, can be taken into account without the measurement problems inherent in intergenerational mobility studies. The disadvantage of Brittain's analysis lies in his small basic sample size of 128 brothers from 55 families. The analysis is not limited to this basic sample, however, and includes surviving sons and daughters of a 5 percent sample of 659 estates closed in Cleveland Probate Court in 1964–5. One of the more innovative analyses of this study, moreover, used the daughters' economic status as measured by their husbands—i.e., the sons-in-law. The relationship between the parents' and the son-in-law's economic status was as strong as that between the parents' and the son's economic status. Daughters, however, showed an unexplained tendency to end up slightly less well-off than their brothers.

The analysis is sophisticated both with respect to statistical techniques and to explanations of the methodological problems. Parental characteristics examined in the regression analysis predicting the son's economic status included age and education, occupation where the parent was male, total number of siblings, race, religion, size of parents' estate, and the presence of a will. The descriptive techniques of transitional matrices are used to show that there was no overlap in economic success between those who began with family backgrounds in the top tenth and those who began in the bottom tenth. In addition, the author presents a sophisticated analysis of educational attainment in separating out the effects of education as an intervening variable, reflecting the impact of family background upon later economic success, and the effects of education independent of family background. The conclusion is that educational attainment has a strong independent effect.

The study is an important one in furthering the understanding of social mobility, especially with regard to education. The author proceeds to make policy recommendations suggesting that "public policies aimed at reducing the inequality of educational attainment would have an independent effect alleviating the inequality of economic status" (p. 162). This would be true only under the assumption that changes in the income distribution can come about through manipulating the supply of workers—i.e., the amount of human capital. Brittain's analysis, however, does not provide any evidence that we can ignore the demand side—i.e., the kind of jobs available. Are low wage jobs in the secondary labor market going to be transformed into high wage jobs as more high school graduates enter them? Even in his analysis, there appears to be support for education as a sorting device since his evidence suggests that the parents' education relative to the parents' date of birth may be more important than absolute years of education. Furthermore the effect of parents' education decreases as the parents' date of birth becomes more recent.

SALLY BOULD
University of Delaware
Newark

GEORGE A. COLLIER. *Fields of Tzotzil: The Ecological Bases of Tradition in Highland Chiapas*. Pp. xv, 255. Austin: University of Texas Press, 1976. $9.75.

The theme of George Collier's carefully argued and eclectically conceived study of perduring Mayan village integrity in Chiapas is suggested in its title. For he gives as a virtual law that the traditional village community based on patrilineal descent is promoted where land is scarce and valued but still adequate to maintain a largely self-sufficient village. If land is free and abundant, the strong patrilineal descent village is unnecessary and unlikely to appear. Nor can it survive amid infertile, dwarf plots, ever shrinking in relation to a growing village population. The first rather narrow set of conditions is most likely to produce the durable, dynamic traditional Mayan village, quick to defend its rights and extend its modest holdings. By village is meant not the largish *municipio* or Spanish township, but the smaller hamlet within it usually consisting of a score or less exogamous, patronymic lineages.

The most significant contribution of this book is that the hamlet is identified as the core of a vital ethnicity able to cope with a variety of challenges. These challenges are internal and external. The internal ones include land transfer and inheritance procedures, and a growing population threatening a limited supply of land. External challenges are presently posed by state and national bureaucracies and scheming *ladinos*, always eager to exploit Mayan labor and to extend or maintain ranching domains which growing villages desire. Ethnicity is not a barrier imposing isolation or simple distinction on a group, but the necessary essence of hamlet collective identity, enabling it to realize effective interaction with the outside world. Fortunately, examples illustrate precisely how this happens.

Collier is relentlessly eclectic and he disparages environmental determinism. He draws attention to the weakness of studies which rise out of such a viewpoint. But there is a lot of determinism in this book, for it is land, available or scarce, fertile or exhausted, which seems to determine the fate of the marginal, traditional Chiapas hamlet and its structure of descent and inheritance. In showing how such a hamlet can survive and grow or disintegrate and vanish, *The Fields of Tzotil* does much to bring up to date the long history of the Middle American Indian village, at least in one region. But reference to many interpretations recalls how varied and dramatic this history has been and foretells that while Collier is convincing about what he has observed first hand in field work, that each region and epoch, when studied separately, will likely yield its own unique findings.

PHILIP EVANSON
Temple University
Philadelphia

ALEXANDER GERSCHENKRON. *An Economic Spurt That Failed: Four Lectures in Austrian History.* Pp. x, 172. Princeton, N.J.: Princeton University Press, 1977. $12.50.

Based on research in the Austrian archives, Alexander Gerschenkron's *An Economic Spurt That Failed* is the revised and enlarged product of two Janeway Lectures (Princeton). While perhaps not consciously intended as such, the book constitutes, in fact, a practical application to (Cisleithanian) Austria of the author's views on industrialization under varying "degrees of economic backwardness," as developed in his 1967 presidential address to the Economic History Association ("The Discipline and I," *Journal of Economic History,* XXVII (December 1967), pp. 443–59).

As in his other studies, Gerschenkron deals with the problem of an economic "spurt," but this time with a spurt that was not a spurt: the prologue and postscript to the two investment bills of June 1901, by which the ministry of Ernest von Koerber sought to strengthen the railway links with Trieste and to build the inland waterways necessary for uninterrupted communication by water with Hamburg and St. Petersburg. While the railroads were built, the average annual investment in the waterways project between 1904 and 1917 was less than one-half of one percent of the total budget of the Austrian state for 1901, not the sort of expenditure from which spurts erupt.

Gerschenkron defines a spurt as the product of a "substitution" or innovation for one of the so-called prerequisites to a sustained rate of industrial growth in the model country of industrial development. The intended innovation in Austria was to use the state as an active agent of economic development: in Koerber's words, "to place the full power of the State in the service of culture and national economy" (p. 24).

This was also the objective of Latin American and Balkan progressists in the period just before and after 1900. But Gerschenkron takes no note of this fact, insisting instead that what Austria lacked—unlike mid-nineteenth-century France and fin-de-siècle Russia—was an industrialization ideology. Such an ideology failed to win the approval of Austro-Marxists. But it was also insufficiently strong among the entrepreneurs and bankers, upon whom Koerber urged the formation of an Economic Party, to coalesce around the goal of economic development.

Another major obstacle to the spurt was the obstruction of Koerber's minister of finance, the economist Eugen von Boehm-Bawerk. Fearful that an inflationary investment policy would upset the currency and jealous of incursions into its own sphere of action, the ministry of finance opposed a policy of state investment in industrial development despite the fact that such action might have created the jobs with which to counteract the depression of 1900–1905. Moreover, Koerber himself was reluctant to take big risks partly because he, too, may have been a victim of fiscalism—but I would add, of a fiscalism that dates back to the eighteenth, perhaps even the seventeenth, century, wherefore the need to study the failed spurt in the framework of the long term.

Interested in spurts, events, and event makers, Gerschenkron generally neglects long-term problems, although he has pinpointed the long-term obstacles to economic development in Cisleithania (Austria without the northeastern Austrian provinces): the great distance of industrial centers from the sea, the dispersion of natural resources, the eastward flow of the Danube River through economically less developed countries, the heavy taxes levied on joint stock companies, the prestige of a landed aristocracy, that was involved in some banking and industrial activities but apprehensive of the threat presented by industrialization to their social position, and the consequent reluctance of banks to invest in industry.

Persuaded more or less that a successful industrialization spurt would have aided Austria in coping with its multitudinous political and ethnic conflicts, Gerschenkron has presented, in essence, a counterfactual history. At the same time, he maintains that "counterfactual history should be essentially regarded as an instrument for the elucidation of relatively short-term changes, preferably in situations in which the political factor may be largely neglected." ("The Discipline and I," p. 457.) But in Austria, the political factor could not be neglected, wherefore the failure of the Economic Party.

TRAIAN STOIANOVICH
Rutgers University
New Brunswick
New Jersey

BOYD GIBBONS. *Wye Island*. Pp. ix, 227. Baltimore: Johns Hopkins University Press, 1977. $10.95.

The setting for the controversy described in the present volume is Wye Island, a previously relatively isolated part of the upper eastern shore of Maryland. The story deals with the problem of accommodating increased land use and human value systems. The issues raised and the feelings of the characters are generally familiar. The locale could have been any one of a number of places facing problems of development, land subdivision, or environmental preservation. In this particular case, the protagonists are the development company of James Rouse and assorted long time and relatively new residents of the area.

The book is not theoretical. The methodology is that of the social historian, largely ethnographic and based on interview and observation, as well as the examination of local records. The author's fascination with the human condition and individual human beings leads him to offer detailed characterization of almost all major, and many peripheral, actors who have in some way impinged on the current dispute. The development of character description helps contribute to the reader's understanding of the complexity of issues involved. At times, one has the feeling that the description is overdone, but there are valuable insights to be gained from it, as well as lessons for individuals who themselves contemplate doing a study based on observation.

Students of land planning research will be interested in the statements and assumptions about planning that Gibbons attributes to various participants in the controversy. Many of these statements, because of the nature of their content, must remain at the level of assumption. Others would make interesting experiments or research projects for the future. Academicians and nonacademicians will both find the book appealing. The content can be related to concepts in various disciplines as well as to very practical concerns.

Some readers may be disappointed that the author did not conclude the book by attempting to tie together the many variables and questions that emerged in the controversy into a theoretical framework. Yet, if the book is viewed as mainly a sensitizing exploratory work on issues in the land use-environment controversy, then this criticism will be dismissed in favor of the richness of the basic data presented.

In order to stimulate the thinking of an audience, broader than that which will be touched by the book, the author should consider a film documentary based upon his work.

WILLIAM A. PEARMAN
Millersville State College
Millersville
Pennsylvania

ALBERT O. HIRSCHMAN, *The Passions and the Interests: Political Arguments for Capitalism Before its Triumph*. Pp. vii, 153. Princeton, N.J.: Princeton University Press, 1977. $10.00. Paperbound, $2.95.

Almost without thinking, contemporary students of capitalism go to Adam Smith, *The Wealth of Nations* (1776), as a sourcebook of arguments regarding the "invisible hand" guiding a free market economy, private enterprise, untouched by the visible hand of government regulation and intervention, and, more generally, the case for unfettered private gain. In this volume—a gem of intellectual historiography—Albert O. Hirschman, a political economist and permanent member of the Institute for Advanced Study in Princeton, argues that the rise of the spirit of capitalism has its origins in discussions of statecraft and political philosophy that antedate Smith's *Wealth of Nations* by several centuries. As the somewhat cryptic title indicates, Hirschman is much concerned with the philosophic etymology of "passions" and "interests," for it is, he suggests, the ultimate tensions between the two which give rise to the historic defense of capitalism. In this regard, and as a central thesis of his extended essay, Hirschman contends that principal justification for capitalism may be found not in the idea that individual pursuit of private gain leads to large-scale, community-wide benefits (à la Adam Smith and Max Weber), but, instead, in the idea that individual interests (in material advantage) could be used as a countervailing force to check individual passions (such as ambition, lust for power, or sexual lust).

Hirschman constructs an historical justification for man's innate proclivities toward capital and monetary gain—a justification based upon a theory of countervailing forces or powers. The analytic distinction between passions and interests, the author argues, was important historically, for the two were not regarded as synonymous until the eighteenth century. From the writings of St. Augustine onward, the focus of a number of philosophers lay in trying to curb the inevitable, excessive passions of man. Often their answer came through the imposition of law and rule: in the construction of political institutions or edifices. But, Hirschman argues, the more effective response was to pit passion against passion. And, over the centuries, certain passions were regarded as less dangerous and destructive than others. Consequently, the passion toward economic advantage and material accumulation is transformed into a positive force strong enough to stem the more injurious vices and passions of man. The *interest* of rulers (an important component of classical statecraft) became the *interests* of various groups among the ruled; and with this transformation, the passion for material gain became an economic *interest* for individuals in a society.

Out of such argument—interests taming passions—comes the idea that an interest in material wealth and acquisition may have a beneficial effect for all of society. The political benefits (for example, in the areas of commerce and economic growth) of following individual interests were many, according to Baron Charles Louis de Montesquieu and Sir James Steuart. It was only Adam Smith—the most celebrated apologist for capitalism—who was to narrow the defense to more strictly economic themes. In fact, as Hirschman points out, Smith, himself, was not unaware of the ideas of countervailing interests and passions developed by his intellectual precursors.

This is, without question, a significant essay in political economy. Not only would it appeal to students of economic thought, but also to political philosophers and psychologists concerned with human nature, drives, and motivation.

ROBERT G. SEDDIG

Allegheny College
Meadville
Pennsylvania

JUAN MARTINEZ-ALIER. *Haciendas, Plantations and Collective Farms*. Pp. viii, 185. Totowa, N.J.: Frank Cass, 1977. $19.50.

Martinez-Alier provides an innovative theoretical perspective for scholars interested in landlord-peasant relations. The book, which incorporates a number of articles that have previously appeared in academic journals, focuses on sheep-farming haciendas in highland Peru and on sugar estates in Cuba, both before and after the implementation of land reform. His discussion of labor relations, land reform, and political activity dispels some misconceptions, including those held by specialists in the field. For example, Martinez-Alier demonstrates that the social relations of sheep haciendas in Peru in no way ressembled the type of debt-peonage or serfdom found in medieval Europe or other parts of Latin America. On the contrary, peasant-laborers attached to such sheep estates, and also associated with nearby communal villages, were able to exercise a high degree of economic independence by herding their own animals and periodically encroaching on the landowner's property. Such peasants, whose social position was much more advantageous than that of wage laborers or peasants outside of the hacienda system, maintained their own language and ethnic identity as a tool in their ongoing and often successful struggle against local landowners and the government agencies that have recently replaced them. In the case of Cuba, the author shows that sugar cane was primarily cultivated by large tenants with a high degree of security of tenure, using wage laborers, thus counteracting the image that the large foreign companies which ran the sugar mills, were directly involved in the growing, as well as the processing, of cane. He also discusses the relationship between cane growers, mill owners, and wage laborers during and after the Castro revolt.

A series of case studies are preceded by an introductory chapter, in which the author discusses the concepts of land rent, exploitation, and surplus. His main thesis is that the radical distinction between traditional peasants and a modern rural proletariat, so frequently made by social scientists, fails to account for the fact that landowners often convert their day laborers into sharecroppers or small cash tenants, or vice versa. Previous theories have thus been incapable of explaining why seemingly "proletarian" plantation workers have petitioned for land distribution while seemingly typical peasants with "strong roots to the soil" have organized labor unions. This central idea, already apparent in his earlier writings on southern Spain, has been further developed in the present book. Martinez-Alier uses an economic analysis partly derived from neoclassical theory and foreshadowed by Chayanov, a well-known Russian rural economist, to show that it is frequently more profitable for commercial landowning farmers to use sharecroppers instead of laborers. However, political and ideological factors must also be taken into account to explain why landowners do not always act in their own best interest. Martinez-Alier is especially perceptive in showing how the widespread use of wage labor, itself an unintended consequence of laws protecting tenancy, can lead to high rates of rural unemployment and the subsequent social upheavals which those tenancy laws were originally designed to avoid. Unfortunately the author does not extend his analysis to small-scale peasant farmers owning their own plots, a topic which he deems to lie outside of his field of interest.

The main drawback of this book is that the different sections, especially the last chapter on socialist Cuba, are not well tied together in a unified whole. Despite a common theoretical approach running throughout his book, it resembles a patchwork of separate articles. Nevertheless, Martinez-Alier's work will be a landmark in the study of agrarian societies with labor-intensive farms.

FRANS J. SCHRYER
University of Guelph
Ontario
Canada

BILL WARREN, *Inflation and Wages in Underdeveloped Countries*. Pp. ix, 285. Totowa, N.J.: 1977. $30.00.

This book is an empirical study of the relations among inflation, wage and profit shares of value added, profit margins, real wages, and material costs for manufacturing in the 1940s and 1950s in the developing countries of India, Peru and Turkey. The topic is of importance because of the widespread assumption that inflation leads to greater nonwage income and therefore savings in developing countries, in addition to the obvious implications for income distribution. The methodology is modest, with neither mathematical modeling nor statistical hypothesis testing. The movements of each of the variables just mentioned are simply considered for each of eight inflationary episodes.

The results question some conventional wisdom in this area. Leaving aside exceptional periods (e.g., initial wartime disruptions or complete trade liberalizations), the labor shares rose and the profit margins fell with inflation. This pattern reflected a greater rise in unit material costs and in nominal wages than in prices of industrial goods due to short-run relative supply inelasticity in agriculture, as compared to manufacturing and to the oligopolistic market structure of manufacturing. Demand pressures quickly raised the flexible agricultural prices (and, thus, prices of materials and of food), given the short-run inelastic agricultural supply. These demand pressures did not, however, increase prices as much in the modern industrial sector, owing to the short-run supply elasticity and relative inflexible oligopolistic pricing in that sector. Money wages in manufacturing were institutionally determined by government policies and union pressures, with a substantial cost-of-living (and, therefore, agricultural, through the price of food) orientation, despite the existence of surplus labor. Manufacturing prices responded to rising material and labor costs less than proportionately in what Warren terms "defensive inflation." Thus inflation did not result in an increased surplus for reinvestment in the hands of the owners of the manufacturing sector.

This study has its shortcomings. The lack of explicit mathematical modeling and of explicit multivariate hypothesis testing makes the presentation at times tedious and insufficiently structured so that the reader cannot be confident of all of the author's claims. Nevertheless it is a thoughtful analysis, within an implicit general equilibrium framework, which comes to some provocative conclusions after careful consideration of the existing data. It should be of interest to those who are concerned about inflation, savings, distribution, and interactions between agriculture and manufacturing in developing economies, as well as to specialists on India, Peru, and Turkey.

JERE R. BEHRMAN
University of Pennsylvania
Philadelphia

OTHER BOOKS

ANDERSON, R. D. *France 1870–1914: Politics and Society*. Pp. vii, 215. Boston, Mass.: Routledge & Kegan Paul, 1977. $12.50.

APTER, DAVID E. *Introduction to Political Analysis*. Pp. viii, 553. Englewood Cliffs, N.J.: Prentice-Hall, 1977. $12.95.

BAKER, JEAN H. *Ambivalent Americans: The Know-Nothing Party in Maryland*. Pp. vii, 206. Baltimore, Md.: Johns Hopkins University Press, 1977. $14.00.

BELKNAP, ROBERT L. and RICHARD KUHNS. *Tradition and Innovation: General Education and the Reintegration of the University*. Pp. 130. New York: Columbia University Press, 1977. $12.00. Paperbound, $4.00.

BENNETT, CORWIN. *Spaces for People: Human Factors in Design*. Pp. v, 195. Englewood Cliffs, N.J.: Prentice-Hall, 1977. $9.95. Paperbound, $3.95.

BIRCH, R. C. *1776: The American Challenge*. Pp. iv, 122. Seminar Studies in History. New York: Longman, 1977. $2.50. Paperbound.

BLOODWORTH, DENNIS and CHINO PING BLOODWORTH. *The Chinese Machiavelli: 3000 Years of Chinese Statecraft*. Pp. 348. New York: Dell, 1977. $2.25. Paperbound.

BOURDIEU, PIERRE and JEAN-CLAUDE PASSERON. *Reproduction in Education Society and Culture*. Pp. 256. Beverly Hills, Calif.: Sage, 1977. $15.00. Paperbound, $6.95.

BRODEY, WARREN M. *Family Dance: Building Positive Relationships Through Family Therapy*. Pp. 160. New York: Doubleday, 1977. $2.95. Paperbound.

BRUNNER, HEINRICH. *Cuban Sugar Policy from 1963 to 1970*. Pp. vii, 163. Pittsburgh: University of Pittsburgh Press, 1977. $9.95.

CAMPBELL, RITA RICARDO. *Social Security: Promise and Reality*. Pp. ix, 351. Stanford, Calif.: Hoover Institution Press, 1977. $14.95.

CANTOR, MILTON and BRUCE LAURIE, eds. *Class, Sex, and the Woman Worker*. Pp. ix, 253. Westport, Conn.: Greenwood Press, 1977. $14.95.

CARJA, ION. *Tom: Emperor of the Mountains*. Pp. 33. New York: Vantage Press, 1977. $4.50.

CARSTEN, F. L. *Fascist Movements in Austria: From Schönerer to Hitler*. Pp. 360. Beverly Hills, Calif.: Sage, 1977. $17.50. Paperbound, $7.50.

CARTER, JIMMY. *A Government as Good as its People*. Pp. 262. New York: Simon & Schuster, 1977. $8.95.

CHALIAND, GÉRARD. *Revolution in the Third World: Myths and Prospects*. Pp. x, 195. New York: The Viking Press, 1976. $11.95.

CIPOLLA, CARLO M., ed. *The Middle Ages: The Fontana Economic History of Europe*, vol. I. Pp. 389. New York: Barnes & Noble, 1976. No Price.

CLARK, DENNIS J. *Irish Blood: Northern Ireland and the American Conscience*. Pp. ix,

97. Port Washington, N.Y.: Kennikat Press, 1977. $7.95.

CLARK, JOHN P. *The Philosophical Anarchism of William Godwin*. Pp. vii, 343. Princeton, N.J.: Princeton University Press, 1977. $16.50.

CLEVELAND, HARLAN. *The Third Try at World Order: U.S. Policy for an Interdependent World*. Pp. iii, 119, New York: Aspen Institute for Humanistic Studies, 1977. No price.

COHEN, DOROTHY H. and MARGUERITA RUDOLPH. *Kindergarten and Early Schooling*. Pp. iii, 432. Englewood Cliffs, N.J.: Prentice-Hall, 1977. $11.95.

COHEN, SHIRLEY. *Special People: A Brighter Future for Everyone with Physical, Mental, and Emotional Disabilities*. Pp. xiii, 177. Englewood Cliffs, N.J.: Prentice-Hall, 1977. $8.95. Paperbound, $3.95.

COHEN, WILLIAM B., ed. *Robert Delavignette on the French Empire*. Pp. vii, 148. Chicago: University of Chicago Press, 1977. $13.00.

Computer Based Aids to Parliamentary Work. Pp. 85. New York: UNIPUB, 1976. $10.00. Paperbound.

CONDE, ROBERTO CORTES and STANLEY J. STEIN, eds. *Latin America: A Guide to Economic History 1830–1930*. Pp. 685. Berkeley: University of California Press, 1977. No price.

CONNELL, JOHN et al. *Migration from Rural Areas: The Evidence from Village Studies*. Pp. iv, 228. New York: Oxford University Press, 1977. $7.00.

COVENEY, P. J., ed. *France in Crisis, 1620–1675*. Pp. vii, 273. Totowa, N.J.: Rowman & Littlefield, 1977. $19.50.

COWLING, MAURICE. *The Impact of Hitler: British Politics and British Policy, 1933–1940*. Pp. ix, 445. Chicago: University of Chicago Press, 1977. $7.95. Paperbound.

DE CARMOY, GUY. *Energy for Europe: Economic and Political Implications*. Pp. 120. Washington, D.C.: American Enterprise Institute for Public Policy Research, 1977. $3.25. Paperbound.

DENTLER, ROBERT A. *Urban Problems: Perspectives and Solutions*. Pp. vii, 438. Chicago, Ill.: Rand McNally, 1976. No price.

DIAMOND, EDWIN. *The Tin Kazoo: Television, Politics, and the News*. Pp. viii, 269. Cambridge, Mass.: MIT Press, 1977. $4.95. Paperbound.

DIAMOND, IRENE. *Sex Roles in the State House*. Pp. ix, 214. New Haven, Conn.: Yale University Press, 1977. $12.50.

DONAHUE, WILMA T., MARIE MAGUIRE THOMPSON, and D. J. CURREN, eds. *Congregate Housing for Older People: An Urgent Need, A Growing Demand*. Pp. iii, 221. Washington, D.C.: U.S. Department of Health, Education and Welfare, 1976. No price.

DZIEWANOWSKI, M. K. *Poland in the Twentieth Century*. Pp. vii, 309. New York: Columbia University Press, 1977. $14.95.

EICHELBERGER, CLARK M. *Organizing for Peace: A Personal History of the Founding of the United Nations*. Pp. vii, 317. New York: Harper & Row, 1977, $12.50.

ERNST, ELDON G., *Without Help or Hindrance: Religious Identity in American Culture*. Pp. 240. Philadelphia, Pa.: Westminster Press, 1977. $6.95. Paperbound.

ESMAN, MILTON J., ed. *Ethnic Conflict in the Western World*. Pp. 399. Ithaca, N.Y.: Cornell University Press, 1977. $17.50.

FAULKNER, HAROLD U. *The Decline of Laissez Faire, 1897–1917*. The Economic History of the United States, vol. VII. Pp. 464. White Plains, N.Y.: M. E. Sharpe, 1977. $9.95. Paperbound.

FELTHAM, R. G. *Diplomatic Handbook*. 2nd ed. Pp. vi, 138. New York: Longman, 1977. $6.95. Paperbound.

FONTANA, ANDREA. *The Last Frontier: The Social Meaning of Growing Old*. Pp. 216. Beverly Hills, Calif.: Sage, 1977. $11.00. Paperbound, $6.00.

Foreign Relations of the United States, 1950: National Security Affairs; Foreign Economic Policy, vol. I. Pp. 111, 945. Washington, D.C.: U.S. Government Printing Office, 1977. $11.00.

Foreign Relations of the United States 1949. Eastern Europe: The Soviet Union, vol. V. Pp. iii, 1011. Washington, D.C.: U.S. Government Printing Office, 1976. $11.25.

Foreign Relations of the United States, 1949: The Near East, South Africa, and Africa, vol. VI. Pp. 111, 1852. Washington, D.C.: U.S. Government Printing Office, 1977. $16.50.

FORSYTH, FREDERICK. *The Making of an African Legend: The Biafra Story*. Pp. 285. New York: Penguin Books, 1977. $1.95. Paperbound.

FREESE, ARTHUR S. *Help for Your Grief: Turning Emotional Loss into Growth*. Pp. 207. New York: Schocken Books, 1977. $9.95.

FRIEDMAN, EDWARD. *Backward Toward Revolution: The Chinese Revolutionary Party*. Pp. 254. Berkeley, Calif.: University of California Press, 1977. $3.85. Paperbound.

FRIEDMAN, LAWRENCE M. *Law and Society: An Introduction*. Pp. ix, 177. Englewood Cliffs, N.J.: Prentice-Hall, 1977. $7.95. Paperbound, $3.95.

GALNOOR, ITZHAK, ed. *Government Secrecy*

in Democracies. Pp. vii, 317. New York: Harper & Row, 1977. $5.95. Paperbound.

GATES, PAUL W. *The Farmer's Age: Agriculture, 1815–1860.* The Economic History of the United States, vol. III. Pp. 496. White Plains, N.Y.: M. E. Sharpe, 1977. $10.95. Paperbound.

GEORGE, SUSAN. *How the Other Half Dies: The Real Reasons for World Hunger.* Pp. vii, 308. Montclair, N.J.: Allanheld Osmun, 1977. $12.50. Paperbound, $4.95.

GOLDMAN, RALPH M. *Contemporary Perspectives on Politics.* Pp. v, 454. New Brunswick, N.J.: Transaction Books, 1976. $14.95.

GOLDSTEIN, HERMAN. *Policing A Free Society.* Pp. 384. Cambridge, Mass.: Ballinger, 1977. $15.00.

GRANATSTEIN, J. L. and J. M. HITSMAN. *Broken Promises: A History of Conscription in Canada.* Pp. 281. New York: Oxford University Press, 1977. $8.50. Paperbound.

GREENBERG, EDWARD S. *The American Political System: A Radical Approach.* Pp. v, 501. Cambridge, Mass.: Winthrop, 1977. $7.95. Paperbound.

GRIFFITHS, TONY. *Contemporary Australia.* Pp. 165. New York: St. Martin's Press, 1977. $14.95.

GRONLUND, NORMAN E., ed. *Constructing Achievement Tests.* 2nd ed. Pp. ix, 150. Englewood Cliffs, N.J.: Prentice-Hall, 1977. $4.95. Paperbound.

GROSSMAN, MENDEL. *With A Camera in the Ghetto.* Edited by Zvi and Alexander Sened. Pp. 112. New York: Schocken Books, 1977. $12.95.

Guidelines for Developing an Effective National Food Control System. Prepared in Collaboration with the United Nations Environment Programme. Pp. 169. New York: UNIPUB. 1976. $12.00. Paperbound.

HALL, RICHARD H. *Organizations: Structure and Process.* 2nd ed. Pp. v, 356. Englewood Cliffs, N.J.: Prentice-Hall, 1977. $11.95.

HAMER, D. A. *The Politics of Electoral Pressure: A Study in the History of Victorian Reform Agitations.* Pp. vii, 386. Atlantic Highlands, N.J.: Humanities Press, 1977. $20.00.

HARRINGTON, MICHAEL. *Fragments of the Century.* Pp. 246. New York: Simon & Schuster, 1977. $3.95. Paperbound.

HARRINGTON, MICHAEL. *The Twilight of Capitalism.* Pp. 446. New York: Simon & Schuster, 1976. $4.95. Paperbound.

HAUG, RARIE R and JACQUES DOFNY, eds. *Work and Technology.* Pp. 258. Beverly Hills, Calif.: Sage, 1977. $12.00. Paperbound, $6.00.

HEIKOFF, JOSEPH M. *Coastal Resources Management: Institutions and Programs.* Pp. v, 287. Ann Arbor, Mich.: Ann Arbor Science, 1977. $16.50.

HEIMAN, GEORGE, ed. *Associations and Law: The Classical and Early Christian Stages.* Pp. 160. Buffalo, N.Y.: University of Toronto Press, 1977. $15.00.

HENDRICKS, JON and C. DAVIS HENDRICKS. *Aging in Mass Society: Myths and Realities.* Pp. vii, 426. Cambridge, Mass.: Winthrop, 1977. $13.95.

HENLEY, NANCY M. *Body Politics: Power, Sex, and Nonverbal Communication.* Pp. vii, 214. Englewood Cliffs N.J.: Prentice-Hall, 1977. $9.95. Paperbound, $3.95.

HENSLIN, JAMES M., ed. *Deviant Life Styles.* Pp. 380. New Brunswick, N.J.: Transaction Books, 1977. $12.95.

HÜFNER, KLAUS and JENS NAUMAN. *The United Nations System International Bibliography: Learned Journals and Monographs 1945–1965,* vol. I. Pp. viii, 519. New York: UNIPUB, 1976. $39.00.

HUMMEL, RALPH P. *The Bureaucratic Experience.* Pp. viii, 238. New York: St. Martin's Press, 1977. $12.95.

IL SUNG, KIM. *On Juche in Our Revolution.* Pp. vii, 537. New York: Guardian Associates. 1977. $4.95. Paperbound.

IRWIN, GRAHAM W. *Africans Abroad: A Documentary History of the Black Diaspora in Asia, Latin America, and the Caribbean During the Age of Slavery.* Pp. v, 408. New York: Columbia University Press, 1977. $20.00. Paperbound, $7.50.

ISAAK, ROBERT A. *American Democracy and World Power.* Pp. vii, 216. New York: St. Martin's Press, 1977. $12.95.

JARMAN, RUFUS. *The Energy Merchant.* Pp. 279. New York: Richard Rosen, 1977. No price.

JOHNSON, WALTER, CAROL EVANS, and C. ERIC SEARS, eds. *The Papers of Adlai E. Stevenson: Continuing Education and the Unfinished Business of American Society 1957–1961,* vol. VII. Pp. vii, 655. Boston, Mass.: Little, Brown, 1977. $22.50.

JONES, DOROTHY M. *Aleuts in Transition: A Comparison of Two Villages.* Pp. v, 125. Seattle: University of Washington Press, 1976. $9.50.

KALISH, RICHARD A., ed. *The Later Years: Social Applications of Gerontology.* Pp. v, 402. Monterey, Calif.: Brooks, Cole, 1977. No price.

KISSINGER, HENRY A. *American Foreign Policy.* 3rd ed. Pp. 445. New York: W. W. Norton, 1977. $9.95. Paperbound, $4.95.

KOCHAN, LIONEL. *The Jew and His History.* Pp. 164. New York: Schocken Books, 1977. $15.00.

KOHL, JAMES and JOHN LITT. *Urban Guerrilla Warfare in Latin America.* Pp. ix, 425. Cambridge, Mass.: MIT Press, 1977. $4.95. Paperbound.

KONCZACKI, Z. A. and J. M. KONCZACKI, eds. *An Economic History of Tropical Africa: The Pre-Colonial Period,* vol. I. Pp. vii, 310. Totowa, N.J.: Frank Cass, 1977. $25.00.

KOTZ, NICK and MARY LYNN KOTZ. *A Passion for Equality: George Wiley and the Movement.* Pp. 372. New York: W. W. Norton, 1977. $8.95.

LADNER, JOYCE A. *Mixed Families: Adopting Across Racial Boundaries.* Pp. 312. New York: Doubleday, 1977. $10.00.

LANDIS, JEDSON T and MARY G. LANDIS, eds. *Building A Successful Marriage.* 7th ed. Pp. vii, 556. Englewood Cliffs, N.J.: Prentice-Hall, 1977. $12.95.

LANGBEIN, JOHN, H. *Comparative Criminal Procedure: Germany.* Pp. 172. St. Paul, Minn.: West, 1977. $4.95. Paperbound.

LEFEBVRE, VLADIMIR A. *The Structure of Awareness: Toward a Symbolic Language of Human Reflexion.* Pp. 200. Beverly Hills, Calif.: Sage, 1977. $11.00. Paperbound, $6.00.

LEVIN, ARTHUR, ed. *Health Services: The Local Perspective.* Pp. vii, 262. New York: Academy of Political Science. $6.50. Paperbound.

LIEBERT, ROBERT M., RITA WICKS POULOUS, and GLORIA STRAUSS MARMOR. *Developmental Psychology.* 2nd ed. Pp. v, 572. Englewood Cliffs, N.J.: Prentice-Hall, 1977. $14.95.

LIEBERT, ROLAND J. and ALLEN W. IMMERSHEIN, eds. *Power, Paradigms, and Community Research.* Pp. 344. Beverly Hills, Calif.: Sage, 1977. $12.00. Paperbound, $6.00.

LIGHT, DONALD JR. and JOHN SPIEGEL, eds. *The Dynamics of University Protest.* Pp. vii, 198. Chicago, Ill.: Nelson-Hall, 1977. $12.00.

LINDER, MARC. *Anti-Samuelson: Basic Ideological Concepts, Crises and Keynesianism,* vol. I. Pp. v, 395. New York: Urizen Books, 1977. $5.95. Paperbound.

LINDER, MARC. *Anti-Samuelson: Money and Credit Value and Price Theory Factors of Production in the World Market,* vol. II. Pp. 472. New York: Urizen Books, 1977. $5.95. Paperbound.

LOW, DONALD A. *That Sunny Dome: A Portrait of Regency Britian.* Pp. vii, 208. Totowa, N.J.: Rowman & Littlefield, 1977. $10.00.

LOYE, DAVID. *The Leadership Passion: A Psychology of Ideology.* Pp. ix, 249. San Francisco, Calif: Jossey-Bass, 1977. $12.95.

LUKACS, GEORG. *The Young Hegel: Studies in the Relations between Dialectics and Economics.* Pp. v, 576. Cambridge, Mass.: MIT Press, 1977. $9.95. Paperbound.

LYNN, KENNETH S. *A Divided People.* Pp. xi, 113. Westport, Conn.: Greenwood Press, 1977. $11.95.

MACAVOY, PAUL W., ed. *Federal-State Regulation of the Pricing and Marketing of Insurance.* Pp. 105. Washington, D.C.: American Enterprise Institute for Public Policy Research. 1977. $3.25. Paperbound.

MADDOX, ROBERT J. *The Unknown War With Russia: Wilson's Siberian Intervention.* Pp. ix, 156. San Rafael, Calif: Presidio Press, 1977. $9.95.

MAGID, ALVIN. *Men in the Middle: Leadership and Role Conflict in A Nigerian Society.* Pp. vii, 292. New York: Holmes & Meier, 1976. $25.00.

MAINE, HENRY SUMNER. *Popular Government.* Pp. 254. Indianapolis, Ind.: Liberty Classics, 1976. $7.95. Paperbound, $1.95.

MARQUAND, DAVID. *Ramsay Macdonald.* Pp. vii, 903. Totowa, N.J.: Rowman & Littlefield, 1977. $25.00.

MARVICK, ELIZABETH WIRTH, ed. *Psychopolitical Analysis: Selected Writings of Nathan Leites.* Pp. 384. New York: Halsted Press, 1977. $20.00.

MAZUZAN, GEORGE T. *Warren R. Austin at the U.N., 1946–1953.* Pp. ix, 233. Kent, Ohio: Kent State University Press, 1977. $10.00.

MCLAUGHLIN, CHARLES CAPEN. *The Papers of Frederick Law Olmsted: The Formative Years 1822–1852,* vol. I. Baltimore, Md.: Johns Hopkins University Press, 1977. $20.00.

MENENDEZ, ALBERT J. *Religion at the Polls.* Pp. 248. Philadelphia, Pa.: Westminster Press, 1977. $5.95. Paperbound.

MEYER, LORENZO. *Mexico and the United States in the Oil Controversy, 1917–1942.* Pp. xi, 367. Austin: University of Texas Press, 1977. $19.95.

MILIBAND, RALPH. *Marxism and Politics.* Pp. viii, 199. New York: Oxford University Press, 1977. $10.00.

MITCHELL, BROADUS. *Depression Decade: From New Era Through New Deal, 1929–1941.* The Economic History of the United States, vol. IX. Pp. 496. White Plains, N.Y.: M. E. Sharpe, 1977. $10.95. Paperbound.

MONAT, ALAN and RICHARD S. LAZARUS. *Stress and Coping.* Pp. vii, 426. New York: Columbia University Press, 1977. $20.00. Paperbound, $10.00.

MONTGOMERY, PETER G. *Humanity at the Helm: A Blueprint for World Unification.*

Pp. vii, 190. Ardmore, Pa.: Dorrance, 1977. $6.95.

MOON, MARILYN and EUGENE SMOLENSKY, eds. *Improving Measures of Economic Well Being*. Pp. ix, 239. New York: Academic Press, 1977. $16.00.

MOONEY, CHRISTOPHER F. *Religion and the American Dream: The Search for Freedom Under God*. Pp. 144. Philadelphia, Pa.: Westminster Press, 1977. $4.95. Paperbound.

MORGAN, PATRICK M. *Deterrence: A Conceptual Analysis*. Pp. 216. Beverly Hills, Calif.: Sage, 1977. $11.00. Paperbound, $6.00.

MORRISON, ELEANOR S. and VERA BOROSAGE, eds. *Human Sexuality: Contemporary Perspectives*. 2nd ed. Pp. iii. 504. Palo Alto, Calif.: Mayfield, 1977. No price.

MUCHOW, DAVID J. *The Vanishing Congress: Where Has All the Power Gone?* Pp. ii, 276. Washington, D.C.: North American International, 1976. $10.00.

MURPHY, WALTER F. and JOSEPH TANENHAUS. *Comparative Constitutional Law: Cases and Commentaries*. Pp. ix, 754. New York: St. Martin's Press, 1977. $20.00.

NAGEL, STUART S., ed. *Modeling the Criminal Justice System*. Pp. 320. Beverly Hills, Calif.: Sage, 1977. $17.50. Paperbound, $7.50.

NOONAN, JOHN T., JR. *The Antelope: The Ordeal of the Recaptured Africans in the Administrations of James Monroe and John Quincy Adams*. Pp. 205. Berkeley: University of California Press, 1977. $10.00.

NETTELS, CURTIS P. *The Emergence of A National Economy, 1775–1815*. The Economic History of the United States, vol. II. Pp. 464. White Plains, N.Y.: M. E. Sharpe, 1977. $9.95. Paperbound.

NEWCOMB, JOAN I. *John F. Kennedy: An Annotated Bibliography*. Pp. iii, 143. Metuchen, N.J.: Scarecrow Press, 1977. $6.00.

OSKAMP, STUART. *Attitudes and Opinions*. Pp. iii, 466. Englewood Cliffs, N.J.: Prentice-Hall, 1977. $14.95.

OTERO, LUIS LENERO, ed. *Beyond the Nuclear Family Model: Cross-Cultural Perspectives*. Pp. 226. Beverly Hills, Calif.: Sage, 1977. $12.00. Paperbound, $6.00.

OTT, DAVID J. and ATTIAT F. OTT. *Federal Budget Policy. 3rd ed.* Pp. ix, 178. Washington, D.C.: The Brookings Institution, 1977. $9.95. Paperbound, $3.95.

PARSONS, TALCOTT. *Social Systems and the Evolution of Action Theory*. Pp. ix, 420. New York: The Free Press, 1977. $15.95.

PENNOCK, J. ROLAND and JOHN W. CHAPMAN, eds. *Human Nature in Politics*. Pp. viii, 348. New York: New York University Press, 1977. $17.50.

PINE, VANDERLYN R. *Introduction to Social Statistics*. Pp. v, 415. Englewood Cliffs, N.J.: Prentice-Hall, 1977. $13.95.

PLATT, ANTHONY M. *The Child Savers: The Invention of Delinquency*. 2nd ed. Pp. ix, 240. Chicago: University of Chicago Press, 1977. $3.95. Paperbound.

PLISCHKE, ELMER. *Microstates in World Affairs: Policy Problems and Options*. Pp. 153. Washington, D.C.: American Enterprise Institute for Public Policy Research, 1977. $3.00. Paperbound.

RATCLIFFE, BARRIE M. and W. H. CHALONER, eds. *A French Sociologist Looks At Britian: Gustave d'Eichthal and British Society in 1828*. Pp. 169. Totowa, N.J.: Rowman & Littlefield. 1977. $12.50.

RENSHON, STANLEY ALLEN, ed. *Handbook of Political Socialization: Theory and Research*. Pp. v, 547. New York: The Free Press, 1977. $19.95.

RICHMOND, J. C. B. *Egypt 1798–1952*. Pp. vii, 243. New York: Columbia University Press, 1977. $15.00.

ROBERTS, NEAL ALISON. *The Government Land Developers*. Pp. vii, 249. Lexington, Mass.: D. C. Heath, 1977. $18.00.

ROGERS, DOROTHY. *Issues in Adolescent Psychology*. 3rd ed. Pp. iii, 485. Englewood Cliffs, N.J.: Prentice-Hall, 1977. $8.95. Paperbound.

ROSE, LEO E. *The Politics of Bhutan*. Pp. 237. Ithaca, N.Y.: Cornell University Press, 1977. $19.50.

ROSE, PETER I., MYRON GLAZER, and PENINA MIGDAL GLAZER. *Sociology Inquiring into Society*. Pp. 603. San Francisco, Calif.: Canfield Press, 1977. No price.

ROSENFELD, ERWIN and HARRIET GELLER. *Afro-Asian Culture Studies*. 2nd ed. Pp. 469. Woodbury, N.Y.: Barron's Educational Series, 1976. $4.40. Paperbound.

RUBEN, BRENT D., ed. *Communication Yearbook 1*. Pp. xi, 656. New Brunswick, N.J.: Transaction Books, 1977. $24.95.

RUMMEL, R. J. *Field Theory Evolving*. Pp. 533. Beverly Hills, Calif.: Sage, 1977. $29.95.

RUSSELL, FRANCIS. *A City in Terror: The 1919 Boston Police Strike*. Pp. v, 256. New York: Penguin Books, 1977. $3.95. Paperbound.

SACHS, MOSHE Y., ed. *The United Nations: A Handbook on the United Nations, its Structure, History, Purposes, Activities and Agencies*. Pp. v, 246. New York: John Wiley & Sons, 1977. $9.95.

SCALAPINO, ROBERT A., ed. *The Foreign Policy of Modern Japan*. Pp. 445. Berkeley: University of California Press, 1977. $21.50. Paperbound, $5.45.

SCHIESEL, MARTIN J. *The Politics of Efficiency: Municipal Administration and Reform in America: 1880–1920*. Pp. 268. Berkeley: University of California Press, 1977. $11.75.

SCHLAGHECK, JAMES L. *The Political Economic, and Labor Climate in Brazil*. Pp. iii, 116. Latin American Studies, no. 4. Philadelphia: University of Pennsylvania Press, 1977. No price.

SCHRAMM, WILBUR. *Big Media, Little Media: Tools and Technologies for Instruction*. Pp. 315. Beverly Hills, Calif.: Sage, 1977. $17.50. Paperbound, $7.50.

SCRIBNER, JAY D., ed. *The Politics of Education: The Seventy-sixth Yearbook of the National Society for the Study of Education*. Pp. vii, 367. Chicago: University of Chicago Press, 1977. $12.00.

SHANAS, ETHEL and MARVIN B. SUSSMAN, eds. *Family, Bureaucracy, and the Elderly*. Pp. v, 233. Durham, N.C.: Duke University Press, 1977. $12.75.

SHANNON, FRED A. *The Farmer's Last Frontier: Agriculture, 1860–1897*. The Economic History of the United States, vol. V. Pp. 464. White Plains, N.Y.: M. E. Sharpe, 1977. $9.95. Paperbound.

SHAPIRO, R. DIANE. *Foundation for Sociology: A Self-Learning Text*. Pp. v, 407. Chicago, Ill.: Rand McNally 1977. $7.95. Paperbound.

SHAVER, KELLY G. *Principles of Social Psychology*. Pp. vii, 636. Cambridge, Mass.: Winthrop, 1977. $14.95.

SIFF, TED and ALAN WEIL, eds. *Ruling Congress: How the House and Senate Rules Govern the Legislative Process*. Pp. 299. New York: Penguin Books, 1977. $2.95. Paperbound.

SINAI, ANNE and ALLEN POLLACK, eds. *The Hashemite Kingdom of Jordan and the West Bank*. Pp. 371. New York: AAAPME, 1977. $6.95. Paperbound.

SIRACUSA, JOSEPH M., ed. *The American Diplomatic Revolution: A Documentary History of the Cold War 1941–1947*. Pp. 263. Port Washington, N.Y.: Kennikat Press, 1977. $12.95. Paperbound, $7.95.

SMITH, JONATHAN RILEY. *What Were the Crusades?* Pp. 92. Totowa, N.J.: Rowan & Littlefield, 1977. $9.50.

SMOLKA, RICHARD G. *Election Day Registration: The Minnesota and Wisconsin Experience in 1976*. Pp. 69. Washington, D.C.: American Enterprise Institute for Public Policy Research. 1977. $2.75. Paperbound.

SOBEL, ROBERT, ed. *Biographical Directory of the United States Executive Branch, 1774–1977*. 2nd ed., rev. Pp. x, 503. Westport, Conn.: Greenwood Press, 1977. $29.95.

SOBOUL, ALBERT. *A Short History of the French Revolution, 1789–1799*. Pp. 197. Berkeley: University of California Press, 1977. $12.00. Paperbound, $2.95.

SORRENTINO, ANTHONY. *Organizing Against Crime: Redeveloping the Neighborhood*. Pp. 272. New York: Human Sciences Press, 1977. No price.

SOULE, GEORGE. *Prosperity Decade: From War to Depression, 1917–1929*. The Economic History of the United States, vol. VIII. Pp. 400. White Plains, N.Y.: M. E. Sharpe, 1977. $8.95. Paperbound.

SPANNAUS, NANCY and CHRISTOPHER WHITE, eds. *The Political Economy of the American Revolution*. Pp. v, 470. Philadelphia, Pa.: University Editions, 1977. $4.95. Paperbound.

SPIEGEL-RÖSING, INA and DEREK DE SOLLA PRICE, eds. *Science, Technology and Society: A Cross-Disciplinary Perspective*. Pp. 607. Beverly Hills, Calif.: Sage, 1977. $29.95.

Spines Thesaurus: A Controlled and Structured Vocabulary of Science and Technology for Policy-Making, Management and Development. Pp. 666. New York: UNIPUB, 1976. $54.50. Set. 3 vols. in 4 parts.

SPIRA, THOMAS. *German-Hungarian Relations and the Swabian Problem*. Pp. viii, 382. New York: Columbia University Press, 1977. $18.50.

STOLER, MARK A. *The Politics of the Second Front: American Military Planning and Diplomacy in Coalition Warfare, 1941–1943*. Pp. xiii, 244. Westport, Conn.: Greenwood Press, 1977. $16.95.

STEINTRAGER, JAMES. *Bentham*. Pp. 133. Ithaca. N.Y.: Cornell University Press, 1977. $11.50.

STEINERT, MARLIS G. *Hitler's War and the Germans*. Pp. vii, 387. Athens, Ohio: Ohio University Press, 1977. $20.00.

TAYLOR, GEORGE ROGERS. *The Transportation Revolution, 1815–1860*. The Economic History of the United States, vol. IV. Pp. 520. White Plains, N.Y.: M. E. Sharpe, 1977. $10.95. Paperbound.

TEITLER, G. *The Genesis of the Professional Officers' Corps*. Pp. 246. Beverly Hills, Calif.: Sage, 1977. $13.50.

THOMA, HENRY F., ed. *The American Prospect: Insights into Our Next 100 Years*. Pp. v, 159. Boston, Mass.: Houghton Mifflin, 1977. $7.95. Paperbound, $3.95.

TODARO, MICHAEL P. *Economic Development in the Third World*. Pp. vi, 440. New York: Longman, 1977. $14.95.

TOWNSEND, JOHN OMAN. *The Making of the Modern State*. Pp. 212. New York: St. Martin's Press, 1977. $16.95.

TURK, HERMAN. *Organizations in Modern Life*. Pp. ix, 283. San Francisco, Calif.: Jossey-Bass, 1977. $15.00.

ULLMANN, WALTER. *Medieval Foundations of Renaissance Humanism*. Pp. vii, 212. Ithaca, N.Y.: Cornell University Press, 1977. $12.50.

WATTS, WILLIAM and JORGE I. DOMINGUEZ. *The United States and Cuba: Old Issues and New Directions*. Pp. 53. Washington, D.C.: Potomac Associates, 1977. $4.00. Paperbound.

WATTS, WILLIAM and LLOYD A. FREE. *Aspirations and Social Concerns: Crime, Blacks, Inequality, and Women*. Pp. 50. Washington, D.C.: Potomac Associates, 1977. $2.50. Paperbound.

WEPPNER, ROBERT. S., ed. *Street Ethnography*, vol. I. Pp. 288. Beverly Hills, Calif.: Sage, 1977. $17.50. Paperbound, $7.50.

WETTIG, GERHARD. *Broadcasting and Détente: Eastern Policies and their Implication for East-West Relations*. Pp. v, 110. New York: St. Martin's Press, 1977. $9.95.

WHEELER, MICHAEL. *Lies, Damn Lies, and Statistics: The Manipulation of Public Opinion in America*. Pp. 320. New York: Dell, 1976. $2.50. Paperbound.

WILLIE, CHARLES V., ed. *Black, Brown, White Relations: Race Relations in the 1970s*. Pp. 235. New Brunswick, N.J.: Transaction Books, 1977. $12.95. Paperbound, $4.95.

WOOD, W. D. and PRADEEP KUMAR, eds. *The Current Industrial Relations Scene in Canada 1977*. Irregular pagination. Ontario, Ca.: McGill-Queen's University Press, 1977. $40.00. Paperbound.

WOODSWORTH, DAVID E. *Social Security and National Policy: Sweden, Yugoslavia, Japan*. Pp. 156. Ontario, Ca: McGill-Queen's University Press, 1977. $8.50. Paperbound, $3.95.

WORICK, W. WAYNE and WARREN E. SCHALLER. *Alcohol, Tobacco, and Drugs: Their Use and Abuse*. Pp. v, 170. Englewood Cliffs, N.J.: Prentice-Hall, 1977. $7.95. Paperbound, $4.95.

ZIEGER, ROBERT H. *Madison's Battery Workers, 1934–1952: A History of Federal Labor Union 19587*. Pp. v, 126. Ithaca, N.Y.: Cornell University Press, 1977. $4.50. Paperbound.

ZIRING, LAWRENCE, RALPH BRAIBANTI, and W. HOWARD WRIGGINS, eds. *Pakistan: The Long View*. Pp. xi, 485. Durham. N.C.: Duke University Press, 1977. $19.75.

INDEX

INDEX

The American Academy of Political and Social Science

3937 Chestnut Street **Philadelphia, Pennsylvania 19104**

Origin and Purpose. The Academy was organized December 14, 1889, to promote the progress of political and social science, especially through publications and meetings. The Academy does not take sides in controverted questions, but seeks to gather and present reliable information to assist the public in forming an intelligent and accurate judgment.

Meetings. The Academy holds an annual meeting in the spring extending over two days.

Publications. THE ANNALS is the bimonthly publication of The Academy. Each issue contains articles on some prominent social or political problem, written at the invitation of the editors. Also, monographs are published from time to time, numbers of which are distributed to pertinent professional organizations. These volumes constitute important reference works on the topics with which they deal, and they are extensively cited by authorities throughout the United States and abroad. The papers presented at the meetings of The Academy are included in THE ANNALS.

Membership. Each member of The Academy receives THE ANNALS and may attend the meetings of The Academy. Annual dues: Regular Membership—$18.00 (clothbound, $23.00). Special Membership—contributing, $40.00; sustaining, $60.00; patron, $100. A life membership is $500. Add $2.00 to above rates for membership outside the U.S.A. Dues are payable in U.S. dollars in advance. Special members receive a certificate suitable for framing and may choose either paper or clothbound copies of THE ANNALS.

Single copies of THE ANNALS may be obtained by nonmembers of The Academy for $4.50 ($5.50 clothbound) and by members for $4.00 ($5.00 clothbound). A discount of 5 percent is allowed on orders for 10 to 24 copies of any one issue, and of 10 percent on orders for 25 or more copies. These discounts apply only when orders are placed directly with The Academy and not through agencies. The price to all bookstores and to all dealers is $4.50 per copy ($5.00, clothbound) less 20 percent, with no quantity discount. Orders for 5 books or less must be prepaid (add $1.00 for postage and handling). Orders for 6 books or more must be invoiced.

All correspondence concerning The Academy or THE ANNALS should be addressed to the Academy offices, 3937 Chestnut Street, Philadelphia, Pa. 19104.